DAVID GLASGOW FARRAGUT
OUR FIRST ADMIRAL

DAVID GLASGOW FARRAGUT
OUR FIRST ADMIRAL

CHARLES LEE LEWIS

NAVAL INSTITUTE PRESS
ANNAPOLIS, MARYLAND

This book has been brought to publication with the generous
assistance of Marguerite and Gerry Lenfest.

Naval Institute Press
291 Wood Road
Annapolis, MD 21402

© 1943 by the United States Naval Institute

All rights reserved. No part of this book may be reproduced or utilized in any form or by any means, electronic or mechanical, including photocopying and recording, or by any information storage and retrieval system, without permission in writing from the publisher.

First Naval Institute Press paperback edition published in 2014.
ISBN: 978-1-59114-432-8 (paperback)
ISBN: 978-1-61251-299-0 (ebook)

♾ Print editions meet the requirements of ANSI/NISO z39.48-1992 (Permanence of Paper).
Printed in the United States of America.

9 8 7 6 5 4 3 2 1

IN MEMORIAM
ROBERT THOMAS QUARLES

PREFACE

THE FAVORABLE reception of *David Glasgow Farragut: Admiral in the Making*, dealing with the life of our great naval leader up to the beginning of the Civil War, has encouraged me to complete his biography in a second volume. Though this second part of his life was only about one sixth of the former portion in length of time, it surpassed the other in thrilling deeds and significant achievements.

As in the preparation of the first volume, I have found much hitherto unpublished material relating to this later period of Farragut's life. For this new material I wish to express my most hearty thanks to Dr. Ellsworth Eliot, Jr., who permitted me to examine his very large and valuable collection of Farragut manuscripts and to quote freely therefrom; to Mr. George T. Keating, who allowed me complete freedom in the use of photostatic copies of the Note Book and the Diary of Farragut, which relate chiefly to the Battle of Mobile Bay; to the Henry E. Huntington Library and Art Gallery for furnishing me with microfilms of numerous important letters; to Captain H. A. Baldridge, U. S. Navy (Retired), Curator of the U. S. Naval Academy, for the free use of the Zabriskie Collection of manuscripts and of other miscellaneous papers in the Naval Academy Museum; and to Captain D. W. Knox, U. S. Navy (Retired), Officer-in-Charge, Naval Records and Library, Navy Department, and to his assistants, who aided me greatly in finding material which was not published in the *Official Records of the Union and Confederate Navies in the War of the Rebellion*.

For similar assistance, my thanks go also to the Manuscript Division of the Library of Congress, The National Archives, New York Historical Society, New York Public Library, Tennessee State Library, Tennessee Historical Society, Public Library of the City of Boston, Library of the U. S. Military Academy, and Library of the U. S. Naval Academy. There are, besides, literally dozens of individuals who have helped me greatly and cheerfully by answering my letters of inquiry. They are too numerous even to list by name. But I do wish to mention personally Mr. Louis H. Bolander, Assistant Librarian of the Naval Academy Library, who has rendered me invaluable aid in tracking down elusive bits of information and in many other ways. The grandniece of Admiral Farragut, Mrs. George G. Hall, and her husband have continued to answer my numerous letters of inquiry as they did so patiently during the writing of the first volume. Mr. Albert Mordell, author and journalist of Philadelphia, and Mr. Robert Thomas Quarles, Junior, of the staff of the Tennessee Historical Society and the Tennessee State Library called to my attention extremely useful material, which otherwise would have eluded me. My colleague, Assistant Professor Richard West, Jr., author of *The Second Admiral: A Life of David Dixon Porter,* who is writing a biography of Gideon Welles, has been of great assistance to me.

It is hoped that the notes will not be found too voluminous. The Civil War was a very controversial period, and it is sometimes very difficult to reach even an approximation of the truth. The reader, therefore, will find the citations of authority unusually numerous; at times, the statements of the opposing sides will be set down for the reader's consideration. In the notes will also be found unusually interesting details, for which no room could well be found in the text. If the reader finds no interest in the notes, they can be easily disregarded, as they were placed in the back of the book for that very reason. The appendix contains fuller information than is usually found, in biographies, concerning statues and other memorials, portraits and paintings of battles, and poems inspired by Our First Admiral. This will be useful, at least for reference.

The reader will also find in this biography an unusually large number of quotations, usually brief, from letters and other primary source material. Most of these were written by Farragut; the others chiefly by those who knew him intimately. It has been thought that in this way more light would be thrown on Farragut's character than could be secured from a mere recital of his achievements, and that the period of the Civil War would be made more real to the reader by thus kindling his imagination. Newspapers and some additional secondary source material have been used in the same manner and for the same purpose.

As in the previous volume, the aim has been to portray Farragut as a human being with his faults and his virtues. No attempt has been made to make him illustrate any preconceived theory as to what constitutes greatness in a naval leader. The reader will be expected to form his own estimate of the nature and degree of Farragut's greatness, after finishing the book. Whether he ranks him very high or comparatively low in the scale of naval leaders, it is believed that no reader will place him "in the roll of common men." In any case, he will have discovered how a brave, patriotic man conducted himself during this extraordinarily interesting period of our history, how he faced obstacles and difficulties of every imaginable sort during the weeks and sometimes months of preparation, and how he met the test of battle itself by courageously making decisions in the very climax of conflict and then by fighting his way through to victory. Those who are thrilled with stories of adventure and high courage will find in Farragut's career full justification for Meredith's glowing lines:

> "Oh! while Atlantic's breast
>   Bears a white sail,
> While the Gulf's towering crest
>   Tops a green vale,
> Men thy bold deeds shall tell,
>   Old Heart of Oak,
> Daring Dave Farragut,
>   Thunderbolt stroke!"

C.L.L.

Annapolis, Maryland
September 8, 1942

CONTENTS

CHAPTER	PAGE
I. The Call to Arms	1
II. Rendezvous in the Gulf	15
III. The Victory over Mud	25
IV. Final Plans and Preparations	33
V. Barriers to New Orleans	38
VI. Bombs Bursting in Air	44
VII. Crashing through the Barriers	55
VIII. The Capture of the Queen of the Gulf	65
IX. On to Vicksburg	78
X. Running the Vicksburg Batteries	91
XI. Meeting of the Fleets	105
XII. The *Arkansas* and Baton Rouge	124
XIII. Blockading the Gulf Ports	135
XIV. Disasters in the Gulf	148
XV. Passing the Batteries of Port Hudson	165
XVI. Patrolling the Mississippi	183
XVII. The Siege and Capture of Port Hudson	198
XVIII. Farragut Has a Furlough	211
XIX. Watchful Waiting	221
XX. The *Tennessee* Enters the Bay	241
XXI. The Monitors Arrive	252
XXII. Forcing the Entrance to Mobile Bay	263

CONTENTS

CHAPTER		PAGE
XXIII.	The Capture of the *Tennessee*	273
XXIV.	The Surrender of the Forts	283
XXV.	Farragut's Health Fails	297
XXVI.	The War Ends	312
XXVII.	Admiral of the Navy	327
XXVIII.	The European Cruise	336
XXIX.	"The Last Scene of All"	366
XXX.	"What Would Farragut Have Done?"	379
	Appendix: Statues, Pictures, and Poems	391
	Sources and Bibliography	404
	Notes	415
	Index	495

ILLUSTRATIONS

PAGE

The Farragut Residence in Hastings-on-Hudson 2
From a drawing

Captain David Glasgow Farragut, U. S. Navy 3
From a photograph by E. Anthony

Secretary of the Navy Gideon Welles 8
From an unidentified contemporary photograph

Gustavus Vasa Fox, Assistant Secretary of the Navy 9
From an engraving by H. B. Hall in *Fox's Mission to Russia*

The *Hartford* under Sail and Steam 16
From a sketch in *Harper's Weekly*, May 17, 1862

U. S. Steam Sloop *Hartford* 17
From a painting by E. Arnold, made in New Orleans, 1862, now in the National Museum

Commander David Dixon Porter, U. S. Navy 54
From an engraving of the portrait by Alonzo Chappel

Farragut's Fleet Passing Forts Jackson and St. Philip below New Orleans 55
From a lithograph by C. Parsons in the collection of President Franklin Delano Roosevelt

Farragut as Captain and Rear-Admiral 78
From photographs by E. Jacobs, C. D. Fredricks & Co., and Brady

Map of the Mississippi River from Vicksburg to Baton Rouge 79
From *Official Records of the Union and Confederate Navies in the War of the Rebellion*

ILLUSTRATIONS

PAGE

Rear-Admiral David Glasgow Farragut, U. S. Navy 124
From a photograph by E. Jacobs, New Orleans

Rear-Admiral Farragut 125
From a photograph by C. D. Fredricks & Co., New York

Passage of the Batteries of Port Hudson 166
From the painting made by E. Arnold in 1864, now in the National Museum

Cadet Loyall Farragut, U. S. Military Academy 167
From a photograph furnished by the U. S. Military Academy

Mrs. David Glasgow Farragut 212
From a photograph by Anthony & Co.

Rear-Admiral Farragut 213
From a photograph by Brady

Rear-Admiral Farragut and Captain Percival Drayton at the Wheel of the *Hartford* 248
From an unidentified contemporary photograph

Sword Presented to Farragut by the Union League Club, New York 249
From a photograph furnished by the National Museum, Washington

Formation of Farragut's Fleet, Battle of Mobile Bay 260
From the original drawing in the Library of Congress

Battle of Mobile Bay, Passing Fort Morgan and the *Tennessee* 264
From a lithograph in the collection of President Franklin D. Roosevelt, after the painting by J. O. Davidson

American Naval Officer Going into Action—New Style Invented by Commodore Farragut 265
From a caricature in *Frank Leslie's Illustrated Newspaper*, September 10, 1864

An August Morning, Battle of Mobile Bay 274
From the painting by William H. Overend in the Wadsworth Atheneum, Hartford, Connecticut

ILLUSTRATIONS

PAGE

Capture of the *Tennessee*, Battle of Mobile Bay 275
    From the painting by Xanthus Smith in Naval Academy Museum

Rear-Admiral Farragut, Commodore Palmer, and Brigadier-General Granger 312
    From photographs by McPherson & Oliver, Bogardus, and an unknown photographer

Vice-Admiral D. G. Farragut, U. S. Navy 313
    From a photograph by Brady

Admiral Farragut and Lieutenant-Commander John C. Watson 334
    From an unidentified contemporary photograph

Admiral Farragut on the *Franklin* during the European Cruise 335
    From an original photograph owned by Mr. and Mrs. George G. Hall

Admiral Farragut 350
    From photographs by Leon Bravy, Gurney & Son, and Beque-Sebastianutti

Admiral Farragut 351
    From an engraving of a photograph, said to be the last

The Farragut Funeral Procession in New York 376
    From *Harper's Weekly*, October 15, 1870

The Farragut Statue by Virginia Ream in Washington .. 377
    From a photograph by the L. C. Handy Studios, Washington

The Farragut Statue by Augustus Saint-Gaudens in New York 392
    After a photograph in Saint-Gaudens' *Reminiscences*

Admiral D. G. Farragut, U. S. Navy 393
    From the portrait by Henry A. Loop, owned by Dr. John J. Loughlin, New York

Admiral D. G. Farragut, U. S. Navy 400
    From the portrait by John F. Weir in the University Club, New York

ILLUSTRATIONS

PAGE

The Farragut Memorial Window 401
From a photograph of the central panel of the stained glass window in the Chapel of the U. S. Naval Academy, designed by Frederick Wilson, and presented by the Naval Academy Graduates Association in 1920

I

THE CALL TO ARMS

1

IT WAS Maytime in the year 1861. The Farraguts had arrived in the beautiful village of Hastings-on-Hudson, some fifteen miles north of the city of New York. They had learned of the place through Captain A. M. Pennock, U. S. Navy, the husband of Mrs. Farragut's cousin Margaret Loyall, who had resided there for awhile before the war.[1] It was a peaceful retreat for the harassed family, after their recent cruel separation from relatives and the sudden breaking of long pleasant associations in Norfolk, after a tiresome and somewhat terrifying journey north, and after the hurlyburly of preparations for war in the great metropolis where they had spent a few days with friends.

The six rooms occupied by the Farragut family constituted one half of a double house, now known as 60 Main Street.[2] The low rental of $150 a year pleased an officer whose income was then limited, as he was not on active duty and his future employment was quite uncertain. But Mrs. Farragut soon made a comfortable new home for her husband and sixteen year old son. Here she was to remain most of the time during the war, suffering the anguish of separation from her husband and, for a time, from her son "in peril on the sea." Here she was also to experience joy and exultation over her husband's victories and his rise to fame. Here the family was in time to form a new circle of friends; but the associations could never be as intimate and as cordial as the former ones in Norfolk, and Mrs. Farragut, though quite loyal to her husband's choice to the end, naturally was to pine for her old Southern home and kindred.

After establishing his family in their new home, Farragut wrote[3] the recently appointed Secretary of the Navy, Gideon

Welles, to inform him of his change of address and the reasons for his hurried departure from Norfolk. He had no further communication with the Navy Department until some seven weeks later when he returned his oath of allegiance, after it had been duly executed. In this he bound himself to serve the United States "honestly and faithfully, without any mental reservation, against all their enemies or opposers whatsoever."[4]

Three weeks afterwards Farragut went to Washington, and called upon Captain Charles Henry Davis, then Assistant to Captain Hiram Paulding, the Chief of the Bureau of Detail in the Navy Department. "Farragut . . . was here this morning," Davis wrote his wife on July 16.[5] "I was glad to see him." He had come to know Farragut intimately three years before when he took the *Saint Mary's* into the Mare Island Navy Yard for Farragut to refit her, and had then formed a very high opinion of him as an officer and a man. There is no evidence that Farragut met Secretary Welles. The particular purpose of his visit to the Navy Department is not certain, but Loyall Farragut relates[6] that in an unfinished letter his father requested the command of a fast war vessel with which he would endeavor to capture the *Sumter*, concerning the movements of which vessel he "had a theory." Apparently, this letter was never sent, but instead he decided to go and make a personal application for such a command. The *Sumter* under command of Captain Raphael Semmes had run the blockade off the mouth of the Mississippi River on June 30 and was causing consternation among merchantmen on the Atlantic.

Farragut appears to have returned home before the Battle of Bull Run, fought on July 21, and he thus missed the unique experience in Washington when the Government and the people of the Capital had the first rude awakening to the terror and the stark reality of war. To them there was little of the humor implied in the line from Benet's "John Brown's Body,"—"The Congressmen came out to see Bull Run."

Farragut's appearance in person at the Navy Department and the favorable opinion of Captain Davis gained for him no early active employment. For two whole months longer he was

Courtesy of Mrs. Edmund M. Devoe

THE FARRAGUT RESIDENCE IN HASTINGS-ON-HUDSON

From a drawing furnished by Mrs. Edmund M. Devoe and her sister, Miss M. Ella Dorland, the present owners of the house.

Captain David Glasgow Farragut, U.S.N.
After a photograph by E. Anthony, New York, early in 1862.
From author's collection.

to remain idle on the banks of the Hudson. There were two reasons for this. At that time there were not naval vessels enough to give commands to all officers, particularly in the higher ranks, and furthermore the Navy Department, according to Welles, "was moving with cautious, vigilant, and wary steps, careful and guarded whom to trust, and in the employment of Southern officers particularly circumspect."[7] Even in the quiet village of Hastings, the tongues of gossipers began to wag because Farragut, who hated above all things idleness and inactivity, took long walks over the surrounding beautiful hills. The villagers looked askance at the genial athletic old man, and repeated stories more dreadful than any Washington Irving had ever imagined about the gentle folks of the Hudson valley. This stranger from Norfolk, they concluded, was an agent of the Southern Confederacy, and on his long rambles he was perfecting plans for destroying the Croton Aqueduct in order to cut off the water supply of New York City. The aqueduct, indeed, ran only about thirty feet in rear of the Farragut cottage.[8]

Farragut could only wait with as much patience as he could muster until the Navy Department decided to call him into active service. Many evenings were pleasantly occupied in the observatory which the astronomer, Henry Draper, had built in Hastings in 1860. Many other evenings he spent in playing chess with Doctor Todd of Dobbs Ferry and Doctor Carter of the village.[8] Mrs. Farragut, a voracious reader, often read to her husband, whose eyes were very weak. Like him, she was fond of conversation and an excellent hostess. Life in such a household could never be dull. Horace Greeley then resided in Hastings, and he and Farragut probably met though there is no record of such a meeting. Politically, there would have been little in common between them. Farragut would not have agreed with Greeley's famous declaration in the New York *Tribune:* "If the cotton States shall decide that they can do better out of the Union than in it, we insist on letting them go in peace."

Meanwhile nothing very spectacular was happening on the sea in the war. After the loss of the Pensacola Navy Yard, Fort

Sumter, and the Norfolk Navy Yard, the Secretary of the Navy began to make preparations for carrying out an ambitious plan. There was to be a blockade of all Southern ports, which would involve also the control of the Potomac River. Combined naval and military expeditions were to be sent to capture strategic points on the Southern coast and on the Mississippi River. Finally, all Confederate cruisers and privateers on the high seas were to be relentlessly pursued and captured. The summer of 1861 was spent largely, therefore, in overhauling ships and fitting out those which could be purchased, and in training the personnel to man these ships as soon as they were ready. The first naval achievement of any consequence was the capture of Hatteras Inlet on August 26 by an expedition commanded by Flag-Officer Silas H. Stringham, accompanied by a small force of troops under Major-General Benjamin F. Butler. Farragut kept in close touch with the course of the war, and began to wonder, as the pleasant summer weeks passed, if Fate was again to play him the same trick it did during the War with Mexico when he was afforded no duty commensurate with his ability and previous experience.

It was, accordingly, with hands trembling with excitement and hope that Farragut opened a letter from Secretary Welles early in September.[9] His interest ebbed when he read that he was appointed to be a member of a board which was to convene in Washington on the following 16th. No greater was his pleasure the next day when another letter[9] arrived, which modified his orders and directed him to report to Commodore Hiram Paulding, then Commandant of the Brooklyn Navy Yard. Under him he was to serve on a board with Commodore Charles H. Bell, Surgeons Charles Chase and L. B. Hunter, and Philip Hamilton, Esquire as Judge Advocate.[10] The work of this board Welles thought "delicate and responsible, requiring sagacity, just discrimination, impartiality, and decision, for they were to take the Register and pass on the merits of each and every officer on the active list of the navy."[11] It was October 18 when the board first convened and Farragut commenced his first duty, such as it was, just about six months after the commencement of the war.

His impatience with duty under such an officer as Paulding, who as a victim of panic had abandoned the Norfolk Navy Yard to the Confederates, was accentuated by the news of a successful expedition of a fleet of fifty ships, including transports which carried about 13,000 troops under Brigadier-General Thomas W. Sherman. On November 7, this powerful fleet, commanded by Flag-Officer Samuel F. Du Pont, reduced Forts Walker and Beauregard and captured Port Royal, South Carolina. On the following day, Captain Charles Wilkes of the U.S.S. *San Jacinto* provoked trouble which almost led to war with Great Britain by stopping the British mail steamer *Trent* in West Indian waters and removing from her James M. Mason and John Slidell, Confederate commissioners to England and France respectively. Important events were taking place, and Farragut sat day after day turning the pages of the *Navy Register* and listening to the chatter of old commodores and medicos about dropping some poor devil from the service. It was maddening to a man of Farragut's temperament! To break the monotony of this drudgery he visited the shipyards in the vicinity of New York where naval vessels were under construction. The keel of the *Monitor* was laid on October 25 at Green Point, Long Island. Paulding was a member of the board which finally approved of her construction. Farragut was not favorably impressed; he never liked ironclads.

2

Meanwhile a plan was taking shape in Washington in the Navy Department which was to give to Farragut an opportunity for action beyond his fondest dreams. To get possession of the Mississippi River all the way to the Gulf of Mexico was one of the prime objects of the Lincoln administration; but the "idea of a naval conquest of New Orleans from the Gulf was not entertained by the army or the administration," declared Secretary Welles.[12] All plans called for a combined army and navy campaign down the river from Cairo, Illinois, as a base. This was the opinion as late as July 31, 1861. But between that date and the Port Royal expedition early in November, Welles had considered in a "speculative and uncertain"[13] way the practicability of capturing New Orleans from the south. Assistant Secretary of the Navy Gustavus Vasa Fox, who had become familiar with the Mississippi while he was in the merchant service, had the very decided opinion that the forts below New Orleans could be passed by a fleet without military assistance.[13] After the success at Port Royal, President Lincoln was made acquainted with the proposed plan of attack. Though interested, he was not at first impressed with its being better than the campaign down the river; but after further discussion, he was convinced and "came into the project."[14]

"About this time," Welles wrote,[14] "Commander D. D. Porter returned with the steam frigate *Powhatan* from an irregular cruise on which he had been improperly sent." After failing to carry out "the plan on which he had been surreptitiously dispatched"[14] by Secretary of State Seward to relieve Fort Pickens, he had been ordered to the Gulf Squadron and had been stationed off one of the mouths of the Mississippi River.[15] "On his return," continued Welles,[14] "the Navy Department, having decided to make a naval attack on the forts and the city, was glad to avail itself of his recent observations, and of whatever information he possessed in regard to the river and the forts. He was therefore questioned and soon taken into our confidence. He entered with zeal into the views of the Department but expressed great doubts whether the forts could be passed until reduced or seriously damaged. This he said might be effected by a flotilla of bomb vessels with mortars which could in forty-eight hours[16] demolish the forts or render them untenable. Commander Porter's proposition was a departure from the original plan of the Navy Department, and was strongly objected to by the Assistant Secretary."

The statement of Welles is corroborated by Montgomery Blair who declared that Fox, his brother-in-law, talked over the plan of capturing New Orleans from the south with him and that "Porter was also taken into council"[17] at his suggestion. He also wrote that Porter thought "the bombardment and reduction of Forts Jackson and St. Philip a necessary preliminary to the ascent of the fleet."[17]

But according to Porter's account,[18] he initiated the whole plan, and the details of what happened are almost wholly at variance with those set down by Welles and Blair and Fox. Porter had no such plan in mind on July 5, 1861 when he wrote a long letter from the Gulf of Mexico to Assistant Secretary Fox, in which he made not the slightest mention of any such attack on New Orleans.[19] "Porter never claimed to Blair or Grimes who knew at the time my suggestion as to attacking New Orleans," wrote Fox to Welles,[20] "but he did claim to agree with Barnard that the forts must first be reduced. He did not hear of the scheme until I had got Barnard's views which were finally put into writing. And it was probably this opinion of Barnard that led him to suggest the mortar boats. You had adopted the plan which was finally carried out before Porter was taken into the counsels of the Department." The score then is at least three to one against Porter's claim.

In any case, after a conference with Porter, a meeting was arranged by Welles to be held at the home of General George B. McClellan on the corner of H and 14th Street on the evening of the 15th of November. President Lincoln, General McClellan, Welles, Fox, and Porter were present.[21] When McClellan was made to understand that not an army of 50,000 men, as he had supposed, but only about 10,000 troops would be required to garrison the forts and hold the city after the fleet had captured them, "he came readily into the arrangement."[21] But the general decidedly approved Porter's proposal for a bomb flotilla as "absolutely essential for success,"[22] perhaps because this plan would insure the employment of troops in the capture of the forts. Fox still held doggedly to his original contention that "the steamers could pass the forts without reducing or even bombarding them. But in deference to military authority and the confident assertions of Commander Porter, the proposition of the latter for a mortar flotilla was adopted as an auxiliary force, which might render assistance and be of no detriment to the expedition," according to Welles.[22] After the final adoption of the plan, extreme secrecy was enjoined and the Navy Department was authorized to work out the details of the expedition. Thereupon the much bewhiskered gentlemen bade their not so heavily bearded host good night.

3

Now that a plan had been agreed upon, a much more difficult problem confronted Secretary Welles—the selection of a flag-officer to command the fleet which was to carry out the plan. The duty which this leader was to perform was unusual and, in the opinion of Mr. Welles,[23] "required courage, audacity, tact, and fearless energy, with great self-reliance, decisive judgment, and ability to discriminate and act under trying and extraordinary circumstances." The plan was kept a profound secret, and in the selection of a commanding officer for that particular mission it was made known merely that Flag-Officer William W. McKean, in command of the Gulf Squadron, was ill and a successor had to be found.

It is somewhat uncertain as to who first suggested the name of Farragut. Montgomery Blair claims[24] that, in looking over the *Navy Register* with the Secretary of the Navy, his brother-in-law Fox first called attention to Farragut's fitness. His principal reason for choosing him, Blair added, was the way he had cleared out from Norfolk after Virginia seceded. "This argued, in Mr. Fox's opinion, great superiority of character, clear perceptions of duty, and firm resolution in the performance of it."[24] But Welles declared that Farragut became a marked man in his mind when he was informed of the circumstances under which he left Norfolk.[25] These circumstances he had known since the receipt of Farragut's letter of the 1st of May. "I had met and been favorably impressed by Captain Farragut," Welles later wrote,[26] "some fifteen years previously during the Mexican War, when I was officiating in the Navy Department as chief of a naval bureau. He at that time made what was considered a remarkable proposition to the Secretary of the Navy, John Y. Mason, which was a plan to take the Castle of San Juan d'Ulloa. I was present when he stated and urged his plan. It was characterized by the earnest, resolute, and brave daring which at a later day was distinctly brought out in our great civil conflict.

Courtesy of F. H. Meserve, New York

SECRETARY OF THE NAVY GIDEON WELLES
From a contemporary unidentified photograph, called to the author's attention by Richard S. West, Jr.

GUSTAVUS VASA FOX, ASSISTANT SECRETARY OF THE NAVY
After an old engraving by H. B. Hall in *Fox's Mission to Russia*

Secretary Mason heard him patiently, but dismissed him with his project as visionary and impracticable. The officer and the interview I remembered." Thus after many years the bread which Farragut had cast upon the waters was to return to him.

Captains Joe Smith, Shubrick, Foote, and Dahlgren, in whom Welles confided, all spoke well of Farragut. Smith, who had been Chief of the Bureau of Yards and Docks while Farragut was Commandant of the Mare Island Navy Yard, replied to Welles's query, "I consider him a bold, impetuous man, of a great deal of courage and energy, but his capabilities and power to command a squadron are a subject to be determined only by trial."[27] Welles also records that Commander D. D. Porter was consulted and that he expressed confidence in Farragut. "As Porter himself was to take a conspicuous part in the expedition," added Welles,[28] "it had an important influence." He also mentioned that Farragut's early connection with Commodore David Porter was in his favor. Montgomery Blair added these significant and interesting details: "He [Farragut] had close relations with Porter, who was then regarded by Mr. Fox, as the great commander, and the command would have been given unhesitatingly to him if his rank had admitted of it. As this could not be done, Porter was given a command in the expedition to bring his influence to bear on Farragut in carrying out the programme, into which he entered warmly."[29] After the war, Welles admitted that in 1861 Farragut "was not more prominent than others of his grade," and declared, "Those great qualities which have since been brought out were dormant. He had a good but not a conspicuous record. All who knew him gave him the credit of being a good officer, of good sense and good habits, who had faithfully and correctly discharged his duty in every position to which he had been assigned."[30]

If the old sailors could have been consulted, Farragut would have been immediately chosen. They knew and accurately gauged their officers, according to Rear-Admiral Winfield Scott Schley. "It often happened in the long hours of the watch that the deck officer would consult with the quartermasters, always old and experienced seamen, about the weather or matters touching the qualities of the ship, etc. In one of these confidences, James Barnes, an old and competent quartermaster, said that 'the men for'd had heard that the Commodore [McKean] was ill and had to be sent home.' Almost immediately he volunteered the suggestion that if he had anything to do with it, he 'would pick out Cap'n Davy Farragut' to take his place. He added that if 'Davy Farragut came down there, it wouldn't be long till the fur was flying.' "[31]

The next step was to sound out Farragut to learn what his "ideas, feelings, and views"[32] were before the Secretary of the Navy committed himself to his choice. Because of Farragut's relations with the Porter family and because of Porter's being "let into the secret of the expedition,"[32] he was sent to New York "to ascertain, in personal interviews and conversations on naval matters and belligerent operations generally the views of Captain Farragut on the subject of such a programme and naval attack as was proposed by the Navy Department, without advising him of our object or letting him know that the Department had any purpose in Porter's inquiries or knew of them."[32]

The interview between Porter and Farragut took place in the Pierpont House in Brooklyn about the middle of December. The two men afforded a striking contrast in appearance and personality. "I found Captain Farragut," recorded Porter,[33] "the same active man I had seen ten years before. Time had added grey hairs to his head, and a few lines of intelligence, generally called 'crows' feet,' round his eyes. Otherwise he seemed unchanged. He had the same genial smile that always characterized him and the same affable manner which he possessed since I first knew him when I was quite a child and he a married man." Farragut was clean-shaven of face. This suggests some of his dominant traits: frankness, straight-forwardness, self-reliance, and hatred of the petty contrivances and chicanery to which many men resort for gaining advancement and position. One could not be so sure of what was behind the unusually thick black beard of the younger Porter, whose character will be further revealed in the interview, of which he flippantly wrote, "I often laugh over the scene that took place at Brooklyn when I called to see Farragut."[33]

After some preliminaries, Porter led the conversation round to Farragut's opinion of the naval officers who had resigned to join the Confederate Navy. Farragut replied, "Those damned fellows will catch it yet!" "I am glad to hear you talk that way," Porter said, and then asked, "Would you accept a command, such as no officer in our navy ever held, to go and fight those fellows whose conduct you so reprobate?" "What do you mean?" inquired Farragut. "I will tell you nothing until you have answered my question," answered black-bearded Porter, and then going quite beyond his instructions he added, "I am empowered to offer you the best command in the navy, if you will go in against the rebels and fight them to the last." To this Farragut slowly and sadly rejoined, "I cannot fight against Norfolk." "Then," said Porter, "you are not the man I came after, for Norfolk will be the very place to be attacked first, and that den of traitors must be wiped out." He was putting Farragut through a most cruel test, for his wife's relations and his former most intimate friends lived in Norfolk. The conversation went on and on for two hours, Porter endeavoring to convince poor Farragut that it was not a crime to fight against one's kindred. Finally the harassed man, torn between sympathy for his own people in the South and the obligation of his oath of allegiance to serve the United States "honestly and faithfully without any mental reservation, against all their enemies," made his decision. Jumping from his seat, he exclaimed, "I will take the command; only don't you trifle with me!" What kind of man was Porter who could afterwards "often laugh" at putting an honest loyal man on the rack in such an unnecessarily cruel fashion?

Porter, highly pleased with the successful outcome of his mission, bade Farragut goodbye with "You will hear in twenty-four hours what your fate will be," and departed to communicate the results to Fox.[34]

Of this famous interview, Farragut wrote very simply, "My

first intimation of that attack [on New Orleans] was a message through him [Porter] from the Department to know if I thought New Orleans could be taken, to which I replied in the affirmative. The next message was to know if I thought I could take it, to which I answered that I thought so and, if furnished with the proper means, was willing to try."[35]

4

With Farragut's selection practically decided, Welles wrote[36] him to proceed to Washington as soon as Captain Samuel Mercer arrived to relieve him. Farragut, accordingly, came to the Capital, arriving early enough on Saturday morning, December 21, to take breakfast at the home of Postmaster General Montgomery Blair.[37] Fox was also present, under instructions from Welles "to have a free, social, and discretionary talk with him."[38] After breakfast, Fox explained the plan to Farragut, with the objective to be gained and the forces to be used. "What is your opinion of it?" he then asked Farragut. Without the slightest hesitation, he replied briefly, "It will succeed." Fox then placed before him the list of the ships which were being fitted out for the expedition, and asked if they were enough. The instant reply was, "I will engage to run by the forts and capture New Orleans with two-thirds of the number." Fox smiled with satisfaction at Farragut's enthusiasm and said, "More vessels will be added to these, and you are to command the expedition." Farragut made no effort to conceal his delight and satisfaction. He was tremendously relieved to know that he was not to be sent to attack Norfolk, though his own brother's family lived in New Orleans and his sister resided at Pascagoula, Mississippi, and he was to fight against the husband of his wife's cousin, Captain John Mitchell, in command of the Confederate naval forces below New Orleans. So elated was Farragut over this favorable turn of Fortune's wheel that, when he had left, Blair, as he stroked his long sideburn, said to Fox, "Don't you think Farragut is too enthusiastic?" "No," answered the long-whiskered, bald-headed Assistant Secretary, "I was most favorably impressed with him, and I am sure he will succeed."

Welles was not present at this first momentous meeting with Farragut, and he has left no record of his first interview with the naval leader of whom he was to grow so fond. But in a letter which Farragut that day wrote[39] to his wife, he states that he had seen both Fox and Welles. So he probably went straight to the Secretary after the conference at Blair's. After warning his wife to burn his letter and observe "perfect silence," he told her the great news, "I am to have a flag in the Gulf and the rest depends upon myself." Welles did relate, however, that Farragut enthusiastically approved of the plan and accepted the command. As to the mortar flotilla, the Secretary reported Farragut to have said, "I would not have advised this, as these vessels will be likely to warn the enemy of our intentions, and I do not place much reliance upon them. But some of them have already been procured, and they may be more efficient and of greater benefit than I anticipate. So I willingly adopt the flotilla as a part of my command. To obey orders is my first duty; to take any risk that may be imposed upon me by the Government to obtain a great result I consider obligatory." At the conclusion of the interview, Farragut said, "I expect to pass the forts and restore New Orleans to the Government, or never return. I may not come back, but the city will be ours."[40] Welles was greatly pleased with Farragut's very evident self-reliance and belief in his ability to fulfill the expectation of the Government, and on the 23d of December he officially notified him to hold himself in readiness to take command of the West Gulf Squadron.

After Farragut was chosen, several doubted the wisdom of the Secretary's choice. Senator Hale wanted to know if Welles was certain of the loyalty of an officer of Southern birth and residence who had a Southern wife.[41] Neither the President nor any member of his Cabinet knew Farragut except, perhaps, Seward who was cordially disliked by Welles and not consulted. When informed of Farragut's appointment, Seward asked

Welles if it would not have been better to transfer Du Pont to that command.[42] That officer was then much in favor because of his capture of Port Royal. Some naval officers told Welles that they considered Farragut a daring, dashing fellow but of doubtful "discretion and ability to command a squadron judiciously."[42] After his choice had been gloriously vindicated, Welles set down in his diary of September 2, 1864: "Had any other man than myself been Secretary of the Navy, it is not probable that either Farragut or Foote would have had a squadron. . . . Neither had the showy name, the scholastic attainments, the wealth, the courtly talent, of Du Pont. But both were heroes." Later still he wrote of Du Pont: "[He] has ability, pride, and intrigue, but he has not the great essentials of a naval commander,—heroic valor, unselfish energy, and devotion to the country. Thinks of himself more than of the country and the service. No more accomplished officer could command our European Squadron, but he is not made for such terrific encounters as that of Farragut at Mobile and New Orleans, and as are necessary to resist Sumter and capture Charleston. He has too much pride to be a coward,—would sooner die than show the white feather,—but the innate fearless moral courage of Farragut or John Rodgers is not his."[43]

II

RENDEZVOUS IN THE GULF

1

WITH THE Secretary's letter[1] in his pocket, instructing him to hold himself in readiness to command a squadron of which the *Hartford* was to be the flagship, Farragut returned home to make preparations for taking over his new duties. On the day after Christmas he was in New York, looking for Captain Henry H. Bell, whom he wished to be his flag captain. Porter, who had talked more or less indiscreetly with Bell during his recent visit[2] to New York, had learned that he would like the post, and had so informed Farragut. Bell could not be located, and so Farragut with hands "so cold I can scarcly [sic] write" dashed off a note,[3] repeating the offer he had written him from Washington and instructing him to communicate with him at Willard's Hotel in the Capital. At six o'clock the same afternoon he and Mrs. Farragut with their seventeen year old son left by train for Philadelphia. Here the following day he inspected the *Hartford,* then being fitted out. She was soon to become his home for many, many months. He and Bell were to live in the poop cabin. After looking her over, he decided not to spend much in personal comforts as he expected only "hard service"[4] on this cruise.

On the 28th, the Farraguts continued their journey to Washington, where they remained until the 9th of January of the new year. Farragut then received his official appointment[5] to command the Western Gulf Blockading Squadron which was to operate from the mouth of the Rio Grande to the eastern shore of St. Andrew's Bay in "West Florida." He was to proceed to Philadelphia where he was to hoist his flag on the *Hartford* when she was ready for service. Further instructions would then be sent him.

One day during this stay in Washington, Farragut accompanied by Senator McDougal of California took his son Loyall to call upon President Lincoln in the White House. "This was the first and only time that I ever saw Mr. Lincoln," wrote[6] Loyall Farragut many years afterwards. "I remember well his tall, ungainly figure clothed in a long linen duster and his sad and kindly face as he stood with his elbow resting on a high desk, listening to my father's appeal." The purpose of the interview was to secure for Loyall an appointment as a midshipman in the United States Naval Academy. "Mr. President," said Captain Farragut, "I am about to depart on desperate service. I have devoted my whole life to the service of my country. It will be a great comfort to know that my son has received the appointment." Lincoln, after a short pause, replied, "Well! put in the application in writing and paint it in the most glowing colors." Then with a smile he shook hands cordially and withdrew to his inner office. Young Farragut did not get the appointment.

2

After receiving his orders, Farragut went back to Philadelphia to hasten the preparations for the sailing of the *Hartford*. Here his family remained with him at the Continental Hotel until he put to sea near the close of January. His flagship was then a comparatively new ship, having been launched in Boston in 1858. Her first cruise had been made to China the following year. She was one of four similar ships built about the same time: *Hartford, Richmond, Pensacola,* and *Brooklyn*.[7] Farragut had had a very unhappy cruise on the *Brooklyn* just before the war, and was thoroughly familiar with that type of steam sloop. A war with England being expected[8] at the time they were built, they were constructed with gun decks high above the water for ocean fighting even in a rough sea, a type of warfare, however, in which none of them were destined to participate. The length of the *Hartford* was 225 feet, her beam 44 feet, her draft 16 feet and 3 inches, and her tonnage 2,900. With the sails and spars of a full rigged ship plus her direct-acting engines, she could develop a speed of thirteen and one half knots

THE *Hartford* UNDER SAIL AND STEAM
From a sketch in *Harper's Weekly*, May 17, 1862.

U. S. Steam Sloop *Hartford*

From a painting by E. Arnold, made in 1862 at New Orleans and now in the National Museum in Washington.

Courtesy of United States National Museum

if conditions were favorable; under steam alone she could make only eight knots. Farragut placed on her six additional 9-inch Dahlgren shell guns, making a total of twenty-two besides two rifled 30-pounders on the poop and forecastle.[9] Later a 30-pounder Sawyer rifle was also placed on the forecastle,[10] and the fore and main tops were protected with quarter-inch rims of boiler-iron,[11] behind which howitzers were placed. The *Hartford* had very graceful lines, and with full sails spread to the breeze she was beautiful to behold. Farragut and his officers and men became greatly attached to her, and Mrs. Farragut called her "dear old *Hartford*."[12]

On the 19th of January,[13] the flagship was commissioned at the Philadelphia Navy Yard, and the square blue flag[14] of Flag-Officer Farragut was hoisted over her. Captain Henry H. Bell had accepted the post of fleet captain, and Captain Richard Wainwright was captain of the ship. On the 23rd she pushed her way down the Delaware through the ice to receive powder from Fort Mifflin,[13] two days later Farragut went aboard her, and then she "stood down and out to sea,"[13] with her prow pointed southward. The crew suffered much from the severe wintry weather, and when the ship arrived at Hampton Roads on the 29th, several were on the sick list with bad colds.[15] "You can better imagine my feelings," Farragut wrote his wife,[16] "at entering Hampton Roads as an enemy of Norfolk than I can. But, thank God, I had nothing to do with making it so."

3

At Hampton Roads, Farragut received additional men[17] for his crew who had recently arrived by steamer from Boston, and found awaiting him two long official letters of January 20th and 25th, containing final instructions. The first dispatch named specifically the thirty vessels which were to be turned over to him by Flag-Officer W. W. McKean to constitute the "Western Gulf Blockading Squadron."[18] It stated also that the bomb vessels and the armed vessels to tow them would be attached to the squadron, and that their commanding officer, D. D. Porter, would "be directed to report"[18] to him. "Completely ready, you will collect such vessels as can be spared from the blockade," ordered Welles, "and proceed up the Mississippi River and reduce the defenses which guard the approaches to New Orleans, when you will appear off that city and take possession of it under the guns of your squadron, and hoist the American flag thereon, keeping possession until troops can be sent to you."[18] If the expedition from Cairo had not by that time descended the river, he was to "take advantage of the panic to push a strong force up the river to take all their defenses in the rear." "You will also reduce the fortifications which defend Mobile Bay and turn them over to the army to hold,"[18] Welles threw in for good measure. As even more vessels would be attached to his squadron than Farragut considered sufficient, "the Department and the country will require of you success."[18] With a grand flourish, Welles brought his first letter to a close with these resounding words: "Destroy the armed barriers which these deluded people have raised up against the power of the United States Government, and shoot down those who war against the Union, but cultivate with cordiality the first returning reason which is sure to follow your success."[18]

The second letter[19] emphasized the importance of carrying on a vigorous blockade to prevent foreign governments from aiding or relieving the enemy on any excuse or pretext whatsoever. The squadron must be spread therefore so as effectively to guard the whole coast from the Mexican border to the eastward of Pensacola. McKean with his base at Key West was to command the "Eastern Gulf Blockading Squadron" and blockade to the eastward as far as Cape Canaveral on the Florida Coast.

After reading these instructions, Farragut wrote[20] Welles that he would endeavor to carry out the "wishes of the Department," and that there would be "no lack of exertion" on his part in the service of his country. To Fox he wrote,[21] the same day, a much longer letter, expressing general satisfaction with the forces assigned to his command, but adding, "My greatest anxiety now is to have proper comforts for the sick and wounded, for somebody will be hurt."[21] He then went into details regarding the fitting out of a hospital ship. "I am familiar with these operations," he continued, "as I was a quiet looker-on in Vera Cruz, when the French attacked that place; and made many notes of all their arrangements. They had a frigate well fitted for the purpose with every facility for getting the men on board without torment."[21] More medical officers would be needed; sailors must not be allowed to bleed to death for want of tourniquets, he warned. He had no illusions as to the realities and needs of a naval battle.

When he had gotten in ordnance stores sent down from Annapolis[22] and had received sailing orders[23] from Welles, Farragut put to sea again on the 2d of February. Two days later he was off Port Royal communicating with Flag-Officer Du Pont, burying on shore a member of his crew who had just died, and securing coal for the *Hartford*. His ship, he reported, had performed very well on the voyage, though she was slow under steam and "will do nothing against the wind."[24] On the 6th, the *Hartford* was off again to the southward,[25] and making rather slow speed against head winds, the sturdy vessel sailed into Key West five days later. Here Farragut found the *Pensacola,* one of the vessels to constitute his squadron, and six of Porter's bomb vessels. He had some bad news to relate to the Secretary,[26] to the effect that some of the gunboats were in such a state that they would have to be sent north for repairs, and that none of the vessels attached to his squadron were suitable for service in shallow waters. He complained also of the inefficiency of the *Hartford's* crew, but hoped that Commander Wainwright and his officers would be able to get them in condition in due time. The need for vessels of not more than five feet draft seemed so imperative to Farragut that he wrote a second letter to Welles the same day, begging him to send two or three such vessels on each of which two or three 20-pound rifles could be placed.[27] He wrote to Fox also that these vessels of lighter draft "are almost indispensable," and that one of the greatest difficulties to be met on the Southern coast was the shallowness of the waters.[28] There were suggestions, as well, about the delivery of coal, and the need of medical officers and mechanics. It was the beginning of the continual begging for more suitable ships, more men, and better and more adequate supplies which Farragut found it necessary to keep up throughout his service in the Gulf.

With a fresh supply of coal in her bunkers, the *Hartford* ran over to Havana on February 15. Here then lay some French and Spanish ships belonging to the allied fleet which had gathered in the West Indies to force Mexico to pay her debts, though France had the ulterior plan of placing Maximilian on the Mexican throne. A number of Confederate vessels were in the harbor also, waiting for an opportunity to make a dash into some Southern port. Farragut went to Havana to consult with the American Consul relative to the enforcement of the blockade. Arriving off Morro Castle after dark, when the port regulations did not permit entrance into the harbor, he boldly steamed in to show his contempt for the unfriendliness of the authorities to the United States. "Who are you?" came a hail. Farragut answered through his speaking trumpet, "United States Flagship *Hartford*, from Key West bound for Havana harbor." "Louder! Louder!" cried the voice in Spanish, which Farragut well understood. Lowering his speaking trumpet with a gesture of impatience, Farragut ordered, "Give her four bells, Captain Wainwright,"—in other words, "Full speed ahead." The next day he courteously saluted the Governor General and the various commodores of the allied fleet, though there was not a vessel in the harbor whose commander would not have taken pleasure in sinking the *Hartford*. When at sea again on the 17th, Farragut drew a long breath and remarked to Captain Bell, "Well, thank God! I am more than pleased to be out of that infernal hole. I've been mad clear through, and if it had not been for the work ahead, nothing would have suited me better than giving those fellows a dose of 9-inch shells. We may have to do it yet before this war is over."[29]

This experience may have reminded Farragut, while at Havana, to write his old friend, Captain A. A. Harwood,[30] Chief of the Bureau of Ordnance, and make a large requisition for ordnance stores in addition to those taken on at Fortress Monroe. When at sea, he wrote[31] again to the Secretary about the need for light draft ships. American Consul Shufeldt had told him that small vessels continually arrived loaded with cotton from the South, which had come out through "little places that it would not be supposed anything larger than a rowboat could pass."[31] Small light draft blockaders alone could stop them, he declared. On the afternoon of February 20, the long voyage of the *Hartford* came to an end with her arrival at Ship Island.

4

This rendezvous was a small island, lying about thirty miles to the south of Biloxi, Mississippi. It was so named because its shape suggested that of a ship with bow pointed towards Lake Borgne and New Orleans and stern toward Pascagoula Bay and Mobile. When a boy, Farragut had often sailed near this low barren island in making voyages through Mississippi Sound with his father from New Orleans to his plantation at Pascagoula.

Fortunately Farragut found Flag-Officer McKean at Ship Island on his arrival, and so no time was lost in arranging with him the details of the transfer of the ships to his command. The day following his arrival he wrote Welles urging the immediate sending of more coal, of which there were then only 400 tons at that base, and requesting machine tools to make ordinary repairs to engines which were repeatedly breaking down.[32] The next day he sent Halter, an assistant of the Coast Survey, to make soundings and place buoys at Southwest Pass and Pass à l'Outre, leading into the Mississippi.[33] That day he also sent Captain Thomas T. Craven with the *Brooklyn* to seize the telegraphic operator and his apparatus at the head of the passes in the Mississippi, and to cut all communications with New Orleans. He was ordered also to capture all the river pilots at that place and bring them to Ship Island. He was to take with him all the vessels on blockade at the mouth of the river whose draft would permit them to enter freely, and then remain on the alert against surprise on that station until he received further orders.[34] Soon a constant stream of orders was on the way by steam dispatch boat to various captains of ships to meet the *Hartford* at Southwest Pass. By February 25, the *Vincennes*,

Preble, Colorado, Brooklyn, Winona, and *Kineo* had gathered there; but communications in those days were relatively slow and many days were to pass before the entire fleet was assembled.

Farragut prepared an extraordinarily detailed general order, giving instructions for the preparation of the vessels for service in the Mississippi. All topgallant masts were to be taken down and all the spars and rigging were to be landed that could be spared. "Send down the topgallant masts, rig in the flying jib-boom, and land all the spars and rigging except what are necessary for the three topsails, foresail, jib, and spanker," the orders read in detail. "Trice up the topmast stays, or land the whiskers, and bring all the rigging into the bowsprit, so that there shall be nothing in the range of the direct fire ahead."[35] One or two guns were to be mounted on the poop and topgallant forecastle, and howitzers were to be placed in the foretop and maintop. Grapnels were to be always ready for towing off fireships. Each vessel was to be trimmed a few inches by the head so that, if she touched bottom, she would not swing head down the river. If machinery were injured, she must "back and fill down under sail" and in no case "attempt to turn the ship's head downstream." "No vessel," Farragut admonished, "must withdraw from battle under any circumstances without the consent of the flag-officer." Dozens of other details were covered; such as, fire fighting, stopping of shot holes during battle, boarding an enemy vessel, and handling the guns most efficiently. "I wish you to understand," he warned, "that the day is at hand when you will be called upon to meet the enemy in the worst form for our profession. You must be prepared to execute all those duties to which you have been so long trained in the Navy."[35] Every one of Farragut's captains, upon reading this first general order, must have stood a little more erect as his face grew sterner. Thus Farragut commenced to develop morale in his fleet.

Meanwhile a party was sent ashore at Biloxi, which, as Farragut expressed it in a letter to his wife, "robbed the post office of a few papers."[36] In these he read with great satisfaction of the fall of Fort Donelson on the Tennessee River and the capture of Nashville, and of the apparent demoralization in New Orleans, which led him to believe that the time was opportune for an attack on that city.

On March 2, the *Pensacola* arrived at Ship Island just ahead of a norther which blew for nearly twenty-four hours. This arrival was very fortunate as her engines were in such a state that the engineer reported that he was afraid they would literally break to pieces.[37] Among the dispatches brought by the *Pensacola* was a confidential letter[38] from Welles enclosing sketches of the defenses below New Orleans prepared by the Engineer Department and a long memorandum on the forts by Brigadier-General John G. Barnard. "The most important operation of the war is confided to yourself and your brave associates," reminded Secretary Welles. Eighteen thousand troops were on the way to cooperate, and six more ships of war were being ordered to join him with all "practicable dispatch." "You will, however, carry out your instructions with regard to the Mississippi and Mobile without any delay beyond that imposed upon you by your own careful preparation," declared Welles, who concluded, "The Department relies upon your skill to give direction to the powerful force placed at your disposal, and upon your personal character to infuse a hearty cooperation amongst your officers free from unworthy jealousies. If successful, you open the way to the sea for the great West, never again to be closed. The rebellion will be riven in the centre, and the Flag to which you have been so faithful will recover its supremacy in every State."

The gunboat *Kennebec*, Lieutenant Commanding John H. Russell, came in on March 5, and the same day Captain Alden arrived with the *Richmond* after barely escaping shipwreck on Florida Reef. That day Farragut wrote Fox, "The moment Captain Porter arrives with his Mortar Fleet, I will collect my vessels, which are pretty close around me, and dash up the river, but I do not wish to make a display before I am ready, as I wish to keep up the delusion that Mobile is the first object of attack."[39]

Porter was then at Key West where he had arrived on the 28th of February in the ex-revenue cutter *Harriet Lane*, his flagship. Here he found his twenty mortar schooners.[40] Delayed by the slow arrival of all his seven towing steamers, he finally set out for Ship Island on March 6 in the *Harriet Lane* with two of his steamers and the mortar boats under their own sail. Five days later all had reached the rendezvous in safety.[41] Farragut meanwhile had gone impatiently, on March 7, to the mouth of the Mississippi to begin operations, but Porter on his arrival very ungenerously wrote to Fox, "Farragut is not ready for us yet."[41]

During the two weeks Farragut had been at Ship Island, he had spent many weary hours in the cabin of the *Hartford* reading official dispatches or listening to his clerk read them when his weak eyes made this necessary. Then all of these communications had to be answered. They were concerned with the organization of the fleet with which he expected to force his way to New Orleans. Orders had to be dispatched to those selected for this service in order that they might gather off the mouth of the Mississippi. Other vessels had to be shifted from one station to another in the blockade of more than a thousand miles of coast line which had been assigned to his squadron. For this purpose he had available only about thirty vessels, less than half of which had steam propulsion; and they had to be placed carefully. There was no end to the letters to be written concerning shipments of coal and other provisions, repairs to ships, and matters of discipline. An example of the last, was the unpleasant duty of carrying out the detachment of Captain T. O. Selfridge from the command of the *Mississippi* because he had not attacked the Confederate ram *Manassas* when she went aground inside Pass à l'Outre and remained there thirty hours in sight of his vessel.[42] Numerous letters from American consuls in Mexican and other ports informing the government of ships that were loading to run the blockade were relayed to Farragut through the Secretary of the Navy. All of this monotonous labor had to be done, and there seemed no end to it. Before one great pile of papers was finished, a dispatch boat always arrived with more. This was to prove to be Farragut's heaviest burden during his wearisome campaigns on the Mississippi. He much preferred fighting to writing.

III

THE VICTORY OVER MUD

1

For a while it looked as though all of Farragut's well laid plans would be disrupted by mud, strange as it may sound. This was not that "General Mud" which armies frequently have to contend with; rather it might be called "Admiral Mud." Mud had become a dangerous barrier, the first line of defense for the Confederates, because the Delta of the Mississippi, which extends like a scrawny chicken's foot down into the Gulf of Mexico, had five passes or mouths, at the entrance to each of which was a bar formed by the enormous deposits made there by Old Man River. These bars were continually shifting, pilots were constantly sounding in order to retain a correct knowledge of the channels, and dredging had to be often resorted to in order to keep them open to navigation. The war had interfered with this careful supervision, and Farragut unexpectedly soon realized that he had a tremendous job on his hands to get his heavier ships across these bars.

Farragut first attempted to get the *Brooklyn* into Pass à l'Outre. For three days every possible exertion was made to get her over. She drew only sixteen feet of water, but for many weeks there had been no daily passing of large ships which had formerly kept the channel open for vessels of her draft. She accordingly went aground and for seventeen hours lay on the bar. Much discouraged, Farragut decided to give up the attempt and pulled her off with the *Hartford*. He and Captain Craven then proceeded around to the westward side of the Delta and made an attempt at Southwest Pass. Here the *Brooklyn* passed through, only grounding once for an hour, and the next day, which turned out to be a lucky March 13, the *Hartford* also succeeded in getting over the bar into the river.[1]

Farragut then proceeded to the head of the passes where they converge in the main stream of the mighty river, and anchored off Pilot Town. This was then a miserable village of some dozen houses on a mud bank, built on piles with the river flowing underneath. Among its inhabitants were two German fishermen and an Italian "pickler of oysters by trade and a big scamp by looks," who gave the place a cosmopolitan character.[2] It had already been captured by the gunboats and preparations had been made for stores and hospital facilities. Farragut proudly announced to Welles, "Our flag is now, I hope, permanently hoisted on Louisiana soil."[3] From this point, Fleet Captain Bell made a reconnaissance on March 12 up the river with the gunboats *Winona, Kineo,* and *Kennebec,* chased two steamers which turned round and fled upon being sighted, and proceeded almost to a point within sight of the forts.[4]

2

But Farragut had won only the first round in the contest with mud. While engaged at Pass à l'Outre with the *Brooklyn,* he wrote[5] his wife: ". . . Success is the only thing listened to in this war, and I know that I must sink or swim by that rule. Two of my best friends have done me a great injury by telling the Department that the *Colorado* can be gotten over the bar into the river, and so I was compelled to try it, and take precious time to do it. If I had been left to myself, I would have been in before this." Alden was one who advised it could be done,[6] and probably the other friend was her commander, Captain Theodorus Bailey. That Farragut had impressed his captains with his energy is shown by Porter's statement to Fox, "Farragut is zealous, they say, and will try to get them all over if he bursts his boiler, but I don't think they will lighten the ships much by merely scraping the outside paint blisters off."[7] This was long range criticism, for Porter was still at Ship Island when he wrote the letter, and it was two days later when he first advised Farragut of the arrival of the mortar fleet.[8]

It became necessary to send the *Colorado,* drawing twenty-three feet, the *Pensacola,* and the *Mississippi* back to Ship

Island to be lightened.[9] On March 17, Farragut himself went there in the gunboat *Winona*[10] to oversee the operations and attend to other duties of the squadron. Here with the advice of Alden, Porter, and Bailey, Farragut decided it was impossible to lighten the *Colorado* enough to get her into the river, but that she should be taken to the entrance to Southwest Pass where she could furnish extra guns and men to the other ships of the fleet. But another attempt was to be made with the *Mississippi* and the *Pensacola*,[11] which were to be lightened of everything but coal enough to steam with, as they drew about eighteen feet. Then they would have to be pulled through at least a foot of mud by tugs.[12]

On the 19th, Porter began towing his mortar flotilla into the river through Pass à l'Outre, and in a couple of days his whole squadron including the seven gunboats had joined Farragut's two sloops and four gunboats already inside.[13] Farragut, still at Ship Island on the 21st where he had been detained by a gale of wind, wrote Fox a letter, ending with this interesting revelation of his state of mind: ". . . I am fully aware of what I have to encounter, and will endeavor to prepare for it in the best manner; but it is a hand to hand business, and the hardest must fend off; but it is just what I like; something *decided,* comes up to the old saying, 'a golden chain or a wooden leg' or still more likely 'Death or Victory.' I have no fears but all will do their duty, and if Fortune does not frown upon us, we will be in the land of promise in less than ten days. . . . If I succeed I will have my reward. God grant that we may, more for the sake of my country than myself."[14] Two days later, he expressed his feelings to his wife. "I have now attained," he wrote, "what I have been looking for all my life—a flag—and having attained it, all that is necessary to complete the scene is a victory. If I die in the attempt, it will only be what every officer has to expect. He who dies in doing his duty to his country, and at peace with his God, has played out the drama of life to the best advantage."[15]

Farragut returned to Southwest Pass in the little gunboat *Miami* on the 24th. Four days previous, Major-General Benjamin F. Butler reached Ship Island. Most of his troops had already arrived ten days before.[16] Farragut had a very pleasant conference with the bald-headed, eagle-beaked, cross-eyed general, whom he found to have no plan but "to follow in my wake and hold what I can take."[15]

After two days of unsuccessful attempts, Captain Alden got the *Richmond* across the bar on March 24.[17] But the real struggle came in trying to get the old *Mississippi* and the *Pensacola* into the river. It took ten days of pulling and hauling to get the first one over and about two weeks for the latter. At the last, a southerly wind helped materially. The assistance of Porter's towing steamers was invaluable, and Farragut gave him full credit in a letter to Fox.[18] But Porter wrote sharp criticisms of the commanding officers of both these vessels, calling them old fogies. Farragut, he declared, should have required "greater promptitude in his captains."[18] "It is very difficult for a man of his age finding himself commanding so large a force for the first time in his life who would have done better," he admitted, "but I am free to say that this matter throughout has not been well managed."[19] Younger men, he thought, should be in command of the ships; "then an elderly Flag-Officer could get support."[19] Still in a later letter to Fox, he wrote, "There is no professional energy among the younger men here."[20]

3

When Fox read Farragut's letters from Key West, asking for light draft vessels, he did not understand that they were to be used in the blockade, and sat down on February 24 and wrote Porter confidentially, "A cold shudder ran through me.... I trust we have made no mistake in our man, but his dispatches are very discouraging. *It is not too late to rectify our mistake.* You must frankly give me your views from Ship Island, for the cause of our country is above all personal considerations. ... I shall have no peace until I hear from you."[21] Welles replied[22] to Farragut's request personally under the same misapprehensions as to the intended use of the shallow draft vessels, and stated that no such ships were available and that they would be "totally unfit to attack the enemy's works." In closing, he reminded him that many more vessels had been added to his squadron than had been thought necessary when he was in Washington.

Fox's peace of mind was destined to be long disturbed, for it was just a month later, March 28, when Porter found time to reply with an enormously long letter, marked "Private and Confidential."[23] But probably by the time this long epistle reached Fox his confidence in Farragut had been restored, and he may have felt ashamed that he had ever written such a letter. Porter began by stating, "If as you suppose there is any want of the proper qualities in the Flag-Officer, it is too late now to rectify the mistake; but as yet I see no reason why he should not be competent to do all that is expected of him. I never thought Farragut a Nelson, or a Collingwood; I only consider him the best of his rank and so consider him still; but men of his age in a seafaring life are not fit for the command of important enterprises, they lack the vigor of youth." He continued with an account of the delay in getting the larger vessels into the river, and went into great detail describing his assistance and the lack of intelligence of everybody else except Baldwin and Renshaw, two of his own officers. He had not learned what Farragut's plans were. "He talks very much at random at times," Porter added critically, "and rather underrates the difficulties before him, without fairly comprehending them. I know what they are and appreciate them, and as he is impressible hope to make him appreciate them also." Coal was the greatest need, and for the lack of it he blamed Farragut's predecessor, McKean, and also Farragut. "I only considered Farragut the best of his rank," he repeated; "his administrative abilities are not of the first order." Then he remarked seriously, not jestingly, "I have great hopes of the mortars if all else fails." And so the letter rambles on interminably about all sorts of things, general and personal. "The Flag will be urged to move at once, the moment we get the bar clear of the ships," he threw in reassuringly, toward the end.

In a second rather long letter[24] to Fox ten days later Porter wrote even more depreciatingly of Farragut, "Again I say he is physically and mentally the best of his rank, except perhaps Du Pont, Goldsborough, and Foote. He is full of zeal and anxiety, but has no administrative qualities, wants stability, and loses too much time in talking. Everyone likes him personally. He is as brave as anyone, but is neither a Nelson nor a Collingwood." With complete confidence in his mortars, he added, "If I can get all my shells here shortly, I think the game is ours."

It was fortunate that, during the delays and disappointments incident to the struggle against mud, Farragut did not know what Fox and his own subordinate officer, Porter, were writing about him "confidentially." It was also fortunate that communications were then so slow that both lack of confidence in Farragut and undermining criticism mixed with praise from Porter were all buried under an avalanche of victory before any harmful results ensued.

Knowing of this correspondence, Farragut probably could not have written to his wife these brave words.[25] "The defeat of our army at Corinth, which I saw in the rebel papers, will give us a much harder fight; men are easily elated or depressed by victory. But as to being prepared for defeat, I certainly am not. Any man who is prepared for defeat would be half defeated before he commenced. I hope for success; shall do all in my power to secure it, and trust to God for the rest. I trust in Him as a merciful being; but really in war it seems as if we hardly ought to expect mercy, when men are destroying one another upon questions of which He alone is the judge. Motive seems to constitute right and wrong."[25]

During those trying days it was mud and coal that gave Farragut most concern—too much of the one and too little of the other. The Navy Department handled the problem of supplies so clumsily and dilatorily that, even if Farragut had conquered the mud two weeks earlier than he did, he would have been stuck in the river for lack of coal. Great was his relief, therefore, when toward the end of the first week in April vessels began to arrive loaded with this precious fuel.²⁶ Even that late he was greatly concerned over the lack of medical supplies, when he was informed that there was not enough material in the whole fleet to dress two hundred wounded men.²⁷ This was not his fault for he had made large requisitions for such articles at Hampton Roads, and had written to the Navy Department repeatedly for medical supplies and more surgeons.

With his fleet all safely through the passes, except the *Colorado*, Farragut had the river completely blocked; but that did not mean that New Orleans was entirely cut off from all connection by water with the Gulf. From Lake Pontchartrain small ships could pass into Lake Borgne and thence to sea, and from the Gulf ships could enter Barataria Bay and then proceed through winding channels and lakes to places near the city. Farragut had suggested to Fox from Havana that he capture Fort Livingston and thus close up the latter avenue of approach; but the answer was in the negative. Farragut's idea was to capture the fort while waiting for Porter's flotilla. In his reply, Fox warned, "Our friend Foote will be ahead of you, if he continues his successes in the West as he is about to move down the river with his ironclad boats and thirty mortar boats. A success at Fort Livingston would cause some delay and might tend to strengthen the other forts."²⁸ Farragut received this letter about the time he learned through other sources of Foote's success²⁹ at Island No. 10, and it made him all the more anxious to take New Orleans as soon as possible.

But Farragut had to worry also about the blockade. When two vessels ran out from New Orleans, only three days after his arrival at Ship Island, Welles wrote him a letter filled with "surprise and regret."³⁰ But shortly afterwards his gunboats on their way to the rendezvous captured four Confederate schooners laden with cotton, and this he proudly reported to the Secretary.³¹ He also wrote to explain how useless his sailing vessels were and how much he was in need of light draft ships to blockade Berwick Bay.³²

With so many details to attend to, with so many obstacles to be overcome, and with practically no workshops for repairs to the ships, the wonder is that in six weeks after his arrival at Ship Island he had organized a fighting fleet without materially weakening the blockade, and had gotten it into the Mississippi ready for a dash towards New Orleans.

IV

FINAL PLANS AND PREPARATIONS

1

IT IS NOW time to take a look at Farragut's fleet assembled at the head of the passes. There were seventeen men-of-war, excluding Porter's flotilla. The largest were four ship rigged screw steamer sloops of approximately 3,000 tons. They had a length of 225 feet and were armed with twenty-four 9-inch Dahlgren smoothbores, except the *Brooklyn* which carried only twenty-two. They had also two rifles each, 6-inch, or 20-pounder, or 30-pounder, and carried two or more howitzers. The old sidewheeler *Mississippi*, though as long as the *Hartford*, had a tonnage of only 1,732 and carried but one 10-inch and fifteen 8-inch smoothbores and one 20-pounder rifle.[1] Three of the largest class of the screw steamer gunboats had a tonnage of slightly over 1,000, a length of about 200 feet, and an armament of ten, nine, and six guns respectively, varying from 11-inch smoothbores to 30-pounder rifles. The remaining nine screw steamer gunboats, of about 500 tons, were 158 feet long, and carried one 11-inch Dahlgren smoothbore and one or two light rifles. The total armament of the fleet was twelve 11-inch, two 10-inch, ninety-six 9-inch, twenty-three 8-inch, and eight 32-pounders, all smoothbore guns, and two 6-inch, eight 30-pounders, and fourteen 20-pounders, all rifles. The howitzers, sixteen in number, were either 24- or 12-pounders. The grand total of guns amounted to 165, raised to 181 by the howitzers.

Porter's mortar flotilla, twenty in number, each carried one 13-inch mortar. Fifteen of them were armed also with two 32-pounders each, while eleven had two 12-pounder howitzers. His seven steam gunboats, all but one of which were sidewheelers, had a total armament of twenty-seven guns, from

11-inch to 6-inch in calibre.² These gunboats were somewhat larger than Farragut's smallest vessels.

The ships had immediately begun to make final preparations for battle, the most ingenious of which were provisions for the protection of the crews and ships as far as possible from all hazards. A remarkable suggestion originated with Engineer Moore³ of the *Richmond*. This involved the arranging of the sheet cables on the sides of the ship so as to form a kind of chain armor for the engines. This idea was at once adopted by all the captains of the other ships. The chain cables were suspended from an iron rod which was fastened with eye-bolts to the ship's side about eight feet above the water. By placing one strand or bight of cable over the next one so that the large links, an inch and a half in diameter, overlapped, a coat of mail was devised extending about two feet below the water line.⁴ Great quantities of sand were taken on board—as much as 150 tons by the crew of the *Richmond* one night.⁵ This was placed in bags, which were stacked about the engines and machinery, down in the storerooms, against the water line in the holds to protect the surgeons, in the bows and under the topgallant forecastle to stop raking shots, and between the guns and against the bulwarks. Even the propeller well was filled with sand or coal. The latter, together with bags of wet ashes and even bags of clothes, was piled here and there where it might serve as some protection. Large nettings, made of 2-inch ropes, were arranged to cover the decks and protect the men from falling spars and splinters. The ships, including guns and rigging, were either painted a mud color⁵ or merely rubbed all over with mud¹³; while the decks and gun carriages of some were whitewashed so that the handspikes, tackle falls, and ammunition could be more readily seen during a night attack.⁶ At the main hatch, arrangements were made for lowering the wounded to the berth-deck. Grapnels and chains were provided in the whale boats for towing fire ships away from the vessels. All ships which had not already done so at Ship Island removed all unnecessary spars, rigging, and boats and landed them at Pilot Town.⁷

Farragut was here and there in the fleet from early dawn to

dark. Sometimes as early as six o'clock he would be rowed alongside a ship and, hailing the watch officer, would inquire if all was well.[4] Such enthusiasm became contagious. All his men were impressed with his energy, his winning smile and charming manner, and his jovial, talkative friendliness. At a dinner which Captain Alden gave on the *Richmond*, Surgeon Foltz, who was present, recorded that "the Flag-Officer, who was among the number, did the talking for half the company."[8] A midshipman remembered all his life how Farragut told him that he always celebrated his birthday by turning a handspring, and would not consider that he was an old man as long as he could do that.[4] Those immediately associated with him fairly worshiped him, and all admired his determination and self-confidence.[12]

Fleet Captain Henry H. Bell, stern of face which was smooth-shaven like that of Farragut, was an excellent organizer and administrator of details, and he took upon his broad shoulders many of the Flag-Officer's burdens. The last of March, Bell had made a second reconnaissance with two gunboats, going up the river to the extreme range of the forts, and examined closely the defenses for half an hour in spite of the shells which fell within a half cable's length of his vessel.[10] Captain Theodorus Bailey, a real sea dog without fear, also had Farragut's complete confidence, and because the *Colorado* could not get into the river, Farragut made him second in command of the fleet and commander of the first division of the gunboats.[9]

On the morning of April 5, the *Iroquois* with Farragut, Captain Bell, and Mr. Osbon on board, accompanied by four other gunboats, steamed up the river, and after three hours came in sight of the forts and the boom of eight dismasted vessels chained together across the stream.[11] The gunboats were fired on, and the sailors were amused at the way some of the "quarter-deck party" ducked and bobbed and dodged. Farragut, like an old bulldog, stood immovable on the horse-block with his glass in hand. "There comes one!" he would cry. "There! There!!" As the shot splashed in the water near, he would add nonchalantly, "Ah, too short; finely lined though!"[12]

2

After about a week of final preparation, the fleet began to move up the Mississippi on April 14, and in two days all had arrived, including mortar flotilla, below the Confederate defenses.[13] Shortly afterwards, a French squadron came down from New Orleans on the way out to sea. According to Surgeon Foltz, their admiral signaled with reference to the forts, "You will find them very strong." In reply Farragut signaled, "I shall take them by audacity." Foltz thought that the French were touched by the word "l'audace," though their sympathies were with French-speaking New Orleans.[14]

On the 17th of April, Farragut issued very important orders. According to these, Captain Bailey was to keep his division of six gunboats: *Oneida, Varuna, Katahdin, Kineo, Wissahickon,* and *Cayuga* in their order of sailing in line ahead. During the attack he was to endeavor to get a sufficient number of his gunboats past the forts to protect the landing of troops above them, and from there he was to enfilade the forts and aid in their capture, "should they not surrender at the first bombardment."[15] An important general order was issued the same day directing vessels, in case of alarm, not to get under way and not to commence firing without orders from the Flag-Officer. There was also to be a blackout of all lights at night.[16] At daylight that day a fire raft had floated down the river, and though towed away from the ships, it had caused much alarm and confusion. Probably this occasioned the general order and another[17] distributed at the same time directing how the boats of the fleet should be provided for dealing with fire rafts, which were to be kept in midchannel while the vessels were to be anchored close inshore. Early that evening another fire raft came down, and these orders were immediately carried out. That day also numbers were assigned to be painted on the smokestacks of the gunboats so that they could more easily be recognized in battle.[18]

Meanwhile members of the Coast Survey had surveyed and triangulated about seven miles of the river below the forts, marking accurately the positions for the mortar vessels to be

FINAL PLANS AND PREPARATIONS 37

placed; and on April 16, Porter brought three of them up to try the range.[19] In reply, Fort Jackson became active—a little white smoke, bang-whiz-whiz-crack-splash and then a white circle on the muddy surface of the water.[20] The test was complete. The next day all the little mortar schooners were towed into position near the western bank of the stream just below the bend where they were protected from view from Fort Jackson, 2,850 yards away from the nearest bomb vessel, by a thick woodland filled with interwoven vines. To further conceal the little vessels, branches of trees were tied to their masts. These also concealed observers at the mastheads.[19]

The stage was thus set for the play to begin. The occasional firing by the gunboats and the deep throated answers from the forts on the 16th and the 17th were merely the tuning of the orchestra for the tremendous crescendos which were soon to follow.

By that time Farragut had not prepared any written detailed plan of battle. According to Welles's orders,[21] the forts were first to be reduced, and Porter was to have a try at this with his mortar flotilla. If that failed, Farragut no doubt knew already what he would do, but no plan was put on paper until the 20th of April. He had been carefully reading and studying the descriptive memorandum relating to Forts Jackson and St. Philip, prepared by Brigadier-General Barnard and forwarded to him by Secretary Welles. "Would it be prudent, however," read Farragut in this official paper, "supposing these works to be at all formidably armed, to force a passage, leaving them behind intact, while the fleet advanced on New Orleans? I think not, unless, perchance, in conjunction with an attack to be made on the city by a large land force from Lake Borgne or Pontchartrain. . . . To pass these works merely with a fleet and appear before New Orleans is merely a raid, no capture."[22] Soon Farragut would have to give his answer to Barnard's question and put his answer to the cold test of actual trial.

V

BARRIERS TO NEW ORLEANS

1

AFTER CONQUERING "Admiral Mud" and getting the fleet into the river, Farragut had yet to overcome stronger barriers to New Orleans. About twenty miles above the head of the passes, the great river turns from its southeasterly course and flows for a mile or two to the northeast before resuming its former course. At this second bend was located Fort Jackson on the southern bank; across the stream but slightly above was Fort St. Philip. There they stood like giant wardens guarding the passage to the upper reaches of the Mississippi and the largest and richest city of the Confederacy.

To a balloonist, Fort Jackson would have looked like a great five pointed star which had fallen into the marshes beside the river bank. But closer inspection would have revealed that each of its sides was one hundred ten yards long and that its brick scarp walls and bastions stood twenty-two feet high above the bottom of a great ditch, extending around the fort, in which there stood five or six feet of muddy water. The nearest point of the fort was about one hundred yards from the levee, where the width of the river was only approximately seven hundred yards. In the center of the fort were barracks, strongly constructed of timbers and earth, intended to be as nearly bombproof as possible. Safer, however, were the shelters in the galleries of the fort and in the casemates where some of the guns were placed. But most were mounted on the walls behind parapets, and a few were in earth works, called "The Water Battery," just outside and below the fort. Only sixteen of the ninety-five guns were in the casemates.[1]

Fort St. Philip, quite irregular in shape, occupied a somewhat quadilateral space about one hundred fifty by one hundred yards. Its brick walls were about seventeen feet in height from the bottom of its surrounding ditch. It was neither as strongly built nor as heavily armed as was Fort Jackson, for it had only 52 guns, even including those of the two water batteries which flanked the fort.[2] About half the guns of the two forts were lighter than 32-pounders. Only thirty-nine were heavier than 32's, even including the seven mortars which were to match Porter's twenty. Farragut's entire attacking fleet carried one hundred sixty-nine guns heavier than 32's. The forts, which were garrisoned by a total of 1100 men, were a part of the coast defenses under the command of the handsome Brigadier-General Johnson K. Duncan, C. S. Army, whose headquarters were at Fort Jackson.[3]

Between the two forts was first constructed a kind of raft of great cypress trees forty feet long and four to five feet in diameter at the larger end. These were securely fastened to strong, heavy 2½-inch chain cables which were attached to trees, crab capstans, and large anchors buried in the ground. Then the whole raft was further secured by being chained to numerous anchors upstream. This was a most difficult undertaking because of the swift current, the shifting sand of the river bottom, and the great depth of 130 feet in midstream. The ever increasing accumulation of driftwood caused the great raft to sag in the middle; and early in March the chains gave way, and all the labor and expense were lost. Then another obstruction was devised, consisting of a line of schooners anchored at intervals with bows upstream. These were all securely chained together amidships and at stem and stern. But as if resenting man's puny attempts to chain the mighty stream and obstruct her free passage to the sea, a storm broke this to pieces in April. Undaunted, the city council of New Orleans appropriated $100,000 to reconstruct the obstruction. This was accomplished by using a part of the first raft and eight schooners, which were anchored and chained as before; but this was not so strong and so satisfactory a barrier as the original one had been.[4]

The Confederates also had a nondescript fleet above the forts. This consisted of a heterogeneous collection of about a dozen armed vessels and several other unarmed small craft. Six converted towboats were dubbed river-defense gunboats. Each carried one or two 32-pounder pivot guns and had thin iron casing round her bows, forming a sort of ram. They were commanded by Captain John A. Stevenson, C. S. Army, whose pet aversion was an order from a naval officer. Also more or less on their own were two Louisiana State gunboats. These were the converted sidewheeler sea steamers, *The Governor Moore* and *The General Quitman*, each armed with two 32-pounders. Belonging strictly to the Confederate Navy were the somewhat rickety steamer *Jackson* with a 32-pounder forward and another aft; the *McRae*, which was the converted sea steamer *Marques de la Habana*, armed with six light 32-pounder smoothbore broadside guns and a 9-inch shellgun pivoted amidships; and the iron-plated ram *Manassas*, a converted tugboat, which carried one 32-pounder that could be poked out pugnaciously through the bow. The *Manassas* looked somewhat like a submarine half submerged except for the smoke pouring from her rakish stacks.[5] Her turtle back was formed of oak twelve inches thick, covered with one and a half inches of iron; and her bow was a solid mass of twenty feet of wood overlaid with iron plates all riveted together to form a dangerous ram.[6]

The most powerful vessel potentially was the *Louisiana*. She was an ironclad with a rectangular sloping casemate of the *Merrimac* type, which was protected by two layers of "T railroad iron, the lower layer being firmly bolted to the woodwork, and the upper layer driven into it from the end so as to form a nearly solid plate."[7] She was well armed with three 9-inch and four 8-inch smoothbores, and two 7-inch and seven 30-pounder rifles. This vessel would indeed have proved a formidable obstacle to Farragut's fleet, if her propelling machinery had not turned out to be defective as she was being taken from New Orleans down to the forts on Sunday, April 20. She was then still not finished and workmen, in spite of its being the Sabbath, were busily hammering away at the iron plating on the forecastle and upper deck, calking the wheelhouses, mounting the guns, and trying to repair the faulty propellers.[8] Towboats eventually brought her safely down stream to a mooring about half a mile above Fort St. Philip where she came to rest with bow down stream. On board her was Commander John K. Mitchell, C. S. Navy,[9] who had been sent down to undertake the hopeless task of bringing order out of chaos in the fleet.

There was also an interior line of fortifications nearer the city of New Orleans, which however were not strong enough to keep an enemy fleet from advancing up the Mississippi after it had broken through the exterior line at Forts Jackson and St. Philip.

2

Much stronger defenses might have been prepared below New Orleans if the authorities there and at Richmond had earlier realized the danger of an attack from the south. A kind of naval Bull Run, early in October, 1861, had lulled the Confederates into a feeling of false security. When stout-hearted old Commodore George N. Hollins, who had fought as a midshipman under Decatur in the *President,* learned that the "Black Republicans"[10] had brought the *Richmond* and four smaller vessels up to the head of the passes, he dashed down with the *Manassas* and six steamers and put them all to flight. The *Vincennes,* in her unseemly haste at making a speedy departure, threw overboard all her guns but four and the *Richmond* had several planks stove in as an evidence of her close encounter with the Confederate ram.[11]

Consequently when news reached New Orleans "through circuitous channels"[12] that preparations were being made to invade Louisiana, Major-General Mansfield Lovell, C. S. Army, who was in command of the entire defenses of New Orleans, wrote[13] President Davis late in October that he believed the attack in the Gulf would be directed at Mobile. But on December 25, the general wrote Secretary of War Benjamin that, because of the gathering of enemy forces at Ship Island, he would organize the defenses of the city as rapidly as possible.[14] Yet four days later he wrote the Secretary that he thought operations there were only a blind to draw the attention of the Confederates away from Mobile, the real point of attack.[15] As late as the 27th of February, "Lord Lovell," as he came to be called facetiously by the Federals, wrote Benjamin, ". . . I regard Butler's Ship Island expedition as a harmless menace so far as New Orleans is concerned. A Black Republican dynasty will never give an old Breckinridge Democrat like Butler command of any expedition which they had had any idea would result in such a glorious success as the capture of New Orleans."[16]

Only on March 10 did General Lovell admit to Benjamin[17] that he had been entirely mistaken. Farragut's ships were then all in the river, and Lovell, fingering his long mustache, thought regretfully of the twenty-two heavy guns he had been ordered[18] to send into Tennessee and to Charleston, South Carolina, late in 1861, and of the 5,000 men he had dispatched to Corinth the following February.[19] After it was much too late he made feverish efforts to secure heavy guns from Pensacola and elsewhere, but with little success. Late in March, the government in Richmond thought the peril at Memphis and Vicksburg greater than that at New Orleans, and changed the destination of ten or twelve heavy guns from New Orleans to Vicksburg.[20] Lovell's calls for cannon from Alabama and West Florida were all in vain, and he wrote despairingly to Benjamin, "I cannot get heavy guns from Mobile. The enemy is in large force out the mouth of the river. Please order commanding officer at Mobile to send immediately."[20]

Incredible as it may seem, as late as April 17 there was an exchange of telegrams between Governor Thomas O. Moore of Louisiana and President Jefferson Davis,[21] concerning the *Louisiana* which had actually been ordered by Secretary of the Navy Mallory up the Mississippi to reinforce the squadron at Fort Pillow. This order, which had raised a furor of opposition in New Orleans, shows how completely out of touch the government in Richmond was with the real situation at New Orleans and with the impending disaster there. Indeed, the *Louisiana* could not have moved up the river against the current, even if obedience to the Secretary's order had been attempted.

Beset as New Orleans was from above and below, it was not

easy to decide where the weak Confederate naval forces might be used to the greatest advantage. Early in April, after the fall of Island No. 10, old Commodore Hollins brought the *McRae* down to New Orleans, and General Lovell telegraphed the Secretary of War to try to get Hollins placed in command there long enough to strike a blow at the Union fleet.[22] Hollins' plan was to rush his four additional gunboats down from Fort Pillow to aid in the attack. Some forty coal boats were to be loaded with light firewood which was highly combustible. Taking full advantage of the current, the Confederate vessels were to rush down, towing the fire rafts, which would then be fired and pushed against the Union ships. In the confusion which he expected to produce among Farragut's wooden vessels, Hollins hoped to sink several by ramming and to destroy others by fire. He waited in vain for a reply. Eventually he was ordered to Richmond as president of a board to examine midshipmen, and Farragut was spared an attack which might possibly have caused injuries to his fleet serious enough to disrupt his entire campaign.

Fate thus seemed to play a hand in the lack of preparations by the Confederates for the storm which was about to break upon the defenses of the great city on the Mississippi. "Whom the gods would destroy they first make mad."

VI

BOMBS BURSTING IN AIR

1

PORTER's confident promise to the Navy Department four months previous that his bomb vessels could reduce Forts Jackson and St. Philip in forty-eight hours was now to be subjected to the acid test of battle.

Before daylight, at six o'clock on April 18, Porter's steamers commenced towing four bombers at a time to their designated positions. Meanwhile the gunboats *Iroquois*, *Cayuga*, and *Wissahickon* were moved up by Farragut within range of the forts to draw the greater part of the Confederate fire away from the bombers.[1] Nine o'clock came; the men had finished their morning coffee; shells had been rammed into the big 11-inch and 9-inch guns on the gunboats, and the short, squat mortars had been loaded with their 13-inch shells. Every preparation finished, the gunners stood expectantly waiting for the opening gun. Finally at about 9:45 it came[2] suddenly like a clap of thunder, and all then joined in the mighty chorus. The air soon became filled with bombs and shells, describing graceful curves in the direction of the forts. Many whose fuses were too short burst in the air, others fell with great splashes of muddy water into the marshes around, and some exploded in the forts. This continued without ceasing until noon.

Meanwhile the gunboats *Sciota* and *Kennebec* had secured permission from Farragut to move into action. A 120-pounder shell had passed through the cabin of one mortar schooner and another had received a 10-inch shot near the water line; so Porter had moved them back two hundred yards.[3] Many of the wooden quarters in Fort Jackson had been set on fire and some had been destroyed.

The bombardment continued in the afternoon. At one o'clock

Page 44

there was great shouting when the *Iroquois* shot away the flagstaff on Fort Jackson.[4] Then the wooden citadel on the fort, in which several fires had already been started but all extinguished, caught fire again and a great pillar of flame and smoke arose, and continued to burn on into the night.[5] In mid afternoon news came up the river that Butler's troops had arrived there and that "Norfolk and the *Merrimack* are taken."[6] Then followed "three hearty cheers and a general ha! ha! and all sorts of questions which no one could answer."[6] So ended the first day's bombardment. Over 1,400 bombshells[7] and a great quantity of shells from the gunboats had been expended. Some guns on Fort Jackson had been disabled and the officers and many of the men had lost their bedding and clothes in the fires.[8]

The bombs began to fall earlier the next morning, at 6:30; but Farragut's five supporting gunboats did not go into action until two hours later.[9] Captain Bell thought the enemy fired "beautifully and with effect."[9] About nine o'clock one of the mortar schooners was sunk by a rifle shot which passed through her deck, magazine, and bottom. Two men only were wounded.[10] In the early afternoon the *Oneida* was badly damaged when struck by two 10-inch solid shot. Nine men were seriously wounded.[11] The weather was unseasonably hot, with barely enough wind stirring to drive the smoke away. But hour after hour the guns were monotonously loaded and fired. Considerable damage was done Fort Jackson. A shell passed through one of the casemates. Seven guns were disabled, two of which were in the water battery.[12] The bombardment continued on and on intermittently through most of the night.

At 7:40 on the morning of Sunday, April 20, Captain Porter went on board the *Hartford* with a deserter who had just come down the river in a small skiff.[13] There had been a shower of rain and the weather was cloudy, with a strong cold north wind—a marked change from the preceding day. Porter's mood was as gloomy as the weather. After bombarding for two days, the forty-eight hours he had prescribed, he had begun to despair of being able to take the forts and was losing confidence in his mortars.[14] The deserter had told him a story of havoc wrought on Fort Jackson, but he believed the fellow was lying. Meanwhile the mortars continued pounding away.

2

Farragut was not favorably impressed with the deserter's report either, and at ten o'clock signaled his commanding officers to come on board the *Hartford*.[15] All the commanders obeyed the signal except De Camp, Nichols, and Russell who commanded the gunboats which that day were covering the mortar vessels. Porter was not present; Farragut had had ample opportunity only that morning to discuss the situation with him.[15] Lieutenant J. M. Wainwright, commanding the *Harriet Lane*, Porter's flagship, claimed that he was present.[16] When all were seated in the Flag-Officer's cabin, Farragut for the first time laid before them his plan of operations, which he demonstrated with charts of the river and the forts. After some discussion, Commander James Alden of the *Richmond* asked, "Flag-Officer, may I read a communication which Commander Porter has requested me to present?" Farragut assented, and Alden then read a rather long memorandum of about nine hundred words, setting forth in detail Porter's ideas as to how New Orleans should be captured. Two methods of attack were suggested: to run the batteries by night or in a fog or to anchor the larger ships "close alongside" the forts with the gunboats constantly moving about and the mortars at their stations, all pouring shell, shrapnel, grape, canister, and bombs into the forts until they were reduced. The memorandum raised several objections to running past the forts, the principal one being that an enemy would be left in the rear and the mortars would be left behind. This was, of course, a purely personal objection. Porter strongly contended for capturing the forts first.[17] Alden finished, slowly folded the paper, and put it back in his pocket. Then Bell suggested, "Would it not be proper to leave the document with the Flag-Officer?" Alden agreed, and handed it to Farragut.

There was some further discussion in which Farragut informed his officers that Porter had that morning given his consent that the boom be broken that night. As to the memorandum, the Flag-Officer argued that, if his fleet got above the forts, the mortars would be in no danger below, and that he could not use troops effectively unless he ran the forts and covered their landing from the Gulf above. To the commanders who declared that it was "a hazardous thing to go above" where they would be out of reach of supplies, Farragut replied, silencing all opposition, "Our ammunition is being rapidly consumed, without a supply at hand; something must be done immediately. I believe in celerity."[18]

There was a general feeling among the officers of the fleet that the ships could not pass the forts. Farragut's surgeon, Jonathan M. Foltz, who referred to the Flag-Officer in his diary as "a smart little sailor man" and "a bold, brave officer, full of fight but [who] evidently does not know what he is going about," recorded, after Captain Bell's reconnaissance of March 28, "Captain Bell, Captain Russell, and Mr. Osbon, the correspondent of the New York *Herald*, who has seen much of naval war, agree as to the strength of the forts. They are impassable by ships alone, they say. If the attempt is made, we shall probably have another disaster at a moment when all north of us is progressing so favorably. Wherever my brave brother officers and shipmates will go I will go to take care of them, but I pray God that we will not be led to defeat."[19]

Farragut, it is evident, had to take upon his own shoulders the sole responsibility for deciding to run past the forts before they had been reduced. He had the courage to make this choice when he had little or no support from his officers. So on the same day the council was held, April 20, he issued the following order, which is so interesting as to justify full quotation: "The Flag-Officer, having heard all the opinions expressed by the different commanders, is of the opinion that whatever is to be done will have to be done quickly, or we will be again reduced to a blockading squadron without the means of carrying on the bombardment, as we have nearly expended all the shells and fuzes and material for making cartridges. He has always entertained the same opinions which are expressed by

Commander Porter—that is, that there are three[20] modes of attack, and the question is, which is the one to be adopted? His own opinion is that a combination of two should be made, viz.: The forts should be run, and when a force is once above the forts to protect the troops, they should be landed at Quarantine from the Gulf side by bringing them through the bayou, and then our forces should move up the river, mutually aiding each other, as it can be done to advantage.

"When in the opinion of the Flag-Officer, the propitious time has arrived, the signal will be made to weigh and advance to the conflict. If, in his opinion, at the time of arriving at the respective positions of the different divisions of the fleet we have the advantage, he will make the signal for 'Close action,' No. 8, and abide the result—conquer or to be conquered—drop anchor or keep underway, as in his opinion is best. Unless the signal above mentioned is made, it will be understood that the first order of sailing will be formed after leaving Fort St. Philip. and we will proceed up the river in accordance with the original opinion expressed. The programme of the order of sailing accompanies this general order, and the commanders will hold themselves in readiness for the service as indicated."[21]

Farragut seems to have been greatly concerned about his lack of ammunition, and that same day he wrote Mr. Welles a letter which would have confounded that earnest Puritan, had it reached him before the news of victory. Farragut informed him bluntly that he was not half supplied with anything. "My shells, fuzes, cylinder cloth and yarn to make the cylinders are all out," he complained; and his fleet indeed had not yet begun to fight. "I asked for the shells I wanted and other ordnance stores, and I am told that my demand is out of the question, and now I find myself dependent upon the Army for everything; and General Butler has been most generous. . . . I have not a solid shot in my ship, and none in the squadron except a few on board the *Richmond*. We have only a few grape and canister; the fuzes of sufficient length were fired away during the first day," he continued.[22] Poor Mr. Welles; if that letter had reached him before the victorious news, he would have torn off his newest glossiest wig and trampled it under foot in his consternation and agitation.

3

The booming of the mortars continued during this eventful April 20th. In the afternoon there was a lessening of fire while ammunition was replenished. At eight o'clock in the evening the firing increased,[23] and the sky was filled with a truly wonderful pyrotechnic display.

At nine o'clock Captain Bell went on board the gunboat *Itasca* with orders to take that ship and the *Pinola* up the river to destroy the schooner raft and make a passage for the fleet. The attempt was made about midnight. They were discovered, and the gunboats would have been destroyed, had not the mortars kept the Confederate gunners occupied.[24] Everything went wrong. After two petards and a barrel of powder had been placed on one of the hulks, the mechanism for exploding them failed to work. Meanwhile the *Itasca* released the chains from one hulk and then drifted ashore. At 12:30 an officer from the *Pinola* came on board the *Hartford* to report the trouble, and assistance was dispatched.[25] "I never felt such anxiety in my life," wrote[26] Farragut to his wife. "I was as glad to see Bell on his return as if he had been my boy. I was up all night, and could not sleep until he got back to the ship."

Farragut had other disturbances to keep him awake that night. At 2:30 in the morning a fire raft was discovered coming down the river. Bells sounded on the ships for "fire quarters."[27] There was considerable confusion among the gunboats as they maneuvered to avoid the raft. The *Kineo* fouled the *Sciota* and knocked her mainmast down, and both then drifted down on the *Mississippi*.[28] The *Iroquois* was run into by the *Westfield*.[29] It was indeed fortunate that Commodore Hollins had not been permitted to try his bold stroke. As the fire raft drifted down between the *Hartford* and the *Richmond,* the flames were shooting up from it as high as the masts, and the heat was so intense that one could hardly look over the side until it passed. Fifty boats were required to tow it ashore.[30]

All day long on the 21st the mortars and three protecting gunboats kept up the monotonous bombardment. The gunners shivered in the cold northeast wind. Farragut, in a bad humor, sat in his cabin after a sleepless night and dictated a report, ending with complaints, to Mr. Welles. He needed more anchors and cables, which his ships were continuously losing; he desperately needed more medical supplies and more ammunition, for which he had made requisition before leaving Hampton Roads and again at Ship Island.[31] With that out of his system and a letter to his wife written, he felt better and took a much needed nap, sitting upright in his chair, from sheer exhaustion. Two more of Porter's mortars were slightly damaged, and he prudently shifted the berths of three of them.[32] More guns were disabled in Fort Jackson, but as before these were repaired as far as practical. General Duncan and his weary garrison were cheered by the news of the arrival during the previous evening of the *Louisiana,* which he expected would drive the mortars off and permit him to make some needed repairs.[33]

After another night of incessant fire from the mortars, the day dawned clear and warm. The masts were taken out of five of the gunboats; only their smokestacks were to be seen above the bulwarks. General Butler's transports with 7,000 troops arrived and anchored below the fleet. During the morning another mortar schooner was hit, and about noon the gunboat *Oneida* was struck by an 8-inch shell which burst on the quarter-deck, wounding six men.[34] General Duncan spent the day trying vainly to get Commander Mitchell to move the *Louisiana* below the boom close in on the Fort St. Philip shore.[33] Mitchell refused to endanger his ironclad to mortar fire, as one bombshell dropped on the grating covering his casemate would have been disastrous. This was her Achilles' heel. Fort St. Philip was still practically undamaged. Only the platform of one 24-pounder had been slightly damaged.[35]

Farragut had planned to make the attack the following morning, and issued a general order for the vessels to take their positions for ascending the river.[36] But at 9 o'clock in the evening he wrote Porter regretfully that he had just learned from

Captain Smith that his carpenter and assistants were on the gunboat *Sciota* down the river and that he did not wish to go into battle without them. "So I do not wish you to calculate on my early start as I proposed," Farragut added,[37] and the attack was postponed. During the night the bombing slackened and became only desultory. At 1:30 in the morning, a fire raft was sighted, and all the fire bells started ringing. It was towed safely ashore where it set the trees on fire for half a mile and made a beautiful spectacle for those on watch.[38]

The following morning, April 23, was warm with hardly a breeze stirring. The crews were disappointed, for the word had gotten round that this was to be *the day*. Porter came on board the *Hartford*, discouraged but still keen on continuing the bombardment.[39] "Look here, David," said Farragut, "we'll demonstrate the practical value of mortar work." "Mr. Osbon," he then directed, turning to his clerk, "get me two small flags, a white one and a red one, and go to the mizzen topmasthead and watch where the mortar shells fall. If inside the fort, wave the red flag. If outside, wave the white one." With a smile, he added to Porter, "You recommended Mr. Osbon to me, so you will have confidence in his observations. Now go aboard your vessel, select a tallyman, and when all is ready, Mr. Osbon will wave his flags and the count will begin." When the test was over, the "outs" had it by a large majority. "There, David," said Farragut when Porter returned to the *Hartford*, "there's the score. I guess we'll go up the river to-night."[39]

But Porter slipped into his official report of April 30, 1862 to Secretary Welles, covering twelve printed pages, this amazing sentence: "On the 23d I urged Flag-Officer Farragut to commence the attack with the ships at night, as I feared the mortars would not hold out."[40] Ten days later he wrote Fox, asking that this sentence be cut out of the report. "Though this is so," he declared, "it won't do in a public dispatch to say so."[41] It was not removed. Welles thought the report should have come to him through Farragut, Porter's commanding officer, and after the war scathingly criticised Porter, declaring that Farragut "needed no urging from any one to move—certainly not from one who from the first had advised that the forts should be reduced before the passage of the fleet was attempted."[42] After the war, Fox wrote that the delay of six days awaiting Porter's reduction of the forts "unquestionably augmented the defenses at New Orleans."[43] "The arrival of the first mortar vessel at Key West," he continued, "indicated to the Rebels the point of attack. How precious then were the hours which the Commander delayed the ascent in compliment to the mortars is shown by the fact that the *Louisiana* which Porter represented as the most formidable ironclad in the world was *almost ready* and we had not a single ironclad. . . . The fire rafts, the naval defenses, the rams, obstructions, etc., which really constituted the peril to Farragut's fleet were unquestionably immensely increased by every hour's delay to try the effects of the bombardment."[43]

In the afternoon, Farragut visited each vessel to make sure his orders were understood and to see if all was in readiness.[44] During that day he had issued another general order, stating that the hoisting of two perpendicular red lights to the peak of the *Hartford* would be the signal to get underway and proceed up the river. He explained that his division would be the red, that of Captain Bailey the blue, and that of Commander Bell the red and blue. The leading division was ordered not to use its port guns, and his division was not to use the starboard batteries in passing the forts for fear of firing into each other.[45]

At about six o'clock that evening, the vessels began to take their positions for next day's battle. Bailey's division then anchored in column on the right hand side of the stream, looking up the river; the other divisions, on the opposite side in formation.[46] On the *Cayuga*, which was to lead the column, the officers and crew were mustered on the quarter-deck, where Captain Bailey and Captain Harrison addressed them. About 8 o'clock Captain Caldwell of the *Itasca* and Acting Master Jones went in a 10-oared boat up the river to inspect the boom; three hours later they reported that there was a clear passage.[47] On Fort Jackson, Duncan by evening was convinced that an attack was imminent, because the mortars had slackened fire in the afternoon and seemed to have exhausted their ammunition. He had again tried to get Mitchell to move the *Louisiana* but in vain. He was told that the vessel would be ready for service by the evening of the 24th, but he replied that this would probably be too late.[48]

At 9 o'clock, Lieutenant Francis A. Roe of the *Pensacola* was jotting down in his diary:[49] ". . . I see no want of determination on the part of our people. But I look for a bloody conflict. These may be the last lines I shall ever write. But I have an unflinching trust in God that we shall plant the Union flag upon the enemy's forts by noon to-morrow. I trust in Almighty God for the results." "If I fall, I leave my darlings to the care of my country," he concluded in good Nelsonian style. The fainthearted did not put on paper their feelings that evening, as far as the records show.

Farragut was standing with his clerk on the quarter-deck the same evening. He suddenly turned toward him and asked, "What do you estimate our casualties will be, Mr. Osbon?" "Flag-Officer," he replied. "I have been thinking of that, and I believe we will lose a hundred." There were about 4,000 men in the fleet, and his estimate was a low percentage. "No more than that?" Farragut asked. "How do you calculate on so small a number?" "Well," Osbon rejoined, "most of us are pretty low in the water, and, being near, the enemy will shoot high. Then, too, we will be moving and it will be dark, with dense smoke. Another thing, gunners ashore are never as accurate as gunners aboard a vessel. I believe a hundred men will cover our loss." Farragut looked at his clerk steadily for a moment, and then remarked rather sadly, "I wish I could think so. I wish I could be as sure of it as you are." The Flag-Officer then walked up and down the quarter-deck for a turn or two, while Osbon scrutinized the sky to determine what the weather might be in the early morning of the morrow. As he looked, he saw a great bald eagle circling above the fleet. "Look there, Flag-Officer," he cried, pointing to the great bird, "that is our national emblem. It is a sign of victory."[50]

Though the mortars had burned all the woodwork in Fort Jackson and torn up things generally, they had done "comparatively little harm to the strength of either fort."[51] A total of about 7,500 bombs had by that time been fired at Fort Jackson alone, 1,080 had exploded in the air, 3,339 had fallen in the ditches and surrounding marshes, 1,113 had struck in the solid grounds of the fort and levees, and the rest were unaccounted for in Porter's estimates.[52] In the fort, four guns had been dismounted and eleven carriages had been injured. Of the results of the bombs bursting in air, General Butler sardonically declared, "Eight days more were consumed in waiting for that superbly useless bombardment, which Farragut never believed in from the hour when it was first brought to his attention to the time when the last mortar was fired."[53] A greater soldier than Butler and a less prejudiced authority, General Viscount Wolseley, wrote: "I may, therefore, venture the opinion, based on the evidence of the Confederate side that the bombardment, considering the enormous numbers of large shells actually exploded within Fort Jackson, had comparatively little effect in preventing that fort from contributing its share toward the result of the operation. . . . Had it been necessary to silence by mortar fire the guns of Fort Jackson and the water-battery before the ships ran the gauntlet between Fort Jackson and Fort St. Philip, Farragut would never have achieved his splendid success."[54]

That evening, when hammocks were piped down, the crews were told that they might sleep until midnight. Then they were to be awakened quietly with none of the usual noisy signals. The officers in the wardrooms were unusually solemn at the evening meal. They could not help thinking who might be missing at the next meal. Quietly they soon went to their staterooms, and most of them wrote a few lines to their nearest relatives. The lights were turned out early and quiet settled down on each ship—such a quiet as is found on board a ship only before a battle.[55]

COMMANDER DAVID D. PORTER, U.S.N.
From an engraving of the portrait by Alonzo Chappel after a photograph from life. From author's collection.

FARRAGUT'S FLEET PASSING FORTS JACKSON AND ST. PHILIP BELOW NEW ORLEANS
From a lithograph by C. Parsons in the collection of President Franklin D. Roosevelt.

Courtesy of United States Navy Department, Naval Records and Library

VII

CRASHING THROUGH THE BARRIERS

1

AT ONE O'CLOCK on the morning of April 24, the quartermasters and their mates with hooded lanterns began to make their rounds. "All hands!"¹ they said quietly, as each man was roused from his slumbers. The night was very dark and the air was chilly. The men went briskly to work stowing hammocks and making everything shipshape for weighing anchor. At the stroke of two, Signal Officer Osbon hoisted to the mizzen peak of the *Hartford* two red lanterns.² These dull red lights announced to every other ship that the decisive hour was at hand. This was the signal to weigh anchor. At about 3 o'clock Bailey's division was under way. Thirty minutes later the vessels near the left bank were also³ moving slowly up the river. By this time the men were at their battle stations, many stripped to the waist with their monkey-jackets tied loosely round their necks. Quietly the gunners stood about their guns, which had been cast loose and loaded, ready for action.⁴ Down below the engineers had not been idle, and there was a heavy pressure of steam on. This would be needed; the current there was running at the rate of four miles an hour.⁵

Captain Bailey in the *Cayuga* led his division of vessels: *Pensacola, Mississippi, Oneida, Varuna, Katahdin, Kineo,* and *Wissahickon.* Edging a little to starboard to give Farragut's ships room,⁶ Bailey passed through the barrier about half past three. Soon thereafter his leading gunboat was discovered; the moon had just risen and the vessel could be plainly seen crossing her disk.⁷ The little *Cayuga* was leading the big *Pensacola* and the other vessels like a pilot fish.⁸ The guns of both Jackson and St. Philip opened on her at 3:40. The exploding shells almost blinded young Lieutenant George H. Perkins, piloting her from the forecastle. Seeing that the guns were aimed at midstream, he steered close under the walls of Fort St. Philip,[9] and the *Cayuga* replied with grape and canister.

Meanwhile Farragut in the *Hartford* was leading the *Brooklyn* and *Richmond,* followed by Bell's gunboats, *Sciota, Iroquois, Kennebec, Pinola, Itasca,* and *Winona.* The Flag-Officer's original plan had been to steam up the river in two columns abreast, Bailey then to dash past St. Philip while he took care of Fort Jackson. But on account of the narrowness of the opening in the obstruction, it was decided there would be fewer chances of getting foul of the hulks and the raft as well as of each other if the vessels moved through in a single column.[10] All of Bailey's division were, therefore, to get through the opening in the barrier ahead of Farragut's ship. This was not quite accomplished, for near the opening the *Brooklyn,* second in the left column, collided with the *Kineo,* seventh of the right and leading division.[11]

The *Hartford* felt her way carefully through the passage, successfully avoiding collision with all obstructions. Soon after getting through she was discovered, and at 3:40 she too was under fire from Fort Jackson. By that time Porter's mortars were filling the heavens with the deafening noise of bursting shells which crisscrossed picturesquely like little comets with trains of fire. His gunboats and the old sailing ship *Portsmouth* had been moved up, and were pouring shells into the water battery. "It was as if the artillery of heaven were playing upon earth," Farragut thought.[12] The guns in the forts were firing shot, shell, hot shot, and grape. Through the darkness and the smoke, the gunners could scarcely see the vessels and aimed at the flashes of their guns.[13] But so far not a gun had been fired on the *Hartford;* Farragut had ordered that no ammunition be wasted.

Farragut had meanwhile climbed into the port mizzen rigging to see better, and stood with his feet on the ratlines and his back against the shrouds, as calm and undisturbed as if he were leaning against the garden gate and enjoying a beautiful sunset. Twice he sent Signal Officer Osbon to find out if all the gun divisions were ready. Then he called down to him, "Go forward and see if the bow guns will bear." Suddenly a shell struck the mainmast. Osbon shouted to Farragut, "We can't afford to lose you, Flag-Officer. They'll get you up there, sure." "Flag-Officer," Osbon continued, "they'll break my opera glasses, if you stay up there." He had loaned Farragut a pair of small opera glasses. Holding the glasses out to him, Farragut replied quite seriously, "Oh, damn the glasses!" But Osbon, now serious, insisted, "It's you we want. Come down." Soon Farragut did so, and almost immediately afterwards a shell exploded where he had stood and cut away some of the rigging.[14] Finally the *Hartford* reached a point from which the guns bore effectively, the order was given to commence firing, and her broadsides roared defiantly at Fort Jackson.

Because of the smoke and darkness, Captain Craven in the *Brooklyn*, next in column, lost sight of the *Hartford*, got off his course, and soon found his ship running over one of the large hulks in the barrier. On she went, and became entangled with a part of the raft of logs. Then she swung athwart the stream and her bow grazed the shore on the right bank. Here she received a severe pounding from Fort St. Philip.[15] Turning up stream, she passed the fort, less than a hundred yards distant, with her broadsides of grape and canister roaring, and the leadsman in the starboard chains shouting, "Thirteen feet, sir." Above the fort she set the River Defense gunboat *Warrior* afire with one broadside, and fired ineffectively at the *Louisiana* which sent a 9-inch shell into her bow about a foot above the water line. It did not explode; otherwise the *Brooklyn* would probably have gone to the bottom. Again losing all sense of direction in the smoke, darkness, and confusion of battle, Craven soon found his vessel on the opposite side of the river under the fire of Fort Jackson and almost ashore. Immediately, the *Manassas* was bearing down on her. When ten feet away, the ram discharged her single gun, the shot penetrating the *Brooklyn* about five feet above the water line; and a moment later the *Manassas* rammed the Union vessel, jarring her fore and aft but not penetrating her chain armor. As the whale-like vessel fell astern, a leadsman in the chains on the *Brooklyn* threw his lead at a couple of men standing in a scuttle forward of the smokestack on the ram and knocked one of them overboard. As day began to dawn, the *Brooklyn* found herself above the forts.[15]

Meanwhile the *Hartford* also had been having some exciting experiences. She too had been carried by the current across toward Fort St. Philip, and after passing that fort at close range she had run ashore just above the upper water battery, while trying to avoid a fire raft.[16] The tug *Mosher* then pushed the raft alongside the *Hartford*, and in a moment the ship was blazing all along the port side "halfway up to the main and mizzen tops."[17] For awhile Farragut thought it was all up with him.[18] As Lieutenant Albert Kautz was crossing the deck, he passed close to the Flag-Officer, and saw him raise his clasped hands above his head and heard him exclaim, "My God, is it to end in this way?"[19] Signal Officer Osbon tried something quite original. Noticing some 20-pound rifle shells, he rolled some of them across the deck. It was so hot there that he covered his head with his coat as he knelt down to uncap the shells. Farragut, seeing the kneeling figure, said, "Come, Mr. Osbon, this is no time for prayer!" Having just gotten the cap off of the third shell, he replied, "Flag-Officer, if you'll wait a second, you'll get the quickest answer to prayer ever you heard of." Then he rolled the three shells over the side into the burning raft. Instantly there was a terrific noise and a big hole in her.[20] Meanwhile the *Hartford's* fire department, under the able direction of Lieutenant Thornton, had gone into action and soon had the fire under control. The flagship then backed off shore into deep water, and continued upstream.

The *Richmond* followed in her turn, with the crew lying flat on the deck and not replying to the Confederate fire until she was almost abreast of Fort Jackson. Then the gunners jumped to their feet and opened with grape and canister when near enough to throw a stone into the fort.[21] "Load and fire at will" was the order from the quarter-deck. The ship throbbed with the beat of her engines and trembled with the shock from the firing of the big guns. The captain of a gun crew was decapitated; as his body fell, the lockstring in his hand was pulled and the gun was discharged. An exploding shell tore off the right arm of a junior officer. A master's mate, with a message for the captain, went up the ladder to the topgallant forecastle; as he touched his cap to the commander, he was struck in the forehead and fell dead, the message undelivered.[22] Crossing the river, the *Richmond* gave Fort St. Philip a few parting broadsides, and she too was then above the forts.

Meanwhile the two large vessels in Bailey's division were battling their way up the river. Because of weak eyesight, Captain Morris intrusted the piloting of the *Pensacola* to Lieutenant F. A. Roe. After passing Fort Jackson, the ship veered across stream and engaged St. Philip in almost a yardarm conflict, so short was the range. The signal quartermaster on the bridge by Lieutenant Roe's side lost a leg. Roe had the right leg of his pantaloons cut away to the knee and the skirt of his coat was cut in strips, though his body was untouched. Finally he lost his bearings and the current carried his vessel over to Fort Jackson, but he caught a glimpse of the shore and turned upstream again just in time.[23] The old sidewheeler *Mississippi* was piloted through the darkness and the thick smoke by another young executive officer, Lieutenant George Dewey.[24] She had a perilous encounter with the ram *Manassas*, which inflicted an extensive wound on the port quarter below the water line.[24]

Bailey's gunboats all got through the barrier and past the forts, and all of Bell's division except three were equally successful. The *Kennebec* became entangled in the raft and struck one of the schooner hulks. This so delayed the gunboat that her commander deemed it imprudent to continue upstream during daylight.[25] Abreast of Fort Jackson, the *Itasca* received a 42-pound shot in her boiler, and floated out of action down the river.[26] The *Winona* was also delayed by getting entangled in the raft, attempted to pass the forts after day broke, and with many casualties was forced to retire down stream.[27]

2

After the ships passed the forts, there was still considerable fighting. The little *Cayuga* was so far in advance of the rest of Bailey's division that young Lieutenant Perkins' heart "jumped into his mouth" after his gunboat had passed the forts and he could not see any Union vessels following. But instead he noted a flock of Confederate gunboats bearing down upon him.[28] "The enemy were so thick," wrote Captain Bailey, "that it was like duck shooting; what missed one rebel hit another."[29] The 11-inch Dahlgren, fired at a range of thirty yards, drove one attacker ashore where she was burned; and the Parrott gun on the forecastle drove another away. Bailey was getting ready to repel boarders from a third,[30] when the *Varuna* came dashing in and fired both starboard and port at everything she passed. Four Confederate vessels were quickly put out of action; one had her boiler explode, and three drifted ashore in flames.[31] In the confusion, the *Varuna* fired also into the *Cayuga*.[32] Then the *Oneida*, *Pensacola*, and *Brooklyn* came up and joined in the melee.

The *Manassas* gave Farragut's fleet a great deal of annoyance. The ram was reported to have been seen at very close range by the *Oneida*, *Cayuga*, *Pinola*, *Richmond*, *Pensacola*, *Iroquois*, and *Wissahickon*. In each case, she slipped off into the darkness and no harm was done. Farragut mistakenly thought it was the *Manassas* that pushed the fire raft against the *Hartford*. Only the *Brooklyn* and the *Mississippi* were struck by the ram, but neither was dangerously injured. At dawn, the *Manassas* turned upstream and went to aid the *McRae* which was fighting four gunboats.[33] Her commander, Lieutenant T. B. Huger, had just been mortally wounded, and the famous Lieutenant "Savvy" Read[34] had taken command. As the *Manassas* approached, the gunboats retired; but then two large vessels came down to attack her.[35] Farragut had seen the ram, and had directed Captain Melancton Smith to run her down. The *Mississippi* rushed at her at full speed. When she was less than fifty yards distant, the *Manassas* put her helm hard aport, dodged her antagonist, and ran ashore. Broadsides were poured into her, and Lieutenant Warley ordered his crew to escape into the swamp. Eventually she slipped off the bank, floated down stream, and sank.[35]

The Confederate vessel, *Governor Moore*, commanded by Lieutenant Beverly Kennon, discovered an enemy vessel proceeding rapidly upstream, and escaped from the vessels surrounding her and went in pursuit. At daybreak she was about one hundred yards from the vessel and six hundred yards ahead of several pursuers. Relentlessly the *Governor Moore* gained in spite of her dreadful loss of life. When abreast of Quarantine, seven miles above the forts, the two vessels were so close that Kennon could not depress his bow gun enough to rake the enemy; so he pointed the gun through his own deck and thus raked her fore and aft with two shells. Soon thereafter the *Governor Moore* rammed the vessel; then backing clear, she rammed a second time. The enemy vessel, which turned out to be the *Varuna*, then made for the shore which she reached just as she sank with her stern in the reeds. By that time the *Governor Moore* had lost a third of her crew, but she turned bravely down stream to continue the fight instead of escaping up the river to New Orleans. The *Oneida*, followed by two or three other vessels, was approaching. They opened fire, and sent their boats to rescue the crew of the *Varuna*. The *Governor Moore* was soon disabled and run ashore, where Kennon set her afire and surrendered himself and the remnants of his crew. "The pennant and remains of the ensign were never hauled down. The flames that lit our decks stood faithful sentinels over their halyards until they, like the ship, were entirely consumed," proudly wrote her commander.[36]

On the way upstream, the *Cayuga* at daylight discovered a regiment encamped on shore about three and a half miles above the forts, and opened on them with canister at close range. Perkins shouted to the commanding officers to come on board and deliver up their swords. Down came their colors and at five o'clock Colonel Szymanski delivered over his sword—an odd surrender of seven hundred troops on land to a gunboat.[37]

3

The *Hartford* moved up to Quarantine with that "unspeakable calmness that only an American man-of-war can exhibit,"[38] thought Lieutenant Roe. Loud cheers greeted the flagship, and the other ships on their arrival. As they passed the sunken *Varuna* whose flag was still flying from her masthead, they dipped their colors and gave her three cheers.[38] The flags fluttering from each masthead and peak never looked "prouder, more beautiful in the balmy morning breeze" than at that hour of victory.[38] Farragut ordered the fleet to anchor. Marines were sent ashore to take possession of the buildings over which white flags were already flying.[39] The men washed the sweat and powder grime from their hands and faces, and went to a late breakfast. Then the bloody decks were washed down, and preparations were made to bury the dead. But for the loss of their shipmates, all would have been happy indeed. The heavy burden of dread and uncertainty had been lifted. They had succeeded; Farragut had taken them through the barrier to New Orleans. No officer felt the relief more keenly than Captain Craven. He had been one of those who had looked upon the attack as "a most desperate undertaking" and had thought that "but few of our number would be left to witness our most terrible disaster." But now he could write his wife, "The Lord of Hosts was still with us, and though no one can tell how it was done, by His Divine Providence we passed through this fiery ordeal."[40]

The casualties in Farragut's fleet were 37 killed and 149 wounded[41]—nearly double Osbon's estimate of the preceding evening. During the previous bombardment of several days the losses had been 2 killed and 30 wounded.[42] The *Hartford* received eighteen damaging shots and had two guns disabled. The *Brooklyn* was struck sixteen times; the *Richmond*, thirteen; the *Mississippi*, eleven; and the *Pensacola*, nine. But none of the shots were dangerously near the water line. The *Cayuga* was struck forty-two times, but only her masts and smokestack were much injured. The *Itasca* was put out of action with a shot in her boiler. Though the *Kineo* was struck by nine shot, she was more seriously injured by her collision with the *Brooklyn*. The *Manassas* injured both the *Mississippi* and the *Brooklyn* by ramming. She cut away from the sidewheeler four strakes of planking seven feet long and four inches deep and sheered off the heads of fifty copper bolts on her port quarter. She broke three strakes of plank at the water line in the *Brooklyn* and caused a bad leak extending five feet below the water.[43]

The Confederate casualties in Fort Jackson were 9 killed and 33 wounded; in Fort St. Philip, 2 killed and 4 wounded.[44] The losses on the Confederate ships, as far as records show, were 73 killed and 73 wounded, one of whom afterwards died.[45] The casualties on the other ships which were run ashore and burned were probably not large. However, the *Warrior* received a broadside of eleven 5-second shells from the *Brooklyn* which exploded and literally drove her ashore, instantly setting her on fire.[46] These frail river steamers were hardly more than targets for the Union vessels. Altogether eight Confederate ships were destroyed.[47] Only two river gunboats escaped up the river. The captain of one of these, the *Defiance*, was drunk that day and would not render any satisfactory assistance.[47]

The *Louisiana*, not being able to move, remained under the guns of Fort St. Philip. She was practically uninjured, though she had received the heavy fire of the larger vessels at close range. Her commander, Charles F. McIntosh, was mortally wounded. Farragut felt great compassion for "poor Charlie McIntosh," whom he had known intimately in Norfolk before the war. In a letter to Mrs. Farragut he related that a member of the City Council of New Orleans, after its capture, with whom he conversed as to McIntosh's condition, said, "Well, sir, he knew his task was a difficult one, and said to me, before he left, that their work would be no child's play; that he knew his enemy, and that you were as brave as you were skillful."[48] For Flag-Officer John Mitchell, his cousin-in-law, who was also on the *Louisiana*, Farragut had not a word of pity. They were spared the embarrassment of meeting after Mitchell's surrender later. John Wilkinson, executive officer of the Confederate ironclad, who had served under Farragut, also had a high opinion of his old commander. "Most of us," he wrote, "belonging to that little naval fleet, knew that Admiral Farragut would dare to attempt what any man would."[49] The *McRae* had also reached the protection of Fort St. Philip. After participating in hot and close fighting, she ran ashore with damaged steering gear, but a towboat took her off and safely down to the fort.[50]

After the battle was over, Farragut wrote Porter, "We had a rough time of it . . . but thank God the number of killed and wounded was very small considering. This ship had only two killed and eight wounded."[51] Without exultation, he then dwelt on the difficulties and his plan to continue upstream. After giving instructions for General Butler, he concluded generously, "You supported us most nobly." General Butler was the first to congratulate him, that same day. "Allow me to congratulate you and your command upon the bold, daring, brilliant, and successful passage of the Forts by your fleet this morning," he wrote. "A more gallant exploit it has never fallen to the lot of man to witness."[52]

"Farragut's splendid achievement was made possible," in the opinion of Lord Wolseley, "first, by the inadequate previous preparation of the naval part of the New Orleans defenses; secondly, by the want of harmonious working between the Confederate naval and military forces; and, lastly, by his own clear appreciation of the moral effect he would produce by forcing his way past the defenses of Fort Jackson and Fort St. Philip and by his appearance before New Orleans. . . . In other words, Admiral Farragut's attack was based on a knowledge of the superior importance in war of moral over material force. One can hardly offer a higher compliment to any naval or military commander."[53]

When in Tunis nearly fifty years before with Consul Folsom, the latter had presented Midshipman Farragut a Turkish ataghan, the scabbard of which was ornamented with an embossed scene representing a frigate passing between the fire of two forts—a strangely prophetic coincidence.[54]

VIII

THE CAPTURE OF THE QUEEN OF THE GULF

1

THE PEOPLE of New Orleans were to suffer a cruel disillusionment. Though Governor Moore, on April 1, telegraphed President Davis to send arms immediately "in God's name, in the name of my State,"[1] the same day the *Daily True Delta* was reassuring its readers as to the strength of the forts and the discipline of the garrisons. Though the enemy might attack, there were "no fears of a bad result to our side," it declared. The *Crescent* of that day felt secure behind the "appliances of war" and thought that even the Southern climate would "check the rapacity of the Hessian invaders." Two weeks later, the *Bee* declared that the Yankees would "never confront the hideous perils of a New Orleans epidemic."[2] There seemed to have been a general feeling in New Orleans during those pleasant days of early April that "nothing afloat could pass the forts; nothing that walked could get through our swamps."[3] The evening of the first day of Porter's bombardment, there was "vivid excitement on Canal and St. Charles streets,"[4] and for the next day or two wild rumors were afloat and people congregated in the streets to hear the latest "from below.' The *Daily True Delta* called upon the citizens to "prepare to meet the coming issue with unblenched faces."[5] "The hour is rapidly approaching when the question will be solved whether or not New Orleans will be a conquered city," it added dolefully. "The issue is now to do or die. Who will be so craven as to falter?"

But as the forts held out from day to day, the people commenced to feel more secure. This was heightened by the publication in the press on April 24 of a dispatch from General

Duncan of the previous day, who declared "an abiding faith in our ultimate success." "They must soon exhaust themselves," he concluded; "if not, we can stand it as long as they can." This appeared in the *Daily True Delta* under this headline: "Glorious News from the Forts."[6] In the *Crescent* of this date, the editor wrote of New Orleans eloquently: "It requires no prophet's eye to look forward to the future of her destiny and see her sitting in splendor, the Metropolis of the Valley and the Queen of the Gulf."[7]

The ink was hardly dry on these newspapers when a rumor reached the city that "several of the enemy's gunboats had succeeded in passing the forts."[8] At 9:30 church bells began to ring the signal for all military organizations to assemble at their armories. The police commandeered vehicles to convey ammunition from the Marine Hospital to the river. Business houses were closed; children were sent home weeping from school.[9] At the wharves the boats got up steam for a sudden departure up the river. General Lovell hurriedly arrived from the forts, convinced that all was lost. All cotton was ordered to be burned and all government supplies to be removed.[10] All the dreary afternoon, drays bumped over the cobble stones to the water front, dumped their cotton, and returned for more. By evening the sky was red for miles around with the leaping flames. The glare was seen even across Lake Pontchartrain, and "set men and women weeping and wailing."[11] The great fire burned on and on through the night, and when it stopped, 13,000 bales of cotton had been consumed in this burnt offering to Mars.[12]

The next morning the city was in a frenzy of excitement. In vain did the *Daily True Delta* with pitiable bombast editorialize on the "Insanity of Trepidation," "Culpable Official Neglect," and "Undying Love of Our Institutions and Country."[13] In vain did the *Crescent* ask, "Have we fallen so low—are we so poor in spirit—that a few gunboats of an enemy shall shake us in our fidelity and resolution?"[14] In vain did the *Bee* urge the people to refrain from "undue excitement."[15] The people knew better. The Union fleet was coming up the river, and the city would be at its mercy. The crowds, red-eyed after a sleepless night, were tired, frightened, and angry. They had been living in a fool's paradise, and felt they had been deceived and betrayed.[16] Boats began to leave crowded with passengers and freight. Some were being burned to prevent their falling into the hands of the enemy. The spirit of license spread to the crowd: barrels and hogsheads of rice, meat, sugar, molasses, and tobacco were broken open and the people helped themselves.[17] A poor fellow who looked like a spy was swung up to a lamp post at the corner of Magazine and Common streets, and he was saved, pale as a ghost, only by the opportune passing of a patrol of the Foreign Legion.[18]

Meanwhile Farragut's fleet was steaming up the river, twelve ships strong. Two gunboats had been left at Quarantine to cooperate with General Butler. At daylight, about five o'clock, the ships had gotten underway. Proceeding slowly and carefully, they did not reach English Turn until about five hours later. Soon the evidence of the panic in New Orleans began to be manifest in cotton-laden ships on fire floating down the river. To Farragut, this "destruction of property was awful."[19] More than twenty blazing ships and more than a thousand burning bales of cotton floated past before New Orleans came in sight.[20] Rounding English Turn, the fleet was confronted with the Chalmette fortifications, the last barrier to the city, near the scene of General Jackson's famous victory over the British. They were earthen embankments facing each other across the river, and at that time they were armed with five and nine 32-pounders respectively.[21]

Resistance was made at Chalmette "through a sense of duty but without any expectation of success."[21] The *Cayuga*, again leading the fleet, received the first fire of the batteries which caused her to fall back. The *Hartford* moved up and at a range of about half a mile "gave them such a fire 'as they never dreamed of in their philosophy.' "[22] Soon the *Pensacola* appeared on the scene and with a tremendous broadside took the starboard battery off Farragut's hands. Then the *Brooklyn* ranged up and took on the battery on the left bank. Other vessels arrived and tried to get in a few shots. Farragut's greatest fear was that his ships might fire into each other, and he and Captain Wainwright shouted themselves hoarse to the men to be careful.[22] In twenty minutes the guns were silenced and the gunners were driven into the woods to escape capture. It was then nearly noon; the fleet reformed and swept on up the river under a full head of steam, one column hugging the port shore and the other moving near the wharves on the New Orleans side.[23]

Below Slaughterhouse Point a rifled fieldpiece fired on the *Richmond* from a large white building on the right hand side of the river, which was then demolished by one broadside from the Union vessel. A few Minie rifle balls struck the bridge of the *Pensacola,* which answered with a broadside, "doing terrible execution" upon "hundreds of innocent people."[23] George Washington Cable, then a small boy, saw the fleet come "into full view, silent, grim, and terrible; black with men, heavy with deadly portent; the long banished Stars and Stripes flying against the frowning sky. . . . The crowds on the levee howled and screamed with rage. The swarming decks answered never a word; but one old tar on the *Hartford,* standing with lanyard in hand beside a great pivot-gun, so plain to view that you could see him smile, silently patted its big black breech and blandly grinned."[24] At one o'clock the *Hartford* came to anchor,[25] and the others soon thereafter. The rain was pouring down in torrents, accompanied with thunder and lightning.[26] This rendered even more wretched the thousands of citizens crowding the levees and the ruined wharves. They gazed as though fascinated at the "dusky, long, morose, demon-like Yankee steamers like evil messengers of woe"[27] lying in front of the city. The falling rain did not quench the smoldering fires which were consuming great piles of cotton and coal, ships, and docks. Soon the unfinished ram *Mississippi,* which completed might have been a terror to Farragut's fleet, came floating down all ablaze—a sad grim sight to the watching crowds.

The river had risen almost to the top of the levees, and the guns of the fleet commanded the city, in which there were then only some 3,000 poorly organized militia armed mainly with shotguns. The Queen of the Gulf was at the mercy of Farragut, with his ships anchored in nearly bow and quarter line and their broadsides trained on the city. At three o'clock he sent Captain Bailey ashore to demand the surrender of the city from the authorities. Accompanied by Lieutenant Perkins, he was rowed to the wharf at the foot of Laurel Street in a small boat under a flag of truce. Here the corpulent red faced captain and the handsome young lieutenant[28] were received by the hooting and the shouting of a crowd whom the heavy rainstorm had not driven indoors. On the way to the City Hall, a mob followed them, many with weapons in their hands, cheering for Jeff Davis and Beauregard and groaning at the name of Lincoln. Some began to throw things at the Union officers and shout, "Hang them! hang them!"[29] At that critical moment, two respected citizens, one a member of the City Council, rescued them from the furious mob and conducted them to the mayor's office. "So through the gates of death those two men walked to the City Hall to demand the town's surrender. It was one of the bravest deeds I ever saw done," wrote George Washington Cable[30] long afterwards, who as a lad was one of that mob.

With Mayor John T. Monroe were some of the most prominent citizens of the city, including Pierre Soulé. To the demand for the surrender, the mayor replied to Captain Bailey that New Orleans was under martial law and that he would have to negotiate with General Lovell. After about half an hour that lithe, brown-haired general of forty-odd years arrived. He was a showy horseman, riding with so long a stirrup leather that he merely stood astride the saddle straight as a spear.[30] His answer was, "I'll never surrender"; but he added that he would remove his troops from the city as soon as possible, and then the mayor would take over and do what he pleased. Meanwhile the mob was putting on a show; they kicked at the doors and swore they would hang the officers. Soulé and others went out and made speeches to them on one side of the building, while Bailey and Perkins were hustled out another way to a closed carriage and driven to the wharf whence they returned to report to Farragut.[30] They were fortunate in suffering no more injury than a subjection to insult and blackguarding, for passions were running high that day. When the *Mississippi* moved in close to the wharf and the band played "The Star-Spangled Banner," some of the crowd cheered and waved their hats. At that moment a troop of cavalry came riding up the street and fired a volley into the crowd of helpless men, women, and children.[31] Farragut fully realized the tenseness of the situation. That evening every man in the fleet was armed with a revolver and a cutlass to overcome any attempt at boarding during the night.[32]

2

After the thrilling experiences of this memorable homecoming to the city of his boyhood, Farragut sat down in the quiet of his cabin and penned this beautiful letter to his wife and son: "I am so agitated that I can scarcely write, and shall only tell you that it has pleased Almighty God to preserve my life through a fire such as the world has scarcely known. I shall return properly my thanks, as well as those of the fleet, for His goodness and mercy. He has permitted me to make a name for my dear boy's inheritance, as well as for my comfort and that of my family. . . . Jim [his Negro servant] escaped, but the other two servants were wounded. I took the city at meridian to-day. Such vandalism I never witnessed as the destruction of property. All the beautiful steamers and ships were set on fire and consumed. . . ."[33]

At six o'clock the following morning, Marion A. Baker, the mayor's private secretary, went on board the *Hartford* to explain to Farragut that his request would be considered by the council at ten o'clock. The Flag-Officer received Baker, whom he had known a long time, with kindness, answered all his questions about the passage of the forts, and took him all over the flagship, showing him how the boilers had been protected and where the ship's sides had been scarred by shots. With Baker standing beside him on the spot where he stood during the battle,

Farragut said, "It was the most terrific conflict I had ever been in. I seemed to be breathing flame."[34]

Baker returned with a brief note from Farragut, asking the mayor to announce that no flag but that of the United States would be permitted to fly in the presence of the Union fleet so long as he had the power to prevent it.[35] Later at ten o'clock, he sent Lieutenant Albert Kautz with a longer letter, making another demand for the surrender of the city, the hoisting of the United States flag over the City Hall, Mint, and Custom House, and the removal of other flags from public buildings. These demands were to be met by twelve o'clock.[36] Kautz was accompanied ashore by Midshipman John H. Read and a guard of twenty marines under the command of Second Lieutenant George Heisler. They too were met by a menacing mob, and on the advice of an officer of the City Guards, the marines were sent back to the ship. Kautz, with Read and a non-commissioned marine on whose bayonet a handkerchief was tied, then made his way to the City Hall through the same jeering and insulting crowds that Bailey and Perkins had encountered.[37]

At about the same time, Captain Morris, under orders from Farragut, sent a force of marines from the *Pensacola* in two boats to seize the Mint and hoist the American flag over it.[38] While Kautz was conferring with the mayor, a gang of men arrived with an American flag. When they saw the Union officers, they tore the flag into shreds and threw them into the window. A man named Mumford had lowered the flag from the Mint.[39] When Farragut some days afterwards reported the incident to Butler, the general snapped his cross-eyes, and said, "I will make an example of that fellow by hanging him." Farragut smilingly remarked, "You know, General, you will have to catch him before you can hang him." Butler very seriously replied, "I know that, but I will catch him, and then hang him." He kept his word; Mumford was hanged.[40]

As on the previous day, Kautz and his companions were spirited away through a rear entrance while the mob was being harangued in front, and were driven to the wharf at full speed. The long reply which was carried back to Farragut from the mayor was in effect a surrender of the city to "the power of brutal force," but a refusal to hoist the American flag or to order it to be hoisted. As to lowering the flag of Louisiana, he was ambiguously evasive.[41]

That afternoon the *Hartford, Richmond, Brooklyn, Pensacola,* and *Oneida* proceeded up the river about twenty miles to destroy the batteries at Carrollton. The *Mississippi* and two gunboats had been sent the previous day down to cooperate with Butler and Porter. Farragut returned with his ships the next morning, with several prizes which had been captured on the excursion. Just about noon the *McRae,* flying the Confederate flag, arrived under a flag of truce with wounded from the forts.[42] It was Sunday. Thousands of people gathered on the levees. Some cheered for Jeff Davis; some waved their handkerchiefs and gave three cheers for the Union.

The next morning Farragut reopened his negotiations with the mayor. Captain Bell was sent with a very strong letter[43] to the City Hall, threatening to fire upon the city if the authorities refused to lower the Louisiana flag, and warning the mayor to remove the women and children from the city within forty-eight hours. Bell also, for his safety, was conveyed by the chief of police in a carriage back to his boat. The mayor still refused to lower the flag, and contended that "there is no possible exit from this city for a population which still exceeds in number 140,000, and you must therefore be aware of the utter inanity of such a notification. Our women and children cannot escape from your shells if it be your pleasure to murder them on a question of mere etiquette."[44] To the *Crescent,* Farragut was a "creature of accidental success," who would not be satisfied until the people of New Orleans had been made to lick "the very dust."[45]

The mayor's written reply was taken by Baker and Soulé on board the *Hartford* early on the morning of the 29th. Bailey and Bell were present at the interview. Soulé gave a long discussion of the international law involved. Farragut listened patiently. When Soulé had finished, he replied, "I am a plain sailor, and it is not expected that I should understand the nice points of international usage. I am simply here as the commander of the fleet, and I aim only to do my duty in this capacity."[46] Farragut had indeed raised an international problem. The foreign consuls, whom he had notified of the possibility of his being compelled to fire on the city and of the advisability of removing their families to safety, signed their names to a letter of vigorous protest.[47]

Realizing that he could not wisely force Mayor Monroe to lower the Louisiana flag, Farragut decided to send Bell ashore with a final letter to the mayor, accompanied by all the marines of the fleet, with the express purpose of hauling down the flag from the City Hall. First he hoisted the American flag over the Custom House; then he proceeded to the City Hall and announced his purpose to the mayor. Directed by an excited red-bearded man, Bell with Lieutenant Kautz and Boatswain's Mate George Russell ascended to the roof and reached the flagstaff, and Russell lowered the flag.[48] "In the street beneath gleamed the bayonets of a body of marines," according to Cable. "A howitzer pointed up and another down the street. All around swarmed the mob. Just then Mayor Monroe—lest the officer above should be fired upon, and the howitzers open upon the crowd—came out alone and stood just before one of the howitzers, tall, slender, with folded arms, eyeing the gunner. Down sank the flag. Captain Bell, tall and stiff, marched off with it rolled under his arm, and the howitzers clanking behind. Then cheer after cheer rang out for Monroe. And now, I dare say, every one is well pleased that, after all, New Orleans never lowered her colors with her own hands."[49] As to this episode, Farragut wrote Welles, "I sent on shore and hoisted the American flag on the custom-house, and hauled down the Louisiana State flag from the city hall, as the mayor had avowed that there was no man in New Orleans who dared to haul it down, and my own convictions are that, if such an individual could have been found, he would have been assassinated."[50]

3

Early on the morning of April 29, the *Cayuga* returned with the welcome news that Forts Jackson and St. Philip had surrendered, and that the ram *Louisiana* had been blown up.[51] These results had been achieved almost entirely by watchful waiting, once the fleet had passed the forts. At first, Porter was very much alarmed about what the *Louisiana* might do to his gunboats as well as the mortars, which he ordered down to their old positions where they continued to bombard during the 24th without reply from the forts. In his concern, Porter thought he saw the *Louisiana* "moving about quite lively,"[52] though as a matter of fact she did not move from her anchorage.[53] He wrote to Flag-Officer McKean, "I ask all the assistance you can give us in the shape of steamers with heavy guns and solid shot. There is no time for delay; we may otherwise meet with disaster. . . ."[54] To Welles he described how formidable the *Louisiana* was, and complainingly added, "This is one of the ill effects of leaving an enemy in the rear." But he assured the Secretary, "I shall at all events take such steps as will prevent her destroying anything."[55] To Farragut he wrote, "I congratulate you on your victory. . . . My hopes and predictions were at last realized. . . . You will find the forts harder to take now than before."[56] These excerpts show quite well how Porter could trim his sails to whatever wind blew his way.

General Butler shared Porter's alarm. Writing to his wife at the base on Ship Island, he declared, "This I deem wholly an unmilitary proceeding on his [Farragut's] part to run off and leave forts behind him unredeemed, but such is the race for the glory of capturing New Orleans between him and Commodore Foote that thus we go."[57]

Soon after the passage of Farragut's fleet, Porter sent Lieutenant Commanding Guest under a flag of truce to demand the surrender of the forts. General Duncan replied simply, "The demand is inadmissible." The next day Porter ordered the mortars below to refit, and dispatched schooners to blockade the bayous in rear of Fort Jackson and two steamers in rear of Fort St. Philip to assist Butler in landing troops.[58]

On the 26th, Commander Mitchell communicated under a flag of truce with the Union gunboats, and learned that New Orleans had surrendered. That afternoon at 4 o'clock this was confirmed when the wreck of the ram *Mississippi* floated down past the forts. The bad news seemed to take the heart out of the defenders. The next morning the landing of troops above Fort St. Philip was observed, and at noon a gunboat with a white flag came up with a written demand for the surrender of the forts. This demand was also refused. But at midnight that same night the garrison of Fort Jackson mutinied in mass; they had had enough. So the next day, after a consultation between Commander Mitchell and the commanding officers of the forts, a flag of truce was sent to the *Harriet Lane,* Porter's flagship, to accept his terms.[59]

Porter steamed up to the forts, accompanied by the steamers *Westfield, Winona,* and *Kennebec,* and received the Confederate army officers, who joined him in the cabin of the *Harriet Lane* to draw up the capitulation.[60] Butler, to his chagrin, was not present; he had gone up to New Orleans to secure light-draft transportation for his troops.[61] At about 10:45 in the midst of the conference, there was a loud explosion, accompanied by considerable surprise and some consternation on the *Harriet Lane.*[62] It was caused by the blowing up of the *Louisiana,* which Mitchell had set on fire. Porter called him an "archtraitor"[63] for destroying his vessel while the conference was being held under flags of truce, and treated him very harshly as a prisoner of war. Porter, however, had made the mistake of not including Mitchell in his negotiations, and as he was independent of the command of the army officers, he felt free to dispose of the *Louisiana* as he thought best.

When Butler took possession of the forts, he found them "substantially as defensible as before the bombardment,"— particularly Fort St. Philip which was "quite uninjured."[64] A controversial rivalry arose between Butler and Porter as to their contributions to the fall of the forts, during which Porter gave old Butler this whacking knockout blow: "Butler did it all!!! So I see it stated by that blackguard reporter of the *Herald* who acted as Farragut's secretary and signal officer, and who had his nose everywhere. If you could have seen the trouble I had getting old Butler and his soldiers up to the forts, to take charge of them (after we took possession) you would laugh at the old fool's pretensions. But he actually asserts that it was his presence (30 miles off) which induced the forts to surrender, and this *Herald* fellow tries to make it appear so, and says that no harm was done to the forts and that they were as good as new."[65]

Indeed Farragut had more reason for feeling aggrieved at the newspapers, for the Washington *Daily National Intelligencer* of April 28 declared, "New Orleans has been captured by the mortar fleet under the command of Commodore Porter," and the New York *Herald* and the *World* of April 30 and the *National Intelligencer* of May 1 reported "that New Orleans is now in Captain Porter's quiet possession." All of this was very annoying to Captain Craven, who wrote his wife, "This is all as I suspected it would be, and as I ventured to say, more than six weeks ago to Captain Farragut, that it would be. 'Porter's mortar boats and Butler's expedition' have been all the talk ever since last November, and one of my remarks when in consultation one night upon the proper mode of attack was, 'Should we be so fortunate as to succeed, it will appear in all of our journals as Commander Porter's victory; but should we unfortunately fail, it will be published as the defeat of the Gulf Squadron under Flag-Officer Farragut.' "[66]

It was four days after Farragut passed the forts when the first news was published in Northern papers, reports having been received by way of Mobile and Petersburg, Virginia newspapers and by telegraph from Fortress Monroe. The New York *Herald* of April 28 carried this headline: "New Orleans Taken. Splendid Victory of the Union Forces in the Southwest. All the Forts on the Lower Mississippi Captured. Tremendous Destruction of Property in New Orleans. The Probable Capture of the Ironclad Boat *Louisiana*. The Rebels Run Off with the Fifteen Millions of Specie Said to Be in the Banks of the City." Some of this, which was mere supposition, had not then happened.

There was an editorial on the importance of the news, which merely mentioned Farragut's name without comment. Other papers of that date carried the same story, but with less fanfare. The New York *World* declared that the capture "reflects great credit upon the gallant commander who directed it," but nowhere mentioned his name. It was not until May 2 that the New York *Herald* gave any consideration to Farragut, and not until May 17 that *Harper's Weekly* carried a photograph of him.[67] The first official announcement of the victory came by telegraph to Secretary Welles from Captain Bailey on May 8 when he arrived at Fortress Monroe on his way to Washington with dispatches.[68]

Though recognition of Farragut was slow, the realization of the importance of his achievement was immediate, not only in the North but also in the South,[69] where the success of Farragut's campaign meant not alone the loss of a great city but even the loss of the war. There is good evidence that the failure of Napoleon III to recognize the Confederacy and take some positive step towards bringing the war to a close even without English cooperation was due to Farragut's capture of New Orleans. If Farragut had failed, it is not unlikely that, a few months later after McClellan's army suffered such a crushing defeat in Virginia, England too would have taken steps towards bringing about peace with the establishment of the Confederate States of America as an independent nation.[70] If this be true, then Farragut's capture of the Queen of the Gulf becomes an important turning point in the course of the Civil War.

IX

ON TO VICKSBURG

1

Though Farragut had written Fox two months before the capture of New Orleans, "If I get a successful entrance, I shall not stop until I meet Foote,"[1] yet after his success, he was torn between two desires. The day after passing the forts, he wrote Welles that as soon as they were captured his purpose was "immediately to ascend to meet Flag-Officer Foote."[2] But four days later he wrote the Secretary, "As soon as I see General Butler safely in possession of this place, I will sail for Mobile with the fleet."[3] The same day he wrote Mrs. Farragut, "I will be off for Mobile in a few days, and put it to them there. I have done all I promised, and all I was expected to do. So, thanks to God, I hope I have acquitted myself to the satisfaction of my friends as well as my country."[4] In a letter to Porter that day he closed with this: "We must get ready to strike at Mobile as soon as possible, nothing like keeping up the stampede upon them."[5] But the very next day he wrote his wife, "I am now going up the river to meet Foote—where, I know not—and then I shall resume my duties on the coast, keep moving, and keep up the stampede I have upon them."[6] Possibly he had meanwhile taken another look at the Secretary's orders of January 20, 1862, which explicitly required, "If the Mississippi expedition from Cairo shall not have descended the river, you will take advantage of the panic to push a strong force up the river to take all their defenses in the rear. You will also reduce the fortifications which defend Mobile Bay and turn them over to the army to hold."[7]

Farragut had quite decided to continue up the Mississippi, when on May 1 Porter arrived in the steamer *Harriet Lane,* and Butler also with troops which he began to land that afternoon.[8]

Courtesy of Curator, U. S. Naval Academy

CAPTAIN D. G. FARRAGUT, U.S.N.

From a photograph by E. Jacobs, New Orleans, made after city's capture.

REAR-ADMIRAL FARRAGUT

From a photograph by C. D. Fredricks & Co., New York. From author's collection. This was the uniform of the regulations of July 31, 1862.

Courtesy of F. H. Meserve, New York

REAR-ADMIRAL FARRAGUT
From a photograph by Brady.

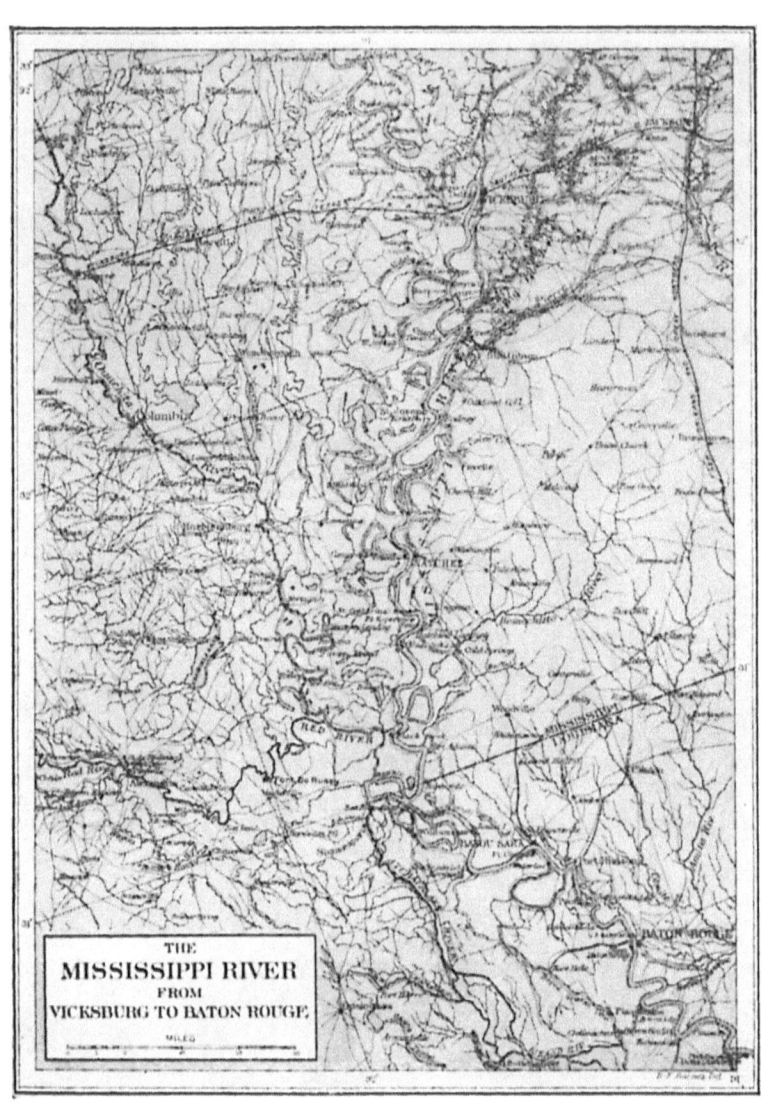

From *Official Records of the Union and Confederate Navies in the War of the Rebellion.*

The same day Farragut ordered Porter to proceed to Ship Island with his flotilla and there await the Flag-Officer's arrival with the heavy ships. But Porter was warned not to attempt any operations until Farragut was ready, for the Confederates were reported to have "at least two rams or ironclad batteries at Mobile, and they might destroy the small vessels if they entered the bay."[9] In conclusion, he asked Porter to send one of his vessels to take possession of the fort at the entrance to Barataria Bay. No definite time was set for operations against Mobile, but at that time Farragut thought that he would soon be able to finish his campaign in the Mississippi and return to the Gulf. There is no evidence that Porter tried to persuade him to attack Mobile before ascending further up the river.[10] Indeed, the contrary is true, if we are to believe Porter, who wrote, "Carefully as the project of capturing Vicksburg was planned, it was not executed. Why, I do not know. I presume Farragut delayed his advance from New Orleans until he could secure the necessary troops to hold Vicksburg. I urged pushing on to Vicksburg, instead of which I was pushed on to Ship Island, a delightful retreat where General Butler used to send rebellious women who hooted at the Union flag."[11]

Farragut had an experience about that time with one New Orleans woman, whom General Butler might not have treated with so much consideration. He and his Fleet Surgeon, Jonathan M. Foltz, entered a streetcar, and Farragut took his seat next to a well dressed woman and her small daughter. The car was somewhat crowded and Foltz remained standing near by. The beautiful child, just beginning to talk, stroked the gold braid on the Flag-Officer's coat, and said, "Look, Mamma! Pretty!" Farragut, who was fond of children, laughingly patted her head and remarked, "You are a dear little girl." At that remark, the mother turned round and spat in Farragut's face. She jerked the child away, poured out a torrent of denunciation, and seemed in her passionate hatred about to attack him like a wildcat. Foltz grasped her by the wrists and began to express his indignation of such conduct. But Farragut took him by the arm, and said very calmly, "Remember that this city is under the guns of my fleet. Many lives may be sacrificed and the city destroyed just because of this foolish woman, for she can easily provoke a riot. We must not think of ourselves but of the innocent who would suffer with the guilty." Meanwhile he was wiping his face with his handkerchief, and the woman, overhearing what had been said about the guns of the fleet, became frightened and made no answer to inquiries from people who had heard the angry voices and came running up to the slowly moving car.[12] What would Ben Butler have done to her?

Farragut may have thought of what might happen to his own relatives, some of whom for all he knew were then in New Orleans, as it was the home of his brother William's family.[13] But none of them had then come to see him. "It is a strange thought that I am here among my relatives," he wrote Mrs. Farragut, "and yet not one has dared say, 'I am happy to see you.' There is a reign of terror in this doomed city; but, although I am abused as one who wished to kill all the women and children, I still see a feeling of respect for me."[14]

2

There was no delay by Farragut in beginning operations above New Orleans. The day after Butler's arrival with troops, Captain Craven in the *Brooklyn* with three gunboats was dispatched up the river.[15] On that day a signal was made for all commanding officers to come on board the flagship. Craven related[16] that, at the interview "with the little man," Farragut said, "I want to send three or four vessels up to Vicksburg at once to destroy the railroad. Who is ready to go right off?" Alden answered, "I cannot start before to-morrow, as I have no pilot and some of my engineers are below in the *Tennessee*." Craven replied that the *Brooklyn* was ready. "Well, now, Craven," said Farragut, "I want you to start right off. Go up to Vicksburg, destroy the railroad, and wait there until I come up."

The day following Craven's departure, Farragut, having been informed that on account of the high stage of the river the *Brooklyn* would likely run aground above Baton Rouge, wrote her commander not to proceed above that place, which he was to capture. He was then to send three or four gunboats on up to Vicksburg under Commander S. P. Lee.[17] Farragut further ordered Craven to return to New Orleans as soon as he captured Baton Rouge, provided the Flag-Officer did not join him. Then he added, almost certainly referring to the attack on Mobile, "We must attend to another work in a few days; in fact, every day is a great loss."[17] Before these orders reached him, Craven passed Baton Rouge without attempting its capture and, arriving about twenty miles below Natchez, turned back because of a breakdown of the machinery of the *Itasca* and the *Sciota* and the smallness of his coal supply.[18] On the way down, he met the *Oneida*, *Kennebec*, and *Pinola* under Commander Lee, and was greatly relieved at Farragut's order for he had been in constant fear of running the *Brooklyn* aground. The seven vessels accordingly anchored, on the afternoon of May 7, near Tunica Island above Baton Rouge.[19]

Meanwhile Farragut had learned that the Confederates had eighteen gunboats at Memphis, and were building an ironclad in that vicinity. So he gave up the idea of intrusting the Mississippi campaign to his gunboats while he reduced the forts at the entrance to Mobile Bay with his larger vessels, and wrote Welles that he would not attack Mobile until he received reenforcements.[20] "I am anxious to reduce that place," he concluded, "as soon as possible, as I understand they are building an ironclad ram there of great dimensions, so that time presses."[20]

Sending the *Iroquois* up the river on May 6 with orders to take possession of Baton Rouge, Farragut followed the next day in the *Hartford* accompanied by the *Richmond*.[21] By the *Itasca*, which he met going down to be coaled, he sent orders for the *Mississippi* also to join him at Baton Rouge. Here he arrived in the afternoon of the 9th, and found that the American flag had been hoisted over the arsenal that morning at 9 o'clock by Commander James S. Palmer of the *Iroquois*, after an exchange of notes with Mayor Bryan. Baton Rouge was then a small town of about 7,000 inhabitants.[21] Here he found also the *Brooklyn*, just arrived, and that evening the *Wissahickon* came in from New Orleans. He was disappointed in learning that his gunboats were still in that vicinity. On the day of his departure from New Orleans he had written Fox of his delay by "a thousand things," and had declared that the *"Oneida* with seven or eight gunboats is at Vicksburg by this time." As to Mobile he wrote, "The last news was that they were blocking up the channel to Mobile—by sinking vessels. I shall push down there as soon as I get back from up the river." He also reported that the *Mississippi* and all his gunboats were in need of repairs.[22]

The very next day Commander Lee was ordered to take five gunboats up the river and capture Natchez, some sixty miles above Baton Rouge.[23] This was accomplished on May 13, and the *Brooklyn* and another gunboat arrived there the same evening on what Craven called "a wild-goose chase."[24] Early the following day the *Richmond* with two steamers transporting 1,200 troops under command of Brigadier-General Thomas Williams started up stream. Two hours later the *Hartford* followed. Delayed by engine trouble, she was overtaken by the *Itasca*. This was fortunate, for that evening the *Hartford* ran aground at Tunica Bend. In vain, she tried to back off. Rolling the ship, caused by the crew running from port to starboard and back several times, was also of no avail. After the *Itasca* tried vainly to haul her off, Farragut decided to send the gunboat to St. Francisville for a ferryboat and a lighter. His ship was really in great danger, for the river was higher than it had ever been known to be, and a sudden fall might soon leave the *Hartford* grounded indefinitely. All the next day, coal and guns were transferred to the *Itasca,* shot and shell to the ferryboat, and the rest of the coal to the lighter. About 10:30 on the following day, the *Itasca* pulled the *Hartford* off "to the great joy of everyone on board and my humble gratitude to the Great Ruler of Events," according to Captain Bell.[25]

While the *Hartford* was stuck in the mud of the Mississippi, Lincoln wrote to Congress on the 14th of May, strongly recommending that a vote of thanks be given Farragut for his capture of New Orleans. If he had known this, he might have been somewhat cheered in his anxiety as to the fate of his flagship. The thanks were not voted, however, until nearly two months later, and not received by Farragut until another month later still.²⁶

Arriving at Natchez early on the Sunday afternoon of May 18, Farragut found the *Brooklyn, Richmond,* and *Iroquois* there. Lee's six gunboats had departed for Vicksburg two days previous, accompanied by the steamers *Burton* and *Ceres* with General Williams' troops.²⁵ At noon that very Sunday, Lee's squadron arrived just below Vicksburg, and a letter was sent to "The Authorities at Vicksburg" demanding the surrender of the city.²⁷ A very confident reply was returned by Colonel James L. Autrey, Military Governor, the high point of which was, "Mississippians don't know, and refuse to learn, how to surrender to an enemy. If Commodore Farragut or Brigadier-General Butler can teach them, let them come and try."²⁷

The following day, the *Hartford, Richmond,* and *Itasca* moved up twenty miles above Natchez to await the transport *Laurel Hill* with seven more companies of troops. Here that afternoon the *Kennebec* arrived from below Vicksburg with disquieting news from Lee as to the rapidity of the current and the strong defenses situated on bluffs two to three hundred feet above the river, which could be approached only head on or in line ahead because of the bend in the river. Bell advised Farragut to leave his heavy ships and go up to Vicksburg in a gunboat to examine the situation personally.²⁸ Farragut agreed, and joined Lee on May 20, leaving orders for the remainder of his fleet to follow up to Grand Gulf, about fifty miles from Vicksburg, and there await his return.²⁹

§

Farragut, on learning that there were ten guns mounted just below Vicksburg and two above, under which two gunboats were lying, ordered five of his gunboats to go up and cut out or destroy the two Confederate vessels. Commanders Lee, Caldwell, and Nichols considered the attempt "impractical or madness,"³⁰ and Lee went so far as to say that anyone who wanted to try it could have his gunboat. Commanders DeCamp and Donaldson alone were willing to attempt the attack. Farragut was greatly disturbed over the lack of fighting spirit among his gunboat commanders, for the enemy had been defiant and needed to be "chastised."[30]

General Williams was of the opinion that his 1,400 troops were inadequate to capture the town and the forts, as he understood that 8,000 men were concentrated there.[30] After two days, Farragut reluctantly came to the conclusion that the guns of his ships could not effectively reach the defenses on the bluffs, and that his military force was not large enough either to take or to hold the town, to the defense of which 20,000 troops could be quickly brought from the vicinity. A bombardment of the place was, therefore, useless. So he decided to leave the gunboats on blockade until the Battle of Corinth should be decided. To Butler he wrote further that he was "unwilling to risk the large ships" beyond Grand Gulf, "which is the most dangerous part of the river."[31] Of this decision Williams also wrote Butler that Farragut "goes down the river this afternoon to join his flagship near Natchez preparatory to a movement on Mobile."[32]

Farragut returned to his fleet below Grand Gulf on May 23, a wet and dreary day. Something meanwhile had led him to change his mind, for within three hours after his return all his vessels were underway not down the river but upstream towards Vicksburg.[33] His sudden change of plan was not due to Fox's telegram to Farragut of May 16: "Carry out your instructions of January 20 about ascending the Mississippi River, as it is of the utmost importance,"[34] which had been rushed off to him from Hampton Roads in triplicate on the *Dacotah, Ocean Queen,* and *Coatzacoalcos.*[35] He did not receive this telegram until his return to New Orleans later[36] on May 30.

Could this have been a case of mental telepathy? Both Fox and Welles had by that time worked themselves into a state of nervous apprehension as to what was happening on the Mississippi. This is reflected in a letter to Farragut from Fox on May 12, a somewhat belated letter of congratulation upon his capture of New Orleans. Secretary Welles also delayed congratulating Farragut until May 10, strange as it now seems.[37]

After praising Farragut's achievement "which has rendered your name immortal," Fox wrote, "The rebellion seems caving in all around and I think we will have very little difficulty in taking the whole coast. The only anxiety we feel is to know if you have followed your instructions and pushed a strong force up the river, to meet the Western Flotilla. We only hear of you at Baton Rouge. The opening of the Mississippi is of more importance than Mobile, and if your ships reach Memphis in the next few days, Beauregard's army is cut off from escape. We listen most anxiously for word that your forces are near there."[38] These were certainly extravagant expectations, displaying complete ignorance of the obstacles to be overcome in ascending the river and the probable results of such a movement upon Beauregard at Corinth.

In a letter to Farragut three days later, Fox again called attention to the "confidential instructions with regard to ascending the Mississippi after the fall of New Orleans."[39] Then the day following the dispatch of the telegram, he wrote a long letter explaining that in the New York papers of the previous day "it was stated, via Natchez and Cairo, that your squadron had returned to New Orleans, instead of continuing their course up the river to Memphis." The probability of the truth of this statement, he declared, had distressed Lincoln so much that the telegram had been sent. "It is of paramount importance that you go up and clear the river with the utmost expedition. Mobile, Pensacola, and, in fact, the whole coast sinks into insignificance compared with this." He had hardly slept during the past three weeks, he plaintively added.[40] The same day Fox wrote Porter, "Somebody has made a most serious blunder, in persuading the Flag-Officer to go at Mobile instead of obeying his instructions to go up the Mississippi River." This was followed by an expression of exaggerated fears of a defeat by the Confederate rams at Memphis of the gunboats under command of Davis, who had replaced Foote, and of the consequent retreat of General Halleck with the loss of "St. Louis, Cairo, and everything." "How important," he sighed, "to obey instructions predicated upon a knowledge of the whole ground."[41]

Before Porter had time to receive this letter and to learn of the Navy Department's ardent feelings about opening the Mississippi, he wrote very indiscreetly to Fox, ". . . I never expect to hear of Farragut again. I have an idea he will ground on the bars of the Mississippi, and remain there for the rest of the season. He went up without good pilots in those large ships where gunboats was [sic] all he wanted. He went up at a high stage of the river, and if the water falls he is done for, and you may make up your mind to fit out a new squadron. If you can get one up without having an old fogy in it, what a blessing it will be to the country. When I think of what a splendid thing we had of it here, I collapse. I proposed to leave the *Mississippi* and *Pensacola* at New Orleans, and make a dash right at Mobile with the rest of the ships."[42] After making an attack on Captain Bell whom he recommended to be ordered home because "he is pig-headed and slow and has a bad influence on Farragut," he went on at great length to show why Mobile should have been attacked before the Confederates had time to strengthen their forts and other defenses.[42]

Fortunately for Porter, by the time Fox received this letter, he and Welles had come to have their doubts as to the wisdom of the campaign which they were forcing Farragut to carry on up the Mississippi. These long letters had eased Porter's mind somewhat, while he was eating his heart out at Ship Island, under the impression that Farragut had somehow cheated him out of glory and distinction. In a letter to his daughter Georgy he wrote "a burlesque description of the Battle of New Orleans, illustrated with caricatures of several participants. A mild little duck and a crowing rooster represented Farragut before and after the battle."[43]

Welles kept up the pressure on Farragut with a letter of May 19, which informed him that President Lincoln required him to use his utmost exertions to join Flag-Officer Davis's squadron above Vicksburg.[44] Three days later the Secretary wrote with relief that he had learned that Farragut had gone up the Mississippi, and evidently he and Fox were then permitted to recover some of their lost sleep.[45] It was, therefore, fortunate for Farragut that he changed his mind and decided to take his entire fleet up to Vicksburg.

4

The *Hartford* anchored four miles below Vicksburg at four o'clock in the afternoon of May 24. Present there then were the three large vessels and eight gunboats. Just one hour later, Farragut took his commanding officers on a reconnaissance of the defenses in the *Kennebec*. Approaching within two miles of the town, they observed three or four guns on a plateau one hundred feet above the water, which commanded the river for two miles up and down stream. Below the town they saw four guns in excavated breastworks facing across and up the river; and on top of the bluffs, two hundred feet high and three hundred yards back from the river, were six or more guns of large size. Only one gunboat was seen lying under the bluff at the upper end of the town.[46]

The next day, Sunday, Farragut was ill, and in the late afternoon Captain Bell went with General Williams and his staff in the *Kennebec* to make another reconnaissance. On returning at sunset, they went on board the *Hartford,* and Farragut held a council of all his captains and General Williams in his cabin. The General declared that with his 1,400 effective troops he could accomplish nothing unless the ships first silenced the batteries. Then he might possibly climb the bluffs, spike the guns, and return to the ships. Bell, Craven, Wainwright, Lee, Russell, Nichols, and Donaldson all agreed that the ships' guns could not reach the highest batteries and silence them, and that therefore the attack should not be made. DeCamp thought the enemy should be attacked because they had replied "insultingly"[46] to Lee's demand to surrender. Palmer wanted to go in and "smash them up," but "thought we should not, if we could not."[46] Caldwell thought the town should be attacked and destroyed. "Alden thought we should attack, and should not attack, and hid his face in his hands"[46]—bushy black mustache and all. Farragut wanted to punish the enemy by destroying the town, but was restrained by his better judgment and acquiesced in the opinion of the majority. Six gunboats were ordered to blockade the river and cut off supplies, and occasionally bombard the defenses.

The rest of the fleet and the army transports started down stream the next day, for the river had begun to fall and grounding under such conditions might have meant the loss of one of the larger ships.[46] At Grand Gulf the troop transports were fired upon, and in retaliation the *Brooklyn* and two of the gunboats shelled the town. A white flag finally appeared, and a group of citizens laid all the blame on irresponsible guerrillas. At Baton Rouge, no American flag was seen, and while Farragut was writing the mayor, Chief Engineer James B. Kimball went ashore in a dingey to get his laundry. Near the landing, a body of cavalry fired upon the boat, wounding Kimball and two of the oarsmen. The *Hartford* and *Kennebec* gave the town a shelling, and citizens came aboard under a flag of truce to explain that the horsemen were guerrillas over whom they had no control. Farragut decided to land General Williams' soldiers there, and leave them under the protection of a couple of gunboats. The *Hartford* and the *Brooklyn* then proceeded down the river to New Orleans where they arrived on the afternoon of the 30th of May. The *Richmond* had arrived three days before, making a twelve to thirteen knots no-stop run from Vicksburg.[47]

5

When Farragut read the telegram and pile of letters from Fox and Welles, his heart sank with the realization that he would have to do a lot of explaining. The same day he wrote an unusually long letter to Welles and a shorter one to Fox and on June 3 another letter to Welles,[48] giving an account of his operations and the reasons for his return to New Orleans. He called attention to the necessity of coaling and making repairs at New Orleans after passing the forts, of the slowness of proceeding up the river against a strong current without dependable pilots and with transports, of the impossibility of taking and holding Vicksburg with the small military force available, of the difficulty of transporting coal and other supplies so far from New Orleans and the danger to transports of capture by guerrillas or destruction by guns placed at strategic places along the river, and of the danger of running ships aground and of being trapped upstream by the falling water. "Thus, sir," he declared in the letter to Welles, "you have my account of my cruise up the river; one of greater anxiety I never had. The elements of destruction to the Navy in this river are beyond anything I ever encountered." He closed with a warning that the gunboats which he had left below Vicksburg would not be able to resist the ironclad *Arkansas* if she came down to attack them, that all his vessels were badly in need of repairs and the time of half his men was out and they were clamoring to go home, that he had been compelled to neglect proper oversight of the ships of his squadron on blockade in the Gulf, and that if his vessels ascended the river again while the water was falling, "they will never descend until next spring, if at all."

Much of this he repeated to Fox, whom he warned, "If I do not receive additional vessels, the Department may be assured that we will be liable to disaster above, as they are preparing one of the largest rams."[48] "Why cannot the Department spare us a monitor?" he asked. "It would be most gratefully received, as worth all the gunboats in the river."

In answer to the expectation of the Navy Department that his fleet would go to Memphis, Farragut answered in his second letter to Welles that he had no conception that this was ever contemplated, and that he thought this was practical only in time of peace when supplies could be obtained along the river. Vicksburg was only about half way to Memphis, and at that time the ironclad gunboats under Flag-Officer Charles H. Davis, who had succeeded Foote, were held up by the Confederate squadron and the strong defenses of Fort Pillow, about fifty miles above Memphis. Rather gloomily Farragut concluded, "As soon as provisions and anchors are obtained, we will take our departure for up the river, and endeavor to carry out, as far as practicable, the orders conveyed in your different dispatches."[48]

To his wife Farragut revealed his real feelings. "They will keep us in this river until the vessels break down," he complained,[49] "and all the little reputation we have made has evaporated. . . . I am expected to take New Orleans and go up and release Foote from his perilous situation at Fort Pillow, when he is backed by the army and has ironclad boats built for the river service, while our ships are to be periled by getting aground and remaining there till next year; or, what is more likely, be burned to prevent them falling into the enemy's hands. A beautiful prospect for the 'hero of New Orleans!' Well, I will do my duty to the best of my ability, and let the rest take care of itself." In another letter he wrote her, "I had a most anxious time up the river. It wore upon my health more than I could imagine. My anxiety was intense. Only think—500 miles up a river, knowing too that the enemy calculated I would never get back in my ship! It was amusing, however, when I did return, to receive the congratulations of my friends. They had it reported that my legs were shot off, and that I was a prisoner at Jackson! . . . I did not pass Vicksburg; not because it was too strongly fortified, not because we could not have passed it easily enough, but we would have been cut off from our supplies of coal and provisions. . . . I find, the more you do the more is expected of you—that is, the work becomes more complicated and I am now worked to death."[50]

X

RUNNING THE VICKSBURG BATTERIES

1

FINDING THE Navy Department so wedded to the Mississippi campaign, Farragut immediately commenced preparations to return with a stronger force and rejoin his gunboats below Vicksburg. When General Butler learned of the batteries there which Farragut's guns could not reach, he suggested that some of Porter's mortars be sent up to bombard them, and offered to send an army of 7,000 men to cooperate in taking the town.[1] Farragut wrote to Porter explaining the plan, and requesting him to send from six to ten of his mortars up to New Orleans. He made clear his realization of the difficulties involved, but philosophically concluded, "I presume it is our duty to meet them and do our duty to the extent of our ability."[2] This was followed by a second shorter dispatch on June 3, "I have received stringent orders from the Department to send a large force up the river. I therefore desire that you will send to me without delay ten of your mortar boats with steamers enough to tow them as high up the river as may be required."[3]

Only the day before, Porter had written Fox, "Tell the ladies there are no jealousies out here that I know of, but kind brotherly feeling which should always exist in the navy. There is glory enough for all. . . . Do lay aside the red tape and let me know (as there is nobody else) what is to be done here for the public service, in the absence of Farragut. There is no chance of seeing him this summer, or until August. Give me the Monitor and four gunboats, besides what I have, 6,000 more shell, and orders to take the forts at Mobile, and if I do not take them, I will eat them. . . ."[4] Just how he expected to eat them without taking them is left to the imagination. The degree of "kind brotherly feeling" which Porter felt for some of the officers of the fleet may be learned from a letter he wrote Fox the previous week in which he complained of Farragut's lack of system, recommended that Fleet Captain Bell, who was "universally disliked" and had "a bad influence on Farragut," be ordered home, and declared sweepingly, "Had the drunken, worthless fellows in Farragut's squadron been treated as they deserved, you would have had a ship load coming home."[5] In this letter also he suggested that communications be sent direct to him, as "Farragut has not time to read his own letters."[5] "Now Mobile will give us trouble," he wrote Montgomery C. Meigs; "they are working like beavers to get it ready for defense, while Farragut is losing time in New Orleans, has sent me down here with positive orders to attempt nothing until he arrives. . . . He had better have let me stay there to hurry him up, as I have been doing all along. I am anxiously expecting him, and get sick waiting."[6] Could this be called another expression of "kind brotherly feeling"?

It is possible that Butler, who was then at swords' points with Porter about the division of glory incident to the capture of Forts Jackson and St. Philip, suggested that the latter be brought up the Mississippi with his mortars in order to forestall his gathering any laurels at the entrance of Mobile Bay. Butler wrote to Farragut on June 2, inquiring if Porter had been ordered to attack the defenses of Mobile. Farragut replied in the negative, but revealed an uneasiness that Porter might attempt something there before he could cooperate with him.[7]

It must have been with mixed feelings of surprise and disappointment that Porter read Farragut's orders. But he acted with characteristic energy, in twenty minutes dispatching twenty instead of ten mortars under sail with a fair wind to Pass à l'Outre. With the hope that Farragut might change his mind and decide not to go up the Mississippi, he wrote him, requesting that orders of confirmation be sent him there. Then he continued at great length, showing that General Butler's proposed aid would be of no assistance and that he should stay in New Orleans where his troops were needed. Then coming to the real point of his letter, he declared, "Mobile is so ripe now that it would fall to us like a mellow pear, while we I fear will fall like a mellow pear before the difficulties above us in the river." He predicted failure for the expedition and loss of the *Pensacola* while they were "up river." "If we miss taking Mobile now," he sadly lamented, "we won't get it. Two ironclads are indispensable to go up the river."[8]

Farragut remained fixed in his decision, and sent no further orders to Porter, for that same day he had written him of his "stringent orders" and repeated his request for ten mortars.[3] After Porter arrived in New Orleans, he wrote an amazing letter[9] to Fox, stating, "No one was more surprised than myself that Farragut had received orders to go up the river.... When Farragut wrote to me to come up with the Bomb Flotilla, I thought this some wild scheme got up by himself and Butler." But in his first letter to Porter, Farragut had written that the Department was urging him to go up, and in the second letter he had told Porter that his orders were "stringent." Porter continued in his letter to Fox with a detailed criticism of Farragut's conduct of the river campaign. He had been too slow about everything, Porter thought. "He is amiable and yielding and he has a 'skeleton in his closet' who won't let him say his soul is his own," he declared. This "skeleton" was probably Bell, though a very live and vigorous one. Immediately following, Porter complained, "Bell is trying to persuade Farragut not to take the mortars up, but Farragut has left it to me, and I shall take the *whole* of them." As to the return to New Orleans, he reported that "in justice to Alden I must say that he opposed the return strongly and was for going through 'whether or no.'" But he was the first to get back to New Orleans with the *Richmond;* and according to Bell's diary, "Captain Alden thought we should attack, and should not attack, and hid his face in his hands"[10] —not a manifestation of a very positive attitude. Porter further stated that Butler's going up with 5,000 troops was nonsense, and ended with the optimistic statement, "On the 20th Vicksburg will be on fire, I hope."[9] This hope was not to be realized.

Porter was to learn that it was much easier to criticize Farragut for moving slowly up the Mississippi than it was to make rapid progress up it himself.

2

After a week in New Orleans, Farragut started back up the river at 5:30 on the morning of June 8 with the *Hartford* and the *Richmond,* the *Brooklyn* and the gunboat *Pinola* following later the same day.[11] Butler modified his plan, and sent reenforcements to General Williams at Baton Rouge so that the latter could take 3,000 men on the expedition. He had the good sense to foresee that there was to be no glory gained at Vicksburg with even 5,000 men. Farragut had to stop at Baton Rouge several days while General Williams was getting his troops ready and embarked, and while the mortars were being towed upstream. He doubtless had missed the fearless Bailey who had been sent home with dispatches after the capture of New Orleans because he was ill and required an operation. In the midst of his duties at Baton Rouge Farragut wrote his old friend a sympathetic letter. "I am up the Mississippi again, and when I will go down God only knows," he confided, adding that the Department expected him to go with his "dilapidated vessels" a thousand miles against a strong current more easily than Davis could come down with gunboats especially constructed for river navigation.[12]

That day the *Itasca* arrived with the news that she and another gunboat had been sent down from the squadron to find out if Grand Gulf was being heavily fortified, and had received an affirmative demonstration with the loss of three men killed and twenty wounded and many shot holes through their hulls, none of which fortunately were below the water line. Commander Palmer, who had succeeded Lee in command of the gunboats, had then dropped down the river and shelled the batteries and on June 11 had destroyed the town by fire.[13]

Welcome rumors reached Farragut, on the 12th, that Beauregard had evacuated Corinth and that Memphis had been captured. If true, he probably would not have to take his squadron further north than Vicksburg. The rumors were confirmed two days later. Beauregard had been forced out of Corinth by General Halleck on May 29, and this made it necessary for the Confederates to abandon Fort Pillow on June 4 and Memphis two days later, after Davis's squadron had defeated the Confederate gunboats there. Not so pleasant was the news which a deserter brought Farragut that the Confederate ram being built on the Yazoo was nearly ready for service and would mount twenty guns. Farragut was also beginning to worry over the appearance of fever, dysentery, and diarrhoea among his officers and men.[14]

The *Brooklyn* and the *Richmond* went on up the river and joined the gunboats below Vicksburg on the 18th; but the *Hartford* tarried, for the mortar boats were still being towed up and the transports were not ready to move. The next day Farragut got under way with a mortar boat in tow. Everything went well until the afternoon of the third day when suddenly the *Hartford* went aground ten miles north of Union Point below Natchez.[15] Farragut had to go through another anxious experience which had previously threatened "an attack of nervous fever."[16] He never left the deck except to get a cup of tea, though the vessel was aground all night. Meanwhile General Williams's eight troopships and a gunboat had come up, and after much pulling and tugging, the *Hartford* was jerked off the bar at eight-thirty the next morning. "I several times made up my mind to spend the summer there—rather that the ship would," Farragut admitted to his wife. "I always feel that I am responsible for the ship that bears my flag; but, thank God! I was patient and did not suffer as I did before, for I knew that I had done all I could to prevent her from being up the river so high, but was commanded to go. . . . It is a sad thing to think of leaving your ship on a mud-bank, 500 miles from the natural element of a sailor."[16]

While Farragut was stuck in the mud down the river, Porter became greatly disturbed over something or other and wrote Fox, ". . . I would be very much pleased if the Department would relieve me from this command or all connection with the Gulf Squadron. I have no reasons to assign, and am willing to serve anywhere else in a yawl boat."[17] He had arrived in the *Octorara* only the previous day. Is it possible that a good look at those high bluffs at Vicksburg had made him feel that there was little chance of gaining any glory there? Or was he annoyed at Farragut's delay in arriving? He must have known what was detaining the *Hartford*, slowly moving upstream like an old duck taking care of her ducklings. Indeed some of those sixteen ducklings were Porter's own mortars.

At 5:00 A.M. on June 25, the *Hartford* came to anchor seven miles below Vicksburg. Already there were the *Brooklyn* and the *Richmond*, four gunboats, and six steamers and sixteen mortar boats of Porter's flotilla. Later in the day the troopships came in, under guard of three gunboats.[18]

On the previous day, Lieutenant-Colonel Alfred W. Ellet's squadron of four rams and a tender arrived above Vicksburg from Memphis where they had cooperated with Davis's fleet. Immediately Ellet sent a message by four men across the swampy land of the river bend, informing Farragut of his arrival and his readiness to aid in any way possible.[19] Farragut sent a courteous reply, suggesting that the rams could be of greatest assistance in protecting communications between the mouth of the Yazoo River and Vicksburg, and that word might be sent to Flag-Officer Davis that an attack would be made in a day or two and that, if his forces were present, "they would add greatly to the chances of success without much loss of life, which is always desirable in such cases."[20]

3

The west bank of the Mississippi is very low from New Orleans all the way to the mouth of the Red River. The east bank is low also for about one hundred fifty miles, above which point there is a series of bluffs extending the remaining two hundred fifty miles to Vicksburg. On these bluffs batteries could be easily erected, which, if sufficiently strong, could command the passage of the river. They could not be permanently reduced except by the aid of the army, as there was extensive land in the rear over which armies could be maneuvered, and such defenses could not be isolated by the passage of naval vessels as Forts Jackson and St. Philip had been below New Orleans. Vicksburg was protected by batteries, on high bluffs located on the outer bank of a large horseshoe bend, which could rake ships attempting to force their way upstream. Other batteries on the bluffs two hundred feet above the river could pour a destructive plunging fire down upon enemy warships, whose guns could not be sufficiently elevated to reply effectively.

These Confederate batteries then mounted twenty-nine guns, two of which were 10-inch Columbiads and the rest, old style 42 and 32-pounders.[21] The battery just below the Marine Hospital was commanded by Captain Todd, President Lincoln's brother-in-law.[22] There were 10,000 men under Major-General Breckinridge in near-supporting distance, as a land attack was expected; but they were not called upon, and only one brigade was under fire during the attack.[21]

Farragut published a general order on June 25, the day of his arrival, explaining in detail his plan of attack, which he expected to make on the morning of June 27. On the previous day, as was his custom before going into battle, he wrote this letter to his wife: "Here we are once more in front of Vicksburg, by a peremptory order of the Department and President of the United States, 'to clear the river through.' With God's assistance, I intend to try it as soon as the mortars are ready, which will be in an hour or two. The work is rough. Their batteries are beyond our reach on the heights. It must be done in the daytime, as the river is too difficult to navigate by night. I trust that God will smile upon our efforts, as He has done before. I think more should have been left to my discretion; but I hope for the best, and pray God to protect our poor sailors from harm. If it is His pleasure to take me, may He protect my wife and boy from the rigors of a wicked world."[23]

The attack, however, was postponed one day. Meanwhile Porter's mortars continued the bombardment, on the batteries and the town, which had been begun in force the previous day. Owing to some imperfection in his fuzes, it had taken him two days to get his ranges.[24] On the 28th the signal to get under way was made at 2:00 A.M. As at the passage of Forts Jackson and St. Philip, this signal was two vertical red lights hoisted at the mizzen.[25] The fleet was in two columns. Colors were hoisted at all the mastheads. The *Richmond* in mid stream was followed by the *Hartford* and *Brooklyn*. The *Richmond* led because her chase guns were better adapted for attacking forts directly ahead.[26] In a column to the left and near the river bank were eight gunboats, led by the *Iroquois* and *Oneida*, which were in advance of the *Richmond* so their fire would not be blanketed by that vessel. The *Wissahickon* and *Sciota*, next in column, were to fire between the *Richmond* and the *Hartford;* and the *Winona* and *Pinola*, between the *Hartford* and the *Brooklyn*. The *Kennebec* and *Katahdin* were to bring up the rear.[27]

The mortars, stationed on opposite sides of the river, opened in full force at four o'clock. About the same time the leading gunboats were engaged with the enemy, firing at the flash of the guns as it was then too dark to see the batteries.[28] The dense smoke so bewildered the gunners that they were as likely to fire at the explosion of a bombshell as at the flash of a gun.[29] The *Richmond* was in the thick of the Confederate fire by four-thirty. The hills seemed ablaze with the batteries; shots came crashing through the bulwarks and exploded among the men crowded about the guns, sending "brains and blood flying all over the decks."[30] The *Wissahickon* and *Sciota* were also suffering casualties, the latter receiving much damage to her hull and rigging.[31] The *Hartford* went into action about a quarter after four, one division of guns attempting to reach the batteries on the highest ridge. But the Confederate gunners would lie down until the broadside passed over and then, rushing back to their guns, open upon the next ship that passed. A perfect hailstorm of shells from mortars and fleet seemed to be falling on the slopes where there were no guns at all. "It was provoking," Bell thought.[32] The lower batteries were silenced temporarily by the broadsides from the other two divisions.[32] The *Hartford* was struck but not seriously damaged. Captain Wainwright's cabin was cut to pieces. One man was killed and eleven wounded. Farragut had a narrow escape. He was at his favorite post, standing in the mizzen rigging. The captain of a gun on the poop-deck hailed him to come down as he wished to fire a gun in his direction. Hardly had he descended when a shell cut away all the mizzen rigging just above where he had stood. He escaped with only a blow on the head which did not break the skin. The same shot cut the halyards and lowered his flag to half mast. This brought grave alarm to the other vessels where it was thought he had been killed.[33]

About five o'clock the sun rose red and fiery. By that time, the leading vessels had passed out of range of the guns. The *Hartford* was being raked by a battery above the town. The crew thought it had been completely silenced as they passed and had given three cheers when its flag was reported to have been struck. But when the *Hartford* had passed, two heavy rifles opened on her, and did considerably more damage to the ship. But there were no more casualties. In a few minutes the flagship was round the bend out of sight behind the trees; and she came to at a quarter after six, three or four miles above Vicksburg.[34] Five minutes later, Farragut's captains came on board. All the fleet were there except the *Wissahickon*, which had passed on up to the mouth of the Yazoo, and the *Brooklyn*, *Kennebec*, and *Katahdin*, which had failed to get through. The officers and men "spliced the main brace" and went to their well earned breakfast with increased appetite.

4

After consultation with his officers, Farragut wrote a telegram and a brief report to Welles and letters to Davis and Halleck. These were intrusted to Lieutenant-Colonel Ellet of the Ram Fleet, who had boarded the *Hartford* before she came to anchor and offered to carry dispatches up the river. At ten o'clock a ram was off for Memphis with them. The telegram announced: "Fleet passed up above Vicksburg this morning, silenced the battery while passing, but received their raking fire as soon as passed. I have communicated with General Halleck and Commodore Davis, asking for an army force."[35] This was received at Memphis in the late afternoon of July 2. The letters to Welles, Halleck, and Davis amplified this statement: "I passed up the river this morning, but to no purpose,"[36] unless Halleck and Davis will cooperate with forces sufficient to take and hold Vicksburg. Twelve or fifteen thousand men would be needed, he thought, to carry out "the peremptory order of the President"[37] to clear the river.

The following day was Sunday, and Farragut signaled his fleet to "return thanks to Almighty God for His Mercies."[38] The losses had not been heavy: eight men killed and thirty-six wounded in the vessels which passed the batteries.[39] Porter had eight killed and eight or ten wounded, the *Jackson* receiving a shot in her wheelhouse and the *Clifton* one through her boiler.[40] His five steamers had been moved up in advance of the mortars and were exposed rather recklessly to the fire of the batteries. There were no casualties in the mortars. "The Mortar Flotilla have never done better service than at Vicksburg," Farragut wrote Welles, "notwithstanding the imperfections of their fuzes. I have no doubt that they did the forts on the heights great damage."[41] This was perhaps exaggerated praise, for Porter admitted in his own report that some of the batteries were out of range. "I regret," he declared, "that the mortars were not able to reach these batteries."[42]

Porter was not so generous to Farragut. The same day the Flag-Officer was praising his work to Welles, Porter was writing confidentially to Fox that General Williams could have landed his troops and captured the main forts "without scarcely the loss of a man." "I can destroy the forts in twenty-four hours," he extravagantly claimed. "Our mortar practice has been terrible to them, almost every shell falling into their works and killing those who dared to remain there.... Those mortars are great things. In ten minutes after they got going they silenced every battery." Then he complained that "we in the mortar fleet are living on half rations, no flour served, no bread, no butter, no sugar, no molasses, and a storeship with all these articles lying close alongside of us. But we are outsiders and not expected to eat. I have an infirmity of temper which never permits me to forget nor to forgive, and the only pleasure I have is in knowing that a day of *Reckoning* will come."[43] He also complained that the failure of the *Brooklyn* to advance upstream had left his steamers unsupported; hence his damages and casualties. "But for the mortars we would all have been sunk," he declared.

As for the Confederates, they claimed that, in the bombardment and attack, "no gun was disabled, no battery injured, and only thirteen were killed or injured,"[44] and that they had expected a land attack and had 10,000 troops near at hand to meet any such attempt. All the cooperation General Williams gave Farragut was the placing of a battery of artillery on the point of land in the bend opposite the upper forts to distract the raking fire from the ships. He had one of his guns dismounted and a horse and a man killed.[45] On the day of the attack, General Earl Van Dorn telegraphed President Davis: "Bombardment heavy yesterday and this morning. No flinching. Houses perforated; none burned yet. Contest will commence when enemy attempt to land; he will probably try it. Crippled several boats. They only amuse our men by firing on them occasionally. There are about forty vessels of war and mortar boats, all sound and fury, and to brave men contemptible. Will keep you advised."[46]

Farragut worried greatly when the *Brooklyn* and the last two gunboats did not appear above Vicksburg. He feared that some great misfortune had overtaken them. Soon after anchoring, he sent a messenger across the bend to find out from Captain Thomas T. Craven what had happened. "What is the difficulty?" he inquired. "I hope your ship is not disabled and that your casualties have not been great, but I am most anxious to hear the worst."[47] In Craven's reply, he laid the blame on Porter, declaring, "After you left us, and Porter stopped throwing his shells, the rascals who had been thoroughly driven from their guns returned, and as I was trying to silence the only two guns remaining in action, it seemed as if a thousand new hands had come to demolish us."[48] The next day Farragut wrote him a curt note asking for an official report, giving his "reasons for not following the flagship up the river."[49] Without delay, Craven prepared his report which declared that Porter's steamers obstructed the passage of the *Brooklyn* "in such a manner as to oblige us to stop our engines, and thus delayed our progress," that the mortar boats ceased firing and the batteries renewed the action with fury, and that he found himself unsupported and retired out of action as advised in the Flag-Officer's general order of June 25, as follows: "Should the action be continued by the enemy, the ships and the *Iroquois* and *Oneida* will stop their engines and drop down the river again." He also declared that on the evening before the engagement, both in Farragut's cabin and on the quarter-deck, he had inquired, "Is it your wish or desire for me to leave any batteries behind me that have not been silenced," and the Flag-Officer had replied, "No, sir; not on any account."[50]

This brought forth an angry reply from Farragut. He could not recollect, he declared, ever saying to Craven that he was not to leave a battery in his rear unsilenced. He did recall that Craven asked to be allowed to act at his own discretion as to increasing or diminishing the distance from the starboard shore so as to reach the batteries on the hill. To this he had agreed, not wishing to embarrass him in such little matters. As to his general order, he pointed out that Craven had not quoted the whole sentence, which was, "When the vessels reach the bend in the river, the *Wissahickon, Sciota, Winona*, and *Pinola* will continue on and pass up, but should the action be continued by the enemy, the ships and *Iroquois* and *Oneida* will stop their engines and drop down the river again, keeping up their fire until directed otherwise." "Now, sir," he asked Craven, "did you ever reach the bend of the river? I can answer for you that you were never within a mile and a half of it." In conclusion, he wrote, "My signals were all ready, but it so happened that the smoke and want of daylight prevented the signals being used, but I trusted to our early education 'that no man did wrong who got his ship alongside the enemy,' and that every man would follow his file leader, so I went ahead, believing that all would do likewise, and no one regrets more deeply than I do that they did not."[51]

Craven's anger boiled over on reading Farragut's letter, and he replied that at the passing of Forts Jackson and St. Philip the Flag-Officer had given the command of one of the columns to his junior, that he had later been similarly discriminated against at Baton Rouge, and that in the recent attack a junior commander had been given a post which should have been assigned to him. "Yesterday," he continued, "you were pleased to address such a letter to me as no officer possessing the least particle of self-respect could receive submissively without degrading himself to the level of a serf." He therefore requested to be relieved of his command.[52]

The same day Farragut replied, giving a temperate explanation of Craven's assignments to duty, and finally granting him permission to return home after transferring the command of the *Brooklyn* to Commander H. H. Bell.[53] The correspondence between him and Craven he forwarded to Secretary Welles, with a letter in which he sadly wrote, "I can assure the Department that nothing can be more painful to me than such difficulties in my squadron, but the morale must be preserved. I cannot permit an officer to fall short of the mark without knowing why, and where the explanations are not in accordance with a commonsense reading of the instructions and my own knowledge of the facts, I can but censure."[54] Perhaps the climate and the lack of interest of Farragut and his officers in this futile expedition contributed to causing this unfortunate incident. "All of us are anxious to see an end of this river war," Farragut wrote his wife. "God grant it may be over soon, or we shall have to spend the rest of the year in this hottest of holes."[55]

Porter disliked Craven whom he thought disposed to play senior officer when the opportunity arose. "Captain Craven don't hesitate to take responsibility when it suits him to do so," he wrote Farragut, "and I don't see why in this instance he would not have consulted the exigencies of the service."[56] Bell was very sorry for Craven, whom he visited on the *Brooklyn* on this very unfortunate first of July. "Bad state of feeling there," he recorded in his diary. "Craven had received a sharp reprimand from flag-officer, which he considered unmerited and insulting, and would not be comforted. Poor fellow; I felt sadly for him, and said all I could to mitigate his anger, or wounded spirit; for he is an honest, straightforward, spirited Christian, having great professional pride; is poor, has a large family, and fondly calculates upon promotion, which no man better deserves, though I fear he has marred his prospects."[57] As to his being sent to command the *Brooklyn,* Bell added, "This is a heavy blow to me and interferes with my calculations for getting free of the river, as there is every prospect of the fleet summering between its steep banks, smitten with insects, heat intolerable, fevers, chills, and dysentery, and inglorious inactivity, losing all that the fleet has won in honor and reputation. I incline to the belief that persons in the mortar fleet have been instrumental in establishing this state of things in the Gulf fleet."[57]

XI

MEETING OF THE FLEETS

1

JULY THE first was a memorable day to Farragut not only because of the climax of the Craven episode but also because of the arrival of Davis's fleet. At about eight o'clock while he and his men were still at breakfast the fleet was sighted coming down stream round the point. To the salt-water sailors, the ironclads *Benton, Carondelet, Cincinnati,* and *Louisville* were "curious looking things" which seemed "like great turtles."[1] These were followed in fifteen minutes by four river steamers, three tugs, four mortar boats, and two hospital boats.[2] The river soon became crowded with vessels, and the little tenders were flying about like birds. The only warlike note was the occasional sound of Porter's mortars down the river.[3] The only fly in the ointment was the absence of any troops. "Bah!" Bell jotted down in his diary, "Grant was at Memphis with few troops; Halleck he [Davis] does not know where."[4]

Farragut was pleased that he had allowed Alden to persuade him to wait for Davis above Vicksburg instead of returning immediately to join the ships left below.[5] He dearly loved excitement. There was much cheering back and forth, and at nine o'clock Flag-Officer Davis came on board the *Hartford.* He then wore a long handle-bar mustache and peculiar monkey-like whiskers which left his chin bare. He and Farragut had been half way round the United States since their last meeting at Port Royal. They had been good friends since Davis's pleasant visit at the Mare Island Navy Yard when Farragut was commandant there before the war.[6] The rather cold scholarly Davis expressed himself as delighted and the warm-hearted, rather voluble Farragut outdid himself in hospitality. "You may suppose that our greetings were cordial and hearty,—given and

Page 105

taken with both hands, not one," Davis wrote his wife.[7] "You may conceive the interest of this occasion and its importance, historical and military," he declared. ". . . To the majority of the men and volunteer officers, everything was strange and wonderful. My own people almost lost their senses. Captain Phelps and myself were very much amused at their bewilderment, at the first sight of regular men-of-war. Our own gunboats were objects of great curiosity, also, to the men-of-war's men; so were the little tugs. When I passed through the fleets in the *Jessie Benton* to Flag-Officer Farragut's ship, to make the first call, with the red flag indicating my rank and presence, the higher decks and ports of every vessel were crowded."[7]

The next morning, Bell, deeply grieved at the "probability of Craven getting the worst of it in these bad times,"[8] went aboard the *Brooklyn* to take over the command. Craven departed with "nine hearty cheers from all hands."[8] They felt unjustifiably that the whole ship and crew had been mistreated by Farragut, and supported Craven to a man. The *Brooklyn* was continuing to be an unlucky ship to Farragut; it was during the command of this vessel that he had had so much trouble shortly before the war.[9]

That afternoon Davis moved his mortars down and fired on Vicksburg. Below the city some 2,000 Confederates with artillery made an unsuccessful attack upon Porter's mortars.[10] Both divisions of bombers kept up an intermittent bombardment all the next day. At twelve o'clock in the night the mortars ushered in the 4th of July with a national salute of 34 guns, and all the vessels of the fleet joined in except the *Richmond* which refrained because of the large number of sick and wounded on board.[10] In the morning, all the vessels were dressed with a flag at each masthead, and at noon the vessels mounting enough guns to authorize a salute each fired twenty-one guns in celebration of American independence.[11]

During the day, Davis invited Farragut to go with him in his flagship *Benton* down the river to try out the Confederate batteries. The *Benton* was a queer looking converted snag-boat. The space between the two hulls had been planked so as to form a continuous bottom with a beam of 45 feet. Her length was 200 feet. She had a slanting casemate covered with iron three and a half inches thick with ports for seven 32-pounders, and two 9-inch and seven 7-inch rifles.[12] Arriving at a good position, Davis opened fire on the upper shore battery. The Confederates had recently received a new Whitworth rifle, which they were pleased to try out on so big a target. Soon they put a shell through one of the *Benton's* bow ports which burst, killing or disabling several men. Farragut became excited and shouted, "Damn it, Davis, I must go on deck! I feel as though I were shut up here in an iron pot, and I can't stand it!"[13] So out on deck he went, but finally to please Davis he compromised by going into the pilot house.

On this holiday, Farragut wrote Welles that he was still lying above Vicksburg waiting for news from Memphis as to whether any troops would be sent. General Williams, he reported, was digging away at a mile and a quarter canal across the river bend, through which supplies might be conveyed. By the time it was finished, he thought the river would have fallen so much that the canal would be useless. The water was already down sixteen feet, and Farragut was afraid he would not be able to get his large vessels down the river during the summer. He was troubled also by reports of mobile artillery which was fortifying the bluffs at Grand Gulf, Fort Adams, and Ellis Cliffs; this necessitated gunboats to convoy all the transports.[14] A reply from General Halleck was then on the way, explaining that "the scattered and weakened condition" of his army made it impossible for him "at the present to detach any troops to cooperate" at Vicksburg. "In a few weeks" probably he could assist. "Allow me to congratulate you on your great success," he concluded.[15] Welles afterwards wrote, "Halleck was good for nothing then, nor is he now. . . ."[16]

The same day that Farragut received Halleck's disappointing telegram, Davis had a letter from Grant with the report that Richmond had been taken. "Should this be true," Farragut wrote Welles, "no doubt but that Vicksburg will soon fall, but it must be by troops coming down in the rear."[17] Two days later he learned that he had been misinformed about Richmond.[18] After the wounding of General Joseph E. Johnston in the Battle of Seven Pines, General Robert E. Lee had taken command and in the Seven Days campaign he administered a decisive defeat to General McClellan and saved Richmond. This defeat alarmed the government at Washington, and Welles telegraphed Farragut to send Porter with the *Octorara* and twelve mortar boats to Hampton Roads without delay.[19] Farragut dispatched Porter with the promise, "The moment this place surrenders, we will be off for Mobile."[20] This was an extravagant hope. "How strange to send nearly 2,000 miles for mortar boats," he wrote to Bell.[21] He also expressed his discouragement because the withdrawal of the mortars would cheer up the Confederates at Vicksburg, and he had no hopes of Halleck acting in "less than several weeks."[21]

Meanwhile the hot July days went by rather lazily with a little desultory bombing occasionally and an answering shot from the batteries. The steam ram *Sumter* came down to join Davis, and the gunboat *Wissahickon* returned to Farragut's fleet from the mouth of the Yazoo. The hospital ship *Monarch* arrived and took the sick and wounded from the *Richmond* up to Memphis.[22] Damages to the hulls and rigging of the ships were repaired. The *Hartford* had one hole near the water line.

2

Farragut was getting restless, and after Porter's mortars departed down the river on July 10, he decided to write a straightforward letter to Welles, requesting permission to return with his squadron to the Gulf Coast. Davis, he pointed out, had a squadron present which was adequate to blockade Vicksburg until the army arrived to reduce it, the only way in which it could be taken. He admitted that the *Arkansas* was in the Yazoo but declared, "I do not think she will ever come forth."[23] His services outside were needed to supervise the blockade from Pensacola to Brazos. Besides, there was the danger of low water preventing his larger vessels from going down at all until the next spring if they delayed much longer.[23] He did not mention the mounting sick lists, but did so in two letters the following day to the Secretary. There were sixty-eight ill on the *Brooklyn* alone of dysentery, diarrhoea, dengue, and malaria, and not enough quinine in the whole squadron for one vessel.[24] These conditions were somewhat alleviated by the arrival soon afterwards of the hospital steamer *Red Rover,* one of the largest and most beautiful steamers on the river, with splendid accommodations for the sick.[25]

The very day Farragut was writing these letters of distress, Congress, more than two months after the event, was voting its thanks to him and his men for the capture of New Orleans.

On Sunday, the 13th, Farragut wrote Bell that as soon as coal arrived he was going to "take a crack at the forts at the head of the bend."[26] Meanwhile an expedition up the Yazoo to investigate the *Arkansas* was to push off the following day, if possible. The *Essex,* as formidable as the *Benton,* had arrived under command of William D. Porter, D. D. Porter's brother.[27] Davis had consented to send an ironclad, and General Williams was requested to come over and consult about sending a regiment along.[28] Two gunboats were to be sent down the river as far as the mouth of the Red River on a cruise of observation, and were then to convoy the supply steamer *Tennessee.*[29]

On the same day, Porter, having just arrived at New Orleans, was writing Farragut a gloomy letter about the large quantities of lead, beef, bacon, flour, and cattle which were reported to have been transported across the Mississippi in ten days together with 3,000 troops in two weeks. Heavy guns would soon be in position at Grand Gulf and on other bluffs. The river, he thought, "is nearer to being closed up at this moment than it has been since we came into it. Vicksburg, the finest strategical point on the river, is neglected by the army at Memphis."[30] A copy of this letter he enclosed to one to Welles from Hampton Roads, in which he wrote of Farragut's ignorance of conditions below Vicksburg and of General Butler's failure to send enough troops to take Vicksburg. But in the same sentence he added, "The number of troops on our side was quite enough to undertake an assault of the place."[31] Porter seemed to have forgotten completely that before the expedition had gone up the river, he had written to Fox that Butler's cooperation with 5,000 men "was nonsense."[32]

This is an example of what Fox had in mind, when he wrote after the war, "He [Porter] came back disparaging the old hero, who, when the fire of battle came near, towered head and shoulders above such men, and this Porter could not forgive. He felt that he should have been the naval hero of the war and from this action [at Forts Jackson and St. Philip] he laid his plans to succeed chiefly by misrepresentations, by championing the younger officers, and creating one of those odious cliques."[33]

Farragut was not so ignorant of conditions below, as Porter thus unfairly wrote Welles, for as late as July 10, the day before Porter left Vicksburg, he had received a long report from Lieutenant Commanding George Henry Preble of the *Katahdin*, just returned from convoy duty, which gave substantially the same information as that furnished by Porter.[34]

Porter even more violently attacked General Butler in a letter of the same day from Hampton Roads to Fox, in which he painted "Butler rule" in New Orleans in the blackest colors. "New Orleans will either be in the hands of the Rebels in forty days," he prophesied, "or it will be burnt. Rest assured of that unless another man is sent in Butler's place. They [Confederates] are great fools for not wishing to keep him there, as he is supplying the Rebels with all they want by way of Pearl River (salt, shoes, blankets, flour, etc.) for which he charges license, which goes, God knows where! This is literally true."[35]

Farragut wrote Bell, on July 13, that he intended to telegraph Welles to learn "if they intend us to spend the rest of the year up here."[36] There is no record of this telegram; but the following day, before it could possibly have reached Welles and before Farragut's letter of July 10 to the Secretary could have been received, Welles called upon Secretary of War Stanton to find out whether Halleck was going to cooperate at Vicksburg. This was another instance of what might be called mental telepathy or thought transference. Stanton immediately telegraphed Halleck to know "whether you have or intend to have any land force to cooperate in the operation at Vicksburg."[37] An immediate reply was requested. It did not come until the following day, and was as follows: "I cannot at present give Commodore Farragut any aid against Vicksburg. I am sending reinforcements to General Curtis in Arkansas and to General Buell in Tennessee and Kentucky."[37]

Welles, either impatient at the delay or convinced that the reply would be in the negative, went ahead and wrote Farragut on July 14 that, owing to the changed circumstances after the evacuation of Corinth and the inability of the army to cooperate, it is thought that great objects can be accomplished by your proceeding to the Gulf and operating at such point or points on the Southern coast as you may deem advisable, leaving Flag-Officer Davis in possession and control of the Mississippi as far down as may be expedient."[38] He was directed to leave an ample force with Davis and an adequate one at New Orleans, and then to move his fleet below Vicksburg "with as little injury and loss of life as possible. Nothing is to be gained by a contest with the batteries of the enemy."[38] He was to send home vessels absolutely in need of repairs and the men whose terms of service were about to expire as well as "take all necessary precautions for the health of the squadron."[38] But before Farragut could receive this most welcome letter, an occurrence subjected him to more annoyance and mental anguish than he had suffered in a long time.

3

On the morning of the 14th of July, Farragut held a conference on the *Hartford* with Flag-Officer Davis, General Williams, and Colonel Alfred W. Ellet concerning the proposed expedition to the Yazoo River.[39] Lieutenant Isaac N. Brown, C.S.N. had been working with all his resources for the past six weeks to complete the ram *Arkansas* at Yazoo City, twenty miles below which was a raft for protection from attack. The ram was 165 feet in length and 35 in beam, and had a draft of eleven and one half feet. Her casemate, covered with railroad iron four and one half inches thick, was pierced for ten heavy guns, three in each broadside and two forward and two aft. In general appearance she was low, long, and rakish, and chocolate in color.[40] Because of the narrowness of the *Yazoo*, it was decided at the conference to send, the next morning, the ironclad gunboat *Carondelet*,[41] the wooden gunboat *Tyler,* and the Ellet ram *Queen of the West.* The latter, armed only with her ram, carried a company of sharpshooters.

It so happened that Brown also had chosen that day for an attempted run through the fleets to Vicksburg, with the hope of eventually forcing his way down to the Gulf and thence to Mobile.[42] As the sun rose clear and fiery, the *Arkansas* was discovered coming down stream near the mouth of the Yazoo. The Union vessels soon turned and fled, hotly pursued by the Confederate ram, exchanging shots as opportunity offered. The *Carondelet* was soon run ashore badly damaged with four killed, eight wounded, and eight missing.[43] The *Queen of the West* and the *Tyler* put on all steam possible and managed to keep about two hundred yards ahead of the *Arkansas* which continued toward Vicksburg. The firing was heard by the fleets of Davis and Farragut, but was thought to indicate an engagement between the gunboats and some mobile artillery said to be on the river banks above Vicksburg. None of the vessels got up steam, loaded their guns, or made any preparations for an emergency.

Suddenly about a quarter after seven the little *Tyler* and the *Queen of the West* were seen rounding the point with smoke belching from their funnels, closely followed by the *Arkansas* like a pair of rabbits pursued by a bear. The first had suffered the loss of eight killed and seventeen wounded.[44] Immediately the Union ships beat to quarters and made all possible haste to load their guns with solid shot, but steam could not be gotten up in time to move and they had to lie and take the fire of the *Arkansas,* which was then fairly upon them. The Ellet ram *Lancaster* received a shot through her boiler and scalding steam forced ten or twelve men overboard where some were drowned. The *Richmond* fired a whole broadside into the ram with no apparent effect, but escaped injury from the return fire of her stern guns.[45] The *Arkansas* fired two shots at the *Hartford* in exchange for a broadside. She was then followed by the *Benton* and the gunboat *Cincinnati,* but escaped to the cover of the batteries.[46] It was truly remarkable that more damage was not done the Union vessels crowding the river.

The *Arkansas* was badly battered, though not seriously injured. Her smokestack was so perforated that hardly enough steam could be kept up to steer her, the pilot house was shattered, and the shield had been penetrated by two shells, one of which killed eleven men and wounded seven. It had been a terrible experience for the men, the heat in the shield being 120 degrees and in the fire room 130 degrees. The arrival of the ram was received in Vicksburg with the cheers of the townsmen and soldiers, but those who went aboard the vessel were quickly silenced by the appearance of the gun deck. "Blood and brains bespattered everything, whilst arms, legs, and several headless trunks were strewn about," wrote one of the officers.[47] There were twelve dead and eighteen wounded out of a crew of 232 men.[48] But greatly elated, General Van Dorn telegraphed President Davis of the successful passage of the *Arkansas,* which would, he declared, "soon be repaired, and then ho! for New Orleans."[49]

Farragut was at first determined to go immediately and destroy the ram as soon as the fleet could get up steam.[50] "If you remember what I have previously told you of Commodore Farragut," Davis confided to his wife, "you may imagine his excitement at this scene of mortification and rebel triumph. He desired to make it worse by putting his whole command in all sorts of perilous positions, and treated my reason as very cold and repulsive. The contrast between us was very striking, though perfectly friendly."[51] After a conference with Davis, Farragut agreed to wait until the late afternoon. Hurried preparations were then made for action. The little tugs kept scurrying about with dispatches from the Flag-Officer to the various commanders. The heat was suffocating until about four o'clock when there was a violent thunderstorm with a downpour of rain. With so much to be done, it was nearly seven o'clock when the whole fleet got under way in two columns,[52] in the same order in which the vessels had come up the river. Farragut issued a general order to cover this, in which he stated, "They will keep their positions as far as practicable and have a good lookout for signals; but no one will do wrong who lays his vessel alongside of the enemy or tackles with the ram. The ram must be destroyed."[53]

It was twilight by the time the fleet was under way, and when it reached the upper battery darkness was settling down. Davis ordered the *Benton, Louisville,* and *Cincinnati* down to draw the fire from the upper battery.[54] The ram *Sumter* accompanied Farragut.[55] A few well directed broadsides at the flashes of the Confederate guns just about silenced them. But the ram could not be discovered, though the port column passed within thirty yards of the shore. "I looked with all the eyes in my head to no purpose," Farragut complained. "We could see nothing but the flash of the enemy's guns to fire at."[56]

The *Winona* was so disabled that she had to run ashore to keep from sinking. The *Sumter* received two shots below her armor, causing a troublesome leak.[56] The crew of the *Brooklyn* gave the ships three rousing cheers of welcome as they arrived, and at nine o'clock Bell came aboard the *Hartford.* He found the Flag-Officer in low spirits, deeply mortified and vexed at his failure. "I was dissuaded against my judgment," said Farragut, "from coming down in the morning. Then there was unexpected delay in getting under way after signal was made."[57] "It is a terrible business," replied Bell after the manner of Job's comforter, "and fraught with great danger. The ram must be attacked with resolution and be destroyed, or she will destroy us."[57] Bell had been thoroughly alarmed by the arrival of the *Arkansas* at Vicksburg. He ordered the remaining mortar boats to be moved down stream, and one which was aground was fired and blown up. The transports also were ordered to drop down the river; while the storeships *Kensington* and *Kuhn* were directed to observe results and then to proceed to New Orleans with the news.[57] It had been a disastrous day. Davis's fleet had casualties of 13 killed, 34 wounded, and 10 missing;[58] Farragut had lost 5 killed and 16 wounded.[59]

4

The next day was a melancholy one, with heavy rain and wind squalls. In the morning, Farragut had a conference with Bell, Alden, De Camp, and Renshaw. "I want to go up with the three larger ships and the ram *Sumter* to-night and attack the *Arkansas*," said Farragut. "What do you think about it, Bell?" He replied, "Flag-Officer, I am opposed to the night attack for the reason that the one just made was a failure. A low object against the bank cannot be seen. Besides, to-night will be dark and unsettled and the wind too fresh to work the ships in the current and narrow channel where we cannot turn. I favor a day attack." Alden added, "It is the specialty of the ironclads and rams of Davis's fleet, and they should do it." But Farragut remarked, "I cannot control them, and can only trust to my own vessels." Alden then left, saying, "I am ready for anything you and Bell agree upon."[60]

Farragut accordingly gave up the idea of a night attack. But preparations were made—splinter nettings on the starboard side and extra stands of grape and canister for each gun. The carpenters prepared the *Sumter* to ram the *Arkansas*. All hands were ordered to lie under arms; two gunboats moved about on guard against surprise throughout the stormy night.[61] During the afternoon the *Arkansas* got up steam and moved saucily across the river opposite the town and then turned round and returned. The crews were called to quarters on the Union ships; shell was drawn from the guns which were then reloaded with solid shot.[62] Farragut was determined not to be surprised a second time. "She is getting her steam up now," Farragut wrote Davis; "whether she means to come down or not, I do not know. While this is on my mind, I cannot rest. God bless you, and may you destroy him if he goes up."[63]

Later in the day, Farragut again wrote Davis that the country would hold them both responsible for any disaster resulting from the ram's escape, but that he would be expected to destroy the *Arkansas* with his ironclads more easily than he with his wooden vessels. He was willing to do his part, however, in a combined attack, and proposed that they meet off Vicksburg at daylight and fight it out to a finish with the forts and the ram. Let him name the day and hour, and he would be there with his fleet to keep the batteries under control while Davis destroyed the ram.[64]

During this dreary day of worry and anxiety for Farragut, Congress passed in Washington the act creating the grade of rear-admiral, under which he was soon commissioned first to enjoy that rank.[65] But he was not to learn of this for many weeks—not until after the *Arkansas* was disposed of.

The following day, Farragut received a reply from Davis, counseling patience, prudence, vigilance, and self-control. "The *Arkansas* is harmless in her present position," he wrote, "and will be more easily destroyed, should she come out from under the batteries than while enjoying their protection."[66] Farragut answered with two letters, trying diplomatically to stir him into action, by pointing out the dangers which might arise if the *Arkansas* slipped past them during the night.[67] Davis's reply was brief. "I have watched eight rams for a month, and now find it no hard task to watch one. I think patience as great a virtue as boldness."[68]

Farragut had conservatives among his officers also. That morning at a council of war on the *Hartford*, at which Bell, Alden, Palmer, and Lee were present, Farragut showed his impatience with Davis's attitude and the unreadiness of the *Sumter*. But Bell suggested, "You might lose, Flag-Officer, everything from here to Fort Jackson as a consequence of defeat under the forts with a loss of ships, or even their propellers, as we have no reserve except the *Pensacola* and *Mississippi* at New Orleans."[69]

Some time during this day of hope deferred, Farragut wrote to Welles the most difficult dispatch he had yet written him. He began, "It is with deep mortification that I announce to the Department that, notwithstanding my prediction to the contrary, the ironclad ram *Arkansas* has at length made her appearance and took us all by surprise."[70] Without attempting to shift the blame, he set down a "plain unvarnished tale" of what had happened, and then declared, "Be assured, sir, however, that I shall leave no stone unturned to destroy her."[70]

In distant Washington that day, Mr. Welles issued his famous general order, carrying out the Act of Congress of July 4, 1862, which abolished the spirit ration in the navy. Spirituous liquors were to be used only for medical purposes. Beginning the following September 1, each member of the crew was to be paid five cents a day in lieu of his spirit ration.[71]

Day after day, Farragut and Davis continued to exchange letters, the former advising action and the latter counseling watchful waiting.[72] "I feel that there is no rest for the wicked until she is destroyed," wrote Farragut. The anxiety which they felt, wrote the scholarly Davis, "is like 'the watch the King keeps to maintain the peace.' It is an old ache that, like a chronic disease, does not prevent sleeping and eating."[72] He more fully revealed himself to his wife, throwing interesting light on Farragut's character and at the same time revealing his own. "He writes me that he wants to go in 'regardless of consequences,'" Davis complained. ". . . This is the language of a Hotspur, and not of one that hath a rule over his own spirit; with such counsels, we shall soon be like a city that is broken down and without walls. . . . Yet you must not think that Farragut and I differ unkindly. Nothing can exceed his kindness, candor, and liberality; our old ties have been strengthened by our present intercourse. He is a man who unites with a bold and impetuous spirit an affectionate temper, and a generous and candid nature."[73]

It was all quite maddening to Farragut. Morale among his officers was beginning to weaken under the strain. "Bell considers himself the oracle," Renshaw wrote D. D. Porter, "and Farragut, I believe, thinks him infallible. I think Bell as inflated an ass as I know—personal courage he may have, but apart from that he is as indecisive a know nothing as the navy produces. I pity Farragut for I really believe he will be disgraced forever if he longer listens to such advice. . . . Farragut is not fit to command, that's certain—he appears to be half crazy since Tuesday [July 15]—here we are without coal—but little provisions—and less ammunition—and at this moment no arrangements have been made to get any."⁷⁴ But Farragut remained considerate and understanding with respect to his men. In writing to Welles rather pathetically of the ever increasing sickness among them, he declared, "I am in consequence of all these things obliged to be less ardent in following up my blows. When men are well, you may push them through a great deal; but when prostrated by sickness and a debilitating climate, we must take more time for everything. I find it even a terrible fatigue to coal ship."⁷⁵

5

At last, Farragut could stand it no longer, and though somewhat ill himself, on Monday morning, July 21, he went across the bend to see Davis personally.⁷⁶ For hours they conferred during this hottest day of the summer.⁷⁷ The previous day Colonel Ellet had written Davis, offering to command one of his rams personally in an attack on the *Arkansas,* if he and Farragut would attack the batteries.⁷⁸ And so Davis finally agreed to participate in such an engagement early the following morning. Three o'clock was appointed for the time to begin.⁷⁹ Farragut then returned to the *Hartford* to complete his preparations.

About daylight the next day the *Benton, Cincinnati,* and *Louisville* moved down and opened fire on the upper batteries, while the ironclad *Essex* and Ellet's ram *Queen of the West* made an attempt to destroy the *Arkansas.* The more powerful *Essex,* with an armor of one inch, attempted to ram the *Arkansas,* but Brown let go her bowline and the current drifted her stern on; so the *Essex* only grazed her side and ran ashore where she lay at least ten minutes and received a hard pounding by the batteries, with three shots through her armor, one of which killed one man and wounded three.⁸⁰ Ellet succeeded in striking the Confederate ram a heavy blow without injuring her much. His vessel was cut to pieces with round shot and grape, though his men miraculously escaped injury.[81] The *Essex* fired into the *Arkansas,* and Porter made extravagant claims as to the damages he did. But the only serious injury was caused by a shot entering one of the gunports which killed six men and wounded six.[82] "The failure [was] so complete that it was almost ridiculous," General Van Dorn telegraphed President Davis.[83] Flag-Officer Davis had written rather boastfully to Farragut, "We shall either drive her [*Arkansas*] down to you, destroy her, or force her to come up the river; in the latter case we are ready for her. I beg you not to think of passing the lower forts."[84]

Farragut's part in the attack was indeed small. At daylight, the remainder of Porter's mortars opened fire and at five o'clock, ten minutes after firing began above, Farragut got under way, the ironclad *Sumter* steaming about a mile in advance. About 5:40 the fleet was in position to commence action, and then fired only two minutes, the *Essex* having meanwhile dropped down the river.[85] "Flag-Officer Davis was determined that, as Commander W. D. Porter thought his vessel, the *Essex,* was shot-proof, he would make an attack on the ram and drive her down to us or destroy her," Farragut reported. "He had also determined to let the *Sumter* run at her, and to let Colonel Ellet also attack her with one of his rams. . . . It was stipulated that I was not to pass up the river, but be ready to receive her if she attempted to come down. Unfortunately, the attack was a failure. . . . The *Sumter,* from some misunderstanding, did not go in."[86]

Davis was displeased at the failure of the *Sumter* to participate.[87] The understanding was that she was to move up to the attack while Farragut's fleet covered the lower batteries.[88] Lieutenant S. L. Phelps, Davis's acting fleet captain, was greatly displeased with Farragut's conduct throughout the *Arkansas* episode, and wrote a highly critical letter about him to his former commanding officer, Flag-Officer Foote. He claimed that a deserter reached Farragut at ten o'clock the night before the *Arkansas* appeared, with news that she was coming down the next morning; but that the information was not sent to him and no preparations were made. He declared that his fleet was in action three quarters of an hour before Farragut got under way at twilight that day to run the batteries, and that all the delay was due solely to his fleet. As to the attack on the 22nd, he wrote that, in spite of the previous eagerness which Farragut had expressed to destroy "the horned enemy," when he was only restrained by Davis and some of his own officers from taking his fleet up under formidable batteries to destroy the ram, his participation in the joint attack was strangely inadequate. His fleet did not begin the attack on the lower batteries simultaneously with the action above, and the *Sumter* did not come up to assist. "I am told," he concluded, "that Commander [sic] Davis's letter was construed as a request to make no attack on the lower batteries. Knowing the plan, as I have described it to you, however imperfectly, is it possible to render it in that manner? Can a gallant man so construe it? Could a man who has to be held back with curb and check rein so read it? It was no part of the plan to pass those batteries, but to attack them, at 1,200 or 1,500 yards, from below. The whole thing was a fizzle. Every day we heard great things threatened only to realize fizzles. I fear that both S. P. Lee and Palmer had too much influence with Commander [sic] Farragut in the matter of the attacks on the *Arkansas*, but that does not excuse his great talk and little action. I tell you, my old commander, I would rather have your little finger at the head than he who led the attack at New Orleans."[89]

Farragut's version was as follows: "You will perceive from Flag-Officer Davis's letter of the evening before, the lower fleet were to have no share in the affair until the ram was driven down to us, and the *Sumter* was expected to 'do her whole duty' by 'ramming' the *Arkansas*. This I fully impressed verbally upon Captain Erben, and told him to take his station at the point above, ready to attack as soon as the *Essex* made her appearance, but he failed to take his part, and never gave me any explanation. He may, however, have rendered some account to his commanding officer."[90]

Fortunately for Farragut he was soon to be released from

this most unpleasant situation. The day following the attempt to destroy the ram, he received this welcome telegram from Welles: "Go down river at discretion. Not expected to remain up during the season. Messenger on the way with dispatches."[91] Whereupon Farragut wrote his wife, "At last the Department appears to have waked up to the fact that we have no business up this river and have sent me orders to drop down and go to sea for which I am most thankful, although it is most mortifying to leave the ram behind me undestroyed."[92]

At a conference the next day with Bell, Alden, Lee, and Crosby, Farragut was advised against another attempt to destroy the *Arkansas* under the batteries of Vicksburg.[93] So he yielded to necessity, and admitted in a letter to Welles that to attack the ram "under the forts with the present amount of work before us would be madness."[94] He then informed Davis that he intended to start down the river with his ships the next day "at the furthest."[95] So eager was everybody to get away that there was no delay, and at two o'clock on the morrow Farragut's fleet was ready to weigh anchor. Davis wished General Williams's troops to remain to keep communications open across the bend with the *Essex* and *Sumter*, which he planned to keep below Vicksburg to blockade the *Arkansas*;[96] but Williams had had more than enough of campaigning in the fever-breeding swamps. Only 800 of his 3,200 men were fit for duty; the rest were either dead or ill of fever.[97] Davis felt obliged, therefore, to order the *Essex* and *Sumter* also down stream, Commander W. D. Porter being instructed to take charge of the river between Baton Rouge and Vicksburg. "The embarrassment of my present situation is one of the vicissitudes of war," Davis wrote philosophically. "We are having a dark hour like those who have gone before us. Our trust is in God and the justice of our cause."[98]

Farragut's fleet proceeded down the river in two columns. The *Brooklyn*, *Hartford*, and *Richmond* were followed by the gunboats in the starboard column. Six troop transports towing the mortar boats constituted the other column.[99] The *Essex* and *Sumter* acted as a rear guard. If the ram was sighted in pursuit, they were in the daytime to hoist signal No. 5 and at night two red lights or two perpendicular white lights. The fleet would then round to and come to their assistance.[100] Marines were stationed in the forecastle and poop as sharpshooters. All craft were thus completely cleared from below Vicksburg. "The whole of the lower fleet and all the troops have disappeared down the river," triumphantly telegraphed General Van Dorn to President Davis. "The upper fleet in movement, but still at anchorage."[101] On July 31, Davis moved all his fleet up to the mouth of the Yazoo, and left Vicksburg and the vicinity to the ram *Arkansas*, which had been mainly responsible for this loss of two or three hundred miles of the river by the Union naval forces.[102]

Farragut's flotilla passed down the river with no untoward accidents or incidents. General Williams's troops were left at Baton Rouge, and the General took up his headquarters in the State House. About noon on the 28th, Farragut arrived at New Orleans with his three larger vessels and four gunboats, the others having been left at Baton Rouge to protect the troops.

Fortunately for Farragut, he did not delay his departure from Vicksburg, for after Welles heard of the escape of the *Arkansas* to Vicksburg he sent Farragut this telegram on the day after he left for New Orleans: "The Department learns with regret of the escape of the rebel steamer *Arkansas*, owing to the unprepared condition of the naval vessels. That vessel must be destroyed at all hazards."[103] This would have held Farragut there indefinitely. Welles followed the telegram with a letter. "I need not say to you that the escape of this vessel and the attending circumstances have been the cause of serious mortification to the Department and the country," wrote the irate Secretary. "It is an absolute necessity that the neglect or apparent neglect of the squadron on that occasion should be wiped out by the capture or destruction of the *Arkansas*, which I trust will have been effected before this reaches you. . . . It is not to be supposed that you will leave Vicksburg until this is accomplished."[104] This letter would have given Farragut great embarrassment, if it had not reached him after the *Arkansas* had been destroyed.

What Welles thought of the *Arkansas* affair he set down in his diary as follows: ". . . The most disreputable naval affair of the war was the descent of the steam ram *Arkansas* through both squadrons till she hauled in under the batteries of Vicksburg, and there the two flag-officers abandoned the place and the ironclad ram, Farragut and his force going down to New Orleans, and Davis proceeding with his flotilla up the river."[105] Farragut's fortunes indeed reached their lowest ebb during the war in the summer of 1862.

XII

THE *ARKANSAS* AND BATON ROUGE

1

WHEN Farragut arrived at New Orleans, he had hopes of soon getting the bulk of his fleet out into the Gulf where the sea air would restore his sick to health.¹ New Orleans was certainly not a summer resort. Some nights on board the ships in the river, the mosquitoes came in swarms and the men were forced to walk the decks to keep from being eaten alive,—sleep was out of the question.² Farragut himself, the old sea dog, longed for the tangy salt air in his nostrils; but this was to be denied him many weeks, for he was not yet through with the *Arkansas*. He sent the remnants of the mortar boats and steamers which Porter had left at New Orleans for repairs off to a rendezvous at Pensacola, and five officers with scurvy were ordered home.³ The gunboat *Oneida* was dispatched to blockade duty off Mobile,⁴ and the *Richmond* to Pensacola for repairs.⁵ The gunboats *Kineo* and *Katahdin* had been left at Baton Rouge to cooperate with General Williams and patrol the Mississippi up to the mouth of the Red River, assisting the *Essex* and the *Sumter*. To Commander William D. Porter of the *Essex*, Farragut wrote that his brother David had written him an excellent letter on the importance of a careful patrol of that portion of the river. This letter, he naïvely added, he had sent to Secretary Welles, not knowing that D. D. Porter had himself sent copies to both Welles and Fox.⁶

On the 1st of August, Farragut received an alarming dispatch from W. D. Porter with the news that General Breckinridge was advancing on Baton Rouge with 6,000 men, and that the *Arkansas* was on the way down to aid in the attack. "I would

Courtesy of Curator, United States Naval Academy

REAR-ADMIRAL D. G. FARRAGUT, U. S. NAVY

From a photograph by E. Jacobs, New Orleans, presented by Farragut to Paymaster B. F. D. Fitch, U.S.N. and by Fitch's daughter to the Naval Academy Museum. The artist, N. M. Miller, based his portrait of Farragut in Memorial Hall, U. S. Naval Academy, on this rare photograph.

Courtesy of Miss Mary E. Brooks

REAR-ADMIRAL D. G. FARRAGUT, U. S. NAVY
From a photograph by C. D. Fredricks & Co., New York, presented by Farragut to his colored steward, John H. Brooks.

like you to send up one of your steam gunboats that will work," he begged; "both of these here are on the doctor's list."[7] Two days previous he had written Butler of the threatening state of affairs in that vicinity, and had requested a powerful steam tug for towing the *Essex* upstream. He had also suggested that Baton Rouge be fortified immediately on both the land and the river side.[8] Butler enclosed this message in a letter to Farragut, urging him to send one of the double-ender steamers to clear out Red River and declaring that he did not have proper guns for fortifying Baton Rouge. "If the fleet cannot hold the river against the enemy's rams or other boats," he mournfully concluded, "the quicker we abandon Louisiana the better."[9] The next day Butler wrote Farragut again, stating that he had reliable information that the Confederates were placing field guns between New Orleans and Baton Rouge to sink his transports and that General Williams was expecting an attack, and he requested that a gunboat be sent up to investigate.[10] Farragut was up most of that night getting the *Cayuga* off on this mission, only to learn the following day, on the arrival of two river boats, that no evidence of the enemy had been seen.

Accordingly on August 4, Farragut wrote W. D. Porter a reassuring letter, declaring that he did not believe the story that Breckinridge was about to attack Baton Rouge. Porter, he complained, should be up at the mouth of Red River to stop the passage of arms, cattle, and other provisions. "If the ram ever gets down here," he confidently asserted, "I have an abiding confidence that it will be the last of her, as she will have no forts to shelter her."[11]

But the reports, though exaggerated, were based on facts. On the morning of August 3 at two o'clock, the *Arkansas* cast off her lines and started to Baton Rouge to aid Breckinridge in retaking the town and raising the blockade of the lower Mississippi. When about twenty-two miles from Baton Rouge, near midnight, one of her engines broke down and the rest of the night was spent in making repairs. Arriving next day in sight of the *Essex* and gunboats, the ram was stopped again by a breakdown of her engine, which was not repaired until nightfall.[12] Lieutenant Henry K. Stevens had succeeded Lieutenant Brown in command of the *Arkansas*. One of his lieutenants was the famous Charles W. ("Savvy") Read.

At two o'clock on the morning of August 5, General Breckinridge with about 6,000 men[13] made the expected attack on Baton Rouge. General Williams was killed with a minie ball through his heart and several officers were wounded; about 250 of his 2,500 effective troops were either killed or wounded. Complete disaster was averted only by the shells from the *Essex* and the gunboats, which were directed by an officer on the State House.[14] News of the attack and of the presence of the *Arkansas* reached Farragut by the steamer *Tennessee* at midnight, and he immediately issued orders for the *Brooklyn* and the gunboats whose machinery was not being overhauled to get ready to accompany him up the river at daylight. The *Hartford* was off at five-thirty; but it took the *Brooklyn* five hours longer to get under way, as a hundred of her crew who were on liberty in the city had to be rounded up.[15]

When Farragut arrived at Baton Rouge at noon on the 7th with his two large vessels and four gunboats, he was greeted with the good news that the *Arkansas* had been destroyed.[16] "It is one of the happiest moments of my life," he announced to Welles with relief, ". . . not because I held the ironclad in such terror, but because the community did."[16] Bill Porter, in his customary blustering fashion, on the day before the Confederate attack said to some of his officers that the *Arkansas* kept him uneasy. "After I get my breakfast to-morrow, I will go up and destroy her."[17] So after Breckinridge's attack was broken up, the *Essex* proceeded up the river in company with the *Cayuga* to deal with the ram. Moving out to attack the approaching Union ironclad, the *Arkansas* broke a connecting rod of her engine, became unmanageable, and drifted ashore with her vulnerable stern exposed.[18] Only one gun could be brought to bear; this was fired and then the vessel was abandoned, set on fire in several places, cut from her moorings, and allowed to drift down the river. "She was no trophy won by the *Essex*, nor did she receive injury at Baton Rouge from the

THE ARKANSAS AND BATON ROUGE 127

hands of any of her adversaries," wrote General Van Dorn with pride mingled with sadness. ". . . With every gun shotted, our flag floating from her bow, and not a man on board, the *Arkansas* bore down upon the enemy and gave him battle. The guns were discharged as the flames reached them, and when her last shot was fired, the explosion of her magazine ended the brief but glorious career of the *Arkansas*. 'It was beautiful,' said Lieutenant Stevens, while the tears stood in his eyes, 'to see her, when abandoned by commander and crew and dedicated to sacrifice, fighting the battle on her own hook.' "[19] "After all hands were ashore," wrote Lieutenant "Savvy" Read, "the *Essex* fired upon the disabled vessel most furiously."[20]

2

Porter, however, made extravagant claims. "I steamed up the river and at 10 A.M. attacked the rebel ram *Arkansas* and blew her up," he wrote Farragut. "There is not now a fragment of her left."[21] In particular, he declared that a shot first disabled her rudder and a shell then ignited cotton on board and set her afire.[22] His story grew in picturesque details each time he told it. Farragut at first believed his claims, and incorporated the details in his report to Welles.[23] He even wrote Porter a letter of congratulation, stating, "I am glad that you have had your revenge in a single-handed combat."[24] But two days later he wrote Welles a correction of Porter's statements.[25] Yet he wrote Mrs. Farragut that he thought Porter was entitled to credit indirectly for destroying the ram, for the Confederates would not have set fire to their vessel if Porter had not made the attack.[26]

Farragut might have felt less consideration for Porter at this time, if he had known of a letter which he had written the Secretary of the Navy, after the manner of his brother David, on August 1, reporting his attack on the *Arkansas* under the guns of Vicksburg. In this letter he laid the blame for his failure on the lack of cooperation from Flag-Officers Davis and Farragut.[27] When this was published in the newspapers, it called for vigorous letters of protest from the usually calm, dignified Davis and the hitherto overly generous Farragut. Davis charged Porter "with a misstatement of facts, so well known, so directly observed and actively participated in by hundreds of people, that this statement cannot be regarded as otherwise than deliberate."[28] Farragut went to great length in explaining what really happened and why. "The published report of Commodore Porter is a most extraordinary document," he rather temperately commented, ". . . I do not object to Commodore Porter's desire to win his promotion, for the exploits of my brother officers always give me pleasure, but I do object to his throwing any share of his failure on me, when I feel assured that it was caused by the unmanageableness of his vessel."[29] To Mrs. Farragut he wrote with less restraint, "Now I suppose you never read a bigger lie than his [W. D. Porter's] account of that fight."[30]

Welles, then somewhat at outs with Davis and Farragut, was at first inclined to believe Porter, whom he set down in his diary as "a bold, brave man, but reckless in many respects, and unpopular, perhaps not without reason, in the service. He has been earnest and vigorous on the Mississippi. . . . His courage in destroying the *Arkansas* was manifest. Both the flag officers were delinquent in the matter of that vessel at Vicksburg, and I so wrote each of them. Admiral Farragut cannot conceal his joy that she is destroyed but is not ready to do full justice to Porter."[31] A month later Welles set down this very different impression: ". . . Received a letter from Commo. W. D. Porter stating his arrival in New York after many signal exploits— capturing the ironclad steamer *Arkansas*, running Bayou Sara, etc. Charges from Admirals Farragut and Davis, accusing him of misrepresentation and worse, have preceded him. The War Department has sent me an inexcusable letter, abusing the military, which Porter has written, and which Stanton cannot notice. I have been compelled to reprove him and to send him before the Retiring Board. Like all the Porters, he is a courageous, daring, troublesome, reckless officer. . . ."[32]

Bill Porter's brother, David Dixon, with much more success, made capital out of the *Arkansas* affair. He arrived at Hampton

Roads shortly after the news of this ram's initial success had reached Washington. "It is nothing more than I expected," he wrote critically to Assistant Secretary Fox. "If you will look at the chart I sent on, you will see there was one flag-officer too many. I saw enough to convince me that Davis should not have been one of them, he deserves to lose his command."[33] A few days later he wrote Fox from Newport, Rhode Island, ". . . I believe Farragut has gone down and left the *Arkansas*. What events have followed his first turning back from Vicksburg! See the order in your book to 'push' up a strong force and take all their defences in the rear. That error has lost us all."[34] After two days, this followed: ". . . Bad business leaving that *Arkansas* up river, she will give them some trouble yet, all of which might have been avoided—you can't think how glad I am that my connection with that party is dissolved I hope forever, and I trust that I may never be so hampered again as I was then."[35] Porter was thus sniping at two officers who were superior to him in rank and command, and it is hardly a coincidence that, in a few weeks, he took over the command of Davis's squadron.

It is interesting to note that near this date Farragut was writing his wife, "Don't give yourself any uneasiness about any one's trying to undermine me. I can see as much as any one, but don't choose to act upon it until the time comes. I fortify myself as well as I can, and trust to my honesty for the rest. Some will try to injure me, but I defy them. There is a feeling among some to get home. They have had fighting enough. Bell and some few others stick to me. Bell is my main dependence, though Alden and Palmer are good friends. Some are bitter against me, no doubt, because I tell them when I think they don't do their duty. You know my fault is not oppression, but being too lenient; but a man *must* do his work, particularly when that work is *fighting*, and if he doesn't I'll tell him of it. I don't want such men under my command, and am only too glad for them to go home and get their 'rights.' I have several of that stripe here; but they have too much good sense to apply to go home because I tell them of their faults. I have no doubt they will try to injure me, and may do it in the dark; but let them come out in the open daylight, and you will see in what a color I will put them before the country...."³⁶

This was probably in answer to a letter which Mrs. Farragut had written about Craven, who had been relieved of his command and had returned home to get his "rights." There is no indication that the Porters were then involved in her uneasiness. But if Farragut had known what D. D. Porter had been repeatedly writing to Fox, he would probably have been greatly disturbed. In a letter to his wife just a week previous, he touched upon a matter relating to the Porter family. "I told you about the Journal and Commodore Porter," he wrote. "Now, darling, remember that, although I am ready and desire to do anything that is right and grateful to Commodore Porter, I wish his relations (who think I owe them something) to know that my adoption by the Commodore was for *kindness rendered to his Father by mine,* by taking him to his house, and my mother nursing him in his sickness, until she herself was taken sick, and they both died and were buried on the same day. I had to tell Commodore Porter's brother one day of it for his presumption when he just pretended to have heard something of it."³⁷

3

At daylight on August 9, the *Hartford, Brooklyn,* and *Cayuga* got under way and proceeded down stream. The *Essex, Sumter, Oneida, Kineo,* and *Katahdin* were left at Baton Rouge.³⁸ Citizens at Donaldsonville had repeatedly fired upon transports in spite of warnings that such would lead to the destruction of the town. Commander Renshaw, on the way down the previous day with the steam double-ender gunboats, was ordered to inform the authorities to move the women and children out as Farragut intended to destroy the town.³⁹ Accordingly, on arrival off the place, the ships fired several shell into the town, and an expedition then went ashore and set fire to the hotels and the wharf buildings and the home of a certain captain of guerrillas. The most valuable portion of the town was thus destroyed.⁴⁰ The ships then continued down to New Orleans.

On the afternoon following his arrival, Commander Richard

Wainwright, who had commanded the *Hartford* since she sailed from Philadelphia, died of fever. He had been ill for two weeks, but his case was considered a light one until three days before his death.[41] Funeral services were conducted by the Reverend Doctor Laycock the next afternoon, and the remains were sent home on board the U.S.S. *Miami*.[42]

Farragut, about ready to leave New Orleans for Ship Island and Pensacola to make arrangements for attacking the forts at the entrance of Mobile Bay[43] and happy that he was leaving "no terror"[43] behind him, had a distinct unpleasantness with General Butler. He inquired by letter of Farragut if he had found him and his officers always willing and prompt to aid the naval operations to the extent of their means and ability.[44] Farragut replied courteously at length in the affirmative, with only this exception: "That you have not been willing to accord to the navy its due share in the operations of taking New Orleans and at Baton Rouge, I confess there have been some doubts expressed. For example, in your address to your command you told them of their taking New Orleans with the assistance of the navy, and did not notice the assistance of the navy at Baton Rouge in the preservation of your command at that place."[45] In his second letter, it developed that Butler was particularly aggrieved because no mention had been made of his army in connection with the capture of New Orleans except in Porter's words, "I sent General Butler in the *Miami* round in the rear of the forts." Also, he complained, "I am not aware that the navy 'preserved' my army at Baton Rouge."[46] Farragut wrote a final letter the next day, explaining the part played by the naval forces at Baton Rouge,[47] and the correspondence ended.

That afternoon General Butler saluted Farragut with fifteen guns, which were returned by the *Hartford* gun for gun; and that evening an army band came on board and serenaded him.[48] This was not done by Butler because of their recent epistolary passage at arms, but in recognition of the receipt of the news that Farragut had been promoted to rear-admiral, a rank created by Congress on the previous July 16. Farragut was thus raised from number 31 on the list of captains to ranking rear-admiral, though his pay remained at $5,000, the same it had been as a captain commanding a squadron, that is, as a flag-officer.[49]

Farragut wrote Butler a sincere note of appreciation of the salute. "I hope that I may be able to return it at some no distant day with interest," he graciously replied. "I feel proud of it because my country seems to think I have won it, and I feel proud of it because the thousands of my brave companions in arms who shared in the perils of the day were not forgotten in the resolution of Congress which accompanied my commission. These things are gratifying, and I only trust that I may continue to enjoy them, and that by our combined movements upon Mobile we may be able to add to our country's obligation to its Army and Navy, for be assured that no one will be more happy than myself to share with the Army the honors of taking that or any other place."[50] Farragut was referring to a certified copy of the joint resolution of Congress, which was approved July 11, and sent him with his commission as rear-admiral. Congress tendered its thanks to him and the officers and men under his command "for their successful operations on the lower Mississippi River, and for their gallantry displayed in the capture of Forts Jackson and St. Philip and the city of New Orleans, and in the destruction of the enemy's gunboats and armed flotilla."[51]

Fortunately the thanks of Congress and promotion to rear-admiral were awarded to Farragut before the news of the *Arkansas* episode reached Washington. Though Welles was much displeased over that affair, he wrote his new rear-admiral this very gracious complimentary letter, which accompanied the commission: "The highly satisfactory manner in which you accomplished the great and primary object which the Department had in view in selecting you for your present command continues to elicit admiration. Our navy has performed wonders during this war, but conspicuous above and beyond all was that of capturing New Orleans with the preliminary attending circumstances. For this achievement you well have come to the thanks and highest naval honors the country can bestow, and it gives me sincere gratification, personally as well as officially, to forward you the evidence of their grateful regard."[52]

At nine o'clock on the morning of August 13, the *Pensacola, Brooklyn*, and *Mississippi* recognized Farragut's promotion by giving him a fifteen guns salute. In less than an hour afterwards the *Hartford* and *Brooklyn* were under way for the Gulf. At eleven o'clock all hands were mustered, and a copy of the thanks of Congress was read to them.[53] Farragut also published the following general order: "The commander in chief feels happy in acknowledging the honors paid him by the officers of his command, and still more so that the Government should have, in conveying to him the agreeable intelligence of his promotion, accompanied it by that resolution of Congress in which the people and Government acknowledge the gallantry of the officers and men of this fleet for the handsome manner in which they overcame the rebels in their multifarious forms of forts, floating ironclad batteries, rams, gunboats, etc., and thereby showing a full appreciation of your merits and abilities. Your admiral feels assured that you will never disappoint these high expectations. A new field is now open before you. To your ordinary duties is added the contest with the elements. Let it be your pride to show the world that danger has no greater terror for you in one form than in another; that you are as ready to meet the enemy in the one shape as in the other, and that you, with your wooden vessels, have never been alarmed by fire rafts, torpedoes, chain booms, ironclad rams, ironclad gunboats, or forts. The same Great Power preserves you in the presence of all."[54]

This vibrant elation, springing from the official recognition of his services, is evident also in a letter written the following day to Mrs. Farragut. "Yesterday I hoisted my flag at the main," he announced to her with pride, "and the whole fleet cheered, which I returned with a most dignified salute. I called all hands, and read the act of Congress complimentary of their achievements. I got underway, and stood down the river, leaving a general order to be read to the fleet. I stopped at the forts to let the men see what they had done to deserve the resolutions."[55]

At last Farragut was returning to the Gulf, and, as he fondly believed, was soon to begin operations against Mobile, which he had wished to commence three months before. Instead he had been compelled to go up the Mississippi, where his two expeditions had been almost entirely fruitless, for the Confederates still practically controlled the Mississippi from the mouth of the Red River to Vicksburg.

XIII

BLOCKADING THE GULF PORTS

1

THOUGH Farragut left New Orleans, happier than he had been for many weeks because of the recognition he had recently received from the government and the opportunity of at last closing up the entrances to Mobile Bay by capturing their defenses, he was to experience hope long deferred.

On the morning of August 17, the *Hartford* arrived at Ship Island; and two days later in the early afternoon she was exchanging signal numbers with the seven vessels blockading off Mobile Bay, under command of Captain Robert B. Hitchcock in the *Susquehanna*. After giving Farragut a rear-admiral's salute, Hitchcock came on board the flagship for a conference.[1] About two weeks before he had written both Fox and Welles, complaining of lack of communications with Farragut and of his need for more fast steamers to make the blockade more effective.[2] Farragut made only one immediate change; he dispatched the sailing brig *Bohio* to the mouth of the Rio Grande to join the 1600 ton sidewheeler *De Sota* of nine guns, recently ordered to that station.[3]

Early on the morning of the 20th, the *Hartford* slipped into the harbor of Pensacola and anchored off the Navy Yard,[4] near the *Brooklyn* which had preceded her. Farragut immediately wrote to Welles and Rear-Admiral Joseph Smith, Chief of the Bureau of Yards and Docks, requesting that he repair the buildings of the Navy Yard and move the machinery from Ship Island in order to repair his ships as quickly as possible and "get off for Mobile." "The *Brooklyn*," he confided, "will have to have a temporary repair of her side where the ram [*Manassas*] ran into her. The damage is very great, and very little more force would have sunk her."[5] All but two or three vessels in the whole fleet were in need of a month or two of repairs.[6]

Hardly had Farragut left New Orleans when Butler became alarmed and ordered Baton Rouge to be evacuated. The gunboat *Sumter* had been run ashore and abandoned by Lieutenant Henry Erben, and then burned by the Confederates. "Depend upon it, sir, that this feeling of timidity or prudence, as they are pleased to term it, must be suppressed," Farragut exclaimed.[7] Commodore Henry W. Morris, whom he had left in charge of naval forces in the lower Mississippi, was ordered to continue to keep gunboats off Baton Rouge to cooperate with the *Essex*.[8] To General Butler he replied, "So you have evacuated Baton Rouge and have sent here for more troops for New Orleans. You must be expecting an attack, but I cannot think it possible that it will be made upon you." Then he dolefully asks, "What will we do for troops when the attack comes off on Mobile?"[9]

Problems of the blockade were also beginning to engross Farragut. Though one of the early letters of instructions from Welles had begun with the injunction: "The importance of a vigorous blockade at every point, to be under your command, cannot be too strongly impressed or felt,"[10] yet he had been so occupied with the campaign against New Orleans and the attempts to open the Mississippi that he had been unable, so far from the Gulf, to supervise the work of the blockaders and look after their needs. Indeed the vessels which had been left for the blockade after his fighting fleet had been organized could hardly have been expected to do much but lay to off a Confederate port. There were three sidewheelers and two small screw steamers; the dozen or so remaining vessels were sailing ships,[11] which evidently could not stop blockade runners. Even steam vessels like the *Susquehanna* and the *Kanawha* could not keep blockade runners out of Mobile Bay. For example, on July 25, the *Cuba* eluded these two vessels and ran in with a "full cargo of arms, ammunition, medicines, and blankets."[12] The blockaders were placed off Galveston, Matagorda, Corpus Christi, Sabine Pass, Berwick Bay, Mississippi Sound, and the entrances to Mobile Bay. By the middle of July three or four more screw steamers and an equal number of sailing ships had been added to the list.

The sailing ship *Santee* was sent home by Farragut because of scurvy in her crew.[13] Also home went the bark *Midnight* which had been on duty off the coast of Texas for nine months with fresh provisions for only twenty-four days, and had arrived off Southwest Pass with "40 cases of scurvy, dysentery, and diarrhoea."[14] The supplying of proper provisions and coal to the blockaders was a serious problem in itself which could not be neglected. Farragut complained to Welles that the price of coal had increased from $4.50 a ton to $8.00, though ships could secure return cargoes at New Orleans. "This may not be any of my business," he caustically wrote," but when my country is bleeding at every pore I feel it my duty to prevent impositions as far as practicable." He also inquired why the coal vessels could not bring out potatoes and other vegetables to prevent scurvy among his men.[15]

2

In spite of all these handicaps, several captures were made. By the first of November, 1862, about fifty-four blockade runners had been taken. The *Kanawha* and *Hatteras* were most successful, each having captured six prizes. Most of the vessels had been outward bound with cargoes of cotton for Havana. Turpentine, resin, rice, corn meal, staves, flour, sugar, molasses, salt, and munitions were also found on some of these ships. Most of them were small sailing vessels. Occasionally a cargo would be worth as much as $10,000, like that of the *Water Witch* which the bark *Arthur* captured.[16] Her commander, Lieutenant Kittredge, captured three other vessels off Corpus Christi, and Farragut wrote him, "Your operations against the rebels give me much gratification,"[17] not knowing that the enterprising officer had been made a prisoner while ashore reconnoitering.

Great care had to be exercised in dealing with ships flying a neutral flag, and Farragut warned his blockaders of the delicate situation likely to arise in stopping vessels at the mouth of the Rio Grande and off the port of Brazos Santiago. Vessels carrying contraband of war, however, were subject to capture.[18] The problem was made more difficult by Confederate vessels frequently masquerading under the English flag. But if the vessel carried powder, cartridge boxes, and muskets along with her cargo of tea, coffee, and paper, as did the English steamer *Ann* of London, which was captured after she had landed a part of her cargo near Fort Morgan, there could be no question as to the legality of her capture.[19] But troublesome cases did arise. There was the Confederate steamer *General Rusk*, fraudulently placed under the English flag, whose name was then changed to the *Blanche*. After making one successful voyage to Havana and back to Galveston, she was destroyed on her second voyage in neutral waters on the coast of Cuba by the Union steamer *Montgomery*. This brought forth vigorous complaints from both the Spanish and English governments, and the court-martial of Commander Charles Hunter and his dismissal from the service,[20] to the great annoyance of Farragut.

A much more serious case was that of the Confederate cruiser *Florida*. On the afternoon of September 4, this vessel under command of Lieutenant John N. Maffitt, C. S. Navy approached the entrance to Mobile Bay with most of her crew ill of yellow fever, which they had picked up in the West Indies. Maffitt himself was so weak from the disease that he had to be supported when it was necessary for him to stand. Forced by the yellow fever to run the blockade into a Confederate port and obliged to do so by daylight for the lack of a pilot, he decided to try to get into Mobile Bay disguised under English colors.[21] Fortunately for him, on that day the *Susquehanna* and three of the gunboats on the blockade were at Pensacola for repairs or coal. The *Cayuga* was out of sight on a special mission, the *Oneida* had just finished minor boiler repairs and did not have up full steam, and the *Winona* was just returning to her station from chasing a strange sail.[22] Resembling the English gunboats which frequently inspected the blockade and flying an English red ensign, the *Florida* completely deceived Commander Preble of the *Oneida* until she failed to answer his hail or to stop to request permission to pass through the blockade. The *Oneida* then began firing on the *Florida*, which was running on a parallel course not more than one hundred yards distant, and making fourteen knots to the blockader's seven. Maffitt could not man his guns, but merely made a dash for the entrance, which he successfully reached, though his vessel was considerably damaged by four effective shots.[21]

For this "inexcusable neglect in permitting the armed steamer *Oreto*, in broad daylight to run the blockade,"[23] Preble was dismissed from the service; but after nine months he was reappointed to the same rank by President Lincoln. Farragut was greatly embarrassed by the affair, and in reporting the event wrote, "Why Captain Preble did not fire into her after she failed to stop or answer his hail, I cannot imagine."[24] But he did not approve the severe punishment which was given Preble, after he learned more complete details of what happened. He then wrote Welles that he was sure that Preble's hesitation in firing arose from a desire to "avoid giving offense to foreign nations in enforcing our blockade."[25] This letter had much to do with Preble's reinstatement.

After the *Florida* incident, Farragut ordered Commander Alden to bring the *Richmond* from Ship Island and assume the command of the blockading forces off Mobile Bay.[26] Ten days previous Captain James S. Palmer had replaced Lieutenant Commanding James S. Thornton, who had been acting in command of the *Hartford* since the death of Wainwright.[27] "I have tried Palmer in the fiery furnace," Farragut wrote his wife, "and he is as true as steel."[28]

While Farragut was at Pensacola, his son Loyall arrived to serve as his clerk on the *Hartford*.[29] He was then approaching his nineteenth birthday. His mother had begun to fear that he might be drafted into the army.[30] After the capture of Norfolk, Mrs. Farragut's mother went to Hastings-on-Hudson for a long visit with her daughter.[31] But relations with other members of the family were not cordial. "When you write to Norfolk," Farragut wrote his wife, "ask that beloved sister of ours to take Mr. Foster's advice and search her Bible and tell me where she found authority to hold up to *my son* the example of a rebel child against his Father—was it Absalom? It has often been wondered at that the ancients should have made the Furies females, but I think a few months of Civil War will make it plain to any man that they were right. . . . Give my love to your dear Mother."[32]

3

It was about this time that Farragut saw immediate prospects of operations against Mobile Bay slip away from him. Near the first of September, he received a letter from Welles congratulating him on the destruction of the *Arkansas*.[33] Farragut was particularly pleased with its conclusion in which the Secretary stated that he realized that at such a great distance it was necessary to act without being able to communicate with the Department. "I have entire confidence," he added, "that in such emergencies your decision will be wise, energetic, and correct."[33] Feeling very happy and quite satisfied with himself after reading Mr. Welles's letter, Farragut wrote his wife, only the day before his mood was changed by the *Florida:* "The health of myself and all on board is excellent, the temperature is delightful, and my crew are getting back to their accustomed tone. I received letters from the Department by this mail, entirely different from the last. They talk about my 'wisdom,' 'judgment,' etc., but when the *Arkansas* was at Vicksburg, I was to 'destroy her at all hazards.' I would have given my admiral's commission to have gotten up to the *Arkansas*. I wanted a wooden ship to do it. The ironclads are cowardly things, and I don't want them to succeed in the world."[34]

Welles's letter dealt chiefly with the importance of holding New Orleans and the lower Mississippi. The unsettled state of affairs there, the lack of sufficient military force, and the bad state of repairs in Farragut's fleet made it inexpedient to attempt any concentration of "an adequate force" for the reduction of Mobile defenses.[33] This was a real disappointment to Farragut. Only a few days before, he had written General Butler that he hoped to have the repairs on his vessels completed in two weeks, and that the moment he was ready he would send him word. "Then you can decide," he wrote hopefully, "as to the assistance you can give."[35]

Farragut continued to dally with the idea of forcing his way into Mobile Bay, even after the *Florida* entered. To Welles he reported, "They have now three 10-gun gunboats in Mobile, and will require a large force to blockade them, and I think it will be cheaper to run the forts if I can secure an outlet through Grant's Pass. I will soon have my vessels in condition to try it."[36] But a later pessimistic letter from Fox further discouraged him. "Our armies have been outgeneraled," he mournfully wrote, "and the rebels are in Maryland in force."[37] This referred to Lee's brilliant defeat of Pope at Second Manassas and his invasion of Maryland, which had not reached its culmination in the Battle of Antietam at the time Fox was penning this lamentation. The *New Ironsides* and more monitors would soon be ready but they would have to be sent against Charleston, through which so many munitions were going to the Confederates. "I notice you speak of Mobile," Fox casually remarked. "We don't think you have force enough, and we do not expect you to run risks, crippled as you are. It would be a magnificent diversion for the country at this juncture, but act on your own judgment and do not give way to any unnecessary risks. We only expect a blockade now and the preservation of New Orleans."[37]

This bad news led Farragut to write his wife: "If your generals go on so badly as they have lately, I don't see how this war is ever to end—until we destroy one another. England, and in fact all Europe, has looked long for the day when the glory of the United States should depart. I still hope some man will rise up who is able to conduct the army to victory."[38] Just a fortnight before, he had written her buoyantly, "As to 'intervention,' I don't believe it, and, if it does come, you will find the United States not so easy a nut to crack as they imagine. We have no dread of 'rams' or 'he-goats,' and, if our editors had less, the country would be better off. Now they scare everybody to death."[39]

But at that very time, the famous interchange of letters between Prime Minister Palmerston and Lord John Russell with regard to the advisability of taking steps towards the recognition of the independence of the Confederate States, because of the defeats of the Union armies and the prospect of Washington and Baltimore being captured, was being carried on. Only with the changed military situation did that danger of intervention pass away, near the first of October.[40]

4

Carrying out a suggestion from Welles that more attention should be given to the coast of Texas, Farragut sent Acting Master Frederick Crocker with the *Kensington* and the *Rachel Seaman* to attempt the capture of Sabine Pass.[41] This was successfully accomplished on September 24 along with eight prizes[42] taken in the vicinity. One of these was the *West Florida* from New Orleans, sailing under a provisional British register. Her captain bore this unusual pass from General Butler: "The *West Florida*, schooner, has been loaded with the present cargo and cleared for Matamoras for the purpose of bringing out cotton from Texas. She proposes to make the Sabine Pass, exchange her cargo for cotton, and then make a port in Cuba or New Orleans, as may be best. The owner, a loyal citizen, has property here to insure his good faith. You will therefore aid what I understand to be the policy of my Government in getting cotton to foreign ports by passing this vessel. This course of trade should be secret, of course, to be successful. You will not, therefore, allow any information of this pass of this vessel to be made public but report that matter, with a copy of this letter, to Admiral Farragut or your superior officer."[43]

When this came to Farragut's notice, he wrote a vigorous protest against the "extraordinary document." "If the Government require of the Army any such policy as indicated in the enclosed document," he declared, "we shall be at issue all the time, for under my present instructions I shall capture all vessels with passes, except those employed in transporting provisions, etc., for the Army and Navy."[44] Earlier in the summer, before the capture of Sabine Pass, Commander George F.

Emmons of the *Hatteras* had taken the Confederate steamer *Indian No. 2*, bearing this pass from Butler: "Mr. E. H. Skaggs has permission to bring the steamer *Indian No. 2* from the mouth of Sabine to this city [New Orleans] with a load of cattle and provisions."[45] Skaggs turned out to be "a professed gambler and speculator," and cheated the navy out of $5,000 through a fraudulent bill of sale, to the annoyance of Farragut.[46]

Another expedition to the coast of Texas with four gunboats under Commander W. B. Renshaw was dispatched to attempt the capture of Galveston. He succeeded in closing that port on October 5,[47] and the northern portion of the coast of Texas was definitely closed to commerce by sea. About this time, the bark *W. G. Anderson* left the blockade at the mouth of the Rio Grande and returned to Pensacola because her crew had become afflicted with scurvy, and the steamer *Albatross* returned from the same station with numerous cases of yellow fever which was prevalent down there. "I have the coast of Texas lined with vessels," wrote Farragut to Welles, "all trying to do something. If I had a military force, I would go down and take every place from the Mississippi River to the Rio Grande."[48]

5

Rough weather sometimes also had to be reckoned with. On September 22, for example, there was a storm which blew away the smokestack and main topmast of the *Kennebec* and so strained the *Winona* that she leaked fore and aft. She managed to reach Pensacola but could hardly have been kept afloat four hours longer. "It is storming now," Farragut wrote his wife while the wind was still howling; "I suppose the true equinoctial gale, and these are the times that try the commander of a squadron. I could not sleep last night, thinking of the blockaders. It is rough work, lying off a port month in and month out. I am very indulgent when I can be so. I have six vessels off Mobile, so that one can always come in for coal. They are all the time breaking down and coming in for repairs."[49]

The continuous need for repairs, particularly to the engines of Farragut's vessels, was the main topic of many a letter to Welles and Fox. "My whole time is taken up repairing vessels," he complained.[50] "We have our navy yards filled with broken-down vessels, and we know your wants and will exert ourselves to help you, but the more we send the more they seem to come back," echoed Fox.[51] What Farragut earnestly begged for were vessels of greater speed and lighter draft. "It is a most mortifying fact that we have no vessel with sufficient speed to catch any of the fast steamers that run the blockade," he ruefully admitted to Welles.[52]

When the *Brooklyn* was finally completely repaired at Pensacola and made seaworthy, she was sent to the blockade off Mobile Bay on October 5. Bell, who had taken temporary control of her when Craven left for home, had remained in command at the special request of Farragut,[53] who had great confidence in him. Recently he had been promoted to Commodore, and in recognition of this advancement in rank Farragut placed him in command of the blockade of Mobile Bay and vicinity, from Ship Island to Pensacola, with some eight or ten ships under his immediate command.[54] With this arrangement completed, Farragut felt more secure, inasmuch as the *Florida* was still in Mobile Bay and Welles had warned him several weeks before that "an ample force should be stationed off Mobile to repel any attacks from the enemy's vessels in that quarter and to maintain an efficient and stringent blockade."[55]

Still the blockade runners slipped in and out. Sometimes it was through pure carelessness of the commander of a blockader, as in the case of Lieutenant Selim E. Woodworth of the *Jackson,* who passed "two steamers in the Sound and never took notice of them, but thought they were going to Pascagoula." As a matter of fact they were the blockade runners *Cuba* and *Clio* bound to sea which were next reported in Havana. Farragut ordered a court of inquiry for Woodworth.[56] According to consular reports forwarded by Welles to Farragut, over 7,000 bales of cotton had been shipped from Matamoras, Mexico, alone, and many small sailing vessels from St. Thomas and Cuba conveyed contraband to that port.[57] "It is impossible to prevent these fast steamers from running the blockade in very dark nights," Farragut admitted to Fox. "You are lying still and the vessel is upon you before you see her, going twelve or fourteen knots, and before you can get your men to aim a gun she is past you."[56]

The blockade runners tried all sorts of tricks. The *Caroline*, under English colors, was chased six hours off Mobile on October 28, 1862 by the *Montgomery*, Commander Charles Hunter, and hove to only after having been struck twice. She was commanded by a Captain Forbes, who claimed when brought on board the *Hartford* that he was bound for Matamoras and not Mobile. "I do not take you for running the blockade," Farragut is reported to have told him, "but for your damned poor navigation. Any man bound for Matamoras from Havana and coming within twelve miles of Mobile light has no business to have a steamer."[58] Forbes was sent North as a "dangerous person," and the vessel was dispatched as a prize to Philadelphia, where it was converted into the gunboat *Arizona* and then returned to the Gulf.

6

For some time Farragut had had in mind making a tour of the coast to see how his blockaders were getting along, but the possibility of attacking the forts guarding the entrance to Mobile Bay held him to Pensacola.[59] He fondled the idea suggested in a recent letter[87] from Fox that an attack on Mobile Bay would be "a magnificent diversion for the country" because matters were going so badly for the Union armies. This Farragut repeated in a letter to Butler, asking him if he had troops to spare to attack Fort Gaines in the rear. "Now is the time to create a diversion," he wrote. "I will be ready in five or six days for anything as far as my force goes."[60] But a few days later, he expressed doubt as to his ability to reduce the forts with his present force. "If the Department can spare me two more steam sloops of the *Housatonic* class, I think that, in conjunction with the army, I could take Forts Gaines and Morgan.

If an ironclad can be spared, so much the better," he declared.[61] His former dislike of ironclads seems to have been disappearing, particularly if he had them in his own fleet.

But Farragut still banked on his wooden vessels. "I agree with you that this is the time for a diversion by an attack on Mobile," he wrote Fox. "At Mobile . . .", he continued, "they have three or four ironclads in construction and no doubt they would be very formidable in shoal water, where our ships cannot operate—but let them come outside of the shallows and I flatter myself I will show you how far wood can stand against iron—particularly anything built in shallow water."[62] To keep Butler primed for a possible attack on the forts at Mobile Bay, he wrote him again a few days later, "I shall be ready to go ahead at Gaines the moment you can furnish the troops."[63] By that time, Farragut knew who was in command of the Confederate naval forces at Mobile. "Frank Buchanan is at Mobile," he wrote Mrs. Farragut, "and is an Admiral. I suppose he was promoted for his conduct on board the *Merrimac*."[64]

By the end of October, Farragut was beginning to worry again about the *Florida's* breaking out through the blockade, and he wrote to Bell to be vigilant, as he had been informed by deserters that she was ready to come out. "I want to be at them," he declared extravagantly, "and as soon as I can get an interview with Butler I think, if he don't give me the soldiers, I will go it alone."[65] He also suggested that Bell send in two launches and two or three smaller boats on a very dark night and board the *Florida* and capture her.

Farragut finally came to the realization that he was not soon to receive any real reinforcements for his fighting fleet in the Gulf. The campaigns in Virginia had turned out so disastrously that a large number of Union war vessels were still detained in the James River. The successful raiding of the *Alabama* under Captain Raphael Semmes had forced the Navy Department to "send out a dozen vessels in pursuit."[66] There had been delay in the completion of ironclads, and these were all allotted to the fleet off Charleston.[51] Only after the enemy was entirely cut off from the Atlantic were these monitors to be sent into the Gulf.⁶⁶ So Farragut decided at last to go to New Orleans and find out from Butler whether he could give him any aid in an attack on the guardian forts at the entrance to Mobile Bay. He could also see at first hand what the conditions were in the lower Mississippi, and perhaps later make a tour of inspection of the blockade of the coast of Texas.

Accordingly, on the morning of November 7, the *Hartford* went to sea with the *Richmond*, visited the *Brooklyn* on the Mobile Bay blockade that afternoon, and a little past noon two days later was at New Orleans receiving salutes from the English corvette *Rinaldo* and the French war vessel *Catinat*.⁶⁷ After three months of rather monotonous service in the Gulf, Farragut was back again at New Orleans, disappointed in his hope and expectation of being able to seal up Mobile Bay. The health of his crews, however, had been restored, his ships were in a better state of repairs, and the blockade seemed to be operating more efficiently.

At New Orleans, Farragut had an unpleasant experience with the crew of the *Rinaldo*. This was the ship which had carried Mason and Slidell to England after they had been released by the American government, and her men were quite sympathetic toward the Confederates. Both her officers and men were treated very kindly and hospitably by the citizens of New Orleans, and many visitors were received in turn on board the vessel. The Englishmen learned Confederate songs which they often sang in the evenings. On one occasion as Farragut was going ashore from the *Hartford*, lying near the *Rinaldo*, the chorus of "Bonnie Blue Flag" was heard coming from the English vessel. "We must have a stop put to that," said Farragut, turning to Captain Palmer, who was not much impressed until Farragut added, "If it isn't stopped, we shall have to drop down and blow him out of the water." When Captain Hewitt of the *Rinaldo* learned that the singing was an annoyance, he put a stop to it by threatening to anchor several miles down the river where his men would not be able to enjoy going ashore in New Orleans.⁶⁸

XIV

DISASTERS IN THE GULF

1

FARRAGUT FOUND the New Orleans area in a chaotic condition. General Butler's available forces were operating to the west of the city in the region of the lower Atchafalaya River, Bayou Teche, and Grand Lake; with these Commander Thomas McKean Buchanan was trying to cooperate with some small gunboats.[1] Butler promised that, as soon as this campaign was finished, Farragut was to have some troops and light draft steamers for the Mobile expedition; but he urged that an attack be made on Port Hudson first.[2] Accordingly, four gunboats were sent to make a reconnaissance of the place. After making careful observations, Lieutenant Commanding George M. Ransom reported that "the fortifications of Port Hudson are now made, by the peculiar advantages of situation, capable of resisting more effectually than Vicksburg the passage of any vessel or fleet."[3] A few days later General Weitzel informed Butler and Farragut that Port Hudson was held by at least 12,000 Confederates and that it would be unwise to attack it with less than an equal number of men. Not having half that many soldiers to spare, Butler abandoned the idea of making an attack.[4]

Farragut then asked for 1,500 or 2,000 men to attack Fort Gaines, and another 1,000 for Galveston. Butler would not make good his promise of troops for Mobile Bay but agreed to send a regiment to Galveston the following week.[4]

2

A very dangerous situation was then developing at Galveston. As early as mid-October Farragut had requested of Butler a small body of troops to hold this place which had been captured by Commander Renshaw. Three days later he repeated the request to Butler.⁵ To this the General replied, "I think I will spare a regiment and some pieces of artillery to hold Galveston, if that will be sufficient."⁶ But week after week he procrastinated; no troops went to Galveston. Meanwhile Renshaw grew uneasy. He had provisions, he wrote Farragut, to last only eighteen days. Immediately the *Kensington* was dispatched with supplies.⁷ Then a few days later Farragut ordered Bell to send more provisions to Galveston by the steamer *Tennessee*.⁸ But Renshaw became more alarmed over the probability of an attack by the Confederates, who he thought were going to place two 100-pounder rifles on river boats with bulwarks of cotton bales.⁹ Later he reported that two of his boats' crews with officers had been captured while ashore scouting, and he repeated his fears of the enemy's heavy rifles. Farragut tried to reassure him by reminding him that he had four gunboats, armed with 8-, 9-, and 11-inch guns. "Are you willing, captain," asked Farragut, "that I should make such a statement to the honorable Secretary—that we have abandoned the ports of Texas because of reports that they were making preparations to drive us out? I trust not. The gunboats must hold Galveston until the army arrives." In reply to Renshaw's request for a 100-pounder, he promised to send him a rifle gun as soon as he had one to spare, "but I do not think it essential to your safety." In conclusion, he referred to the supplies recently sent, and complained, "You should have sent requisitions for such articles as you required, as we are at a loss to know what articles or quantities to send."¹⁰

Meanwhile Renshaw poured out his complaints to the supposedly sympathetic D. D. Porter, in whose mortar fleet he had been an officer. Referring to Farragut as "brainless" and to his orders as "the braying of this ass," he wrote that when he met Porter again he would unfold to him specimens of composition, in reply to dispatches of his, "involving such *deep thought,* such profound professional reasoning that must unquestionably lead you to think your old friend is entirely bereft of reason and comprehension." "Let's drop this nonsensical style," he continued, "and in plain straightforward words tell you that, since

I have been down here, notwithstanding his [Farragut's] being weeks before informed of my *wants*, he has twice allowed me to run down my provisions—once to five day's rations, and then only was saved the mortification of being obliged to abandon this important place, by the energy of Law whom I sent in the *Clifton* to tell him I would be in a state of starvation in ten days. It would take a week for me to give you an idea of what I have gone through with since coming down here. At this moment, I am hourly expecting an attack from the rebels. ... I have bust [sic] my 100-pd. rifle—we have but two 30-pounders among us—Magruder has two 84-pounders—first rate guns—one shot from which in the *right* place would sink the *Clifton* or *Westfield* and without our being able to reach the devil that did the deed. I have told Farra *guts* this fact—no use, I was writing to an Ass. Good night—I will finish, when the steamer comes. If I am not looking through the bars of some *fine prison at Houston*. Seriously, I am almost hourly expecting an attack, and don't feel *satisfied* that I can hold my own. If they come, the result will tell how far my opinion was correct."[11]

3

When Farragut learned that D. D. Porter had been appointed, near the first of October, to take Commodore Davis's command of the squadron in the upper Mississippi, he commenced to worry about his own status at New Orleans and in the lower Mississippi. "I think they will soon get me out of this," he wrote confidentially to Bell, "as the Mississippi will not work well with me at this end of the river, nor do I desire it more than Porter. I only feel a little curious to know whom he will nominate for my successor in the river, if he don't take it all himself."[12] A few days afterwards he wrote his wife, "So soon as the river rises, we will have Porter down from above, who now commands the upper squadron, and then I shall probably go outside. I do not think the Government wishes me here after Porter arrives; but I am agreeable, if they will only let me do something to keep the boys up to their work. We shall spoil unless we have a fight occasionally. Blockading is hard service, and difficult to carry out with perfect success, as has been effectually shown at Charleston, where they run to Nassau regularly once a week."[13] "No doubt they will want to move me soon," he wrote her again a week later, "not because they find fault with me, but because room is wanted for some favorite to win his spurs. But they shall never say that I backed out. I will do my duty, and obey my instructions. Don't think that I hold on from ambitious motives. I know too well the history of all revolutions, not to know that I now have everything to lose and nothing to gain. My country has rewarded me for my services, and it is not for me to say I *will* or I *won't* continue in command, but to be, as I always am, ready to do my duty and stay or go as I am directed."[14]

General Butler heard a rumor that Farragut was to be replaced, and wrote to Fox about it. "Whence did you surmise that Farragut was to be relieved?" asked Fox in reply. "We never heard the rumor here. The hero of that unequalled dash, despising the great obstacles, gave us victory, glory, and New Orleans, and is not to be forgotten or removed except at his own pleasure, and probably not even then. If he is with you, I beg that you will assure him that we never heard of any such rumor this way."[15] Before Butler received this letter, he learned that he and not Farragut was to be relieved from his command. Indeed, several days before it was written his successor had been appointed.

One of the last official letters that Farragut wrote to Butler while he was still in command at New Orleans was one of vigorous complaint. "While no one appreciates more highly than myself the energetic, persevering, and skilful merchant," Farragut pointed out, "I must confess that no one has a greater abhorrence and detestation of the unscrupulous speculator who takes advantage of every necessity of his fellow-beings, and regardless of consequences, by bribery and corruption forces his trade into the enemy's country, drawing down dishonor upon the cause as well as the country we serve, and upon us who are exerting every nerve to sustain our honor among nations, and even claim the respect of our enemies, however unwilling they may be to yield to it." He then outlined to General Butler the case of the schooner *L. L. Davis* whose cargo was owned by a Mr. Wyer of New Orleans, who claimed that the ship was going to Matamoras, though instead it went to the Confederate port of Pontchatoula. Farragut wanted him to be punished according to law. "This and similar things are the theme of public discussion," he added, "and bring discredit upon the whole of us, for it is said publicly that it could not be done without the connivance of the authorities, a charge which I am sure we all desire to avoid by a fair investigation."[16]

The problem of trade in the Gulf ports was a complicated one during the war. For example, there were certain cotton merchants in Mobile who wished to pretend to run the blockade with their cotton and then deliver it to the blockaders as Union property with permission to continue the voyage to New Orleans. Farragut informed them that no permits could be issued for such a procedure, but that all such cotton would have to be taken to Ship Island and proved to be Union property before it could be liberated. "These men say they must go to Washington and Richmond and for the sake of humanity to try to make some arrangement by which they can get some means of getting shoes and clothing for their Negroes this winter or they will perish," Farragut wrote Bell.[17] "I happen to know the fact that there is great distress among the families at Pascagoula," he asserted, "as I have a widowed sister in the same place who made strong appeals to me of the same kind recently."[18] But there had been so much abuse of Butler's scheme of granting permits for trade between New Orleans and Confederate ports that he was forced to take precautions.

4

On Monday, December 15, six transports arrived at New Orleans with General N. P. Banks's army of about 20,000 men. The General arrived with orders to relieve Butler, and with instructions to open the Mississippi River and reduce "Fort Morgan or Mobile City in order to control that bay and harbor."[19] Farragut was to cooperate with him in these expeditions. After capturing Vicksburg, he was to send a force east to destroy the railroads at Jackson and Marion and thus cut communications between northern Mississippi and Mobile and Atlanta. Still another naval and military expedition was to ascend the Red River and provide an outlet for the sugar and cotton of northern Louisiana. Then, as it would almost seem in jest, the orders continued, "These instructions are not intended to tie your hands or to hamper your operations in the slightest degree."[19] These were from General Halleck, then commander-in-chief of all the Union armies. It seems fantastic that he, who had accomplished so little in Tennessee and northern Mississippi, could have been placed in a position to order Banks or any other general to work miracles with inadequate forces.

Banks bore a letter from President Lincoln to Farragut, reading: "This will introduce Major-General Banks. He is in command of a considerable land force for operating in the South, and I shall be glad for you to cooperate with him and give him such assistance as you can consistently with your orders from the Navy Department."[20] Farragut was duly flattered. "General Banks's arrival here upsets everything," he informed Mrs. Farragut. "Butler is relieved, and goes home. How the change will work I know not. I think it will be a good opportunity to enter upon a milder system of administration; but I am satisfied that Butler was the man to begin. Banks brought me an autograph letter from the President, and says the President told him to rely on my 'judgment,' 'discretion,' etc., and we are likely to get along very well. He has troops to open the Mississippi and occupy Texas. We shall have a new rule in Sodom."[21] Banks advised Lincoln of his arrival and of the delivery of his letter to Farragut. "He was much gratified to receive it," the General confided, "and promised a hearty and cordial cooperation. He is earnest for work and full of enthusiasm. I was delighted with him and feel assured that we shall act together without difficulty."[22]

The handsome, smooth-shaven Banks, who had given up the Speakership of the House of Representatives to be a major-general and had already had considerable experience in active service, presented a contrast to Butler not only in appearance but also in genial manners and social graces. For "Beast" Butler the people of New Orleans were to have Banks the "Dancing Master," a nickname soon bestowed upon him for the elaborate balls he sponsored in an effort to win the good will of the aristocrats of that Southern metropolis.

Farragut had never been able to get one soldier from Butler for Galveston much less any for Mobile Bay. But when he recommended to Banks the occupation of Baton Rouge, he approved at once and ordered his transports with 10,000 men to proceed up the river early on the morning after their arrival without disembarking at New Orleans. This expedition, supported by the *Richmond* and four gunboats, accomplished its mission without opposition on the morning of December 17, and the American flag was again raised over the State House.[23] Farragut was so impressed with Banks's aggressiveness that he ordered Bell to leave the blockade of Mobile Bay to Commodore Hitchcock and to bring the *Brooklyn* to New Orleans. "I hear that Porter is knocking at the upper door at Vicksburg, and we must go to work at the lower door, Port Hudson," he declared.[24] Later he wrote again, "I trust your ship is not so much out of order as to delay you beyond this week. General Banks talks of being at Vicksburg in a fortnight, but of course he does not know the difficulties to be encountered."[25]

With considerable satisfaction Farragut was at last able to report also to Welles that Banks had sent 1,000 troops to Galveston.[26] He had, a week or ten days before, written Renshaw that Banks had arrived, and would send 1,000 or 2,000 troops immediately. He also informed him that he had a 50-pounder rifle which he would send down as soon as he could get it mounted.[27]

5

Just when the future seemed brighter and conditions better in the Gulf than they had for many months, disaster began to follow disaster. Early in December, Farragut wrote his wife that he had a great many irons in the fire and that he had "to look sharp" to keep some of them from burning. "I have all the coast except Mobile Bay," he too boastfully added.[28] He was about to lose an important part of that coast.

The *Brooklyn* arrived at New Orleans at noon on the day after Christmas. During the holidays preparations for the expedition against Port Hudson apparently were not being feverishly pushed by the aggressive Banks, and Farragut was still in New Orleans on January 3. That afternoon at four o'clock Bell was dining with Farragut on the *Hartford*, when a telegram was delivered from Southwest Pass with bad news from a steamer which had just arrived from Galveston. The two officers could hardly have been more astonished and more concerned if a bombshell had just exploded on the deck of the *Hartford*. Farragut's eyes blinked as he read that on New Year's Day Renshaw's gunboats had been attacked by four Confederate ships, the *Harriet Lane* had been boarded and captured, and the *Westfield* had been blown up to keep her from falling into the enemy's hands. Commander Renshaw had been killed. The three remaining blockaders had been driven away from Galveston, and the port entirely taken over by General Magruder's forces.

When Farragut and Bell had recovered somewhat from the shock, the latter declared, "I am ready for any service, Admiral." Farragut answered, "Then, go down to Galveston as soon as you can." Sixty of the *Brooklyn's* crew were "on shore on a debauch," and an officer was immediately sent to round them up and get them on board that night. But it was eleven the next morning when the *Brooklyn* got under way with the *Sciota* for Galveston.[29]

Only 260 troops of the 42nd Massachusetts Volunteers had reached Renshaw before the attack. But after capturing Galveston, he had written Farragut an extraordinarily long report, in which he declared that two or three hundred men with some half dozen pieces of artillery would be sufficient.[30] "I am grieved to see this 'nightmare' that appears to seize upon our officers," Farragut wrote Alden up at Baton Rouge. "All our disaster at

Galveston has been caused by it. Poor Renshaw, who has paid the forfeit of his life, was a martyr to it. He had become so nervous that he had made up his mind to blow up his vessel rather than have her taken, and did not look to see that he was destroying himself by the act. I cannot talk about it, as the Department puts a gag law upon officers against prejudicing cases of this kind, but the moral effect must be most terrible if we don't retake it again. . . . If the *Lane* gets out, she will be as bad as the *Alabama*. . . . There appears to be a vein of ill luck upon us, so look out for it. They will now be emboldened by their success and try it again. I expect Buchanan to try it at Mobile next."[31]

The Confederates began their attack before dawn. The decks of the *Harriet Lane* were swept by a destructive fire from sharpshooters placed behind cotton bales on two Confederate steamers. A 68-pounder rifle, the only heavy gun the Confederates had, burst at the third fire. One of the Confederate steamers was rammed and sunk in shallow water; but the other one rammed the *Harriet Lane*, which was then boarded. Commander Jonathan Wainwright was killed and ten other men were either killed or wounded. The *Owasco*, attemping to assist the *Harriet Lane*, was driven away when the Confederates turned the *Lane's* guns upon her. The flagship *Westfield* ran aground hard and fast. A white flag was hoisted on the *Harriet Lane* and a boat bearing a flag of truce, with a Confederate officer and the acting master of the *Lane*, came over to the gunboat *Clifton* with the proposition that all the vessels surrender but one which would be permitted to leave the harbor with all the crews; otherwise the Confederates would continue the engagement, using the *Harriet Lane* and three other steamers which had just appeared. When the proposal was taken to Renshaw, he refused the conditions and ordered his gunboats to retire from the harbor. His own vessel, the *Westfield*, was blown up by a premature explosion, causing his death and that of about fifteen of his officers and men. Lieutenant Commander Richard L. Law, left as commanding officer, then abandoned the blockade and sailed away to New Orleans with the remaining vessels.[32] For this, he was court-martialed and suspended from the service for three years.[33] The Confederates were immensely encouraged by their success, and on January 5 Major-General J. Bankhead Magruder issued a proclamation formally announcing that "the harbor of Galveston is open for trade to all friendly nations."[34]

When Bell arrived off Galveston on January 7, he saw the wreck of the *Westfield,* and in the harbor the mastheads of the captured *Harriet Lane,* two barks, two schooners, and two bay steamers. There was also great activity in the construction of defensive earthworks at strategic points. Three days later after other vessels had arrived, he made a rather half-hearted attack on these defenses, at long range because of the shallow water, with the *Brooklyn* and two gunboats.[35] He then settled down to a blockade of the port.

Fox was greatly disturbed over the disaster, which he called "the most melancholy affair ever recorded in the history of our gallant navy," in a letter to the harassed Farragut. "Five naval vessels driven off by a couple of steam scows with one gun which burst at the third fire and the attack made by soldiers," he continued. "The worst feature has followed I am afraid and occasions the Government services embarrassment, viz., Lieutenant-Commander Law after being driven out voluntarily abandoned the blockade. If Bell had immediately pushed in and retaken the city no questions could have arisen."[36] To Porter the same day he gave free rein to his pen: "The disgraceful affair at Galveston has shaken the public confidence in our prestige. Five gunboats were sunk and dispersed by two river steamboats armed with one gun and filled only with soldiers; the attack of the enemy being known the day before. It is too cowardly to place on paper. Poor Wainwright did well. Renshaw —bah—he is dead."[37]

Welles was more restrained. ". . . Get as yet no official report of the disaster at Galveston," he recorded in his diary on January 24. "Farragut has prompt, energetic, excellent qualities, but no fondness for written details or self-laudation; does but one thing at a time, but does that strong and well; is better fitted to lead an expedition through danger and difficulty than to command an extensive blockade; is a good officer in a great emergency, will more willingly take great risks in order to obtain great results than any officer in high position in either Navy or Army, and, unlike most of them, prefers that others should tell the story of his well-doing rather than relate it himself. . . ."[38]

Farragut and Banks received a lot of criticism. An example of what was going the rounds is found in a letter to Postmaster General Montgomery Blair from a certain William Alexander of New Orleans, who had resided sixteen years in Texas. After pointing out how easy it was to mass Confederate forces near Galveston in a few hours because of its rail connection with Houston, a railroad center, he declared, "It was selected by Admiral Farragut as a point to be taken and by General Banks as a point to be occupied. The result is already before you. Now, if Napoleon Ist were at the head of our Government, he would disgrace Farragut for taking a place without military value to us, and for attacking at a point where our enemies wish us to attempt to make an entrance into the state, and leaving the railroad bridge from the mainland to the inland unbroken; and he would at least have removed Banks for suffering a small force to be landed where so long as the bridge stood they would be entirely at the mercy of the enemy. These officers, through neglect or ignorance of facts they could have easily mustered, have caused defeat and loss. I suppose that some petty naval officer will be made the scape-goat, and that Farragut and Banks will escape even an enquiry."[39]

6

A second disaster followed before Farragut had time to begin to recover from the first blow. He went to call on General Banks on the evening of January 14, and the General handed him a telegram from Southwest Pass, announcing the loss of the sidewheeler *Hatteras*, carrying about 125 officers and men and 8 guns.[40] She was one of the five gunboats Farragut had hurried down to the assistance of Bell off Galveston. Before the war she had been an excursion steamer on the Delaware River; and it was sadly ironical that a vessel which had formerly given so much pleasure should have come to such a tragic end.

January 11 was a beautiful, clear Sunday, off Galveston. At three o'clock in the afternoon a sail to the southeastward was sighted from the masthead of the *Brooklyn,* and the *Hatteras* was ordered to chase the stranger. At sunset the little sidewheeler was last seen, about twelve miles to the south, chugging along in pursuit. At about seven o'clock when it was quite dark, the *Hatteras* came within hail of the suspicious vessel. "What steamer is that?" inquired Lieutenant-Commander H. C. Blake. "Her Britannic Majesty's ship *Vixen,*" was the reply. As a boat was being piped away to investigate, a second reply came from the stranger, "We are the Confederate steamer *Alabama.*" A broadside followed, and after a hot engagement of thirteen minutes, the *Hatteras* in a sinking condition signaled her defeat. The crew were scarcely removed when she went down. The flashes of guns had been seen and the sound of heavy firing had been heard on the *Brooklyn,* which in company with the *Sciota* and *Cayuga* made all possible speed to the rescue. They hunted in vain all that night. At eleven o'clock the next morning they discovered two masts standing out of the water, from one of which the United States pendant was flying, according to Bell's diary, "playfully and unconscious."[41]

On the 15th of January, Farragut sat down and wrote Mr. Welles, "It becomes my painful duty to report still another disaster off Galveston." After relating the details, he informed the Secretary that he had warned his officers commanding at Ship Island, Mobile Bay, and Pensacola to be "on the lookout for the pirate in case she makes any attempt to depredate upon our coast."[42] "I was sadly grieved for the loss of vessel, officers, and men," he wrote Bell. "Independent of all other considerations, I can badly spare them. Still, had she been taken in the capture of Galveston, it would not thus have grieved me."[43] He thus reproached Bell for the failure of his mission.

It was not until January 20 that Bell issued a proclamation announcing that the coast of Texas was still under blockade.[44]

He continued to procrastinate in endeavoring to retake the place. Though Farragut showed his displeasure with the delay, he did not take Bell personally to task. But when writing to Welles he was more critical. "As Commodore Bell did not attack the place the moment he had the first four or five boats, he has missed his chance, as they have been very industrious in throwing up earthworks and placing the guns of the *Westfield* and *Harriet Lane* in battery. The shameful conduct of our forces at Galveston has been one of the severest blows of the war to the Navy; the prestige of the gunboats is gone in that quarter until it is again reestablished by some corresponding good conduct on our part."[45] When Welles finally wrote Farragut a whole month after the Galveston disaster, he was highly critical of Bell. "The recapture or destruction of the *Harriet Lane* should have been the first object of his attention," he declared, and requested a copy of Farragut's orders to Bell.[46] In forwarding this to Welles, Farragut defended Bell and explained the delay.[47]

7

There were still other losses. On January 14, Lieutenant-Commander Thomas McKean Buchanan was killed by a Minie ball in an attack on the Confederate steamer *Cotton* and the batteries on the Bayou Teche to the west of New Orleans.[48] Farragut declared that he was "one of the most gallant young officers" he had in his command.[49] The Confederates, however, were defeated, and forced to burn their steamer.

Two days later, what Farragut had been fearing, happened off Mobile Bay. The *Florida* escaped through the blockade. The night was dark and stormy, but at two o'clock the stars came out, though a light mist still covered the water. Forty minutes later, the *Florida* had passed two of the seven blockaders undetected, when flames from the coal dust flared above her stacks and caused her discovery. She dashed on at full speed between the *Susquehanna* and the fast steamer *Cuyler*. The captain of the latter jumped out of bed, but before he reached the deck half dressed on that cold January morning, just enough time had elapsed to give the hare the start of the hounds. The

Cuyler hung on in pursuit all that day until dark when she lost sight of the fleeing *Florida*.[50] "From fancying myself near promotion in the morning," Commander George F. Emmons wrote, "I gradually dwindled down to a court of enquiry at dark."[50] Captain S. F. Hazard, commanding the *Oneida,* was indeed ordered to appear before a court of inquiry for failure to aid in the interception of the *Florida,* but his health broke down and he was surveyed and sent home.[51]

"Pa's eyes have given out, so I will finish his letter," wrote Loyall Farragut to his mother. "Pa has been very much worried at these things but still he bears it like a philosopher; he knows that he has done all in his power to avert it with the vessels he has; if the government had only let him take Mobile when he wished to, the *Oreto* would have never run out. I suppose you will say, 'You think the South is going to succeed'; we haven't the least idea of it; we hope still for the best."[52] "I had to bear him these bad tidings," wrote Captain Thornton A. Jenkins, who had been detached from the command of the *Oneida* the day before the *Florida* escaped and had been ordered to New Orleans to become Farragut's fleet captain. "Though no stoic, he bore the news as one accustomed to misfortune."[53]

The appearance of the *Alabama* off Galveston and the escape of the *Florida* from Mobile Bay demoralized Farragut's blockaders. No vessel could safely cruise by herself, and it was feared that all the small blockaders would "be gobbled up" before the raiders could be destroyed.[54] The *Alabama* was reported more than once to be hovering about the mouth of the Mississippi, and Farragut sent the old *Mississippi* down to guard the vessels in the vicinity of Southwest Pass. Some even feared that New Orleans might be attacked from the south.[55] Farragut did not share in these fears, but wrote Welles that he was waiting on the Army in order to carry out operations up the river.[56]

After the Galveston affair, he had written the Secretary that he had been compelled to withdraw four or five vessels from the Mississippi to the coast of Texas, and he begged for more ships of war to be sent as soon as possible, as he did not want to hazard an attack on Port Hudson with "less than three ships besides the gunboats" and that he ought to have four or five.[57] Of Commander Alden at Baton Rouge he inquired, "What do you think of the works at Port Hudson? Don't you think our soldiers ought to whip them out there without our assistance?"[58]

In this disturbed state of mind, Farragut wrote his wife," . . . You are right about Porter. We all came to the same conclusion here, that they did not want Farragut's fleet. Not one word has ever been written to me on the subject of going up the river or attacking Mobile. No; it was intended to give a chance for others to win their spurs and God knows I have never interfered with any one, but always do my duty according to my understanding of it. They lie, when they say, 'I am not ready to act with Banks or to do anything else that the vessels under my command can do.' I have never required more than sufficient time to get up steam to go anywhere and have always told the generals so, but they are not ready and God only knows when they will be, but that is no concern of mine. . . . You are right in supposing, my dearest, that I was distressed at the death of Renshaw and Wainwright, although had they lived they would have gone home my bitter enemies, because I foresaw and told them that they were demoralized and but to have lived under such circumstances would have been ten times worse than death. . . . No, my dear, the Government has sins enough, but they are not answerable for the loss of Galveston; it was the bad conduct of the *Navy alone* that caused it and most of them have paid the forfeit with their lives and some of the rest will pay with their commissions."[59]

Another serious loss was inflicted on Farragut's blockaders off Sabine Pass on the morning of January 21, when two "cotton-fortified" Confederate steamers, with a 6-inch rifle and two 12-pounders between them, captured the full-rigged ship *Morning Light* and the schooner *Velocity*, together totaling eleven guns and one hundred seven men. On the approach of the *New London* and the *Cayuga* the next day, the Confederates were forced to burn the *Morning Light* which they had not been able to get into port and from which they had been able to remove only her supplies and ammunition.[60]

On account of all these calamities in the Gulf, even Commodore William Smith, in command of the Pensacola Navy Yard, became alarmed over a report that Pensacola was to be attacked by 5,000 or 6,000 cavalry; while he had only twenty-two marines and eight landsmen with whom he might defend the yard. "I wish I could think this yard as safe from an attack as the Admiral does," he despondently wrote Captain Thornton Jenkins.[61] Farragut himself became quite uneasy over the possibility of the Confederate ironclads breaking out of Mobile Bay and destroying his blockaders right and left.[62] "No doubt Buchanan will make a dash at us soon," he wrote Bell.[63] Accordingly, he decided to visit Ship Island, the blockade off Mobile Bay, and Pensacola. On the way, the *Hartford* went aground on the bar at Southwest Pass; and after a day and a half, just as she had gotten over, a telegram came from General Banks, asking Farragut to return to New Orleans because of disquieting news from Vicksburg.[64] Hence he abandoned his visit of inspection and returned to New Orleans.

With a heavy heart he wrote to Welles of the dangerous reduction of his fighting force. The *Susquehanna* was still on blockade off Mobile Bay with a cylinder cracked and a piston rod bent;[65] the bottoms of the boilers of the *Brooklyn* and *Mississippi* were so thin that they had to be continually patched;[64] the *Cuyler* and *Oneida* were off chasing the *Alabama*, and were temporarily appropriated by Commodore Wilkes;[66] for active operations in the Mississippi there were available only the *Hartford, Richmond, Essex,* and three gunboats;[66] the *Brooklyn* was held to the blockade of Galveston, and the *Mississippi* was required for the protection of the Mississippi Passes; and Pensacola had to be defended only by the guns of the *Potomac, Anderson,* and *Sam Houston*.[67] From mid-November, 1862 to the first of March following, the number of prizes taken by his blockaders had fallen to a dozen or so, and all of these had been captured before the epidemic of disasters commenced.

During this period of disaster, Farragut never lost sight of the strategic importance of sealing up Mobile Bay. "Mobile can be taken at any moment and by the wooden ships, whenever I have 1,500 or 2,000 men to threaten Gaines in the rear," he wrote Fox two days before Christmas, 1862; "but my implied orders (I have no others) are to assist the army to attack Port Hudson and Vicksburg. . . . Had I my own way, it would be to attack Mobile first and then have my whole available force free for the river and Texas and the Rio Grande."[68] "As to Mobile," he declared two weeks afterwards to his wife, "I would have had it long since, or been thrashed out of it. I feel no fears on the subject; but they do not wish the ships risked, for fear that we might not be able to hold the Mississippi."[69]

XV

PASSING THE BATTERIES OF PORT HUDSON

1

JUST WHAT impelled General Banks to telegraph Farragut to return so soon from Southwest Pass to New Orleans is not at all clear. Nothing unusual had happened recently up the Mississippi except that early in February Ellet had run the Vicksburg batteries in the *Queen of the West* and destroyed about $200,000 worth of Confederate property near the mouth of the Red River. Banks was not on the point of beginning operations against Port Hudson. Farragut had consulted him before he departed on his proposed inspection tour, and had found him ready only for an expedition on the right bank of the river through Plaquemine and the Atchafalaya River, in which he could aid him only with the light draft gunboats.[1] Banks was beginning to realize how foolish he had been on his arrival to talk of being in Vicksburg in a fortnight.

On his return to New Orleans, Farragut wrote to his wife, "... We are doing nothing but await the great events, except now and then an expedition with small draft gunboats on the bayous. But Banks is not willing to move in the great attack yet awhile. They do not want us up above yet. They don't want our rank. Bell is still at Galveston, having a watchful time of it. Every one is calling on me to send them vessels; which reminds me of the remark of the musician, 'It is very easy to say blow! blow! but where the devil is the wind to come from?' Pensacola writes, 'We are to be attacked, and want more force.' Ship Island the same. Mobile the same. And yet I am losing my vessels every day, and getting none in return. Our disaster at Galveston has thrown us back and done more injury to the Navy than all the events of the war."[2]

The truth was that Banks, after a visit to Baton Rouge, had already informed General Halleck that the force at Port Hudson was too large for him to attack with his available troops.[3] But Farragut did not know this. After waiting several weeks for the General to decide on a plan of action, he was very angry when he read in the New York *Journal of Commerce* that the operations on the Mississippi had been delayed because his fleet was not ready for service. The implication of the article was that the information had come from the War Department. On a letter which Farragut wrote Welles, explaining that in spite of recent losses his force was "kept ready for action at all times," was this endorsement: "Have never doubted the readiness of Admiral Farragut to act, and the article referred to had not its origin in this Department."[4] To Mrs. Farragut the Admiral wrote, "You will no doubt hear more of 'Why don't Farragut's fleet move up the river?' Tell them, because the army is not ready. Farragut waits upon Banks as to when or where he will go."[5]

The Confederates had, meanwhile, not been idle but had turned Port Hudson into a veritable fortress. Repeated reconnaissances of it had been made by the *Essex*. On the last one, an unsuccessful attempt was made by the enemy to blow the vessel up with a demijohn mine anchored off Profit Island.[6]

The unmerited criticism of Farragut's inaction led him to consider a movement up the river without Bank's cooperation. On the evening of January 20, Captain Thornton Jenkins reported on the *Hartford* as flag captain. Farragut, having cleared all others out of his cabin, said to him, "I wish to have some confidential talk with you upon a subject which I have had in mind for a long time." Jenkins having shown his interest in what the Admiral was about to reveal, Farragut continued, "I have never hinted it to any one, nor does the Department know anything of my thoughts. The first object to be accomplished, which led me to think seriously about it, is to cripple the Southern armies by cutting off their supplies from Texas. Texas at

PASSAGE OF THE BATTERIES OF PORT HUDSON

From the painting made by E. Arnold in "1864 under the direction of Commodore Palmer," and now in the National Museum, Washington, D.C.

Courtesy of United States National Museum

Courtesy of United States Military Academy
CADET LOYALL FARRAGUT, U. S. MILITARY ACADEMY

this time is, and must continue to the end of the war to be, their main dependence for beef cattle, sheep, and Indian corn. If we can get a few vessels above Port Hudson the thing will not be an entire failure, and I am pretty confident it can be done."[7]

With this plan in mind, Farragut wrote Bell a few days afterwards that he wanted him and three gunboats at New Orleans in ten days.[8] But the loss of the *Morning Light* and the *Velocity* at Sabine Pass caused Bell to consider it unwise for him to leave the blockade, and he so informed Farragut.[9] A few days afterwards, the latter wrote again, ". . . We will want you in the *Brooklyn* up here as soon as possible, as I shall have to pass Port Hudson for the purpose of acting against Red River and such other places as the enemy may think of fortifying below Vicksburg."[10] He concluded, however, by leaving it to Bell's judgment as to when he would leave the blockade. Farragut waited nearly two weeks and then ordered Bell to come to New Orleans.[11] The next day he wrote again, repeating the orders and slipping in this semi-critical sentence: "If you could only retake Galveston, it would gain your spurs."[12] To these orders Bell replied ten days later that he could not come until the *Owasco* arrived, and that he thought the gunboats alone were insufficient for the blockade of Galveston.[13]

Farragut's misfortunes in the Gulf and his comparative inactivity week after week did not cause Welles to lose confidence in him. In expressing his disapproval of Du Pont's failure to gain any results before Charleston, he wrote in his diary for February 10, 1863: ". . . It is not what we have talked of, not what we expected of him; is not like the firm and impetuous but sagacious and resolute Farragut."[14]

While waiting from day to day, like Mr. Micawber, "for something to turn up," Farragut amused himself with the social events which General Banks sponsored in New Orleans. "Loyall and I went to the opera last night," he informed Mrs. Farragut. "Do not be shocked. It was a concert given by the young ladies of New Orleans to raise money for the poor. We all thought we ought to go. So I took a box for myself and staff. It was a beautiful sight, and the singing, I suppose, was very fine. But you know two facts: I am no judge, and I am no admirer of operatic music. I could but feel, however, that I was giving my money to those who would not give me a Christian burial if they could help it. Still, poor creatures! I feel as if I could say, 'Lord, forgive them, for they know not what they do.' "[15] He was not pleased with conditions in New Orleans. "I scarcely know what to hope," he wrote his wife a day later. "I do not see any improvement in the moral condition of the country. Those who can seem to be doing all they can to swindle the Government. And it appears to be as bad in the Confederacy as with us, judging from the papers."[16]

2

Farragut's long period of inactivity was brought to a sudden close by disasters to Porter's squadron in the upper Mississippi. So successful had been the raid of the ram *Queen of the West* that Porter decided to send down his brand-new ironclad *Indianola*. She had two 11-inch Dahlgren rifles besides other guns, carried provisions for sixty days, and towed two barges laden with coal. She passed the batteries without damage on the night of Friday, February 13, but the bad luck of that ill omened day was only deferred a few days.[17] On the 14th, the *Queen* ran aground while being attacked by a battery on the Red River, and was captured.[18] The prize and the ram *Webb* then pursued the *Indianola*, which had been lying off the mouth of the Red River. The chase extended above Grand Gulf to a point about thirty-five miles below Vicksburg, where the Union vessel was overhauled about nine o'clock on the evening of the 24th. In a confused night attack, the *Indianola* was rammed several times; and rendered unmanageable, she surrendered in a sinking condition. Two nights later the partly submerged vessel was blown up after the Confederate rams had been frightened away by what they thought was an enemy gunboat but what turned out to be a dummy launched by Porter.[19]

When Farragut learned of what had happened above Port Hudson, he said to Captain Jenkins, "The time has come; there can be no more delay. I must go—army or no army."[20] He convinced the reluctant Banks that it was his duty to cooperate, at least to the extent of making a reconnaissance in force while the fleet ran the batteries at Port Hudson. His chief objective was to cut off all Confederate supplies from the Red River.[21]

Bell was once again ordered to New Orleans "as soon as possible," though Farragut informed him that he feared he would not arrive in time to aid him "in the good work."[22] Farragut, however, did not then need him so badly, for the *Lackawanna* had joined the blockade off Mobile Bay and the *Monongahela* had arrived at New Orleans.

Knowing Porter as well as he did and having had losses of his own recently, Farragut must have taken some satisfaction in penning the following to Bell: "Porter has allowed his boats to come down one at a time, and they have been captured by the enemy, which compels me to go up and recapture the whole, or be sunk in the attempt. The whole country will be in arms if we do not do something."[23] With even more satisfaction he wrote to Fox, "I was much grieved that Porter should have allowed the boats to come down one at a time—but I confess that the capture of the *Indianola* by two common river boats with no one killed has astonished me; I never thought much of ironclads but my opinion of them is declining daily."[24]

Commander Charles H. B. Caldwell was ordered to take the *Essex* to Baton Rouge and assume the command of the mortars there. These he was to move up to a position from which they could most effectively shell the batteries of Port Hudson.[25] Commodore Henry Morris was placed in command of all naval affairs in the lower Mississippi and the vicinity of New Orleans.[26] With these arrangements completed, the *Hartford, Richmond,* and *Monongahela* proceeded up to Baton Rouge, where they arrived on March 11 and there found the *Essex,* three gunboats, six mortar schooners, and a dozen or more transports and river steamers. That afternoon two other gunboats arrived from a reconnaissance of Port Hudson.

The following day, running rigging was taken down, splinter nettings were placed on the starboard side, and everything put in readiness for an engagement. Barricades were placed around the steam and engine room bulkheads, and bulwarks of hammocks were made around the topgallant forecastle.[27] Chain cables were swung from the extreme ends on each side to keep off the "cotton-clad" steamers, and other chain cables were placed vertically to protect the boilers, as at the passing of Forts Jackson and St. Philip. Boat howitzers were placed in the tops to be used at short range.[28] As usual, Farragut allowed no detail of protection to his men and ships to be overlooked.

While these preparations were being made, General Banks held a review of his troops, 10,000 in number. Admiral Farragut and several of his officers were invited to accompany the General along the line on horseback. Several ditches, which seemed to the naval contingent to have been dug to test their horsemanship, had to be jumped. But only one man was unhorsed, and he was one of Banks's aids. Farragut was mounted on a bob-tailed horse, and as the cavalcade passed the 24th Connecticut Regiment its band struck up the familiar air, "I Bet My Money on the Bob-Tailed Nag."[28]

3

Port Hudson is about one hundred thirty-five miles above New Orleans, and is located on the east bank of the river, facing an abrupt bend of over ninety degrees. Extending down the river a mile and a half from the town were seven batteries of several field-pieces and nineteen heavy guns, many of which were rifles. These were placed upon bluffs from eighty to one hundred feet high. The channel ran close to the east bank.[29] Such was the formidable obstruction which the Confederates had prepared to the navigation of the river from the south. These batteries, together with those at Vicksburg, protected a long stretch of the Mississippi including the Red River, and thus permitted the unobstructed passage of large quantities of supplies of all kinds from the southwest to the armies of the Confederacy.

The batteries were manned by about 16,000 men. Banks thought his enemy had between 25,000 and 30,000, from "the best information we have." The Confederates were very successful in spreading exaggerated reports, greatly to Farragut's continued disgust at the credulity of the Union generals and many of his own officers. Banks had about 12,000 men, including one Negro regiment and nine companies of cavalry and some light artillery. He had been obliged to leave 5,000 men at Baton Rouge to protect that important base. Many of his troops were new levies, and some of his officers were inexperienced. One colonel had to resort to this unmilitary command in disembarking his men: "Break ranks, boys, and get ashore the best way you can."[30] All the army, except those who could be crowded into three transports, marched up the Bayou Sara road toward Port Hudson on March 13.[31]

Farragut's general order for passing Port Hudson specified that each of the three larger ships, *Hartford, Richmond,* and *Monongahela,* was to lash a gunboat to her aft port side, leaving the port battery as free as possible to attack Confederate guns at the bend on that side. Each was to keep a little on the starboard quarter of her leader so that her chase guns might be fired without danger from premature explosions of shrapnel or shell. He explained that the objective was to pass the batteries with the least possible damage to the ships so that they might immediately continue operations up the Mississippi and Red Rivers. Directions were then given for retirement down stream, if a vessel were so disabled as to make it impossible for her to pass the batteries. Then he concluded with the often quoted inspiring words: "I expect all to go by who are able, and I think the best protection against the enemy's fire is a well-directed fire from our own guns—shell and shrapnel at a distance and grape when within 400 or 500 yards."[32] No gunboat was lashed to the *Mississippi,* Farragut declared, because he had only three available and besides one could not be secured alongside her to advantage, as she was a side-wheeler.[33] The *Albatross, Genesee,* and *Kineo* were so employed. The *Pinola* had to be left at Baton Rouge to aid in its protection.

4

At four o'clock in the afternoon of Friday, March 13, an unlucky day to begin the attempt, the fleet steamed fifteen miles above Baton Rouge and came to anchor for the night. At five o'clock the next morning the vessels were under way again. It was cloudy and a heavy mist hung over the great river. But three hours later when the fleet arrived just above Profit Island, the mist had lifted sufficiently for Port Hudson to be plainly seen with the batteries perched high on the yellowish clay banks. Three or four Confederate steamers were observed moving about the river, on the wheelhouse of one of which could still be read the name, *Queen of the West*.[34]

Farragut called a council of war at ten o'clock on the *Hartford*. He conversed freely with his officers and found that his instructions were well understood. In particular, he consulted Commander Caldwell of the *Essex*, who had preceded the fleet with the mortars, as to information concerning the batteries and the Confederate ships. Then he directed the mortar boats to test their ranges, and seeing that the distance was too great, he ordered them to move up a half a mile nearer. They were well concealed by the thickly forested river bank.[35]

While making these observations, Farragut was standing on the poop deck surrounded by Captain Jenkins, fleet captain, Captain Palmer, commanding the *Hartford*, Lieutenant J. Crittenden Watson, flag lieutenant, and some younger officers. "He was at this time in the full pride of his manhood," wrote John C. Parker, who accompanied Commander Caldwell on board the flagship, "and presented a perfect picture of an ideal sailor. Rather undersized, his figure was faultless, and dressed with the neatness and care customary in the navy, he appeared much younger than he was. His smooth face with its prominent features was as clearly cut as a cameo in which was blended firmness with gentleness. He always wore the regulation service cap, and his face as it lighted with a smile when returning the salute of the officers from the *Essex* made an indelible impression, a mental photograph which time has never effaced."[36]

When it became dark about seven o'clock, the ships were formed in column for the attack. The *Albatross* lashed to the *Hartford* led, followed by the *Genesee* and *Richmond*, and *Kineo* and *Monongahela* with the *Mississippi* alone bringing up the rear. After supper, Farragut and his son Loyall went on deck to watch the last preparations for the coming battle. Presently an army tug was seen approaching with lights flaring and whistle blowing. This greatly ruffled Farragut's feelings, as he had hoped to move up the river unperceived. After much wig-wagging with the signal torch, it was learned that General Banks would have a force at the crossroads in rear of Port Hudson at midnight which would endeavor to create a diversion in favor of the fleet.[37] Farragut remarked to Loyall, "Banks had as well be in New Orleans or at Baton Rouge for all the good he is doing us."[38]

Shortly before nine o'clock the Admiral said quietly to his son, "Go below and inform Captain Jenkins and Captain Palmer, with my compliments, that I am ready to get under way." Loyall Farragut found Jenkins sitting at his writing table with a lighted candle near him. He had apparently just finished writing a letter to his family and was absorbed in his thoughts, but he promptly obeyed the summons. Captain Palmer began to button up his coat, and then pulled on his kid gloves. To Loyall Farragut the ship's captain was an awesome person. He was a very dignified and punctilious officer. With his freshly shaven face and his high collar in place, he always stepped out of his cabin as if about to enter a ball-room. "Make the pre-concerted signal to the fleet to get under way and follow the flag," Palmer ordered. With the assistance of Signal Quartermaster Knowles, young Farragut suspended a red lantern over the stern of the *Hartford*, and the ships began quietly to get under way.

Somewhat excited and at a loss for something to say, Loyall remarked to his father, "Captain Jenkins looked very serious when I called him." Farragut, placing his hand on his son's shoulder, replied, "Well, my son, Captain Jenkins has a family, and is no doubt thinking of the desperate nature of the work before us." Loyall said nothing more, but he thought of his mother far away on the Hudson and knew that his father's thoughts were of her too.

In the darkness there was some delay with the *Monongahela* and the *Mississippi* in gaining their stations. Farragut impatiently paced the deck, occasionally making a remark to Jenkins or Palmer. Finally about ten o'clock all were in order and steamed slowly ahead. The stars shone brightly, and the outline of the shore was visible. An almost unnatural quiet prevailed, broken only by the pulsation of the engine and the noise of the screw. "I felt as if we were going over Niagara Falls," declared Loyall Farragut.[39] The men stood at their guns with arms bared ready for action. The divisional officers moved about giving last instructions to the captains of gun crews in low, earnest tones. The marines in full accoutrement stood by to man the after guns or repel boarders. Young Farragut noticed Engineer Speights standing at the bell leading to the engine-room, and thought how much depended on his coolness, for a wrong bell might bring sudden disaster to the ship.[40] The pilot, Mr. Correll, in the mizzentop above the smoke of battle, conveyed his orders to the wheel through a trumpet attached to a tube.[41] Down in the engine-room, the men were already busily engaged, and would see nothing of the impending battle unless the fortune of war sent a shot or shell crashing through the steam chest or boiler, when they would be in grave peril.[40]

Earlier in the evening, Fleet Surgeon J. M. Foltz had requested Farragut to permit his son to assist below with the wounded in the best protected part of the ship. "No, that will not do," answered the Admiral. "It is true our only child is on board by chance, and he is not in the service; but, being here, he will act as one of my aids, to assist in conveying my orders during the battle, and we will trust in Providence and *la fortune de la guerre*." Foltz made the same suggestion to Loyall, but he replied, "I want to be stationed on deck, and see the fight."[42] It was a very trying experience to have his son thus subjected to danger, and as the ship was going into action, while he was in the midst of the anxieties of a commander of a fleet, he gave his son some practical suggestions as to how to staunch a wound and use a tourniquet.[43]

The Confederates were not to be taken by surprise. In each battery were silent men, watching the dark forms of the Union ships gliding slowly up the placid river. The guns remained silent until the vessels were within a range of about 800 yards.[44] Then suddenly a rocket flared up on the west bank and exploded, another flashed along the surface of the river, and a third ascended perfectly high in the air before exploding.[45] Immediately an 8-inch rifle from one of the batteries opened fire, accompanied by a loud rebel yell.[44] Soon all the batteries joined in with a mighty chorus. A great fire suddenly blazed up on the west side of the river, fed by pine knots and other combustibles placed there, and thus served to outline the dark hulls of Farragut's ships to the gunners on the heights.[46]

It was then about a quarter past eleven. The *Hartford* answered the challenge with the Sawyer rifle on the forecastle and then with a broadside as soon as the guns could be brought to bear. The understanding on the *Mississippi* was that the enemy's fire was not to be returned as that would uncover the ships' positions. When the *Hartford* commenced firing, Midshipman Batcheller who was standing beside the executive officer, Lieutenant George Dewey, on the deck of the *Mississippi* exclaimed, "There! just as I expected. I knew the old sea dog would bark. He couldn't help it."[46] As the Admiral was walking about in his quiet but active way watching the firing, he stepped on a tarpaulin covering the small hatchway aft leading to the relieving tackles. The canvas gave way; Loyall saw him fall and was almost paralyzed with fear, thinking he had been shot. But instinctively he caught hold of his father, and saved him from a dangerous fall.[40]

The spectacle was magnificent but awe-inspiring. The *Essex* and the mortars had also joined in; and the deep, hollow roar of the latter could be distinguished from all the other sounds.[40] The burning fuses of their 13-inch shells looked like globes of golden flame or small meteors describing graceful curves across the dark heavenly blackboard. Dazzling fires flashed from the ports of the *Essex* and *Hartford* and other ships coming into range, as their guns were discharged at the flashes springing from the batteries on the bluffs. The broadsides were fired not simultaneously, for this would strain the ship; but beginning with the forward gun, the guns were discharged in rapid succession as fast as the ticking of a watch.[45] All these dreadful noises, mingled with the hissing, screaming, whistling, shrieking, and howling of the Confederate projectiles, made a combination rivaling Pandemonium.

Soon the *Hartford* was enveloped in smoke from keel to trucks, and the pilot called through his speaking tube from the mizzentop that he could not see ahead. The ship immediately ceased firing, and none too soon for, when the smoke cleared, the pilot shouted down that the ship was running ashore under the batteries and the bowsprit of the *Richmond* was looming up over the *Hartford's* quarter.[40] The Confederates thought Farragut's ships were making a bold dash at the batteries in order to fire broadsides at point blank range, to which their "brave cannoniers" replied at a distance of a hundred fifty yards in "more than thunder tones."[44] The little *Albatross* was ordered to back the *Hartford* around. The suspense was terrible. Farragut impatiently shouted, "Back! back on the *Albatross!*" Loyall Farragut, carried away by the excitement of the moment, repeated the command in his youthful voice, "Back! back on the *Albatross!*"[40] The ship was really in great danger. A Confederate officer trained a gun loaded with grape on the group of officers on the poop deck, but it misfired and they were saved.[42] Soon the *Hartford* swung around, and forged ahead upstream. Then there was a report, "Ram on the port bow, sir!" "Man the port battery, and call away the boarders!" ordered Captain Palmer. Farragut seized his cutlass lying on the signal locker, and exclaimed, "I am going to have a hand in this myself," springing forward with the old spirit of 1812. But no ram appeared.[40]

In a few minutes the *Hartford* was rounding the bend, replying with only two rifles on the poop deck to the upper batteries, and at 12:15 with a cheering crew she came to anchor above the town.[40] Her losses had been remarkably small, one man killed and two slightly wounded.[47] Though the ship had been repeatedly hit, she was not seriously damaged. Some of the shots had been freakish. One had smashed through a partition and a bureau, and cut a box of socks completely in two.

Another was found resting peacefully in an engineer's bunk in the steerage.[40]

5

The other ships were not so fortunate. The *Richmond* followed the *Hartford* successfully through the perilous night almost to the bend, before disaster befell her. Her gallant executive officer, Lieutenant-Commander A. Boyd Cummings, had just had his leg taken off by a round shot. He had been standing on the bridge by Captain Alden's side, cheering the men at the guns, and was thrown violently to the deck below.[48] "Quick, boys," he cried to those who came to his aid, "pick me up, put a tourniquet on my leg, send my letters to my wife, tell them I fell in doing my duty." When taken below, he said to the surgeons, "If there are others worse hurt, attend to them first."[49]

As the *Richmond* began to round the bend, she received a shot in her boilers and another through her steam drum. About the same time, the *Genesee*, her consort, got a shot in her machinery, and was set on fire. "Torpedoes were exploding all around us, throwing water as high as the tops," according to the exaggerated account in the *Richmond's* journal. "We were, for a few minutes, at the rebels' mercy; their shell were causing great havoc on our decks; the groans of the wounded and the shrieks of the dying were awful. The decks were covered with blood. We got afire in the starboard bulwarks, which was soon put out. We found we could not go up; we turned her head down stream."[50] Alden, who developed a phobia for torpedoes, reported to Welles, "Just before the accident to our steam pipe, a torpedo exploded close under our stern, throwing the water up thirty feet, bursting in the cabin windows and doing other important injury."[51] When Cummings was told that the noise he heard was from escaping steam, and that the ship had turned back he complained, "I would rather lose the other leg than go back. Can nothing be done? There is a south wind. Where are the sails?"[49] The casualties were out of all proportion to the gory details of the *Richmond's* journal—three killed and twelve wounded, only two or three of whom were seriously hurt.[52]

The *Monongahela* made her way nearly to the turning point, when she went aground with such force as to break loose from the *Kineo*, whose rudder had been rendered useless by a shot. A hawser was secured to her again, but it was thirty minutes before the ship was pulled off. Meanwhile she was subjected to a severe fire which killed six men and wounded twenty-one. Among the latter was Captain J. P. McKinstry, who had the bridge shot from under him and was thrown to the deck below and seriously bruised. The *Monongahela*, badly cut up, was lucky to be able to make her escape back down the river.[53]

The worst fate befell the old side-wheeler *Mississippi*. When she reached the last and most formidable batteries, she too went aground on the west shore. For thirty-five minutes the engine was reversed in vain. Then the pilot declared that it would be impossible to get the vessel off. The captain decided to abandon ship, as three batteries had the range of the doomed vessel, and their shot were frequently hulling her. The crew was then landed, the sick and wounded being first attended to. The ship was set on fire in four different places between decks, and Captain Melancton Smith, accompanied by his executive officer, Lieutenant George Dewey, left the ship in a small boat and passed safely through the fire of the batteries to the *Richmond*. Of Dewey, his captain wrote, "I consider that I should be neglecting a most important duty should I omit to mention the coolness of my executive officer, Mr. Dewey."[54] The whole ship's company acted in a praiseworthy manner; there was no confusion in abandoning ship, but this was accomplished as orderly as though the men were being mustered for Sunday morning inspection.[41]

Farragut was greatly concerned when his other ships failed to follow him round the bend. "I remember well," wrote Meredith, "that just as the ship came to an anchor after the battle we were sending up rockets from the poop deck, in the vain endeavor to open communication with the fleet below. The light fell on Farragut's face as he stood there looking anxiously down the river with his arm on the shoulder of . . . his son . . . , and I shall never forget the expression of anxiety and woe in the

PASSING THE BATTERIES OF PORT HUDSON   179

old hero's face. If he could only know what had happened to his fleet."⁵⁸ This feeling of anxiety was increased when across the point of land a vessel was seen to be on fire. The burning ship afforded a grand and fearful scene, lighting up the whole river for several miles. After awhile, the ship slipped off the bank, swung around, and slowly drifted down the river.

"As the fire would reach her large guns, they would go off— one after another with deep and solemn sound—like minute guns at sea," wrote Colonel Robert Farquharson of the 41st Tennessee Infantry to his wife. "Then a shell would explode—then another —and another—and another. Then the slow and majestic movement of the ship—enveloped with flame. You could fancy phantom gunners flitting about on the fiery decks—and thus she floated down the broad father of waters for eight or ten miles until, at last, the all consuming element reached her magazines when with a roar equal to a thousand thunders what was left of the gallant *Mississippi* was received into the bosom of her majestic godmother. . . . Then arose cheer after cheer from many a brave heart. For myself, I felt extremely sad—I don't know why—but I was in poor spirit for rejoicing. If the good ship had been blown up with all on board, colors flying, in a fair stand up fight, I believe I could have cheered as loud as anybody; but that terrible, horrible, lingering agony of Indian-like torture set me to moralizing and in my heart for the thousandth time I cursed the infernal Abolition instigators of this war."⁵⁹

This is how the burning *Mississippi* appeared to those aboard the *Richmond*: "At length it was reported that the *Mississippi* was coming down, and we all turned out to see the sight. It was a most magnificent spectacle. From the midships to the stern the noble vessel was enveloped in a sheet of flame, while firewreaths ran up the shrouds, played around the mainmast, twisted and writhed like fiery serpents. Onward she came, keeping near to the right bank, still bow foremost, as regularly as if she was steered by a pilot. It was indeed a wonderful sight. Captain Smith, her recent commander, and several of her officers, who had by this time arrived on board the *Richmond*.

assembled on the poop deck, their emotions almost too great for words."[60]

It was about half past four when the *Mississippi* blew up. The ships below, particularly the *Richmond,* were engaged all night in picking up survivors from the stricken vessel.[50] There was not much sleep for anybody in the fleet that night. Farragut went to his cabin shortly after midnight. There Loyall found him later in bed but not asleep. They had a little chat. Farragut told him that he hoped to communicate by signal with the army or the ships below the next day. He was greatly distressed over the failure of the other ships to pass the batteries, but said that he knew his officers well enough to be sure their failure had been unavoidable. When young Loyall finally climbed into his hammock after the most exciting evening he was ever to experience, it was a long time before he fell asleep from sheer exhaustion.[37]

6

Sunday morning dawned quite peaceful and bright in complete contrast to the darkness and ear-splitting noises of the preceding night. All hands set to work to care for the wounded and cleanse the decks of the blood of battle. The carpenters were particularly busy making coffins for the dead, and repairing damages to the ships.[50] From the deck of the *Hartford* Loyall Farragut saw Confederate cavalrymen watering their horses on the Port Hudson side of the river, and an occasional gleam of a sabre on the opposite side, indicating that it would be difficult to communicate by land with the other ships. Early in the morning the *Hartford* dropped down almost in range of the batteries, and fired, as by previous arrangement, three signal guns to announce her successful passage above Port Hudson. Farragut had no idea of attempting to rejoin his ships below, but was determined to blockade the mouth of the Red River and patrol the Mississippi.[40]

The first news of the passage of Port Hudson reached New York on March 23 through military channels from Baton Rouge. "Commodore (sic) Farragut, leading in the *Hartford,* passed the Port Hudson batteries last night at 11 o'clock with his fleet," the telegram read. "Steamer *Mississippi* ran aground, was abandoned, and burned. Firing on both sides rapid and severe. Army within five miles of enemy's works, in good spirits, and bound to win. Cavalry skirmishes only fighting yet."[61] Banks's forces seem to have gotten no nearer than five miles from the enemy, remaining under arms all night but not firing a gun. The following evening they started back to Baton Rouge, probably still "in good spirits" but not "bound to win." Banks, as an excuse for not participating more actively, wrote somewhat vaguely about "the premature commencement of the action."[62]

Farragut's total casualties were 113, of whom 35 were killed and 78 wounded.[63] The heaviest losses had been, of course, on the *Mississippi*. Of her 297 officers and men, 64 were reported killed or missing;[55] 48 were captured;[56] and 4 were severely wounded.[57] The Confederate losses were surprisingly small—1 killed and 8 wounded.[64] No guns were hit and very little damage was done to the parapets. The projectiles either buried themselves in the soft earth, or passed harmlessly over the batteries. "Open mud forts can fight gunboats with an advantage," boasted Confederate Lieutenant Broom, "when defended by stout hearts and cool heads."[44]

Farragut was somewhat uneasy as to what Welles would think of the loss of the *Mississippi*, and he inserted in his report, in the midst of praise of his officers, a paragraph defending his operations. "If in this effort to come up and cut off the enemy's supplies from Red River and recapture the *Indianola*, misfortune has befallen some of our vessels," he explained, "I can only plead my zeal to serve my country, and the chances of war, and I felt that my orders of October 2, 1862 fully justified me in doing what I should have done two months ago, but for the disasters at Galveston and Sabine Pass, the strong force of the enemy at Mobile, and the inadequacy of my force to meet all these contingencies."[35] But he had nothing to fear. Fox even wrote a letter of commendation to Captain Melancton Smith, an unusual procedure when an officer has lost his ship. "We feel no regret here at the attempt," Fox assured him, "for the unflinching qualities displayed make us forget Galveston."[65] Welles wrote Farragut, the same day, upon the receipt of his report, congratulating him "upon the gallant passage of the Port Hudson batteries." He could "find no fault" with the others who were "not successful in following their leader."[66] Fox wrote him that President Lincoln approved of his course, for he had always believed in "cutting the rebels in two" by getting control of the Mississippi. "The President says look out or Grand Gulf will be as strong as Vicksburg," he confided. "No particular orders can be given to you," he admitted;" only I pray take care of yourself and get back as soon as you shall deem it best."[67]

"In speaking of the loss of the *Mississippi*, Farragut said that he was sorry to lose a good vessel and so many brave men," related Dewey, "but that you could not make an omelet without breaking eggs. When Captain Smith, who was as serious as Cromwell and withal extremely sensitive, heard this remark, he appeared hurt; for he said, in his sober fashion: 'He calls us an omelet.' "[68]

XVI

PATROLLING THE MISSISSIPPI

1

FARRAGUT did not waste any time after passing Port Hudson. Not being able to communicate with the rest of his fleet on Sunday, he proceeded up the river at five-thirty the following morning with the *Hartford* and the little *Albatross*. Two hours later two of the original crew of the *Queen of the West*, who had been hiding in the woods, were received on board, and Farragut learned for the first time of the destruction of the *Indianola*.[1] About noon his vessels anchored at the mouth of the Red River. All the Confederate gunboats had fled at his approach, and seeing nothing to shoot at, he exercised his crew at target practice.[2] The effect of Farragut's appearance on the transport of Confederate supplies was immediate. "Great God! how unfortunate!" wrote a commissary in General Richard Taylor's Department. "Four steamers arrived today from Shreveport. One had 300,000 pounds of bacon; three others are reported coming down with loads. Five others are below with full cargoes designed for Port Hudson, but it is reported that the Federal gunboats are blockading the river."[3] When Farragut passed Port Hudson, the Confederate garrison had only ten days' allowance of corn.[4]

The next morning at four o'clock Farragut pushed on up the river, and after a long day's struggle against the current of the muddy swollen Mississippi, the *Hartford* arrived in the late afternoon with her consort off Natchez.[1] One party went ashore below the town and cut the telegraph communications with Port Hudson.[2] Another under a flag of truce took a message to the mayor warning him that, if there was any more firing on United States vessels, Farragut would be forced to shell the town.⁵ The following evening found his ships anchored for the night a few miles below Grand Gulf.

As they approached that place the next morning, several Negroes were observed on the levee, gesticulating and pointing at the bluffs up the river. One old woman was particularly noticed as she waved her bandanna dramatically. Soon a battery of four rifled guns came into view. When they commenced a brisk fire, the *Hartford* signaled her small duckling to take cover on her port side, and the two vessels pushed on up under full steam. The *Hartford* answered with her heavy guns, but did no damage except to a battery flagstaff.⁶ But she had her hull and rigging cut badly and a shot in her mizzenmast.⁷ When the vessel was nearly out of range, Captain Jenkins said to Farragut, "Admiral, this ship goes entirely too slow." At that moment, an exploding shell threw up a small geyser near where they stood, and Farragut agreed briefly, "I should think she *was*—just at this moment." But the engagement also had its tragic side. Two men were killed and six wounded.⁸ The dead were, as was the custom, given the place of honor on the quarter-deck, and their bodies covered with a flag. Here Loyall Farragut found his father pacing back and forth before them, "not ashamed to show his deep emotion."⁹

Ten miles above Grand Gulf, Farragut passed the partially submerged shattered wreck of the *Indianola* on the right bank of the river, and at four o'clock in the afternoon he anchored twelve miles below Vicksburg under the protection of the bluffs on the Mississippi side three miles below Warrenton.² He immediately sent a telegram to Welles, and wrote a long letter to Mrs. Farragut, the first he had written her since running the batteries of Port Hudson. "We came through in safety," he informed her feelingly; "your dear Boy and myself are well; he has won his spurs and will be gazetted for the first time in his life, but I hope not the last. He was cool under fire and bore himself well." "You know my creed," he added. "I never send others in advance when there is a doubt and being the one on whom the country has bestowed its greatest honors, I thought I ought to take the risks which belong to it; so I took the lead. I knew they would try to destroy the flagship and I was determined to follow out my idea that the best way to prevent it was to hurt them the most." "One of my greatest troubles on earth is the pain and anxiety I inflict upon one of the best of wives and most devoted of women," he affectionately concluded. "Oh, that it yet be in my power to compensate you for the pain I have caused you. Send my love to your mother and sisters and all the family and let them know that we are well."[10]

2

The next day Farragut informed General Grant of his arrival, and enclosed a dispatch from General Banks. He explained to Grant the purpose of his expedition up the river and requested coal for his vessels. "I shall be most happy to avail myself of the earliest moment to have a consultation with yourself and Rear-Admiral Porter," he suggested.[11] Farragut wrote Porter also a similar letter,[12] but the latter was not then on his flagship above Vicksburg.

Operations against this stronghold had been moving slowly and unsuccessfully. The day before Christmas, Porter had arrived with his squadron at the mouth of the Yazoo, accompanying an army commanded by General Sherman. A few days later a disastrous attack was attempted on Chickasaw Bluffs above Vicksburg. On January 11, Arkansas Post some fifty miles up the Arkansas River was taken, but the victory was of no strategic importance. Welles was displeased. "The accounts from Porter above Vicksburg are not satisfactory," he set down in his diary. "He is fertile in expedients, some of which are costly without adequate results. His dispatches are full of verbosity of promises, and the mail which brings them also brings ludicrous letters and caricatures to Heap, a clerk who is his brother-in-law, filled with laughable and burlesque accounts of amusing and ridiculous proceedings. These may be excusable as a means of amusement to keep up his spirits and those of his men, but I should be glad to witness, or hear of something more substantial and of energies employed in what is really useful. Porter has capabilities and I am expecting much of him, but he is by no means an Admiral Foote."[13] A week after the capture of Arkansas Post, Grant arrived and took over the command; but two months had passed without any real progress toward capturing Vicksburg.

On March 16, Porter took five of his ironclads and four mortar boats, followed by small transports laden with a division of troops commanded by Sherman, on another expedition. They were to pass through a network of bayous from the Mississippi to the Big Sunflower River and thence into the Yazoo River, and so arrive above Haynes's Bluff, the capture of which would open up Vicksburg for an attack in the rear. Slowly but successfully the expedition moved along for four days; but on the second day following Farragut's arrival, Porter's vessels were attacked by a large force of Confederates who felled great trees across the bayou in front and in the rear of the squadron. Porter sent a message of distress to Sherman, made arrangements for defending his vessels as long as possible, and drew up a general order for blowing them up to keep them from falling into the hands of the Confederates. Fortunately Sherman received Porter's message, disembarked some of his troops by night, splashed through the swamps by the light of torches, and rescued the beleaguered flotilla the next afternoon, the General covered with mud riding up on an old horse with a rope bridle. After the rescue, the whole expedition returned to the Mississippi without accomplishing anything.[14]

The same day Porter was extricated from his peril, he answered Farragut's dispatch which had been carried up to him. "I will do all I can to send you coal," he promised, "if I can get out of this creek, where I have been fighting for four days without eating or sleeping." He advised Farragut not to attempt to run the batteries of Vicksburg; but Farragut had had no intention of doing this. "Your services at Red River will be a Godsend," Porter declared; "it is worth to us the loss of the *Mississippi,* and is at this moment the severest blow that could be struck at the South." After much more advice, which Porter enjoyed giving, he rather gloomily concluded, "The sharpshooters are plugging away at us, and I have to sit down in a hot corner. General Sherman is driving the rebels before him, and I hope to-night to have a good sleep."[15]

The same day Porter was writing Farragut from his "hot corner," the latter wrote him again, expressing regret at not finding him near Vicksburg and at his secretary's following him up the river with his letter to bother him on the expedition. He explained that coal had been sent down by General Grant, but requested that Porter send two of the Ellet rams and one ironclad to assist in blockading the mouth of Red River. Finally, he suggested that, if Grant thought he could not take Vicksburg, it would be a good plan to move down the river and take Grand Gulf, and from there go down and attack Port Hudson in conjunction with General Banks from below. He agreed to furnish all the assistance possible with his vessels both above and below Port Hudson.[16]

Though Farragut wrote two letters to Grant that day, he felt a delicacy in making this suggestion to him personally. He thanked the General for the barge of coal, and suggested that they make a joint attack on the new casemated battery near Warrenton. He also mentioned how much trouble the battery at Grand Gulf had given his vessels as they came up the river.[17] In the second letter, he indirectly hinted at the plan he had mentioned to Porter by informing Grant that General Banks did not think he had sufficient men to attack Port Hudson with any chance of success. He also repeated his request to Porter for two rams and an ironclad.[18] In reply, Grant declared that it was "a matter of the utmost importance to cut off trade with the Red River country" and thought that, if Porter were present, he might spare one or more of his rams to aid in the patrolling of the river.[19] He also entrusted to Farragut a letter for General Banks, describing pessimistically the campaign then in progress against Vicksburg. He was hoping, he declared, that Banks would be able to capture Port Hudson and then move on up to Grand Gulf; but he said nothing about cooperating with him there.[20] In a letter to Farragut next day, however, he outlined a plan similar to that which Farragut had suggested to Porter. It involved sending 20,000 men to aid Banks to capture Port

Hudson. The combined forces could then move up the east bank of the river, presumably taking Grand Gulf on the way, and participate in operations against Vicksburg.[21]

Meanwhile Brigadier-General Alfred W. Ellet, commanding the ram flotilla, learned that Farragut wished reinforcements, and with the gallantry and love of action for which the Ellets were noteworthy he offered to send down two of his rams. Before daylight on the morning of March 25 the attempt to join Farragut was made by the *Switzerland* and the *Lancaster*, commanded by Colonel Charles R. Ellet and Lieutenant-Colonel John A. Ellet respectively. The *Switzerland* succeeded in spite of a plunging shot which exploded her boiler; but the *Lancaster* was struck near the water line and sunk at the lower end of the canal, with the loss of four wounded and five drowned.[22]

Porter was very angry when he heard what had happened, and wrote Ellet, demanding to know by what authority the rams had been sent past the batteries at Vicksburg.[23] Ellet wrote a temperate, manly reply, giving the details of the expedition and taking upon himself full responsibility for the vessels being sent.[24] Farragut felt it his duty to write Porter a long letter "for two purposes—first, to exonerate myself from any charge of a disposition to interfere with your command, and, secondly, with a hope to excuse General Ellet any feeling to do that which he thought would be disagreeable to you; but, on the contrary, all who surrounded him at the time thought, and so expressed themselves, that it would be in accordance with your wishes if you were present." Farragut, however, admitted that the night was not dark enough, and that the attempt was made too late in the morning for its completion before daylight. But he made plain to Porter that he desired the two rams and the ironclad to continue the blockade of the Red River, when he returned below Port Hudson to resume his duties in command of the blockading squadron in the Gulf.[25]

Grant had agreed to send two regiments to assist in destroying the Warrenton batteries, and Farragut made arrangements to transport them across the river.[26] But the misfortune which befell the rams so delayed the undertaking that the Confederates had time to send reinforcements, and the plan was given up after a visit of Grant on board the *Hartford*. This first meeting of Farragut and Grant took place on the afternoon of March 26. The log of the *Hartford* is annoyingly brief in recording this historic event, stating simply, "Major-General Grant came on board."[27] Grant does not mention it in his *Personal Memoirs*, nor does Farragut refer to it in any of his letters home. But one may be sure that Farragut very hospitably received the little black-bearded general, dressed in a uniform which looked as though he had been sleeping in it, and that the best cigars and wines and liquors on the *Hartford* were placed before him. That very morning, Farragut had started to pay Grant a visit, but on reaching Biggs's Plantation, about half way across the point of land, he became so weary that he could go no further.[28] Grant, in turn, found the eleven miles a long, hard walk, and on his return so reported it to Porter, who was enjoying the comforts of the flagship *Black Hawk* so much after his trials and tribulations in the bayous and swamps that he did not go over to see Farragut at all. "I have been so much confined to the ship since I have been here that I have almost lost the use of my legs," he wrote him as an excuse.[29]

But Farragut continued to communicate with Porter by letter, endeavoring to persuade him to send down one or two ironclads. In one letter, he frankly admitted that the Galveston affair was "the greatest blow that the navy has sustained during the war."[30] Grant favored the sending of the ironclads. "We should have vessels sufficient below to patrol the whole river from Warrenton to the Red River," he wrote Farragut. "I will have a consultation with Admiral Porter on the subject."[31] When Farragut pressed Porter for a decision on the question,[32] he replied that he could take the ram *Switzerland* with him but that he had no ironclads then fit for service; otherwise he would "with great pleasure" give him "one or two ironclads."[33] Still he hoped that Farragut would remain at Red River as long as possible, for "it is death to these people; they get all their grub from there."[33] Two days later, he promised to send a force down to the Red River before Farragut returned below Port Hudson.[34] After Farragut had departed, Porter received a letter from Welles which must have aroused his jealous nature. "The occupation of the river between Vicksburg and Port Hudson is the severest blow that can be struck upon the enemy, is worth all the risk encountered by Rear-Admiral Farragut, and in the opinion of this Department is of far greater importance than the flanking expeditions, which thus far have prevented the consummation of this most desirable object. I desire that you will consult with Rear-Admiral Farragut and decide how this object can best be obtained."[35] When he recalled how he had recently disregarded Farragut's repeated requests for aid, he must have felt guilty of neglect of duty.

3

Before returning down the river, Farragut sent his son Loyall home by way of Cairo. "I am too devoted a father to have my son with me in troubles of this kind," he wrote Mrs. Farragut. "The anxieties of a father should not be added to those of the commander."[36] On March 25, Loyall left the *Hartford*,[37] spent a couple of days on Porter's flagship enjoying fresh butter and mush and cream and amusing himself with Porter's ménage which included eight dogs in his cabin,[38] and then proceeded home to join his mother in New York.[39] Two days after his son's departure, Farragut wrote him a letter filled with fatherly counsel. "You have seen much in a short time," he declared, "and know what your Father's sufferings have been for the honors he has gained—that his life has not been spent on a Bed of Roses. But, my son, follow your Father's rule to the best of your ability, do as *little wrong* as the weakness of your feeble nature will permit and as *much good* as you can—pray to God to give you a good understanding and keep you from evil and protect you from harm." Then somewhat fatalistically he concluded, "I know you will always be affectionate to your Mother and make amends for your Father's absence and take care of her when he is gone, for you know we must all fade away by turn. God grant that you may both enjoy a long and happy life and be free from this terrible affliction, Civil War, which these miserable Politicians have brought upon our once so happy country."[40]

From January to March, 1863, Mrs. Farragut visited her family in Norfolk. "I am glad that you have been to Norfolk and still more so that your family all treated you well," Farragut wrote her. After expressing his pleasure at the safe arrival of Loyall with her, he added, "He ought not to be with me, nor ought I to have him. He is so much afraid of my doing wrongly and I so much afraid of his getting hurt. He hears everything that is said among the officers and men as to the enemy and fears that I do not take the necessary precautions, while I laugh at him and ask him what else I have to think of. 'Well,' he says, 'Pa, you know I am so much afraid that you will be blamed.' But, my darling, you need give yourself no fear on account of what his morals suffered with me at New Orleans; he is an excelent (sic) good Boy and I never hear his name mentioned except with respect."[41] Of his wife's visit in Virginia, Farragut wrote Bell, "She has paid her visit to Norfolk and thinks she deserves quite as much credit for her heroism as I did in passing the forts, for they were exulting over my defeat and told her they would soon have me a prisoner; but she stood it like a philosopher and told them that she did not believe they would take me, and laughed at them. Now that I am back again, she will be relieved."[42]

Very early on the morning of March 28, the *Hartford* got under way and stood down the river,[43] Farragut taking his last look at the forbidding bluffs protecting Vicksburg. He was not to return to the place, in the vicinity of which he had been subjected to so much physical danger and mental anxiety. In passing Warrenton, the *Hartford* exchanged several parting shots with the batteries, which Farragut was forced to leave little damaged from his three attacks, though his flagship bore many scars in both hull and rigging.[44] That night there was a cold March rain with thunder and lightning; it developed into a howling gale, which swamped and broke adrift the fourth cutter.[45] But the *Hartford* was securely anchored below Warrenton awaiting the *Albatross.* After midnight a steamer was reported coming down the river. All hands were called to quarters and both batteries were "cast loose" for action. Thirty minutes later the vessel drifted past and went ashore on the starboard quarter. She turned out to be the Confederate steamer *Vicksburg,* which had been blown from her moorings at Vicksburg by the storm.[43] The next night, the *Albatross,* with a barge load of provisions which Porter had previously floated down, slipped by the Warrenton batteries without damage and joined Farragut.[45]

At four o'clock on the morning of the 31st, the Confederates burned the steamer *Vicksburg* just twenty minutes before the ram *Switzerland* ran past the batteries at Warrenton. Two hours later the three vessels were steaming down the river. They anchored below New Carthage near the spot where Farragut thought he had seen the wreck of the *Indianola* in order to complete her destruction;[43] but he was misinformed by some Negroes who stated that during the recent storm she had slipped off into deep water and disappeared. This was Porter's fake gunboat, however, and so Farragut missed the *Indianola* which was practically submerged on the other side of the river.[46] At nightfall he continued downstream, and after two hours was running the Grand Gulf batteries.[43] "Seven heavy shells were seen to take effect, one raking the *Hartford* from stem to stern," reported Brigadier-General John S. Bowen, C.S. Army, in command of the batteries.[47] This was an exaggeration, though the flagship was struck once, and one man was killed when hit by a fragment of an iron hammock stanchion.[48] The *Switzerland* was struck twice without material damage, and the *Albatross* not at all.

In the late afternoon of All Fools' Day, Farragut arrived with his little squadron at the mouth of the Red River, having destroyed a couple of flatboats en route.[49] After remaining in that vicinity four days without intercepting any Confederate vessels, he proceeded down to Port Hudson to endeavor to communicate with the rest of his fleet. Arriving about five miles above that place after nightfall, the *Hartford* fired three guns at two minute intervals and then three rockets; but the only reply was from lights on the river bank, which were apparently Confederate signals.[49]

Not having succeeded in establishing communications by signal, Farragut sent his secretary, Edward C. Gabaudan, accompanied by a Negro, to communicate with General Banks and Commodore Morris in New Orleans.[50] They set out at eight o'clock on the evening of April 7 in a skiff camouflaged to resemble a floating tree trunk. At one point their craft drifted so near the river bank that sentinels could be heard talking. They actually rowed out a distance to investigate the floating object but were convinced it was only a log. Thirty minutes afterwards another skiff with two Negroes bearing dispatches started down the river. About two hours later two rockets were observed, which were thought to be a signal from the *Essex* that the skiffs had arrived.[51] But this was an error, for they passed all the vessels below Port Hudson unobserved and arrived alongside the *Richmond* at Baton Rouge, the first at half past two in the morning and the second at daylight.[52]

Farragut was back again off the Red River mouth just before noon on the 9th, and captured the steamer *J. D. Clarke* with Major Howard of the Confederate Commissary Department on board. He missed capturing a second steamer by about five minutes. The next week was spent in destroying all boats on the river down as far as Bayou Sara that might be used in transporting cattle, hogs, and other food supplies across the river.[53]

On the 15th, Farragut returned to Port Hudson, by appointment, to attempt communications by signal from a platform on the topgallant mast, across the point of land. The *Richmond* had arrived, and the two ships signaled with great success. During the day, Gabaudan with four officers and two Negroes made his way across the marshy land and rejoined his ship, and the next day the officers returned and a party of five men carried the mail across to Farragut and returned in safety after being chased by a large number of Confederates.[54] In this way important dispatches were exchanged, some of which Farragut had been afraid to intrust to the skiffs. With a great pile of letters to read, Farragut returned to the Red River again.

4

On April 15, Welles sent this "confidential" telegram to Porter: "The Department wishes you to occupy the river below Vicksburg so that Admiral Farragut may return to his station."[55] His reasons for telegraphing Porter are revealed in this item in his diary, two days later: ". . . Am in hopes that side issues and byplay on the Mississippi are about over and that there will be some concentrated action. Porter should go below Vicksburg and not remain above, thereby detaining Farragut, who is below, from great and responsible duties at New Orleans and on the Gulf. The weak and sensitive feeling of being outranked and made subordinate in command should never influence an officer in such an emergency. Porter has great vanity and great jealousy but knows his duty, and I am surprised he does not perform it. Wrote him a fortnight since a letter which he cannot misunderstand and which will not, I hope, wound his pride."[56] Welles and Fox had begun to worry over the possibility that Buchanan would come out of Mobile Bay and attack the blockading fleet while Farragut was away.[57]

Before Welles's urgent telegram had reached him, Porter passed the batteries of Vicksburg, on the night of April 16, with seven ironclads, a wooden gunboat, and the tug *Ivy* to cooperate with Grant in an attack on Grand Gulf. Of the three transports, to be used below in ferrying Grant's troops, one was sunk, another was disabled but towed to safety, and the third passed down unharmed. The total casualties were only fourteen wounded. "All kinds of missiles were flying through the air," Porter colorfully wrote Fox, "—the screaming of shot resembling something to be heard only in the infernal regions. . . . It was a jolly scene throughout, and I reckon the city of Vicksburg never got a better hammering. We all drifted by slowly, and opened on them with shell, shrapnell, and canister, as hard as we could fire." Then he added this extraordinary detail:

"I could hear the bricks falling on the floor of the houses. . . ."[58]

Porter wrote Fox again, a week later, ". . . I am anxious to relieve Farragut, though he is on his own beat, and is in a measure responsible for all the trouble at Port Hudson and Red River."[59] This was a very broad statement, which he makes no attempt to explain. On the 29th, his fleet bombarded the batteries of Grand Gulf for five hours and thirty-five minutes, lost 24 killed and 56 wounded, killed 2 Confederates and wounded 18, temporarily disabled one gun, and tore up the earthen works.[60] The next day Grant began transporting his 30,000 men across the river just below Grand Gulf. They first moved against Port Gibson. This was captured, and the Confederates were thereby forced to evacuate Grand Gulf on May 3. "We had a hard fight for these forts," reported Porter to Welles, "and it is with great pleasure that I report that the Navy holds the door to Vicksburg." Then he continued very unfairly to Grant, "I hear nothing of our army as yet,"[61] when he knew that Grant had caused the evacuation of the forts and made it possible for him to "capture" the place.

5

Farragut, becoming impatient at not receiving any ironclads from Porter, finally sent Ellet in the ram *Switzerland* to Grand Gulf with a letter for Porter who it was rumored had passed below Vicksburg with some of his fleet. He had been informed by General Banks of the capture of Butte-à-la-Rose and Opelousas, the sinking of the captured *Queen of the West*, the destruction of two other Confederate vessels, and the capture of 2,000 men with 20 siege guns and 1,000 small arms and 10,000 head of cattle. The Confederates had then deserted the Atchafalaya River and moved all their guns and ships up the Red River to make a last stand at Alexandria, upon which Banks was advancing. All this information Farragut wrote to Porter with the urgent request that he send him a couple of ironclads so that he could move up the Red River, cut off General Kirby Smith with reinforcements, and cooperate with Banks in the attack on Alexandria.[62] He sent a letter to Grant also, in which he informed him that he had sent a "most imploring appeal" to

Porter for the ironclads, that his fuel was nearly exhausted, and that he would soon be forced to return to New Orleans. He also enclosed a letter to Grant from Banks. "Its soiled condition," he explained, "is owing to the secretary being compelled to carry it in his mouth when pursued by the enemy's pickets on his return to the ship across the peninsula."[63]

Meanwhile Grant had abandoned his base and boldly advanced toward Jackson, Mississippi, in a brilliant maneuver which resulted in the defeat of General Johnston, the driving of General Pemberton back into Vicksburg, the capture of Haynes's Bluff, and the ultimate capture of Vicksburg after a siege of two months. Porter's fleet was no longer needed below Vicksburg; so, flushed with his victory in "capturing" Grand Gulf, he decided to answer Farragut's request in person, and add to his laurels by "capturing" Alexandria on the Red River.

Accordingly, about two o'clock on the morning of May 4, a light was seen from the *Hartford* moving down the river. Drums were beat calling the men to quarters. But the approaching ship turned out to be Porter's flagship *Benton*, followed by three gunboats, the ram *Switzerland*, and the tug *Ivy*. After communicating with Farragut and securing thirty volunteers from the *Hartford*, Porter steamed up the Red River in the afternoon, with the ram *Switzerland* leading.[64]

The next day Farragut went down to communicate with the *Richmond* below Port Hudson and to make arrangements for turning over the command of the *Hartford* to Captain Palmer so that he could return to New Orleans.[65] Having informed Porter of these arrangements, he left the *Hartford* early on the morning of May 8. The sailors with eyes "wet with tears they would fain conceal" manned the rigging and gave such cheers as were "seldom given by our noble sailors to any person."[66] Farragut then went on board the little gunboat *Sachem*, accompanied by Captain Jenkins, Fleet Surgeon Foltz, the Admiral's secretary Gabaudan, Jenkins's clerk, and Lieutenant S. M. Eaton of the Army Signal Corps.[67] The *Sachem* proceeded up the Red River to the mouth of the narrow but deep Atchafalaya. Veering from bank to bank and running into floating trees, the little gunboat slowly made its way southward to Grand Lake and Brashear City, whence the last leg of the journey to New Orleans was made by rail.[68]

The arrival of Farragut on May 11 took the city of New Orleans by storm, and newsboys were soon making the streets ring with "Extra! Extra! Arrival of Admiral Farragut, the Game Cock! Capture of Alexandria! Capture of Port Gibson! General Grant with fifty thousand men below Vicksburg."[68] Part of this was false and some of it mere exaggeration, but there was enough that was true to cast gloom over the spirits of the Confederates in the city. They had heard and believed that Farragut had been trapped with his flagship, "The Black Devil," as they called the *Hartford*.

Farragut sat down in comfort in General Banks's luxurious headquarters, and wrote to his wife of his recent experiences. "You say you think I am getting too ambitious," he began. "You do me great injustice in supposing I am detained here a day by ambition. I am much more apt to lose than win honors by what I do. My country has a right to my services as long as she wants them. She has done everything for me, and I must do all for her. Gladly would I go home; but you see how it is. Du Pont is being blamed. It may be my turn to-morrow. All I can do is my best. The worst of it is, that people begin to think I fight for pleasure. God knows there is not a more humble poor creature in the community than myself. . . . I shall go to church to-morrow, and try to return suitable thanks for the many blessings that have been bestowed upon me."[69]

XVII

THE SIEGE AND CAPTURE OF PORT HUDSON

1

AT NEW ORLEANS Farragut found that Commodore Morris had "conducted the affairs of the squadron with as much ability" as he himself "could have done" in supplying the vessels and keeping up the blockade. Eight of the blockaders were in need of extensive repairs; three required new boilers—a condition which Farragut thought was due to bad engineering.[1] "I hope Port Hudson will soon fall," he wrote Mrs. Farragut, "and that will finish my river work." As soon as Mobile and Galveston were taken, he would ask to be relieved. "They make a great deal of me here; I don't know why, unless it is because I did not get my head knocked off," he modestly added. Then he plaintively wrote that he was looking "for Du Pont's attack on Charleston with intense anxiety" and hoping for "the success of Grant at Vicksburg," for he was "growing old fast" and wanted rest.[2]

Farragut had to write to Welles a letter defending the conduct of his special friend, Captain Bell. The Secretary had written, asking that a court of inquiry be held on Bell's failure to put forth all possible effort to capture Galveston. A complaint had also been received by Welles that Bell had too freely entertained Confederate officers on the *Brooklyn* when they had come on board under a flag of truce, and that he had wished to show them too much official respect.[3] Farragut replied that "the Government does not possess a more patriotic, zealous, and untiring officer" than Commodore Bell, and "as the rebels are now considered in all matters of intercourse as belligerents, I see no reason why he should not have been courteous to them, and I doubt if he did more."[4] He also wrote to Bell, informing him of the report and warning him to be careful not to be too indulgent to the Confederates for he apparently had personal enemies on board the *Brooklyn*.[5]

The American Consul at Havana reported to Welles on April 29 that blockade running between Cuba and Mobile was fairly frequent,[6] and Farragut had the "infinite satisfaction" of informing Welles that, between March 25 and May 18, Captain Goldsborough's vessels off Mobile Bay had captured ten prizes and destroyed four others.[7]

2

After the capture of Alexandria, Banks decided to move up to Vicksburg and aid Grant, but Farragut urged the capture of Port Hudson, where the garrison had been greatly reduced. "It is generally believed that they are evacuating it," he concluded persuasively.[8] Porter had meanwhile hurried back up the river, fearing that he would not be present at the surrender of Vicksburg. Then Banks changed his mind about going to the aid of Grant, and agreed to co-operate with Farragut in taking Port Hudson. General Grover's division, which had been operating west of the Mississippi, was ordered to march through Simmesport south of the Red River and cross the Mississippi to Bayou Sara, and invest Port Hudson on the north. Meanwhile General Augur's division was proceeding up from Baton Rouge, and on May 23 Port Hudson was completely encircled by approximately 14,000 men.[9]

Since the 8th of May the *Essex*, the *Richmond*, and the four bombers had been firing sporadically on the fortifications.[10] Farragut joined them on the afternoon of May 23 with his flag on the *Monongahela*. Also present by that time were the gunboats *Kineo* and *Genesee*. Next morning the usual Sunday services were held to the accompaniment of heavy firing in the rear of Port Hudson, and a general bombardment by the whole fleet began in the afternoon. This continued the two following days with Banks's artillery of about ninety guns joining in the terrific din, the men sweating at the guns in the excessive heat.

At daylight on the 27th, Banks began an attack with light

artillery, followed a couple of hours later with heavy guns. This was to be the prelude to a general assault on the works. Farragut's ships aided as much as possible with the assistance of the *Hartford* above; but they were somewhat handicapped by the danger of firing into Banks's army. Though shells fell all around the vessels, sometimes throwing the spray as high as the tops, little damage was done.[10] The battle continued furiously all day, but every attempt to storm the breastworks failed, though many men gained a temporary footing on the parapets. The losses were heavy, and Banks asked for a suspension of hostilities until two o'clock next day so that his dead and wounded might be brought in.[11] Both Farragut and Banks had underestimated the strength of the garrison. "Port Hudson will be ours to-day," Banks had signaled to Captain Palmer on the *Hartford*.[12] "It seems to me that you have only to make the assault and they must fall," Farragut had confidently written Banks.[13] The casualties had mounted to about 2,000 men; among the killed were seven or eight colonels and Brigadier-General T. W. Sherman.[14]

3

At the time Farragut was thus actively engaged at Port Hudson, Welles was thinking of him as a possible successor to Du Pont, who had failed to bring his operations against Charleston to a successful issue. "Du Pont is proud and will not willingly relinquish his command, although he has in a half-defiant way said if his course was not approved I must find another," Welles put down in his diary. "I am at a loss as to his successor. Farragut, if not employed elsewhere, would be the man, and the country would accept the change with favor."[15] Nearly three weeks before, Du Pont had written Farragut a very friendly letter, informing him that he was getting ready for an attack on Charleston and that the "new and untried monitors" might be in better shape for use in the Gulf when he was through with them. He then criticized the recent promotion of Dahlgren to rear-admiral, which seemed to him to demonstrate "that a navy officer who remains on shore does better than if he went to sea, and the inventor of a gun is much in advance of him who fights it." "You and I," he continued, "seem left alone in our work afloat and must expect the vicissitudes of long service. I have followed you with great interest and sympathized in the many irons you were obliged to have in the fire at one time and how much you have had to annoy you. We have all had some ebb tide on us."[16] Could he have had a premonition that Dahlgren would be the officer to supersede him? This is what happened on July 6, 1863.

4

During the next two weeks, Banks's army gradually recovered from its first setback, and made preparations for a second attempt. The bombers and the ironclad *Essex* continued to shell the batteries at varying intervals. One morning the *Essex* was struck fifteen times, but no one was injured. Banks set up a battery of four 9-inch siege guns, and requested forty men from the gun crews of the *Richmond* to man them.[17] He requested also 32-pounders from the mortars, and hand grenades; but the latter could not be provided. The weather continued hot; some days the air was heavy and stifling until a downpour of rain would bring relief for awhile. The sick lists daily grew longer. There was a rumor that President Davis was dead.[18] The Confederates reoccupied all the ground west of the Mississippi recently taken by Banks, and cavalry appeared across the river opposite Bayou Sara.[14] The Atchafalaya was again blocked and Palmer had to beg Porter for coal. Banks's flanking campaign had been largely a waste of time, sweat, and blood.

One day while Lieutenant Winfield Scott Schley, Executive Officer of the *Richmond,* was in temporary command, he attacked the citadel of the fortifications with his long rifle. It was a still, suffocating day, and the signal flags hung limp from the mastheads. In the midst of the smoke of battle, the quartermaster reported a signal flying, but declared that he could not distinguish the flags. The *Richmond* continued to fire until the enemy ceased replying, and then dropped down to her station. Schley then went on board the flagship to report the result of the action. He found Farragut on the quarter-deck. After returning his salute, the Admiral said, "Captain, you begin early in your life to disobey orders. Did you not see the signal flying for near an hour to withdraw from action?" Schley, very much embarrassed, made a stammering explanation, to which Farragut replied, "I want none of this Nelson business in my squadron about not seeing signals." He then invited the lieutenant into his cabin, and when the door was closed, in a different tone and manner, he smilingly explained, "I have censured you, sir, on the quarter-deck for what appeared to be a disregard of my orders. I desire now to commend you and your officers and men for doing what you believed right under the circumstances. Do it again whenever in your judgment it is necessary to carry out your conception of duty. Will you take a glass of wine, sir?"[19]

As the hot June days passed, Farragut saw his ammunition fast becoming exhausted. "You must remember," he reminded Banks on the 11th, "we have been bombarding this place five weeks, and we are now upon our last 500 shells, so that it will not be in my power to bombard more than three or four hours each night at intervals of five minutes."[20] The next day, Banks replied, "We are ready for the assault to-morrow, but may postpone it till next day; we shall carry the works without fail when we attempt it."[21] The attack was postponed, though a tremendous bombardment by the fleet and Banks's artillery was carried on for an hour ending at noon. Then a summons to surrender was sent to Major-General Frank Gardner, who replied that his duty required him to defend the place.[22] As during the previous night, the bombers continued their monotonous booming; and at daylight the Sunday morning peace was broken by a long-continued roar of artillery which sounded like distant thunder. "From the fleet in the river and from every gun in position on shore came the quick flash and angry roar of threatening annihilation," reported Colonel William R. Miles, C.S.A. "The air grew thick with smoke and hoarse with sound."[23] After this artillery preparation, an assault was attempted. One whole division was misdirected by its guides; the commanding officer of another was severely wounded. Banks was again disastrously repulsed, with casualties bringing the total of the campaign up to 4,000.²⁴ The daily ration of the Confederate soldiers had been reduced to three ears of corn and a half pound of fresh beef; but their fighting spirit had not been reduced.²⁵

5

Banks then settled down to a regular siege which was to last almost a month longer. To occupy his time, Farragut wrote a long letter to Welles, criticizing the *Monongahela,* then his flagship, as "a remarkable specimen" of inadequately armed vessel of war for her tonnage and her speed and her unsteadiness. He particularly opposed the placing of pivot guns on vessels of her size.²⁶ She had a tonnage of 1,378 and carried only twelve guns. He wanted his ships to carry all the guns possible.

Farragut was soon to be relieved from the monotony of an occasional bombardment of the Confederate batteries. Word came that an attack had been made on Plaquemine below Baton Rouge and several transports had been burned. Leaving Captain Alden in command at Port Hudson, Farragut, though unwell, hurried down the river in the recently criticized *Monongahela.* When he arrived on the 18th, he found that a small troop of 150 Texas cavalrymen²⁷ had attacked the place and burned a steamboat and a smaller bayou boat. The gunboat *Winona* had then arrived and shelled them out of the town. After reading a lecture to the mayor, who declared the soldiers were all strangers to him, Farragut dropped down the river to Donaldsonville, where he found the gunboats *Kineo* and *Winona* confident they had the situation well in hand.

There he received a letter from Mrs. Farragut, informing him that it was reported "from Washington direct" that Dahlgren was to relieve him, though he was to be allowed to retain full pay.²⁸ This did not improve the state of his health, for he did not know that the report was false. He would have felt much better, had he known that a letter from the Secretary was on the way, filled with unrestrained praise of his campaign above Port Hudson. Everything he had done had pleased Welles, who wrote, "You have carried out the wishes of the

Department, well served your country and her cause, and inflicted serious injury upon those in arms against the Governernment. I congratulate you upon these achievements." "It is hoped," he continued, "that affairs have arrived at such a state as to admit of your giving your attention to other important interests on the Gulf coast, and I trust that your future operations may be as successful and as gratifying as your past."[29] There was no thought of his supersedure in Welles's mind. But the same day he wrote him another letter, suggesting that he might come North for recreation "for a reasonable period, and the Department would be pleased to see you."[30] This may have given rise to the false rumor.

Before Farragut could return to his fleet below Port Hudson, he received a telegram on the 20th from General Emory in New Orleans, stating that communications with Brashear City had been cut, that he feared an attack on New Orleans, and that he then had only 400 men with whom to defend the city.[31] Farragut hurried on down to New Orleans, where he learned that in the early morning of the 23d Brashear City had been captured by a force of 8,000 or 10,000 men under General Richard Taylor, who it was supposed had begun to move on New Orleans, distant only one hundred miles. It was feared that there would be a rising in the city, when the army appeared across the river. "We will forget our humanity in such a case," declared Farragut, his Irish blood up, "and therefore I trust it will not occur." He had the guns of the *Portsmouth, Pensacola, Monongahela*, and several smaller vessels with which to defend New Orleans or to fire upon it, if there was an uprising.[32]

Instead of attacking New Orleans, the Confederates marched northward, and on the 28th attacked Donaldsonville with 5,000 men. Farragut had been advised, and ordered up the *Monongahela* to assist the three gunboats gathered there. The enemy was repulsed, a storming party which entered the fort was captured, and about a hundred men were killed.[33] This reassured Farragut that he could easily defend New Orleans with the naval forces he had available there; but others were not so sure.

"There are rumors of a contemplated rising of 11,000 men

secretly organized with aid from outside, and Farragut has been urged to remain to protect the city with his fleet," Surgeon Foltz recorded in his diary. "He says: 'We are ready for them. Let them come.' He will destroy the city if necessary. . . . June 30. The revolt in the city is fixed upon for to-night. July 1. The night passed quietly. In our house we made no preparations for resistance, and if the city is taken we will be taken prisoners, or killed in the tumult as the ships open fire on the town, but we submit our fate to God. July 2. Admiral Farragut left last night for Port Hudson, in the *Tennessee*. The citizens of New Orleans look confident and defiant and all hands say that they are 'buying rope to hang the Yankees.' Rebel money has risen twenty per cent."[34] Farragut, convinced that his preparations were adequate, hurried back to his fleet up the river, where he arrived in the early afternoon of July 2.

6

Farragut found that the siege of Port Hudson, since the last unsuccessful assault, had been very quiet as compared with the excitement which General Dick Taylor had aroused from Baton Rouge to New Orleans. Any unusual incident up there was greeted with enthusiasm. For example, one hot afternoon in the midst of a bombardment, a beautiful large goose came swimming down the river near the *Richmond*. Out of a gunport jumped a gunner, caught the surprised goose, and was back again helping to load his gun before he was scarcely missed.[35] That same afternoon, Lieutenant L. A. Schirmer, C.S.A. performed an act of heroism. When a flag to the left of Battery Eleven was shot down, he fixed it to a light pole and, jumping on the parapet, planted the improvised flagstaff. Again it was shot down, and regardless of sharpshooters he raised it again. The third time it fell, he raised it up and waved it defiantly as he put it in place while his comrades cheered him with all their might.[36]

On July 3 Farragut issued this order to his commanding officers: "To-morrow being the anniversary of our independence, the ships will display an American ensign at each masthead and fire a national salute at 12 o'clock meridian, following the movements of the flagship."[37] That July 3, 1863 was a momentous day in the Civil War. That afternoon was the third and last day of the bloody battle of Gettysburg. On that day also began the negotiations for the surrender of Vicksburg, which was carried out the following day.

Farragut, still unwell, wrote a pessimistic letter, on the 4th, to Morris in New Orleans. He could not estimate, he declared, how long it would take Banks to reduce Port Hudson. Deserters reported that the garrison were eating their mules, and that there were only 2,500 men fit for duty. "Our men are apparently on the top of the works," Farragut complained. "Why they do not go in I cannot tell." His fleet could not fire for fear of injuring Banks's troops.[38]

Down in New Orleans some pens were scratching pessimistically also on that day. General Emory informed Farragut that he was sure the enemy had 13,000 men with "numerous artillery," and were slowly but steadily advancing upon New Orleans. To Banks, he wrote unashamed, "You can only save this city by sending me reinforcements immediately and at any cost. It is a choice between Port Hudson and New Orleans."[39] He was not alone in his funk. On July 3, Surgeon Foltz added these items in his diary: ". . . It is said in New Orleans that to-morrow the Confederate flag will wave over the city. Captains Morris and Jenkins fear a rising in the city to-night. July 4. Slept last night on a smoldering volcano. At dusk I rode out to Ridge Cemetery and met but a single carriage, and that filled with Army officers. All the doors and windows of the houses were closed and not a white man was to be seen on the streets; only women and children. The city reminded me of Buenos Aires after the defeat of Rosas. At nine o'clock all was still as death. All our troops slept on their arms, but the night passed quietly, and also to-day, and toward evening the city was cheerful. The crisis had passed. This evening there was a procession of 5,000 Negroes, all able-bodied men organized in regiments, but not armed. Some 10,000 Negro women, men, and boys surrounded them, frantic with delight at being free men. This was the first

Negro procession ever seen in New Orleans. It won't be the last."[40]

Farragut sent General Emory a long letter in reply, advising him and trying to bolster up his courage.[41] He also wrote Captain Jenkins that Vicksburg had surrendered and that Banks thought Port Hudson would fall in a day or two.[42] Captain Palmer thought that the reason the garrisons at Vicksburg and Port Hudson held out so stubbornly was their diet of mule meat.[43] Perhaps, the Federal troops might have fought better on scantier rations. About two o'clock on July 6, Farragut called on General Banks at his headquarters, where he found him and Major-General Thomas Kilby Smith still at dinner. There was plenty of champagne and ice as well as food. After Farragut left, Smith remarked, "I imagine rather a clever man and a fine officer."[44]

Farragut was aroused from sleep at four o'clock on July 7 with a dispatch, which had been inspired by a telegram from General Emory to the commanding officer at Donaldsonville, warning him of an imminent attack on that place. Farragut sent word to Banks that he would go down and investigate that afternoon, but regretfully, for he had planned to suggest that he go up the following day under a flag of truce to demand the surrender of Port Hudson. He thought that Gardner might be more willing to surrender to the navy than the army, because Banks had Negro regiments among his troops.[45] At seven o'clock the same morning, Farragut received dispatches from Grant confirming the news that Vicksburg had fallen. With the good tidings was the disquieting, though false, report that Lee's army had taken Harrisburg and Carlisle and had certainly, by then, captured both Baltimore and Philadelphia.[46] All hands ran aloft and gave cheer after cheer for Grant. At midday every vessel that carried a gun fired the national salute, and two batteries from General Banks's army were moved to the edge of the bluff and fired a hundred guns. The Confederates did not know what to make of the yelling and saluting.[47]

In the early afternoon, Farragut had his flag hoisted on the little *Tennessee,* which then steamed down the river to see what was wrong at Donaldsonville.⁴⁷ On that same morning Captain Jenkins had started from New Orleans in the *Monongahela* for Port Hudson to take command of the *Richmond*, Captain Alden having gone home on account of the illness of his wife. Jenkins was ill of a fever, but Farragut had written him to "come if he could crawl."⁴⁸ About twelve miles below Donaldsonville, the *Monongahela* was fired upon by newly placed Confederate batteries, and in the engagement Captain Abner Read, standing by the side of Captain Jenkins, was mortally wounded. Lieutenant George Dewey, executive officer, displayed his usual coolness and courage.⁴⁹ Poor Read, a much loved and excellent officer, died five days later in Baton Rouge. Of him, Farragut wrote, paraphrasing Shakespeare, "The country could well have spared a better man."⁵⁰

7

The garrison at Port Hudson finally exhausted its supply even of mule meat, and General Gardner surrendered to Banks at two o'clock on the afternoon of July 8. The Federals were overjoyed; they had, by no means, been having a picnic. "The heat, especially in the trenches, became almost insupportable, the stenches quite so, the brooks dried up, the creek lost itself in the pestilential swamp, the springs gave out, and the river fell, exposing to the tropical sun a wide margin of festering ooze," graphically wrote Lieutenant-Colonel R. B. Irwin.⁵¹ At the end, hardly half of the army was well enough to be on duty. During the siege, Banks had employed about 20,000 men. The garrison at the time of surrender numbered only about 6,000; 200 had been killed and an equal number had died of disease, while about 400 had been wounded.⁵² Banks's casualties amounted to over 4,000, of whom 700 were killed.⁵³

All the preliminaries for the surrender were arranged by Banks without giving the Navy any recognition at all. After the arrangements had been completed, he sent a dispatch to Farragut, forwarded by Jenkins down the river to him, which informed him of the surrender.⁵⁴ The formal surrender took place early on the morning of the 9th, with military music, lowering and raising of flags, stacking of arms, and the generous

THE SIEGE AND CAPTURE OF PORT HUDSON

return of General Gardner's sword to him in the presence of his men in recognition of their heroic defense.[55]

In these ceremonies, Farragut who had contributed so much to the final capture of Port Hudson had no part. It would have gladdened his heart to have seen the *Hartford* come down proudly that morning and join the fleet[56] from which she had so long been separated. But on that day he proceeded down the river from Donaldsonville with the *Monongahela, Essex, Kineo, Tennessee,* and *New London,* and had a spirited engagement with the four batteries recently erected on the levee. These were silenced with the loss of only one man killed, and the next day the flotilla arrived at new Orleans bearing the news of the fall of Port Hudson—news which the Confederate sympathizers refused to believe but which was received with unbounded joy by the Union people.[57] Just at sundown the following day the *Hartford* and the *Albatross* arrived, and crowds flocked to the river front to see the flagship which had been so often reported destroyed. That night there was great rejoicing in the city over the capture of Vicksburg and Port Hudson, the Negroes being out in full force with a torchlight procession.[58]

Farragut had been quite right about New Orleans. It had never been in any real danger. With the completion of Banks's operations at Port Hudson, he hurried two divisions onto transports and proceeded to Donaldsonville to drive General Taylor out of the Berwick Bay region. By the 21st the Confederates had retired across the Bay, taking with them all the spoils they could carry. In September they were forced on toward Opelousas.[59]

"I am happy at last in being able to give you 'glad tidings of great joy,'" Farragut wrote Bell in a long letter, detailing the Union successes on the Mississippi, at Gettysburg, and elsewhere. "I shall soon turn over the river to Porter and then make a short trip North; perhaps return and wind up the concern, unless the good people at home have some one else to whom they want to give a chance, and God knows I would not deprive him of it."[60] The favorable turn of events had cured his illness. "I continue my health," he wrote Mrs. Farragut, "my vessels are all repairing, and I am trying everybody by court-martial to clear the calendar. . . . We have done our part of the work assigned to us, and all has worked well. My last dash past Port Hudson was the best thing I ever did, except taking New Orleans. It assisted materially in the fall of Vicksburg and Port Hudson."[61]

On July 15, Farragut wrote Porter, turning over to his command the Mississippi down to New Orleans; but Porter delayed until he could receive explicit orders from the Navy Department.[62] On the 16th of July, the merchant steamer *Imperial* from St. Louis arrived at New Orleans; this demonstrated that the Mississippi was at last open to navigation throughout its course. "The Father of Waters rolled unvexed to the sea," declared Lincoln.[63] This was, however, an exaggeration, as guerrilla sharpshooters were to greatly "vex" river boats for many months to come.

While Farragut was waiting for Porter to appear, he went into the Gulf in the *Tennessee* on a five days' tour of inspection of Ship Island, Pensacola, and the Mobile blockade.[64] Commodore Morris was so ill he had to be sent home, and to take command of the squadron in Farragut's absence Bell was ordered up from the Galveston blockade. Meanwhile Farragut received a congratulatory letter from Fox. "You smashed in the door in an unsurpassed movement and the success above became a certainty," he wrote. ". . . Some of the *young* officers only saw in it a rash act. . . . We hope soon to welcome you here where you will find a nation ready to acknowledge how well you have performed every duty imposed by this unfortunate rebellion."[65]

On the morning of August 1, Porter finally arrived at New Orleans on the *Black Hawk*. There was much saluting, the transfer of command was made with felicitations on board the *Hartford*, and in the late afternoon Farragut's flagship hove up anchor, steamed up the river and turned round, and then stood down the Mississippi, to the ringing of church bells[66] and echoing cheers from the fleet.[67] Farragut was off on his first visit home in more than eighteen months of hard service.

XVIII

FARRAGUT HAS A FURLOUGH

1

THE *Hartford* crossed the bar at Southwest Pass in the early morning of August 2,[1] and after an uneventful passage of nine days arrived at New York. In the early afternoon of the 12th she came to off the Navy Yard.[2] The *Richmond* had preceded her by one day,[3] and the *Brooklyn* came in two weeks later. Two gunboats had been dispatched to Philadelphia and two others to Baltimore.[4] All were greatly in need of repairs. The *Hartford*, which was less injured than the others, required new masts and bowsprit and repairs to her lower rigging and hull above the water line. During her nineteen months of actual service, she had been struck two hundred and forty times by shot and shell.[5]

Mrs. Farragut, accompanied by Loyall, arrived at the Metropolitan Hotel, the day before the *Hartford* came in, to meet her "gallant husband."[6] It was a very happy family reunion after long months of painful anxiety and separation. When Loyall returned from service with his father, he had been given an appointment to West Point, had passed the entrance examination, and was soon to enter the Military Academy on the first of September.[7] They had much to talk about. Mrs. Farragut had made a recent visit to relatives in Norfolk, and she had many stories to tell relating to their former friends and acquaintances in the old home town. Farragut, in turn, had an unlimited supply of anecdotes about his war experiences. He had hardly seen any of his relatives in New Orleans and Pascagoula. His sister, Mrs. Gurlie, at Pascagoula was then a widow,[8] and had written him of the distress which the war had brought. In May, his nephews in New Orleans, sons of his brother William, had been obliged to leave for Pascagoula as "registered enemies." His nephew William's wife had to remain behind as she was enceinte. Farragut wrote his wife that he was very sorry for her and gave her money for her confinement.[9]

The New York *Herald*[10] saluted Farragut's arrival home with headlines and a column and a half on the front page, containing a description of the *Hartford* and a detailed account of her engagements in the war. On the editorial page, "The Situation" referred to "the valiant actions of the American Viking, Farragut, on board the *Hartford,* which have won for him a name not inferior to the naval commanders of any nation of the present day."[11]

Welles answered Farragut's telegram, announcing his arrival, with congratulations and praise. "A respite from the labors and responsibilities which have been imposed upon you and which you have borne so heroically under difficulties and embarrassments which only the Department can know and appreciate was due you," the Secretary generously wrote, "and I welcome you home to an interval of repose." He told Farragut to suit his convenience about reporting in Washington, and advised him to wait until the weather was less oppressive.[12] Farragut greatly appreciated such consideration, for he found New York even hotter than New Orleans had been at the time of his departure. He was also deeply appreciative of a letter welcoming his return to New York, which was signed by eighty-one of her prominent citizens, who wished to express their feeling of indebtedness to him for his great achievement, "the results of which have given increased admiration for the Navy, and a new lustre to the national flag."[13]

As soon as he could get away from New York, Farragut retired to the quiet of his home in Hastings-on-the-Hudson and there enjoyed the peace for which he had yearned. From here, on August 27, Loyall Farragut departed for West Point,—"a great trial to me," his mother wrote, "as I feel as if it is really 'the flight from his nest.' Other separations have always been attended with a hope of his return."[14] It was fortunate that she had the Admiral with her at such a time when her loneliness would have been extreme. To occupy her time, she had been

Courtesy of Curator, United States Naval Academy

MRS. DAVID GLASGOW FARRAGUT

From a photograph by Anthony & Co., New York, presented by Mrs. Farragut, Nov. 24, 1869, to Dr. Samuel Jones, Chicago, and now in the Naval Academy Museum.

REAR-ADMIRAL D. G. FARRAGUT, U. S. NAVY
From a photograph by Brady, furnished by the L. C. Handy Studios, Washington, D. C. This was the uniform of the regulations of Jan. 28, 1864.

thinking of writing a biography of her husband, and had written to the publisher, George W. Childs, about it. He was enthusiastic. "Such a book as you could prepare in regard to your excellent and noble husband would have a very large sale, and I would be glad to publish it," he assured her, and to encourage her declared that he had paid $66,000 in royalties to Dr. Kane and his heirs for his *Arctic Explorations*.[15] But the plan never materialized.

While he was resting, Farragut wrote[16] a long letter to Bell, who had taken over the command of the fleet in his absence, telling him how sorry he was that he could not also come home with the others and how disappointed Mrs. Bell was. After giving some not very promising news about the operations before Charleston, he added, "When I visit Washington, I will endeavor to place the affair of your entertaining the rebels in its true light. I trust that you will never consider yourself under any obligation to me for doing you a simple act of justice." Then his eyes having given out, Mrs. Farragut finished the letter.[17]

2

The weather became more pleasant, and Farragut went to Washington, where on Friday, September 11, he made a call "of a most cheerful and friendly character" on Mr. Welles.[18] While he was at the Navy Department, dispatches were received from Commodore Bell, stating that General Banks had applied for aid and co-operation in an attack on Sabine Pass, and that he had answered the call. After reading the dispatch, Farragut laid down the paper and said to the Secretary: "The expedition will be a failure. The army officers have an impression that naval vessels can do anything; this call is made for boats to accompany an army expedition; it is expected the navy will capture the batteries, and, the army being there in force with a general in command, they will take the credit. But there will be no credit in the case, and you may expect to hear of disaster. These boats which Bell has given them cannot encounter batteries; they might co-operate with and assist the army, but that is evidently not the object. The soldiers should land and attack in the rear, and the vessels aid them in front. But that is not the army plan. The soldiers are not to land until the navy had done an impossibility. Therefore there will be disaster."[19] Eleven days later news came verifying Farragut's prediction. The expedition had failed and the gunboats *Clifton* and *Sachem,* half of the naval force, had been captured.

On the day following Farragut's call, Welles invited him and "a few friends" to dinner. That evening he jotted down in his diary this high praise of the Admiral: "The more I see and know of Farragut the better I like him. He has the qualities I supposed when he was selected. The ardor and sincerity which struck me during the Mexican War when he wished to take Vera Cruz, with the unassuming and the unpresuming gentleness of a true hero."[18]

Farragut was back in New York the following Monday, taking a look at his ships to see what progress was being made in their repairs.[20] Some days afterwards Welles was talking with Lincoln about the failures of the generals who had commanded the armies of the Potomac. Then the conversation turned to the naval commanders. "[Lincoln] thought there had not been, take it all in all, so good an appointment in either branch of the service as Farragut, whom he did not know or recollect when I gave him command," Welles recorded. "Du Pont he classed, and has often, with McClellan, but Porter he considers a busy schemer, bold but not of high qualities as a chief. For some reason he has not so high an appreciation of Porter as I think he deserves, but no man surpasses Farragut in his estimation."[21]

3

Farragut informed Welles, on October 6, that the *Richmond* would be ready for sea in two or three days, but that it would be probably more than three weeks before the *Hartford* was ready. "I can sail in the *Richmond,* if such is the wish of the Department," he suggested.[22] Welles replied that he was not to go on the *Richmond,* but that it was hoped that the *Hartford* might be ready in time for him to reach his station by the last of the month.[23] Farragut was becoming restive. "I am run to death with the attention of the good people," he confessed to Bell, "but I am beginning to give out, as I am not able to bear my honors. I have not been able to have a day at home in a week." Since the failure at Sabine Pass, he was eager to get back and look after the interests of his fleet. He warned Bell that the Army was making "a foolish attempt" to get supreme command everywhere by placing a general in command who was senior to the naval officer stationed there.[24]

"I am very anxious to get out to my station," Farragut informed Fox, "as I perceive that General Banks is beginning to take the field, and it may be in my power to render him assistance." He suggested that some of the monitors, recently added to Porter's fleet, might be sent down the river to aid him in attacking Fort Morgan, and begged him to send gunboats of under eight feet draft to New Orleans as soon as possible. As to monitors, he complained, "They tell me that they will not steer, the moment they stop the propeller, but all these things will be corrected by degrees and they will always be great things for harbor work." He preferred ships with broadside batteries, though the turreted monitors he thought were all right for slow, deliberate firing.[25]

Farragut was pleased that the Secretary did not wish him to return to the Gulf with only one ship, for he would be expected to do something down there with nothing. "They are trying to force the Department to send me to Charleston," he wrote Bell, "but I think Dahlgren is too firm in favor for me to fear that."[24] Du Pont, whom Dahlgren had superseded, was at his home "near Wilmington" in a morbid state of mind over his failure to take Charleston. He wrote Welles, complaining of his treatment, and the latter set down in his diary of October 31: ". . . He [Du Pont] was for a time the great naval hero, but Farragut has eclipsed him. He has seen Farragut toasted and complimented, dined and extolled by our countrymen and by foreigners, until his envy and vexation could no longer be repressed. . . . He has too much pride to be a coward—would sooner die than show the white feather—but the innate, fearless moral courage of Farragut or John Rodgers is not his."[26]

Poor Bill Porter still nursed a grievance against Farragut regarding the *Arkansas* affair, and about this time he wrote a letter to his old mother, attacking Farragut, which concluded: "My counsel will be on in a few days and we will wind up the 'concern' and I hope that Gallient Hossifer Rear Admiral Pharigoot of Uncle Psalms Navey."[27] But Farragut was not wound up, nor was the 'concern,' though the latter ended with Porter's death in New York the following May 1.

Farragut was not to reach his station, not even leave New York, by the last of October, as Welles had hoped. On the 30th, he wrote Bell from the Astor House of his disappointment and of a probable further delay of three weeks. "You know what it is to get a vessel in the hands of the machinists," he explained. Then he dwelt on the great difficulty in finding light draft vessels for operating in shallow waters, and of the lack of monitors for use against Mobile which were not to be had until Charleston was taken. "I was glad to see that you were still taking prizes off the coast of Texas and Mobile," he added. "I told the madam that you would get enough to pay for the house, etc.—her only fear was that you would not want to come home, so I promised *to make* you."[28]

While he was waiting, time did not hang heavy on Farragut's hands. His popularity continued to increase. On the 5th of November, the Chamber of Commerce of New York City adopted resolutions of congratulation, which were beautifully engrossed on parchment and presented to him. These accorded him the highest praise for the service he had rendered to the merchants of the United States. "In forcing the passage of the Mississippi River under the guns of Forts St. Philip and Jackson, through narrow channels and against rapid currents, and through a fleet of fire-ships, rams, and men-of-war, and wresting from the enemies of the country the great port of New Orleans, Admiral Farragut has achieved one of the most celebrated victories of any time, has added a new and lustrous page to the naval history of the United States, and has proved himself a worthy successor of those earlier heroes of the republic who shrank from no obstacle, and whose daring was always superior to the difficulties and dangers of their undertaking," sonorously declared the resolutions. Looking to the future, they continued, "The Chamber of Commerce watches with profound interest the course of the Admiral, and will hail with joy and hope the day when, at the head of some noble squadron, he may again lead the victorious way to the restoration of other cities to the national rule."[29]

Farragut, in reply, expressed his sincere thanks and declared he would "gratefully cherish these kind sentiments of interest and hope for the success of the fleet" he had the honor to command. As to the capture of New Orleans, he modestly wrote, "That we did our duty to the best of our ability, I believe; that a kind Providence smiled upon us and enabled us to overcome obstacles before which the stoutest of hearts would have otherwise quailed, I am certain. I trust the recipient of these honors will ever remember the injunction of the poet:

> 'If thou hast strength, 'twas Heaven that strength bestowed,
> For know, vain man, that valor belongs to God.
> 'Tis man's to fight, but God's to give success.' "[30]

When Farragut was in New York, he stopped at the Astor House. Here he was frequently visited by the Russian Admiral in command of the fleet which was spending the winter in New York harbor. Farragut had known the Russian commander when they were serving as young officers in the Mediterranean, and a warm friendship had grown up between them. One day after dinner in the presence of Thurlow Weed, Farragut asked the Russian Admiral, "Why are you spending the winter here in idleness?" "I am here," he replied, "under sealed orders, to be broken only in a contingency that has not yet occurred." Other vessels, he declared, were at San Francisco with similar orders. During the ensuing conversation, the Russian admitted, "I have received orders to break the seals, if during the Rebellion the United States becomes involved in a war with foreign nations." Strict confidence was then requested.[31]

Farragut began to think that the repairs on the *Hartford* would never be completed. On November 20, he wrote Mr. Welles that, from the best information he could obtain, it would be another three weeks before either the *Hartford* or the *Brooklyn* was ready. He particularly regretted not being able to cooperate with Banks.[32] Ten days later he reported to Fox that he had been to the Navy Yard that day and found the *Hartford* coming out of the dock, and that she would be ready for her crew in four or five days. He hoped to sail in ten days if no new difficulty arose. He was quite disappointed at not being at his station to move with Banks against Galveston. "Oh, that I was only there to assist him in the recapture of that port!"[33]

4

Captain Percival Drayton was on duty in New York at the time of Farragut's furlough, and they soon became rather intimate friends. Drayton introduced him to his circle, and to one lady in particular he sent the Admiral's carte de visite photograph, "which," he wrote, "is very good, the one with the cap however the most agreeable."[34] Farragut grew to like Drayton so well that he eventually asked him to be his fleet captain. Though he liked his duties in New York and did not wish to leave his friends there, he accepted. "I cannot help feeling that in time of war an officer's place is afloat," he wrote.[35] Drayton belonged to an old South Carolina family, and when he participated in the attack on Port Royal under Du Pont, his brother, Brigadier-General Thomas F. Drayton, was in command of the Confederate forces defending that place. Captain Drayton was tall and commanding in appearance and, though gentlemanly and courteous, he was thoughtful and reserved. He made a good listener to Farragut's ready flow of talk. With his full beard and rather austere face, he looked more like a clergyman than a fighting man. In appearance he was quite the opposite of Captain James S. Palmer, whom he succeeded.[36]

On the 9th of December, the Farraguts were at a party at the Welleses. Admiral Lesoffsky and his wife were there, and also Mrs. D. D. Porter. "I was very much mortified to find that your wife was at the Secretary's party when I was there and no one told me of it and I did not know her," Farragut explained to Porter. "I was appointed to wait upon the Russian Admiral's wife because she did not speak English and I was so occupied all the evening."³⁷ Farragut's preoccupation with Madame Lesoffsky afforded a great deal of amusement to Mrs. Farragut and Mrs. Welles. "How much I should like to joke with you about the Admiral's touching devotion to the young *Russian bride*, the night of that delightful party at your house," wrote Mrs. Farragut to Mrs. Welles. "My *heart broken* expression was so *apparent* in spite of my efforts to look as young as Madame Lesoffsky!"³⁸

On the afternoon of December 15, the *Hartford* went into commission, the officers reported for duty, and about one hundred fifty of her crew were received on board.³⁹ Eight days later the ship was still short sixty-nine seamen and an equal number of ordinary seamen, and it seemed to Farragut that he might be detained for another month.⁴⁰ Christmas came and was celebrated by the Admiral and his wife and son, home from West Point. Five days later, an urgent letter came from Mr. Welles, enclosing a telegram from General Hurlbut at Memphis, stating that a deserter from Mobile had brought out the information that Buchanan intended to break through the blockade off Mobile Bay on January 20. Mr. Welles asked Farragut to use every possible exertion to hasten his departure, and authorized the transfer of enough men from the *Niagara* to complete his crew.⁴¹ This Farragut had suggested a whole week previous; but even a Secretary of the Navy must celebrate Christmas.

New Year's Day came and passed; the *Hartford* was still delayed in transferring the men from the *Niagara*. Farragut wrote a last note to Fox, who had inquired how many monitors he would need against the forts at Mobile. "Just as many as you can spare; two would answer me well, more would do better," he replied.⁴² He found time also to write a letter to his son. He had just received his report from General Totten. Loyall had received sixteen demerits for the term. "That is nothing," Farragut wrote, "but still I would never allow them to give me a demerit if I did not deserve it. . . . Don't mind the disagreeable things, of course; you will soon get used to them and you will have a pleasant time in the summer.... They all say you give yourself more trouble than there is a necessity for but remember one thing, my dear boy, so long as you do nothing dishonorable, your father will stand by you to the last, and I feel no fears on that subject.... Don't let your lessons disquiet you; you can get them easy enough; it only requires you bend your mind to it. I forgot to give you some money the other day and so mother sent it to you. God bless and preserve you, my dear boy, and keep you in the straight path you have thus far walked, free from vice and immorality and keep you a dutiful son to your mother; if it should be God's will to take your father, you will be her support and comfort.... Buchanan has a vessel which he says is superior to the *Merrimac* with which he intends to attack us in a short time. So we are to have no child's play."[43]

In the early afternoon of January 5, the *Hartford* finally put to sea in a heavy snowstorm.[44] After leaving Sandy Hook, she ran into a northwester which lasted for three days; but six days and a half later she arrived at Key West.[45] In less than a week the snow and cold of New York were exchanged for heat and mosquitoes—"a thing perhaps difficult for you to realize in New York at this season," wrote Drayton. He was all right, his only trouble being too much appetite for life on shipboard where there was too little opportunity for exercise. "Farragut hurt his foot a little before leaving New York," he added, "and has been quite lame. The symptoms are strong, however, of gout, which he, however, won't listen to, but which, as he prides himself on never drinking water, looks to me very probable. He is very temperate, confining himself to Bordeaux at dinner but I suppose that in sufficient quantities may do the business. Being so near Havana, cigars are as you may suppose plenty, and I actually smoked one myself yesterday after a dinner on shore, and did not find that it disagreed with me, so perhaps I may some of these days take up again that vile habit."[46]

In the early morning of January 17, the *Hartford* came to anchor in the harbor of Pensacola.[47] Farragut was back at his station.

XIX

WATCHFUL WAITING

1

WHEN FARRAGUT arrived at Pensacola, he found everybody suffering from "Ram Fever."[1] It was prevalent among the Union officers in the Gulf of Mexico, and had even spread to the Navy Department. Was it not "Ram Fever" in Washington which had hurried Farragut away from New York in a snow storm? A telegram had been received that Buchanan's *Tennessee*, "a ram more formidable than the *Merrimac*," would be ready for sea not later than the 20th of January.[2] In September, Bell had written Goldsborough, then in command of the Mobile blockade, that he had information that the Confederates had five rams at Mobile. "Look out for a surprise," he had warned.[3] Two days before Farragut's arrival at Pensacola, Bell wrote to Porter that he had information of a Confederate plan to recapture New Orleans. The Mobile rams were to attack and break through the blockading vessels, and then proceed up the Mississippi and take New Orleans with the aid of troops in Louisiana and Mississippi and the gunboats in the Red River. "I have nothing but the *Pensacola* and the river steamboats to defend this point with," despairingly wrote Bell, commanding at New Orleans, "all the gunboats here having their machinery apart undergoing repairs."[4]

Farragut soon learned that the situation was not really alarming. Refugees, who came daily into Pensacola, informed him that the *Tennessee* had not yet been gotten over Dog River Bar, that she drew two feet more water than was ever to be found on that bar, and that Buchanan was endeavoring to float her over with camels. But he was disturbed, when he visited the Mobile blockade, to find only the *Richmond* present, the six gunboats being at Pensacola for either coal or repairs.[5]

He accordingly wrote Porter, again requesting two of his monitors and small vessels of light draft for operating in the shallow waters of Texas.[6]

Farragut had long had rather definite information about the *Tennessee*. She was launched at Selma on the Alabama River about one hundred fifty miles north of Mobile on February 8, 1863, and then floated down the river near the first of March.[7] But on February 25, through a deserter, the commanding officer of the blockaders off Mobile Bay had obtained quite accurate information as to her size, the thickness of her armor, and the size and number of her guns.[8] As the machinery, armor, and guns were furnished her after she reached Mobile, this information must have been based in part on her plans. When completed, she was indeed a powerful man-of-war. Two hundred nine feet in length and forty-eight feet in beam, she carried her battery in a casemate about seventy-eight feet long with sides sloping at an angle of thirty-three degrees, armored with six inches of iron on the forward end and five inches elsewhere over wooden sides about two feet thick. She was armed with two 7-inch Brooke rifles on pivots and four 6.4-inch Brooke rifles in broadside. Her ram, covered with wrought-iron plates, projected about two feet. Her engines, brought overland from the steamboat *Alonzo Child* on the Yazoo River, were entirely inadequate and could develop only six nautical miles an hour.[9]

Farragut's information regarding the rams *Tuscaloosa* and *Huntsville*, similar to but smaller than the *Tennessee*, was not so accurate. They were to have two and a half inches of armor and four guns. Both rams were reported to him as being "ready for service" on December 2, 1863;[10] but as a matter of fact their armor was never sufficiently completed for them to go into battle, though they were launched at Selma ahead of the *Tennessee*. Equally exaggerated was the information about the *Nashville* which was built at Montgomery and floated down to Mobile. Her armor was never completed, though she was reported to Farragut, on December 2, as nearly ready for service, with five and a half inches of armor and four guns. At the same time, the ram *Baltic* was said to be ready, with two and a half inches of armor and six guns; but as she was a converted vessel, her hull was "as rotten as punk"[11] and she had to be laid up as unseaworthy.

At the time of Farragut's return to the Gulf, the only Confederate vessels at Mobile which were ready to operate in the bay were the three small gunboats *Selma, Gaines,* and *Morgan.* The *Selma* was a converted river steamer, and the other two had been hastily built early in the war at Mobile. They were unarmored except for a light plating around the boilers. The *Morgan*, which was the largest, was about two hundred feet long and carried two 7-inch rifles and four 32-pounders. The *Gaines* had one 8-inch rifle and five 32-pounders, while the *Selma* was armed with one 6-inch rifle and three 8-inch shell guns. Detailed, though exaggerated, information regarding the armament of these gunboats and of the *Baltic* was in the hands of the Navy Department as early as August, 1862.[12] But the data was inaccurate as to the number of guns as late as December, 1863.[13] In June, that year, Farragut admitted, "As to Admiral Buchanan's preparations, I have not been able to fathom them."[14]

2

On the morning of January 20, Farragut and his staff went aboard the gunboat *Octorara* and, accompanied by the *Itasca*, made a reconnaissance of Forts Morgan and Gaines at a distance of about three miles. It being a beautiful day with the air unusually clear, the forts could be seen quite distinctly. "I could count the guns and the men who stood by them," Farragut wrote; "could see the piles that had been driven across from Fort Gaines to the channel opposite Fort Morgan."[15] Unfortunately Farragut did not state the number of the guns in the forts, about which there has been a great difference of opinion.

These two forts guarded the chief entrance into Mobile Bay, between Mobile Point and Dauphin Island, three miles to the west. About thirty miles to the north was the city of Mobile situated on the northern shore of the bay which varies in width from six to fifteen miles, the lower end being the wider. On Mobile Point was located Fort Morgan, a pentagonal bastioned work of brick, with some exterior water batteries. Though some reports declared the total number of its guns to be as many as 125, the true figure[16] was 45, only eleven of which were rifled guns. The garrison of nearly 650 officers and men was commanded by Brigadier-General R. L. Page, who had formerly been an officer in the United States Navy.[16]

On the eastern extremity of Dauphin Island across the channel from Fort Morgan was the smaller brick fortress, Fort Gaines, with an armament of twenty-six guns and a garrison of about 850 officers and men.[17]

In addition to the piles which Farragut saw in the shallow water to the east of Fort Gaines, mines, or torpedoes as they then were called, had been planted, which reduced the channel for the free passage of ships from about 2,000 to approximately 250 yards under the guns of Fort Morgan.[18] Farragut did not mention the torpedoes, though the reports were that at least thirty had already been planted.[19] Authorities disagree as to the total number which obstructed the channel at the time of the Battle of Mobile Bay. Two hundred is the number given by Lieutenant-Colonel V. Sheliha, C. S. Army, Chief of the Engineer Department. ". . . Forty-six torpedoes of General Rains' pattern have been placed in the main ship channel between Fort Morgan and the west bank," he reported. "We have now one hundred thirty-four torpedoes of Singer's make and forty-six of Brigadier-General Rains', three rows and in echelon, placed in the channel."[20] According to Colonel A. J. Myer, U. S. Army, the torpedoes extended from the end of the piles at the edge of the main channel four hundred yards to a small "black buoy" about half a mile from Fort Morgan, and were arranged "in three lines and in quincunx order."[21] He does not, however, give even their approximate number.

3

Convinced that Buchanan could not raise the blockade and that the state of alarm had been caused by the circulation of false rumors, Farragut departed, after his reconnaissance of the forts, for New Orleans to inspect the repairs being made on the *Lackawanna* and seven gunboats.[22] In mid afternoon of the 22nd of January, the *Hartford* anchored again off the Crescent City, as Bell hauled down his broad pennant from the *Pensacola* and saluted with fifteen guns.[23]

"Here we are once more, my dear boy, at this place," Farragut wrote his son; "but oh, how changed! Masked balls are the order of the day. They must be having a fine time, but the 'ram fever' still exists."[24] "Dancing Master" Banks was meeting with more success in his campaign in New Orleans than in his military operations in the field. His plan was to amuse the lighthearted Creoles and thereby make them more sympathetic to the Union cause.[25] Captain Drayton thought that "the taking of Galveston and Mobile" would make "a stronger diversion in our favor than all the opera singers and balls that could be supplied in the next ten years."[25]

Farragut found himself caught in the whirl of New Orleans society. His barge, "the last new thing in steam tugs" which had been made from the launch of the *Mississippi*, was often to be seen whisking him from the *Hartford* to the city with "the utmost rapidity," reported Drayton.[26] On the Monday evening following his return there was a "promenade concert" sponsored by General Banks and his staff. But Drayton noted that the only ladies belonging to "la crème" of New Orleans society who were present were Mrs. Norman Jackson and a young lady friend. The following day Farragut and Drayton dined with Mrs. Jackson, whom Drayton thought "very pretty and just sesech enough to be amusing."[25] The next Friday the Admiral dined with a Mrs. Wright, a Northern lady.

On the evening of February 2, Farragut went to a grand ball given by the Plumlys at the St. Charles Hotel, accompanied by Drayton, Palmer, Watson, and Brownell. The ball room, decorated with flags, seemed to Farragut "equal to the East Room at the President's House."[27] He explained to Mrs. Farragut that he danced only three dances, with Mrs. Banks, Mrs. Wright, and Mrs. Plumly, and "then warmed up with the Spanish country dance with Mrs. Wright again," whom he "found looking on, a little afraid to undertake it."[27] Farragut praised Mrs. Banks because she made herself agreeable to every one. "The General is as fond of fun as I am," he added. "I think we were the amusement of all beholders in the Spanish dance—he enjoyed it as much as I did."[27] Farragut had such a good time that he did not return on board at eleven with Palmer and Drayton, who declared he was too young for them; but stayed on until half past one. "I stayed late to accommodate Watson who wished to attend to his young ladies at supper," he wrote apologetically to Mrs. Farragut.[27]

His son Loyall inherited his father's love of dancing, and was appointed manager of the dances at West Point for the summer of 1864. "Only do not neglect your studies and I don't care how much you dance," wrote Farragut. "I was always fond of it, and I think it a most innocent amusement and one that always takes you into the best society, teaches you ease of manner and grace of person." Then he described to his son the recent dance he had attended in New Orleans. "You ought to have seen General Banks and myself leading off a Spanish Country Dance.... There was a California girl there who went it with the real Spanish swing. I had a time of it at New Orleans, and more to my liking they did not require me to make speeches, and as to talking and dancing you know I am at home. They tried to get me at the schools but I had not the time."[28]

Being a Southern woman, Mrs. Farragut would not have enjoyed the social life of New Orleans at that time. Before the capture of the city, she seems to have considered joining her husband in the Gulf, as Mrs. Butler did the General; but he advised her to postpone coming until she knew the result of "an important event" which was soon to occur—the attack on Forts Jackson and St. Philip.[29] Afterwards, circumstances led her to resign herself to separation from him. While he was enjoying himself in New Orleans, she was having a very sad experience in Norfolk. Her brother-in-law, Frank Zantzinger, had gotten into serious difficulty. He had been accused of smuggling seventy-five barrels of liquor into the city, under the guise of "goods of military necessity," of falsely invoicing goods and suborning his clerks to swear falsely, and of bribing a revenue officer.[30] Mrs. Farragut wrote to General Butler, who was then in command of that district, on behalf of her brother-in-law; but he replied coldly in a matter of fact letter.[31] Zantzinger, and his associate, Daniels, were found guilty and ordered to be "confined at hard labor on bread and water in the exterior trenches at Bermuda Hundreds, and wherever the army may elsewhere be building fortifications and digging rifle pits, during the campaign and until further orders."[32]

Farragut was finding his relatives a problem also. His sister, Mrs. Gurlie, wrote from Pascagoula, suggesting that she pay him a visit and informing him that his nephew Glasgow was ill in Pascagoula and that the other nephew, William, was in the Confederate army. She wished to come to New Orleans, but he had to write that he was soon leaving and would not be able to help her.[33] His sister replied that she would stay where she was but begged him not to let the Negroes come over to Pascagoula. "I promised her that I would not," he wrote Loyall.[34]

There were other matters than social and family obligations to claim Farragut's time and attention. He redeemed his pledge to Mrs. Bell by arranging for her husband to go home on furlough. On the 27th of January Bell turned over the command of the *Pensacola* to Captain James S. Palmer, who became Farragut's first divisional officer of the West Gulf Blockading Squadron as well as commander of the naval station at New Orleans.[35] This meant the parting of the ways for Farragut and Bell, who had been his constant stalwart supporter since the *Hartford* set forth from Philadelphia on the New Orleans campaign. Like Farragut, Bell was born in a Southern state and married a daughter of Virginia, and he was thus forced to make the same decision at the outbreak of the war. His native state was North Carolina; Farragut's was Tennessee. Twelve of Farragut's twenty-two ship commanders in the campaign against New Orleans were born in slave-holding states.[36] After Bell went home, he was never again to be associated with Farragut in naval service. In 1865 he became the commander of the East India Squadron and met his death by accidental drowning in Japanese waters.

Captain Palmer was pleased with his new command, as he had many friends and acquaintances in New Orleans.[37] Drayton had taken over Palmer's duties as fleet captain, and on February 9 he became also captain of the *Hartford*.[38] "Drayton is my Captain," Farragut wrote his son, "and we live like Father and Son—we are all very happy."[39] Farragut had to look over a great mass of reports, applications, orders, and requests, which constantly poured in from the sixty odd vessels of his squadron, and also answer them and write his reports to the Navy Department. In this he was greatly assisted by Drayton who energetically introduced system and order where there had been hitherto little or none.[40] Farragut besides was beginning to pay the penalty of popularity—letters from admirers. "About half of Farragut's letters are for autographs," Drayton complained, "and what is I think a little impudent Cartes de Visite, the latter being an article which costs money and can be bought currently."[41] Later Drayton wrote of these applications for the Admiral's photograph, "Like a prudent man he keeps none of the latter on hand."[42]

Farragut kept his eye particularly on the blockade of the Texas coast, while waiting for the completion of the repairs to his ships and for reinforcements, and watched developments also in Mobile Bay. He was in great need of light draft vessels. The four which had been purchased for him in New York had not arrived, and the four which Porter had at last sent down had to be coppered before being used in the salt water of the Gulf "where the worm bites worse than anywhere in the world," Farragut declared.[43] After about two weeks in New Orleans, he returned to his headquarters at Pensacola to be within easy reach of the blockade off Mobile Bay.

4

Before leaving New Orleans, Farragut learned from General Banks of Sherman's campaign against Atlanta, which was just getting under way. Having neither sufficient naval force nor any available aid from Banks, he decided that he could assist Sherman by pretending an attempt to force an entrance into Mobile Bay.[44] This he thought would keep large forces at Mobile for its defense, which otherwise might join General Johnston's army in fighting Sherman. Accordingly, on the 13th of February he had his six mortars towed to the west of Dauphin Island to attack Fort Powell on Shell Island. The mortars were supported by the *Octorara* and three other gunboats. Fort Powell defended Grant's Pass, which was a channel for light draft vessels between Dauphin Island and Cedar Point.[45] This fort was armed with six or seven rifled guns.[45]

The threatened attack had the desired effect for General Dabney H. Maury immediately wrote very pessimistically to Secretary of War Seddon that he feared Fort Powell could not long resist and that the passage between Forts Morgan and Gaines was "very liable to be forced." His effective force for manning all the forts and defending the city was 10,000 men, and he begged 6,000 or 7,000 additional troops immediately.[46]

Farragut was then quite unwell. A ride on horseback with Drayton and the picturesque refugee Hungarian, General Asboth, at Pensacola had been too much for him. "Although a most active man for his age, that age is over sixty," Drayton explained, "and as he will drink wine he has to be a little careful."[47] The weather had been remarkably good since Farragut's return to the Gulf—warm and quite clear.[48] But about the time the attack on Fort Powell was to begin, the weather changed; it became very hazy for a few days and then a cold norther blew for three days, which held up the attack.[49] By that time General Maury had concluded that the operations were "a feint to detain troops" at Mobile, but he still feared Farragut would endeavor to force his way through Grant's Pass and occupy the lower bay.[50]

In spite of his rheumatism or gout, Farragut went in the *Hartford* over to Ship Island on the 18th, where he waited for the storm to blow itself out.[51] Then he and Drayton boarded the little side-wheeler gunboat *Calhoun* and on February 22 proceeded to inspect the bombardment of Fort Powell.[52] There they found the mortars hammering away at the fort, but at too great a range to do much damage. The water was so shallow that none of the vessels could get nearer than 4,000 yards, and even then they were "at least a foot in the mud."[53] Though the *Calhoun* drew only eight and a half feet, she went aground and stuck so fast that it took two of the other gunboats to get her off again. After a week of these ineffective operations, ammunition began to run low. The weather became thick with a strong north wind which threatened to "blow the water out of the Sound"[54] and leave the mortars all aground. So Farragut had them pulled out into deeper water, and returned to Ship Island for more ammunition. On the 29th, the extra day of that leap year, he returned to continue the sham attack, convinced that there was no hope of reducing the fort with the forces then available.[54]

Farragut had very definite information that Buchanan was still attempting to get the *Tennessee* over the Dog River Bar into the bay,[55] and he declared that, if he had 2,000 troops to attack Fort Gaines in the rear, he would run into the bay with the meager forces he then had. Not even the *Brooklyn* had arrived from New York. With one ironclad he thought he could go up the bay and destroy the *Tennessee*, lying helpless on the bar;[56] but Porter had written that his ironclads would not be ready before March or April,[57] and Dahlgren was being no more speedy than Du Pont had been in capturing Charleston and releasing monitors for Farragut's use. Much to the Admiral's surprise, about eight o'clock on the morning of March 1, "the *Tennessee* made her appearance coming down the bay." As soon as he was satisfied that it was really the *Tennessee*, he set off in the little *Glasgow* in a gale from the north northwest to join the *Hartford* at Ship Island. When the weather moderated, he hastened to join the blockaders off Fort Morgan to see what Buchanan had up his sleeve.[58]

That ended the attack on Grant's Pass, from which the mortars were soon withdrawn.[59] The results had been indeed small. In the fort, two men were wounded, and a 7-inch Brooke gun burst after having been fired fifty-five times.[60] The mortars had one man wounded, and on the gunboat *Jackson* one Sawyer rifle cracked and another burst.[61] The score was about even.

5

The unexpected appearance of the *Tennessee* caused Farragut himself to develop a sudden acute case of "Ram Fever." A letter with the bad news was dashed off to Captain Jenkins in command of the eleven gunboats and three larger vessels off Mobile Bay, informing him that the *Hartford* was coming to his assistance.[59] Another letter went to General Asboth at Pensacola, warning him of the possibility of a night attack on that place, "as they have two or three of these vessels." "I am also expecting ironclads from the North, but God knows when they will arrive," Farragut added pessimistically.[62] The next day he wrote his son about seeing the long ram which moved very slowly. "If good for anything, she ought to be very formidable," he admitted.[63] In a letter to Banks the same day, he wondered hopefully if the *Tennessee* had gone down in the gale which swept the bay, and explained how the problem of Mobile Bay had now become more difficult and why the attack on Fort Morgan would have to be delayed until the ironclads arrived. "But it is a consolation to us to know that it was neither our wish nor fault that Mobile was not taken last year or last month," he concluded with feeling.[64]

The *Hartford* was with the blockaders off Mobile Bay on March 3, where two days later Farragut reported to Fox that it was not known what had happened to the Confederate ram in the storm but that steamers had been seen rushing to her assistance, and all were then seen moving up the bay.[65] The next day he informed Palmer that some were claiming that the *Tennessee* had not yet crossed over the bar, "but I saw a vessel that I do not believe could be anything but the *Tennessee*. . . . A very intelligent man who had worked on her pronounced her to be the *Tennessee* the moment he saw her."[66] But on the 9th, Farragut had to admit to Welles that he had been mistaken. He thought he might have seen the *Huntsville* or the *Tuscaloosa*,[67] but they were quite smaller than the *Tennes-*

see and Farragut declared that the vessel he saw was at least three hundred feet long.[66] Besides there is no record that these vessels were cruising in the bay on that day. It was a strange error. In justice to Farragut, it should be remembered that his eyes were weak.

The *Tennessee* was indeed still above Dog River Bar, for the first attempt to get her across with camels had failed as they raised her only twenty-two inches and four feet was the lowest calculation for clearing the bar. When Farragut thought he saw her in the bay, the Confederates were hard at work on six sectional docks with which to float her.[68] The fear of the *Tennessee* was thus for the time being removed, but there were alarming reports of a torpedo boat having been seen near Fort Morgan, which might come out at night and sink one of the blockaders as had happened to the *Housatonic* off Charleston.[69]

Farragut continued his watchful waiting at Pensacola, on the whole, a monotonous experience. Out of the ordinary, however, was the Hungarian refugee and old companion of Kossuth, General Alexander Asboth, in command of the army there. In appearance he resembled Don Quixote. A great admirer of horses and dogs, he always had about him half a dozen or more of the largest specimens of the latter he could find. When Farragut and Drayton dined with him, the first course was chocolate soup, just ordinary chocolate ladled out of a tureen like soup. "I have seen a good many strange customs," commented Drayton, "but both the admiral and self agreed that this was beyond both of our experiences."[69]

There were the miscellaneous affairs of the blockade to keep Farragut and his staff occupied. The problem of supplies remained an ever present one, particularly food. The health of the crews constantly suffered from the lack of fresh provisions. "They do not receive one quarter of the vegetables necessary for health, and have only had fresh beef sixteen days in six months," Farragut complained to the Chief of the Bureau of Provisions and Clothing.[70] He was continuously begging for more potatoes for his men.[71] Blockade runners now and then were captured, particularly off Sabine Pass and Galveston where a dozen or so were taken in February and March.[72] The blockade of Mobile was so tight that few vessels were able to run through the main channel.[73] But some small schooners continued to slip through the shallow waters of Pelican Pass below Dauphin Island.[74]

6

Farragut, having recovered from his rheumatism, or "horseback ride," as Drayton facetiously called his illness,[75] became very restive because of inactivity. "Doing nothing has made me so fat that my clothes are all getting too small for me," he wrote his son.[76] For weeks he had been wanting to make an inspection of the blockade of the coast of Texas down as far as the mouth of the Rio Grande.[77] But fear that the *Tennessee* might make a sortie had kept him at Pensacola within reach of the blockaders off Mobile Bay. At last, he decided he could with safety leave for awhile, and on April 2 he and his staff were transferred to the U.S.S. *Tennessee* which immediately sailed for New Orleans.[78] The vessel was a large side-wheel passenger steamer, formerly a Confederate blockade runner, which had large comfortable staterooms for both Farragut and Drayton and was "as steady in rough weather as a church," the latter declared.[79] She arrived in New Orleans a day ahead of a howling gale which would have put her seaworthiness to a severe test.

During the gale, while the rain was falling in torrents with flashes of lightning and heavy peals of thunder, Farragut wrote his wife that he was thankful to be in port and not out at sea, though his cabin was "all afloat with rain running down from the heretofore undiscovered leaks." "I am here in this city of attraction—at least for our young officers," he announced. "It is the most difficult thing in the world to keep them away from it, and, when they once get here, to get them away again. I confess blockading is a most disagreeable business; but, if we had nothing but agreeable things to do in war, everybody would be in the Navy, and on one would be worthy of reward or promotion. This is a state of civil war, and God has dealt with us most generously thus far. My duty is arduous mentally only." "I suppose you saw the notice of me as 'Jack the Giant-Killer,' declaring that, when I had taken Mobile, they would give me a suitable force to take Charleston, and then run me for President of the United States!" he continued. "As if a man who had toiled up the ladder of life for fifty-two years, and reached to top round of his profession, did not need a little rest. My own opinion is, that, if I survived those two engagements, there is little doubt that a presidential campaign would finish me. No, after I have finished my work, I hope to be allowed to spend the remainder of my days in peace and quiet with my family on the banks of the Hudson. It is for man to plan, and God to rule, and I am perfectly submissive to His will, but hope He will grant my prayer. I expected from the beginning to fight to the end of this war, or to my end, and I am still ready and willing to do so if my health will permit."[80]

"This city, although not so gay as when Banks and the army were present, is still much of a vanity fair," wrote the rather austere Drayton, "and the admiral, who I think at least enjoys its life and dissipations as much as any one, never tires of abusing it for the demoralization it produces on the fleet. As for him, I can't keep him on board in the evening and he takes me to many places I would be very glad to keep out of. We went last evening to a party at Mrs. Banks', where there were plenty of nice people, but few if any Creoles among them. She is beautifully lodged in what the natives call a stolen house, but worth committing a slight sin to obtain, and surrounded as it is now with orange blossoms and all kinds of sweet smelling plants, is the perfection of Southern elegance and comfort."[79]

The next evening Farragut dined with a Mr. Goodman. Of this he wrote Mrs. Farragut, "I am up early this morning in consequence of dining out yesterday and drinking champagne, and so I seize the moment to drop you a line by the Mail Steamer for I have not had a moment before to write—in fact I am worked to death here. . . . I am very well—weigh 150, at least 20 lbs. more than my ordinary weight."[81]

Since the first of March, General Banks had been engaged

in another expedition in the region of the Red River, aided by a large naval force under Porter. It was planned to capture Shreveport. On the day after Drayton and Farragut had dined so pleasantly with Mrs. Banks, the advance force constituting about half of her husband's army of 40,000 men was defeated by 9,000 men under General Richard Taylor, son of old "Rough and Ready" Zachary Taylor, and the next day the whole Union army was forced to retreat by Generals Taylor and Kirby Smith with a combined force of about 20,000 men. In retiring down the river, Porter's large squadron was caught by the falling water above the shoals near Alexandria, where it was held for over a month in desperate danger of destruction by the Confederates, until it was released by an ingenious system of dams constructed by an army engineer. This was the second time Porter owed his salvation to the Army.[82] Of Porter's peril, Farragut wrote Banks, "I am deeply pained at the sad result. We can illy afford the loss of one ironclad at this time, when the Rebels appear to be redoubling their exertions at every point. I hope Porter will not be compelled to lose his vessels."[83] To Porter he wrote reassuringly, "Never mind. You'll come out all right yet. Fortune is an uncertain wench, but she generally sticks to those who fight it out with her. She loves perseverance and courage and they will accomplish much even against her *will*, but although things look well for the Rebels just now and from that very cause, that they are devoting soul and body to the war. We have been doing everything else. But my hope is in God and that he will yet put the right man in the right place. I trust it is Grant—that must be the great battle whenever it comes and they appear to be preparing to fight it soon. I wrote to Palmer to send you all the tin clads. They are the only boats we have that can operate in the Red River."[84]

The news of disaster on the Red River was slow in reaching New Orleans, and the tableaux, sponsored by Mrs. Banks, were presented as scheduled the following Tuesday evening at the Opera House for the Louisiana Soldiers Benefit. In the tableau, entitled "Spirit of 1866," Mrs. Banks was the Goddess of Liberty surrounded by the States.[85] In this entertainment, the General's wife had as a co-sponsor "a Mrs. ――― of New York, rather a highflyer, although not of the crème at home," according to Drayton. "She is, however, a nice person," he continued, "and as her husband is said to be quite rich, no one can understand her intention of spending the summer here, notwithstanding the possession of one of the finest houses in the city, for the time being. The ready answer of the residents or of those above suspicion, however, in all such cases is, that they are after cotton, or, as it is expressed, belong to the cotton stealing association, most of the bags seized being marked C.S.A. It seems that it was generally thought that this late expedition up the Red River was to have yielded largely in the staple, but unfortunately Banks, occupied with the political organization of this state, delayed his departure so much that Porter got ahead, and it is said has cleared out every available bale."[86]

The day following the tableaux, Farragut and Drayton dined with Mr. Wright, owner of the Horse Fair. "Coming on top of a good deal of indiscriminate eating and drinking," this dinner "rather used the Admiral up, which I did not much wonder at, when reminded by him of what he had eaten, for among the articles were the following ones all served as courses and with the highest seasoned sauces, shrimp soup, lobster salad, soft shell crabs, shrimps, ice cream, and strawberries," declared Drayton.[87]

After ten days spent in inspecting the repairs being made on eleven of his vessels at New Orleans,[88] Farragut departed in the *Tennessee* for the coast of Texas. Everything was found in good condition there except the ships' engines. Some of the vessels had not been in port for six months, and when steam was kept up month after month with no opportunity to clean the boilers and make necessary repairs they could not be kept in condition. Though Farragut had seventy-five or eighty vessels in his squadron, fully one fourth were constantly undergoing repairs. It was a difficult trying service for the ships as well as for the men who manned them. Captain Marchand, in command off Galveston, had kept the *Harriet Lane* closely watched, and she had not been able to break out. During the month of

April seven blockade runners had been captured; but the light draft sailing vessels continued to dodge in and out of the numerous inlets along the coast.[89]

After a week's cruise, Farragut returned to New Orleans. By coincidence he was in the city on the second anniversary of the successful operations which led to its capture, and he celebrated the event by writing, on April 24, a very revealing letter to his son. "This night two years ago was the anxious night of my life, when I felt as if the fate of my country, and my own life and reputation were all on the wheel of fortune, to be turned by the finger of the All-Wise," he confided. "It was only left to do or die," he continued. "God was my leader, and we passed through a fiery furnace where none but He could have carried us. It is the second anniversary of the passage of Forts Jackson and St. Philip, and, being Sunday, it seemed a fit occasion for going to church and offering up our prayers and thanks to the Dispenser of all things for His blessings and mercies during the last two years."[90]

Gloom had settled over New Orleans since Farragut's recent departure. The news of Banks's "Bull Run" had arrived with reports of the loss of three or four thousand killed, wounded, and missing and the capture of the whole wagon train and twenty guns, the best in his army. "When you get a command," Farragut admonished his son, "don't put your baggage in the way so that you can not get your troops or guns out except by stampeding." "I write flat on my back," he concluded personally. "I am just getting over a boil that would humble the greatest hero that ever fought a ram."[90]

7

In the late afternoon of April 26, Farragut arrived at Pensacola, and hoisted again his flag on the *Hartford*.[91] Admiral Buchanan did not know that he had been away for three weeks. But it would have made little difference if he had known, for he had the misfortune of having two of the sectional docks destroyed accidentally by fire and his workmen were busy replacing them when Farragut returned.[92]

But there were other worries for Farragut. So great were the profits to be made from cotton which could be gotten through the Confederate lines that all sorts of fantastic schemes were devised for that purpose. One man offered to Farragut to run out of Mobile Bay both of the gunboats *Morgan* and *Gaines*, loaded with cotton, Farragut to have the gunboats and he the possession of the cotton. A similar proposition was made by another with respect to the *Harriet Lane* in Galveston.[93] Farragut instructed Captain Marchand to attempt to get the *Harriet Lane* out in this way;[94] but on the night of April 30 this vessel and three or four other steamers ran through the blockade and escaped to Havana, loaded with cotton to be exchanged for munitions.[95] This revealed that the offer to Farragut was fraudulent,[96] and also showed the inefficiency of the blockade off that port.[97]

Farragut also had to remove Captain W. W. Walker from the command of the *Ossipee*. While commanding the blockade off Mobile Bay, Walker had assumed the authority to send vessels of the squadron with their prizes to Key West and had issued orders contradictory to those of Farragut. Only two small gunboats, on one occasion, had thus been left on the blockade, where they were exposed to the hazard of being destroyed by the enemy.[98]

Shortly before Walker was ordered home,[99] Acting Ensign Charles E. Clark was sent to the *Hartford* with a requisition for some articles. When he entered Farragut's cabin, Drayton and Lieutenant Watson began to question him. He was so absorbed in gazing with admiration and affection at Farragut's "strong yet kindly face" that he found it difficult to answer their questions rationally. Suddenly, Farragut, who was seated at his desk, glanced at young Clark and exclaimed, "Brass plate, eh? What's that for?" "To cover the socket of the after 11-inch pivot, sir," he replied with pleasure at being spoken to by the Admiral. "There's nothing in the Ordnance Manual providing for that," Farragut explained. "No, sir, but you see, on board the *Ossipee*—." "What?" inquired Farragut, "so that's where you come from, is it? There's a great deal too much brass already on board that *Ossipee*, young man!" He waved his hand as if to clear the young officer out of his cabin. With the persistence and indiscretion of youth, Clark continued, "But, Admiral, you see, Captain Walker—." That finished the interview. The young ensign hastened toward the companionway in fear that his ears were going to be cut off. "This was the only marked attention I ever received from the great Admiral," related Clark, who afterwards himself became a rear admiral. "I once heard a speaker at a banquet in Philadelphia refer to me as one of Farragut's eaglets, and was inwardly amused as I reflected that I might at least lay claim to having been pushed from the nest of the parent bird."[100]

Fearing that the *Tennessee* might soon get over the bar into the bay, Farragut wrote Mr. Welles a long letter on May 2, explaining the situation and begging him to order the Eads ironclads on the Mississippi to his squadron. "If I saw any great importance that these vessels would be to Admiral Porter, I would not ask for them," he wrote, "but I do not, nor do I see the least hope of my getting any from the North, as each of the admirals commanding the Atlantic squadrons have never yet thought they had force enough."[101] If Porter had lost his ten ironclads on the Red River, as then appeared likely, he would have been unable to send Farragut any assistance. Fortunately the dam successfully released his flotilla between the 9th and the 12th of May from its perilous position above the Alexandria rapids.[102] The Eads double turreted monitors, however, were not ready when Porter went up the Red River, and accordingly were still at Cairo.

Then came news of another disaster on the coast of Texas, where on May 6 the side-wheelers *Granite City* and *Wave* together with a boat and its crew from the steamer *New London* were captured near the Sabine River. Lying without steam and with no precautions against attack, they were overpowered by about three hundred Confederate infantrymen and four pieces of artillery. "It is very mortifying to see my vessels behave so badly, but I have none else but these volunteer officers to send in them," Farragut commented sadly.[103]

On that same day, by contrast, Lee was winning his first round with Grant in the battle of Chancellorsville. Farragut did not know this, but Buchanan with his telegraph connections learned of it almost immediately and was greatly encouraged. "I feel confident he [Lee] will succeed in Virginia," he wrote. "Johnston will soon be engaged. All are sanguine of his success also." He was likewise optimistic of early success in getting the *Tennessee* over the bar; the camels, as he called them, were finished and were being placed under the ironclad.[104] Thus the tides of victory ebbed and flowed, as the spirits of the people, North and South, rose and fell.

Farragut learned, on May 2, that his sister, Mrs. Gurlie, was at Biloxi and wished to come over to Ship Island. He gave directions that she was to be taken good care of and sent to him at Pensacola. From there he would send her to New Orleans. "I wish she would remain at Pascagoula," Farragut wrote his wife, "for I know she is only coming to beg for those nieces and nephews of hers who are eating her out of house and home. My life is now one of anxiety and I can not leave here to go and see her."[105] This sister had given him a Holy Virgin which had been blessed by the archbishop who told her he was good to the priests. This pleased him very much for he had been accused of robbing the church at Point Coupée. The Holy Virgin was like one which was given Farragut by Rose Hughes, an ardent Roman Catholic and devoted maid in the Farragut family for many years.[106] Mrs. Gurlie did not make the visit, and there is no record that she ever saw her brother again. Farragut's attitude toward his sister does not quite accord with his feelings, when he wrote Mrs. Farragut shortly after the capture of New Orleans, "It is a strange thought that I am here among my relatives, and yet not one has dared to say 'I am happy to see you.' "[107]

XX

THE *TENNESSEE* ENTERS THE BAY

1

FARRAGUT was fully informed of the progress being made in getting the *Tennessee* into the bay. As to going to the assistance of Porter on the Red River, he wrote Welles, "I cannot leave here, as I am hourly expecting the rebel ram *Tennessee* out of Mobile Bay."[1] Three days afterwards he wrote a long letter to the Secretary, explaining the danger of his situation when the *Tennessee* got across the bar. He felt that public opinion in the South after the recent success of the ironclad *Albemarle* in North Carolina waters and the disastrous campaign of Banks and Porter would practically force Buchanan to take the offensive with his four ironclads and three wooden gunboats. He thought the *Nashville* was finished with the exception of the plating, and described the armor and armament of the other ironclads, under the impression that the *Tuscaloosa* and *Huntsville* were also completed. "Thus you perceive," he pointed out, "that I am in hourly expectation of being attacked by almost an equal number of vessels, ironclads against wooden vessels, and a most unequal contest it will be, as the *Tennessee* is represented as impervious to all their experiments at Mobile, so that our only hope is to run her down, which we shall certainly do all in our power to accomplish; but should we be unsuccessful, the panic in this part of the country will be beyond all control. They will imagine that New Orleans and Pensacola must fall." New Orleans he thought well defended, as Forts Jackson and St. Philip each had two XV-inch guns, but he felt that Pensacola would be in danger of capture. "I fully understand and appreciate my situation," he declared. "The experience I had of the fight between the *Arkansas* and Admiral Davis's vessels on the Mississippi showed plainly how unequal the contest is between ironclads and wooden vessels in loss of life, unless you succeed in destroying the ironclad. I, therefore, deeply regret that the Department has not been able to give us one of the many ironclads that are off Charleston and on the Mississippi." He concluded, "Be assured, sir, that the Navy will do its duty, let the issue come when it may, or I am greatly deceived. I think you have many ready and willing to make any sacrifice their country can require of them. All I ask of them is to do their whole duty; the result belongs to God."[2]

Farragut wrote also to Captain Marchand about the situation, and ordered him to turn over the command of the blockade of the Texas coast to Commander Woolsey and to join him at Pensacola with the *Lackawanna* "so that I can have the use of your ship and your head in a case of great importance."[3] Before receiving Farragut's orders, Marchand had reported to him the recent capture of seven blockade running schooners.[4]

In great depression of spirits, Farragut wrote his son: "The enemy seem to be bending their whole soul and body to the war, and whipping us in every direction. What a disgrace that, with their slender means, they should, after three years, contend with us from one end of the country to the other, after we had taken nearly half of their land! I trust that the telegrams from the North are not correct. The rebels say they have defeated Grant; but I do not believe it, and my opinion is, that if they whip him to-day they will have to repeat it tomorrow." Finishing the letter the next day, he added pessimistically, "While I was writing, my mail schooner arrived from New Orleans, bringing continued bad news—that Grant is hemmed in, and Porter working to get out of Red River. The rebels had a jubilee yesterday at Fort Morgan in honor of the capture of Steele by Price. I expect Porter to save Banks—I am very much afraid the army will be captured. I get right sick every now and then, at the bad news." He then ended on a personal note, "So you are destined, my son, to be satisfied with that old sword which Pinkham gave me. It has been my trusty companion through most of the dangers of my life. I hope you will always value it highly."[5]

Drayton shared in Farragut's pessimism. "They say some ironclads are coming out to us," he wrote; "if they don't soon, and 'Buck' gets out, I doubt if we can, with all our ramming, do him much harm, and if he does us any, I believe the stampede in New Orleans will be such as to risk us the city. Fortune has certainly deserted us, whether through our own fault or her fickleness I don't know, but I think a good deal of the first."[6]

2

On the night of May 17-18, the *Tennessee* was sufficiently raised by the floating docks to clear the bar, and was successfully towed into the bay by two steamers. According to Buchanan's long cherished plan, she was to proceed the same night down the bay and break through the blockade, and then capture Fort Pickens and Pensacola. But much time was consumed in transferring ammunition and coal to the ram, and after she had proceeded a considerable distance and the docks were removed from her, the tide had fallen so much that she was left aground. So her presence was revealed next morning to the blockaders, and the element of surprise was lost.[7] If Buchanan had been accurately informed as to the strength and distribution of the Union naval forces, he might have attemped his plan by daylight. That morning Farragut was at Pensacola with the *Hartford* and four or five gunboats. On the blockade off Mobile Bay were the *Richmond* and eight gunboats, which were not strong enough to stop the *Tennessee* from coming out. The *Monongahela* was still under repairs in New Orleans; the *Brooklyn* was en route from New York, and did not reach Key West until the 22nd of May.[8] Buchanan thus missed his golden opportunity for attempting his plan—an opportunity which was not to return.

Farragut did not learn that the *Tennessee* was in the bay until the evening of the 20th.[9] After making some final arrangements for the defense of Pensacola, he sailed the next day to join his fleet off Fort Morgan.[10] "Well, here we are again, my son, off this disagreeable place, blockading," he wrote Loyall. "One thing appears to be certain, that I can get none of the ironclads. They want them all for Washington. We will trust in God, as we have always done before. You can only know by your own feelings what suspense I must be in, at this distance from the impending battles in Virginia."[11] By next day he had received better news, and wrote, "We ought to pray for the preservation of Grant's life."[12] His courage rose as he was confronted by danger. "Our fellows are beginning to understand that war means fighting," he continued. "It is the duty of an officer to save his men as much as possible; but in almost all cases there has to be a certain amount of sacrifice of life. I have a fine set of vessels here just now, and am anxious for my friend Buchanan to come out."[12] In the afternoon of the 24th, Farragut and his staff went aboard the little gunboat *Metacomet* which steamed close inshore[13] to take a good look at Buchanan's fleet. The *Tennessee*, bearing the blue flag of Admiral Buchanan as well as the Confederate ensign, appeared to be what the refugees and spies had reported. A torpedo fixture on her bow, however, was an unreported detail. Farragut at once decided to add this feature to his vessels as well as "heavy iron cutters" on their bows. He reluctantly used the torpedo. "I have always deemed it unworthy of a chivalrous nation; but it does not do to give your enemy such a decided superiority over you," he declared to Welles.[14] He took this occasion to remind the Secretary of his request for ironclads from the Mississippi, to which there had been no response.[14]

Drayton took a half-humorous attitude toward the *Tennessee* which was expected "to come out on a bender any fine night." "In the meantime, there is one comfort at least should we be the party sunk," he jokingly added, "and that is that down will go at the same time a mass of papers and reports that it is disgusting to look at, and which it would almost be a relief to get rid of even at such a cost."[15]

Besides the *Tennessee*, Farragut and his staff saw at Fort Morgan the *Baltic, Morgan, Gaines,* and *Selma*.[16] Also small boats could be seen industriously laying down torpedoes in the channel.[17]

Day after day went by, night after night; but Buchanan did

not attempt a dash through the blockaders. During this time of anxious waiting, Farragut wrote his wife this characteristic bit of philosophy concerning religion in time of war: ". . . It amuses me to see the effect of religion. Everybody relying upon God, until it comes to fighting—then they rely upon men—even my darling wife. Now you know *Grant cannot* make his men fight if they are not so disposed and all his courage and strategy amount to nothing; remember, my darling, these lines. Victory or success is with God—he must give Grant the Power over his officers and men to fight and himself the gift of foresight into results and the daring to undertake. Now, as I believe God is on our side, I think he will sooner or later give us the proper instrument to carry us through the fiery furnace."[18]

3

Though Farragut was then unaware of it, his affairs were on the point of taking a turn for the better. General Sherman, on the 4th of June, wrote General Canby, in command in West Mississippi, that he wished him to make a strong feint or a real attack on Mobile by way of Pascagoula in connection with Admiral Farragut's fleet.[19] Sherman wrote from Allatoona Creek, well along on his way toward Atlanta, though the bloody battle of Kennesaw Mountain was still before him. Grant had long had in mind an attack on Mobile by land. After the capture of Vicksburg, he had proposed to land an army at Mobile with Farragut's cooperation and from there to advance against Atlanta. But the plan was not approved.[20] Again after the Chattanooga campaign, he asked to be allowed to lead his men south against Mobile.[21] "I had tried for more than two years to have an expedition sent against Mobile when its possession by us would have been of great advantage," he wrote in his memoirs.[22] As it happened, the day after Sherman's letter to Canby, Grant wrote Halleck from Cold Harbor, "The object of sending troops to Mobile now would not be so much to assist General Sherman against Johnston as to secure for him a base of supplies after his work is done. Mobile is also important to us and would be a great loss to the enemy."[23] This interest of the army in Mobile is what Farragut had been hoping for in vain for many months.

About the same time, Welles ordered the monitor *Manhattan* at New York to "proceed with all possible dispatch" to join Farragut,[24] though she did not leave the Capes of the Delaware in tow of the *Bienville* until June 20.[25] Farragut's letter of May 25 regarding the arrival of the *Tennessee* at Fort Morgan had awakened Welles to a realization of the danger. He had been acting as though the Confederate ram could never get over Dog River Bar. He also, finally, wrote to Porter, "It is of the greatest importance that some of the new ironclads building on the Mississippi should be sent without fail to Rear-Admiral Farragut. Are not some of them ready? If not, can you not hurry them forward?"[26]

Suffering from rheumatism and mental anxiety incident to the fruitless and nearly disastrous Red River expedition, Porter answered Welles petulantly, ". . . .The only two iron vessels lately finished are the *Winnebago* and *Chickasaw*. . . . They would break to pieces in the least swell, and they are not fitted to go anywhere but in the smoothest water, such as may be found in rivers. I would not take the responsibility of sending them to Admiral Farragut without express orders to that effect. They are very vulnerable and unfit to cope with anything carrying heavy guns, or to engage fortifications. They are all manned and fitted, though having been sent off in a hurry, will require some few ordnance stores. I doubt if they would ever reach Mobile. . . ."[27] This required another letter from Welles, again ordering the monitors to be sent;[28] and at last on June 30 Porter issued orders for them to proceed down the Mississippi from Mound City to New Orleans.[29] Everything that he stated about the unseaworthiness and weakness of these monitors turned out to be a gross exaggeration. Could his jealousy of Farragut have led him to withhold these reinforcements when they were sorely needed? He had recently made a complete failure. Did he wish to see Farragut meet disaster? In any case, his delay caused a loss of weeks of precious time.

Farragut, ignorant of the orders which eventually were to bring monitors and troops to his assistance, continued the monotonous routine of the blockade which he did not dare to leave. This monotony was broken shortly after daylight on the 6th of June by the capture of the famous blockade runner *Donegal* by the gunboat *Metacomet* under command of James Jouett. She was trying to get into Mobile Bay with munitions of war.[30] So tedious was this constant watching that Farragut was reduced to mentioning in his letters to his wife anything unusual on shipboard; as, a dinner he gave to four of his captains at which was served "a fine turkey" and "a gopher"—not a rodent but a large terrapin of that region.[31] The weather was growing hotter, and quinine was much in demand. Though the ships were lying two miles from the nearest land, the mosquitoes flew out to visit them in swarms.[32] Farragut noticed in the *Scientific American* that steel shot were said to penetrate ironclad armor more easily, and as he had only common cast-iron solid shot to fire at 6-inch armor, he wrote to the Chief of the Bureau of Ordnance to send him steel shot, if he could possibly procure them, and to send them at the earliest possible moment.[33] Hearing of a Confederate plan for capturing one of the blockaders in Mississippi Sound by getting a boat's crew ashore through a flag of truce and then getting them drunk, Farragut wrote a letter of warning. "Mark the moral," he declared, "that our men are such drunkards that they can calculate with almost certainty on it to capture our vessels." He then cited two instances of the loss of ships on the coast of Texas. "In one case the officer says he left the deck for not over ten minutes in charge of the best man he had, the acting boatswain of the *Kineo,* and when he came on deck the whole prize crew were beastly drunk, and the boatswain so crazy that he jumped overboard and was the only man saved from prison. The rest were captured."[34]

Still thinking that Buchanan was only waiting for a dark night and smooth water to make a sortie, Farragut issued a general order on the 14th of June, explaining that in such emergency the *Richmond* and the other vessels to the eastward which composed the right wing were to attack him on the flank and try to prevent him from getting back inside the bar. The larger ships were to keep close together and attempt to override the *Tennessee,* striking her just abaft the casemate and firing at the water line and ports when within a few yards' distance. The *Brooklyn* and the other vessels to the westward were to attack the other flank in the same way. This was to be understood as the plan of attack which would be followed without signals, for they might not be understood in the confusion of a night action.[35]

But Buchanan had given up the idea of trying to come out and attack Farragut's large fleet, then numbering seventeen vessels, which included the *Hartford, Richmond, Monongahela,* and *Brooklyn*.[36] The last arrived only on May 31.[37] Buchanan himself had begun to worry about an attack by Farragut, which he expected would soon be made.[36]

4

Just after noon on June 17, the little side-wheeler dispatch steamer *Glasgow* chugged in from New Orleans with Major-General Canby and his staff on board. Canby, who had superseded Banks after his recent disaster, came to confer with Farragut about operations against Mobile. He was stern of face, and Drayton thought him the most taciturn man he had ever met. Having taken over the command of an army which had become completely demoralized, he may have felt that sternness of mien and taciturnity might get better results than the social graces of "Dancing Master" Banks had obtained. "Banks I at one time had a pretty good opinion of," Drayton declared, "but he proved himself on this last expedition so utterly inefficient and helpless, as to have become a perfect laughing stock to the whole soldiery, and this with his lending himself to Cotton and all other speculators has pretty much finished him with all respectable people in that part of the world. Then he was also giving suppers to fast women and behaving in a most indecorous manner, especially for one of his antecedents and bringing up."[38] Canby, losing no time, returned to New Orleans the next day, and reported to General Halleck that Farragut would cooperate to the extent of his

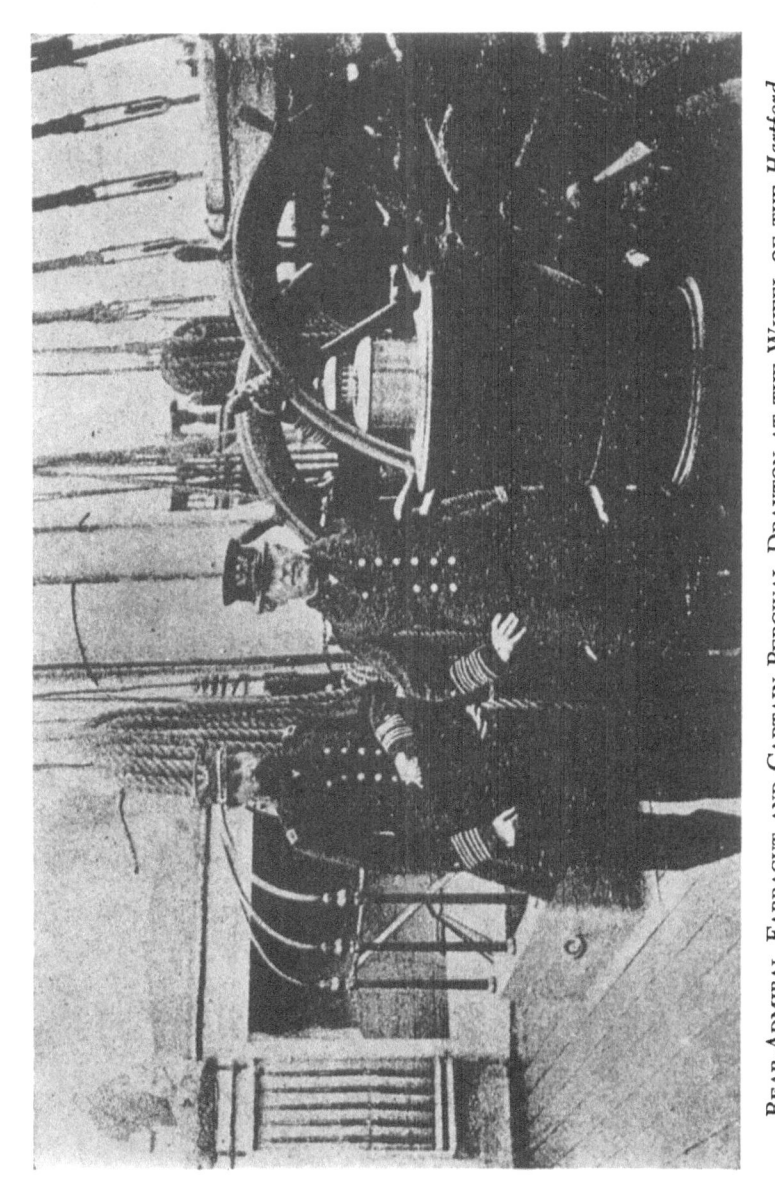

REAR-ADMIRAL FARRAGUT AND CAPTAIN PERCIVAL DRAYTON AT THE WHEEL OF THE *Hartford*
From an old photograph.

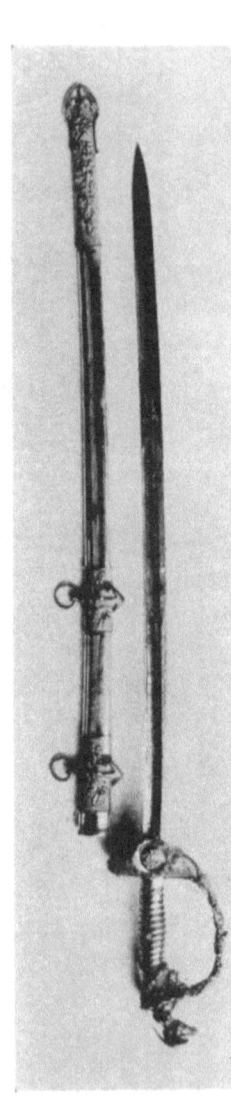

Courtesy of U. S. National Museum

SWORD PRESENTED TO REAR-ADMIRAL D. G. FARRAGUT, U. S. NAVY

"as a token of their appreciation of his gallant services in defense of his country," by members of the Union League Club of New York, April 23, 1864, and later presented to the National Museum.

power, and that he would prepare immediately for a demonstration against Mobile.³⁹

The *Glasgow* also brought a letter from Brigadier-General Bowen, Provost-Marshal-General in New Orleans, informing Farragut that a sword, presented to him by the Union League Club of New York, had arrived. Bowen regretted that the presentation could not be made "on the waters of the Mississippi, and in front of the city you compelled to return to its allegiance."⁴⁰ In the language of the committee, it had been presented "as a slight token of the high esteem in which you are held here by all, and an evidence of our appreciation of the brilliant services you have rendered to our common country."⁴¹ Fearing that the sword might be lost and wishing to deliver it personally to Farragut, Bowen kept it at New Orleans and forwarded only the scroll of presentation. "We have not yet seen it," wrote Drayton, "but it is said to be very handsome."³⁸ It was indeed a beautiful sword with a scabbard of massive silver and gold and a hilt with Farragut's initials set in diamonds.⁴¹ Farragut replied to Bowen that he would have appreciated a public presentation but could not leave the blockade where he was guarding the interests of the country, "and literally watching its enemies, who like hawks are ready to pounce upon us at the first unguarded moment."⁴² To the Committee on Presentation he expressed his full appreciation of the honor the Union League had conferred upon him. "Next to the feeling of having done your duty," he declared, "is that of knowing that your efforts are appreciated by your countrymen."⁴³

Farragut began to grow very tired of waiting for something to happen, and wrote his wife that he wished from the bottom of his heart that Buchanan would come out. "This question has to be settled, iron versus wood," he confessed; "and there never was a better chance to settle the question as to the seagoing qualities of ironclad ships. We are to-day ready to try anything that comes along, be it wood or iron, in reasonable quantities. Anything is preferable to lying on our oars."⁴⁴ He fully realized that he could not go in and attack the *Tennessee*, however, without the assistance of monitors, and he was in despair of ever receiving any of these. So was Drayton, who complained, "This squadron is as much lost sight of as if it belonged to the Danes, and now the best part of the season is passed, and we must soon expect yellow fever and hurricanes."[45] The fever had already broken out in Pensacola, and some cases had been reported in New Orleans.[46] The monitor *Manhattan* was being slowly towed down the Atlantic coast; the *Tecumseh* had not yet started.

The Confederates were even more uncomfortable from the heat and the mosquitoes in the forts and in the confined quarters on board the *Tennessee*. There was a rumor that Farragut was soon to attack by land and sea. General Page, commanding Fort Morgan, was pessimistic and thought he did not have enough soldiers to man his guns. Buchanan, since his failure to surprise Farragut's vessels the night the *Tennessee* first got into the bay, seemed to Page to look "humbled and thoughtful."[47]

A bit of diversion came on the night of June 30, when a blockade runner, attempting to get into Mobile Bay, was run ashore partly under the guns of Fort Morgan. Early the next morning Farragut sent six of his gunboats in to shell the vessel, and during the course of the day all the smaller units of his fleet fired at her without doing great damage as the guns of Fort Morgan kept them at long range. The attack was continued the following day, Farragut boarding the *Glasgow* and going in close to observe the operations.[48] During the next two days the firing continued at the doomed ship, though time was taken out to celebrate Independence Day, all the ships in the fleet firing seventeen guns at midday with flags flying from all the mastheads.[49] The blockade runner was still undestroyed on the 5th, and that evening an expedition of three boats under command of Farragut's flag-lieutenant, J. Crittendon Watson, was sent in to burn the vessel. "Well, as you may suppose," Farragut wrote his son, "it was an anxious night for me; for I am almost as fond of Watson as yourself ,and interested in the others. I thought it was to be a hand-to-hand fight, if any. I sat up till midnight, and then thought they had found the enemy in too great force, and had given it up; so I lay down to rest. About half an hour later the rebel was reported to be on fire, and I was happy, because I had heard no firing and knew the surprise had been perfect. And so it turned out. The rebels scampered off as our fellows climbed on board. The boats returned about 2 o'clock A.M., all safe—no one hurt. I was anxious until their return. But no one knows what my feelings are; I am always calm and quiet."[50] The blockade runner which was thus destroyed was the *Ivanhoe;* but her cargo was all saved by the Confederates.[51]

That 5th of July was Farragut's sixty-third birthday. "He was just about my height and build, though after the summer of 1864 he grew much stouter," wrote Watson. "Up to that year he had on several successive birthdays tested his suppleness by holding with his right hand his left foot by the toe of the left shoe while he hopped through the bight or loop, forwards and backwards. He was a most accomplished fencer and was not averse to testing his skill with the single stick against the most proficient seaman on board. When he spent an evening on shore he always wore his sword, feeling perfectly confident of his ability to protect himself with it from possible attacks in passing through the slums or along the wharves. Farragut was a very religious man. He loved to have me read to him from the Bible. He made it very evident that he always believed the issue was with God, while recognizing that he must do his best."[52]

War-weary, Farragut wrote his wife the day following his birthday, realizing that he was an old man, "Would to God this war was over that I could but spend in peace with you all the few remaining years of my life—but there is no peace for the wicked. I always regretted that you did not let me purchase that house on Sixteenth Street, but when you see one to suit you, purchase and for gracious sake do not deny yourself a horse and carriage. I know it will give you trouble to take care of it. . . . Don't you trouble yourself about the war on my account; I am in the hands of a Merciful Providence."[53]

XXI

THE MONITORS ARRIVE

1

THE NEWS that the monitors were coming reached Major-General Dabney H. Maury in Mobile before Farragut was informed,[1] as Welles delayed until January 25 to write him of the departure of the *Manhattan* and of his orders to Porter to send him the *Winnebago* and *Chickasaw*.[2] So it was with some surprise and great satisfaction that Farragut wrote the Secretary on July 8, "I am most happy to announce the arrival of the U. S. ironclad *Manhattan*, in tow of the *Bienville*, at Pensacola, but needing some repairs, coal, etc. I hope to announce her arrival at this place soon. If she is what she is represented, we are all right."[3]

The same day, Major-Generals Canby and Granger, accompanied by Captain Palmer, arrived from New Orleans for a conference with Farragut,[4] who now became hopeful that he would at last get troops sufficient in number to land in rear of the forts and cut off the enemy's communications.[5] Becoming restless and eager for the arrival of the *Manhattan* off Mobile Bay, he shifted his flag to the *Tennessee* in the late afternoon of the 11th[6] and dispatched Drayton with the *Hartford* to Pensacola, unwilling himself to break his watch on the other *Tennessee*, Buchanan's ram, though she was not likely to come out while the moonlight nights lasted. The day after Drayton's arrival at Pensacola to investigate what was delaying the monitor, when he was looking forward to a quiet night's sleep, to his disgust and horror he was suddenly summoned on board the *Manhattan*, with the news that she was on fire. Fortunately a steamer which had come in that day for ammunition had a steam pump, and with its aid the fire was extinguished before much damage was done. But Drayton did not get back to his

THE MONITORS ARRIVE

ship and the anticipated quiet sleep until midnight.[7] The destruction of this ironclad for which they had hoped and waited so long would have been a heavy blow to their morale.

Believing that the day for action was approaching, Farragut published general orders for his fleet on the 12th of July. These specified in detail the preparations all ships were to make. They began with these magnetic words: "Strip your vessels and prepare for the conflict. Send down all your superfluous spars and rigging. Trice up or remove the whiskers." This last sentence might have also been applied to the many bearded men in the fleet; such as, Drayton, Jenkins, and others. "Put up the splinter nets on the starboard side," he continued, "and barricade the wheel and steersmen with sails and hammocks. Lay chains or sandbags on the deck over the machinery, to resist a plunging fire. Hang the sheet chains over the side, or make any other arrangement for security that your ingenuity may suggest. Land your starboard boats or lower and tow them on the port side, and lower the port boats down to the water's edge. Place a leadsman and the pilot in the port quarter boat, or the one most convenient to the commander." The orders then went on to explain how the attack would be made. "The vessels will run past the forts in couples, lashed side by side, as hereinafter designated. The flagship will lead and steer from Sand Island N. by E. by compass, until abreast of Fort Morgan; then N. by W., and the others, as designated in the drawing, will follow in due order until ordered to anchor; but the bow and quarter line must be preserved to give the chase guns a fair range, and each vessel must be kept astern of the broadside of the next ahead; each vessel will keep a little on the starboard quarter of his next ahead, and when abreast of the fort, will keep directly astern, and as we pass the fort will take the same distance on the port quarter of the next ahead, to enable the stern guns to fire clear of the next vessel astern."

As usual Farragut was leaving nothing to chance; all details were being provided for. "It will be the object of the admiral to get as close to the fort as possible before opening fire," he further explained. "The ships, however, will open fire the moment the enemy opens upon us, with their chase and other guns, as fast as they can be brought to bear. Use short fuzes for the shell and shrapnel, and as soon as within 300 or 400 yards give them grape. It is understood that heretofore we have fired too high, but with grapeshot it is necessary to elevate a little above the object, as grape will dribble from the muzzle of the gun." He provided for ill fortune also. "If one or more of the vessels be disabled, their partners must carry them through, if possible; but if they can not, then the next astern must render the required assistance; but as the admiral contemplates moving with the flood tide, it will only require sufficient power to keep the crippled vessels in the channel." Then came a last bit of advice about the guns. "Vessels that can must place guns upon the poop and topgallant forecastle and in the tops on the starboard side. Should the enemy fire grape, they will remove the men from the topgallant forecastle and poop to the guns below until out of grape range. The howitzers must keep up a constant fire from the time they can reach with shrapnel until out of its range."[8]

Nothing was stated as to how or where the monitor *Manhattan* was to be used. Farragut had not seen that vessel nor had a conference with her commander. By that time he knew also that the *Chickasaw* and *Winnebago* had arrived at New Orleans and would soon be ready to join him.[9] Before any of them arrived, however, he had decided how he would use them. "I propose to go in according to programme—14 vessels, two and two, as at Port Hudson," he wrote Captain Palmer in New Orleans on July 18; "low steam; flood tide in the morning, with a light southwest wind; ironclads on the eastern side, to attack the *Tennessee*, and gunboats to attack rebel gunboats as soon as past the forts. Ships run up into deep water, seven vessels outside to assist the Army in landing on the beach and to flank the enemy; five or six in the Sound to assist the Army to land on Dauphin Island. The signal to land will be the signal to form line, third order of steaming, and run in."[10]

Palmer had written, requesting to participate in the approaching battle, but Farragut answered that he thought it would be necessary for him to remain at New Orleans. Commodore Theodorus Bailey, who had commanded the leading gunboats at the attack on Forts Jackson and St. Philip and was then in command of the East Gulf Blockading Squadron, wrote Welles in February asking that Farragut be directed to send for him and a part of his squadron for the attack on Mobile.[11] The request was approved by Welles and forwarded to Farragut.[12] In March, Bailey wrote also to Farragut, "Nothing will please me more than to hoist once more the square red flag and lead the van of your squadron into Mobile Bay, to the capture of forts Morgan and Gaines, as well as the city. Put me down for two chances, as the jackass said to the monkey at the lion's ball. I appreciate your kind invitation to join you when the big fight is to come off, and will be ready with the *San Jacinto* and what gunboats may be in hand at the time you notify me."[13] But in July Farragut wrote him again, "I am all ready so soon as the soldiers arrive to stop up the back door of each fort. I can form no idea when we will make the attack, and will find it difficult to let you know so as not to take you from your station at such an important time."[14] So Bailey did not join Farragut.

Only one of the commanders of ships in the New Orleans campaign was with Farragut at Mobile Bay. He was Captain James Alden. As it turned out, it would have been better if Alden had not been on hand. Of the prominent officers who were closely associated with Farragut several were, like him, of Southern birth; such as, Percival Drayton from South Carolina, Thornton Jenkins from Virginia, James E. Jouett from Kentucky, Henry H. Bell from North Carolina, and Dr. James C. Palmer from Maryland.

2

Farragut's spirits had risen as the battle approached, and he was in a mood to rejoice greatly over Semmes's defeat. "The victory of the *Kearsarge* over the *Alabama* raised me up. I would sooner have fought that fight than any ever fought on the ocean," he exclaimed to his son. "Only think! it was fought like a tournament, in full view of thousands of French and English, with a perfect confidence, on the part of all but the Union people, that we would be whipped. People came from Paris to witness the fight. Why, my poor little good-for-nothing *Hatteras* would have whipped her in fifteen minutes, but for an unlucky shot in her boiler. She struck the *Alabama* two shots for one, while she floated. But the triumph of the *Kearsarge* was grand. Winslow had my old first lieutenant of the *Hartford*, Thornton, in the *Kearsarge*. He is as brave as a lion, and as cool as a parson. I go for Winslow's promotion."[15]

As he saw the summer days slipping by, Farragut wrote General Canby that time was very precious and urged him to bring his force through Mississippi Sound and land it in the rear of Fort Gaines, where it would be completely protected by the gunboats.[16] Though the troops which had been intended by Canby for the attack on Mobile had been sent to the Army of the Potomac, he still had available enough men to cooperate with Farragut.[17] Accordingly, the next day he replied that he would send 2,000 men on seagoing vessels to conceal their destination, and that they would leave in company with the two monitors.[18] Meanwhile the *Manhattan* had joined the fleet, and Farragut reported to Welles that, as soon as the other two monitors and the army forces arrived, he would commence operations.[19] He would not wait for the monitor *Tecumseh*, which he then knew was on the way down the Atlantic coast to join him.[20]

The Confederates also were preparing for the eventful day. Commander Catesby ap R. Jones, in trying to encourage his uncle, General Richard L. Page, down at Fort Morgan, wrote that he thought Farragut's present force, including the monitor, would be beaten off by the guns of Fort Morgan. "Fire slowly and deliberately," he counseled, "taking care not to throw away a shot. Use hot shot and shell against the wooden vessels, aiming always at the water line, and at base of turret with precision." But he was of the opinion that no attack would be made until other monitors arrived.[21] On the morning of the 28th, from the deck of the *Hartford*, the *Tennessee* was observed cruising around in the bay and engaging in target practice.[22]

On the same day the *Tecumseh* arrived at Pensacola with her two towing vessels both crippled en route. Injuries to her own engines had delayed her six days at Port Royal.[23] Commander T. A. M. Craven, brother to Captain T. T. Craven, who commanded the *Brooklyn* in the New Orleans campaign and on the Mississippi, was her commanding officer.

On the 29th of July, Farragut issued General Order No. 11 to answer some questions which had arisen or might arise. "Should any vessel be disabled to such a degree that her consort is unable to keep her in her station, she will drop out of line to the westward and not embarrass the vessels next astern by attempting to regain her station," he explained.[24] "Should she repair damages so as to be able to reenter the line of battle, she will take her station in the rear as close to the last vessel as possible. So soon as the vessels have passed the fort and kept away N.W., they can cast off the gunboats at the discretion of the senior officer of the two vessels, and allow them to proceed up the bay to cut off the enemy's gunboats that may be attempting to escape up to Mobile." Then came this advice about torpedoes, or mines: "There are certain black buoys placed by the enemy from the piles on the west side of the channel across it toward Fort Morgan. It being understood that there are torpedoes and other obstructions between the buoys, the vessels will take care to pass to the eastward of the eastern-most buoy, which is clear of all obstructions. So soon as the vessels arrive opposite the end of the piles, it will be best to stop the propeller of the ship and let her drift the distance past by her headway and the tide, and those having side-wheel gunboats will continue on by the aid of their paddle wheels, which are not likely to foul the enemy's drag ropes."[25] Farragut did not know that the rope obstructions had proved a failure, having been swept away by the current.[26]

Before the issuance of General Order No. 11, Farragut instructed his carpenter to make some little boat-shaped blocks of wood. With these he experimented on a table on which the points of the compass were indicated, to determine the best relative positions for his vessels in entering the bay. "I used to help him maneuver the little blocks so as to concentrate and maintain as heavy a fire as possible upon Fort Morgan when we should be going in, and also, after these General Orders were issued, we played with the blocks preparatory to practicing the ships in keeping close order when under way, at varying speeds," wrote Rear Admiral John C. Watson.[27]

3

August began with "execrable weather" which might have swamped the *Manhattan*, if she had not been anchored in a snug harbor close in to the northward of Sand Island. Just then the double-turreted monitor *Winnebago* arrived from New Orleans at this safe anchorage.[28] The other double-turreted monitor *Chickasaw* fortunately reached the protection of Petit Bois Pass in Mississippi Sound. The *Winnebago* came alone and, though the water was rough, she was not inconvenienced.[29] Porter's doleful prophecy about the unseaworthiness of the vessels was not fulfilled. These double-turreted monitors were armed with four 11-inch guns, two in each turret. They had a length of 257 feet, a beam of 57 feet, and a tonnage of 970. The *Manhattan* and the *Tecumseh* each had two 15-inch guns in a single turret. As compared to the others, they had a tonnage of 1,034, a length of 190 feet, and a beam of 37 feet and 8 inches.[30]

Realizing that he would soon engage in battle, Farragut wrote a letter to his son, in which he declared, "I know Buchanan and Page, who commands the fort, will do all in their power to destroy us, and we will reciprocate the compliment. I hope to give them a fair fight, if I once get inside. I expect nothing from them but that they will try to blow me up if they can."[31] Feeling that this might be a last letter to Loyall, he concluded, "With such a mother, you could not fail to have proper sentiments of religion and virtue. I feel that I have done my duty by you both, as far as the weakness of my nature would allow.

I have been devoted to you both, and, when it pleases God to take me hence. I shall feel that I have done my duty. I am not conscious of ever having wronged any one, and have tried to do as much good as I could. Take care of your mother if I should go, and may God bless and preserve you both."[31]

The evening of August 1, Major-General Gordon Granger dined with Farragut on the *Hartford*. The somewhat bald, black-bearded general was very soldierly in his bearing. He and Farragut got along well together, and their plans for cooperation were perfected that evening.[32] The transports with the troops arrived the next day. There were 2,400 men, including two light and two heavy batteries, a battalion of engineers, and 1,500 infantry.[33] The *Chickasaw* also arrived that day, and joined the other monitors[34] in their secure harbor where Farragut immediately visited them.[32]

Two days later, a detachment of signal officers under command of Major Frank W. Marston was distributed among the larger vessels of the fleet to communicate with Granger's forces after the fleet had entered the bay. Lieutenant John C. Kinney with eight men was assigned to the *Hartford*.[35] That day all of Farragut's captains came on board for a last conference before the attack, which he had planned to make the following day.[36] There was some doubt of this, however, on account of the failure of the *Tecumseh* to arrive from Pensacola. She was then two days behind schedule. and Jenkins in the *Richmond* and Jouett in the *Metacomet* had been sent over to hurry her along.

Jenkins received four letters from Farragut and Drayton, on August 2 and 3, urging the utmost haste. She did not arrive, and Farragut postponed the attack one day, much against his will for the weather had been quite favorable for two or three days and he could not expect a kind fortune to smile upon him indefinitely. "Every day is an irretrievable loss," he complained. "The soldiers, by agreement, are landing to-day back of Dauphin Island, and could I have gone in this morning, we would have taken them by surprise. Four deserters came off from Gaines last night, and they say they do not expect any landing there; but they are working like beavers on Morgan. I have consented

Diagram to supersede the previous one

Brooklyn and Octorara	00 0	Tecumseh
Hartford & Metacomet	00 0	Manhattan
Richmond and Port Royal	00 0	Winnebago
Lackawanna & Seminole	00 0	Chickasaw
Monongahela & Kennebec	00	
Ossipee and Itasca	00	
Oneida and Galena	00	

Flag Ship Hartford, Aug 4. 1864
The above diagram will be observed in forming line of Battle tomorrow morning or whenever this Fleet goes in

D. G. Farragut
Rear Admiral

Courtesy of Manuscript Division, Library of Congress

FORMATION OF FARRAGUT'S FLEET, BATTLE OF MOBILE BAY
From the original diagram in the Library of Congress.

THE MONITORS ARRIVE

to let Alden go ahead, as he has four chase guns and a cowcatcher or torpedo catcher. I send the *Bienville* to tow the *Tecumseh*. Send out the *Metacomet* and come out yourself to-morrow morning. I can lose no more days. I must go in day after to-morrow morning at daylight or a little after. It is a bad time, but when you do not take fortune at her offer, you must take her as you can find her. I have had the wind just right, and I expect it will change by the time I can go in."[37]

Farragut, on the following day, issued some special instructions on the use of the ironclads. "As the monitors are slower than the wooden vessels," he wrote, "I desire that as soon as a signal is made from this vessel in the morning, or if a signal cannot be seen, you perceive any movement which shows that the fleet is about moving, you will get under way and proceed toward the fort, endeavoring to keep at about a mile distance until we are coming up and begin to fire, when you can move nearer, so as to make it certain that when abreast of the fort we have our ironclads as an offset to those of the enemy, which otherwise might run us down. The service that I look for from the ironclads is, first, to neutralize as much as possible the fire of the guns which rake our approach; next to look out for the ironclads when we are abreast of the forts; and, lastly, to occupy the attention of those batteries which would rake us while running up the bay. After the wooden vessels have passed the fort, the *Winnebago* and *Chickasaw* will follow them. The commanding officers of the *Tecumseh* and *Manhattan* will endeavor to destroy the *Tennessee*, exercising their own judgment as to the time they shall remain behind for that purpose."[38]

Also on this last day of preparation, a final diagram was issued, which showed in detail how the line of battle would be formed the following morning.[39] At four thirty on that afternoon, a sail was reported from the masthead of the *Oneida*, which turned out to be the *Bienville* laboriously towing the *Tecumseh*, and accompanied by the *Metacomet*. About an hour later the ironclad was at anchor near the *Hartford*.[40] The monitors had, at last, all arrived.

That morning in the privacy of his cabin, Farragut penned

this farewell message to his wife: "My dearest Wife, I write and leave this letter for you. I am going into Mobile Bay in the morning if 'God is my leader' as I hope He is, and in Him I place my trust; if He thinks it is the proper place for me to die, I am ready to submit to His will, in that as all other things. My great mortification is that my vessels, the ironclads, were not ready to have gone in yesterday. The Army landed last night and are in full view of us this morning and the *Tecumseh* has not yet arrived from Pensacola. God bless and preserve you, my darling, and my dear Boy, if anything should happen to me and may His blessings also rest upon your dear Mother and all your sisters and their children. Your devoted and affectionate husband, who never for one moment forgot his love, duty, or fidelity to you, his devoted and best of wives. D. G. Farragut."[41]

XXII

FORCING THE ENTRANCE TO MOBILE BAY

1

IT RAINED hard near sundown on August 4, but by midnight it was clear and hot, with a very light breeze just rippling the surface of the water. Farragut, after so many weeks of anxious watching and waiting, was not well and slept restlessly. About three o'clock he called his faithful Negro steward, John H. Brooks, and sent him to investigate the weather. The Admiral was greatly pleased when he soon returned with the report that, though it was cloudy, the wind was southwest. This was just what he wanted, as it would blow the smoke of battle directly into the eyes of the gunners in Fort Morgan. Friday, the sailor's unlucky day, was bringing good weather; it was an omen of victory. So Farragut said quietly to Brooks, "We will go in, this morning."[1] At about this time, some one on watch on the deck of the *Manhattan* saw a comet flash across the heavens towards the northeast. Another omen of victory.[2]

Soon throughout the fleet were heard the boatswains' shrill pipes and the calls, "All hands!" and "Up all hammocks!" Last preparations for battle, and an early breakfast were quickly finished, as the vessels took their places according to plan, in the following order: *Brooklyn* with the *Octorara* lashed to her port side, *Hartford* paired off similarly with the *Metacomet*, *Richmond* and *Port Royal*, *Lackawanna* and *Seminole*, *Monongahela* and *Kennebec*, *Ossipee* and *Itasca*, and *Oneida* with the *Galena*. The vessels lashed to the three leading ships were sidewheelers, which were less likely to be fouled by obstructions and somewhat less likely to strike submerged torpedoes, or mines.[3] To the starboard, the monitors formed column with the

Tecumseh leading and followed by the *Manhattan, Winnebago,* and *Chickasaw*. Four small gunboats were stationed to the southeast of Fort Morgan; while six other light gunboats invested Fort Powell and blocked Grant's Pass.[4]

Forming column took time and was not completed until about five-thirty. Farragut was then just finishing a cup of coffee with Captain Drayton and Fleet-Surgeon Palmer, and remarked casually, "Well, Drayton, we might as well get under way."[5]

Farragut had agreed to allow Alden in the *Brooklyn* to lead the line "only at the urgent request of the captains and commanding officers."[6] She was the only vessel with four chase guns and "an ingenious arrangement for picking up torpedoes," affixed to the jib boom. Farragut thought that "exposure is one of the penalties of rank in the navy"[6] and, as the battle developed, he greatly regretted he had yielded to the wishes of his officers. In 1856 Alden had assisted Superintendent A. D. Bache in the preparation of the chart of Mobile Bay.[7] Farragut did not refer to this, and it probably had nothing to do with his permitting Alden to take the lead.

By six o'clock the fleet was moving on a northerly course toward the entrance to the bay. Forty minutes later it was daylight, and flags were hoisted from peak, staff, and every masthead. Farragut's blue pennant gracefully floated from the *Hartford's* mizzen.[8] To one of the crew with the artist's appreciative eye the beautiful flags of the advancing fleet presented a scene "worthy of the brush of an Angelo or Raphael."[9]

By six-thirty the two leading monitors were engaged at long range with Fort Morgan. About thirty minutes later the fort opened fire at a range of half a mile on the *Brooklyn,* which replied immediately. Five minutes afterwards the *Hartford* was in action, the starboard 100-pounder Parrott on the topgallant forecastle being the first to fire.[10] The engagement became general as other ships came within effective range.[11] In spite of the favorable wind, Farragut's vision was soon obscured by the smoke, and he climbed up in the port main rigging for a better

BATTLE OF MOBILE BAY, PASSING FORT MORGAN AND THE *Tennessee*

From a lithograph in the collection of President Franklin D. Roosevelt, after the painting by J. O. Davidson.

Courtesy of United States Navy Department, Naval Records and Library

AMERICAN NAVAL OFFICER GOING INTO ACTION—NEW STYLE
INVENTED BY COMMODORE FARRAGUT

From a caricature in *Frank Leslie's Illustrated Newspaper,*
September 10, 1864.

view, ascending step by step "until he found himself partly above the futtock bands and holding on to the futtock shrouds."[12] Fearing that the Admiral might be wounded and hurled to the deck or thrown into the sea, Captain Drayton directed Quartermaster Knowles to climb aloft and secure him to the rigging.[13] Though Farragut said, "Never mind; I am all right," Knowles went ahead, and fastened a piece of lead line to one of the forward shrouds, passed it around the Admiral, and made it fast to the after shroud.[12] Captain Drayton remained on the poop deck, surrounded by the staff, Watson, Yates, McKinley, and Brownell. Signal Quartermaster Knowles returned there also to perform his duties. The three old sailors, McFarland, Wood, and Jassin, who had been on the *Hartford* in all her engagements, were at the wheel, proud in the knowledge that upon their coolness depended the safety of the ship. Just above Farragut stood his trusty pilot, Martin Freeman, in the top, within easy reach, connected through a speaking-tube with the deck; while Captain Jouett stood on the starboard wheelhouse of the *Metacomet*, lashed alongside, where the Admiral could communicate easily with him.[12]

The other vessels had their own organizations, which were not so complicated as that of the flagship.[14] Many young officers and sailors were under fire for the first time. For example, on the *Lackawanna* were some young fellows just out of the Naval Academy who afforded considerable amusement at first. They left their stations and ran fore and aft, bumping into one another in an effort to dodge the Confederate shells. But the laughter of the veteran officers brought them to their senses, and sent them ashamed back to the guns.[15] In marked contrast was the bravery of some of the experienced officers. Captain Stevens of the *Winnebago*, as his monitor went into close action, was seen to be walking back and forth between the two turrets, giving orders to the gunners of one and then to those of the other.[16] Captain Perkins, then only twenty-seven years old, was on top of one of the turrets of the *Chickasaw*, which he commanded, waving his cap and dancing about in his excitement, under the full fire of the fort.[17] On the poop deck of the *Galena* a Negro seaman promenaded back and forth, singing a hymn, with his hands raised to heaven.[18]

2

Everything went along according to plan until seven twenty-five, when the battle suddenly took a turn which might easily have brought disaster, if Farragut had not been in a position to see clearly what had happened and if he had not had the capacity to decide wisely and quickly on a course of action. At that time, one of the Army flagmen on the *Brooklyn* was seen to be signaling.[18] As these men had come aboard Farragut's ships in order to communicate with General Granger's army after the fleet had passed Fort Morgan, the Admiral, at the commencement of the engagement, had ordered Major F. W. Marston, Lieutenant John C. Kinney, and the five flagmen on the *Hartford* to go below and assist the surgeons. But for some strange reason Alden was using the Army signaling instead of the Navy, and no one on the *Hartford* understood the signals coming from the *Brooklyn*. Accordingly, the Army signal officers and their men were hurriedly summoned on deck. Lieutenant Kinney ran to the forecastle, and took this message from the *Brooklyn:* "The monitors are right ahead. We cannot go on without passing them. What shall we do?" Five minutes later, Farragut had this simple reply signaled to Alden: "Go ahead."[19]

Farragut's general orders required all the vessels to pass "inside the buoys"[20] next to Fort Morgan. Instead of keeping his course to the starboard of the column of wooden ships, as ordered, Craven had turned the *Tecumseh* to port, and that monitor, closely followed by others, had gotten directly in the course of the *Brooklyn* and, because of slower speed,[21] was impeding the progress of the advancing column of wooden ships. At seven-thirty, as Lieutenant Kinney was climbing up to the foretopgallant crosstrees so that he could get above the smoke from the *Hartford's* bow guns and see the signals more clearly on the *Brooklyn*, he was amazed to see the *Tecumseh* careen to one side, and almost instantly sink.[22] Five minutes later this signal came from the *Brooklyn:* "Our best monitor has been sunk."[23]

According to Farragut's own record, when the *Tecumseh* approached the buoy indicating the eastern limit of the torpedo field, Craven said to the pilot, "The Admiral ordered me to go inside that buoy, but it must be a mistake."[24] The pilot replied that there was plenty of water inside, "but he ran just his breadth of beam to the westward, struck a torpedo, and went down in two minutes."[24]

At that time, Engineer Harrie Webster had come up into the turret of the *Manhattan* from the engine room where the temperature was 150 degrees Fahrenheit to get some fresh air and take his turn with the handling levers of the turret. Through a gun port he saw the *Tecumseh* go down, "her stern lifted high in the air with the propeller still revolving, and the ship pitched out of sight like an arrow twanged from a bow."[25] Though orders to reverse engines were shouted to the men below, "the bubbling water around our bows and the huge swirls on either hand told us that we were passing directly over the struggling wretches fighting with death in the *Tecumseh.*" "The effect on our men," he further declared, "was in some cases terrible. One of the firemen lost his mind completely and never recovered."[25]

When the *Tecumseh* went down, she was only about one hundred yards from the Confederate ironclad *Tennessee,*[26] which had been moved down just inside the line of torpedoes, as Farragut's fleet approached.[27] Her bow gun was loaded and trained on the approaching monitor, which probably left her prescribed course to attack the *Tennessee* more quickly. "Do not fire, Mr. Wharton," ordered Captain Johnston on the *Tennessee,* "until the vessels are in actual contact." "Aye, aye, sir," coolly responded Wharton, stepping up to the breech of the bow gun. At that instant, the *Tecumseh* reeled to port and went down head foremost, screw visible in the air.[28] Immense bubbles of steam as large as cauldrons rose to the surface. The crew of the *Tennessee* gazed through the portholes at the catastrophe, speaking together only in whispers.[29]

As the *Tecumseh* was sinking, Craven and his pilot, John

Collins, in endeavoring to escape met at the small hatchway in the floor of the pilot house leading down into the turret. Only one man could pass through at a time, and there was no other exit from the pilot house, which was placed on top of the turret. The pilot said to Craven, "Go ahead, captain!" "No, sir!" replied the gallant officer. "After you, pilot! I leave my ship last." Collins reached the turret, escaped through one of the sliding hatches in its top, and was rescued. Captain Craven went down with his ship.[30] Only twenty-one of the one hundred fourteen officers and men on the *Tecumseh* escaped death.[31] Four swam ashore and were captured, seven escaped in one of the *Tecumseh's* boats, and ten were rescued by a boat which Farragut ordered to go to their aid from the *Metacomet*. The boat was commanded by Acting Master Henry Clay Nields.[32] When General Page in Fort Morgan saw the boat on her errand of mercy, he gave these directions: "Pass the order not to fire on that boat; she is saving drowning men."[33] The men on the *Tennessee* also withheld their fire from Nields' boat. "The muzzle of our gun was slowly raised," wrote Wharton, "and the bolt intended for the *Tecumseh* swept harmlessly over their heads [in the rescue boat] and far down in the line of foes."[34]

3

This catastrophe, which happened in less time than it has taken to describe it, was witnessed by Farragut himself in the port main rigging. Five minutes after Alden had signaled the loss of the monitor, Farragut answered by signal at seven-forty: "Tell the monitors to go ahead and then take your place."[35] Like his famous ancestor, whom Priscilla chided with "Why don't you speak for yourself, John?", Captain Alden was lacking in self-assertiveness, and seemed to be paralyzed into inaction by what he called "assassination in its worst form,"[36] and was not eager for the "immortal fame"[36] just gained by Craven and his men. Shoal water had been reported to him, and "a row of suspicious-looking buoys was discovered directly under"[36] his bows. Apparently he too had gotten somewhat off the course which he was supposed to follow and was leading the column into the mine, or torpedo field, when disaster came. So he began backing to get clear of the torpedoes.[36] He had cast off the *Octorara,* his consort, before the *Tecumseh* sank, and this made it more difficult for him to turn the *Brooklyn* quickly away from danger.[37] Meanwhile the vessels in the rear were pressing on those in the van. In the uncertainty and confusion, their fire had slackened, while the guns of Fort Morgan had increased in rapidity and effectiveness of fire. A first class disaster was in the making.

Confronted with the most momentous decision of his life, Farragut reverently offered this silent prayer: "O God, who created man and gave him reason, direct me what to do. Shall I go on?" Then his spiritual ear heard a voice which commanded, "Go on!"[38] Determined to take the lead, as he had wished to do in the beginning, he gave the necessary orders, and the *Hartford* was quickly placed on her new course. She was followed by the other ships, whose officers believed "that they were going to a noble death with their commander in chief."[39] Farragut believed there were torpedoes ahead, but hoped they had been in the water long enough to be rendered innocuous. In any case, he was "determined to take the chance of their explosion."[39]

As the *Hartford* passed on the port side of the *Brooklyn,* Alden reported that there was "a heavy line of torpedoes across the channel." "Damn the torpedoes!" Farragut is reported to have shouted. Then to his own captain, he added, "Four bells! Captain Drayton, go ahead!" and to the captain of the *Metacomet* alongside, "Jouett, full speed!"[40] Good fortune attended such daring, and not a single torpedo was exploded as the column of ships followed the *Hartford* to the northwestward into Mobile Bay.

In a statement after the battle, in which Farragut thanked his officers and men, he mentioned the fact that he "had led in." Alden took offense at this, and went on board the flagship to protest. Holding out a copy of the statement, he inquired of Farragut in an angry tone, "Do you mean to say that this is so?" The Admiral, avoiding an open quarrel, conducted him to his cabin, where no one could hear what was said. Relations were strained between them afterwards, and it has been reported that Farragut considered taking some action. But the *Brooklyn* was ordered to Boston early in September for repairs, and no official action was ever taken.[41]

Though the *Hartford* had been struck in the foremast and port rigging, no serious injuries had been received when she took the lead. Soon thereafter she was beyond the range of the guns of Fort Morgan.[42] How the ships escaped all the torpedoes is somewhat of a mystery. Some had deteriorated in the water, but after the battle a few were removed which were still quite dangerous. Some of Farragut's officers are reported to have declared, though not officially, that they heard primers snapping as the ships passed over the torpedo field.[42] It has also been suggested that, as the torpedoes were arranged in a quincunx, echelon order, Farragut's change of course to the northwest carried the ships between the lines of torpedoes.[42]

A new danger immediately confronted the *Hartford*. This was the *Tennessee*, which made a vigorous attempt to ram the flagship. Only the superior speed and maneuverability of the *Hartford* saved her from being struck amidships and sunk by the iron prow of the *Tennessee*.[43] Pouring a broadside into the ram, which bounded harmlessly off her iron sides, the *Hartford* advanced on the three wooden gunboats. The *Selma* had been annoying her with a raking fire, which her guns could not effectively return. At about eight o'clock, Farragut ordered Jouett to release the *Metacomet* and pursue the *Selma*.[44] This order Jouett obeyed with great alacrity, for, only ten minutes before, a shell from the *Selma* had exploded in his ship's storeroom and started a fire, which had, however, been extinguished. One man had been killed and another wounded.[45]

The *Tennessee* also made an unsuccessful effort to ram the *Brooklyn*, firing a broadside into her as she passed just clear of her stern by a few yards. The *Brooklyn* gave her a few parting shots from her 60-pound Parrots on the poop, and followed the *Hartford* into the bay.[46] The *Richmond* fired rapidly at the *Tennessee* at ranges from 200 to 75 yards from her thirteen IX-inch guns and 100-pounder rifle, as she passed.[47] The *Lacka-*

wanna in turn also gave her a broadside.[48] The *Monongahela* left the line to attack the ram, which passed on her port side[49] and fired into the *Kennebec* lashed to her, wounding five men.[50] The *Tennessee* then turned and passed between the *Monongahela* and *Ossipee*, delivering a broadside into each vessel.[51] The *Oneida*, rearmost ship in the column, received from Fort Morgan a 7-inch rifle shell, which penetrated through her chain armor into the starboard boiler where it exploded and did serious damage. Another passed through her side just above the water line and exploded in the cabin, cutting both wheel ropes. Then the *Tennessee* passed down her starboard side and fired into her. Her losses were eight killed and thirty wounded, among whom Commander Mullany lost an arm. The *Itasca* assisted the *Galena* in towing her to the fleet's anchorage.[52] As the *Tennessee* passed the *Oneida*, the ram's "primers failed to explode the charges in the guns three times,"[53] and this no doubt saved the vessel from destruction. The monitors, which had been covering the passage of the wooden vessels, came up at that time, opened fire on the *Tennessee*, and took position between her and the *Oneida* to prevent her being rammed.[53]

The *Hartford* anchored about four miles northwest of Fort Morgan at eight thirty-five,[54] where she was joined by the other vessels after they had fought their way through into the bay. It was a grand sight as the ships passed the *Hartford* with flags flying and sailors cheering the victorious Admiral.[55] About that time a heavy northwest squall of wind and rain struck the fleet, making it quite dark.[56] Though the monitors had gone "far to the eastward,"[57] no particular uneasiness was felt for their safety.

Meanwhile the Confederate gunboat *Morgan* retired to the protection of the guns of Fort Morgan, her captain thinking that discretion was the better part of valor, and the *Gaines* in a sinking condition with two killed and three wounded was beached about 500 yards from the fort.[58] Jouett's *Metacomet*, after a hot fight, captured the *Selma*, which surrendered at 9:10, when the *Port Royal* arrived on the scene. The *Selma* had eight killed and seven wounded, among whom was her commander, Lieutenant P. U. Murphey. Jouett and Murphey had been friends before the war, and when the latter came on board the *Metacomet* with his wounded arm in a sling and his sword clutched in the other, he drew himself up and said, "Captain Jouett, the fortunes of war compel me to tender you my sword." To this, Jouett very kindly and quite less formally replied, "Pat, don't make a damned fool of yourself; I have had a bottle on ice for you for the last half hour!" He was then taken below for the surgeon to dress his arm.[59]

Farragut lost one vessel, the supply ship *Philippi*. Against the orders of Captain Drayton, she attemped to follow the fleet in, and was disabled by a shot from Fort Morgan. Running ashore, she was afterwards set on fire by the Confederates, after her officers and crew had escaped. Two men were killed and two were wounded. Her commander, Acting Master James T. Seaver, was "dishonorably dismissed" from the service for his zeal without intelligent discretion.[60]

The losses in Fort Morgan were "slight,"[61] and though 491 projectiles were fired from the guns of the fort, the damage to Farragut's fleet from them might be called equally "slight," the *Oneida* alone suffering severely. Page declared that the guns of the fleet were too much elevated.[61] The range also seems to have been great. General Maury was of the opinion that none of Farragut's ships passed nearer than 800 yards from Fort Morgan.[62] But this is a point about which there has been great difference of opinion.

The first stage of the battle thus came to a victorious end after about two hours of fighting—and severe fighting too. "You may pass through a long career and see many an action," Farragut remarked to one of the junior officers of the *Hartford* during the lull in the battle, "without seeing as much bloodshed as you have this day witnessed."[63] Though he did not then know it, much more blood was to be shed before the morning was over, in a desperate fight with the *Tennessee*.

XXIII

THE CAPTURE OF THE *TENNESSEE*

1

THOUGH THE *Tennessee* had been repeatedly struck by the broadsides of Farragut's fleet, she had received no serious injuries to either armor or machinery. Perforations through her smokestacks had indeed further decreased her slow speed; but the ram was in good condition to continue the engagement. Her officers and men were hot, tired, and hungry, as they had hurried into battle without having had any breakfast, and they eagerly seized the opportunity for enjoying some hardtack and coffee and quenching their thirst as the heat had been intense in the poorly ventilated casemate. Admiral Buchanan, grim faced and silent, paced up and down the deck limping from the wound he had received on the *Merrimac (Virginia)* two years before. He was pondering an important decision. Commander J. D. Johnston, the commanding officer of the *Tennessee,* joined him. His mind made up, Buchanan gave him the simple command, "Follow them up, Johnston; we can't let them off that way."[1] So instead of retiring to the protection of the guns of Fort Morgan, he turned the iron prow of the ram toward Farragut's assembled fleet. As it became apparent what was intended, these suppressed exclamations were heard from officers and men: "The old Admiral has not had his fight out yet. He is heading for that big fleet. He will get his fill of it up there. Well, we'll never come out of there whole." To Buchanan, his attack was not foolhardy and ill-advised. "I determined, by an unexpected dash into the fleet, to attack and do it all the damage in my power," he declared, "to expend all my ammunition and what little coal I had on board, only six hours' steaming, and then, having done all I could with what resources I had, to retire under the guns of the fort, and being without motive power, thus to lay and assist in repulsing the attacks and assaults on the fort."[2]

On the *Hartford*, the anchor had just been gotten under the bow and was about to be hoisted to the cathead.[3] Farragut had descended from his post in the main rigging and was standing on the poop. Drayton, who was near by, remarked, "What we have done has been well done, sir; but it all counts for nothing so long as the *Tennessee* is there under the guns of Fort Morgan." "I know it," rejoined Farragut, "and as soon as it is dark enough for the smoke to prevent Page from distinguishing friend from foe, I intend to go in with the three monitors, myself on board the *Manhattan*."[4] When the *Tennessee* was seen to be moving, Drayton said he thought she was going outside to attack the outer fleet. "Then we must follow him out!" said Farragut. It becoming clear that the ram was really moving up the bay, the Admiral remarked, "No! Buck's coming here. Get under way at once; we must be ready for him."[5]

It was then about a quarter to nine.[6] The crew was hastily called to quarters. The men had had a bit of rest and some refreshment. "On the night before the battle we were sitting on the poop together," wrote Surgeon Palmer, "when I remembered that I wished we had whiskey enough to serve round after the action when the men would be a good deal exhausted. The Admiral answered, 'Well, we'll have to give them good strong coffee instead.'"[7] Soon this signal was flying from the *Hartford*: "Rebel ram coming up the bay toward us."[8] To the *Brooklyn* went another signal by army signalmen: "Hail the monitor and tell her to run alongside of us. Prepare to run down the ram."[9] This was the *Manhattan*. Fleet-Surgeon Palmer, having attended to the few wounded on the flagship, had just entered the dispatch boat *Loyall* to visit the other vessels and assist the surgeons, when the approach of the *Tennessee* was noted. Farragut instructed him to go immediately to all the monitors, which were somewhat separated, with orders to attack the *Tennessee*.[10] The orders were quickly delivered by Palmer. "Happy as my friend Perkins habitually is," wrote Palmer, "I thought he would turn a somersault overboard with joy when

Courtesy of United States Navy Department, Naval Records and Library

AN AUGUST MORNING

From the painting of the engagement between the *Hartford* and the *Tennessee* in the Battle of Mobile Bay by William H. Overend, now in the Wadsworth Atheneum, Hartford, Connecticut.

CAPTURE OF THE *Tennessee*, BATTLE OF MOBILE BAY
From the painting by Xanthus Smith, presented to the Naval Academy Museum by Colonel Henry H. Rogers, Jr.

Courtesy of Curator, United States Naval Academy

THE CAPTURE OF THE *TENNESSEE* 275

I told him, 'The Admiral wants you to go at once and fight that *Tennessee*.' "[11]

Farragut's ships, accordingly, were not taken off guard, as Buchanan had hoped they would be found. The Union captains had orders to attack not only with their guns but also with their bows at full speed. "Then began," declared Farragut, "one of the fiercest naval combats on record."[12]

2

The *Monongahela* was the first to attack the *Tennessee*, attempting to run her down at full speed. In striking the ram, her iron prow was entirely carried away together with the cutwater. Just before she struck, she received two shells in the berth deck, which wounded three men and did extensive damage to the vessel. The *Monongahela* then gave her a broadside at a distance of ten yards, without doing any injury to the ram.[13]

The *Lackawanna* was next to try conclusions with the *Tennessee*. At full speed she struck her at right angles near the after end of the casemate. Her stem was crushed and a considerable leak forward was caused; the only result to the ram appeared to be a heavy list. The two vessels swung head and stern alongside each other. But the *Lackawanna* returned only one gun for two from the *Tennessee*. Some of the Confederates were seen through the gun ports of the ram. They flung "opprobrious language"[14] at the Federals, and the marines answered with musketry; also "a spittoon and a holystone were thrown at them."[14]

Then it came the *Hartford's* turn at the *Tennessee*. As the vessels rushed at each other head on, Farragut jumped into the port mizzen rigging above the poop deck to see the effect of the ramming. Lieutenant Watson seized the tails of his frock coat and tried in vain to hold him back. He then grabbed up a rope's-end, and climbing up to him, said, "If you *will* stand there, you had better secure yourself against falling."[15] Farragut thanked him, and "took a turn around and over the shrouds"[15] and around his body. Watson remained standing near him with a drawn revolver ready to fire on anybody on the ram who might attempt to pick Farragut off. The Admiral was thus only a few feet above the ram, as the port sides of the two vessels rasped against each other, and guns almost touching one another exchanged broadsides.[16] As the ships came together, Drayton ran to the bow of the *Hartford* and shook his lorgnette at the ram, shouting, "The cowardly rascal; he's afraid of a wooden ship"[17] He thought the *Tennessee* had sheered off to avoid striking a square blow. The blow indeed was a glancing one, and the concussion was lightened, because the *Hartford's* port anchor which had not been catted caught on the gunwale of the *Tennessee* and the shank bent so as to bring the flukes nearly parallel with the stock. One shell entered the *Hartford* and exploded, killing and wounding a number of men.[18] Engineer Rodgers on the *Tennessee*, standing near a gun port to get a breath of air, was cursed roundly by one of the *Hartford's* men. Rodgers jabbed him with his bayonet and received a pistol ball through his shoulder from another Union sailor.[19]

The *Hartford* then stood off and began another circuit to get up momentum to override the ram; but the *Lackawanna* crashed into her a little forward of the mizzenmast and cut her down to within two feet of the water.[18] Farragut had descended from the rigging and was standing aft on the poop deck. Instantly he climbed over the side to examine the damage. There was then a cry of alarm from all sides, "Get the Admiral out of the ship!" for it was thought that the vessel was in a sinking condition. Farragut had come to be so loved by his men that, when in danger, they thought first of him and not of themselves. As soon as he found that the flagship would still float, he ordered Drayton to make another attempt to sink the ram.[20]

3

Meanwhile the monitors had been firing at the *Tennessee* with their powerful guns as opportunity was afforded in the general melee. Curiously the Confederate ram and her ironclad foes, as most of Farragut's fleet, bore Indian names in keeping with their savage work. "The *Monongahela* was hardly clear of us," wrote Lieutenant Wharton of the *Tennessee*, "when a hideous-looking monster came creeping up on our port side, whose slowly revolving turret revealed the cavernous depths of a mammoth gun. 'Stand clear of the port side!' I shouted. A moment after, a thundering report shook us all, while a blast of dense, sulphurous smoke covered our portholes, and 440 pounds of iron, impelled by 60 pounds of powder, admitted daylight through our side where, before it struck us, there had been over two feet of solid wood, covered with five inches of solid iron. This was the only 15-inch shot that hit us fair."[21] Also this was one of the six shots fired by the *Manhattan* during the engagement, Commander Nicholson's strange excuse being that the smoke of his own guns interfered and not that his monitor steered badly.[22]

Lieutenant-Commander George H. Perkins skillfully maneuvered the *Chickasaw* to a position close under the stern of the *Tennessee*, where he held on like a bulldog, firing his two 11-inch guns in his forward turret again and again at the stern of the *Tennessee's* casemate, at distances ranging from fifty to ten yards.[23] By this continuous pounding, the after port shutter of one of the gun ports became jammed. While four men with sledge hammers were trying to free the shutter, another shot struck the casemate not far away, and killed two men and wounded Admiral Buchanan, whose leg was broken.[24]

This bad news was carried to Commander Johnston in the pilot house, and he immediately went to see Buchanan. The white-haired old Admiral was grim and silent, bearing his pain stoically. "Well, Johnston," he said, "they have got me again. You'll have to look out for her now; it is your fight." "All right," he replied, "I'll do the best I know how."[25] But there was not much more that he could do with the *Tennessee*. Her defectively exposed wheel chains had been shot away. Relieving tackles had been substituted until they too had been destroyed and the tiller unshipped from the rudder head. The two quarter ports for the after gun also had their shutters jammed. The smokestack had been completely riddled and then knocked down close to the top of the casemate. The gun primers had proved defective, and many favorable opportunities for sinking the wooden vessels at very close range had been lost thereby. After making a hurried examination of the condition of his vessel, Johnston returned with a pessimistic report to Buchanan, and inquired if he did not think they should surrender. "Do the best you can, sir," replied the wounded Admiral, unwilling to commit himself, "and when all is done, surrender."

Returning to the gun deck, Johnston observed a Union vessel bearing down to strike the ram on the port quarter; others were closing in; the after end of the casemate was so shattered that it seemed ready to fall and expose the gun deck to a raking fire. He then decided that it was unfair to his men to further resist, and ordered the ensign to be lowered from the gun scraper which had been stuck up through the grating for a flagstaff. The firing continued. "I then decided," he declared, "although with an almost bursting heart, to hoist the white flag, and returning again onto the shield, placed it in the same spot where but a few moments before had floated the proud flag for whose honor I would so cheerfully have sacrificed my own life if I could possibly have become the only victim; but at the time it would have been impossible to destroy the ship without the certain loss of many valuable lives."[26] The second stage of the Battle of Mobile Bay thus came to an end about ten o'clock after an hour of ferocious fighting. "Old Buck" had had his fight out to the bitter end.

4

The vessel which was charging down on the *Tennessee* was the *Ossipee*. When Commander William E. Le Roy saw the white flag, he stopped his engines, but the momentum carried his ship on and the *Tennessee* received a glancing blow. "This is the United States steamer *Ossipee*," Le Roy hailed. "Hello, Johnston, how are you? Le Roy—don't you know me? I'll send a boat alongside for you." They had been lifelong friends, and when Johnston reached the deck of the *Ossipee*, Le Roy said, "I'm glad to see you, Johnston. Here's some ice-water for you—

THE CAPTURE OF THE *TENNESSEE*

I know you're dry; but I've something better than that for you down below." They went down to his cabin where they renewed their friendship with a bottle of "navy sherry."[27]

The boat sent to the *Tennessee* was under command of Acting Volunteer Lieutenant Pierre Giraud, who had the distinction of receiving Buchanan's sword and the flag of the Confederate ram which were conveyed by him to Farragut.[28] Giraud, the commander of the supply ship *Tennessee,* had participated in the battle as a volunteer on the *Ossipee*. He told Buchanan that Farragut had directed him to ask for his sword, and it was brought from the cabin and given to him by one of the Admiral's aides.[29] The *Tennessee* was then towed by the *Winnebago* up to the anchorage near the *Hartford*.[30]

Farragut did not go on board the ram to call upon the wounded Confederate Admiral. But he invited Johnston on board the flagship, where he expressed his regret at meeting him under such circumstances. Johnston replied, "You are not half as sorry to see me as I am to see you." Drayton, who was present, diplomatically remarked, "You have one consolation, Johnston; no one can say that you have not nobly defended the honor of the Confederate flag to-day." Johnston thanked him, but declared that all the honor was due Buchanan, who "was the true hero of the battle."[31]

Surgeon Conrad of the *Tennessee* went on board the *Hartford* with a request from Buchanan to Farragut that the surgeon be permitted to accompany the wounded Admiral wherever he was sent. "The scene was one of carnage and devastation," according to Conrad. "The spar deck was covered and littered with gun carriages, shattered boats, disabled guns, and a long line of grim corpses dressed in blue lying side by side. The officer accompanying me told me that these men—two whole guns' crews—were all killed by splinters, and, pointing with his hand to a piece of weather-boarding ten feet long and four inches wide, I received my first vivid idea of what 'a splinter' was, or what was meant by 'a splinter.' Descending, we threaded our way, and, ascending the poop, where all of the officers were standing, I was taken up and introduced to Admiral Farragut, whom I found a very quiet, unassuming man, and not in the least flurried by his great victory. In the kindest manner he inquired regarding the severity of the Admiral's wound, and then gave the necessary orders to carry out Admiral Buchanan's request."[32]

Surgeon Palmer was sent by Farragut to see Buchanan who received him politely but coldly. They were both from Maryland. After some conversation, Palmer remarked, "Admiral Farragut will take you aboard the *Hartford,* or send you to any other ship you may prefer." Buchanan replied, "I don't pretend to be Admiral Farragut's friend and have no right to ask favors of him, but I will be satisfied with any decision that may be come to." Palmer returned to the flagship and reported his conversation. Farragut appeared to be hurt at Buchanan's irritated feeling. "He formerly professed friendship for me," he declared. Seeing that it would be embarrassing to bring the two men together, Palmer suggested that a steamer take all the wounded, both Confederate and Union, to Pensacola.[33] Arrangements were accordingly made with General Page for a vessel to pass Fort Morgan under a flag of truce, and the *Metacomet,* on the following day, carried all the wounded to the Pensacola hospital.[34] Buchanan was treated very kindly en route by Jouett. To Lieutenant Murphey of the *Selma,* also a wounded prisoner, Buchanan said at breakfast, "Well, if Jouett had only let me know what he was going to give me for breakfast, I would have surrendered two hours earlier."[35] General Page had requested that Buchanan be sent under parole to Mobile, but Farragut had refused. In his reply, he had asked to bury his dead on shore, and Page had granted the request.[36]

5

Farragut's losses had been heavy. "This was the most desperate battle I ever fought since the days of the old *Essex,*" he recorded in his note book.[37] The total losses suffered in passing Fort Morgan and in capturing the *Tennessee* were 52 killed and 170 wounded, not including the losses with the *Tecumseh.* The *Hartford* with 25 killed and 28 wounded and the *Brooklyn*

THE CAPTURE OF THE *TENNESSEE* 281

with 11 killed and 43 wounded had the heaviest casualty lists. The *Port Royal, Seminole, Itasca,* and the three remaining monitors had no casualties.[38] In addition to the damages to the vessels already mentioned in passing, five of the twenty hits, reported by the carpenter to have struck the *Hartford,* penetrated the hull and did much smashing and wrecking. Similarly, thirteen of the thirty hits penetrated the hull of the *Brooklyn.* The *Octorara* was struck nineteen times; the *Metacomet* eleven times; and the *Richmond* "a number of times in the hull and rigging." Five shot went through the hull of the *Lackawanna,* two of which were only eighteen inches above the water line. Five shells penetrated the *Monongahela* and smashed things terribly; the *Ossipee* had five large holes in her; and the *Galena* had two serious hits from 10-inch guns. The *Kennebec* was badly damaged by a shell from the *Tennessee,* the *Oneida* was put out of action, and the *Tecumseh* was sunk.[39]

The Confederate casualty list was small in Buchanan's fleet: 12 killed and 20 wounded. Two of the killed and nine of the wounded were on the *Tennessee.* Fort Morgan had only one man killed and three wounded. The remainder of the 133 officers and men in the *Tennessee* were captured,[40] as well as the survivors of the crew of 94 men on the *Selma.*[41] Though the *Gaines* was beached, her commanding officer, Lieutenant J. W. Bennett, conveyed her crew of 129 officers and men safely in six small boats to Mobile the following night.[42] The gunboat *Morgan,* during the same night, slipped by the Union fleet and reached the Mobile defenses, hotly pursued and shelled most of the way by Farragut's gunboats.[40]

And so ended this momentous day in Farragut's life and in American history. Worn out with mental strain and physical fatigue, at its close, he dashed off a brief message to his wife. "The Almighty has smiled upon me once more," he wrote with a mixture of exultation and thankfulness. "I am in Mobile Bay. The *Tennessee* and Buchanan are my prisoners." "It was a hard fight," he continued, "but Buck met his fate manfully. After we passed the fort, he came up in the ram to attack me. I made at him, and ran him down, making all the others do the same. We butted and shot at him until he surrendered. The *Selma* was annoying us, but I sent Jouett after him, who in a short time brought his colors down. But, sad to say, the *Tecumseh* was sunk by a torpedo, and poor Craven with his gallant crew went to the bottom. I have lost a number of fine fellows, more than ever before." "They made a gallant fight," he concluded in reference to the Confederates, "but was all to no purpose. My ship is greatly cut up—25 killed and 28 wounded. I escaped, thank God! without a scratch. God bless you, and make you as thankful for this victory as I am."[43]

The following day, Farragut published this general order: "The Admiral returns thanks to the officers and crews of the vessels of the fleet for their gallant conduct during the fight of yesterday. It has never been his good fortune to see men do their duty with more courage and cheerfulness, for although they knew that the enemy was prepared with all devilish means for our destruction, and though they witnessed the almost instantaneous annihilation of our gallant companions in the *Tecumseh* by a torpedo, and the slaughter of their friends, messmates, and gunmates on our deck, still there were no evidences of hesitation in following their commander in chief through the line of torpedoes and obstructions, of which we knew nothing except from the exaggerations of the enemy, who had given out that we should all be blown up as certainly as we attempted to enter. For this noble and implicit confidence in their leader he heartily thanks them. D. G. Farragut."[44]

XXIV

THE SURRENDER OF THE FORTS

1

THE SMALL Fort Powell, defending Grant's Pass, was the first to be captured. Five of Farragut's gunboats bombarded it during the passage of Fort Morgan. The fort replied spiritedly with the four guns which would bear, until the Union fleet had passed into the bay. That afternoon, the *Chickasaw* was sent by Farragut to shell it in the rear.[1] It was then realized that further defense was impossible and Lieutenant-Colonel J. M. Williams commenced preparations for evacuating and destroying the fort. There were no casualties, and all his garrison of about 140 men were brought safely to Cedar Point on the mainland to the westward and thence to Mobile. The fort was blown up that night at ten-thirty, after the guns had been spiked.[2] Early the next morning, the crew of the *Hartford* saw the stars and stripes floating over what had been Fort Powell. The rigging was manned and cheers resounded throughout the fleet.[3] The capture of the fort was important for it enabled supply vessels for the fleet to pass from Mississippi Sound into the bay, though the main channel was still controlled by the guns of Fort Morgan. A few days later, Farragut visited the place, and declared, "It was astonishing to see how completely the blowing up of Powell had demolished it."[4] "It is nothing but a heap of rubbish and ruins, with a deep tunnel-shaped hole in the center, which was filled with water," wrote Acting Master G. P. Pomeroy.[5]

2

The news of Farragut's great victory of August 5 reached New Orleans very quickly, and Major-General Canby wrote a letter of congratulations to Farragut, the following day, on the success of his "glorious operations." He promised also to send at least 2,000 reinforcements immediately to General Granger.[6] The same day Commodore James S. Palmer in New Orleans telegraphed Welles the news of the victory. But the message was not received until ten days later,[7] as it apparently was conveyed partly by ship and was otherwise unaccountably delayed. That day Fox, eager for news from Farragut, telegraphed General Butler, then commanding the Department of Virginia and North Carolina, "Please try and get a Richmond paper to see how Farragut is getting on at Mobile. He went inside about the 1st and is attacking Fort Gaines."[8] The last clause was strangely quite accurate for that very day the *Chickasaw* was bombarding Gaines.

On August 7, Sunday, Farragut published the following very brief general order: "The admiral desires the fleet to return thanks to Almighty God for the signal victory over the enemy on the morning of the 5th instant."[9] That morning Butler replied by telegraph to Fox that the Richmond *Examiner* of the previous day had published a communication from Mobile of August 4 to the effect that an infantry force had been landed on Dauphin Island and that the fleet outside had increased in size. "General Maury calls on all to enroll themselves for battle. Great confidence prevails," the paper added. This message, which reached Fox at four-thirty that afternoon, was not very reassuring.[10]

But there were important developments that day in Mobile Bay. Very early in the morning, a flag of truce approached the *Hartford* with two Confederate officers who brought dispatches from Colonel C. D. Anderson, in command of the garrison of Fort Gaines. He offered to surrender and asked for conditions.[11] "I trust to your magnanimity for obtaining honorable terms," he wrote.[12] After conferring with General Granger, Farragut sent, in the early evening, Captain Drayton and Colonel A. J. Myer on the *Metacomet* under a flag of truce to meet Colonel Anderson at Fort Gaines. They returned with the Colonel and Major W. R. Browne, and an unconditional surrender was signed on board the *Hartford* the same evening.[13] General Page had observed the communications in progress under a flag of truce, and endeavored to find out by signals from Fort Morgan what was meant. "Hold on to your fort," he repeatedly signaled. Not getting any reply, he took a boat and crossed over to the fort, but found that Anderson was on the *Hartford* signing terms of surrender. He left orders that the fort was not to be surrendered and removed Anderson from the command. Then he sadly returned to Fort Morgan, no doubt realizing that he had been too late.[14]

The next morning about seven o'clock, Captain Drayton and Colonel Myer went in the dispatch steamer *Loyall* to receive the surrender of the fort. At nine forty-five the stars and stripes were raised, and were greeted by three hearty cheers from the fleet.[15] About 600 men surrendered;[16] 23 guns were captured.[17] The officers had the privilege of surrendering their swords to either branch of the service they chose; all but one presented them to Drayton, representing the Navy.[18]

It had been a pleasant day for Farragut in spite of the rain, and he celebrated his success with a letter to Mrs. Farragut. "As I told you on the 5th," he wrote with satisfaction, "it pleased God to grant me one of the hardest earned victories of my life, and one momentous to the country, over the rebel ram *Tennessee*. I always said I was the proper man to fight her, because I was one of those who believed I could do it successfully. I was certainly honest in my convictions and determined in my will, but I did not know how formidable the *Tennessee* was. On the 6th, Fort Powell was evacuated and blown up. This morning Gaines surrendered to the Navy; but I would not neglect the Army, so had General Granger in to sign the articles of capitulation with me."[19]

On that day, August 8, the first news of Farragut's great victory in Mobile Bay reached Washington through telegrams to President Lincoln and Assistant Secretary of the Navy Fox from General Butler. The report was based on an official statement in the Richmond papers of the same day, announcing that Farragut's fleet had passed Fort Morgan with the loss of the *Tecumseh*, and that the *Tennessee* had been captured.[20] But the news did not appear in Northern papers until the next day, when it was particularly featured with front page headlines, then unusual, in the New York *Daily Tribune*.[21]

His mind quite relieved at the good report, Fox departed for a vacation that afternoon to New Hampshire. Welles, greatly pleased, recorded in his diary that evening after a busy hot day at the Navy Department: "News of Farragut's having passed Forts Morgan and Gaines was received last night, and sent a thrill of joy through all true hearts." But there was a small fly in the ointment of his pleasure. "It is not, however, appreciated as it should be by the military," he set down regretfully. "The President, I was sorry, spoke of it as important because it would tend to relieve Sherman. This is the narrow view of General Halleck, whom I tried to induce to make a joint demonstration against Mobile one year ago. He has done nothing new and only speaks of the naval achievement as a step for the Army. While I regard the acts and opinions of Halleck as of little worth, I regret that from constant daily intercourse he should be able to imbue the President at times with false and erroneous notions. Halleck never awarded honest credit to the Navy; the President never knowingly deprived them of any merit. Yet I have mentioned the result."[22]

The New York *Herald* tried to scoop the other papers by publishing on August 6 a story that Farragut's fleet had passed the forts on July 30. The number of his ironclads was doubled and mortars were added to the attacking force. According to this account, Farragut was then hammering at the city of Mobile. "What a canard," wrote Drayton in sarcastic comment. "Who says we are not a hopeful people? The fall of Mobile is no doubt hourly looked for, and if 20,000 men take it, they will do well, and our force is three [thousand], and to get this New Orleans has been left almost defenseless."[23]

Though the telegram to Lincoln mentioned the loss of the *Tecumseh*, this was omitted by Butler in the message to Fox. It was not until the following day Welles heard this, when he recorded in his diary, "It is stated that the *Tecumseh* was sunk by Fort Morgan's guns. I discredit this. She may have grounded

THE SURRENDER OF THE FORTS   287

or she may have encountered a torpedo; but most likely it was one of the river boats, though they, being of light draft, would be less likely to keep the channel and encounter the obstructions and torpedoes. If the guns of Fort Morgan sunk an ironclad, it was doubtless one of the river monitors."[24]

3

Fort Morgan still held out resolutely. Serious operations were commenced against it on the 9th; army transports landed troops in its rear under the guns of the *Lackawanna, Itasca,* and *Monongahela.* The monitors moved up into position to shell the fort, and the captured *Tennessee* was towed up into effective range to aid in the attack. A heavy rain squall interfered with operations the next morning, but in the afternoon more troops and provisions were landed.[25] With Fort Morgan invested, a summons was sent to General Page to surrender, but he replied that he would fight as long as he had any means of defense.[26] The Confederates set fire to the gunboat *Gaines,* which was on the beach near the fort, and also burned all the wooden buildings around the fort.[27] It looked like another fight to the finish.

Holding all the high cards, Farragut wrote Canby, "If I did not think Mobile would be an elephant to hold, I would send up the light-draft ironclads and try that city, but I fear we are not in a condition to hold it."[28] By that time General Maury had become quite alarmed as to his ability to hold Mobile, and was sending telegrams repeatedly to Secretary of War Seddon, begging for "some veteran infantry."[29] To General Cooper he wrote in detail of his situation. What he feared most was that General Canby would bring a large force from New Orleans and attack him through Mississippi. Maury had only about 6,000 men.[30] Additional heavy guns were added to the defenses, and more torpedoes were planted in the channels. The unfinished ironclad *Nashville* loaded with stone and brick was sunk right across the main channel. But when Farragut reconnoitered on board the *Metacomet,* accompanied by two monitors and two or three gunboats, some days later, he found the water so shallow that even his gunboats could not get within two miles of the forts protecting the city on the bay side.[31]

The bombardment of Fort Morgan by the monitors and the *Tennessee* continued from day to day. The fort struck back viciously, particularly at the *Tennessee* which was hit one day ten times. But her casemate was not penetrated.[32] It rained nearly every day. This interfered with the operations, but Granger went ahead. "We get along well together," Farragut noted. "Granger is more of a man than I took him for, attends to almost all the work so far as keeping others up to their mark."[33]

Farragut had time to write his wife a longer letter. "We are now tightening the cords around Fort Morgan," he declared. "Page is as surly as a bulldog, and says he will die in the last ditch. He says he can hold out six months, and that we can't knock his fort down." Page had had a distinguished career in the U. S. Navy before the war. His home was in Norfolk where he and Farragut had formerly been neighbors and intimate friends. "My sister writes me a long letter," the Admiral continued, "begging me not to risk my life. How little people know of the risks of life! Drayton made his clerk stay below, because he was a young married man. All my staff—Watson, McKinley, and Brownell—were in an exposed position on the poop deck, but escaped unhurt, while poor Heginbotham was killed. He was a good man, and a loss to Drayton. General Canby and Commodore Palmer came over yesterday from New Orleans to 'see the sights.' They spent the night with me, and visited Forts Gaines and Powell. Of course, you see how the papers are puffing me; but I am like Brownell's old cove, 'All I want is to be let alone,' to live in peace (if I survive this war) with my family." "I have quite a colony here now," he ended humorously, "two forts, a big fleet, and a bay to run about in."[34]

Monotonously the guns on Farragut's ironclads boomed at ranges varying from 1,400 to 1,000 yards, sending a shell into Fort Morgan every fifteen or twenty minutes day and night.[35] Granger's batteries on shore, of 30-pounder rifles at 1,200 yards and of mortars at 500 yards, chimed in from time to time.[36]

THE SURRENDER OF THE FORTS   289

Farragut was quite unwell. He was suffering from "Job's comforters." For a week he could neither walk, sit, nor stand except in great pain on account of boils.[37] He was placed in no better humor by a visit from the son of Vanderbilt. Drayton despised these "loafing curiosity hunters" who "quietly came on board with their baggage" and "a letter from Banks." "I think all the time of the courtier who came to Hotspur for his prisoners," he wrote contemptuously.[38]

By the 21st of August, Granger's infantry had advanced their intrenchments to within two hundred yards of the fort, four IX-inch guns from the fleet had been landed to reinforce the army batteries, and all preparations had been completed for a heavy combined attack at daylight the following morning. At five o'clock, eight of Farragut's wooden vessels moved into position to aid the ironclads. All the big guns opened according to schedule, and continued all that day and night. Farragut thought "a more magnificent fire" had "rarely been kept up for twenty-four hours."[39] The bombardment wrought havoc on the fort, breaching the walls in several places, reducing the interior to a mass of debris, disabling all the guns but two, and endangering the magazines by fires which raged for hours at a time. Realizing that the capture of the fort was a foregone conclusion and fearing the magazines might be exploded, Page ordered some eighty thousand pounds of powder to be carried out and flooded and the guns no longer useful to be spiked during the night.[40]

At six-thirty the following morning, a white flag was seen on the fort, and Farragut immediately sent Drayton to meet General Granger, with instructions to negotiate for an unconditional surrender. After trying unsuccessfully to get his sick sent to Mobile under parole, Page accepted the terms.[41] At a quarter past two that afternoon, the stars and stripes were hoisted over the fort and saluted by one hundred guns from the fleet.[42] The garrison of about 400 effective men were made prisoners, and 45 guns were captured, 15 of which had been spiked.[43] Most of the guns had been rendered unserviceable by the bombardment. Though about 3,000 shells had been thrown into the fort,[44] the Confederate losses were only one man killed and three wounded. Only seven men were wounded in Granger's force of approximately 5,500 men.[45] The casualties had been unusually slight on both sides.

At the surrender General Page said he had no sword and gave up his revolver instead. Several other officers had no swords, and some of those which were surrendered had been broken. It was also reported to Farragut that the guns had been spiked and much property had been destroyed after the white flag had been raised. When he learned about the broken swords and spiked guns, his ire was aroused over this "childish spitefulness,"[46] and he wrote a strong letter of condemnation of Page's conduct to General Canby.[47] But Farragut had been misinformed as to the guns. A commission of three Army officers and one Naval officer was appointed on September 1, 1864 by General Canby to investigate the charges against Page. When they arrived in Mobile Bay on September 7, Farragut wrote in his note book, "I hope they will prove him truthful and honorable, as I do not wish to change an opinion of a man's moral honesty."[48] He had his wish, for the commission decided that no public property in Fort Morgan had been destroyed after the white flag had been raised "about the hour of six o'clock."[49] Farragut had written rather spitefully to Commodore Palmer in New Orleans, "Old Page wishes to be sent North. See what Genl. Canby says on the subject. I have no objections, for I don't believe he will ever come back."[50] In this he was also mistaken, for Page returned to Norfolk after the war and outlived Farragut by many years.

4

By the time of the surrender of Fort Morgan, Farragut was suffering from both physical and mental strain and fatigue. "I was talking to the Admiral to-day," wrote young Lieutenant Perkins to his mother, "—he talks a great deal to me when I go to see him—when, all at once, he fainted away. He is not very well, and is all tired out. It gave me a shock, for it shows how exhausted he is; and his health is not very good anyway. He is a mighty fine old fellow."[51] Farragut's feelings are well set forth in a letter to his wife of about the same date. "I know that few men could have gone through what I have in the last three years, and no one will ever know except yourself perhaps," he declared sadly. "What the fight was to my poor brains, neither you nor any one else will ever be able to comprehend," he continued. "Six months constantly watching day and night for an enemy; to know him to be as brave, as skilful, and as determined as myself, who was pledged to his government and the South to drive me away and raise the blockade and free the Mississippi from our rule. While I was equally pledged to my government that I would capture or destroy the rebel."[52]

An unpleasant aftermath of the entrance into Mobile Bay was the killing of five men and the wounding of nine others through the careless handling of one of the torpedoes after it had been removed from the channel.[53] But in general the fleet settled down to the monotonous routine of blockade duty. There were vessels to be repaired—particularly the *Hartford*, *Brooklyn*, and *Oneida*. There was the eternal problem of supplies. "Why fighting is mere child's play compared to the preparations required for it, and the keeping one's forces supplied with food, coal, ammunition, etc.," wrote Drayton petulantly.[54] Vessels had to be shifted on the blockade, which had been necessarily somewhat neglected during recent weeks. The captured ram *Tennessee* had to be towed to New Orleans by the *Bienville*. "My heart was full of anxiety for her safety," Farragut wrote in his note book, "but she has had a fair wind all night from N.W. to N.E. and I hope she will arrive at the S.W. Pass today—it was a bad night."[55] After her safe arrival in New Orleans, a board appraised her total value at $883,880.[56] This was indeed prize money sufficient to arouse anxiety in any naval officer's heart.

The tedium was somewhat relieved by the reception of congratulatory letters which commenced to reach Farragut. Major-General Daniel Sickles wrote from New York "of the universal rejoicing over your brilliant exploit and the happy effect of this triumph upon the temper of the public—which had been quite despairing of late in view of the general military situation."[57] General Butler wrote how delighted he was when he first heard the news. "In my tent all alone, when the rebel journal was brought in and the official telegram read that you and seventeen of your vessels had passed Fort Morgan," he wrote, "I called out, 'Three cheers for Farragut!' They were given with a will that brought in my staff and orderlies, who thought their general had gone crazy, perhaps, from a stroke, whereas it was only a stroke of good luck, of high daring and noble enterprise, quite as brilliant as anything the sun could do. Let me assure you, Admiral, that those cheers, the first given in the loyal North, are not done ringing yet, but every hilltop is resounding with them as they are caught up from hamlet to hamlet, city to city, of a grateful nation. I speak no language of hyperbole, and only the words of sincere admiration when I say I envy you alone of all men for the place you have in the hearts of your countrymen."[58] In reply, Farragut gave Butler an outline of the Battle of Mobile Bay, because he thought he and Mrs. Butler would take a "lively interest in the fight." As to the surrender of the *Tennessee* and the lowering of the Confederate flag, he declared, "I don't think anybody was very sorry to see it come down—it is one of those things people like to have passed through but have no particular desire to repeat often."[59]

Of great satisfaction to Farragut was a long letter from Welles—the kind which the Secretary found "difficult to pen." "They must be brief and comprehensive, satisfactory to the Navy, the Government, and the country, and not discreditable to the Department," he confided to his diary just after finishing the letter.[60] After a few preliminary sentences, Welles struck his stride with this long flowing sentence: "Again it is my pleasure and my duty to congratulate you and your brave associates on an achievement unequaled in our service by any other commander and only surpassed by that unparalleled naval triumph of the squadron under your command in the spring of 1862, when, proceeding up the Mississippi, you passed Forts Jackson and St. Philip, and, overcoming all obstructions, captured New Orleans and restored unobstructed navigation to the commercial emporium of the great central valley of the Union." Such sentences are indeed "difficult to pen," and if he wrote the letter in the hot August evening in the privacy of his study, he probably was forced to remove his thick warm wig before the final draft was finished. After taking a resounding whack at Admiral Buchanan for deserting "his country in the hour of peril," he recognized the strategic importance of controlling Mobile. He did not forget "the gallant and lamented dead" who went down with the *Tecumseh,* and closed thus formally: "To you and the brave officers and sailors of your squadron who participated in the great achievement the Department tenders its thanks and those of the Government and country."[61]

In replying to Welles, Farragut had this to say about Buchanan: "He, though a rebel and a traitor to the Government that had raised and educated him, had always been considered one of its ablest officers, and no one knew him better or appreciated his capacity more highly than myself, and, I may add, felt more proud of overcoming him in such a contest, if for no other reason than to prove to the world that ramming and sinking a helpless frigate at her anchor is a very different affair from ramming steamers when handled by officers of good capacity." After thus laying low his antagonist a second time, and pointing out the weaknesses of the *Tennessee* as a ram, he concluded in a style similar to that of Welles, "The Department will please accept my thanks for its congratulatory letter. I have directed it to be read at muster on all the ships in my squadron, and I know well that it will be as gratefully appreciated by every officer and man in this fleet as it is by Very respectfully, Your obedient servant, D. G. Farragut."[62]

Farragut's old friend, Commodore Andrew A. Harwood, also found it difficult to compose a letter—wrote one and tore it up in disgust, and then penned this excellent epistle: "I feel now that I would, were I in your situation, like to be greeted on my return by my naval friends, and be told by them that they rejoiced in my glory and success. I believe there are few, if any, who do not congratulate you in their hearts most sincerely; but I desire to put it on record in a friendly way that I am glad of your success, both because I know you deserve it, and because I feel that you are better able to bear your honors meekly than some who might have more luck but have less ballast. May God continue you His blessing."[63]

Though Farragut did not then know it, President Lincoln had just written him a personal letter expressing "the national thanks" for his recent "brilliant success."[64] But the President did not stop with that. He ordered officially that, at noon on September 5, a salute of one hundred guns be given at the Arsenal and Navy Yard at Washington, and a similar salute on September 6 or the day following the reception of the order at each arsenal and navy yard in the United States in celebration of the recent achievements in Mobile Bay.[64] Also he issued a proclamation of thanksgiving to be offered in all places of public workship on the following Sunday for the "glorious achievements" of Farragut in Mobile Bay and of Sherman at Atlanta.[65]

In justification of Welles's feeling that Lincoln did not properly estimate the importance of Farragut's victory, it should be noted that, though the President had known of the successful outcome of the Battle of Mobile Bay for more than three weeks, he gave Farragut no official recognition until Sherman's victory. Then recognition came the very next day after the capture of Atlanta, to Farragut and Sherman in the same official papers.[66]

But American journals were loud in their praise of Farragut. "Few commanders by sea or land have won their way more successfully to the popular heart than Farragut," declared *Leslie's*.[67] "He has that bluff, persistent, daring recklessness that makes the hero. In his bold rush up to New Orleans he gained every point of applause, and now when the moment for attacking Mobile arrives he brushes past two rebel forts in his own style." "He is as great in preparation as in action," wrote the *Army and Navy Journal;* "he makes such novel and admirable use of his means as to baffle all the plans of the enemy; and having prepared himself with all the patience of the merest plodder, he delivers battle with an impetuosity which breaks down all resistance."[68] The same journal later published a letter of August 17 from Farragut's old friend and teacher, Charles Folsom. "My young countryman was the delight of old and young," he recalled. "This had always been among his chief moral dangers; but here [in Tunis] he learned to be proof against petting and flattery. Here, too, he settled his definition of true glory—glory, the idol of his profession—if not in the exact words of Cicero, at least in his own clear thought. Our familiar walks and rides were so many lessons in ancient history; and the lover of historical parallels will be gratified to know that we possibly sometimes stood on the very spot where the boy Hannibal took the oath that consecrated him to the defense of his country. . . . The better his countrymen understand him, the more they will see that his is no false brilliancy; that he is not a flashing meteor, but a star in our national firmament. The past is secure; and whatever mischance may betide him, we shall feel certain that he deserved success."[69]

The poets also were inspired by Farragut's deeds. In the *Army and Navy Journal* of September 3, appeared a rather good poem by "T," beginning,

> "The sea upon the bar is smooth,
> Yet perilous the path
> Where Gaines' and Morgan's bristling guns
> Belch forth their rebel wrath.
> And, close beyond, their ironclads
> Loom in the breaking day;
> But Farragut is leading us,
> And we will clear the way."[70]

This was the best of its ten stanzas. Just a week later *Harper's Weekly* published an anonymous poem, entitled "Farragut," in which was celebrated first in poetry his being "lashed to the mast" in the Battle of Mobile Bay, as follows:

> "Oh, never through all time shall be forgot
> His last brave deed, now told by every lip,
> When on he sailed, amid a storm of shot,
> Lashed in the rigging of his staunch old ship."[71]

A month later, the *Army and Navy Journal* contained an ode by General J. Watts De Peyster, called "Farragut." It was somewhat extravagantly phrased, as these concluding lines show:

"To Farragut all glory! the Sea-King's worthy peer,
Columbia's greatest Seaman, without reproach or fear.
To Farragut all honor! to him the rostrate crown,
Who from her place of strength and pride the Rebel flag tore down;
To Farragut be endless praise, the hero, sailor man,
The boldest captain trod a deck since history began."[72]

In the British press there was a full realization of the strategic element in Farragut's victory. "Next to New Orleans, the city of Mobile was the greatest cotton port in the States," declared the *British Army and Navy Gazette*.[73] "It was lately deriving a considerable trade in blockade-running, and gave abundant supplies to the Confederacy. Now, neither can cotton go out nor guns run in, and Mobile, its inhabitants, and garrison are thrown on the resources of the impoverished and hard-pressed Confederacy. Already a fleet of transports, laden with fresh provisions and ice, has sailed from New York to supply the doughty Admiral, whose feats of arms place him at the head of his profession, and certainly constitute him the first naval officer of the day, as far as actual reputation, won by skill, courage, and hard fighting, goes."

"The achievements in Mobile Bay," wrote the Prince de Joinville from France, "are without parallel, and throw the greatest honor on your flag. All naval men pay a just tribute of admiration to Admiral Farragut."[74]

XXV

FARRAGUT'S HEALTH FAILS

1

"I AM NOW a little embarrassed by my position," Farragut admitted to Welles four days after the surrender of Fort Morgan. "We have taken the forts at the entrance of Mobile Bay, which is all I ever contemplated doing for more reasons than one. I consider an army of twenty or thirty thousand men necessary to take the city of Mobile and almost as many to hold it."[1] Only about four thousand men were then available, and these were hardly enough to make a diversion in favor of General Sherman. But he expressed his willingness to carry out the orders of the Department to the best of his ability. "I fear, however, my health is giving way," he confided. "I have now been down in this Gulf and the Caribbean Sea nearly five years out of six, with the exception of the short time at home last fall, and the last six months have been a severe drag upon me, and I must rest, if it is to be had."[1] In conclusion, he declared that Mobile in his possession would be a constant source of trouble and anxiety as it would be difficult to prevent supplies for the Confederates from passing out of it.

After news of the capture of Fort Morgan arrived, Fox began to urge Welles to recall Farragut immediately and to order him to replace Acting Rear-Admiral S. P. Lee, then in command of the North Atlantic Squadron. Welles hesitated to do so, because he thought the public was expecting the early capture of the city of Mobile, and if Farragut were recalled, the failure to take the city would be laid at the door of the Navy Department. He realized that the port of Wilmington should be closed, but he feared that, if Farragut were transferred to the North Atlantic Squadron, the plan would be advertised to the Confederates who would then begin to strengthen their defenses. Besides, a large force of troops would be necessary, and Secretary Stanton was not inclined to co-operate.[2] So he postponed his decision.

It was not a question of lack of confidence in Farragut—this had never been higher. Welles was then being criticized in the press for slighting Du Pont. "Not one of them awards me any credit for selecting Farragut," he jotted down in his diary. "No one can now hesitate to say which is the real hero; yet three years ago it would have been different. Farragut is earnest, unselfish, devoted to the country and the service. He sees to every movement, forms his line of battle with care and skill, puts himself at the head, carries out his plan, if there is difficulty leads the way, regards no danger himself, dashes by forts and overcomes obstructions."[3] Du Pont he portrayed as presenting an unfavorable contrast in every respect.[3]

Farragut wrote Welles again on September 3 about shifting vessels on the blockade, but did not refer to operations against Mobile or to the state of his health. Two days later he informed Canby that, as his work appeared to be at an end for the time being, he would ask for a respite from duty, as he had not felt well lately. "I never was in favor of taking Mobile, except for the moral effect, as I believe it would be used by our own people to flood rebeldom with all their supplies," he added.[4]

On the very same day, Welles wrote Farragut a long letter, informing him that Grant could spare military forces to cooperate against the defenses at the mouth of the Cape Fear and thus cut off Wilmington from the sea. Details were given as to where the attack would be made and how it would be carried out. "You are selected to command the naval force," he wrote, "and you will endeavor to be at Port Royal by the latter part of September, where further orders will await you."[5] Grant's force was to move by the first of October. Besides Acting Rear-Admiral Lee's squadron he was to have the *New Ironsides* and some half a dozen monitors, and about eighteen wooden vessels. He was also to bring from the Gulf such officers and vessels as could be spared without weakening the necessary efficiency of the blockade. "The operation is an important one," he concluded enthusiastically, "as closing the last port of the rebels, and destroying their credit abroad by preventing the exportation of cotton as well as preventing the reception of munitions and supplies from abroad. The whole subject is committed to your hands so far as the Department is concerned, in the confident expectation that success may attend our arms."[5]

Welles wrote Farragut another letter the same day congratulating him on the capture of Fort Morgan. "In the success which has attended your operations you have illustrated the efficiency and irresistible power of a naval force led by a bold and vigorous mind, and the insufficiency of any batteries to prevent the passage of a fleet thus led and commanded," he wrote in his best style.[6] These congratulations he wished extended to the army "who have so cordially co-operated with you";[6] and this Farragut did in a letter to General Granger two weeks later.[7]

It happened that Farragut replied, the same day, September 5, to Fox's recent letter of congratulation, declaring that he had been ready to go ahead in the capture of the city of Mobile with the aid of the army but that Canby had informed him that he had to use his troops to support Steele in Arkansas, and that it would be at least a month before any would be available. "It appears to me," wrote Farragut pessimistically of the Presidential campaign, "that our party politics are stronger than the patriotism of our people; it is either that or cowardice, I don't know which, for they appear determined not to fight."[9] This was hardly fair to the Army of the Potomac which had fought from the Rapidan to the James that summer, losing more than 60,000 men, which was more than Lee had had at the beginning of the campaign; but there was a feeling of disappointment in the North when Grant settled down to the long siege of Petersburg and Richmond.[8] Farragut was also unfair to Sherman who had recently brought to a successful issue a long campaign ending with the capture of Atlanta.

Farragut then repeated to Fox that he had never approved of taking Mobile without an overwhelming force to hold it, and that he had the place closely watched by a monitor and three gunboats. His vessels, he complained, were all breaking down because of constant use for two or three years. It was fortunate, he thought, that they had gotten inside the bay for they could not have blockaded outside during the winter months. Concerning his health, he was more particular than in the previous letter to Welles. "As to myself," he declared, "I have been on board ship so long that the want of exercise has had a bad effect on me, and a few days after we came in I had an attack of vertigo that I fear to have repeated. It kept me down for two weeks, but I am now beginning to feel more like myself, but I must have rest and exercise; both my mind and body require them. My mind has been too constantly on the stretch for four or five months. After that I will be ready for any services the Government requires of me."[8] To Fox's feelers about Wilmington, he answered that he knew nothing about its defenses, but that he had been told by officers familiar with those waters that vessels of any size could not enter the river because of the shallowness of the water. Eads' light draft monitors might do, if there was any shelter for them outside; but he thought the season was too far advanced for such operations.[9]

That same day, Drayton was confiding to his friend, Hamilton, ". . . The fact is that if I was not in a very healthy condition and living on oatmeal and water, I should have been used up long ago as almost every one else has been, even the Admiral who prides himself on standing everything, but then he will drink a little wine and eat meat at breakfast."[10] A few days later he wrote his friend that he supposed Farragut would go to Pensacola as soon as an important court-martial was finished, and that there had been some talk of his going North but that he did not know whether the *Hartford* would be going.[11]

2

Then misunderstandings and embarrassments began to develop through the slowness of communications. Ten days after Welles had offered Farragut the command of the North Atlantic Squadron, he received Farragut's letter regarding his health. "I am exceedingly embarrassed how to proceed," he set down in his diary.[12] The War Department had at last become definitely interested in closing up Wilmington. "Just at this crisis," Welles continued with a sigh, "Farragut unfortunately fails. It is unavoidable, a necessity. He would not ask relief if not compelled to, and may try to obey the orders, though I think not; and if he offers to, I shall not, under the present aspect of affairs, accept the service from him."[12]

It did not seem to occur to Welles at any time that he might call Farragut to Washington for a conference, before committing himself to this new campaign. The condition of Farragut's health could there have been determined, plans for the campaign could have been formulated, the change of climate and scene and some additional rest might have enabled Farragut then to have accepted the command. Such unseemly haste was, at least, unusual; Farragut had waited more than six months in the Gulf for sufficient military aid to enter Mobile Bay.

Instead of calling Farragut home for a conference, Welles on the 22d of September wrote him that he had learned of the condition of his health with much regret. "In accordance with the views of the Department and the universal wish of the country, the orders of the 5th instant were given to you," he explained; "but a life so precious must not be thrown away by failing to heed the monitions which the greatest powers of physical endurance receive as a warning to rest. The country will again call upon you perhaps to put the finishing blow to the rebellion." He then ordered Farragut to proceed to New York. This letter was addressed to him at Port Royal, South Carolina,[13] where it was supposed that he might soon arrive.

Meanwhile Farragut received the letter of congratulation and the orders to the new command. The first arrived in the mail boat on September 18, a rainy Sunday. Farragut was sick, having had choleramorbus the previous night.[14] The congratulations cheered him considerably on this dreary day. The other letter did not arrive, for some reason, until three days later.[15] The very next day Farragut answered Welles. "I can but express my surprise that I should be selected for so difficult and arduous a service (and that at the short notice of nine days)," he began.[16] He was ordered to be at Port Royal by the end of September, and received the orders on September 20. Somewhat querulous and forgetful of the length of time necessary in transmitting dispatches from Washington to Mobile Bay, Farragut wrote as though Welles had received his letter explaining his failing health before he had dispatched his orders to a new command. Welles, too, must have forgotten the slowness of communications when he ordered Farragut to be at Port Royal by the 1st of October. Farragut might justifiably write, "Judge, sir, my surprise to find myself called upon to repair to Port Royal to organize an expedition of such magnitude at a port one thousand miles distant in nine or ten days."[16]

Then in reply to Welles's request for his "views and wishes in the matter,"[16] Farragut explained that the large vessels would be of no use because their great draft would prevent their getting near enough to the batteries to damage them with their broadside guns, that the monitors of the *Passaic* class would not be able to cross the bar, and that only the light draft wooden vessels would be able to pass inside. They would, however, be destroyed by the Confederate ironclad, referred to in his orders as being "in the river in commission."[16] The light draft monitors, such as the *Chickasaw* and *Winnebago,* could not with safety be conveyed from the Gulf to Wilmington at that season of the year; and if they arrived, they would be helpless except in smooth water. The *Tennessee* could not possibly be repaired and gotten to Wilmington, as suggested by Welles, in several months. None of Farragut's vessels could be employed, as all were in need of extensive repairs, the *Brooklyn* already having been sent North for that reason. The undertaking, he declared, would be attended with many difficulties, great labor, and constant fatigue of body and mind to the commander in chief who undertook it; and he did not feel equal to such a task. Though at all times anxious to serve his country to the best of his ability, he was fully persuaded that, in attempting such an undertaking, he would do credit neither to the country nor himself. In conclusion, he requested to remain at his post, as Canby had written that he hoped to begin operations against Mobile in a week or two; Farragut was "anxious to finish up the work so satisfactorily begun," and would, accordingly, not proceed to Port Royal until he had a reply from the Secretary.[16]

Drayton felt that Farragut had not been rightly treated. "Such unceremonious treatment might perhaps have been looked for in the case of a midshipman," he complained to Mrs. Farragut, "but that the highest officer in rank and by far the most distinguished officer in our Navy should have been treated with so little consideration brought to my mind very forcibly the allusions you had made to Belisarius and others who had been used as long as they were necessary to the government and then thrown aside and treated with the utmost ingratitude because it suited the caprice of a clique of courtiers. There was an outcry to take Wilmington and to quiet this for the moment your husband was called on without any inquiry as to his convenience, wishes, or health."[17] After reviewing at length the whole episode, he stated that he thought the Admiral would be much better off in the Gulf.

3

Always present were the numerous problems of the blockade. With Mobile Bay in Farragut's hands, the attempts to run cotton-laden vessels out of Texas ports became bolder and more ingenious. A letter which President Lincoln wrote General Canby on August 9 gave Farragut a great deal of concern and annoyance. "For satisfactory reasons which concern the public service," wrote Mr. Lincoln, "I have to direct that, if Andrew J. Hamilton, or any person authorized in writing by him, shall come out of either of the ports of Galveston or Sabine Pass with any vessel or vessels freighted with cotton, shipped to the agent of the Treasury Department at New Orleans, the passage of such person, vessels, and cargoes shall not be molested or hindered; but they shall be permitted to pass to the hands of such consignee."[18]

When this was brought to Farragut's attention, he saw the opportunities for corruption and chicanery, and reported the matter to Welles.[19] The Secretary went to the President to inquire as to its purpose. Lincoln, somewhat embarrassed, said he believed it was all right. "How right?" Welles asked. The President replied, "It is one of Seward's arrangements that I guess will come out well enough." Welles was very much perturbed, and recorded in his diary, "There is unmistakable rascality in this cotton order. . . . He [Lincoln] insisted on a blockade at the beginning. Would not listen to closing the ports. Would make it an international, not permit it to be a domestic, question. Now, in violation of international law and of fair and honorable blockade, he and his friends are secretly bringing out cotton from Texas. This is not in good faith, but is prostituting the government and its action."[20]

The September days passed with a visit from General Canby and Commodore Palmer, who came under the impression that Farragut was on the point of departure for the North. He accompanied them through Fort Morgan. One evening they went to see the Confederate torpedo boat. Before the passage of the fleet into the bay, it had been destroyed near Fort Morgan by a boiler explosion which had killed three of its crew.[21] According to Farragut's description,[22] it was shaped like a cigar and had a propeller on the stern and fixtures on the bow for carrying the torpedo. It was constructed of cypress wood covered with one eighth inch iron, its length being thirty-eight feet and diameter seven feet. Its smokestack and boilers were lying near it in five feet of water.

On the 30th, Farragut had General Granger to dinner, and then they walked together on the shore near Fort Morgan. That evening he had another attack of vertigo.[22] "I have to be careful of my head," he wrote the next day to Rear-Admiral Davis. "This blockade duty, with eighty vessels, nearly a thousand miles of coast, etc., etc., has been a terrible pull upon my brain."[23]

In New York, about that time, Thurlow Weed was congratulating Mrs. Farragut on the "great service" her husband was rendering his country and "the glory he is achieving for himself."[24] He had urged the Government, he claimed, to give him the command at Charleston, assuring the President that wherever he went he would do his work thoroughly and gloriously." "His Fame is imperishably established," he assured her.[24] Captain Charles Steedman was writing his wife, ". . . What a glorious achievement that was of the gallant Farragut! If there ever was or ever is or ever will be a naval Amadis de Gaul or Cid, Farragut should be that individual in the pages of history. I hope Congress will make him a full admiral and place his name at the head of our Navy List. That little man has done more to put down the rebellion than any general except Grant and Sherman."[25] In Washington, Lincoln inquired of Welles about Farragut, and said that Halleck and Sherman and the War Department had "some movements on hand' 'and wished to know if Farragut could remain. Welles replied that Farragut preferred to stay in Mobile Bay to coming to Wilmington and would be permitted to remain as long as he desired. The Secretary was angry at being kept in the dark about the plans of the War Department.[26]

In Mobile Bay there was little evidence of any such "movements." "A move on Mobile now would greatly assist Sherman," wrote Drayton, "but it can't be made without men. The weather is very hot and with the yellow fever quite bad in New Orleans on one side and the breakbone fever at Pensacola on the other, we are pretty fortunate that we remain so healthy." In this letter, Drayton enclosed $500 to pay for a breastpin which Tiffany's was making for Admiral Farragut to present to his wife. "The intention was to make the matter a surprise," he declared, "but as in such cases usually occurs, the secret was too much for him, and perhaps he would not have been a good husband had it been otherwise."[27] The pin was designed to bear Farragut's initials in diamonds on it.

Not many letters which Farragut wrote his wife during that unhappy period are now extant. In one, he began, "They must think I am made of iron." After explaining why he had felt obliged not to accept the command of the new expedition, he continued, "Why, even the routine of duty for a fleet of eighty sail of vessels works us all to death; and but that I have the most industrious fleet-captain and secretary, it would never be half done."[28] He wrote a long letter to his son near mid October, devoted largely to advice for the West Pointer. "In regard to your studies," he counseled, "bear in mind, that which is acquired easily does not stick so well by you as that which has required labor. I confess I do not know much about analytical geometry, and I might not have seen the use of steam, telegraphs, and railroads, when I was as young as you are; but I do now fully comprehend the difficulties of keeping them all in order for working. So go along with your age, my boy, and remember also that one of the requisite studies for an officer is *men*. Where your analytical geometry will serve you once, a knowledge of men will serve you daily. As a commander, to get the right men in the right place is one of the questions of success or defeat. Take another lesson from the affair to which you alluded—about contending with the Government. Dr. Franklin said: 'Always stoop your head a little rather than run it against a beam.' It is not necessary to do wrong to avoid a difficulty. To submit to the decisions of the Government is what we all have to do. The object of government is to decide these matters. It may sometimes do injustice, but an unwise decision will recoil on the officials that be sooner or later. Therefore, my son, avoid difficulties with your superiors if possible, but never submit to indignity without becoming remonstrance."[29]

Farragut wrote Welles, the same day, that he was feeling better and that he expected to leave as soon as he could turn over the squadron to Commodore Palmer, his next in seniority in the Gulf. Nothing was said about the prospects of an offensive against Mobile.[30] He had not then received Welles's long letter of October 1, which arrived on the 18th. In this letter the Secretary attempted to smooth Farragut's ruffled feelings about being ordered to Port Royal on such short notice when he was ill. He was assured that, at the time the orders were sent, Welles did not know he was ill. "There being still a great work to be accomplished, the country as well as the Department looked to you as the proper man for its accomplishment," he wrote reassuringly. Farragut was given full permission to remain at his post and co-operate against Mobile when the army was ready, but the Secretary earnestly desired that he would not overtax his physical and mental powers in such an undertaking. "Aware of what you had done and are doing," Welles added, "the Department, in its contemplated demonstration against Wilmington, proposed to take upon itself and to devolve upon others the labor of collecting and placing at your disposal the force which may be essential to make that demonstration effective."[31] If he had only written this in the original orders, Farragut's decision might have been different. In this letter, he learned for the first time that Rear-Admiral D. D. Porter had been given the command of the North Atlantic Squadron.[31] Porter's official orders were dated September 22, 1864, the same date as that of the letter releasing Farragut from that command. Strangely, in that letter to Farragut, which was sent to Port Royal, Welles made no reference to Porter's being given the command.

Farragut replied immediately, "It is, as you may imagine, most painful to me to be compelled to avoid or evade a duty in any manner or shape whatever." He then reviewed the circumstances and conditions which at the time made it necessary for him to request the selection of some other person more able than he. Then he stated that exercise on shore had improved his health, which was "still not good." Also, he defended the conduct of the generals in that department, who had seemed disposed to do what they could to co-operate with him; but their forces had been small and separated over a wide area.[32] "As to my own life," he concluded, "it is of little consequence; its duration is now but short, and nearly all of it has been expended in the service of my country. My great desire is not to overestimate myself and permit my country to suffer by my weakness."[33] It is noteworthy that in this letter Farragut made no reference, either in approval or disapproval, of Porter's appointment.

Farragut interpreted this letter from Welles as orders to remain at his station.[34] The next day he took a ride with General Granger. The horse fell and hurt the Admiral's leg, but "not much," he wrote.[34] Two days afterwards he took another long ride with Granger on Dauphin Island.[34] He became very friendly with the General, and they had their picture taken together at Fort Gaines.[34] By this time, Drayton could write Mrs. Farragut, "We have had lately quite an agreeable change from the extreme heat of the summer, and owing to it his [Farragut's] health has very much improved and now is, I think, as usual."[35] But the day previous Farragut wrote Fox, "I will in a short time I hope by exercise on shore, walking and riding, soon begin to pick up and regain the tone of my stomach and, with that, my head. I am already much stronger than I was, but still suffer with my head." The letter was a long one, covering the indecision of the army about attacking Mobile, the possession of which he thought "would be a great nuisance"; of the relief he felt over the outcome of the Mobile Bay engagement and the destruction of the *Tennessee,* which had kept him "on the constant alarm for so many months"; of Sherman's request that he send gunboats up the Apalachicola River to destroy the arsenal at Columbus—a plan he thought entirely impractical; and of Porter's taking command of the Wilmington expedition. "Porter has had a long respite," he declared, "is fresh and I feel assured will do as well as any man"—not very hearty approval.[36] Porter had not been actively employed since the army rescued his fleet from the disastrous Red River campaign.

Near the close of October, Canby wrote that "no orders will be given in relation to operations from Mobile until after General Sherman's plan of campaign has been fully determined upon."[37] When the orders came a week later, he was advised to move with 15,000 men against Selma, Alabama, to co-operate with Sherman's march to the sea, then about to get under way through Georgia.[38] Farragut was thus deprived of any military aid in the capture of Mobile, but he remained at his post, waiting for orders to go home.

4

A month, however, was to pass before he departed for New York, where he was to become the idol of the city. Mrs. Farragut had written to prepare him for this hero-worship. "Don't believe I can be spoiled by adulation," he answered. "Thank God, I am able to resist that temptation, if no other. I avoid the ports as much as possible, for my own sake as well as for the well-being of my officers and men. They are not all as able to resist the devil—especially in the shape of a bottle—as I am. But my fleet is very sober. I have only a few disposed in that way. I think the Confederates are beginning to be a little down in the mouth out here. They firmly believed they would retake New Orleans in less than six months when I was last there. All that I used to tell them in Norfolk about civil war is upon them now with a vengeance."[39]

In a letter to Welles on the importance of placing the proper officers in command of monitors, Farragut expressed this interesting principle of warfare: ". . . On this point permit me to say that I think the world is sadly mistaken when it supposes that battles are won by this or that kind of gun or vessel. In my humble opinion, the *Kearsarge* would have captured or sunk the *Alabama* as often as they might have met under the same organization and officers. The best gun and the best vessel should certainly be chosen, but the victory three times out of four depends upon those who fight them. I do not believe that the result would have been different if the *Kearsarge* had had nothing but a battery of 8-inch guns and a 100-pounder chase rifle. What signifies the size and caliber of the gun if you do not hit your adversary?"[40]

On the 12th of November, "a fine clear day,"[41] Farragut made a run up the bay to visit the *Chickasaw* and the three gunboats which were maintaining a close blockade on the city of Mobile; here he found conditions satisfactory. Four days later news came that Lincoln had been reelected by a large electoral majority.[41] There had been great fear among Lincoln's supporters, and as late as August 23 the President himself had written in a private memorandum, "This morning, as for some days past, it seems exceedingly probable that this Administration will not be reelected."[42] That month Horace Greeley wrote Mayor Opdyke of New York, "Mr. Lincoln is already beaten. We must have another ticket to save us from utter overthrow. If we had such a ticket as could be had by naming Grant, Butler, or Sherman for President and Farragut for Vice, we could make a fight yet."[43] This, of course, did not materialize. But Farragut had contributed to the nomination of Lincoln. As Seward expressed it in a speech in Washington, "Sherman and Farragut have knocked the bottom out of the Chicago nominations. Gloomy August became a September edged with a few splinters of dawn."[44]

On the 19th of November, Farragut with Drayton, Watson, and McKinley went in the steamer *Glasgow* to pay General Canby a visit in New Orleans. There the Admiral had some hope of meeting Mrs. Farragut, but received instead a letter[45] from her stating that Fox had told her he was soon coming home. There was also a dispatch from Welles, informing him that it is "the wish of the Department that you should feel at liberty to turn over the command of the West Gulf Squadron to the next officer in rank to yourself at any time you may see fit and return to New York on the *Hartford*."[46] Farragut replied that he would turn over his command to Commodore Palmer about the 1st of December.[47]

After celebrating Thanksgiving Day in New Orleans, Farragut returned to the *Hartford* in Mobile Bay. On Monday, November 28, at six o'clock in the morning, the flagship got under way, hoisted the signal "Goodbye" to the squadron, received three cheers from the *Richmond*, and put to sea for Pensacola. In the early afternoon of the 30th, the *Hartford* sailed for New York to the sound of the echoing salutes from Fort Barrancas and all the war vessels in the harbor.[48] With adequate coordination in planning between the War and Navy Departments, and more consideration of Farragut's feelings at the close of an arduous campaign on the part of Mr. Welles, Farragut might have gone home two months earlier. "We are off at last for the North," he joyfully wrote Mrs. Farragut off Pensacola Bar, "with the delightful hope of seeing our beloved ones, wives and sweethearts. May God grant us a quick and pleasant passage. My labors have been incessant up to the last moment. I feel as if I were leaving my charge for a short recreation, but I shall not anticipate evil. God has not only been merciful to me, but blessed me with great success, and I still trust in his mercy."[49] Though he did not know it, Farragut was bidding farewell forever to the scenes of his greatest labors, anxieties, and triumphs; he was never again to see the Gulf of Mexico.

XXVI

THE WAR ENDS

1

WITH GOOD weather, the *Hartford* made excellent time under sail and steam, and arrived at Key West early on the morning of the 4th of December. Rear-Admiral Stribling came aboard, and the *San Jacinto* and the *Hartford* exchanged salutes. It being Sunday, the two admirals went to church together. Early the next day, the *Hartford* sailed for New York. For four days all went well. Then it began to blow hard and a very heavy sea rolled the ship terribly; the waist boats were filled again and again, and finally the barge was torn away and lost. The battle scarred *Hartford*, only temporarily repaired in Mobile Bay, fought through the rolling waves and terrific wind for four days. Very early on the 12th, she made the Barnegat Light, and in the afternoon anchored off Sandy Hook lighthouse.[1] At noon the next day she moved up the bay in charge of the pilot.[2]

Before the *Hartford* came to anchor, Farragut found himself in the hands of the hero-worshippers. The revenue cutter *Bronx*, carrying Collector of the Port Draper and several prominent citizens, bore down on the approaching vessel, which was flying at her mizzen the Admiral's blue pennant. Farragut and Drayton were standing on the poop deck, and "exchanged friendly salutations"[3] with the party, who came on board and were conducted to the Admiral's cabin. They turned out to be a "welcoming committee."[3] Draper delivered a short appropriate speech, praising Farragut's achievements and informing him that on his arrival the leading citizens of New York wished to receive him at a formal meeting at the Custom House and tender him a reception "somewhat worthy"[3] of his great services. Farragut thanked him briefly, and the gentlemen departed, after they were shown

REAR-ADMIRAL FARRAGUT AND COMMODORE J. S. PALMER
From a photograph made by McPherson & Oliver, New Orleans, Nov., 1864. From author's collection.

REAR-ADMIRAL FARRAGUT
From a photograph made by Bogardus, New York. From author's collection.

Courtesy of F. H. Meserve
REAR-ADMIRAL FARRAGUT AND BRIGADIER-GENERAL GRANGER
From a photograph taken at Fort Gaines in August, 1864.

VICE-ADMIRAL D. G. FARRAGUT, U. S. NAVY
From a photograph by Brady, furnished by the L. C. Handy Studios, Washington, D.C.

several curiosities, among which were two chairs in the cabin which had belonged to Admiral Buchanan and General Page.[4]

When the *Hartford* came to off the Battery at a quarter past three, the *Bronx* again came puffing out with the Committee and other prominent citizens and, receiving Farragut and Drayton on board, returned to the wharf at the Battery. Here a crowd had gathered to see the Admiral, and "cheer after cheer arose as he stepped on the pier, and before reaching terra firma the mob had increased to hundreds, and the Admiral had to run the gauntlet of outstretched, welcoming hands, which he good-humoredly shook to the best of his ability before reaching the coach which was in waiting."[3] He was then driven up Broadway and down Wall Street to the Custom House, people on the street being unaware of the distinguished naval officer in "the simple hack,"[3] which was followed by an "omnibus filled with the remainder of the suite."[3] It was long before the day of ticker tape receptions.

At the Custom House, a crowd "wild with enthusiasm"[3] made it difficult for Farragut to reach the Collector's Office, where there were formal introductions, reading of resolutions, and speeches. It was well for him that his health had improved. The laudatory resolutions invited Farragut to become a citizen of New York "so that the man, his achievements, and his fame may belong to the city."[3] The Admiral's reply was brief but sincere and impressive. "I have been devoted to the service of my country since I was eight years of age," he said in part, "and my father was devoted to it before me. I have not specially deserved these demonstrations of your regard. I owe everything, perhaps, to chance, and to the praiseworthy exertions of my brother officers serving with me. That I have been very fortunate is most true, and I am thankful, deeply thankful for it, for my country's sake."[3] This was followed by "great applause,"[3] and three cheers for Farragut, three for Drayton, and three for the "fleet that captured Mobile."[3] The last phrase must have made Farragut and Drayton wince, for the fleet had not captured Mobile.

After Drayton's speech of thanks, composed of only three

short sentences, Colonel A. J. H. Duganne read a poem he had written for the occasion. This was a "stirring ballad, which was listened to with breathless interest throughout, although the modest Admiral wore the appearance of being somewhat overwhelmed with eulogy."[3] His feeling might have been a mixture of fatigue and boredom. The poem had ten stanzas of seventeen lines each. The following last stanza was probably the best:

> "Messmates! at morn we fight:
> This may be our last night;
>   Fill up the can again!
> If we must bravely fall,
> God keep our dear ones all!
> God shield the Admiral,
>   Leading our van again!
> When, o'er yon channel bars,
> Stream out the rocket stars,
> Then, to the signal spars,
>   Up will climb Farragut;
> Listening to cannon-jars,
>   There will be Farragut!
> Wrapped in his battle cloak,
> Woven from fire and smoke,
> God bless his heart of oak;
>   There we'll see Farragut."[3]

A reporter for the *Tribune*, who had been observing the Admiral, was reminded of Sir Gervais Oaks in Cooper's *Two Admirals*. "Hale, hearty, and of rather spare but powerful mold, the Hero of New Orleans and Mobile Bay is apparently between fifty and sixty years of age," he wrote. "He looks as if he dearly loved a joke, steps with the springiness of a boy, and his manner is so perfectly frank and unassuming that it is no wonder that he is beloved by his officers and men."[3]

Finally, after shaking hands with numerous people who were introduced to him, Farragut made an escape from his admirers and was driven to the home of a friend on Twenty-third Street where "Mrs. Farragut was expecting him."[3] He immediately telegraphed his arrival to Secretary Welles, and the same day dispatched a written report of his voyage North.[5] This was accompanied by a statement from Drayton as to the condition of the *Hartford* and the status of her crew.[5] On December 20, the

THE WAR ENDS 315

"dear old *Hartford*" was turned over to Rear-Admiral Paulding at the Navy Yard for repairs and at sunset Farragut's flag was hauled down[6] for the last time on the vessel with whose name his own will be forever associated.

Fox greeted Farragut on his return in a very friendly manner. "It is a source of very great happiness to me that you have come back with the laurels of Nelson without leaving any limbs or eyes for those rascals to console themselves with," he wrote banteringly. "Perhaps if there was not a beautiful wife, I should not think so much about it, but how shocking it would be for us to hand over only part of you."[7] Welles's communications were stiffly official and formal, as though he had been somewhat displeased with Farragut about the Wilmington campaign. Just then that expedition was giving him much concern. There had been great delay in Army co-operation, and the military aid finally had come from General Butler's troops. Though Butler's name was anathema to Porter, they had buried the hatchet; but not very deep. Butler insisted on accompanying the opéra bouffe expedition which had just gotten under way about the middle of December and was to end in complete failure on Christmas Day in spite of Porter's armada of sixty ships and Butler's 7,500 troops.[8] Welles may have wished he had heeded Farragut's advice and not embarked on such an expedition at that season of the year.

2

Farragut found himself again caught in the social whirl of a large city. There was a "series of festivities," as Drayton called them.[9] Meanwhile in Washington a bill was introduced in Congress on December 22, creating the grade of Vice-Admiral. It immediately passed both houses, and was signed the following day by Lincoln, who had recommended it in his annual message. The President at once named Farragut as the first Vice-Admiral, and the Senate confirmed the nomination without delay on December 21.[10] The pay of the Vice-Admiral at sea was set at $7,000; while on shore duty he was to receive $6,000, and $5,000 when waiting orders. *The Army and Navy Journal* highly approved the action of Congress and the President, in establishing the grade of Vice-Admiral and the "promotion of the brave Farragut to that new rank."[11] "In Farragut the ideal sailor, the seaman of Nelson's and Collingwood's days, is revived," it declared; "and the feeling of the people toward him is of the same peculiar character as that which those great and simple-hearted naval heroes of Great Britain evoked in the hearts of their countrymen."

Farragut was invited by Joseph H. Choate to attend the annual dinner of the New England Society on December 22 at the Astor House.[12] It was a brilliant affair. As a glee club finished "New England, I Love Thee," Farragut entered, and the audience rose and greeted him enthusiastically with nine cheers. He was then conducted to a seat on the right of the President of the Society. In the course of the evening William Cullen Bryant, the poet and editor, made an eloquent speech, and Farragut also spoke briefly, beginning, "Gentlemen, I do not know what your expectations may be of Vice-Admiral Farragut, but I have seen enough of Rear-Admiral Farragut to know that he is not very well qualified to make such a speech as you would wish to listen to." In closing, he said he could back up what Bryant had said about the sons of New England pouring out their blood in the South. "God knows they have poured it out freely."[13] Captain Winslow, who destroyed the *Alabama,* was also present and made a short speech, as did Captain Drayton.

Christmas Day was celebrated in New York, where Farragut was joined by his son Loyall on leave from West Point.[14] The Admiral's recent antagonist in Mobile Bay celebrated the day by writing him from his prison in Fort Lafayette, complaining of an article in a recent issue of the *Herald,* in which Farragut was reported to have said that he saw a letter from Buchanan requesting him to use his influence to get him in the Naval Hospital. This Admiral Buchanan hotly denied. "I have no objection to all my acts, public and private, being known to the world," he caustically wrote, "but I have an objection to being misrepresented."[15] Farragut answered coldly and unsympathetically, "I did not say that 'I tried to shoot your leg off,' nor did I say that you had written me a letter asking my intervention to have you removed to the Naval Hospital, as reported in the newspaper." The letter in question, he declared, was written by Mrs. Buchanan.[16]

About this time, Farragut received a letter from the author, James Parton, stating that he had written him two weeks previous, but that, as there had been no reply, he had concluded that his letter had not been received, and so was repeating his request. He desired to write a biography of the Vice-Admiral, but would not attempt to do so without his consent and co-operation. He requested one hour's conversation with him each day for a week or two, a list of officers and others from whom he might secure "interesting information," and permission to copy official orders and reports. "How desirable then that our young men should learn how great things are done, and catch inspiration from those who have done honor to the naval service," he declared enthusiastically. "I think that such a volume as I propose would be useful in this respect. It could do no honor to you, but it might to the country and to the navy, as well as fire some young spirits to endeavor to follow your example. It would be to me a most grateful task, and I think I could do it so as not to offend your modesty. It would be a pleasure to you, I think, to see the services of your gallant officers and men placed on record in a volume accessable (sic) to all the public."[17] Nothing came of the proposal. Farragut may have felt unable then to give the kind of co-operation requested. Parton had published, the preceding year, *General Butler in New Orleans: Being a History of the Department of the Gulf in the Year 1862*. Farragut may not have been pleased with the way the author made him play second fiddle to Butler in that book. Welles expressed his displeasure with Parton's giving Butler and Secretary of War Stanton the credit for initiating the New Orleans expedition.[18]

On the last day of the year, a very substantial recognition of Farragut's services to his country was made by a committee representing the merchants of New York City. The presentation was made at the Custom House at eleven o'clock on that Saturday morning. A letter engrossed on a large sheet of parchment and enclosed in a blue morocco case, lined with white and red satin, was first read and then handed to the Admiral.[19] After praising his achievements in ringing phrases, the letter ended as follows: "The citizens of New York can offer no tribute equal to your claims on their gratitude and affection. Their earnest desire is, to receive you as one of their number, and to be permitted, as fellow citizens, to share in the renown you will bring to the Metropolitan City. This desire is felt in common by the whole community, and, in the hope that it may not be inconsistent with your own views, the grateful duty has been confided to us of placing in your hands the accompanying testimonial."[20] Then to Farragut was handed a large envelope, tied with red, white, and blue ribbons, containing $50,000 in government bonds, which had been purchased with subscriptions made by the "merchant-princes of New York."[19] Farragut responded with modesty as to his accomplishments, but he was profuse in the expression of his thanks for the cordiality of his reception in New York and for this crowning evidence of "the flattering attention" accorded him. "It would be impossible for me, even if I were in the habit of making speeches, to express what I so heartily feel," he said with sincere emotion. "As to becoming a resident and a citizen of New York, nothing would be more grateful to my feelings. I came here, I can hardly say as a refugee but being forced out of the South where I had resided more than forty years; came naturally to this city, as the metropolis of the country, and made my resting-place on the banks of the Hudson. I have every reason to be grateful; you have always extended to me and my family the kindest treatment; and it would be but natural that we should feel a desire to be with you."[20]

3

By this time Farragut was very much in need of quiet and rest, and in the afternoon following the presentation of the testimonial he and Mrs. Farragut went to their home at Hastings-on-Hudson. Here they were given a sincere and beautiful reception. In Union Square near the railroad station a triumphal arch had been erected, which was decorated with evergreens and flags and bore the inscription, "Welcome to Admiral Farragut."[21] Though a deep snow had fallen all that day, a large crowd greeted them as they stepped from the train. They were then driven in a sleigh to the Reformed Dutch Church through other arches at street intersections, which bore the names, "New Orleans" and "Mobile." As the Admiral entered the church, the band played "See, the Conquering Hero Comes."[21] Over the pulpit was an inscription in evergreens, "May God bless and preserve you."[21] After the address welcoming Farragut home again, which was an excellent one because it was brief, he delivered a beautiful response, under such emotion that he found it difficult at times to proceed. "When, nearly four years ago, I came to this village, unknown and without means, a voluntary refugee from my country because I could not participate in measures hostile to the dictates of all loyal duty and to all the associations of my life," he said, "I was received with open arms and with a warmth of friendship and a sympathy of patriotic and social intercourse that have ripened into attachments and associations which can never be effaced, wherever I may be, or whatever may be my future lot. Here, also, when absent on distant duty in a service dear to my heart, my family have found a quiet and agreeable retreat, where the hand of friendship and the kindest attentions were ever extended to them."[21] After shaking hands with every one present, including the children, he and his wife were taken to their residence. The white mantle of snow then covered everything; and over the entrance to their house the neighbors had placed in evergreen letters the name, "Virginia L. Farragut."[21] This simple but beautiful tribute to his wife as the sharer in his honor gave Farragut as much pleasure and satisfaction as all the recognition he had received.

Farragut's rest in Hastings was brief. After remaining only four days, he and Mrs. Farragut went to Washington, accompanied by Captain Drayton.[22] On Saturday following, he called on Mr. Welles, and they went to see the President together.

That evening the Farraguts and Captain Drayton dined with the Secretary and Mrs. Welles.[23] Farragut lives "in society from morning to night," wrote Drayton, "and seems to enjoy the excitement much."[24] On the evening of the 19th of January he and Mrs. Farragut were invited to attend the opera with the President and Mrs. Lincoln. "The former quite won Mrs. F's. heart by his genial manner," Drayton reported. "She would not tell much that occurred for fear of its getting into the papers, as she said, but one joke I must repeat. She remarked how pleasantly distance softened the music. 'Yes,' was the response, 'it is like time on whiskey.' "[24]

In the *Army and Navy Journal,* about this time, there appeared an article by an officer of the West Gulf Blockading Squadron under the nom de plume of "Valeat Quantum," answering a complaint by an anonymous writer which had appeared in the *Journal* of November 19. The allegation was that Farragut's official report, which had been published in various papers, did not give enough credit to the *Brooklyn, Monongahela, Oneida, Port Royal,* and *Ossipee.* The answering article pointed out that the complainant did not know the facts and was doing wrong to bring division into the service with a criticism of Farragut who had accomplished so much for his country.[25]

The following week there appeared an interesting article in the same journal on Farragut. After analyzing a dozen or so notable achievements of naval leaders, the writer declared, "Of all the great admirals who have flourished, there is only one, as a man, a comparison to whom would be just to our Farragut. That one was the Dutch Ruyter. Nelson failed or fell short in many particulars. Among other things, his subservience to the interests and views of the Court of Naples, his connection with Lady Hamilton, his judicial murder of the gallant Carraccioli, are serious blots upon his character. Ruyter, on the other hand, was a Christian republican and born gentleman. . . . He lived a model of Christian simplicity; he died an example of Christian resignation. No aristocratic or mundane idea of Westminster Abbey as a burial place troubled his death scene."[26]

4

The Union naval force on the James below Richmond had been somewhat weakened by sending some vessels to Porter's tremendous fleet, which had at last succeeded on January 15 in making possible the storming and capture of Fort Fisher by General Terry's army of 8,000 men. Commodore John K. Mitchell, in command of the Confederate squadron at Richmond, on the night of January 23 moved down the river to attempt to cut Grant's communications with his supply base at City Point. His force consisted of three ironclads, a gunboat, a torpedo boat, and three torpedo launches. One ironclad passed through the obstructions, but the other two ran aground. The double-turreted monitor *Onondaga* retired, according to Commander William A. Parker, "to obtain an advantageous position."[27] When the news reached Washington, Lincoln sent for Welles, who found Secretary Stanton with the President. Stanton had a dispatch from Grant, asking that Commander Parker be removed from his command. In the course of the conversation, Welles remarked that Farragut was still in Washington, and Lincoln sent for him at Willard's Hotel. Hearing how matters stood, he volunteered to go down and investigate the situation. Lincoln was pleased, and Farragut at once began preparations to depart. At ten o'clock in the evening he set out for Annapolis by special train. Grant telegraphed Fox that he would be glad to see Farragut but that he would be of no service in the present emergency;[28] but the Admiral had already departed by that time to take the steamer at Annapolis.

When Farragut arrived at City Point, he learned that the Confederates at flood tide had gotten the two ironclads off and had retired upstream with the loss of the gunboat and one of the torpedo launches. Another attempt had been made the following night, but it had been frustrated by Federal batteries on shore.[27] Parker had meanwhile been relieved of his command,[29] and Commander William Radford had been ordered up from Norfolk to take his place.[29] Seeing that the emergency had passed, Farragut left for Washington by way of Annapolis on the steamer *Don*, where he arrived on Saturday evening,

January 28. He went directly to Welles's residence, where Mrs. Farragut had been invited to stay during his absence.[30] In making his report, he called the Secretary's attention to the fact that Fox had signed his own name to telegrams to Grant and Parker which Welles had written and sent by Fox to the telegraph office. Farragut was indignant. "I have, on one or two occasions," wrote Welles, "detected something similar in Fox in regard to important orders—where he had been intrusive or obtrusive, evidently to get his name in the history of these times, and perhaps to carry the impression that he was at least a coadjutor with the Secretary in naval operations. Farragut assures me he has observed and detected this disposition and some objectionable acts in Fox, as in this instance, which he thinks should be reproved and corrected, but while I regret these faults I have deemed them venial."[31]

Mrs. Farragut was displeased with the way the Admiral had been hurried away at a moment's notice, and did not approve of the apparent pleasure he had taken in the excursion. Drayton thought that, after the Admiral had occupied such a prominent position for years, he did not like inactivity even though he did have the rank of Vice-Admiral. As senior officer in the navy, he had recently been appointed president of a board which was to recommend officers for promotion.[32] He favored the creation of a Board of Admiralty, and tried in vain to persuade Welles that it would be beneficial to the government and the country.[33] The question of promotions was a serious and difficult one, and Drayton feared that Farragut might find duty at the head of such a board a troublesome one. "There is a disposition to place Porter in advance by Fox," Welles confided to his diary. "Admiral Porter is a man of courage and resource, but has already been greatly advanced, and has some defects and weaknesses."[34] Farragut's board, after much labor, made out a list of officers for promotion and sent it to the Senate for confirmation; but it arrived half an hour late, and the matter had to be held over for the next Congress.[35]

Meanwhile the Farraguts continued to enjoy themselves at

dinner parties, one of which was at the White House. "The Admiral is most certainly going through almost as much risk of life with all his dissipation as he has in his battles," Drayton wrote ruefully, "and I am really afraid that he will seriously impair his health before the winter is over. I have written to tell his wife that because I am away she must not permit him to run wild, and get back to the late hours which through constant lecturing I thought to have somewhat broken in on."[36]

During the festivities incident to Lincoln's second inauguration, the Farraguts were in Washington. At the Capitol, on that rainy morning of March 4, "invited notables trooped in to their reserved seats," according to Sandburg. "General Joe Hooker, rosy, decked out as though for a corps review, strode in representing the army. From a side door stole in a naval figure, women whispering 'The dear old Admiral' as Farragut half slunk with modesty into his seat."[37] "All was confusion and without order—a jumble," Welles wrote sorrowfully. "The Vice-President made a rambling and strange harangue, which was listened to with pain and mortification by all of his friends. I said to Stanton, who was on my right, 'Johnson is either drunk or crazy' "[38] All this was forgotten when Lincoln began his now famous Second Inaugural, ending with the immortal words: "With malice toward none; with charity for all; with firmness in the right, as God gives us to see the right, let us strive on to finish the work we are in; to bind up the nation's wounds; to care for him who shall have borne the battle, and for his widow, and his orphan—to do all which may achieve and cherish a just and lasting peace among ourselves, and with all nations."

The crowd and the confusion at the President's reception was almost too much even for Farragut. "From the midst of this compress mass on that platform at the entrance I heard a voice and saw the hand of a tall naval officer waved toward me, with the call: 'Can't you get us out of this?'" declared Lieutenant Ashmun of the White House Guards. "After a hard struggle he was reached and at his side a much shorter man in full uniform was standing, whom I had not seen until then, and who proved to be Admiral Farragut being released from a very uncomfortable position, to say nothing of the delay in reaching the President."[39]

An incident displaying Farragut's simplicity of character and almost boyish youthfulness of spirit and feeling is related by General James Grant Wilson to have happened in Washington during this March of 1865. "Are you going to Mrs. Lincoln's reception?" asked Mrs. Farragut of Wilson, then a colonel. "Yes," he answered, "and I shall be accompanied by the belle of the capital." The Admiral thereupon joined in with this remark: "Certainly not, Colonel; the prettiest girl in Washington is going with me." So a wager was made, with the agreement that Mrs. Lincoln was to decide the contest between the two beauties. The Admiral appeared at the White House with a triumphant smile, escorting the lovely Miss B——, and when the decision went against her, he was as greatly disappointed as if he had been a young fellow of twenty with his fiancee instead of a married man of 63. "The old hero most amusingly questioned the fairness of the decision," wrote General Wilson, "and insisted that Miss B—— was a greater beauty than Miss K——, that she was *la rosa entre toda*, and that he should have the champagne."[40]

5

Later in March, Admiral and Mrs. Farragut went to Norfolk to visit relatives. Here at noon on April 3, the Admiral heard of the evacuation of Richmond, and he and Brigadier-General George H. Gordon left immediately by steamer for the Virginia capital. Landing at Varina on the James River below Richmond, they arrived by horseback in the city on the morning of the 4th. Order had been restored by General Weitzel's troops but there was yet some confusion, the smoke still rising from the ruins of the areas which had been devastated by fire. They rode to the Capitol, where General Weitzel had his headquarters in the Senate Chamber. "The door opened, and a smooth-faced man, with a keen eye and a firm, quick, resolute step, entered," according to war correspondent Charles C. Coffin. "He wore a plain blue blouse, with three stars on the collar. It was the old hero who opened the way to New Orleans, and who fought the battle of the Mobile forts from the masthead of his vessel—Admiral Farragut. . . . It was a pleasure to take the brave Admiral's hand, answer his eager questions as to what Grant had done. Being latest of all present from Petersburg, I could give him the desired information. 'Thank God it is about over!' said he."[41]

On the return trip down the James that afternoon, Farragut met Lincoln and Porter proceeding up to the city. Porter had managed to have his flagship *Malvern* at City Point, and when Lincoln arrived there, he took him in charge. So it was Porter and not Farragut who accompanied the President in his first visit to the fallen Confederate capital. It was Porter and not the Vice-Admiral who rode with Lincoln and Weitzel through the streets of Richmond with a cavalry escort.[42]

At a reception given Farragut in Norfolk by the Union League and officers of the Army and Navy after the fall of Richmond, he made a short speech in which he reverted to the unhappy weeks preceding the secession of Virginia—an action which caused him to leave his home with his family and go to New York. The speech may have been given near the date of the surrender at Appomattox, for he concluded thus: "I hope, my friends, that this day, with its events, may prove the culminating point of our revolution; and I hope that before long all will be restored to that peace and reunion which has been sought by the Government and desired by everybody; and then you, gentlemen, who have deserved so well of your country by your steady adherence to its Government, will receive the reward which fidelity, and honesty, and moral courage always deserve."[43]

This visit was not a very pleasant one for Farragut. According to tradition, when he went to call on a lady who had been his friend before the war, she did not offer her hand or give him any word of welcome; but stood and looked at him in silence and at last said with mixed sadness and bitterness, "My dear Admiral, between you and me there is a deep gulf." He turned away without replying, and left the house; and there was no more friendship between the families.⁴⁴ This was probably the feeling and attitude of most of the first families of the city, among whom he had previously lived. There was another tradition among them that before the war Farragut had said that "his right arm would wither at his side before he would raise it against the South" and that "if Virginia seceded, he would resign at once his commission in the United States Navy" and tender his sword to the South.⁴⁵ Their bitterness was accentuated, no doubt, by Farragut's having fought against former Norfolk intimate friends, Commander Charles F. McIntosh who had died of his wounds in the New Orleans campaign, and Brigadier-General Richard L. Page who had been captured at the surrender of Fort Morgan. Besides there was Captain John K. Mitchell, husband of his wife's cousin, who was also made a prisoner in the New Orleans campaign. Under such circumstances, the visit of the Farraguts to the old city they had loved so dearly was comparatively brief, and the Admiral was never to return.

XXVII

ADMIRAL OF THE NAVY

1

THE NEWS OF the assassination of Lincoln on the evening of April 14 brought Farragut to Washington. On Tuesday afternoon, April 18, he wrote Mrs. Farragut, "Welles arrived to-day at eleven. I at six only five hours ahead of him. They have the man who attacked Mr. Seward—great gloom exists. All the people in the city are going to see the President in state. I go tomorrow as one of the pallbearers. Will write after the funeral. We made our visit to the White House or to Mr. President Johnson. Mr. and Mrs. Welles send their love to you. God bless you, my dearest wife. D. G. Farragut."[1] "On Wednesday, April 19," according to Sandburg,[2] "arrived sixty clergymen, the Cabinet members, the Supreme Court Justices, important officials from coast to coast, foreign ministers spangled in color and costume, General Grant with white sash across his breast, Admiral Farragut as a model of composure and quiet valor, and new President Andrew Johnson—six hundred dignitaries in all—crowded and squeezed amid the chandeliers and eight grand mirrors of the East Room."

After this sad event, time passed more slowly and less dramatically for the Farraguts. For several weeks they retired to Hastings-on-Hudson for the rest which the Admiral had so long needed. The last of June they went with their son Loyall to attend the Peace Jubilee in Boston.[3] In Faneuil Hall, on the afternoon of July 6, a public reception was given in honor of Farragut and Brigadier-General Robert Anderson, the hero of Fort Sumter.[4] When they appeared on the rostrum, there was much cheering and waving of hats and fluttering of perfumed handkerchiefs, a little brief speech making, and a great deal of handshaking as the entire audience passed across the platform to be presented to the heroes, who shook hands with about twenty-five hundred people and were kissed besides by "at least two hundred ladies, representing all ages."[4] The Admiral and the General "stood all such attacks with composure, if not pleasure."[5]

After enjoying an excursion down the harbor to visit Fort Warren and other notable places, Farragut went in the evening to the Union Club where a dinner was given in his honor, during which Oliver Wendell Holmes read one of his best occasional poems, entitled "A Toast to the Vice-Admiral," which is as follows:

"Now gallant friends and shipmates all,
    Since half our battle's won,
A broadside for our Admiral!
    Load every crystal gun!
Stand ready till I give the word,—
    You won't have time to tire,—
And when that glorious name is heard,
    Then let the main deck fire!

Bow foremost sinks the rebel craft;
    Our eyes not sadly turn
And see the pirates huddling aft
    To drop their raft astern;
Soon o'er the sea-worm's destined prey
    The lifted wave shall close,—
So perish from the face of day
    All Freedom's banded foes!

But ah! what splendors fire the sky!
    What glories greet the morn!
The storm-tost banner streams on high,
    Its heavenly hues new born!
Its red fresh dyed in heroes' blood,
    Its peaceful white more pure,
To float unstained o'er field and flood
    While earth and seas endure!

All shapes that feel the living blast
    Must glide from mortal view,—
Black roll the billows of the past
    Behind the present's blue,—
Fast, fast are lessening in the light
    The names of high renown,—

> Van Tromp's proud besom fades from sight,
>   Old Benhow's half hull down!
>
> Scarce one tall frigate walks the sea,
>   Or skirts the safer shores
> Of all that bore to victory
>   Our stout old Commodores;
> Hull, Bainbridge, Porter,—where are they?
>   The answering billows roll
> Still bright in memory's sunset ray,—
>   God rest each gallant soul!
>
> A brighter name must dim their light
>   With more than noon-tide ray,—
> The Viking of the River Fight—
>   The Conqueror of the Bay!
> For others shape the marble form,
>   The molten image cast,
> But paint him in the battle-storm,
>   Lashed to his flagship's mast!
>
> Now then, your broadsides, shipmates all,
>   With grape well loaded down!
> May garlands filled with sunshine fall
>   To gild his silvered crown!
> I give the name that fits him best,—
>   Ay, better than his own,—
> The Sea King of the Sovereign West,
>   Who made his mast a throne!"[6]

In Cambridge on the following day, the Harvard students received Farragut with hearty cheers, and when a slight accident happened to his carriage, they removed the horses and themselves drew him through the streets to the various college buildings. At the Scientific School, he briefly addressed the students, and that evening there was a brilliant reception to him at the home of Mr. Charles Dean.[7]

Probably it was during this visit to Boston that Farragut had dinner with Congressman Alexander H. Rice. "At one time while a guest at my house," Rice related, "the serving man at table was about to fill his glass with water, when the Admiral quietly passed his hand over the top of it, and playfully remarked, 'None of that inside me to-day, if you please, though I usually like about three or four fathoms under my keel.'"[8]

From Boston, Farragut went on a two weeks' tour of the White Mountains with his wife and son, and then visited his old friend, Rear-Admiral Bailey, Commandant of the Portsmouth Navy Yard, and Mrs. Bailey. After four days, the Farraguts boarded the steam-tug *Port Fire* and departed for the Isle of Shoals and Rye Beach, lustily cheered by the two thousand employees of the yard who had gathered on the wharf, and given a parting salute of fifteen guns from the *Vandalia* as the little tug steamed out of the harbor.[9]

During the summer, Farragut received a letter from the Prince de Joinville, to whom he had sent a copy of the plan of the Battle of Mobile Bay. The Prince declared that he had read and reread all that he could secure about his "gallant deeds." "Since the days of Nelson," he affirmed, "I don't know of more brilliant actions, and the skill and bravery displayed is if possible heightened by the simplicity and modesty shown by yourself and your gallant brothers in arms."[10]

2

There was a deceptive calm in the affairs of the nation during the summer and autumn of 1865. Underneath the surface were the smoldering fires of passion which were to be fanned into hot flames when Congress met early in December to debate the plan of reconstruction in the Southern states.

Ten days after Congress began its session, Farragut went to Washington to see Mr. Welles. The findings of the court on promotions, of which he had been president, had been set aside. Its proceedings Welles thought "a shocking jumble." "I should not be surprised," he wrote down in his diary, "if Farragut's kind and generous heart acquiesced against his better judgment, but I do not know. We had some talk in regard to promotions. It will make lifelong enmities to supersede. Farragut suggests that medals will answer an equal purpose."[11] Vice-Admiral Farragut then went home, feeling no doubt that he was somewhat in the way and entirely useless in Washington. That summer on July 5 he had celebrated his sixty-fourth birthday.

The winter was spent in New York in the home at 113 East 36th Street, which Farragut had purchased with the generous gift of the New York merchants. It was an imposing residence with brown stone front, of the sort then very fashionable in the city.[12] The demands of society occupied much of the Admiral's time. But this he greatly enjoyed, and Mrs. Farragut had developed an interest in society and liked to meet particularly people connected with public affairs. Some of the Admiral's time was devoted to the perplexing problem of the settlement of the prize money due him and his officers and men for the many captures made in the Gulf and the campaigns of New Orleans and Mobile Bay.[13] He read with misgivings the news of the battle then beginning to rage between President Johnson and the radical leaders in Congress. With mixed feelings he read Johnson's Washington's Birthday speech in which he classed Sumner and Stevens with Jeff Davis as traitors to the constitutional form of government of the United States. Probably with a desire to be nearer the scene of action, he and Mrs. Farragut paid a visit to Secretary and Mrs. Welles toward the close of April,[14] about the time the debate on the proposed Fourteenth Amendment began. The Thirteenth Amendment, ratified the preceding December, had freed the slaves; the Fourteenth Amendment, among other things, attempted to assure the Negro the right of suffrage.

One of the reasons for Farragut's visit to Washington was his interest in a bill which Congress passed on Wednesday, May 10. This gave him a secretary, with the rank, sea pay, and allowances of a lieutenant, to aid him in attending to his large correspondence.[15] Another item of legislation under consideration was of much more interest to him. This was the Act of July 25 which was to establish the rank of Admiral with the annual compensation of $10,000. He was immediately named by the President for this high office, the first full Admiral in the United States Navy. The Senate at once confirmed his nomination, his commission being dated July 25, 1866.[16] That evening Farragut and Welles called on General Grant to congratulate him, as he had been made a full General the same day. They then rode on to the Capitol where the Congress was having an evening meeting.[17] The press highly approved these promotions. "They set the final seal of the national approval on the distinguished services rendered by these two officers," declared the *Army and Navy Journal*,[18] "who we believe will both be content to wear the honors they have so gloriously won without being led aside from their legitimate sphere by the seductive but delusive ambition of the Presidency. However considerations of public duty may require a sacrifice of personal wishes in this regard, we may be sure that both of these representative heroes of the war for the Union are placed by their position beyond the influence of personal motives in their action with reference to that office, which is neither to be sought nor declined. Neither of them will ever enter into a partisan strife to obtain it; and if it comes to them at all, it will be through an expression of public sentiment too marked to be lightly disregarded."

Farragut's star was then in the ascendant. That summer a portrait of him by William Page was exhibited in the Somerville Gallery in New York. It represented him as "lashed to the rigging of the *Hartford* in Mobile Bay," and was praised as a masterly work.[19] The portrait was painted from life in the artist's studio on Tenth Street in New York, the Admiral himself showing Page with a small piece of rope just how the quartermaster made him fast to the futtock shrouds.[20] This portrait was purchased by a committee of citizens, and on December 2, 1869 it was given to the Grand Duke Alexis at the Academy of Design in New York for presentation to Czar Alexander II of Russia.[20]

3

Farragut was in sympathy with the conservative policy of reconstruction, and supported his fellow Tennessean, President Johnson, in his attempt to carry it into effect. He was one of the party of influential men who accompanied Johnson in his unusual "Swing around the Circle." Others were General Grant and five more generals including Custer, Admiral Radford, Secretary Welles, Postmaster General Randall, Secretary of State Seward, Mrs. Farragut, Mrs. Welles, and other ladies and gentlemen.[21] The route included Baltimore, Philadelphia, New York, West Point, Albany, Auburn, and Niagara Falls where the party spent Sunday; Buffalo, Cleveland, Toledo, Detroit, and Chicago where Johnson gave an address at the unveiling of a memorial to Stephen A. Douglas, a conservative, whose loyalty to the Union under the Constitution had a strong appeal to the President; and then homeward by way of Springfield, Alton, St. Louis, Indianapolis, Louisville, Cincinnati, Columbus, Pittsburgh and Harrisburg. The special Presidential train started on August 28. In Baltimore, a hundred thousand turned out to greet Johnson and his distinguished associates, and when Seward, the master of ceremonies, presented Grant and Farragut, they were "wildly cheered."[22] In New York there was a monster parade from the Battery up Broadway to the City Hall, and that evening a great banquet at Delmonico's. There was speech making at every stop. The burden of Johnson's appeal was a plea for the restoration of the political and civil rights of the Southern states. "They are our brethren. They are part of ourselves. They are bone of our bone, and flesh of our flesh. . . . We have come together again; and now, after having understood what the feud was, and the great apple of discord removed; having lived under the Constitution of the United States in the past, they ask to live under it in the future."[22] Up the Hudson they went in the *River Queen* to West Point where the President reviewed the cadets, among whom was Farragut's son, Loyall.

On went the "triumphal procession," as General Rawlins wrote his wife,[23] until it reached Cleveland. Here Radical rowdies by prearrangement tried to break up the meeting with hisses and shouts; but Johnson stood his ground and cowed the rowdies, as he shouted, "I have been fighting the South, and they have been whipped and crushed, and they acknowledge their defeat and accept the terms of the Constitution; and now, as I go around the circle, having fought traitors at the South I am prepared to fight traitors at the North."[24] This display of courage shows why fighting men like Grant and Farragut were drawn to his side. Great enthusiastic crowds greeted them in Chicago, though there was some organized Radical opposition. In St. Louis a great crowd gathered in the street near the Southern Hotel and demanded to see the President. He went out on the balcony to say a few words, but made a regular campaign speech with intemperate remarks to his Radical hecklers.

The opposition papers distorted Johnson's speeches, and tried to create the impression that the whole trip was a drunken orgy and that the President was "dead drunk" when he spoke at Cleveland. But the only man who drank heavily on the tour was General Grant. At Cleveland he became "stupidly communicative to Mrs. Farragut"[25] and finally so intoxicated that he was "put on a Detroit-bound steamer to conceal his shame."[18]

At Indianapolis, there was a riot in the public square in which a man was killed and such organized opposition developed that Johnson did not attempt to speak. The reception in Louisville, on the contrary, was very favorable, but here Seward became so ill that his life was despaired of and he had to be sent home on another train. At Pittsburgh, the mob would not permit Johnson to speak; and would only cheer Grant and Farragut. On September 15, the weary party reached Washington, where the President was welcomed by a mammoth demonstration.[26] It had been an amazing experience for the Farraguts. Grant had dropped out at Cincinnati to visit his father.

With the control of both houses of Congress assured by the recent elections, the Radicals gained complete domination of the government, and set about the establishment of a plan of reconstruction in the South, which was to produce what came to be known afterwards as "The Tragic Era." Johnson vetoed every measure but his vetoes were overridden. In the midst of this struggle, Francis P. Blair advised Johnson to reorganize his cabinet, by naming Farragut Secretary of the Navy, Grant Secretary of War, George Peabody Secretary of the Treasury, Horace Greeley Postmaster-General, etc., etc. "No patriot," Blair declared, "can refuse to you his aid in your effort to lift the government above revolutionary faction, to save the Constitu-

ADMIRAL FARRAGUT AND LIEUTENANT-COMMANDER JOHN C. WATSON
From an old photograph.

Courtesy of Mr. and Mrs. George G. Hall

ADMIRAL FARRAGUT ON THE *Franklin* DURING THE EUROPEAN CRUISE
From an original photograph, owned by Mr. and Mrs. George G. Hall.

tion."[27] But loyalty to his old cabinet prevented Johnson from taking a step which might have kept him from being impeached.[27]

Farragut was an intimate friend of George Peabody's, and in March of the year 1867, he and Mrs. Faragut and General and Mrs. Grant were invited by Mr. Peabody to attend the Italian Opera with him in New York. In the note of invitation Peabody enclosed half a dozen of his photographs and requested two each of the Admiral and Mrs. Farragut.[28]

Whether Farragut would have accepted an appointment to Johnson's cabinet, even with such congenial associates, is doubtful, for he had no love of politics. Fortunately he was not confronted with such a decision, and an appointment more to his taste was some weeks afterwards presented to him.

XXVIII

THE EUROPEAN CRUISE

1

ON THE LAST day of May, 1867, Farragut went to Washington to pay a visit to Mr. Welles. On the following Saturday they called on President Johnson and that evening dined at Seward's.[1] On June 4, they went together over to Annapolis to inspect the Naval Academy, where the Board of Visitors were then in session. Vice-Admiral D. D. Porter, then Superintendent of the Naval Academy, received them with all the ceremony due their high rank.[2] Just a week after his arrival in Washington, Farragut returned home with very important orders in his pocket. "In bidding him goodbye, I was more affected than he was aware," Welles wrote sentimentally, "and I perceived that he was to some extent similarly affected. We have both reached that period of life when a parting of two years may be a parting forever on earth."[3] Welles was only a year younger than Farragut. He was telling Farragut goodbye for two years, because the Admiral's new orders placed him in command of the European Squadron.[4]

When Farragut hoisted his flag on the *Franklin* in New York harbor near the middle of June, it was the first four-starred admiral's flag that had ever floated over an American man-of-war.[5] The *Franklin* was a steam frigate of about 4,000 tons, and in time of peace was armed with thirty-nine guns and manned with a crew of seven hundred fifty men. She was commanded by Captain Alexander M. Pennock, husband to Mrs. Farragut's first cousin. The surgeon was J. M. Foltz, who had been Farragut's Fleet Surgeon during the New Orleans campaign.[6] Farragut, when a midshipman, had served in the old ship of the line of the same name in the Mediterranean.

Mrs. Farragut had engaged passage on the steamer *Fulton*

with the expectation of meeting the Admiral abroad; but President Johnson, unsolicited, waived the naval regulation prohibiting wives from cruising with their husbands on men-of-war and telegraphed her his permission to sail on the *Franklin*. Secretary Welles then permitted Mrs. Pennock to accompany her husband.[7] In this way the President showed the Farraguts his deep appreciation of their loyal support of him on his speaking tour.[8]

About ten days before sailing, Farragut gave a brilliant reception on board his flagship to President Johnson, several cabinet members, prominent citizens of New York, and their wives and daughters. The *Franklin* sailed in the afternoon of June 28, and after an uneventful voyage of sixteen days, during which Farragut's sixty-sixth birthday was duly celebrated, she passed over the scene of the recent engagement between the *Alabama* and *Kearsarge* and entered the harbor of Cherbourg, on Bastile Day, a day then not popularly celebrated during the reign of Emperor Louis Napoleon. Here the *Franklin* was saluted by the *Colorado*, commanded by Rear-Admiral Goldsborough, whom Farragut was to relieve of his command. Three other American war vessels were in the harbor,[9] and not long afterwards three others,[10] composing the Midshipmen's Practice Squadron, came in, under command of Commander Stephen B. Luce.

After a week of very bad weather, during which salutes and official visits were exchanged in the rain, the Farraguts, the Pennocks, and some of the officers set out for Paris. The evening after their arrival, Major-General Dix, the American minister, gave a reception in honor of Admiral Farragut. For five days, he and his party then diligently visited the most famous historical and cultural buildings in Paris as well as the great palace at Versailles, and every day went to see the wonders of the Great Exhibition. "I did not see half of the departments," Farragut complained in his journal. "Saw pretty much all the boats and guns, however." He added naively, "Vice-Admiral Halstead was exhibiting a new system of ironclad, with upper decks and tripod masts; upper works for the comfort of the crew. I do not think an ironclad can be so constructed as to float easily with all the appurtenances for sail and steam, and the additional superstructure of decks, having at the same time armor thick enough to resist 15 or 20-inch shot."[11] One day the Admiral was observed gazing with admiration at a huge gun from the Krupp's Foundry, as though he were calculating the hazards of getting a fleet past a fort armed with such guns.

Farragut had hardly returned to his flagship when he received a telegram from the American Minister, informing him that he had been invited to dine with the Emperor. The next day he, accordingly, hurried back to Paris. General Dix accompanied him to the Palace of the Tuileries, where he was cordially received by the Emperor, who shook hands with him and welcomed him to France. "The Emperor was a small man with light blue eyes, a prominent slightly Roman nose, and a sandy Holland complexion; looked ten years younger than his age which was fifty-nine; had the air of a club man, fond of sport; did not have any of the features of the Bonaparte family," according to Surgeon Foltz's impressions.[12]

The Empress was on a visit in England, but was expected to return soon by way of Cherbourg. Indeed that afternoon she arrived on the royal yacht to the accompaniment of thunderous salutes, paid a visit to the *Franklin,* and entertained the senior officers on board her yacht that evening. The Farraguts in Paris thus missed seeing the fascinating Empress Eugénie.

During the dinner, the Emperor led the conversation, inquiring of Farragut as to the seaworthiness of the *Dunderberg,* an ironclad built in the United States for the French government.[13] He then shifted to an invention he had made for propelling ships by a kind of piston. Farragut told him he had not seen it, but had heard it highly spoken of by an English engineer. The Emperor replied modestly that a French scientific commission had pronounced it merely a mechanical contrivance. "Like a German toy," suggested Farragut. "Precisely," said the Emperor; "and not supposed to be of practical use."[14] He did not turn the conversation to Farragut's capture of New Orleans, which had upset his plans for intervention on behalf of the Confederate government, and nothing was said about the Maximilian Affair, only recently liquidated by the Emperor with great loss of prestige.

Returning to Cherbourg, Farragut visited the arsenal and dockyard, and after arranging for the docking and coppering of the *Ticonderoga,* he sailed for St. Petersburg on July 31 in company with the rest of his squadron. Mrs. Farragut and Mrs. Pennock, escorted by some of the officers, traveled overland from Paris through Berlin, and joined the *Franklin* later at Cronstadt.

2

On August 5, en route, according to Farragut's journal, "This being the anniversary of the Mobile Bay fight, I had all the officers in the cabin to take a glass of wine with me."[15] Ten days later the *Franklin* arrived at Cronstadt. Soon there was so much smoke from the exchange of salutes that one could not tell who was firing, nor how many guns. In the midst of the thundering of cannon were heard the cheers of the sailors manning the rigging, each side trying to outdo the other, and the blare of bands on every ship, playing American and Russian national airs. Rear-Admiral Lessovski,[16] Governor of Cronstadt, then came on board and extended to Farragut and his officers and men a cordial welcome, placing a gunboat at his disposal to take the Americans back and forth to St. Petersburg and offering the Admiral the Government House in Cronstadt as his headquarters.

The next day the Swedish commodore of a squadron of four monitors then lying off the city made an official visit on the *Franklin.* The day following, Farragut paid his first call on Admiral Lessovski, and that afternoon gave a grand reception on the *Franklin* to the Russian and Swedish officers. They were shown through the ship and then to the Admiral's cabin where many toasts were drunk in sparkling Veuve Cliquot. The next day was spent in exchanging official calls, and in the evening the Admiral and his staff dined with Governor Lessovski and his family, in the old cottage which was once occupied by Peter the Great.

After calling on General Cassius M. Clay, the American Minister, and the Russian Prime Minister, and other Cabinet Members in St. Petersburg, Farragut was invited to visit the Grand Duke Constantine on August 15 at Pavlosk Summer Palace. His brother, the Czar, was then traveling for his health in Southern Russia. Though Surgeon Foltz described the Grand Duke as being "a thin spare man with German features, who does not look like a man of mark,"[17] Farragut found him "very affable and intelligent,"[18] and enjoyed conversing with him during the dinner, following a walk in the palace gardens and a visit to the armory, which had been converted into a museum where the diamonds and other precious stones, and swords and every imaginable kind of arms pleased Farragut immensely. The Grand Duke showed himself familiar with naval affairs, and considered himself a sailor. The next day he returned the Admiral's visit with his suite, and was received with all the honors due his exalted rank. He showed great interest in everything on board, and invited Farragut to visit his fleet of ironclads. The Admiral replied that he would be greatly pleased to accompany him at any time. "No," said the Grand Duke tactfully, "I want you to go when I am not present, as the honors would be mine, and I wish them to be yours particularly."[19]

Mrs. Farragut had meanwhile arrived, and she and the Admiral accepted the invitation of Governor Lessovski to stay at Government House. With official visits paid, they were free to devote themselves to sightseeing in St. Petersburg, and even made a hurried trip to Moscow and one to Nijni-Novgorod. Mrs. Farragut, it was claimed, was the first American woman to visit the latter city. In Moscow they visited the principal palaces, churches, and public buildings, under the guidance of Colonel Posniak. The Alexander Palace, the Kremlin, the Zoological Garden, and the Great Bell pleased Farragut particularly. "It is impossible to refrain from reflecting," he wrote of all the precious things he had seen in the palaces and churches, "upon the amount of good this wealth might do if properly employed."[20] Nijni-Novgorod, overlooking the Volga, reminded him of Baton Rouge. Here they were lavishly entertained by the Governor and the President of the Board of Trade. Of particular interest was the great fairground where rare and costly articles from the Caspian and other remote regions in the East were displayed for sale and exchange. The dinner that evening in the Merchants' Dining Hall was on a sumptuous scale. Farragut noted especially the great sturgeon, three feet long, which was served, its meat being considered one of the greatest luxuries of the country. After coffee, a band of gypsies sang and performed a dance which reminded Farragut of the Spanish fandango. They were skilful with their hands as well as their feet, for they stole Mrs. Farragut's veil and almost got her watch.[21]

On returning to St. Petersburg, Farragut spent a day at the Hydrographic Department where he was presented a full set of charts by the Minister of Marine, and at the Engineering Department, studying plans of military fortifications. The following evening he and his staff dined with the Minister of Marine on the *Ruric* off Cronstadt. Before leaving St. Petersburg, he visited the Hermitage Museum, the Winter Palace, Kazan Cathedral, and old Paul Palace, which he considered one of the most interesting places in the capital. He also made an excursion twenty miles up the Neva to see a gun foundry. On Sunday he went to the American Episcopal Mission Church, and "heard a very fair sermon from an American minister."[22]

The evening before Farragut left St. Petersburg, Prince Gallitzin, Assistant Secretary of the Navy, gave a dinner in his honor—which was unusual in that Mrs. Farragut and Mrs. Pennock were also invited. At Cronstadt, the Lessovskis honored them with a farewell ball at Government House. The Farraguts and the large party of Americans were received with music, Roman candles, rockets, and cheers for the Americanskis. Russian officers of distinction with their wives were present in great numbers. It was "just five o'clock in the morning"[23] when the weary and somewhat dazed American officers reached their ships. After a day had passed, during which Farragut, none the worse for so much dissipation, visited Fort Constantine and received Prince Lichtenberg with becoming ceremony, he gave a farewell entertainment on the *Franklin,* on the afternoon of the 29th of August. All the officers of high rank, military, naval, and civil, in St. Petersburg and Cronstadt, attended with their families. The ship was handsomely decorated with flags; a table one hundred feet long was set up on the gun deck which was laden with delicacies in a style which would have won the approval of Delmonico himself; and the opposite side of the gun deck, the quarter-deck, and the poop were arranged for dancing. As the guests departed, there were many expressions of regret that "the American Squadron came so seldom to Russia, and whenever it did come was always in such haste to leave!"[23]

Though the *Franklin* left Cronstadt early on the morning of August 30, Farragut had not said a last farewell to Russia. He was yet to visit the Russian ironclad fleet then at summer maneuvers in Trongsund Roads near Viborg, Finland. On his arrival there, he was honored by novel and beautiful salutes, a naval review, unusual fireworks and the singing of peasant songs by sailors, and the usual round of official calls and dinners. A costly banquet was given on the flagship of Vice-Admiral Boutakoff by the Emperor's order and at his expense. The ship had been transformed into a flower garden with hothouse plants, flowers, and fruits, and arbors, grottoes, and arcades. There was a monument to Washington and another to Lincoln.[24] An unusual and impressive compliment was paid Farragut by printing on a beautifully embossed card this extract from the Signal Book of the Russian Imperial Ironclad Squadron, in Russian and in English: "Let us remember the glorious examples of Farragut and his followers at New Orleans and Mobile."[25] These were distributed among the guests.

In the afternoon of the 1st of September, Farragut's little squadron "weighed anchor and proceeded to sea, exchanging salutes with the flagship, and thus, amid cheering from all the ships of the two squadrons, concluded a visit which from first to last had been marked by the interchange of the warmest friendliness."[26]

3

On September 3, the American squadron anchored off Waxholm, Sweden, about fifteen miles from Stockholm, "the Venice of the North." The winding channels between the numberless small islands did not permit a nearer approach to the capital, where a reception to the Americans was given, none the less cordial, if not so lavish as that just experienced in Russia. The setting was, of course, different, as were also the beautiful blond Swedish women. Sightseeing, dinners in honor of Admiral and Mrs. Farragut by the Minister of Marine and King Charles XV at his summer palace, and a dance on board the *Franklin,* which the king could not attend on account of his health, were the high points of the six days' visit. "I was very favorably impressed with the Swedes," wrote Farragut, "and received nothing but kindness from them during my entire stay."[27]

From Stockholm, Mrs. Farragut and her party went by land across to Copenhagen to rejoin the ships. The monotony of the voyage down the Baltic was broken by the pilot's running the *Franklin* aground off Nyborg, where she stuck until flood tide. On Farragut's arrival at the Danish capital, the routine of receptions and entertainments was about the same—a dinner by the American Minister, which Farragut enjoyed immensely because there were no speeches, a "reception and a collation"[28] on the *Franklin,* a magnificent supper in the Tivoli Gardens given by the Minister of War, a presentation at Court and a dinner with King Christian IX at his country palace. Among the toasts, the king proposed the following: "Admiral Farragut, the most renowned of naval captains."[29] This, according to the American Minister, "disconcerted the patriot hero far more than the battle of Mobile or the gantlet of the forts."[29]

Among the places of great interest in Copenhagen, Farragut enjoyed most the remarkable collection of cannon and small arms in the Museum of Northern Antiquities. Previously, his officers had been able to shorten his inspection of old implements of destruction by certain wiles of diplomacy; but in this museum when he discovered a whole battery of breech-loading cannon of wrought iron of the 17th century, he refused to budge in spite of other engagements until he had examined all the guns to his complete satisfaction. He also enjoyed a visit to the Crown Battery, and an exhibition of a torpedo which was exploded by a galvanic battery for his entertainment.

Farragut sought out the daughter of his old friend Gierlew, who as Consul General at Tunis had befriended him in his youth. Finding her in need of financial assistance, he gave her his photograph and "a very substantial token of his regard."[30] She showed Mrs. Farragut a letter which her father had received from young Farragut in 1819 from Pisa, Italy, and had treasured to the day of his death.[31]

Sailing from Copenhagen on September 20, a day of evil omen to sailors, the *Franklin* ran into a storm in the North Sea on the voyage to England. For three days and a half the ship struggled with high wind and raging sea, and the ladies as well as some of the men on board realized how unpleasant cruising might sometimes be, particularly in September in north European waters. One night both the Admiral and Mrs. Farragut were flung from their beds to the cabin floor, and he lashed his astonished but submissive wife to her bed with the swordbelt he had worn in his memorable battles.

4

Anchoring at Gravesend on the Thames, Farragut commenced a very pleasant month's visit in England. On the day before his arrival, a London paper had expressed surprise that Admiral Farragut would visit France, Russia, and the Scandinavian countries, and pass by England. The writer endeavored to account for this slight on the grounds that the American government had advised this because the *Alabama* claims had not been settled. His arrival was, therefore, somewhat timely.

Though Queen Victoria was at Balmoral Castle in Scotland and United States Minister Charles Francis Adams was traveling on the Continent, and London was "considered depopulated"[32] at that season, yet the two weeks Farragut spent there were a continuous round of dinners, entertainments, calls, and as much sightseeing as could be sandwiched in between. Lords of the Admiralty and high ranking army and naval officers and civil officials were his daily associates. The Admiralty Board invited him to be their guest in their annual tour of inspection of the dock-yards of Woolwich, Chatham, and Sheerness, and everywhere he was received with the honors due his rank and with marked kindness and courtesy. A constant stream of eminent people called at his apartments at the Clarendon Hotel to meet "the Nelson of the Age." The Prince and Princess de Joinville entertained the Farraguts at their beautiful country estate, Claremont on the Thames. Three times they dined in state on Park Lane with Her Grace the Duchess Dowager of Somerset, formerly the belle of London, who developed a great liking for the Admiral. When she cordially invited him to dine with her for the fourth time, it is said, though Farragut denied it, that he grasped her hand with both of his and exclaimed, "But, my dear fellow, it is impossible!' and that the Duchess was so delighted with the term of endearment that her disappointment at his refusal was quite removed.[33]

The Farraguts occupied the Queen's box at the Drury Lane Theatre to see Shakespeare's *King John.* The play did not please Farragut. "It seems to be a fatality with me to witness a harrowing tragedy," he complained, "either on the canvas in any picture-gallery I may visit, or enacted on the stage of any theater to which I am specially invited."[34] When he visited the Tower with a party, and some of them lay down and had their necks adjusted on the very block where famous characters of history met their end, he gave them a brief lecture for seeking this vicarious experience "of the horrors of a cruel and vindictive age."[35] But he enjoyed attending a religious service in St. Paul's and visits to Westminster Abbey, the Houses of Parliament, the Zoological Gardens, the Crystal Palace, and Windsor Castle.

Returning at length to the *Franklin,* he went to Shoeburyness to witness experiments to determine the respective destructive effects of the American 15-inch gun and the English 9-inch rifled cannon. The result, he noted, was greater penetration for the English rifle but more crushing power for the American gun.[36] The next day, the *Franklin* weighed anchor for Portsmouth. Only four days were spent at this great maritime city, occupied with exchanging official visits, inspecting the great dock-yard, receiving a deputation of the Admiralty Board from London on the *Franklin,* visiting the *Victory* which is sacred to all Englishmen as Nelson's flagship and the scene of his death at Trafalgar, receiving on board His Royal Highness the Duke of Cambridge and his staff, and dining with Admiral Sir Thomas and Lady Pasley at Admiralty House. Farragut derived most pleasure in observing experiments in ship construction, propulsion, and armament, which he described at length in his journal.

The *Franklin* next called at Plymouth, the birthplace of Sir Francis Drake. Arriving in the harbor on a cold rainy morning, Farragut postponed the official calls until the following day. He then inspected the dock-yard, never seeming to tire of any detail relating to ships and guns. He also went aboard the armored *Agincourt* of 6,621 tons and the *Prince Albert* which had four of Captain Cole's turrets, and also a Prussian ironclad which had arrived after the *Franklin* came in. When three days had passed as pleasantly as the bad weather permitted and with the same friendly courtesy he had enjoyed elsewhere in England, Farragut sailed southward where better weather might be expected.

5

After a delightful voyage of four days, Farragut arrived at Lisbon. In the harbor were four other American men-of-war. On the King's birthday, the second day after the *Franklin* arrived, a salute was given in his honor, and Farragut was presented to King Don Luis I. It was a grand reception at which were present the diplomatic corps and most of the distinguished people of Lisbon, gorgeously uniformed and bemedaled. The King, accompanied by the Queen and his father, moved about the circle of notables to receive their congratulations. He seemed greatly pleased to meet Admiral Farragut, and after the presentation, he inquired, "You wrote a history of the late war, I believe?" Farragut, taken off his guard, managed to reply that he had "not turned author yet" and was about to begin a defense against the accusation, when the American Consul came to the rescue diplomatically with the observation, "Admiral Farragut, your Majesty, has made the history of the war."[37]

After receiving a visit of the Admiral of the Portuguese Navy, the Farraguts with a party went on an excursion to the summer resort of Cintra while the ship was being coaled. Upon their return, an English ironclad fleet of ten vessels, commanded by Rear-Admiral Read Warden, arrived from a practice cruise, and there was a round of official calls and dinners. After three weeks off Lisbon, the *Franklin* sailed just an hour after the English fleet, which gave an impromptu review in honor of Farragut, for the *Franklin* approached as Admiral Warden was commencing his maneuvers.

On rounding Cape St. Vincent, the *Franklin* ran into rough weather which lasted across Trafalgar Bay and through the Straits into the harbor of Gibraltar. Here Mrs. Farragut and Mrs. Pennock, and the Admiral with his staff were shown the great rock fortress, and were wined and dined by the English officers with a warmth of sincere friendship that had hardly been expected. At one dinner, Colonel Maberly departed from the custom of proposing a toast at an English banquet only "To the Queen," and made an eloquent tribute to Farragut "whom every nation was proud to welcome as its guest," and closed with the "fervent hope" that the "reunion of the two sections of that great and glorious republic on the other side of the Atlantic, which we are proud to claim as our own race, would be permanent and enduring."[38]

After making an excursion to Tangier where the Farraguts and their party were nearly mobbed by beggars, they sailed into the Mediterranean and arrived, on the 5th of December, at Carthagena. The *Franklin* was held in quarantine off this old Spanish city for three days before any one was permitted to land. A unique form of welcome was a poem in Spanish by Carolina Coronado, a poetess of Madrid. It was entitled, "To Admiral Farragut upon His Arrival at Carthagena." Printed copies were distributed, the English version of which was as follows:

> "Hail, Farragut, great captain! Thy swift bark,
> At her arrival on the Spanish shores,
> Old Ocean greets with rolling waves; and hark!
> His hollow bed an echoed welcome roars.
>
> Thy name is honored now in every land;
> All nations hail thy flag with loud acclaim;
> Yes! even on the Tagus' lonely strand,
> Men know and sing thy bright, undying fame.
>
> I am the songster, captain, who alone
> Rehearsed thy triumphs in my native land
> When Freedom's star, obscured, more dimly shone,
> And fickle Fortune strengthened Treason's hand.
> Thine and thy country's stars triumphant shine
> To-day; thou need'st no feeble praise of mine."[39]

There being nothing of great interest in Carthagena, Admiral and Mrs. Farragut and some of his staff went to Madrid for a four days' visit. Here he was received with great honor and courtesy, and had another opportunity to see more guns at the Museum of Arts and Arms as well as other places of great historical interest. He and all the members of his party were presented to Queen Isabella and the King Consort. The Queen cordially received the Admiral. "Admiral Farragut," she said, "I am glad to welcome you to Spain; but assure you your name and fame have preceded you to Madrid. I also assure you that I am proud to know that your paternal ancestors came from my dominions."[40] In Madrid, Farragut had the privilege of seeing again the Countess Montijo, mother of the Empress Eugénie, with whom he had danced at Malaga when he was only a midshipman and she was Miss Kirkpatrick, a Scotch lass.

6

A most extraordinary reception was given Farragut on the Island of Minorca, which was next on his itinerary. He had often been to Port Mahon when a midshipman, and had there received invitations to visit persons in the interior who claimed to be relatives. As a youth, he had not had sufficient curiosity to seek them out; but in later life he became more interested in his family history after George Ticknor sent him an old Spanish book containing the poems of Mossen Jaime Febrer, one of which celebrated the exploits of his ancestor, Pedro Ferragut (sic). For the adornment of his plate, Farragut had adopted the design of the horseshoe, found with ecclesiastical and military emblems on different escutcheons of the family. Within the outline of the horseshoe, he added a squadron of men-of-war in battle line, swinging round the circle.[41]

In the midst of the exchange of official calls on Farragut's arrival, a committee of citizens from Ciudadella, the birthplace of the Admiral's father, delivered an invitation personally to him to visit their city.

But Christmas had to be properly celebrated first on board the *Franklin* with religious services, carols, and a bountiful dinner for all hands. Admiral and Mrs. Farragut kept open house all day. On the wardroom and steerage tables were large tureens of eggnog, around which the happy returns of the season were merrily pledged. The following day, the Admiral with Mrs. Farragut, the Pennocks, and several officers from the ship set out to visit his ancestral city.

The news of Farragut's journey had apparently spread to all parts of the island, for crowds had gathered all along the way to see him and cheer him and, if possible, shake hands with him as he passed. Four miles from Ciudadella, the Alcalde was waiting with an official welcome and a handsome barouche in which the Farraguts rode at the head of an imposing procession into the city. The streets, the walls, the balconies, and even the housetops were crowded with people, who filled the air with cheers and shouts of welcome, As the carriage approached the mansion of Signor Don Gabriel Squella, where Farragut was to lodge, the street became so completely blocked with the mass of people that the Admiral had to get out and follow the policemen on foot as they made a passage with difficulty into the house. As an indication of his appreciation of their warm reception, he finally came out on the balcony and bowed his thanks repeatedly. It was midnight, however, before the great crowd dispersed. Meanwhile the most prominent citizens and their families were admitted inside Signor Squella's mansion to meet the great Admiral from America.

At daylight the next morning, the crowd began to gather again. "Had there been an election that day for Governor of the Balearic Islands, or for King of Spain itself, the Admiral would have been chosen without opposition,"[42] declared one of the Admiral's party. Farragut and his suite were conducted to points of interest in the city, and he had scarcely entered the Cathedral when it was packed with people and the organ began to play American melodies. Later the Alcalde and city fathers presented to him a book containing the registry of the baptism of his father and a copy of a law passed that very day making the Admiral a citizen of Ciudadella. That evening a banquet was given in his honor in the palace of the Marquis de Albranca. In the center of the unique and beautiful table decorations was a column of victory bearing the inscription: "El Gran Almirante Farragut." On top of it was a small statuette of Fame blowing a trumpet, which was presented to Mrs. Farragut and afterwards cherished by her as a souvenir of this remarkable visit. The following morning the Admiral departed amid the same crowds and enthusiasm and a similar ceremonial farewell from the Alcalde. This reception pleased and deeply affected Farragut more than any accorded him on his cruise because it was so evidently sincere—not to promote friendly international relations or increase commercial intercourse and profit.

On the evening of the last day of 1867, a grand ball was given by the civil and military authorities of Port Mahon at the Casino. The guests, unlike the custom in the United Sates, paid no attention to the passing of the Old Year at midnight and the birth of a New Year; but continued with the uninterrupted pleasures of the evening. With a farewell dance on the *Franklin* the following Friday, Farragut sailed for Toulon. The visit here was of the usual pattern, though it was more interesting

ADMIRAL D. G. FARRAGUT
From photograph by Leon Bravy, Port Mahon, Island of Minorca, during cruise of the *Franklin*. From author's collection.

Courtesy of F. H. Meserve, N.Y.
ADMIRAL D. G. FARRAGUT
From photograph by Gurney & Son, N.Y.

ADMIRAL D. G. FARRAGUT
From photograph by Beque-Sebastianutti, Triest, during cruise of *Franklin*. From author's collection.

ADMIRAL D. G. FARRAGUT, U.S.N.
From an engraving of a photograph, probably by Gurney & Son, said to be the last taken from life. From author's collection.

to Farragut because of the presence of the French Mediterranean fleet composed of ten powerful armor-clad men-of-war. He, of course, inspected the dock-yards, the old *Muiron* which brought Napoleon home from Egypt, and the *Belle Poule* in which his remains were conveyed from St. Helena to be placed in the great tomb in the Hôtel des Invalides in Paris.

After the prescribed number of salutes, the proper number of calls, dinners, and speeches, and as much sightseeing as the time would permit, the *Franklin* proceeded to Villa Franca, whence the Farraguts, the Pennocks, and the Admiral's staff went to the world famous winter resort at Nice. The high point of this visit was a grand ball in his honor, given by the United States Consul and the American colony at the Casino. Farragut shook hands with the fifteen hundred guests—a tiresome ordeal in itself. It was noticed that he took the hands of the ladies with more alacrity than those of the sterner sex. He led the first quadrille with Madame Gavini, wife of the Préfet. It was a unique crowd of personages that had gathered to do honor to the American hero—the Ex-King of Bavaria, princesses, dukes, earls, countesses, marquesses, baronesses, and other titles of nobility too numerous to mention. The total amount of wealth represented in the ladies' jewels alone would have been amazing. A Russian princess wore diamonds worth 40,000 pounds, and a German baroness was decked out with precious stones worth 30,000 pounds sterling.

Not to be outdone completely, Farragut on the last day of January gave a matinée dance on the *Franklin,* which was the most brilliant entertainment ever given on the flagship. Never before had there been on the ship at one time so many titled persons representing so many different countries of Europe. After two weeks of mingling with titled and wealthy Europeans, Farragut crossed the Gulf of Genoa, and the *Franklin* anchored off Spezia, Italy.

7

After exchanging salutes with the two Italian men-of-war in the harbor and visiting the new unfinished navy yard, the Farraguts with a shore party from the ship went on a grand tour of Italy. At Pisa they saw the Leaning Tower, the Duomo, and the Baptistery, the Admiral recalling his former visit more than fifty years before during his midshipman days. At Florence they had ten crowded days of visiting churches, palaces, art galleries, and museums. In the courtyard of the Bargello, the Admiral suddenly exclaimed. "There's my gun!"[43] Upon closer examination it turned out to be one of the twelve monster cannon, which he had seen in Tunis fifty-two years before. They were called "The Twelve Apostles," because the cascobel of each represented the head of one of the Apostles. The one he had rediscovered in Florence, called "St. Paul," had been made in that city in 1638 and had been brought back home since Farragut had last seen it. The Admiral was reluctant to hurry on to other objects and spoke eloquently of the beautiful finish of the old gun. In the Egyptian Museum, a chariot of the time of Rameses II particularly aroused his interest. Social obligations also made demands upon his time. He dined with King Victor Emanuel in his palace, Florence then being the capital of Italy; he attended a brilliant reception at the residence of the Turkish Ambassador; he was banqueted by the Deputies of the Italian Parliament; and he was honored with a farewell entertainment by American Minister George P. Marsh and Mrs. Marsh, where the most eminent people residing in Florence were presented to him. Many begged him to prolong his stay, but the Admiral replied to all invitations, "No one can stand this sort of dissipation very long without ruining his constitution."[44]

Venice made almost as heavy demands upon Farragut's strength. He arrived during the season of the Carnival. Three days were filled with sightseeing, made somewhat easier by the two state gondolas and a special guide, which were placed at his disposal. So he and his party saw the Palazzo di San Marco, the Cathedral of San Marco, and numerous other churches, museums, and other monuments of Venice's glorious past. The evenings were spent at the opera and in observing the revelries of the Carnival masquers and their gay processions on the Grand Canal.

Farragut arrived at Milan on the anniversary of Washington's

Birthday. Here his party visited the Ambrosian Library, saw Leonardo da Vinci's fresco of the Last Supper, and finally arrived at the great Gothic cathedral. Farragut was by that time very weary and could not be persuaded to climb up and see the view of the fertile fields of Lombardy. That evening he and Mrs. Farragut occupied the Governor's box at the Della Scala Opera House. He did not enjoy the music much, and sighed for "a good English ballad."[45] The next day a special invitation was brought from the Duc de Mignano for the Admiral and his suite to attend a grand ball that evening. But it was Sunday, and Farragut politely declined; he could not be persuaded to "do in Milano as Milano does." The official messenger was astonished at our American customs.

In Genoa, city of palaces, the Farraguts witnessed the processions of the last day of the Carnival on the Corso from an apartment in the Municipal Buildings, placed at their disposal by the mayor. In the evening they were entertained with the opera "Giulietta" at the Teatro Carlo Felici. During the sightseeing in Genoa, they saw Paganini's famous violin and some original letters by Christopher Columbus, a Genoese. On the 27th of February, a banquet was given in Farragut's honor by the city at the Palazzo Doria Tursi. A large crowd, anxious for a look at the famous Americano, greeted him on his arrival at the palace. The mayor proposed the first toast, and made an eloquent tribute to Farragut, with references to the great sea fighter Andrea Doria, Garibaldi, and Christopher Columbus; he ended with "Evviva Farragut! Evviva l'America!"[46] which was received with enthusiastic applause. The Admiral, in a suitable response, spoke in flattering terms of the progress the city had made since his former visit more than half a century before.

Returning to the *Franklin*, Farragut sailed down the coast to Naples, where the great volcano, then quite active, fired the grandest salute he had received as "Italy's welcome to the distinguished head of the American navy."[47] Here was afforded an entertainment quite out of the ordinary. At the invitation of the Superintendent of the Museums of Naples and Pompeii, he and Mrs. Farragut and a large delegation from the ship witnessed the excavation of a room in the house of Balbus at Pompeii. Household furniture, several loaves of bread "considerably overdone," and two skeletons of human beings were uncovered by the removal of the scoriae and pumice stone after nearly 1800 years. The skeletons were of young adults, one a man and the other a woman, at whose feet was the skeleton of a bird, apparently a pigeon. Delicately wrought finger rings worn by the woman were presented to Mrs. Farragut, who afterwards gave them to Dr. Foltz.[48] The guests then proceeded to the Stabian Thermae where the luxurious Pompeians used to enjoy themselves. There refreshments were served by the American colony; and in the building on whose walls were frescoes of the Epicurean Pompeians, dancing was enjoyed to the strains of a band which sounded strange in such surroundings.

After attending a review of the garrison and the National Guard in Naples as a guest of honor, and being banqueted by Admiral Provana, Farragut and his party went up to Rome to see the Eternal City. There, through the assistance of his staff, official visits were reduced to a minimum and he was able to see more leisurely most of the landmarks of the city during his visit of eight days. He was presented to Pope Pius IX, who descended from his papal chair and came forward to welcome him when he was ushered into the throne-room. In a very friendly conversation with Farragut, he referred to the troubles which the United States had suffered. These, he said, he "appreciated the more, as he had his own to contend with." He then expressed his surprise at the "unaccountable friendship existing between the United States and Russia—the one a republic and the other the very opposite." Farragut assured him that the friendship was genuine, and His Holiness replied that he believed it, but that it was nevertheless unaccountable.

The entertainments in Rome in Farragut's honor were given by Americans; namely, Miss Charlotte Cushman, the famous actress, and the Secretary of Legation to the American Embassy, Mr. Hooker, and Mrs. Hooker. The latter sent out eight hundred invitations to the distinguished foreigners residing in Rome, among whom were the American authors, John Pendleton Kennedy and John Lathrop Motley, to the diplomatic corps, and to members of the Roman nobility. In the apartments of the Hookers in the Palazzo Bonaparte, all these bemedaled and bejeweled guests were pleased to file by and shake the hand of the little man who had been born in a log cabin in Tennessee and had become the greatest sea fighter of his age.

Back once again on the *Franklin*, the Admiral gave a farewell dinner to prominent Neapolitans, and on April 6 he sailed away to the southward. Passing through the Straits of Messina, the *Franklin* entered the beautiful sickle-shaped harbor of Messina. where after official honors were exchanged, Farragut went ashore to visit the grave of his old friend, Captain Gordon who was buried there in 1816. This was accomplished with so much interference from hordes of persistent beggars that he retreated to the protection of the ship without attempting any sightseeing, and admired the picturesque city and its surroundings at a comfortable distance. Farragut, being too generous with his soldi, had a similar difficulty with the beggars at Syracuse, which was next visited; but under the protection of his staff he was able to make official calls and with Mrs. Farragut to inspect some of the vestigial remains of the city's historical past and enjoy the views of Mount Etna with its snow clad summit.

The next day the *Franklin* was on her course for Malta. The six days spent at Valetta, the capital of the island fortress formerly controlled by the Knights of St. John, were filled to overflowing with official amenities, balls, military reviews, banquets, the opera, and a bit of sightseeing now and then. The Governor-General, Sir Patrick Grant, and Lady Grant with the assistance of the American Consul, William Winthrop, and the English army and naval officers on the island made Farragut's visit an event long to be remembered. A poem, entitled "Fraternal Greeting," was issued as a broadside. Its very friendly tone may be indicated by the following last stanza:

> "As friend with friend and man with man,
> Oh, let our hearts be thus—
> As David's love to Jonathan
> Be Jonathan's to us!"[49]

While in Malta, Farragut received a letter from an influential politician in New York. "The men now in power are determined, at any cost, to have the Negroes rule in the Southern States," he wrote, "as the only means of their continuing to hold the government." They had impeached the President, he continued, and would probably remove him; then they would pack the Supreme Court, and have their own way unopposed. "The country needs at its head a sober, brave, honest man of simple purpose," he declared, and then begged him to accept the nomination of the Democratic party for the Presidency, because he had the confidence of all the people, even the Conservative Republicans, who were disgusted with their own party and would support him."[50] He also wrote to Mrs. Farragut the same day, "I pray you not to let him refuse it."[50] Before leaving Malta, Farragut replied that he was not qualified for the office of President. "I therefore beg again to assure you that I have no such idea as entering the political arena under any circumstance," he wrote. "I have no ambition to gratify, no aspiration beyond my present position as the Admiral of the United States Navy in the enjoyment of a fair proportion of the confidence and affection of the American people."[50]

When the *Franklin* put to sea from Malta, Vice-Admiral Lord Clarence Paget honored Farragut with a review of the English ironclad squadron, which was just starting on a cruise to the Levant. The sea was running high, and the *Lord Clyde* passed so close to the *Franklin* that Mrs. Farragut thought a collision was unavoidable and retreated to her cabin to await the worst. Farragut was greatly pleased with this naval review, which he declared in his official report "terminated one of the most agreeable visits of our cruise."[51] The *Franklin* then turned her prow toward the Straits of Gibraltar, and Farragut enjoyed a few days of rest and relaxation after the strenuous weeks he had recently spent in the Mediterranean.

8

In ten days, Farragut was back in Lisbon for a month's stay, which was necessitated by duties connected with the other vessels of his squadron. It was a comparatively dull month, but it afforded him an opportunity for more rest which he greatly needed. The opera, bull fights, somewhat quiet dinner parties, a visit from the American Minister from Madrid, and another visit to Cintra occupied the leisure of the ship's company. All were pleased when the time came for departure to the shores of the Netherlands. Farragut's interest in this visit may have been aroused through his intimate associations in Rome with John Lathrop Motley, author of the *Rise and Fall of the Dutch Republic*.

Appropriately, the *Franklin* anchored at the mouth of the River Scheldt off Flushing, the birthplace of De Ruyter, greatest of Dutch sea fighters. This neat and trim little town delighted everybody; besides there was not a beggar to be seen, in striking contrast with the towns of Spain, Italy, and Portugal. Having received an invitation to dine with King Leopold II the following Monday, Farragut with his wife and most of his officers proceeded to Brussels, stopping en route at Antwerp to see the sights of that beautiful old city.

The King received Farragut and his staff with all the ease of a courtly and polished gentleman. Some sixty distinguished persons sat down at the royal banquet, which was superb in every detail. The King and the Admiral became so absorbed in conversation that they forgot to leave the table at the appointed time. "I have never in all my life seen the like of this," said an old field marshall to another guest. "The dinner is over, we are all ready to rise, and we are all tired of the table, but the King cannot leave your Admiral. He has captured all Belgium; we are his prisoners; we shall never get away; we shall all die here. What is there about Farragut that is so fascinating?" "I cannot tell you, unless it is that the Admiral is so natural," replied the person by his side. "No, that is not it," continued the marshal facetiously; "he has magnetized the King. Farragut is a magician."[52]

The following morning the Queen gave a breakfast in honor of Mrs. Farragut, and the King and the Admiral had an opportunity to continue their conversation. The next day Farragut was able to realize a wish he had long cherished. This was an excursion to Waterloo. From the top of the "Belgian Mound" he had a bird's-eye view of the battlefield. After he had finished the visit, he said, "For the first time I thoroughly understand the disposition of the two great armies on that field, and the general plan of the attack and defense."[53]

After a banquet given in his honor by American Minister Sanford, Farragut and some of his officers departed on a visit, by way of Cologne, to the Krupp Works at Essen. Though Mr. Krupp was in St. Petersburg, the Superintendent showed them everything, to Farragut's great astonishment, pleasure, and satisfaction. Upon returning to the *Franklin,* they sailed for Ostend where, on the 22nd of June, Farragut entertained the Belgian King and Queen on board the flagship. Undismayed by a downpour of rain, they came on board with their suite at the appointed time, and so enjoyed the unique entertainment and experience that they remained four hours. For some reason or other, Farragut did not go to Amsterdam and did not meet King William of Holland.

The *Franklin* then crossed over to Southampton, where the Farraguts with others from the ship left for a tour of Scotland. Stopping to see York's great cathedral, they went on to Edinburgh where Farragut had the unusual experience of no official calls or entertainment. After seeing the various historical and literary landmarks in the city, they visited Scott's home at Abbotsford, Farragut taking great delight in examining Rob Roy's long rifle, and then went to see the great novelist's tomb at Dryburgh Abbey. A trip through the Scottish lakes brought them to Glasgow, where Farragut was delighted with the privilege of inspecting two immense shipbuilding yards in which thirteen vessels were then on the stocks. Here the Admiral was in his element, and it was with difficulty that he could be persuaded to leave for the hotel where a banquet had been prepared in his honor by the city authorities. Returning by way of Oxford, he again joined the flagship to look after matters connected with his squadron.

On the 10th of July, Farragut went up to London again to be

present at a banquet, given not to honor him but his countryman, Henry Wadsworth Longfellow. Playing second fiddle in this way was a new experience for Farragut on the cruise. The banquet was given at the Langham Hotel by the American landscape painter, Bierstadt. Among the eighty-seven guests was Gladstone, who made a speech in which he paid high tribute to the American poet. Farragut also spoke, probably very briefly, though his speech has not been preserved.[54] Longfellow had not been inspired by Farragut's naval battles to celebrate them in verse. Indeed he wrote but little on the stirring events of the Civil War. This was probably due to the shock he experienced in the loss of his wife who was burned to death in 1861 and his consequent burying himself in a translation of Dante's *Divine Comedy*.[55]

Near the middle of July, the Prince of Wales and his brother, the Duke of Edinburgh, were received on the *Franklin* with royal honors. After being cordially entertained in many of the beautiful country residences in the vicinity, the Farraguts proceeded in the *Franklin* to Cowes, Isle of Wight, the headquarters of the Yacht Clubs, and anchored near the *Galatea,* commanded by the Duke of Edinburgh. Farragut called on the Duke on board his ship, and then went with him to Osborne House, where he was received by Queen Victoria. "England's gracious Queen" conversed very pleasantly with Farragut about the United States, and he was deeply impressed with the way all the trappings of royalty were concealed beneath the domestic comforts of a home for herself and children. The day following, the Duke sent him pictures of himself, Prince Albert, and Queen Victoria with a friendly little note.[56] Dr. Foltz, who had seen the Queen thirty years before, wrote, "She has not improved in appearance, although she has a jolly red face." He liked the Duke of Edinburgh but thought that "the Prince looks dissipated."[57]

9

On the 19th of July, the *Franklin* sailed again for the Mediterranean with Constantinople as the ultimate destination. Mrs.

Farragut and Mrs. Pennock, accompanied by four officers, left the ship and went overland, through central Europe, to the same destination. The flagship made the first stop at Syra, one of the Greek Cyclades, where the Admiral and his staff were transferred to the *Frolic,* which proceeded to the Dardanelles while the *Franklin* went to Smyrna to await permission to pass through waters then forbidden by Turkey to foreign men-of-war. Even the little *Frolic* had to wait at Chanak Kalessi on the Dardanelles for an official permit from Constantinople. Meanwhile Farragut went ashore, and enjoyed inspecting the immense bronze guns, which hurled stone balls twenty-seven inches in diameter, more than recalling the historical and romantic associations of the area with Hero and Leander, Xerxes, and Lord Byron.

On arriving at the city of the Sultans, Farragut was officially welcomed by American Minister Edward Joy Morris, occupying the diplomatic post once held by Farragut's old patron and friend, Commodore David Porter. Under the guidance of Mr. Morris, Farragut and his officers made a series of calls on the Grand Vizier, the Minister of Foreign Affairs, and the Russian Ambassador at their summer palaces on the shores of the incomparably beautiful Bosporus. Everything pleased Farragut immensely—the friendly cordiality, the Turkish coffee, and the refreshing sherbert; but when the chibouques were brought in, an expression of despair was seen to steal over his face, for he never used tobacco.

Mrs. Farragut arrived with her party only a day after the Admiral. With her was her son Loyall, who had graduated at West Point on June 15 and had joined her in Europe. He accompanied his father on August 13 at his presentation to Sultan Abdul Aziz at his magnificent palace of Beglerbeg on the Asiatic shore of the Bosporus. "We were ushered into a large reception room of the Palace, upholstered and decorated in modern style," wrote Loyall Farragut,[58] "and after being seated were regaled with sherbert, coffee, and pipes. Then came our audience with his Royal Highness. He received us, it appeared to me, in a very diffident and embarrassed manner, although very cordial and courteous. I noticed that he spoke in a very low tone and the interpreter in his obsequiousness seemed to fear to raise his voice above that of his sovereign; consequently the reception did not partake of an hilarious nature!" The interview lasted only ten minutes, during which the Sultan conversed mainly about ironclads.

Banquets were given in honor of Farragut by the Russian Ambassador, the American Minister, and the Grand Vizier, the last in an immense glass conservatory in the midst of most luxurious and beautiful surroundings. "The Turks drank no wine, an example which was not followed strictly by their guests."[59] Mrs. Farragut with the ladies of her party were accorded the unusual privilege of visiting the harems of the Grand Vizier and the Viceroy of Egypt, then spending the summer on the Bosporus. They joined the Admiral and his staff in a visit to the Viceroy's yacht, a magnificent work of naval architecture, a veritable floating palace. The Mosque of St. Sophia, the palace and gardens of the Seraglio, and the famous Bazaars were also visited, not to mention dockyards, military schools, hospitals, ordnance depots, the "Dancing Dervishes" and the "Howling Dervishes" in Scutari where Florence Nightingale ministered to the English soldiers during the Crimean War, the Hippodrome, numerous mosques, etc., etc.

Meanwhile after much interchange of diplomatic opinions and many conferences of the ambassadors of the five great powers in Constantinople, permission was given for the *Franklin* to pass through the Dardanelles, and she arrived on August 21 and came to anchor in the Bosporus off Dolma Baghtche, the Sultan's winter palace. Then followed a long series of visits to the flagship, official and diplomatic, accompanied by many thundering salutes, and a continuous stream of visitors from the city which gave the ship the appearance of the setting of a masqued ball or carnival, so varied and picturesque were the costumes of the many nationalities and races represented.

One day while Farragut was receiving the Grand Vizier and the Minister of Foreign Affairs as personal representatives of the Sultan, who found it "impossible" to visit the "beautiful frigate,"[60] an embarrassing incident occurred. A large deputation of Greeks came on board, and began to distribute copies of a proclamation printed in Greek and English, which welcomed Farragut and his officers and men to Constantinople as friends of the oppressed and supporters of liberty. "May God grant that the American and the Greek nations may rejoice one day over the liberation of this historical country," it concluded, "in the same manner as all adorers of liberty all over the world have hailed the putting down of the rebellion and the emancipation of the slaves, to which you, illustrious Admiral, have so powerfully contributed through your bravery and skill."[61] The officer of the deck stopped the distribution of the proclamation, and Farragut received the deputation in Captain Pennock's cabin, where he lectured them severely for their lack of judgment in circulating such a document while he was entertaining members of the Turkish Cabinet. A little girl about five years old then spoke a panegyric, ending with,

> "Live! live! America,
> Whose name is sweet throughout Greece—
> Live! noble Farragut, Champion of liberty;
> Accept our guileless utterance,
> Our countless, devout prayers."[62]

The somewhat crestfallen Greeks then departed, and after Farragut left Constantinople the leaders were arrested and imprisoned. When the Admiral heard of this in Athens, he requested their release through the American Minister. The Grand Vizier granted the request "exclusively out of deference for the Admiral, otherwise they would have been sent into exile."[62]

Another incident of interest occurred at the Grand Vizier's banquet. Powerful interests in Turkey had prevented Dr. Cyrus W. Hamlin from beginning the erection of buildings for Robert College on a site which had been purchased overlooking the Bosporus about four miles above Constantinople. Secretary Seward had taken up the matter with the Turkish Minister in Washington, who wrote home that, if the matter was not settled at once, serious trouble might follow. It happened that Farragut arrived not long afterwards, and Dr. Hamlin, President of the

College, called on the Admiral and spoke to him about the trouble he was having with the Turkish government. Farragut became very much interested and promised to speak to the Grand Vizier unofficially about the matter at his first opportunity. He was able to do so at the banquet, and very favorable results followed. The Turkish government apparently thought that Farragut's mission was to settle the College problem with possibly an interference in the Cretan Revolution then in progress. So it gave the College more than had been asked, presenting Dr. Hamlin an imperial charter as an American college under the protection of the United States with extraterritorial rights and all the privileges of educational institutions in Turkey.[63]

A third incident happened just as the *Franklin* was leaving Constantinople. The Russian Ambassador came on board to bid Farragut farewell, and when he returned to his steam yacht her rigging was manned, the American flag was hoisted, and three lusty cheers rang out. All of this was returned by the *Franklin*. This extremely friendly leave-taking was telegraphed to all the European capitals, and alarmed journalists ran wild in trying to explain the hidden meaning of this further indication of the growing friendship between Russia and the United States.

Farragut's visit had lasted three weeks during an unseasonable time of year; but all hands voted Constantinople and the Bosporus the most picturesque, the most varied, and the most fascinating region they had visited during the entire cruise.

10

The warmth of Farragut's reception in Athens was exceeded only by the weather, for he arrived in Piraeus on the last day of August. The Temple of Jupiter Olympus, the majestic ruins of the Parthenon and other buildings on the Acropolis, and the Temple of Theseus were visited by moonlight which even increased their mournful beauty. "This is all very grand and very historic," remarked Farragut, "but it nevertheless makes me more than ever thankful that I belong to the present generation."[64]

The Farraguts with such officers as the Admiral might designate were invited to witness the baptism of the infant heir to the throne of Greece, performed in the Cathedral with a great ceremony in which two hundred priests participated. They then went to the Palace to a grand levee where they were cordially received; Farragut had recently met the King in Denmark and the Queen's mother, the Grand Duchess Constantinovna, in St. Petersburg. That evening Farragut met the American missionaries resident in Greece at the home of the American Minister, and the following evening he and Mrs. Farragut were honored by a banquet at the King's palace.

When Farragut returned to his flagship at Piraeus, he received an eloquent address in Greek and English, from the mayor of the town, welcoming him somewhat belatedly to that port and thanking him "as a prominent champion in the cause of constitutional liberty and humanity"[65] for all the aid and sympathy his countrymen had given Greece in her struggle for independence and begging the same assistance in the Cretan Revolution. Here Farragut received on board the members of the Greek Cabinet and several foreign diplomats with much burning of powder in noisy salutes. A few days later, the King, the Grand Duchess, and high ranking officers and members of the King's household were received with full honors. The Grand Duchess, to show her admiration for everything American, wore a necklace of clusters of red, white, and blue precious stones with a bow of ribbons of the same colors, which she gave Mrs. Farragut as a souvenir of the visit—the ribbons and not the necklace.

After making another trip to Athens to attend a banquet in his honor given by the American Minister, Farragut put to sea again. For ten days the *Franklin* had been anchored only a few miles from Salamis, the scene of one of the greatest sea battles in history.

On the way up the Adriatic to Trieste, Farragut's ship passed over the scene of a then recent naval battle, fought near the Island of Lissa between the Austrian and Italian fleets, commanded by Admirals Tegethoff and Persano respectively. The prominent events in Farragut's thirteen days' visit at Trieste were a trip to the Palace of Miramar, former picturesque home of the unfortunate Maximilian and Carlotta; meeting Charles Lever, Irish author of *Charles O'Malley* and other delightful novels; and a banquet in his honor given by Governor-General Moering, at the conclusion of which Surgeon Goracuchi presented Farragut with a copy of a book he had written. On the flyleaf he inscribed: "To the Hero, who has no equal in the history of sea battles. To the Man, whose mind contains a world and seems for all things framed. To the Citizen, whose word is truth and whose wisdom is from Heaven. To Admiral Farragut, with the Author's most respectful acknowledgments."[66]

11

On the homeward voyage of the *Franklin*, she made only one stop. That was at Gibraltar and lasted eleven days, the time being spent in coaling, in exchanging personnel with the ships which were remaining on the European station, and in exchanging official calls and dinners and other entertainments with the Governor and the Army and Navy officers. About noon on October 18, the *Franklin* steamed away from Gibraltar to the dipping of colors by the vessels in the harbor. After a voyage without unusual incident, she anchored on the morning of November 10 off the Battery, whence she had sailed about seventeen months before. Six days later Farragut hauled down his flag, and the extraordinary European cruise came to a close.

The cruise had made a great stir in Europe, where it was variously supposed that Farragut had been sent over to establish an alliance with Russia, an entente cordiale with England, and a league of friendship with Italy; or to interfere with the Cretan Revolution, and force the Dardanelles with the assistance of Russia. But the only instructions, diplomatic or otherwise, he received from Seward were telegraphed him just before his departure. They read as follows: "Do not glide too often to the masthead."[67]

XXIX

"THE LAST SCENE OF ALL"

1

A PLEASANT feature of Farragut's European Cruise was that it kept him out of the United States during the unsuccessful impeachment of President Johnson, the first stages of the military system of reconstruction in the South, and the acrimonious Presidential campaign which had recently come to a close with the election of General Grant. "He had been out of range of the shafts of political malice, out of range of the mud which party hacks have been flinging against so many distinguished officers," wrote the *Army and Navy Journal.* "He can congratulate the successful candidate without having his courtesy misinterpreted, or made the signal for calumny. He has been, as it were, 'up in the shrouds' above the smoke of the political conflict."[1] But even after the election of Grant, there were many serious problems. Virginia, Texas, and Mississippi were still under military rule, and Georgia was to revert to that status the following year.

The very day Farragut arrived in New York, Secretary Welles wrote him a letter, begging him to accept the appointment as Secretary of the Navy, should Grant offer the post to him.[2] Three days later General and Mrs. Grant arrived in New York and many paid court to him at the Metropolitan Hotel, but the *Herald* did not mention Farragut's name among those who called.[3] Upon his return from West Point where his son was a cadet, Grant attended the dinner given by the New York bar at the Astor House on November 17 in honor of Attorney General William M. Evarts. Farragut was also present and made a brief speech.[4] Mr. Welles, along with other members of the Cabinet, had been invited, but he did not attend because it was announced in the *Herald* that Grant would not be present if

Welles came.[5] The latter had been very friendly with President Johnson and opposed Grant as a Presidential candidate.

The following week Admiral and Mrs. Farragut went to visit the Welleses. The evening after their arrival, they dined with President Johnson and his daughter, Mrs. Patterson, and Admiral and Mrs. Radford.[6] Farragut thus belonging clearly to the other camp, it is strange that Welles should even have supposed that Grant would offer the Admiral a Cabinet position. Whether he would have accepted such an offer is extremely doubtful. Welles may have been thinking of his non-political characteristics when he wrote of him, "He is guileless, simple-hearted, and as sincere as he is brave. Mrs. F. is devoted to him, proud of him, and very social."[6]

When Farragut returned to New York, he received a kind of official letter of welcome home from the European Cruise, signed by fifty-four distinguished fellow citizens, including Peter Cooper, William Cullen Bryant, Thurlow Weed, Cyrus W. Field, John Bigelow, and Hamilton Fish. They expressed their pleasure at the honors, conferred upon him all over Europe, which had "enlarged your country's fame in all civilized lands."[7]

Since Farragut's visit to Spain, there had been a revolution which had forced the Queen into exile. Much discussion followed as to who would succeed her. Not more than half in earnest, the *Army and Navy Journal* published what it called "A Hint for the Spaniards," containing the following advice: "Let all parties lay aside their contentions and unite upon our own Admiral Farragut, as the people's choice for king or emperor, whichever they prefer. The Admiral certainly has stronger claims to the Spanish throne than any of the foreign princes whose names have been suggested. He is Spanish by descent, is proud of his old Castilian origin, and talks Spanish like a native. Moreover, he has had an invaluable experience in the practical workings of free institutions, and we will answer for it with our editorial head that he does not prove a despot. So sturdy a republican as he is ought to be acceptable to the democrats, if they find themselves forced to accept a monarchy, and the monarchists are too much divided in opinion to object, so long as their desire for a king is gratified in some sort. . . . By all means, then, let the Spaniards crown him David the First. It would be a severe sacrifice for the Admiral to resign his position at the head of the American Navy, to accept a crown; but he may be willing to sacrifice much for the opportunity to regenerate a nation. With him at their head, the Spaniards will be able to establish relations with this country which will really be more valuable to them than the friendship of half of Europe. They will secure, too, the good will of all the European liberals; they will be put under excellent schooling for the final establishment of a republic; and when the Admiral decides that they are ready for it, we have no doubt that he will save them the trouble of another revolution by inaugurating the republic himself."[8]

The naval surgeons had for some time been endeavoring to secure naval rank with the line officers. Welles had opposed this change. "Admiral Farragut himself, in kindness of heart," the Secretary wrote, "has given them an approving letter that conveyed more than he really intended, which was read on the floor of the House. Vice-Admiral Porter, who is opposed to extending recognition or even justice to the staff, I am told, gave them a favorable letter, but refused to have it made public. Oh the duplicity and moral cowardice of some of our heroes!"[9]

2

Farragut spent the winter in comparative quiet in his home in New York, but went to Washington to attend Grant's inauguration. On that gloomy, drizzly March 4, 1869, he went up to the Capitol, and was on the floor of the Senate with Admirals Goldsborough and Dahlgren and Generals Sherman, Thomas, Hancock, Terry, and Sickles when the inaugural ceremonies began promptly at noon.[10] It was not a happy occasion. Grant had refused to ride with Johnson to the Capitol; so Johnson and his Cabinet transacted their last business at the White House and did not attend the inauguration. "General Grant rode up in a dogcart with Rawlins," spitefully recorded Mr. Welles. "There was a long procession, mostly of Negroes—at least two thirds, I should judge."[11] Farragut probably did not attend the inaugural ball two evenings later, and so escaped the confusion consequent to the lack of system in checking the hats and wraps of the two thousand guests. Pandemonium reigned when they presented their checks—women fainted, the police were called, many valuable coats were "taken," ladies had to go home in their light evening dresses in the cold, and many were still there battling for their coats in the gray dawn.[12]

Grant did not delay in announcing his Cabinet. His nominations were sent in on the afternoon of the 5th. It was an amazing Cabinet. Grant told Farragut that he gave the office of Secretary of State to E. B. Washburne as a compliment.[13] He held it four days, and was succeeded by Hamilton Fish. For Secretary of the Navy he nominated Adolph E. Borie of Philadelphia, who "had made a fortune in profiteering operations during the Civil War" and "knew less about the navy than the average man knows about astronomy."[14] At that time, Grant was very friendly with Vice-Admiral Porter. "When General Grant went to Annapolis, a few days after he was nominated at Chicago," wrote Welles, "Porter fired salutes and made great demonstrations. For two days there was polishing and great exultation. Until about the time of the impeachment movement, Porter had been an open friend and frank but not partisan supporter of the Administration. But when impeachment was decided upon, Porter became suddenly an intense partisan, scandalizing and abusing the President."[15] When, during the campaign that followed, Porter "volunteered his testimony to the effect that Grant was a total abstinence man, it was a bid which was well understood," declared Welles, "and which no man of position, unless a Porter, would make."[16] So when Borie was appointed, Grant telegraphed for Porter to come over on a special train from Annapolis to take charge of the Navy Department. He came with "his pockets filled with general orders which he had been weeks preparing," and he and Borie went arm in arm to the Navy Department, where Porter told Chief Clerk Faxon that he had come to "run the Department."[17] "Borie is dwarfed and overborne by the self-assuming and arrogant Vice-Admiral," lamented poor Mr. Welles.[18] "The department is managed by Admiral Porter; I am only a figurehead," sighed Mr. Borie, wishing he were out of the mess and back in Philadelphia.[19]

"He [Porter] succeeded in humbugging Gen'l Grant," wrote Fox, "persuading him that all the operations of the western gunboats were due to him as well as the inspiration concerning naval affairs at Washington. The consequence was that General Grant, as soon as he became President, found a person to serve Porter as clerk, with the title of Sec'y of the Navy, whilst all the power vested in him (Porter). And the Pres. of the U.S., at the instigation of Admiral Porter threw aside with neglect this Christian hero [Farragut] and to his dying day and even at his funeral 'passed him by' for a man whose true character, long since known, was only made manifest to the President when he became the recipient of the calumnies and ingratitude which Porter sooner or later visits upon all those to whom he is placed under great obligations."[20]

Farragut did not tarry long in Washington. There seemed to be no place for him as Admiral of the Navy in an arrangement by which a subordinate Vice-Admiral was virtually head of the Navy Department. Mr. Welles, on his way back to his old home in Hartford, called on Farragut in New York not long afterwards, and found him slightly recovering from severe illness. "His ailment is mostly nervous," Welles thought, "the result, in a great measure, of official neglect and the condition of things at Washington. He feels acutely the slight that is shown him, and the orders and movements which were calculated to, and I am constrained to believe were intended to, annoy him. He and myself have been subjected to similar slights by Porter, whom we both have favored. I would not permit the Admiral to dwell on these matters which so keenly and sorely affected him, but told him we must for the time being patiently bear with any injustice. . . . He need not fear that his countrymen and posterity would fail to do him justice. My remarks soothed, comforted, and consoled him."[21]

The broad pennant denoting Farragut's rank was a flag with a blue field and four white stars. When Commodore James

"THE LAST SCENE OF ALL" 371

Alden was placed at the head of the Bureau of Navigation under the Borie-Porter regime, he changed Farragut's pennant to one of the same dimensions with alternate stripes of red and white. This annoyed the Admiral very much.[22] Farragut was also appointed Port Admiral of New York, a position which "self-respect and regard for the Navy compelled him to decline."[23] The uniform of the Admiral which he had adopted when the rank was conferred on him was also ordered changed. But Farragut refused to accept the changes in his flag and uniform, and the Secretary ordered them not to be altered during the Admiral's lifetime.[23]

After three months, the opposition to the Porter-Borie administration of the Navy Department became "nation wide,"[24] and Grant permitted Borie to resign. In his place, he appointed George M. Robeson, at Borie's suggestion. John Kean, in a letter to Hamilton Fish, referred to Robeson as "a first-rate judge of wines, a second-rate trout-fisherman, and a third-rate Jersey lawyer."[25] According to Allan Nevins, he "was good-looking, florid, jovial; a bachelor, he was gallant in his attentions to the ladies; previously poor, he soon displayed a surprising affluence."[25] The new Secretary "gradually eased Vice-Admiral Porter from his exceptional position in the Department."[26]

3

In the summer of 1869, Admiral and Mrs. Farragut made a trip to California. He wanted to see the completed Mare Island Navy Yard, which he had commenced eleven years before. A large cavalcade of citizens of Vallejo went out to meet him and escort him to the town. The City Council gave him a reception, with a speech of welcome beginning, "You left us a captain. You are here to-day the High Admiral of the American Navy." Farragut, greatly moved, with his old friends about him, replied that he had done his duty and that "the fiat of the Almighty is seen in the result." He was happy, he concluded, to be among them again and "get a good rest."[27] That evening he was entertained with fireworks and a torchlight procession.

After spending several days inspecting the Navy Yard and looking after the real estate investments he had previously made in the town, he turned homeward with Mrs. Farragut. In Chicago he had a serious heart attack, induced by a severe cold, and for a time his life was despaired of.[27] General Sheridan sent the following telegram to General Sherman: "Admiral Farragut is here and unwell. He is an old man and the Doctor thinks, without desiring to create any alarm, that it would be well to send his son who is at Fort Preble, Portland, Maine, here without delay."[28] But Farragut rallied, and after a few days of careful nursing he recovered his strength sufficiently to continue his journey home.

During the ensuing winter, the Admiral had several other heart attacks, but his powerful constitution enabled him to recover from each. By the end of November he was much better, and began to plan a visit to Washington.[29] Replying to an inquiry from Mr. Welles, who was writing some magazine articles on the late war, he wrote that he had heard that Porter claimed to have originated the idea of attacking New Orleans, that the first he knew of it was through Porter, and that he did not want the mortars which he thought would be in the way but he had acceded to the wishes of the Navy Department. "I hope soon to be able to visit Washington," he added, "when I shall pay my respects to the Honorable Sec'y and endeavor to enlighten him a little on the subject of the imperfections of the navy, notwithstanding a writer in the *Army and Navy Journal* insists that its condition is near perfection."[30]

This visit was not made, but Farragut had considerable correspondence with the Department concerning the alleged misconduct of Paymaster Thomas H. Looker and a critical letter which Admiral Turner had written about him. "A few months after Farragut's return from California, and after his first great sickness," wrote Porter to Turner, "he became very much exercised in mind about a forgery of his name that he asserted had been committed by Paymaster Looker of the Navy, and he wrote several communications to the Department, showing in his weak condition evidently a good deal of distress of mind.

"THE LAST SCENE OF ALL" 373

He also demanded to see a letter which you wrote about him from California. The Secretary to soothe him offered him the superintendence of the Peabody funeral and sent an officer to see him and show him your letter, so he wouldn't have a copy of it. Of course, the Admiral was rather indignant when he read the letter and gave utterance to some little expletives not used in saintly places."[31]

Farragut felt well enough to go to Portland, Maine, in January, 1870 to take charge of the naval ceremony incident to the receiving of the remains of George Peabody, which were conveyed home in the British turreted battleship *Monarch*, accompanied by the U. S. corvette *Plymouth*. The draft of the *Monarch* was too great for her to enter the harbors of Boston or New York. On that occasion, Commander Winfield Scott Schley saw Farragut for the last time, at a public reception in the Preble House. Schley grasped his hand and said, "Admiral, I am glad to see you looking so well, after the alarming reports of your illness." He answered, "Do you really think so? I am very far from being a well man. Do you remember our conversation some years ago, before Port Hudson, when I bantered you about jumping over a squilgee handle?" Schley had to admit he could not recall what was said but that he remembered that the Admiral was then much more active and agile than he, though the difference in their ages was some forty years. "Yes," Farragut continued, "I recollect you then said I belonged to that class of men who would preserve their vigor and vitality until ripe old age, and that, when the break comes, would go in a year. It looks to me now that this may be so. But I shall never forget how I was impressed by what you said."[32]

4

The superintendence of the Peabody funeral was Farragut's last official duty. His health continued gradually but surely to fail. He rarely left his home except for a short drive in Central Park or to attend services in the Church of the Incarnation near his home on the corner of Madison Avenue and 35th Street.[33] His physician advised that he leave New York during the summer and pay a visit to the Pennocks in Portsmouth, New Hampshire, where Commodore Pennock was Commandant of the Navy Yard. Learning of his intention, the Navy Department placed at his disposal the dispatch steamer *Tallapoosa* to convey him and Mrs. Farragut to Portsmouth. To Porter, who claimed that he had suggested the arrangement, Farragut sent a brief but sincere note of thanks for his thoughtfulness. "My physicians are decidedly of the opinion that a change of air will be highly beneficial to me and I do not doubt that this little trip by sea will also be of service,"[34] he wrote.

As though he had a premonition that his death was not far distant, Farragut arose from his sick-bed when he heard the salute being fired in his honor as the *Tallapoosa* approached Portsmouth on July 4, and dressing himself in full uniform, he went on deck. "It would be well if I died *now*, in harness," he said with a sad smile, as he looked up at his blue flag fluttering at the masthead.[35] One day while he was idling about the Navy Yard, he went aboard the old sailing sloop *Dale*, then lying dismantled at the wharf. Walking around a little and letting his eyes dwell fondly on the old ship whose work, like his, was finished, he went sadly ashore again. As he was leaving, he remarked to the old sailor who was the caretaker, "This is the last time I shall ever tread the deck of a man-of-war."[35] Then he slowly climbed the steps leading up to the stately Commandant's Residence, and sat down wearily on the wide white-pillared verandah, breathing deeply the sea-laden air sweeping in from the Atlantic.

Farragut's premonitions of approaching death were well founded. A few days later he became too ill to leave his bed. Fox, the former Assistant Secretary of the Navy, heard of his illness, and came up from Boston on July 24 to see him. "Mrs. F. took me upstairs to see the Admiral who was asleep and very low—with heart disease," he recorded in his diary.[36] A week later he made another trip to see him, and found him "dangerously sick."[36] But Farragut lingered on two weeks longer until August 14, when he died of a paralytic stroke. It was Sunday, and everything seemed very quiet and peaceful on that summer day in the Navy Yard. Just as eight bells was struck at noon, the spirit of the great Admiral "put out to sea." The previous day, when fully conscious, he had received the eucharist.[37] With him at the end were his wife and son, members of the Pennock family, and three physicians.[37] When his Negro steward, John H. Brooks, heard of his death, he wrote in his diary: "Aug. 15. My good friend Admiral D. G. Farragut died yesterday. What a great loss he is to this country. Thank God he died in peace with his Maker. I have lost my best naval friend."[38]

On the following Wednesday, August 17, the city of Portsmouth and the officers and men of the Navy Yard united in honoring Farragut with a public funeral. The city was crowded with people to overflowing. A procession a mile long, composed of marines and sailors, Army and Navy officers, civil officials, patriotic and fraternal societies, and citizens of all ranks of society, followed the flag draped hearse which was drawn by four horses. Bells tolled and minute guns sounded from the Navy Yard and the ships in the harbor; all business was suspended. Funeral services were held in St. John's Church, which was decorated in festoons of black and white crepe with masses of flowers in beautiful designs, one representing a ship made entirely of flowers. On the casket of rosewood with heavy silver trimmings rested the Admiral's full dress uniform and his sword. Farragut's pastor, the Reverend Doctor Henry E. Montgomery, came from New York to assist in conducting the services. Among the distinguished persons present were the Admiral's old friends, General Banks, Mr. Gideon Welles, and Mr. Gustavus Vasa Fox, with whom he had been intimately associated during the late war. After the Episcopal service, Masonic honors were rendered, and then three volleys were fired by the military escort, after which the coffin was placed in a temporary vault in the cemetery near the church.[39] The understanding was that in the autumn the remains were to be removed to Annapolis for burial "in accordance with the expressed wish of the late Admiral."[40]

There was considerable unfavorable comment on the failure

of the government to participate officially in the funeral at Portsmouth. As an excuse the *Army and Navy Journal*[41] cited a section in the Navy Appropriation Act for 1870 which stated that no funeral expenses of a naval officer who died in the United States would be allowed. But when Mrs. Farragut agreed to the request of the leading citizens of New York that her husband be buried in Woodlawn Cemetery in Westchester County near New York City, and when the city decided to give Farragut a public funeral and asked the government to send the frigate *Guerrière* to convey his remains to New York, the request was granted and President Grant and his Cabinet attended the funeral.

Under the supervision of Loyall Farragut, Rear-Admiral Bailey, Commodore Pennock, Major Montgomery and a committee of the Common Council of New York and the Military Order of the Loyal Legion of which Farragut had been president, the coffin was removed from the cemetery of St. John's Church to the steam tug *Speedwell* under an escort of a marine band and four companies of marines. Thence it was taken down the Piscataqua River to the *Guerrière*, to the accompaniment of salutes from the *Vandalia* and shore and station batteries. Captain Thomas H. Stevens of the *Guerrière* received it on board with his flag halfmasted and yards manned, and a salute of seventeen guns. On the voyage south, unfortunately the pilot ran the vessel ashore on Great Point, Nantucket, and the coffin had to be landed at Hyannis and forwarded to New York by the Fall River boat. In the vicinity of the city it was transferred to the sloop of war *Brooklyn*, Farragut's unlucky ship, and brought thus ceremoniously up the harbor.[42]

Great preparations had been made for a grand and solemn procession up West and Canal Streets to Broadway and thence to the Harlem railway station at 47th Street. In the procession, in addition to President Grant and his Cabinet, were the Governor of New York and state officials, the Mayor and municipal officials, two divisions of the National Guard, marines of the Brooklyn Navy Yard, and military, civic, patriotic, and fraternal organizations innumerable.[43] But the weather, which

THE FARRAGUT FUNERAL PROCESSION IN NEW YORK

The Farragut Statue by Virginia Ream in Farragut Square, Washington, D.C.
From a photograph by the L. C. Handy Studios, Washington, D.C.

"THE LAST SCENE OF ALL" 377

is no respecter of persons or events, on that September 30 was very unpropitious. A long continued, tremendous downpour of cold rain drenched everybody. A confusion of orders resulted in reducing the procession at least half, and took away much of the pomp and ceremony and solemnity of the occasion. General Woodward and staff looked brilliant but very wet, and the usually "resplendent plumes of their chapeaux failed to present their wonted appearance."[44] The newspapers incorrectly reported that Mrs. Farragut was in an open carriage; she was not in the procession at all.

The Admiral's remains were laid to rest in a beautiful plot which the trustees of the Woodlawn Cemetery had selected. As General George Meade and General James Grant Wilson turned away from the grave, the former declared with feeling, "I believe that the Admiral was more beloved than any other commander of the late war, either of the Army or Navy."[45]

Here a rather imposing monument was placed, bearing the simple inscription: "Erected By His Wife And Son To The Memory Of David Glasgow Farragut, First Admiral In The United States Navy, Born July 5, 1801, Died August 14, 1870." Here were buried in turn Mrs. Farragut, Loyall Farragut's wife, and lastly Loyall Farragut himself, the last of the family for he had no children [46]

Appropriate in conclusion seems the following poem, "Farragut," by Charles de Kay:

> "After life's long watch and ward,
> Sleep, great Sailor, while the bard
> Chants your daring. When, of late,
> Tempest shook the Bark of State,
> Fierce and deadly, throe on throe,
> Horrid with a phosphor-glow,
> And the mountains rearing gray
> Smote her reeling on her way—
>
> Day and night, who stood on guard,
> Steadfast aye for watch and ward?
> You, great Pilot, who were made
> Quick and cautious, bold and staid;
> Like Decatur, Perry, Jones,
> Mastering men with trumpet tones.

How you met your land's appeal
Knows New Orleans, knows Mobile.

Slumber, free from watch or ward,
Dweller deep in grassy yard
Of still billows! Keep your berth
Narrow in the quiet earth!
As of old the north star shines,
Heaven displays the ancient signs,
On the Ship drives, sure and slow,
Though the Captain sleeps below.

Only sleeps upon his sword;
Slumber earned by watch and ward;
For if timbers crack, and helm
Fail her, and a sea o'erwhelm,
Then his spirit shall inform
Some new queller of the storm,
Who shall bring, though stars are pale,
The Bark in safety through the gale."[47]

XXX
"WHAT WOULD FARRAGUT HAVE DONE?"

1

ADMIRAL GEORGE DEWEY, who served as a lieutenant in Farragut's fleet in the New Orleans campaign and at Port Hudson, after his own victory in Manila Bay, wrote Loyall Farragut, "In all my operations in the Philippines, the example of the Great Admiral, your father, was constantly before me. I often said to myself in great emergencies, 'What would Farragut have done under like emergencies?' And when I entered Manila Bay immediately on arriving off the coast, I felt sure I was doing exactly as he would have done."[1]

The characteristics of Farragut which Dewey had in mind have been abundantly exemplified, it is hoped, in this biography, but perhaps a final summary of them may be useful. Many have attempted to characterize Farragut briefly. Instead of endeavoring to make a synthesis from these, one might quote from several different estimates and note the remarkable agreement of them all.

Not long after the Admiral's death, an editorial in the *Army and Navy Journal* declared, "An unaffected, honest gentleman, a sincere practical Christian, a determined though kindly commander, a captain of proved courage 'who dared to lead where any dared to follow,' it was not surprising that he speedily leaped into position as an idolized popular hero. Nelson, disobeying orders at Copenhagen, or breaking the allied line at Trafalgar with his *Victory,* furnishes the nearest parallel. But Admiral Farragut would never have tolerated a Lady Hamilton or signed himself Bronte. There have been greater marine strategists or, more properly, tacticians, than Nelson and Farragut. Yet each of these heroes was invested with a natural perception of the right course to take, an intuition of the enemy's weak point, which, if not genius, was next allied to it. And both developed a dash and daring which are their distinctive qualities, and were the great causes of the great results. Once satisfied that a course must be pursued, it was utterly impossible to hold Farragut back from it. . . . He was bold, decisive, self-reliant, and directed by intuitional rather than by severe scientific processes."[2]

Rear Admiral Winfield Scott Schley, who was a lieutenant in Farragut's fleet at the siege of Port Hudson and whose family had known Farragut since he was a young officer, wrote of him, "The wide difference that was apparent between this sprightly, kind, mild, and pleasing gentleman, even when under a heavy load of responsibility, and his lion-like character and presence when battle was going on, was the contrast between sunshine and storm. His judgment of men was excellent, as the choice of officers with whom he surrounded himself indicated. The unvarying and complete success he met in everything he undertook in that great war was due largely to his strong personality, unerring purpose, and dashing example. The naval history of the past presents two characters that were much alike in their restless activity, their untiring energy of purpose, their absolute personal intrepidity and self-poise in emergency, and their dogged adherence to the idea that the enemy was to be fought wherever met—Farragut and Nelson. Farragut's private life and high ideals, however, gave him preeminence over his great English compeer."[3]

Another junior officer in Farragut's fleet, afterwards Rear Admiral S. R. Franklin, in a few words thus summed up his estimate of the character of his former commander: "I think Farragut was the pluckiest man I ever knew. I think he was absolutely insensible to fear; indeed, that feeling did not enter into his makeup as a man at all. I do not believe he could appreciate the meaning of the word. I do not mean that he was so influenced in this way as to destroy his judgment, and cause him to take unnecessary risks, for he had a great abundance of naval wisdom, and knew well when to take great chances to accomplish great ends."[4] Another very brief estimate was given in an address by Ex-Governor Alexander H. Rice of Massachusetts at the dedication of the Farragut monument in Marine Park, South Boston. "As a strategist he had something of the quality that Emerson had as a poet," he said of Farragut whom he had known very well personally; "he was not only practical, but mystical; he had keen and faultless sagacity, delicate intuitions, wonderful penetration, and great staying power; and, in the language of our day, the habit of 'getting there.' "[5] In the same vein wrote the *Nation,* "His victories were victories of character rather than intellect. He owed no advantage to juggling device or shrewd ingenuity. His tactics were simple and without novelty. . . . Nothing was left to chance that could be anticipated. When the time for action came, his composure, quickness of perception, resolution, and command of his fleet proved invincible. . . . The lesson of his life is that his success was no accident."[6]

From Mahan's careful analysis of Farragut's character, the following has a direct bearing on Dewey's question: "He had a clear eye for the true key of a military situation, a quick and accurate perception of the right thing to do at a critical moment, a firm grip upon the leading principles of war; but he might have had all of these and yet miserably failed. He was a man of most determined will and character, ready to tread down or fight through any obstacles which stood in the path he saw fit to follow."[7] Mahan, primarily interested in the principles of tactics and strategy, points out how well Farragut understood the importance of getting "in a soldier's rear," the maxim that offense is the best defense, the value of the element of time in winning a naval campaign, the necessity of bearing heavy responsibility in making quick and unexpected decisions, and lastly audacity. Farragut said, "Drayton does not know fear, and would fight the devil himself, but he believes in acting as if the enemy can never be caught unprepared; whereas I believe in judging him by ourselves, and my motto in action is, 'L'audace, et encore de l'audace, et toujours de l'audace!' "[8]

2

Farragut's personal appearance has been touched upon from time to time in this biography as the narration of events permitted. The most complete description, and according to Loyall Farragut the best word picture, of the Admiral at the time of the Battle of Mobile Bay is that by Cyrus Townsend Brady in his *Southerners*. It is worthy of being quoted in full, though it better portrays Farragut's appearance the previous year before he began to put on weight. "He was a rather small man who still preserved his waist and figure, although he had already entered upon his sixty-third year," Brady wrote. "While he was rather small, he yet had broad shoulders and a well-knit frame that showed unusual vigor for one of his age. In reading he wore eye-glasses, and when he removed them a slight contraction of his brows was noticeable, which turned the upper curves of the eyelids into straight lines, giving a singular eagle-like directness to his glance;—if an eagle's eye could be kindly and filled with humor which is the completing quality of greatness. His face, which was rather long, was smooth-shaven. His forehead was round and high. His nose was aquiline, and his upper lip long; the curves of his mouth bespoke an indomitable resolution which the firm, bold chin and resolute jaw confirmed. He was bald on the top of his head, but his black hair, already turning white about the temples, which was allowed to grow long on the left side, was carefully brushed over the denuded spot; in seaman's parlance, 'the after-guard was made to do folk's'l duty.' His naturally very dark complexion was intensified by an exposure of many years to wind and weather, largely in tropic seas. In spite of the dark skin his color came and went like a boy's especially when he laughed or grew excited. His manners were simple, genial, and unaffected; his address easy and pleasant. Fifty years of naval service had given the Admiral the authoritative appearance of long command. There was about him that indefinable stamp of power and its habitual use, or employment, which held the most presumptuous at a proper distance.

At the same time he was easily approachable, too. In his bearing there was dignity without stiffness. When he knitted his brows, as he frequently did on account of slightly impaired vision, and his mind turned to action, his hazel eyes fairly flashed with fire and spirit. In repose there was a twinkle of humor, and good humor, in them, which yet neither invited presumption nor allowed familiarity. The predominant impression that an observer accustomed to reading men would have gathered from his appearance was one of absolute fearlessness. You could see that he was a sailor beyond peradventure; a thousand things indicated it to the observing or experienced eye. He could no more disguise it than he could disguise his character. Yet there were none of the popular accepted signs of his profession about him; nothing of the 'roll like-a-seventy-four-in-a-gale-of-wind' in his manner, nothing of the bluff, burly, bull-like blow-hardness of the so-called Benbow school of sailors, in his appearance. Nor was he of the red-faced, irascible type, which so many ancient seamen affect—especially in novels. He was not full of strange oaths and uncouth phrases, more or less technical. There were about him none of the common affectations of the sea—indeed no affectations of any sort. Here was a cultivated gentleman of the very highest type, an accomplished officer, a lion in his bravery, almost a woman in gentleness."[9]

3

Farragut's attitude toward war also throws a revealing light on his character. "When actually engaged in battle," his son wrote, "he always seemed to enjoy the conflict, and yet there was a gentle and sentimental side to his nature. I have heard him remark with sadness: 'War is a terrible business. It is demoralizing and brings out all the worst characteristics of men; but', he added, 'we must go to war, or more terrible things may follow.' "[10] In the same vein he wrote Mrs. Farragut after the New Orleans campaign, ". . . But oh, what a destroyer is an ambitious man, what wreck and ruin have they brought upon this happiest and loveliest of countries. What a state of things —here everything is desolation and suffering and yet no one can see the end of it. This river will loose (sic) its trade and be cast back fifty years in population and will be ultimately like the sugar and coffee countries."[11]

Six months later Farragut was feeling quite war-weary when he wrote his wife, "We have a rumor to-day that there has been a big fight in Virginia, and that Lee has been defeated after four days' hard fighting. I trust it is true; and, if so, we may be able to see a prospect of an end to this war. As Micawber says, 'I am waiting for something to turn up.' "[12] But Lee won the bloody battle of Fredericksburg, and the war went on and on. A couple of months afterwards, Farragut wrote his wife, ". . . Your ideas of the war are all right; but, notwithstanding that the politicians have done the mischief, I believe it was God's will to have it so. No people could go on with such vice and extravagance as ours, without being brought to a reckoning sooner or later. . . . Civil war, once commenced, will run its course like a violent disease, and frequently changes its character *in toto;* and thus it may be with ours. It is difficult to see the end, and, as you say, all we can do is to perform our duty and pray for the best results."[13]

This attitude toward war was in keeping with Farragut's religion. All his immediate family were Roman Catholic, with the probable exception of his mother. His wife was Episcopalian, and he attended that church regularly with her, though he did not become a member until very late in life.[14] When he was at the Mare Island Navy Yard a few years before the war, he was president of the board of trustees of the Methodist Church at Vallejo, which he and Mrs. Farragut attended, as there was no Episcopal Church in the village. The minister of that church, C. V. Anthony, nearly forty years afterwards wrote the only detailed account of Farragut's religious beliefs in existence.

"Farragut was essentially religious," Anthony declared.[15] "He did not belong to any church, but had a profound regard for all churches, and generously contributed to their support.[16] He always attended Christian worship, unless it was conducted in a language he could not understand. For this reason he did not attend the Roman Catholic church unless upon some rare occasion. He asked a blessing at his own table when others than his own family were present. He certainly never lost an opportunity to speak well of the Christian faith. It is true that he sometimes under excitement used expressions that were inconsistent with a Christian profession; but he could not be said to be, in the ordinary sense, a profane man."

As to this weakness in Farragut's character, Anthony related a very interesting incident. One day his son Loyall, then only nine or ten years old, while with his father at the Navy Yard, used an expression bordering on profanity, though he did not mention the name of God. After Farragut had rebuked his son severely, the boy turned to him and said, "Why, pa, I heard you say the same thing yesterday!" In reply, Farragut explained, "I went to sea when a small boy and have always been associated with rough men. I never had the help of a pious mother, and could never go to Sunday school and church as you can. Now you must go right to the house and to your room, and pray God to forgive you for saying such a naughty thing. And when you have done that, ask God to forgive your father for saying such bad words sometimes." Loyall went to the house and related to his mother what had occurred. She told him to do exactly what his father had asked, and through the half-open door to his room heard this prayer for his father after he had finished asking forgiveness for himself: "Lord, you must forgive my pa for saying bad words sometimes. You know he went to sea when he was a little boy, never had a mother to teach him, couldn't go to church and Sunday school as I do, and—and, Lord, you must forgive my pa, for you know he don't mean anything."[15]

According to Anthony, Farragut did not believe in the divine origin of the Old Testament, though he expressed confidence in the evangelical history and the sincerest admiration for Jesus Christ. "The sufferings of Christ often affected him to tears," he declared, "and many times he bowed his head upon the seat in front of him to hide his emotion. It may be proper here to add that he sometimes exhibited that proof of great courage—the tenderness of a woman. Though he never went to the sacramental altar, he sat an intensely interested beholder, with a look of sadness that indicated deep sympathy with what was being done."[15]

Anthony revealed that, though Farragut was not a total abstainer, he never went into a saloon to drink. "When he had company at his table, he drank wine with them," he wrote. "When he had no company, or company that did not drink, he put about a table spoonful of whiskey into a common goblet, filled it with cold water, and drank it instead of tea or coffee at the dinner hour, and only then.... Whenever other company was present that drank wine, he always said, after they were served, 'Mr. Anthony, I do not offer wine to you because I know you never drink'—a manifestation of real politeness rarely seen among drinking men."[15]

Like many men of strong character, Farragut had a high temper, which, as he grew older, he was better able to control. Captain William C. Bolton, who had been associated with him when he was a junior officer, advised Mrs. Farragut, when her husband was upset by Commodore Perry's treatment of him during the Mexican War,[17] "Now you must tell him to keep quiet and avoid getting into difficulty, which I fear he may do, knowing as I do his ardour of feeling and acute irasibility" (sic).[18] Throughout the Civil War, Farragut's "ardour of feeling" was displayed on several occasions and sometimes his irascibility. But he was not a man to nurse a grudge or to harbor ill will. Having been the protégé of David Porter, who was very friendly to Decatur and hostile to Barron, Farragut naturally sympathized with that side of the unhappy controversy which ended with Decatur's being killed by Barron in a duel. Yet when he was on duty in Norfolk before the war, Farragut brought about, on his own initiative, a reconciliation between Commodore Charles Morris, also one of Decatur's former warm friends, and Commodore Barron, who had been Morris's bitter enemy for many years.[19] In spite of D. D. Porter's unfriendly and unfair criticism of Farragut during the war, as fully revealed in this biography, Farragut developed no particular enmity for him, though he was fully aware of at least some of his attempts to discredit him at the Navy Department.

Throughout his life there were many illustrations of the truth of the statement that Farragut was "a practical Christian," even when he was not a church member. It became his duty on one occasion to reprimand an employee at a navy yard, who had been found guilty of peculations. Through influence in Washington, the man was ordered to be "publicly admonished" instead of being dismissed, as he really merited. In performing this unpleasant duty, Farragut turned to the man and, pointing his finger at him, said solemnly, "Remember the eighth commandment, *Thou shalt not steal.*" This was all that was needed to bring a look of complete misery to the man's face.[20] Farragut hated all dishonesty and sham. After the war, it was intimated to him that one hundred thousand dollars of stock in a certain company would be given him, if he would allow his name to be used as a director of the company. This he politely but firmly refused.[20] On another occasion, he remarked that "he believed in doing things open and aboveboard, as such a policy in the long run would always give one the advantage over an intriguing adversary."[20] When it was reported to him once that some dissatisfied officers in his squadron were working against him, he replied, "I know nothing about it nor do I care to know; but I will give them something else to think about, for I intend to fight a battle in a few days."[20] The battle soon followed. When the Navy Department wished to indicate that some favorites were efficient officers, whom Farragut did not approve, he declared, "Gentlemen, you can no more make a sailor out of a land-lubber by dressing him up in sea-toggery and putting a commission into his pocket than you could make a shoemaker of him by filling him with sherry cobblers."[20] On the other hand, he strongly favored giving promotion to those who merited it. When it was claimed that a certain officer was too young for promotion, which might turn his head, Farragut said, "Well, if he can't stand prosperity, that will be his own fault."[20]

Also worthy of particular note was Farragut's absolute reliance on Divine Providence, which sustained him in the most terrifying crises of battle. Again and again this supreme faith was exemplified in his life, and to this he referred constantly both in his conversation and in his letters. It was the foundation upon which rested both his moral and his physical courage.

4

Farragut's education was fragmentary, though perhaps not more so than that of the average naval officer of his day. What he knew he acquired the hard way, largely through the school of experience. He had a particular aptitude for languages, and was able to speak fluently Spanish, French, Italian, and even Arabic. An amusing story is told of his being called upon, when a very young officer in the Mediterranean, to interpret the strange speech of a bumboat woman. She was talking Arabic, and for his ability to converse with her Farragut was said to be in league with the "Old Boy."[20] On account of weakness of eyesight caused by a sunstroke in Tunis during his midshipman days, he was not able to read very long at a time. His wife, who was very fond of books, often read to him and wrote many of his letters when he was at home. On shipboard he had his junior officers read to him frequently, from the Bible and other books. In his Bible and Prayer Book he had his favorite passages marked.[21] He often quoted freely from the Bible, Shakespeare, and other secular literature in his letters. James Fenimore Cooper was one of his favorite authors.[22]

Farragut was interested in all fields of knowledge. Anthony recalled that he borrowed his copy of *Types of Mankind,* a work on ethnology.[15] Before the war he attended lectures on varied subjects at Yale University and at the Smithsonian Institution in Washington.[23] He also loved conversation and gathered a great mass of information in this way from all kinds of people in all sorts of places at home and abroad. "In conversation he was an animated and interesting talker," wrote Rear Admiral Winfield Scott Schley. "His information and experience were general, and upon almost all subjects—professional, scientific, or political—he was interesting and attractive."[24] Farragut was fond of society, and had many social graces which made him popular and perfectly at ease on any occasion anywhere. He loved dancing and the society of women, but his relationship with them was always such as not to give the slightest occasion for scandal or unhappiness to Mrs. Farragut, to whom he was completely devoted. Singularly, in spite of his Spanish blood, he did not care much for music, particularly the operatic variety.

As to his profession, Farragut kept himself as completely informed as possible about everything new in guns and ships, and maintained this keen interest to the end of his life. "He was a thorough seaman, a thorough man-of-war's man.... He did not neglect all the details which merit and win success," wrote General Sherman to Loyall Farragut.[25] He was somewhat conservative, particularly in later years. "As a sailor of the 'old school,' he instinctively repelled the idea of ironclad protection, and despised submarine engines of defense," the *Army and Navy Journal* pointed out. "... It is no secret that he was both an illogical and strenuous opponent of the Dahlgren theory of ordnance, at first objecting to any change in our ships' batteries and afterwards opposing each increase of calibre as it came along. These were his defects, which honest criticism cannot deny or be blind to—easily ascribed to his long experience with walls of wood and the natural tendency of men to cling to the system and theory of which they have been part. Yet there is no hero in our Valhalla who will be more honored with a more honest respect, a purer reverence, than the nation's first Admiral. And many a day will come and go ere we shall look again upon an example so modest, so brave, so thoroughly patriotic. The clumsy cuirass and the ugly turret are fast banishing the fair broadsides and graceful lines of wood from the seas, and they in their turn may have to give way to the torpedo and the submarine boat. After our mariners of to-day come scientists instead of sailors. But when turning away from the roster of philosophers, chemists, and electricians for the romance and chivalry of the old type, we look backwards, we shall contemplate with pride and enthusiasm the gallant sailors of Farragut's day."[26]

In recalling the influence Farragut had on Dewey—an influence which has been wide and deep on the United States Navy for three quarters of a century, it would be interesting to raise the question as to who particularly influenced Farragut. It has been generally supposed that David Porter had most to do with indoctrinating Farragut with the principles and ideals of the naval profession. This may be true, though it would be difficult to prove it. Farragut was ever ready to acknowledge his indebtedness to Porter for his very friendly patronage during his early years, but he has not left on record any expression of his professional indebtedness to Porter. It is, therefore, very interesting to note that on one occasion after the Civil War, when in conversation with General James Grant Wilson about the naval heroes of the War of 1812, Farragut remarked, "Commodore Hull was as able a seaman as ever sailed a ship. If I have done the country any service afloat, it is in no small degree owing to the ambition and enthusiasm he inspired in me by fair fight with and capture of an English frigate, when I was a youngster serving on the *Essex*. I always envied Isaac Hull that piece of good luck." After all, David Porter lost the *Essex* to the British; Hull in the *Constitution* destroyed the *Guerriére*. Besides, Farragut may have been too near David Porter for hero-worship of him.[27]

The influence of Farragut on the morale of his countrymen in time of war has been beautifully and effectively phrased by Harry Lyman Koopman in these lines:

> "But, if ever in fight it should befall
> That the foe, for a space, shall seem to win,
> Then let his boldest hearts beware,
> For, on a sudden, none knoweth from where,
> A ship shall steer through the fiery din,
> That flieth the stars of the Admiral.
> Ye shall know her by her long white deck,
> Unmarred by battle wreck;
> And in her shrouds, trumpet in hand,
> The Admiral shall stand.
> She heeds not wave nor wind,
> She leaves no wake behind,
> No shot her hull may feel,
> But her black stem sheareth oak and steel;
> And woe worth the proudest foe's renown,
> On whom the *Hartford* beareth down....
> It is the grand old ship,
> Where Farragut, still on guard,
> Keepeth perpetual watch and ward."[28]

APPENDIX

STATUES, PICTURES, AND POEMS

1

ONLY FIVE days after Farragut was buried in Woodlawn Cemetery, the Commandery of the Military Order of the Loyal Legion of the State of New York appointed a committee to initiate the erection of a memorial to the Admiral. The result was a mural tablet bearing a likeness of Farragut in bas relief, sculptured by Launt Thompson, which was placed to the left of the chancel in the Church of the Incarnation in New York, where Farragut worshipped.[1]

In 1874, Congress appropriated $20,000 for the erection of a bronze statue of Farragut to be placed in Washington in Farragut Square. The statue was modeled by Virginia ("Vinnie") Ream,[2] and cast under her direction at the Washington Navy Yard, one of the propellers of the *Hartford* furnishing material. She also designed the granite base with the mortars, which cost an additional $7,000. The entire monument is thirty feet high. Farragut is portrayed holding a telescope, with one foot on a round object around which a cable is coiled. It was unveiled April 25, 1881. A military and naval procession marched past the White House and was reviewed by President Garfield. The statue was presented by Secretary of the Navy Hunt and received by the President. Horace Maynard, late Postmaster General, and Senator Vorhees made addresses.[3] Mrs. Farragut and Loyall were guests at the White House, at the special invitation of Mrs. Garfield.[4]

Just a month later, on May 25, the Augustus Saint-Gaudens statue of Farragut was unveiled in New York in Madison Square. Under the direction of Rear Admiral Melancton Smith, the actual unveiling was done by Quartermaster Knowles, who lashed Farragut to the rigging, and J. B. Millner, another sailor who was on the *Hartford*. The statue was presented by Secretary of the Navy Hunt, and the Honorable Joseph H. Choate, who had been Farragut's friend, delivered the address. "We come together today," he said near the beginning of his speech, "to recall the memory and to crown the statue of one of the dearest of these idols of mankind [naval heroes]—of one who has done more for us than all of them combined—of one whose name will ever stir like a trumpet the hearts of his grateful countrymen."[5] In conclusion, he said, prophetically, "Our frigates may rot in the harbor—our ironclads may rust at the dock, but if ever again the flag is in peril, invincible armies will swarm upon the land, and steel-clad squadrons leap forth upon the sea to maintain it. . . . We can always be sure, then, of fleets and armies enough. But shall we always have a Grant to lead the one, and a Farragut to inspire the other? Will our future soldiers and sailors share, as theirs almost to the last man shared, their devotion, their courage, and their faith? Yes, on this one condition, that every American child learns from his cradle, as Farragut learned from his, that his first and last duty is to his country, that to live for her is honor, and to die for her is glory."[5] Sharing in these impressive ceremonies as honored guests were Mrs. Farragut and her son Loyall.

The bronze figure of Farragut, modeled by the great sculptor Saint-Gaudens and cast in Paris, stands on a pedestal of North River bluestone, which was designed by Stanford White.[6] The figure to the left on the pedestal represents Loyalty; that to the right symbolizes Courage. The inscription, written by Richard Grant White, after giving the main facts and dates of Farragut's career, concludes, "That the memory of a daring and sagacious commander, and gentle, great-souled man, whose life from childhood was given to his country, but who served her supremely in the War for the Union, 1861-1865, may be preserved and honored, and that they who come after him and will owe him so much may see him as he was seen by friend and foe, his countrymen have set up this monument. 1881."[6] The statue of Farragut is of heroic size. "It shows the Admiral in his

The Farragut Statue by Augustus Saint-Gaudens in Madison Square, New York
From a photograph in Saint-Gaudens' *Reminiscences*.

Courtesy of Dr. John J. Loughlin

ADMIRAL D. G. FARRAGUT

From the portrait, painted by Henry A. Loop for the Union League Club of New York, 1871. Now owned by Dr. John J. Loughlin, New York.

navy uniform, his cap straight visored, and the trousers loose, his sword hanging from the belt. In his left hand he holds a marine glass. The right hangs naturally. The skirt of the coat seems to be agitated by the wind. The pose is easy and natural, and the expression admirable in its combination of gravity and penetration. The instant that it was unveiled it achieved the success to which it is in every way entitled. Indeed, there are few, if any, statues in America to be compared with it in naturalness and power."[7] Robert Bridges, at the time Poet Laureate of England, wrote a beautiful poem on the statue, beginning:

> "To live a hero, then to stand
> In bronze serene above the city's throng;
> Hero at sea! and now on land
> Revered by thousands as they rush along."[8]

The city of Boston dedicated a monument to Farragut on June 28, 1893, in Marine Park, South Boston. Preceding the ceremony in the afternoon, there was a large naval and military parade. Ex-Governor Alexander H. Rice made the principal address. Admiral Koznakoff spoke for the Russian Atlantic Squadron, which came up to Boston from New York for the unveiling. The Russian admiral's speech was chiefly a quotation from the general order of Admiral Boutakoff, which he had published to his fleet in August, 1867 after Farragut's visit to Russia. "Twenty-five years have elapsed since that order of the day was issued," he said in conclusion; "but none the less today than then do we respect the memory of Admiral Farragut. And we are therefore glad to see, upon visiting your country, how deeply Farragut's name is respected in his fatherland. Eternal be Farragut's glory, and long live and prosper the nation that does not forget the memory of its heroes!"[9] Governor Rice made a long speech, summarizing Farragut's career and estimating his character and achievements. "Ten thousand [cheers] more for the great sea king himself," he concluded. "Wave round him the flag of the country he loved so much! Let these salvos of artillery be to our ears the echoes of his thundering squadrons! And while chiming bells and martial strains fill the air with melody, let all our hearts renew their tributes of admiration, affection, and gratitude to the peerless admiral, the incorruptible patriot, the altogether noble man."[10]

The sculptor of the Boston statue of Farragut was Henry H. Kitson. It is of heroic size and stands on a pedestal of blue Quincy granite. The entire cost was $22,500. It is a dignified, impressive, and altogether worthy memorial to Farragut.

On Memorial Day, May 30, 1900, an excellent large statue of Farragut by Charles Henry Niehaus was unveiled in Hackley Square, Muskegon, Michigan. The same day, statues of Lincoln, Grant, and Sherman by Niehaus were dedicated in the same square. They were all donated to his native city by Charles H. Hackley. After the military parade, an address was given by Ex-Senator John Patton of Grand Rapids. Niehaus portrays Farragut as though standing with his feet squarely placed on the deck of his ship, bracing himself against the wind, which blows his uniform backwards, and against the roll of his vessel, as he gazes far out to sea.[11]

A statue of Farragut by George F. Bissell was on exhibition at the Louisiana Purchase Exposition at St. Louis in 1904 in the Iowa Building. It is now on the estate of Ex-Governor William Larrabee at Clermont, Iowa. The pose of Farragut is natural but animated. Mr. Larrabee donated a statue of Lincoln to the village of Clermont, one panel of which represents Farragut in the rigging of the *Hartford* at the Battle of Mobile Bay.[12]

Farragut was among the first to be elected to membership in the Hall of Fame of New York University. He received 79 of the 97 votes cast and was fourteenth on the list; Washington was first, the only one chosen unanimously. On May 5, 1927, Farragut's bust by Charles Grafly was unveiled in the Hall of Fame.[13]

In Grace Church, Hastings-on-Hudson, a tablet with the following inscription has been placed: "New York State National Society, Daughters of the Union, 1861-1865, Inc. In Memory of the First Admiral of the United States Navy, David Glasgow Farragut. He gave his 'Prize Money' towards erecting this church. This tablet is placed under the direction of Sarah J. Loomis, Regent, July 4, 1938."[14] Later Mrs. Farragut gave the fount to the church. These stanzas from "A Passing Landmark" by J. Loring Arnold beautifully connect Farragut with this church:

"Its rafters lift like bowsprits high;
Their brackets make one think of prows of ships.
An admiral's prize of gold so much could buy;
For roar of guns, 'Peace' from the Master's lips.

And on the forward deck above,
A stoled and surpliced pilot steers toward God,
Baptizes infancy and marries love
And comforts grief and sanctifies the sod."[14]

2

Among the portraits of Farragut, considerable notice has already been given to the one painted by William Page and afterwards presented to the Czar of Russia.[15] This portrait from life was the basis of the magnificent memorial window in the Naval Academy Chapel, designed by Frederick Wilson, which was presented in 1920 by graduates of the U. S. Naval Academy. Some other portraits of Farragut deserving special mention are by Henry Augustus Loop, N.A., by S. Jerome Uhl in the Army and Navy Club in Washington, by J. F. Weir in the University Club in New York, by Bolling (1869) and by N. M. Miller at the U. S. Naval Academy, by Lloyd Branson in Farragut Hotel, Knoxville, Tennessee, and by U. D. Tenney in the Farragut High School in Portsmouth, New Hampshire, said to have been based on an engraving of Farragut on a $100 treasury note. The portrait by Loop, bearing the date 1871, was painted to order by the Union League Club of New York, and at the request of the Navy Department was exhibited at the Centennial Exposition in Philadelphia in 1876. This three-quarter-length portrait represents Farragut in the undress uniform of a full admiral, with left hand upon his sword hilt, standing on the deck of a ship with the open sea in the background.[16]

Of the numerous photographs of Farragut, the earliest extant appears to be one made by E. Anthony in New York in 1862, when he was a captain. Probably the best pictures of Farragut were made by Brady, though Gurney and Son of New York also made some excellent ones. An extremely interesting photograph, and a very good one too, was made by Leon Bravy at Port Mahon on the Island of Minorca during Farragut's European Cruise in the *Franklin*. From these various photographs, A. H. Ritchie, O'Neill, Augustus Robin, J. C. Buttre, J. A. J. Wilcox, H. W. Smith, George E. Perine, W. J. Jackman, and others have made engravings of great value and interest.

Farragut's naval battles have also inspired painters to produce noteworthy works. The distinguished marine painter, William Frederick De Haas, painted a picture of Farragut's fleet passing the forts below New Orleans. It was exhibited in New York in 1867, and was considered to be a "superb work of art" which deserved "the admiration it receives."[17] Diligent search has failed to reveal any later information concerning the picture, no reproductions of it have been discovered, and its present whereabouts is unknown. Probably the most widely known battle scene connected with Farragut is that, entitled "An August Morning with Farragut," painted by the English artist, W. H. Overend.[18] This picture, portraying the fight between the *Hartford* and the *Tennessee*, is now in Wadsworth Atheneum, Hartford, Connecticut. Farragut's passing the batteries at Port Hudson was painted by Edward Arnold; this picture is in the Smithsonian Institution in Washington.[19] It is said to have been painted under the direction of Captain Palmer, one of Farragut's commanders. Currier and Ives published a popular lithograph of this same engagement. J. O. Davidson also painted this battle as well as the passage of Forts Jackson and St. Philip and the Battle of Mobile Bay. The latter is one of the best pictures of Farragut's last battle. Excellent engravings of the battle with the forts below New Orleans are by George E. Perine and W. Ridgway after C. Parsons. There are many other prints of varying excellence and interest, too numerous to mention. The drawings in *Harper's Weekly* and *Leslie's* are of great interest but, like most war paintings unfortunately, they are often quite inaccurate.

3

The poets began to celebrate Farragut's victories not long after the first was achieved. Among the earliest was "New

APPENDIX 397

Orleans Won Back" by Robert Lowell, the following lines from which refer to the passage of the forts:

> "A flash! Our strong ships snapped the boom
>   To the fire-rafts and the forts,
> To crush and crash, and flash and gloom,
>   And iron beaks fumbling their ports."[20]

The anonymous "New Ballad of Lord Lovell" makes sport of the Confederate General Lovell, as this stanza shows:

> "Oh! tarry, Lord Lovell!" Sir Farragut cried.
>   "Oh! tarry, Lord Lovell!" said he;
> "I rather think not," Lord Lovell replied,
>   "For I'm in a great hurry."[20]

"The Yankee Tars at New Orleans," also anonymous,[21] is devoted more to the praise of Boggs, captain of the *Varuna* which was sunk in the battle, than to Farragut. Surgeon Robert T. Maccoun of the *Mississippi,* who was in the battle below New Orleans, wrote "The Battle of New Orleans of 1862," which was "Respectfully dedicated to Flag-Officer David G. Farragut by an Officer of the Squadron." These two stanzas are perhaps the best:

> "Through the serried lines they go,
> Face to face they brave the foe,
> While their booming broadsides glow
>   Upon the river's tide.
>
> Dark and dreary was the night,
> Fierce and bloody was the fight;
> Naught but fires of death to light
>   The path of victory!"[21]

The most significant poem on the New Orleans campaign was written by Henry Howard Brownell, and is entitled "The River Fight." He first wrote a versification of Farragut's general orders for the battle, which was published in a Hartford paper, with the title, "General Orders." Farragut was greatly pleased with this, and wrote the author his appreciation. Brownell then wrote the longer poem, in which the earlier lines were incorporated. It is a long poem, describing the battle in detail. Perhaps, the following stanzas are the best; at least, they are fairly representative:

"Would you hear of the River Fight?
It was two, of a soft spring night—
    God's stars looked down on all,
And all was clear and bright
But the low fog's chilling breath—
Up the River of Death
    Sailed the Great Admiral.

On our high poop-deck he stood,
    And round him ranged the men
Who have made their birthright good
    Of manhood, once and again—
Lords of helm and of sail,
Tried in tempest and gale,
    Bronzed in battle and wreck—
Bell and Bailey grandly led
Each his Line of the Blue and Red—
Wainwright stood by our starboard rail,
    Thornton fought the deck.

And I mind me of more than they,
    Of the youthful, steadfast ones,
    That have shown them worthy sons
Of the Seamen passed away—
(Tyson conned our helm, that day,
    Watson stood by his guns).

What thought our Admiral then,
Looking down on his men?
    Since the terrible day,
    (Day of renown and tears!)
    When at anchor the *Essex* lay,
    Holding her foes at bay,
When, a boy, by Porter's side he stood
Till deck and plank-shear were dyed with blood,
    'Tis half a hundred years—
    Half a hundred years, to-day!

Who could fail, with him?
Who reckon of life or limb?
    Not a pulse but beat the higher!
There had you seen, by the star-light dim,
Five hundred faces, strong and grim—
    The Flag is going under fire!
Right up by the fort,
With her helm hard-a-port,
    The *Hartford* is going under fire!"[22]

The next poem was not written until Brownell had himself experienced a naval battle. In a friendly correspondence with Farragut, he expressed such a desire, which was fulfilled by his appointment as an acting ensign on the *Hartford* and his subsequent participation in the Battle of Mobile Bay. This battle he celebrated in an even longer poem, called "The Bay Fight." This is the way Brownell describes the crisis in the battle:

> "On, in the whirling shade
>   Of the cannon's sulphury breath,
>   We drew to the Line of Death
> That our devilish Foe had laid—
> Meshed in a horrible net,
>   And baited villainous well,
> Right in our path were set
>   Three hundred traps of hell!
>
> And there, O sight forlorn!
>   There, while the cannon
>   Hurtled and thundered—
>   (Ah, what ill raven
> Flapped o'er the ship that morn!)—
> Caught by the under-death,
> In the drawing of a breath
>   Down went dauntless Craven,
>   He and his hundred!
>
> A moment we saw her turret,
>   A little heel she gave,
> And a thin white spray went o'er her,
>   Like the crest of a breaking wave—
> In that great iron coffin.
>   The channel for their grave,
>   The fort their monument
>   (Seen afar in the offing),
> Ten fathom deep lie Craven,
>   And the bravest of our brave.
>
> Then, in that deadly track,
> A little the ships held back,
>   Closing up in their stations—
> There are minutes that fix the fate
>   Of battles and of nations
>   (Christening the generations),
> When valor were all too late,

> If a moment's doubt be harbored—
> From the main-top, bold and brief,
> Came the word of our grand old Chief—
> 'Go on!' 'twas all he said—
> Our helm was put to starboard,
> And the *Hartford* passed ahead."[23]

Of these two poems, Oliver Wendell Holmes wrote, "They are, to all of our drawing-room battle poems, as the torn flags of our victorious armadas to the stately ensigns that dress their ships in harbor."[24] Brownell dedicated his *War Lyrics and Other Poems*, published in 1866, to Admiral Farragut, in the following very appreciative letter: "Permit me to inscribe to you this book, a part of which is due to the inspiration of your deeds and your example. What you have been in war is known to your country, to her enemies, and to the world; but only those who have had the honor of approaching you nearly can know how great is your love for peace, how real your kindliness, how true your feeling for nature, your interest in art, letters, and science, how genial, even in the roughest times, your sense of wit and humor and of all the amenities of social life. It is in remembrance of these traits, and of the personal friendship you were pleased to accord me, while serving under your command, that I once again write myself, Very respectfully, Your obedient servant, The Author."[25]

This pleased Farragut very much, and he replied in part, "I have always esteemed it one of the happy events of my life that I was able to gratify your enthusiastic desire to witness the grandest as well as most terrible of all nautical events, a great sea-fight! And you were particularly fortunate in its being one in which all the ingenuity of our country had been employed to render it more terrible by the use of almost every implement of destruction known in the world, from the old-fashioned smooth-bore gun to the most diabolical contrivances for the destruction of human life. And permit me to assure you I have fully realized all my anticipations that your pen would faithfully delineate the scene and do justice to the subject; and although your feeling of friendship for your commander should

Courtesy of the University Club, New York City
ADMIRAL D. G. FARRAGUT, U. S. NAVY
From the portrait painted in 1889 by John F. Weir, and now in the University Club, New York.

Courtesy of the Curator, United States Naval Academy

THE FARRAGUT MEMORIAL WINDOW

From a photograph of the central panel of the stained glass window in the Chapel of the U. S. Naval Academy, designed by Frederick Wilson and made by the Gorham Company, New York. Presented by the Naval Academy Graduates Association.

sometimes manifest itself rather partially, it will be forgiven by the world, under the circumstances, and blotted out by the recording angel as was Uncle Toby's sin when he swore his friend should not die, and it will only be remembered with grateful feelings by your Affectionate friend, D. G. Farragut."[26]

Farragut was doubly fortunate in having on the *Hartford* two poets to celebrate the Battle of Mobile Bay. Paymaster William T. Meredith wrote a much shorter, but none the less significant, poem, entitled "Farragut," which in full is as follows:

"Farragut, Farragut,
    Old Heart of Oak,
Daring Dave Farragut,
    Thunderbolt stroke,
Watches the hoary mist
    Lift from the bay,
Till his flag, glory-kissed,
    Greets the young day.

Far, by gray Morgan's walls,
    Looms the black fleet.
Hark, deck to rampart calls
    With the drums' beat!
Buoy your chains overboard,
    While the steam hums;
Men! to the battlement,
    Farragut comes.

See, as the hurricane
    Hurtles in wrath
Squadrons of clouds amain
    Back from its path!
Back to the parapet,
    To the guns' lips,
Thunderbolt Farragut
    Hurls the black ships.

Now through the battle's roar
    Clear the boy sings,
'By the mark fathoms four,'
    While his lead swings.
Steady the wheelmen five
    'Nor' by East keep her,'
'Steady,' but two alive:
    How the shells sweep her!

>   Lashed to the mast that sways
>   Over red decks,
>   Over the flame that plays
>   Round the torn wrecks,
>   Over the dying lips
>   Framed for a cheer,
>   Farragut leads his ships,
>   Guides the line clear.
>
>   On by heights cannon-browed,
>   While the spars quiver;
>   Onward still flames the cloud
>   Where the hulks shiver.
>   See, yon fort's star is set,
>   Storm and fire past.
>   Cheer him, lads—Farragut,
>   Lashed to the mast!
>
>   Oh! while Atlantic's breast
>   Bears a white sail,
>   While the Gulf's towering crest
>   Tops a green vale,
>   Men thy bold deeds shall tell,
>   Old Heart of Oak,
>   Daring Dave Farragut,
>   Thunderbolt stroke!"[27]

Another participant in the Battle of Mobile Bay, Thomas H. Stevens, who commanded the monitor *Winnebago*, wrote "Battle of Mobile Bay," a simple, straightforward, sailor-like ballad, which hardly sustains throughout the high level of the opening lines:

> "Fair broke the morn off Mobile Bay;
> On Morgan's crest its first beams play;
> O'er stately ships, and mirrored deep,
> The blushes of the morning creep."[28]

Several other poems relating to Farragut have been quoted in whole or in part in earlier chapters in this biography. One more deserves consideration. It is *The Great Admiral* by Richard Henry Stoddard. This is a biographic poem, which contains some stirring passages. Its opening and closing stanzas will serve as a conclusion:

"Great men are few, but when
The world demands great men,
Either with sword or pen,
    It does not lack them;
Nor they the iron will
That conquest can not kill,
For, crushed, they conquer still
All who attack them. . . .

Ay! For there is not one
Can do what he has done;
And, History, greater none
    Thou consecratest.
Immortal honor, then,
To this, our man of men,
Whose soul is greatest when
    Our need is greatest."[29]

SOURCES AND BIBLIOGRAPHY

I. MANUSCRIPTS

United States Navy Department, Naval Records and Library
    Letters to Officers, Ships of War
    Officers' Letters
    Captains' Letters
    Appointments, Orders, and Resignations
    Confidential Letters
    Admirals and Commodores, Letters
    Squadron Letters
    Official Letters: Fleet-Surgeon James C. Palmer, U.S.N.
    Official Letters of Farragut's Commanders
    Miscellaneous Letters and Documents

Dr. Ellsworth Eliot, Jr.
    Numerous personal and official letters to, or from, Farragut, Mrs. Farragut, and Loyall Farragut
    Letter Books
    Journal of Farragut for Cruise of the *Franklin* to European Waters
    Typewritten Reminiscences of Loyall Farragut
    Miscellaneous Papers

Library of Congress, Manuscript Division
    David Dixon Porter Papers
    Gideon Welles Papers
    Benjamin F. Butler Papers

The National Archives
    Logbooks of the *Hartford* and other ships of Farragut's squadrons

United States Naval Academy Museum
    The Zabriskie Collection of Farragut Papers
    Miscellaneous Papers

George T. Keating
    Notebook of D. G. Farragut
    Diary of D. G. Farragut

Henry E. Huntington Library and Art Gallery
    Miscellaneous Letters to, or from, Farragut, Thornton Jenkins, Gustavus Vasa Fox, Welles, Nathaniel P. Banks, D. D. Porter, Loyal Farragut, and others.

New York Historical Society
    Correspondence between Gustavus V. Fox and Farragut, Fox and D. D. Porter, and Other Letters
    Diary of Gustavus V. Fox
    Miscellaneous Letters

New York Public Library
  Letters of Captain Percival Drayton, U.S.N.
  Recollections of the Cruise of the U.S.S. *Hartford*, Admiral Farragut's Flagship in Operations on the Mississippi River, in Mobile Bay, etc. . . . by Bartholomew Diggins
  Letter Books of Rear Admiral Thomas Turner, Ten Volumes
Tennessee State Library and Tennessee Historical Society
  Miscellaneous Letters
The Church of the Incarnation, New York
  Records

II. NEWSPAPERS AND MAGAZINES

Academy (London), XLIV.
American Architect (Sept., 1881), X.
Architectural Record, Sept., 1911.
Army and Navy Gazette, II.
Army and Navy Journal, I-VIII.
Army and Navy Register, XXXV.
Atlantic Monthly, May, 1865 and Apr., 1892.
Baltimore *American*, Apr., 1862.
Baltimore *Sun*, Apr., 1862.
Charleston *Mercury*, Aug., 1864.
Coast Artillery Journal, Mar.-Apr., 1941, "Farragut at Mobile Bay."
Continental Monthly (May, 1863), art. by F. H. Gerdes.
Criterion, Apr., 1902.
Current History, New York *Times*, XXXI.
Daily American (Nashville, Tennessee), Sept., 1877.
Dial (Chicago), XIV.
Eclectic Magazine (1864), LXII.
Edinburgh Review, CXXIV, "Battle for New Orleans" by C. C. Chesney.
Everybody's Magazine (Nov., 1917), XXXVII.
Frank Leslie's Illustrated Weekly Newspaper, Apr. and May, 1862 and Sept., 1864.
Galaxy, An Illustrated Magazine of Entertaining Reading (Nov. and Dec., 1871), XII.
Harper's New Monthly Magazine (Mar., 1865) XXX, "Heroic Deeds of Heroic Men" by J. S. C. Abbott, and (Aug., 1867), XXXV.
Harper's Weekly, May, 1862 and Feb., 1864.
Hearst's Magazine, XXII, "Dewey's Autobiography," published serially.
Historical Magazine, ed. by Dawson (July, 1869), XVI (VI in second series).
Independent (Mar., 1901), LIII.
Journal of the Military Service Institution of the United States (July, 1893), XIV.
Journal of the Royal United Service Institution, XXII, "Facts Connected with the Naval Operations during the Civil War in the United States" by Rear Admiral R. V. Hamilton, C. B.
London *Times*, Aug., 1864.

Louisiana Historical Quarterly (Apr., 1941), XXIV.
Magazine of American History (1881), VII and (Mar., 1886), XV.
Methodist Review (Bimonthly), Sept.-Oct., 1894, LXXVI (Poole, LIV and 5th series, X), "Personal Reminiscences of Admiral Farragut" by C. V. Anthony.
Montgomery (Alabama) *Daily Advertiser,* Mar. 8, 1863.
Munsey's Magazine (Feb., 1900), XXII, "Some Famous Admirals" by J. R. Spears.
Nation (Jan., 1880), XXX and (Sept., 1878), XXVII.
National Republic (Feb., 1935), XXII.
New Eclectic Magazine, V.
New Orleans *Bee,* Apr. and May, 1862.
New Orleans *Crescent,* Apr. and May, 1862.
New Orleans *Daily True Delta,* Mar. and Apr., 1862.
New Orleans *Picayune,* Apr., 1862.
New York *Daily Tribune,* Apr., 1862 and Aug. and Dec., 1864.
New York *Evening Post,* Apr., 1862 and Aug. and Dec., 1864.
New York *Herald,* Apr., 1862, Aug., 1863, and Aug., 1864.
New York *Times,* Apr., 1862.
New York *World,* Apr., 1862.
North American Review (Oct., 1879), CXXIX, "Napoleon and the Southern Confederacy" by O. F. Aldis, and (July, 1889), CXLIX.
Outlook, LXX.
Pan American Union, Bulletin, XXXVI.
Philadelphia *Daily News,* Apr., 1862.
Philadelphia *Enquirer,* Apr., 1862.
Philadelphia *Evening Bulletin,* May 13, 1938 and Oct. 1, 1942, "Men and Things" by Albert Mordell.
Putnam's Monthly (Oct., 1908), V, "Farragut at Port Hudson" by Loyall Farragut.
Review of Reviews (Nov., 1900), XXII.
Richmond *Enquirer,* Apr., 1862 and Aug., 1864.
Richmond *Examiner,* Apr., 1862 and Aug., 1864.
Richmond *Sentinel,* Aug., 1864.
Richmond *Whig,* Apr., 1862.
Scribner's Monthly (Feb., 1877), XIII and (June, 1881), XXII.
Southern Historical Society Papers, III, IV, VI, IX, XXIII (1895, "Reminiscent of War Times" from New Orleans *Picayune,* Dec. 1, 1895), XII (Jan. to Dec., 1884, "The Story of the *Arkansas*" by George W. Gift), XIX, XXI, XXXV, I (No. 5, May, 1876).
Southern Magazine (Mar., 1873), new series V (Poole, XII).
Spectator (London), Oct., 1893, LXXI.
St. Nicholas Magazine (July, 1900), XXVII.
United Service. A Monthly Review of Military and Naval Affairs, Dec., 1896 and Jan., 1897, "Life of James Edward Jouett" by Alfred Pirtle; Sept., 1892; Feb., 1889; and Jan., 1881.
United States Naval Institute Proceedings (July-August, 1914), XL; (July-August, 1915), XLI; and (1880), VI, 303.

SOURCES AND BIBLIOGRAPHY 407

United States Naval Institute Proceedings (Dec., 1923), XLIX, "Farragut" by Rear Admiral C. F. Goodrich, U. S. Navy (Retired).
U. S. Naval Institute Proceedings (May, 1927), LIII, "Farragut and Mobile Bay—Personal Reminiscences" by Rear Admiral John C. Watson, U. S. Navy (Retired); "Historic Ships of the Navy—Hartford" by Robert W. Neeser; and "The Grade of Admiral in the U. S. Navy" by Louis H. Bolander.
U. S. Naval Institute Proceedings (July, 1935), LXI, "The Relations between Farragut and Porter" by Richard S. West, Jr.; (May, 1937), "(Private and Confidential) My Dear Fox" by Richard S. West, Jr.
U. S. Naval Institute Proceedings (Oct., 1939), LXV, "Damn the Torpedoes . . . ?" by Lieutenant Colonel Wilfrid Bovey, R.O.; (Nov., 1939), LXV, 1676, letter from the Reverend Thom Williamson, Jr.; (Dec., 1939), LXV, 1776, comment by Rear Admiral Ammen Farenholt (M.C.), U. S. Navy (Retired).
United States Service Magazine (Jan., 1865), III.
Unsere Zeit (1869), II, "David G. Farragut" by K. J. G. R. Doehn.
Washington *Daily National Intelligencer*, Apr. and May, 1862.
Washington *Daily Globe*, passim.

III. BOOKS AND PAMPHLETS

Adams, F. Colburn. *High Old Salts*. Washington, 1870.
Adams, W. H. Davenport. *Farragut and Other Great Commanders*. . . . London and New York, n.d.
Alden, C. S. *George Hamilton Perkins, U.S.N., His Life and Letters*. Boston, 1914.
American Caricatures Pertaining to the Civil War, Anonymous. New York, 1918.
Argument of Counsel before Arbitrators (1872, 1873), n.p., n.d. (Harvard College Library).
Barnes, James. *Farragut*. Boston, 1899.
(Barnes, John S.) *Manuscripts and Prints and Other Memorabilia in the John S. Barnes Memorial Library of the Naval History Society*. New York, 1915.
Barnes, T. W. *Memoir of Thurlow Weed*. Boston, 1884.
Bartlett, John Russell, compiler. *The Literature of the Rebellion. A Catalogue of Books and Pamphlets Relating to the Civil War in the United States*. . . . Boston, 1866.
Batcheller, Oliver A., Commander, U. S. Navy. *War Papers Read before the Commandery of the State of Maine, Military Order of the Loyal Legion of the United States*, "The Battle of Mobile Bay," II. Portland, 1898.
Battles and Leaders of the Civil War, 4 Vols. New York, 1884-1888.
Beebee, M. B. *Four American Naval Heroes: Paul Jones, Oliver H. Perry, Admiral Farragut, and Admiral Dewey*. New York, 1899.
Bennett, Frank M., Lieutenant, U.S.N. *The Monitor and the Navy under Steam*. Boston and New York, 1900.

Bodder, Charles H., pseud. for Charles H. B. Shepherd. *Under Fire with Farragut: The Signal Boy's Story.* New York, 1919.
Boynton, Charles B. *The History of the Navy during the Rebellion*, 2 Vols. New York, 1867.
Brady, Cyrus Townsend. *The Southerners.* . . . New York, 1903.
Brockett, L. P. *Our Great Captains: Grant, Sherman, Thomas, Sheridan, and Farragut.* New York, 1866.
Brownell, Henry Howard. *War Lyrics and Other Poems.* Boston, 1866.
Buenzle, Fred J. *Bluejacket: An Autobiography.* New York, 1939.
Butler, Benjamin Franklin. *Butler's Book: Autobiography and Personal Reminiscences.* . . . Boston, 1892.
(Butler, B. F.) *Private and Official Correspondence of General Benjamin F. Butler during the Period of the Civil War*, Vols. I-V. Privately Issued, 1917.
Chesney, Charles C. *Essays in Military Biography.* New York, 1874.
Chester, Colby M., Rear Admiral, U.S.N. "Showing the Way," in *Military Order of the Loyal Legion of the United States, Commandery of the District of Columbia, War Papers*, No. 79.
Choate, Joseph H. *American Addresses*, "Admiral Farragut," 27-47. New York, 1911.
(Choate, Joseph H.) *Farragut. Mr. Choate's Address, Made at the Request of the Farragut Monument Association, on the Occasion of the Unveiling of the St. Gaudens Statue, May 25, 1881.* New York, 1881.
Cowles, Captain Calvin D., compiler. *Atlas to Accompany the Official Records of the Union and Confederate Armies.* Washington, 1891-1895.
Church, William C. *The Life of John Ericsson.* New York, 1911.
Clark, Charles E., Rear Admiral, U.S.N. *My Fifty Years in the Navy.* Boston, 1917.
Cronin, Cornelius, Gunner, U.S.N. *Recollection of Service in the U. S. Navy.* . . . *While serving in the U. S. Ships Sabine, Brooklyn, and Richmond.* Privately Published, n.d.
Dalzell, George W. *The Flight from the Flag.* Chapel Hill, North Carolina, 1940.
Davis, Captain Charles Henry, U.S.N. *Life of Charles Henry Davis, Rear Admiral, 1807-1877.* Boston and New York, 1899.
Dewey, George. *Autobiography.* New York, 1913.
Dictionary of American Biography. New York, 1928-1937. *passim.*
Dorsey, S. A., editor. *Recollections of Henry Watkins Allen, Brigadier General, Confederate States Army, Ex-Governor of Louisiana.* New York, 1866.
(Drayton, Percival) *Naval Letters from Captain Percival Drayton, 1861-1865.* New York, 1906.
Eggleston, George Cary. *The American Immortals.* New York, 1901.
Ellis, Edward S. *Dewey and Other Naval Commanders.* New York, 1899.
(Farragut, D. G.) *History Set Right. Attack on New Orleans and Its Defenses by the Fleet under Admiral Farragut, April 24, 1862. Corre-*

spondence between Admirals Farragut and Bailey. New York, 1869.
(See also Army and Navy Journal, July 17, 1869.)
Farragut Day: Flagship Hartford Memorial. Official Souvenir Program. Oct. 19, 1897. Hartford, Connecticut.
Farragut Testimonial. . . . New York, 1864.
Farragut, Loyall. The Life of David Glasgow Farragut. First Admiral of the U. S. Navy. New York, 1879.
Farragut, Loyall. "Passing the Port Hudson Batteries," an address delivered Feb. 6, 1884 before the New York Commandery of the Loyal Legion of the United States, in Personal Recollections of the War of the Rebellion . . . , ed. by James Grant Wilson and Titus M. Coan, Series I. New York, 1891.
Fiske, John. The Mississippi Valley in the Civil War. Boston and New York, 1900.
Foltz, Charles S. Surgeon of the Seas. The Adventurous Life of Surgeon General Jonathan M. Foltz in the Days of Wooden Ships. Indianapolis, 1931.
Foster, Joseph. The Soldiers' Memorial. Portsmouth, N.H., n.d.
[Fox] Narrative of the Mission to Russia in 1866 of the Hon. Gustavus Vasa Fox, Assistant-Secretary of the Navy . . . , edited by John D. Champlin. New York, 1873.
Franklin, S. R. Memories of a Rear-Admiral. New York and London, 1898.
Freeman, Douglas Southall. A Calendar of Confederate Papers. . . . Richmond, 1908.
Frothingham, J. P. Sea Fighters from Drake to Farragut. New York, 1892.
Glazier, Willard. Heroes of Three Wars. Philadelphia, 1884.
Goodrich, C. F. Some Rope Yarns from the Old Navy. New York, 1931.
Grant, U. S. Personal Memoirs, 2 Vols. New York, 1885.
Greeley, Horace. The American Conflict: A History of the Great Rebellion in the United States of America. . . . Vol. II. Hartford, 1866.
Grove, K. W. American Naval Heroes, Jones, Perry, Farragut, Dewey. Chicago, c. 1913.
Hamersly, Lewis Randolph. List of Officers of the Navy of the United States and of the Marine Corps, from 1775 to 1900. Edited by Edward W. Callahan. New York, 1901.
Headley, J. T. The Great Rebellion: A History of the Civil War in the United States. 2 Vols. Hartford, Connecticut, 1865.
Headley, P. C. Life and Naval Career of Vice-Admiral David Glascoe (sic) Farragut. New York, 1865.
Headley, P. C. Old Salamander: The Life and Naval Career of Admiral David Glascoe (sic!) Farragut. Boston, 1883.
Henry, R. S. The Story of the Confederacy. Indianapolis, 1931.
(Hicks, Ex-Governor Alexander H.) A Memorial of David Glasgow Farragut from the City of Boston with an Account of the Dedication of the Farragut Statue at Marine Park, South Boston, June 28, 1893. Address by Hicks. Boston, 1896.
Hill, Frederic S. The Romance of the American Navy. . . . New York and London, 1910.

Hill, Frederic S. *Twenty Years at Sea, or Leaves from My Old Logbooks.* Boston and New York, 1893.
Hill, Jim Dan. *Sea Dogs of the Sixties.* Minneapolis, 1935.
Hitchcock, Ripley, editor. *Decisive Battles of America:* "Farragut's Capture of New Orleans" by James K. Hosmer. New York and London, 1909.
Homans, J. E. *Our Three Admirals.* . . . New York, 1899.
Hoppin, James M. *Life of Andrew Hull Foote, Rear Admiral, U. S. Navy.* New York, 1874.
Hunt, William H., Secretary of the Navy. *Address on the Occasion of the Unveiling of the Statue of Admiral Farragut in Madison Square, New York, May 25, 1881.* Boston, 1881.
Hutchinson, W. F. *The Bay Fight. A Sketch of the Battle of Mobile Bay,* read before the Rhode Island Soldiers and Sailors Historical Society, October 4, 1876. Providence, 1879.
Kenyon, W. S. *William Larrabee, Memorial Address.* Cedar Rapids, 1913.
King, Grace. *New Orleans, the Place and the People.* New York, 1895.
Kirkland, Frazar, pseud. for Richard M. Devens. *Pictorial Book of Anecdotes and Incidents of the War of the Rebellion.* Hartford, Connecticut, 1866.
Knox, Captain Dudley W., U.S.N. (Retired). *A History of the United States Navy.* New York, 1936.
Leech, Margaret. *Reveille in Washington.* New York, 1941.
Lewis, Charles Lee. *Admiral Franklin Buchanan: Fearless Man of Action.* Baltimore, 1929.
Lewis, Charles Lee. *Famous American Naval Officers.* Boston, 1924.
Longfellow, Samuel. *Life of Henry Wadsworth Longfellow.* Boston, 1886.
Lossing, Benson J. *Eminent Americans: Comprising Biographies of Leading Statesmen, Patriots, Orators, and Others, Men and Women Who Have Made American History.* New York, 1881.
Lossing, Benson J. *A History of the Civil War.* . . . New York, 1895.
Lossing, Benson J. *Pictorial History of the Civil War in the United States of America,* Vol. II. Hartford, 1870.
Maclay, Edgar S. *History of the United States Navy from 1775 to 1894.* New York, 1894.
Mahan, Alfred Thayer. *Admiral Farragut.* New York and London, 1892.
Mahan, Alfred Thayer. *The Gulf and Inland Waters.* New York, 1883.
McCormick, Robert R. *Ulysses S. Grant: The Great Soldier of America.* New York, 1934.
Meade, Rebecca Paulding. *Life of Hiram Paulding, Rear Admiral, U.S.N.* New York, 1910.
Meredith, W. T. "Admiral Farragut's Passage of Port Hudson," an address delivered Dec. 7, 1892 before the New York Commandery of the Loyal Legion of the United States, in *Personal Recollections of the War of the Rebellion* . . . , Second Series. New York (n.d.)
Milton, G. F. *The Age of Hate: Andrew Johnson.* . . . New York, 1930.
Montgomery, James E. *Our Admiral's Flag Abroad: The Cruise of Ad-*

SOURCES AND BIBLIOGRAPHY 411

miral D. G. Farragut, Commanding the European Squadron in 1867-1868 in the Flagship Franklin. New York, 1869.
Morgan, James Morris and John Philip Marquand. *Prince and Boatswain: Sea Tales from the Recollection of Rear Admiral Charles E. Clark.* Greenfield, Massachusetts, 1915.
Moore, Frank. *The Portrait Gallery of the War.* New York, 1864.
Moore, Frank. *Rebellion Record: A Diary of American Events with Documents, Narratives, Illustrations, Incidents, Poetry, etc.*, 11 Vols. New York, 1864.
(Morris, Charles) *Autobiography of Commodore Charles Morris, U. S. Navy.* Boston, 1880.
Morse, John T., Jr. *Thaddeus Stevens.* Boston, 1899.
(Muskegon, Michigan) *Dedication and Unveiling of the Statues of Lincoln, Grant, Sherman, and Farragut . . . Memorial Day, 1900.* Muskegon, 1900.
Navy Register, 1861-1866.
Neeser, Robert W. *The Statistical and Chronological History of the United States Navy, 1775-1907.* New York, 1909.
Nevins, Allan. *Hamilton Fish: The Inner History of the Grant Administration.* New York, 1936.
Newbolt, Sir Henry John. *The Book of the Blue Sea.* New York, 1914.
(Nicholson, John Page) *Catalogue of Library of Brevet Lieutenant Colonel John Page Nicholson, U. S. Vols. Relating to the War of the Rebellion, 1861-1866.* Philadelphia, 1914.
Nicolay, J. G. and John Hay. *Abraham Lincoln. A History,* Vol. V. New York, 1890.
Official Records of the Union and Confederate Armies. War of the Rebellion, Series I, Vols. VI, XXXIX (Parts I and II), LII (Part I), and XV. Washington, 1880-1900.
Official Records of the Union and Confederate Navies in the War of the Rebellion, Series I, Vols. I, II, IV, VI, VIII, XII, XIII, XVII-XXVI, and Series II, Vol. I. Washington, 1894-1922.
Osbon, B. S., editor. *The Cruise of the U. S. Flagship Hartford, 1862-1863. . . . From the Private Journal of William C. Holton.* New York, 1863. Reprinted in *Magazine of History,* Extra Number 87, Vol. XXII, No. 3 (1922).
Paine, Albert Bigelow. *A Sailor of Fortune: Personal Memories of Captain B. S. Osbon.* New York, 1906.
Parker, Foxhall A., Commodore, U.S.N. *The Battle of Mobile Bay. . . .* Boston, 1878. This was first read as an address before the Military Historical Society of Massachusetts, Dec. 10, 1877.
Parker, John C. "Night with Farragut," in *War Papers and Reminiscences, Commandery of Missouri, Military Order of the Loyal Legion,* Vol. I. St. Louis, 1892.
(Parker, Captain William Harwar) *Confederate Military History, Vol. XII: The Confederate States Navy* by Captain William Harwar Parker. Atlanta, 1899.

Parton, James. *General Butler in New Orleans: Being a History of the Department of the Gulf in the Year 1862.* . . . New York, 1863.

Patton, John. *Address: Unveiling Statue of Farragut, May 30, 1900.* Muskegon, 1900.

Photographic History of the Civil War, edited by F. T. Miller and James Barnes, Vol. VI. New York, 1911.

Pollard, Edward A. *Life of Jefferson Davis, with a Secret History of the Southern Confederacy.* . . . Philadelphia, 1869.

Porter, David Dixon. *An Answer to Misrepresentations.* Washington, 1872.

Porter, David Dixon. *Incidents and Anecdotes of the Civil War.* New York, 1885.

Porter, David Dixon. *The Naval History of the Civil War.* New York, 1886.

(Portrait of Farragut) *The Presentation of the Portraits of General William Whipple, Signer of the Declaration of Independence, and of David Glasgow Farragut, Admiral, U. S. Navy, November 20, 1891 by Storer Post, No. 7, Grand Army of the Republic, Department of New Hampshire.* . . . Portsmouth, N.H., 1891.

Preble, G. H. *History of the Navy Yard at Portsmouth, N.H.* Washington, 1892.

Preble, G. H. *Origin and History of the American Flag.* . . . Philadelphia, 1917.

Prime, R. E. *American Territory in Turkey: or Admiral Farragut's Visit to Constantinople, and the Extraterritoriality of Robert College*, an address before the New York Society of the Order of the Founders and Patriots of America, Feb. 14, 1908. Publications of the Society, 21-35. 1908-1914.

Proceedings of the Court of Inquiry Relative to the Fall of New Orleans, published by order of the Confederate Congress. Richmond, 1864.

Regulations of the Uniform of the United States Navy. Washington, 1862, 1864, 1866, and 1869.

Report of Secretary of the Navy, 1862-1865.

Reports of the Naval Engagements on the Mississippi River Resulting in the Capture of Forts Jackson and St. Philip and the City of New Orleans, and the Destruction of the Rebel Naval Flotilla. Washington, 1862.

Rhodes, J. F. *History of the United States, 1850-1896.* 8 Vols. New York, 1920.

Rice, Alexander H. *A Memorial of David Glasgow Farragut . . . City of Boston . . . Marine Park, June 28, 1893.* Boston, 1894. An address.

Roberts, W. A. *Semmes of the Alabama.* Indianapolis, 1938.

Rowland, Kate M. and Mrs. Morris L. Croxall, editors. *Journal of Julia LeGrand—New Orleans, 1862-1863.* Richmond, 1911.

[Saint-Gaudens] *Reminiscences of Augustus Saint-Gaudens*, edited and amplified by H. Saint-Gaudens. 2 vols. New York, 1913.

Sandburg, Carl. *Abraham Lincoln: The War Years.* 4 Vols. New York, 1936.

SOURCES AND BIBLIOGRAPHY

Scharf, J. T. *History of the Confederate States Navy.* New York, 1887.
Schlesinger, A. M. *Political and Social History of the United States, 1829-1925.* New York, 1925.
Schley, Winfield Scott, Rear Admiral, U.S.N. *Forty-Five Years under the Flag.* New York, 1904.
Sears, Louis M. *John Slidell.* Durham, North Carolina, 1925.
Seitz, D. C. *Horace Greeley.* Indianapolis, 1926.
Semmes, Raphael. *Memoirs of Service Afloat during the War between the States.* Baltimore, 1869.
Sheldon, G. W. *American Painters.* New York, 1879.
(Sherman, General W. T.) *Home Letters of General Sherman,* edited by M. A. De Wolfe Howe. New York, 1909.
(Sherman, General W. T.) *Memoirs of General W. T. Sherman Written by Himself.* . . . Vol. I. New York, 1891.
Shively, J. W. "The U.S.S. *Mississippi* at the Capture of New Orleans, 1862," in *Military Order of the Loyal Legion of the United States, Commandery of the District of Columbia, War Papers, No. 15.* Washington, n.d.
Smith, Gustavus W. *Confederate War Papers.* New York, 1884.
Smith, Walter George. *Life and Letters of Thomas Kilby Smith.* New York and London, 1897.
Soley, James Russell. *Admiral Porter.* New York, 1903.
Soley, James Russell. *The Blockade and the Cruisers.* New York, 1883.
Southwood, Marion (A Lady of New Orleans). *Beauty and Booty: The Watchword of New Orleans.* New York, 1867.
Spears, John Randolph. *David G. Farragut.* Philadelphia, 1905.
Spears, John Randolph. *The History of Our Navy from Its Origin to the Present Day, 1775-1898.* 5 Vols. New York, 1897-1899.
(Steedman, Charles) *Memoir and Correspondence of Rear Admiral Charles Steedman, U. S. Navy,* edited by A. L. Mason. Cambridge, Massachusetts, 1912.
Stevenson, Burton Egbert, editor. *Poems of American History.* Boston and New York, 1908.
Stewart, Paymaster General Edwin, U.S.N. Address on Farragut delivered Feb. 2, 1910 before the New York Commandery of the Loyal Legion of the United States, in *Personal Recollections of the War of the Rebellion* . . . , edited by A. Noel Blakeman. New York and London, 1912. Fourth Series.
Stryker, L. P. *Andrew Johnson, a Study in Courage.* New York, 1929.
Taylor, Gorham Coffin. *Notes of Conversations with a Volunteer Officer in the U. S. Navy on the Passage of the Forts below New Orleans, April 24, 1862.* Privately Printed. New York, 1868.
Taylor, Richard. *Destruction and Reconstruction.* New York, 1879.
Tobin, M. F., compiler. *1862-1902, In Commemoration of Our Fortieth Anniversary.* . . . n.d. (New York).
Tobin, M. F., compiler. *List of Survivors of Farragut's Fleet.* . . . New York, 1900.
Thompson, Robert Means and Richard Wainwright, editors. *Confidential*

Correspondence of Gustavus Vasa Fox, Assistant Secretary of the Navy, 1861-1865. 2 Vols. New York, 1920.
Todd, Helen. *A Man Named Grant.* Boston, 1940.
Walke, H., Rear Admiral, U.S.N. *Naval Scenes and Reminiscences of the Civil War in the United States on the Southern and Western Waters.* New York, 1877.
Walpole, Spencer. *Life of Lord John Russell,* Vol. II. London, 1889 (2nd edition).
Washburn, George. *Fifty Years in Constantinople and Recollections of Robert College.* Boston and New York, 1909.
Watson, John C., Rear Admiral, U.S.N. *Farragut and Mobile Bay—Personal Reminiscences,* War Paper No. 98, read Dec. 16, 1916 to the Military Order of the Loyal Legion of the United States, Commandery of the District of Columbia. Washington, n.d.
Webster, Harrie, Chief Engineer, U.S.N. *The Battle of Mobile Bay in a Monitor,* address read before the California Commandery of the Military Order of the Loyal Legion of the United States, Aug. 29, 1894. War Paper, No. 14. (San Francisco, 1894.)
(Welles, Gideon) *Diary of Gideon Welles, Secretary of the Navy under Lincoln and Johnson.* 3 Vols. Boston and New York, 1911.
West, Richard, Jr. *The Second Admiral. A Life of David Dixon Porter, 1812-1891.* New York, 1937.
[Wilkes] *Commodore Charles Wilkes's Court-Martial.* House of Representatives, 38th Cong., 1st Ses., Ex. Doc. No. 102.
Wilkinson, John. *The Narrative of a Blockade Runner.* New York, 1877.
Willis, Henry A. *The Fifty-Third Regiment, Massachusetts Volunteers, Comprising Also a History of the Siege of Port Hudson.* Fitchburg, Massachusetts, 1889.
Wilson, H. W. *Ironclads in Action.* Boston, 1896.
Wilson, James Grant, editor. *The Memorial History of the City of New York.* . . . 4 Vols. New York, 1893.
Woodward, W. E. *Meet General Grant.* New York, 1928.

NOTES

Loyall Farragut is used below for *The Life of David Glasgow Farragut* . . . by Loyall Farragut; *O. R. Navies*, for *Official Records of the Union and Confederate Navies in the War of the Rebellion;* and *O. R. Armies*, for *Official Records of the Union and Confederate Armies in the War of the Rebellion.*

I. THE CALL TO ARMS

1. *Life and Naval Career of David Glascoe* [sic] *Farragut* by P. C. Headley, 311.
2. "Admiral Farragut and New Orleans" by Gideon Welles in *The Galaxy: An Illustrated Magazine of Entertaining Reading* (November, 1871), XII, 680; and a letter of Jan. 26, 1942 from Mrs. Edmund M. Devoe, who with her sister, Miss M. Ella Dorland, now owns the house, 60 Main Street, in which the Farragut family resided.
3. May 1, 1861. *Captains Letters,* Naval Records and Library, Navy Department.
4. Farragut's oath of allegiance: "I, David G. Farragut, do solemnly swear or affirm (as the case may be) that I will bear true allegiance to the United States of America, and I will serve them honestly and faithfully, without any mental reservation, against all their enemies or opposers whatsoever; that I will observe and obey the orders of the President of the United States and the orders of the officers appointed over me, according to the rules and articles for the government of the Navy of the United States. D. G. Farragut. Sworn to and subscribed before me, at Hastings, Westchester County, New York, this 22nd day of June, 1861. Thos. Smith." Naval Records and Library.
5. *Life of Charles Henry Davis* . . . by his son, Captain Charles Henry Davis, U. S. Navy, 126. While Farragut was Commandant of the Mare Island Navy Yard, Davis brought the *Saint Mary's* in for refitting in March, 1858. Of Farragut he wrote his wife on June 18, 1858: "I have delivered Mr. Folsom's message to Captain Farragut; the latter had often spoken to me of the former, and always in terms of gratitude and affection. He was very glad to hear from Mr. Folsom [Davis's near neighbor in Cambridge, Mass.], and begged me to say to him everything that was kind. He had never forgotten his obligations to him, and never would forget them. . . . Tell Mr. Folsom he may well be proud of his pupil. He is one of the cleverest men in the navy, in both the English and American senses of the word." *Ibid.*, 106, 107. For the relationship between Farragut and Folsom,

see *David Glasgow Farragut: Admiral in the Making* by Charles Lee Lewis, 126-129, 132-134, 139, 337. On July 1-4, Davis wrote his wife: ". . . He [Farragut] is personally popular, his temper is amiable, his sentiments just, his feelings good, and his manners frank though brusque. His character is eminently upright and manly. He has made some enemies and a good many friends during his four years in command. I like him. He has been kind and hospitable towards me, and in some respects he is a pattern of a man and of a navy officer. I consider it a great piece of good fortune that I have had him here during my refitment. He has been generous and agreeable." *Ibid.*, 107.
6. *The Life of David Glasgow Farragut* . . . , 205.
7. *The Galaxy* (November, 1871), XII, 680.
8. Letter from Mrs. Edmund M. Devoe of Jan. 29, 1942; *Admiral Farragut* by Alfred Thayer Mahan, 114; *David G. Farragut* by John R. Spears, 155.
9. Sept. 3, 1861, Naval Records and Library.
10. Report of Secretary of the Navy, Dec. 2, 1861. Board to investigate and report "on such cases as may be referred to it under the 17th and 23d sections of the 'Act Providing for the Organization of the Military Establishment,' approved 3d of August, 1861." Welles to Farragut, Sept. 4, 1861, Naval Records and Library.
11. *The Galaxy* (November, 1871), XII, 680.
12. *Ibid.*, 673.
13. *Ibid.*, 676. According to a letter of Fox to Welles, June 19, 1871, in the Henry E. Huntington Library and Art Gallery, "Port Royal was captured November 7th and immediately afterwards I suggested to you a naval attack upon New Orleans."
14. *The Galaxy*, XII, 677.
15. For an account of Secretary of State William H. Seward's intrigue against Secretary of the Navy Gideon Welles in the attempted relief of Fort Pickens and the strange role played by Commander D. D. Porter see *The Second Admiral: A Life of David Dixon Porter* by Richard West, Jr., 77-93.

For Welles's rather low opinion of Porter's character and his distrust of him as a Southern sympathizer see *The Diary of Gideon Welles*, I, 19, 35-37, and 88, and II, 255. For example, "William [D. Porter] had, not without reason, the reputation of being very untruthful—a failing of the Porters, for David was not always reliable on unimportant matters, but amplified and colored transactions, where he was personally interested especially, but he had not the bad reputation of William. I did not always consider David to be depended upon if he had an end to attain, and he had no hesitation in trampling down a brother officer if it would benefit himself. He had less heart than William" (*Ibid.*, I, 88).
16. Also mentioned in West's *Second Admiral*, 114. This claim was later to confound and embarrass Porter.
17. "Opening the Mississippi" by Montgomery Blair in *The United Serv-*

ice: *A Monthly Review of Military and Naval Affairs* (January, 1881), IV, 38.
18. *Incidents and Anecdotes of the Civil War* by Admiral D. D. Porter, 64-66. This is repeated in West's *Second Admiral*, 114, 115. John R. Spears's *David G. Farragut*, 170, adds that Porter declared to Midshipman John R. Bartlett who visited the *Powhatan* while she was with the Gulf Squadron that if he "had half a dozen good vessels he would undertake to run by the forts and capture New Orleans"; but no authority is cited. Mahan's *Admiral Farragut*, 118, does not give Porter credit for initiating the plan. James R. Soley's *Admiral Porter* (1903) makes out a strong case for Porter, but as this biography was "undertaken in fulfillment of Porter's desire" (West's *Second Admiral*, p. xi), it would naturally be strongly prejudiced in his favor.

Welles, in disposing of the claims of the friends of Ben Butler that he initiated the plan, wrote, "He [D. D. Porter] no more proposed it than that gentleman [Butler]. He did, when let into the confidence of the Department and made aware of its programme, recommend a large force of mortar vessels, and he is entitled to the credit of having proposed that appendage to the squadron. It was not a part of the original programme of the Navy Department" (*The Galaxy*, XII, 819).
19. *Confidential Correspondence of Gustavus Vasa Fox*, edited by Robert M. Thompson and Richard Wainwright, II, 73-79.
20. Aug. 12, 1871, in the Henry E. Huntington Library and Art Gallery.
21. *The Galaxy*, XII, 677. Porter's *Incidents and Anecdotes of the Civil War*, 64-66, declares that, at a previous interview with Welles, Senators Hale and Grimes were present, that immediately afterwards the four men called on Lincoln, and that after Seward came, the six men went to see General McClellan at his headquarters. Fox is thus left out of the picture entirely. But in Porter's *An Answer to Misrepresentations* (Washington, 1872), a pamphlet of 28 pages, he does not mention Seward at all as being present.

Though Porter pretended to be Fox's friend, this is what he wrote of him after the war in his *Private Journal* in two manuscript volumes, entitled on page 35 therein *Journal of Occurrences during the War of the Rebellion, 1860-1865*, from which he drew in writing his *Incidents and Anecdotes of the Civil War* (D. D. Porter Papers in the Manuscript Division, Library of Congress): "Mr. Fox was a vain man. He was vain of his physique, which was excellent, he could knock down a bull. He was vain of his personal appearance. In a photograph I had, he looked like a poet but in nature rather athletic. He was vain of his oratorical powers, but his speeches were very offensive. He thought himself superior to the Secretary and the rest of the Cabinet, in his political talents, whereas if he had thrown away his corks, he would have sank [sic] to the bottom. Such was the man who was selected to advise Secretary Welles, to show Mr. Lenthal how to build ships, teach Dahlgren how to make guns and instruct

Isherwood in the mysteries of the steam engine. He undertook, in fact, to do all this and has fastened upon the navy a class of vessels that would throw discredit on the Feegee Islanders. When I returned home, I found him installed in office, and as he was an old acquaintance, with whom I had been on several pleasure parties and found to be a jolly good fellow, I was in hopes to have had some influence with him. Personally I have no right to complain of his course, for I found him in general obliging; it is only with regard to his treatment of others that I find fault. A short time after my return I proposed to Mr. Fox to get up an expedition against New Orleans. . . . I was not listened to and as it seemed to me that I was making myself a bore I asked for service afloat again to go in search of the *Sumpter* [sic]; but could not get it. . . . I waited round the Navy Department, hoping to see more active measures adopted by the authorities and kept urging them to take New Orleans." Details are then given relating to how the matter was taken to Welles and to Lincoln, which differ from other accounts published by Porter (Vol. I, 166, et seq.). This characterization of Fox was not included in Porter's *Incidents and Anecdotes of the Civil War*.

According to a letter of June 19, 1871 from Fox to Welles, in the Henry E. Huntington Library and Art Gallery, the meeting at the house of General McClellan was attended by Lincoln, Welles, McClellan, and Fox. After the meeting, Fox writes, "With your consent I informed Lieutenant David D. Porter of the contemplated attack and offered him a command in it."

22. *The Galaxy*, XII, 678. McClellan selected Major J. G. Barnard, U. S. Army Engineers to represent him in arranging details for the army's participation. Barnard was familiar with Forts Jackson and St. Philip, having assisted in their reconstruction. He also strongly favored the use of the mortar flotilla and was of the opinion that the forts should not merely be bombarded but reduced before the passage of the fleet up the river (Mahan's *Admiral Farragut*, 120).
23. *The Galaxy*, XII, 679.
24. *The United Service*, IV, 38.
25. *The Diary of Gideon Welles*, II, 134.
26. *The Galaxy*, XII, 681.
27. *The Diary of Gideon Welles*, II, 135.
28. *Ibid.*, II, 116, 117.
29. *The United Service*, IV, 38.
30. *The Galaxy*, XII, 681.
31. *Forty-Five Years under the Flag* by W. S. Schley, 27, 28. Schley was then a lieutenant on the *Potomac*.
32. *The Galaxy*, XII, 682. Porter's *Incidents and Anecdotes of the Civil War*, 66 states, "Mr. Fox named several, but I opposed them all, and finally urged the appointment of Captain D. G. Farragut so strongly that I was sent to New York to communicate with him on the subject."
33. *Private Journal: Journal of Occurrences during the War of the Re-*

bellion, 1860-1865 (Manuscript Division, Library of Congress), I, 181. The account of the interview is based entirely on this journal, and has not been previously published. Porter's story is probably inaccurate and, at best, highly exaggerated.

34. *Ibid.* In Porter's "Opening of the Lower Mississippi" in *Battles and Leaders,* II, 28, he states, "He [Farragut] authorized me to accept for him the Secretary's offer, and I telegraphed the Department: 'Farragut accepts the command, as I was sure he would.' " This telegram is not extant. But in his *Private Journal,* he states that he wrote to Fox.
35. Farragut to Welles, Dec. 7, 1869, as published by Stan. V. Henkels of Philadelphia in Catalogue Number 1342, p. 29.
36. Welles to Farragut, Dec. 15, 1861, and Farragut to Welles, Dec. 17 and 18, 1861, Naval Records and Library.
37. *The United Service,* IV, 39. The entire interview is based on this.
38. *The Galaxy,* XII, 682.
39. Farragut to Mrs. Farragut, Dec. 21, 1861: ". . . Went to see Mr. Fox and Secretary Welles. Now to begin, you must keep your mouth shut and burn my letters for perfect silence is to be observed—the first injunction of the Secretary. I am to have a flag in the Gulf and the rest depends upon myself. . . . I called and got your photograph—how did you like mine—it was good except the squint which is impossible to avoid" (Farragut Papers in collection of Dr. Ellsworth Eliot, Jr.). This letter has been edited in *Loyall Farragut,* 208. Mrs. Farragut did not burn the letter, as directed.
40. *The Galaxy,* XII, 683. Farragut wrote Welles Dec. 7, 1869, ". . . I was ordered to Washington, where the Department informed me I should have all the vessels I desired and many more, including a number of mortar boats. To this I replied that I did not want the *latter,* as they would be more in my way than otherwise, as I felt satisfied they would be an impediment in my mode of attack. I presume that was the origin of my supposed opposition to the mortar boats. But as the Department seemed to think they were indispensable and had provided gunboats to tow and protect them in every emergency, I made no further objections. . . ." (As quoted in Catalogue Number 1342, p. 29, of Stan V. Henkels of Philadelphia).
41. *The Diary of Gideon Welles,* II, 117.
42. *Ibid.,* II, 134. Under this date, Sept. 2, 1864, Welles wrote of Du Pont: ". . . Du Pont is a polished naval officer, selfish, heartless, calculating, scheming, but not a hero by nature, though too proud to be a coward." Another entry states: "Neither Farragut nor David D. Porter were within the charmed circle [of Du Pont]. Du Pont had some jealousy, I saw, of Porter, but none of Farragut. I do not remember to have ever heard a complimentary remark of Farragut from Du Pont, but he evidently considered him a fair fighting officer, of ordinary standing—not one of the élite, not of the Du Pont Navy" (*Ibid.,* II, 119).
43. *Ibid.,* I, 477.

II. RENDEZVOUS IN THE GULF

1. December 23, 1861, Naval Records and Library.
2. *O. R. Navies*, XVIII, 3, Welles to Porter, November 18, 1861.
3. Farragut to Bell, Dec. 26, 1861, Zabriskie Collection, U. S. Naval Academy Museum.
4. *Ibid.*, Dec. 29, 1861, Zabriskie Collection, Naval Academy Museum.
5. *O. R. Navies*, XVIII, 5. The original appointment is in Naval Records and Library, Navy Department.
6. *Reminiscences* (in manuscript) by Loyall Farragut, in collection of Dr. Ellsworth Eliot, Jr.
7. For description of the *Brooklyn* see *David Glasgow Farragut: Admiral in the Making* by Charles Lee Lewis, 270.
8. *Memoir of John A. Dahlgren*, 176. Discussion of a bill for "Additional Sloops of War" in United States Senate, Mar. 3, 1856.
9. Farragut to Bell, Dec. 29, 1861, Zabriskie Collection, Naval Academy Museum.
10. *Loyall Farragut*, 211. A Sawyer was thought by Farragut to be inferior to the Parrott rifle (*Loyall Farragut*, 393).
11. *Ibid.* Also Farragut to Dahlgren, Jan. 15, 1862, *O. R. Navies*, XVIII, 6.
12. The *Hartford* is still afloat, but is now only a shell of her former grandeur. She is at the Washington Navy Yard where she was brought for a proposed reconstruction which the Second World War has postponed. See "Historic Ships of the Navy—Hartford" by Robert W. Neeser in *U. S. Naval Institute Proceedings*, LIII, 538 (May, 1927).
13. Log of the *Hartford*.
14. Log of the *Carondelet*, July 1, 1862, *O. R. Navies*, XXIII, 685.
15. Farragut to Welles, Jan. 29, 1862, *O. R. Navies*, XVIII, 11.
16. Between Feb. 25 and Mar. 5, 1862, collection of Dr. Ellsworth Eliot, Jr.
17. According to a letter to the author from Dr. S. Ralph Harlow of Smith College, July 9, 1861, "My grandfather on my mother's side was Col. Roland G. Usher. He served throughout the Civil War and was stationed for a time at Fortress Monroe. He was at that time a major and was an army paymaster. It was while he was at Old Point Comfort that Farragut's fleet was there. One night Farragut came to my grandfather. He had orders to sail and was leaving for his attack on New Orleans. Farragut told my grandfather that the fleet was on the point of mutiny because they had not been paid for weeks. He said that it would be impossible to sail unless the men were paid off and begged Major Usher to pay the sailors. Of course, my grandfather had no official grounds for advancing this money, though he had at the time a considerable sum on hand, enough to meet Farragut's need. Farragut wanted to sail that very night. My grandfather, on his own initiative, went out with Farragut and paid the sailors off and the fleet sailed for New Orleans. My grandfather got a statement from Farragut and sent in his own to Washington, not

knowing what the reaction would be. Congress voted him their thanks for having taken the initiative in so critical a situation. Later my grandfather became paymaster for the Department of the Gulf and was stationed in New Orleans. Farragut was always most grateful to him for his cooperation on that night." Only the *Hartford* could have been concerned, not the fleet which was then not present. Such a situation might have arisen with respect to the men who had recently arrived from Boston. I have found no confirmation of this story in Official Records.

18. *O. R. Navies*, XVIII, 7, 8, Welles to Farragut, Jan. 20, 1862. This letter had an inclosure to McKean ordering him to turn over a part of his command to Farragut, expressing regret that his health made it necessary for him to come home, and promising him his relief by the *San Jacinto*.
19. *O. R. Navies*, XVIII, 9, 10, Welles to Farragut, Jan. 25, 1862.
20. *Ibid.*, 11, Jan. 30, 1862.
21. *The Correspondence of Gustavus Vasa Fox*, I, 299, 300.
22. *O. R. Navies*, XVIII, 12, Farragut to Welles, Jan. 31, 1862.
23. *Ibid.*, 11, Welles to Farragut, Jan. 30, 1862.
24. *Ibid.*, 13, Farragut to Welles, Feb. 5, 1862.
25. The dates of sailing and arrival are from the log of the *Hartford*.
26. *O. R. Navies*, XVIII, 27, 28, Farragut to Welles, Feb. 12, 1862.
27. *Ibid.*, 28, Farragut to Welles, Feb. 12, 1862.
28. *Correspondence of Gustavus Vasa Fox*, I, 300-302.
29. *A Sailor of Fortune: Personal Memoirs of Captain B. S. Osbon* by Albert Bigelow Paine, 172-174. Osbon was Farragut's clerk on the *Hartford*. Farragut wrote Fox, Feb. 17, 1862, that he exchanged salutes "with all the Flag Officers in port, Spanish and French" (*Correspondence of Fox*, I, 302, 303).
30. *O. R. Navies*, XVIII, 14, Feb. 16, 1862. See also *David Glasgow Farragut: Admiral in the Making* by Charles Lee Lewis, 252. Farragut wrote frequently to Harwood concerning ordnance supplies. In one letter he says, "We expect to make good use of them, but will certainly require a great quantity, shell or otherwise" (*O. R. Navies*, XVIII, 29).
31. *O. R. Navies*, XVIII, 30, 31, Farragut to Welles, Feb. 17, 1862.
32. *Ibid.*, 33, 34, Farragut to Welles, Feb. 21, 1862.
33. *Ibid.*, 35, Farragut to Capt. T. Bailey, Feb. 22, 1862.
34. *Ibid.*, Farragut to Craven, Feb. 22, 1862.
35. *Ibid.*, 48, 49. Henry Howard Brownell turned this official paper into a poem entitled "General Orders," which was published in a Hartford newspaper. When Farragut saw it, he was so pleased that he wrote to the author and a friendship developed which led to his appointment later of the poet as acting ensign on the *Hartford*. This short poem he incorporated in his "The River Fight," and after participating in the Battle of Mobile Bay wrote a poem on the engagement, called "The Bay Fight."

36. Between Feb. 25 and March 5, 1862, collection of Dr. Ellsworth Elliot, Jr.
37. *O. R. Navies*, XVIII, 43, 44, Farragut to Welles, Mar. 3, 1862.
38. *Welles to Farragut*, Feb. 10, 1862, *Confidential Letters*, V, April 1, 1861 to December 5, 1879, Naval Records and Library. For Barnard's memorandum see *O. R. Navies*, XVIII, 15-24.
39. *Correspondence of Fox*, I, 304-306.
40. *Ibid.*, II, 8. Porter states to Fox, Mar. 11, 1862, that there were 21; but the *Horace Beals* did not carry a mortar and instead had two 32-pounders and one 30-pounder rifle (*O. R. Navies*, XVIII, 26).
41. *Correspondence of Fox*, II, 84-89, Porter to Fox, Mar. 11, 1862. According to the journal of the *Richmond* for Feb. 28, 1862, ". . . Commodore Porter came aboard of us this evening and is to accompany us to Ship Island" (*O. R. Navies*, XVIII, 730). The *Richmond* sailed Mar. 1; Porter evidently changed his plans.
42. *Letters to Flag Officers*, I, Naval Records and Library, Welles to Farragut, Feb. 6, 1862; *O. R. Navies*, XVII, 31; *Ibid.*, XVIII, 49 and 57.

III. THE VICTORY OVER MUD

1. *O. R. Navies*, XVIII, 65, Farragut to Welles, Mar. 14, 1862 and *Ibid.*, 67, Farragut to Fox, Mar. 16, 1862 (not published in the *Correspondence of Fox*).
2. New York *Times* and New York *World* of Apr. 29, 1862.
3. *O. R. Navies*, XVIII, 65, Mar. 14, 1862.
4. *Ibid.*, 62, 63, Captain H. H. Bell's report to Farragut, Mar. 13, 1862, and *Ibid.*, 682-684, diary of Captain Bell.
5. Mar. 10, 1862, *Loyall Farragut*, 217.
6. *O. R. Navies*, XVIII, 47, Farragut to Fox, Mar. 5, 1862.
7. *Correspondence of Gustavus Vasa Fox*, II, 84-89, Porter to Fox, Mar. 11, 1862.
8. *O. R. Navies*, XVIII, 64.
9. *Ibid.*, 67, Farragut to Fox, Mar. 16, 1862.
10. *Ibid.*, 717, log of *Hartford*.
11. *Ibid.*, 68, Farragut to Fox, Mar. 16, 1862.
12. *Ibid.*, 71, Farragut to Welles, Mar. 18, 1862.
13. *Ibid.*, 717, log of *Hartford*. Letter of Porter to Welles, Mar. 18, 1862, says it was accomplished in eight hours and apparently not later than the 18th (*Ibid.*, 71, 72).
14. *Correspondence of Fox*, I, 308, Farragut to Fox, Mar. 21, 1862.
15. *Loyall Farragut*, 212, Farragut to his wife, 25 (?), 1862. The date could not have been later than the 24th as he states that he is packed and ready to return to the mouth of the Mississippi. According to the log of the *Hartford* he returned there on Mar. 24 (*O. R. Navies*, XVIII, 717).
16. *O. R. Navies*, XVIII, 56.
17. *Ibid.*, 732, journal of the *Richmond*. In Porter's letter to Fox of Mar. 28 (*Correspondence of Fox*, II, 89-96) he gives the impression that

he assisted the *Richmond* across, but according to the journal of the *Richmond*, which goes into many details, no mention is made of the slightest assistance.
18. *Correspondence of Fox*, I, 310, Farragut to Fox, Apr. 8, 1862. Farragut's gunboats also helped (*O. R. Navies*, XVIII, 92).
19. *Ibid.*, II, 89-96, Porter to Fox, Mar. 28, 1862.
20. *Ibid.*, II, 96-99, Porter to Fox, Apr. 8, 1862.
21. Fox to Porter, Feb. 24, 1862, D. D. Porter Papers, Manuscript Division, Library of Congress.
22. *O. R. Navies*, XVIII, 37, Welles to Farragut, Mar. 24, 1862.
23. *Correspondence of Fox*, II, 89-96, Porter to Fox, Mar. 28, 1862.
24. *Ibid.*, II, 96-99, Porter to Fox, Apr. 8, 1862.
25. *Loyall Farragut*, 218, Apr. 11, 1862.
26. *Ibid.*, 218, Farragut to his wife, Apr. 8, 1862 and *Correspondence of Fox*, I, 310, Farragut to Fox, Apr. 8, 1862.
27. *O. R. Navies*, XVIII, 109, Farragut to Welles, Apr. 8, 1862.
28. *Correspondence of Fox*, I, 306, 307, Fox to Farragut, Mar. 7, 1862.
29. *Loyall Farragut*, 218, Farragut to his wife, Apr. 8, 1862.
30. *O. R. Navies*, XVIII, 189, Mar. 12, 1862.
31. *Ibid.*, 56, 62, 63, 68, 69.
32. *Ibid.*, 71, Farragut to Welles, Mar. 18, 1862.

IV. FINAL PLANS AND PREPARATIONS

1. *O. R. Navies*, XVIII, 690, Captain Bell's diary for Apr. 12, 1862. The different figures given in *O. R. Navies*, Series II, Vol. I, *passim*, and in *Battles and Leaders*, II, 74 probably do not include the guns which were transferred from the *Colorado* to various ships of the fleet. Mahan's *Admiral Farragut*, 127 and Spears' *David G. Farragut*, 180 are inaccurate. The sailing ship *Portsmouth* had sixteen 8-inch guns also, but she took only a small part in the battle.
2. *O. R. Navies*, XVIII, 361-422. The *Horace Beals*, sometimes erroneously called a mortar boat, carried only two 32-pounders and one 30-pounder rifle.
3. *Ibid.*, 155, Farragut's report of May 6, 1862.
4. *Battles and Leaders*, II, 56-58, from an article by Commander John Russell Bartlett, then a midshipman on the *Brooklyn*.
5. *O. R. Navies*, XVIII, 734-736, journal of the *Richmond*.
6. *Ibid.*, 199, Alden's report, Apr. 27, 1862.
7. *Ibid.*, 765-766, diary of Lieutenant Roe of the *Pensacola*.
8. *Surgeon of the Seas* by Charles S. Foltz, 213.
9. *O. R. Navies*, XVIII, 132, 133, Farragut to Bailey, Apr. 17, 1862. The command was given him as early as Apr. 9, 1862 (*Ibid.*, 115, Bailey to John L. Davis).
10. *Ibid.*, 89, Bell to Farragut, Mar. 28, 1862.
11. *Ibid.*, 799, log of the *Iroquois*.
12. *Notes of Conversations with a Volunteer Officer in the U. S. Navy on the Passage of the Forts below New Orleans, Apr. 24, 1862* by Gorham Coffin Taylor, 8.

13. *O. R. Navies*, XVIII, 719, log of the *Hartford*.
14. *Surgeon of the Seas* by Charles S. Foltz, 213.
15. *O. R. Navies*, XVIII, 132, 133. On Feb. 21, 1862, Farragut wrote Welles: ". . . I will try and get together four of the gunboats to enfilade Fort St. Philip, and with the bombs and other vessels I hope to accomplish the great end of my first expedition" (*Ibid.*, 33, 34).
16. *Ibid.*, 131, 132. The original copy in Farragut's hand with several misspelled words, before being edited by his clerk, is in the D. D. Porter Papers, Manuscript Division, Library of Congress.
17. *O. R. Navies*, XVIII, 133.
18. *Ibid.*, 132.
19. *Ibid.*, 362, Porter's report, Apr. 30, 1862.
20. New York *Herald*, Apr. 19, 1862.
21. *O. R. Navies*, XVIII, 7, 8, Welles to Farragut, Jan. 20, 1862.
22. *Ibid.*, 15-23.

V. BARRIERS TO NEW ORLEANS

1. Figures hopelessly disagree in various authorities. Compare the memorandum of Brigadier-General Barnard, *O. R. Navies*, XVIII, 15-18; report of Joseph Harris, U. S. Coast Survey, May 4, 1862, *Ibid.*, 393; *Battles and Leaders*, II, 75; and report of Major-General Lovell, Dec. 5, 1861, *O. R. Armies*, Series I, Vol. VI, 775.
2. *Battles and Leaders*, II, 75. Mahan in his *Admiral Farragut*, 128 gives the total as forty-two guns, without citing his authority.
3. *O. R. Armies*, Ser. I, Vol. VI, 521. Lieutenant-Colonel Edward Higgins commanded Fort Jackson, and Captain M. T. Squires was in command of Fort St. Philip.
4. *O. R. Navies*, XVIII, 522, 523, 562, 564, 775,
5. *Ibid.*, 290-292, report of Commander John K. Mitchell, C.S.N., Aug. 19, 1862.
6. *History of the Confederate States Navy* by J. Thomas Scharf, 264, 265. Scharf says she carried one 68-pounder, but he cites no authority. For a remarkably inaccurate drawing of the *Manassas* see *Harper's Weekly* for June 14, 1862, p. 369.
7. *Battles and Leaders*, II, 48, article by William C. Whittle, Third Lieutenant in the *Louisiana*.
8. For side view and deck plan, see *O. R. Navies*, XVIII, 287, 288. Mitchell's report to Mallory, Aug. 19, 1862, *Ibid.*, 290.
9. Mitchell was the husband of Margaret Loyall, first cousin to Mrs. Farragut.
10. Major-General D. E. Twiggs, C.S.A. to Secretary of War Judah P. Benjamin, Oct. 4, 1861, *O. R. Armies*, Ser. I, Vol. VI, 750.
11. *O. R. Navies*, XVI, 703, Flag Officer McKean to Welles, Oct. 15, 1861.
12. *O. R. Armies*, Ser. I, Vol. VI, 730.
13. *Ibid.*, 761.

14. *Ibid.*, 788.
15. *Ibid.*, 790.
16. *Ibid.*, 832.
17. *Ibid.*, 850.
18. *Ibid.*, 561, 646.
19. *Ibid.*, 828.
20. *Ibid.*, 513 and 867.
21. *O. R. Navies*, XVIII, 323.
22. *O. R. Armies*, Ser. I, Vol. VI, 563. Testimony before the Court of Inquiry into the Capture of New Orleans.

VI. BOMBS BURSTING IN AIR

1. *O. R. Navies*, XVIII, 693, diary of Captain Bell.
2. Porter's official report does not give the time. Other accounts vary from 9:00 to 10:15. See *Ibid.*, 775, 792, 794 and *O. R. Armies*, Ser. I, Vol. VI, 525.
3. *O. R. Navies*, XVIII, 364, Porter to Welles, Apr. 30, 1862. Porter made his report directly to Welles, though it was clearly understood that he was under Farragut's command.
4. *Ibid.*, 736, journal of the *Richmond*.
5. *O. R. Armies*, Ser. I, Vol. VI, 525, General Duncan's report.
6. *O. R. Navies*, XVIII, 693, diary of Captain Bell.
7. *Ibid.*, 364, Porter's report.
8. *O. R. Armies*, Ser. I, Vol. VI, 525, Duncan's report.
9. *O. R. Navies*, XVIII, 694, Captain Bell's diary.
10. *Ibid.*, 365, Porter's report.
11. *Ibid.*, 776, log of *Oneida*.
12. *O. R. Armies*, Ser. I, Vol. VI, 525, General Duncan's report.
13. *O. R. Navies*, XVIII, 720, log of *Hartford* and *Ibid.*, 737, journal of *Richmond*.
14. *Ibid.*, 367, Porter's report.
15. *Ibid.*, 695, diary of Captain Bell.
16. *Ibid.*, 143, 144, J. M. Wainwright to Porter, June 1, 1862. Porter resented not being asked, and in a letter to Fox of May 10, 1862 he wrote: ". . . Farragut has been pleased to consider me an 'outsider,' and has not deigned to invite me to his public councils" (*The Correspondence of Gustavus Vasa Fox*, II, 100).
17. *O. R. Navies*, XVIII, 145, 146. The original copy of this memorandum is in the D. D. Porter Papers, Manuscript Division, Library of Congress.
18. *Ibid.*, 695, diary of Captain Bell. In a letter of June 1, 1862, in reply to one from Porter, Lieutenant J. M. Wainwright wrote that this meeting was held on the afternoon of April 22, that he was "laughingly told" on entering the Flag-Officer's cabin that the signal was not intended for him but that he determined to remain, that there was opposition among those present to Farragut's plan to run the forts, that Farragut said that "Captain Porter urged very strongly the attempt being made, not only on the grounds of its probable

success, but from the fact that the fire of the mortar vessels could not be sustained for a much longer period," that Farragut declared he "entirely agreed with the plan of operations submitted by Porter, and that he had determined to make the attack that night" (*Ibid.*, 143-145). From the contents of this much muddled letter it appears that Porter wrote his subordinate officer, Wainwright, to inquire whether he was "justified by results in advocating so strenuously the advance of the fleet, and what might and would have been the result had my counsel, which was deemed premature, been disregarded." Wainwright then thus nobly rose to the occasion with his amazing letter.

Surgeon Foltz, Farragut's fleet surgeon, records that he and Farragut dined with Alden on the *Richmond* on Apr. 17 and that Farragut "is anxious to make the attack upon the forts without waiting for the action of the mortar fleet. He is brave—impulsive" (*Surgeon of the Seas* by Charles S. Foltz, 213).

19. *Surgeon of the Seas* by Charles S. Foltz, 214.
20. He no doubt includes Porter's first plan to reduce the forts by the use of the mortars alone. This would make three.
21. *O. R. Navies*, XVIII, 160. An original copy, apparently in Farragut's hand, misspelling and all, is in D. D. Porter's Papers, Manuscript Division, Library of Congress.
22. *Ibid.*, 136, 137.
23. *Ibid.*, 737, journal of the *Richmond*.
24. *Ibid.*, 135, 367.
25. *Ibid.*, 720, log of the *Hartford*.
26. *Loyall Farragut*, 226, 227, Apr. 21, 1862.
27. *O. R. Navies*, XVIII, 720, log of the *Hartford*.
28. *Ibid.*, 777, log of the *Oneida*.
29. *Ibid.*, 800, log of the *Iroquois*.
30. *Ibid.*, 738, journal of the *Richmond*.
31. *Ibid.*, 134, 135, Farragut to Welles, Apr. 21, 1862.
32. *Ibid.*, 366, Porter's report of Apr. 30, 1862.
33. *O. R. Armies*, Ser. I, Vol. VI, 526, Gen. Duncan's report.
34. *O. R. Navies*, XVIII, 721, log of the *Hartford*.
35. *O. R. Armies*, Ser. I, Vol. VI, 551, report of Captain M. T. Squires, Apr. 27, 1862.
36. *O. R. Navies*, XVIII, 140.
37. D. D. Porter Papers, Manuscript Division, Library of Congress. Lieutenant J. M. Wainwright's letter of June 1, 1862 says that Farragut came on board the *Harriet Lane* that evening to express "his mortification at the delay." Does it seem probable he would have come after having written a letter? J. M. Wainwright was not a relation to Commander Richard Wainwright of the *Hartford*.
38. *O. R. Navies*, XVIII, 768, diary of Roe of the *Pensacola*.
39. *A Sailor of Fortune: Personal Memoirs of Captain B. S. Osbon* by Albert Bigelow Paine, 183, 184.
40. *O. R. Navies*, XVIII, 367. Charles S. Foltz's *Surgeon of the Seas*,

221, states that a council of all the captains "fixed the hour for the advance at ten o'clock on the night of the 22d; but as the hour approached, an expedition to cut the levee above the forts had been absent 24 hours and another to make sure that the opening in the chain remained clear had not been heard from." No confirmation of this has been found elsewhere.

41. *Correspondence of Gustavus Vasa Fox,* II, 100, Porter to Fox, May 10, 1862.
42. "Admiral Farragut and New Orleans" in *Galaxy,* XII, 827, 828. To see how Porter confused his own statements, compare his article, "The Opening of the Lower Mississippi" in *Battles and Leaders,* II, 38, in which he states that "on the 23d instant" he persuaded Farragut to make "an immediate attack" and that Farragut *then called* a council of the commanders but that the "movement was postponed" because of the absence of the carpenters, with his "Journal of Occurrences during the War of the Rebellion, 1860-65" in the D. D. Porter Papers, Library of Congress, in which he says that he urged Farragut to call a council of officers on April 22, that he proposed to run past the forts, and that Farragut agreed with him.

The letter of Capt. John Guest of Jan. 10, 1872, which was written and printed as a reply to Welles's attack on Porter in the *Galaxy,* is based upon what he had been told by Lieutenant Wainwright (see note 18 above) of an interview in the cabin of the *Harriet Lane* on April 22, at which Farragut, Porter, and Wainwright were present and during which Farragut contended that the bombardment should continue but Porter persuaded him to promise to attack that night. Guest was one of Porter's officers in his flotilla and entirely under his influence then and at the time the letter was written. This letter is quoted in full in D. D. Porter's *An Answer to Misrepresentations* (Washington, 1872), 27.

See also "Farragut's Capture of New Orleans" by William T. Meredith, Late U.S.N. and Secretary to Admiral Farragut, in *Battles and Leaders,* II, 70 et seq. for a presentation of Farragut's side. At the time this was published, Farragut was dead and Meredith could have expected nothing in return from him; when Captain Guest's letter was written, Porter was his superior officer, the highest ranking officer in the navy.
43. Fox to Welles, Aug. 12, 1871, Henry E. Huntington Library and Art Gallery.
44. *O. R. Navies,* XVIII, 156, Farragut's report of May 6, 1862.
45. *Ibid.,* 141. The diagram (*Ibid.,* 164) marks Bailey's pennant red, Farragut's blue, and Bell's red and white. The log of the *Oneida* (*Ibid.,* 778) states that Bailey's divisional flag was red.
46. *Ibid.,* 739, journal of *Richmond* and *Ibid.,* 754, log of *Cayuga.*
47. *Ibid.,* 813, log of *Itasca.*
48. *O. R. Armies,* Ser. I, Vol. VI, 527, 528, Duncan's report.
49. *O. R. Navies,* XVIII, 768.

50. *A Sailor of Fortune: Personal Memoirs of Captain B. S. Osbon* by Albert Bigelow Paine, 186.
51. *O. R. Navies*, XVIII, 339, statement of Lieutenant A. F. Warley, C.S.N., commander of the *Manassas;* diary of Lieutenant Roe of *Pensacola*, who inspected the fort after its capture (*Ibid.*, 772), which states, "The strength of these defenses would make any one believe they were impregnable"; letter of Captain Craven to Mrs. Craven, May 16, 1862, *Ibid.*, 196; Gen. Duncan's report, *O. R. Armies*, Ser. I, Vol. VI, 528; report of Capt. M. T. Squires, in command of Fort St. Philip, *Ibid.*, 552; letter of Col. Edward Higgins in *Battles and Leaders*, II, 36, and Higgins to Bridges, Apr. 30, 1862, *O. R. Armies*, Ser. I, Vol. VI, 549; and Capt. Bailey's report of May 7, 1862, *O. R. Navies*, XVIII, 172.
52. Statistics prepared for Porter, after the fort surrendered, by Mr. Gerdes of the Coast Survey, on a detailed chart, *O. R. Navies*, XVIII, 372, and Gerdes' report, May 4, 1862. In his *Incidents and Anecdotes of the Civil War*, 48, Porter states that the forts "had borne for six days and nights the heavy pelting on their casemates of nearly 17,000 13-inch shells." This was a *heavy* pelting for the casemates alone. In his article in *Battles and Leaders*, II, 38, Porter says that the total was 16,800. But in his report to Welles of Apr. 30, 1862 (*O. R. Armies*, Ser. I, Vol. XV, 461-2) he wrote: "Fort Jackson is a perfect wreck. . . . Over 1800 shells fell in the work proper, to say nothing of those which burst over and around it."
53. *Butler's Book*, 358.
54. "An English View of the Civil War" in *North American Review*, CXLIX, 31.
55. *Twenty Years at Sea, or Leaves from My Old Log-books* by Frederic Stanhope Hill, 173-177. Hill was an acting master on the *Richmond*.

VII. CRASHING THROUGH THE BARRIERS

1. *Twenty Years at Sea, or Leaves from My Old Log-books.* by Frederic Stanhope Hill, 173-177. Hill was an acting master on the *Richmond*.
2. *A Sailor of Fortune: Personal Memoirs of Captain B. S. Osbon* by Albert Bigelow Paine, 188. Farragut's report of May 6, 1862 (*O. R. Navies*, XVIII, 156) states that the signal was made "about five minutes of 2 o'clock a.m."
3. Watches must have been adrift, or records were carelessly made from memory in the logs after the battle, for there is much variation in the time schedule.
4. Hill, *op. cit.*
5. *O. R. Navies*, XVIII, 196-199, Craven to his wife, May 16, 1862.
6. *Ibid.*, 170, 171, Bailey's report of Apr. 25, 1862.
7. *Ibid.*, 196-199, Craven's letter of May 16, 1862; and *Ibid.*, 739, Alden's report of Apr. 27, 1862.
8. *Ibid.*, 768-770, Lieut. Roe's report of Apr. 30, 1862.
9. *George Hamilton Perkins* . . . by Carroll S. Alden, 118-120, Perkins' letter to his homefolks.

10. *Army and Navy Journal* of July 17, 1869, Farragut to Bailey, May 19, 1869 and Bailey to Farragut, Apr. 1, 1869. See also the corrected diagram with Farragut's letter to Sec. of Navy A. E. Borie, May 24, 1869 (*O. R. Navies,* XVIII, 165). General Duncan had the impression that the attack was made "in column of twos, en échelon, so as not to interfere with each other's broadsides" (*Ibid.,* 269). Even in Farragut's report of May 6, 1862, he states, "We then advanced in two columns" (*Ibid.,* 156).
11. *Ibid.,* 792, the log of the *Kineo.*
12. *Ibid.,* 157, Farragut's report of May 6, 1862.
13. *Ibid.,* 269, report of Gen. J. K. Duncan, C.S.A., Apr. 30, 1862, and *Ibid.,* 282, report of Capt. M. T. Squires, C.S.A., Apr. 27, 1862.
14. *A Sailor of Fortune: Personal Memoirs of Captain B. S. Osbon* by Albert Bigelow Paine, 191. Osbon says that he hoisted the flag. "Why do you do that?" asked Farragut, for it was unusual to have the colors flying at night. Osbon replied, "I thought, if we are to go down, it would look well to have our colors flying above the water." "All right," Farragut said, and the *Brooklyn* and *Richmond* soon had their flags flying also. Lieut. Roe's diary of Apr. 24 (*O. R. Navies,* XVIII, 768-770) states that at daylight the stars and stripes were gotten out and hoisted by the quartermaster on the *Pensacola.*
15. *O. R. Navies,* XVIII, 196-199, Craven to his wife, May 16, 1862. Craven's report to Farragut (*Ibid.,* 182, 183) states that it was the "left bank" (probably meaning, going down stream). The accounts in the two letters disagree in many particulars. See also "The *Brooklyn* at the Passage of the Forts" by Commander J. R. Bartlett, in *Battles and Leaders,* II, 65.
16. Note Book of D. G. Farragut, owned by Mr. George T. Keating of New York City. Capt. M. T. Squires' report of Apr. 27, 1862 (*O. R. Navies,* XVIII, 282) states that the 24-pounder in the salient bearing directly on the *Hartford* was broken in two near the trunnions, and the whole battery was manned by green men.
17. *O. R. Navies,* XVIII, 154, Farragut to Fox, Apr. 25, 1862. Farragut was mistaken in stating that the *Manassas* pushed the fire raft against the *Hartford.* See also Farragut's report of May 6, 1862 (*Ibid.,* 156, 157).
18. *Ibid.,* 142, Farragut to Porter, Apr. 24, 1862.
19. *Battles and Leaders,* II, 64.
20. *A Sailor of Fortune: Personal Memoirs of Captain B. S. Osbon* by Albert Bigelow Paine, 196, 197.
21. *O. R. Navies,* XVIII, 739, 740, Captain Alden's journal of Apr. 24, 1862.
22. *Twenty Years at Sea, or Leaves from My Old Log-books* by Frederic Stanhope Hill, 173-177.
23. *O. R. Navies,* XVIII, 768-770, diary of Lieut. Roe.
24. *Ibid.,* 206, report of Capt. M. Smith, Apr. 26, 1862, and *Ibid.,* 207-209, report of Commander Lee of the *Oneida,* Apr. 26, 1862.
25. *Ibid.,* 224, 225, report of Lieut. J. H. Russell, Apr. 29, 1862.

26. *Ibid.*, 225, 226, report of Lieut. C. H. B. Caldwell, Apr. 24, 1862.
27. *Ibid.*, 226, 227, report of E. T. Nichols, Apr. 30, 1862.
28. *George Hamilton Perkins* . . . by Carroll S. Alden, 118-120, letter to homefolks.
29. *O. R. Navies*, XVIII, 150, Bailey to Montgomery Blair, May 8, 1862.
30. *Ibid.*, 170, 171, Capt. Bailey's report of Apr. 25, 1862. Lieut. Perkins states that one of those destroyed was the *Governor Moore* (Alden, *op. cit.*, 118). This was an error. He says that another was the *Manassas*; this was equally untrue.
31. *O. R. Navies*, XVIII, 210, 211, report of C. S. Boggs of the *Varuna*, Apr. 29, 1862.
32. Alden, *op. cit.*, 118-120.
33. *O. R. Navies*, XVIII, 302, 303, report of Lieut. A. Warley of the *Manassas*, June 8, 1862.
34. *Sea Dogs of the Sixties* by Jim Dan Hill, 178 et seq. and *Prince and Boatswain: Sea Tales from the Recollection of Rear Admiral Charles E. Clark*, edited by James Morris Morgan and John Philip Marquand, chapter on Read.
35. *O. R. Navies*, XVIII, 174, 175, report of Capt. H. H. Bell, Apr. 26, 1862; *Ibid.*, 154, Farragut to Fox, Apr. 25, 1862; and *Ibid.*, 156, 157, Farragut to Welles, May 6, 1862.
36. *Ibid.*, 304-308, report of Commander Beverly Kennon, May 4, 1862. Farragut's report of May 6, 1862 (*Ibid.*, 157) is incorrect in stating that the *Varuna* destroyed the *Governor Moore*; she destroyed the River Defense gunboat *Breckinridge*, or possibly the *Stonewall Jackson* (*Ibid.*, 212). Boggs' report of Apr. 29, 1862 (*Ibid.*, 210, 211) accused Kennon of burning "his wounded with his vessel."
37. Alden, *op. cit.*, 120, and Bailey's report of Apr. 25, 1862, *O. R. Navies*, XVIII, 171.
38. *O. R. Navies*, XVIII, 768-770, diary of Lieut. Roe.
39. *Ibid.*, 740, Alden's report of Apr. 27, 1862.
40. *Ibid.*, 196-199, Craven to his wife, May 16, 1862.
41. *Ibid.*, 152, 177-180. Surgeon Foltz's reports, and also reports of various commanding officers. Foltz's reports give totals for Apr. 24 and 25. Casualties were slight for the second day, but not on record. Figures for Apr. 24 are approximate. It is known that one man was killed on the *Hartford* on Apr. 25; Farragut wrote to Porter, Apr. 24, 1862 that his losses then were 2 killed and 8 wounded on the *Hartford* (*Ibid.*, 142). The *Brooklyn* had one killed on the 25th (Roe's diary, *Ibid.*, 768).
42. *Ibid.*, 374, Porter's report of Apr. 30, 1862 and *Ibid.*, 177-180, Foltz's report.
43. Based on various officers' official reports, journals, and ships' logs.
44. *Ibid.*, 283, 284, surgeons' reports. Porter claimed that there were 14 killed and 39 wounded in Fort Jackson alone, in his report of Apr. 30, 1862 (*Ibid.*, 372).
45. *Ibid.*, 302, surgeon's report for the *Louisiana*: one killed and two wounded. Article by Beverly Kennon in *Battles and Leaders*, II, 85

for *Governor Moore:* 57 killed and 17 wounded, though his official report (*O. R. Navies,* XVIII, 307) gave these figures: 57 killed and 7 wounded. The *McRae* had 4 killed and 17 wounded (*Ibid.,* 345). There were no casualties on the *Manassas,* according to Lieut. Warley (*Ibid.,* 337).
46. *Ibid.,* 185, report of the executive officer of the *Brooklyn.*
47. *Ibid.,* 289-301, Commander Mitchell's report of Aug. 19, 1862. Not counted are the unarmed tenders and tugs and two launches armed with one howitzer each.
48. *Loyall Farragut,* 261-263, Apr. 30, 1862.
49. *Narrative of a Blockade Runner,* 38.
50. *O. R. Navies,* XVIII, 333, report of Lieut. Charles W. Read of May 1, 1862.
51. *Ibid.,* 142, Farragut to Porter, Apr. 24, 1862.
52. *Private and Official Correspondence of General Benjamin F. Butler,* I, 420, 421.
53. "An English View of the Civil War" by General Viscount Wolseley in *North American Review* (July, 1889), CXLIX, 34.
54. *Our Admiral's Flag Abroad* by James E. Montgomery, 4, footnote.

VIII. THE CAPTURE OF THE QUEEN OF THE GULF

1. *O. R. Armies,* Ser. I, Vol. VI, 869.
2. New Orleans *Bee,* Apr. 16, 1862.
3. "New Orleans before the Capture" by George Washington Cable in *Battles and Leaders,* II, 19.
4. New Orleans *Bee,* Apr. 19, 1862.
5. New Orleans *Daily True Delta,* Apr. 20, 1862.
6. *Ibid.,* Apr. 24, 1862.
7. New Orleans *Daily Crescent,* Apr. 24, 1862. The *Picayune* was equally versatile in its efforts to keep up the spirits of the citizens.
8. New Orleans *Daily True Delta,* Apr. 25, 1862.
9. Letter of Mary Newman to her sister Alice, May 28, 1862, in B. F. Butler Papers, Library of Congress.
10. *O. R. Armies,* Ser. I, Vol. VI, 597.
11. Cable, in *Battles and Leaders,* II, 19.
12. New Orleans *Bee,* May 16, 1862.
13. New Orleans *Daily True Delta,* Apr. 25, 1862.
14. New Orleans *Daily Crescent,* Apr. 25, 1862.
15. New Orleans *Bee,* Apr. 25, 1862.
16. *Beauty and Booty: The Watchword of New Orleans* by [Marion Southwood], 19.
17. The New Orleans *Bee,* Apr. 26, 1862.
18. Cable in *Battles and Leaders,* II, 19.
19. *O. R. Navies,* XVIII, 158, Farragut to Welles, Apr. 25, 1862.
20. *Ibid.,* 740, journal of Commander Alden.
21. *Ibid.,* 285, report of Brig.-Gen. M. L. Smith, C.S.A., May 6, 1862, and *Ibid.,* 256, report of Gen. Lovell, May 22, 1862.
22. *Ibid.,* 153, Farragut to Fox, Apr. 25, 1862.

23. *Ibid.*, 770, diary of Lieut. Roe.
24. *Battles and Leaders*, II, 19-21.
25. *O. R. Navies*, XVIII, 722, log of the *Hartford*.
26. *Ibid.*, 760, log of the *Brooklyn*.
27. *Southern Historical Society Papers*, XXIII, 183.
28. New Orleans *Democrat*, as quoted in *George Hamilton Perkins* by Carroll S. Alden, 125-127.
29. *Ibid.*, 121-123.
30. Cable in *Battles and Leaders*, II, 19-21.
31. *O. R. Navies*, XVIII, 740, journal of Commander Alden. *Ibid.*, 760, log of the *Brooklyn*, states that they were fired into "by some soldiers standing near."
32. *Ibid.*, 741, journal of Commander Alden.
33. *Loyall Farragut*, 234.
34. "Farragut's Demands for the Surrender of New Orleans" by Marion A. Baker in *Battles and Leaders*, II, 95.
35. *O. R. Navies*, XVIII, 231.
36. *Ibid.*, 230, 231.
37. *Battles and Leaders*, II, 91, 92.
38. *O. R. Navies*, XVIII, 237, 238, Farragut to Morris, Apr. 26, 1862 and *Ibid.*, 771, diary of Lieut. Roe.
39. *Battles and Leaders*, II, 91, 92 and *Butler's Book* by Benjamin F. Butler, 370, 376, 437, 443. For variations of the story, see diary of Lieut. Roe (*O. R. Navies*, XVIII, 771) and *Battles and Leaders*, II, 96 (Baker's account).
40. *Battles and Leaders*, II, 92.
41. *O. R. Navies*, XVIII, 232, Mayor Monroe to Farragut, Apr. 26, 1862.
42. *Ibid.*, 723, log of the *Hartford* and *Ibid.*, 741, log of the *Richmond*.
43. *Ibid.*, 232, 233.
44. *Ibid.*, 234, Mayor Monroe to Farragut, Apr. 28, 1862.
45. New Orleans *Daily Crescent*, Apr. 29, 1862.
46. *Battles and Leaders*, II, 98.
47. *O. R. Navies*, XVIII, 238-240. The notification to the British Consul was mislaid, and not sent until the following day, when it was accompanied by a note explaining that the emergency had passed.
48. *Ibid.*, 697, 698, Captain Bell's diary. Mahan's *Admiral Farragut*, 171, states, without citing authority, that there were 250 marines.
49. "New Orleans before the Capture" in *Battles and Leaders*, II, 21.
50. *O. R. Navies*, XVIII, 159, report of May 6, 1862.
51. *Ibid.*, 697, diary of Captain Bell.
52. *Ibid.*, 358, Porter to Welles, Apr. 25, 1862 and *Ibid.*, 143, Porter to Farragut, Apr. 25, 1862.
53. *Ibid.*, 274, Duncan's report and *Ibid.*, 318, report of Youngblood to Mitchell, Aug. 1, 1862.
54. *Ibid.*, 359, 360, Apr. 25, 1862.
55. *Ibid.*, 358, Apr. 25, 1862.
56. *Ibid.*, 143, Apr. 25, 1862.

57. *Private and Official Correspondence of General Benjamin F. Butler,* I, 422, Apr. 26, 1862.
58. *O. R. Navies,* XVIII, 368, 369, Porter's report to Welles, Apr. 30, 1862.
59. *Ibid.,* 271-274, Duncan's report of Apr. 30, 1862.
60. *Ibid.,* 369, Porter's report to Welles, Apr. 30, 1862.
61. *Private and Official Correspondence of General Benjamin F. Butler,* I, 428, Butler to Stanton, Apr. 29, 1862.
62. There is evidence that Porter's statement (*Battles and Leaders,* II, 51) that the explosion "fairly shook us all out of our seats and threw the *Harriet Lane* over on her side" is an exaggeration. See Mitchell's statement, *Battles and Leaders,* II, 102, and Capt. William C. Whittle's answer to Porter's attack on Mitchell in the Philadelphia *Weekly Times* of Mar. 6, 1886.
63. *O. R. Navies,* XVIII, 371, Porter's report of Apr. 30, 1862. For Mitchell's own vindication, see his report of Aug. 19, 1862 (*Ibid.,* 298, 299).
64. *Private and Official Correspondence of General Benjamin F. Butler,* I, 428, Butler to Stanton, Apr. 29, 1862. This was substantiated by Weitzel's report of May 5, 1862, as quoted in *Loyall Farragut,* 219, footnote.
65. *Correspondence of Gustavus Vasa Fox,* II, 113, Porter to Fox, June 2, 1862.
66. *O. R. Navies,* XVIII, 196, May 16, 1862.
67. Photograph by Holmes, 264 Broadway, N.Y.
68. *O. R. Navies,* XVIII, 149, 150.
69. Richmond *Whig,* Apr. 28, 1862.
70. "Louis Napoleon and the Southern Confederacy" by Owen F. Aldis in *The North American Review* (Oct., 1879), CXXIX, 342-360; *Life of Lord John Russell* by Spencer Walpole, II, 349-351; and *John Slidell* by L. M. Sears, 188-193.

"Mr. Slidell wrote from Paris privately to Mr. Davis: 'If New Orleans had not fallen, our recognition could not have been much longer delayed'" (*Life of Jefferson Davis with a Secret History of the Southern Confederacy . . .* by Edward A. Pollard, 195).

IX. ON TO VICKSBURG

1. *Correspondence of Gustavus Vasa Fox,* I, 303, February 17, 1862.
2. *O. R. Navies,* XVIII, 153, Apr. 25, 1862.
3. *Ibid.,* 148, Apr. 29, 1862.
4. Dr. Ellsworth Eliot, Jr. Collection. This letter is slightly edited in *Loyall Farragut,* 261.
5. D. D. Porter Papers, Library of Congress, Manuscript Division.
6. *Loyall Farragut,* 262.
7. *O. R. Navies,* XVIII, 8. That this was clearly Welles's desire is shown in his letter to Farragut of February 10, 1862 (*Ibid.,* 15) and in the

Diary of Gideon Welles, I, 72 and in the letter of Fox to Farragut of May 15, 1862 (*O. R. Navies*, XVIII, 245).
8. *Ibid.*, 743, journal of *Richmond*, and *Ibid.*, 698, diary of Bell.
9. *Ibid.*, 462.
10. *The Second Admiral: A Life of David Dixon Porter* by Richard West, Jr., 145.
11. *Incidents and Anecdotes of the Civil War*, 95, 96 and "The Opening of the Lower Mississippi" in *Battles and Leaders*, II, 25.
12. *Surgeon of the Seas: The Adventurous Life of Surgeon General Jonathen M. Foltz in the Days of Wooden Ships*, edited by Charles S. Foltz, 258, 259.
13. His two sisters had moved to Pascagoula, Mississippi, before the war.
14. *Loyall Farragut*, 261-263, Apr. 30, 1862.
15. *O. R. Navies*, XVIII, 698, 699, diary of Captain Bell and *Ibid.*, 814, log of the *Itasca*.
16. *Ibid.*, 528, 529, letter to Mrs. Craven, June 3, 1862.
17. *Ibid.*, 465, Farragut to Craven, May 3, 1862. Orders were carried by Lee (*Ibid.*, 531, Craven to his wife, June 3, 1862). Lee, however, did not start until June 5 (Log of *Oneida, Ibid.*, 782 and Farragut to Craven, May 5, 1862, *Ibid.*, 467); he was probably delayed.
18. *Ibid.*, 531, Craven to his wife, June 3, 1862.
19. *Ibid.*, 782, log of the *Oneida*.
20. *Ibid.*, 470, Farragut to Welles, May 6, 1862.
21. *Ibid.*, 700, diary of Bell and *Ibid.*, 744, journal of the *Richmond* and *Ibid.*, 473, Palmer's report of May 9, 1862.
22. *Correspondence of Gustavus Vasa Fox*, I, 311, 312.
23. *O. R. Navies*, XVIII, 489, Palmer's report of May 13 1862.
24. *Ibid.*, 532, Craven to his wife, June 3, 1862.
25. *Ibid.*, 703, Bell's diary.
26. *Ibid.*, 246.
27. *Ibid.*, 491, 492.
28. *Ibid.*, 704, Bell's diary.
29. *Ibid.*, 745, 746, journal of *Richmond*.
30. *Ibid.*, 704, 705, Bell's diary.
31. *Ibid.*, 507, May 22, 1862.
32. *Letters of Benjamin F. Butler*, I, 512.
33. *O. R. Navies*, XVIII, 704, Bell's diary.
34. *Ibid.*, 498.
35. *Ibid.*, 502, Welles to Farragut, May 19, 1862.
36. *Ibid.*, 521, Farragut to Welles, May 30, 1862.
37. *Ibid.*, 245, Welles to Farragut, May 10, 1862.
38. *Ibid.*, 244, 245, Fox to Farragut, May 12, 1862.
39. *Ibid.*, 245, Fox to Farragut, May 15, 1862.
40. *Ibid.*, 498, 499, May 17, 1862.
41. *Correspondence of Gustavus Vasa Fox*, II, 102.
42. *Ibid.*, 105-108.
43. *The Second Admiral* . . . by Richard West, Jr., 146.

NOTES 435

44. *O. R. Navies*, XVIII, 502. West's *Second Admiral*, 151, is clearly in error in stating that Farragut had returned to New Orleans at the time Fox and Welles were writing him their urgent dispatches.
45. *Ibid.*, 506, Welles to Farragut, May 22, 1862.
46. *Ibid.*, 705, 706, Bell's diary, and *Camp, Court, and Siege* by Wickham Hoffman, 37. For photograph of Alden see *Photographic History of the Civil War*, VI, 189.
47. *O. R. Navies*, XVIII, 706, 707, 725, 746, 747, 761, 794, and 810, logs, diaries, and journals of *Hartford*, *Brooklyn*, *Richmond*, *Kineo*, and *Kennebec* and their officers.
48. *Ibid.*, 519-521, Farragut to Welles, May 30, 1862; *Ibid.*, 521, 522, Farragut to Fox, May 30, 1862; and *Loyall Farragut*, 266-268, Farragut to Welles, June 3, 1862.
49. *Loyall Farragut*, 269, 270, June 3, 1862.
50. *Ibid.*, 270, 271.

X. RUNNING THE VICKSBURG BATTERIES

1. *O. R. Navies*, XVIII, 521, Farragut to Welles, May 30, 1862.
2. *Ibid.*, 576, Farragut to Porter, May 31, 1862.
3. D. D. Porter Papers, Library of Congress, and *O. R. Navies*, XVIII, 580.
4. *Correspondence of Gustavus Vasa Fox*, II, 114, 115.
5. *Ibid.*, 103-112.
6. D. D. Porter Papers, Library of Congress.
7. Farragut to Butler, June 2, 1862, Zabriskie Collection in Naval Academy Museum.
8. *Correspondence of Gustavus Vasa Fox*, II, 119, 120. See also Butler to Porter, June 1, 1862, *Letters of General Benjamin F. Butler*, I, 549, 550.
9. *Correspondence of Fox*, II, 117, 118, Porter to Fox, June 7, 1862. "The Relations between Farragut and Porter" by Richard West, Jr. in *U. S. Naval Institute Proceedings* (July, 1935), LXI, 985 et seq. is incomplete and partial to Porter.
10. *O. R. Navies*, XVIII, 706, Bell's diary.
11. *Ibid.*, 708.
12. *Ibid.*, 550, 551, June 11, 1862.
13. *Ibid.*, 545-47, 711, and 802.
14. *Ibid.*, 709, Bell's diary; Farragut to Fox, *Correspondence of Fox*, I, 316; Farragut to his wife, June 15, 1862, *Loyall Farragut*, 271, 272; and Farragut to Welles, June 16, 1862, *O. R. Navies*, XVIII, 561.
15. *O. R. Navies*, XVIII, 710, Bell's diary.
16. *Loyall Farragut*, 271, 272, Farragut to his wife.
17. D. D. Porter Papers, Library of Congress.
18. *O. R. Navies*, XVIII, 711, Bell's diary, and log of *Hartford*, *Ibid.*, 727. Porter says he had 17 mortars in his report to Farragut of July 3, 1862 (*Ibid.*, 639).

19. *Ibid.*, 583; *Battles and Leaders*, I, 454; and *O. R. Navies*, XVIII, 762, log of the *Brooklyn*.
20. *Ibid.*, 584.
21. "The Defense of Vicksburg" by Colonel S. H. Lockett, C.S.A., Chief Engineer of the Defenses, in *Battles and Leaders*, III, 483, and *O. R. Navies*, XVIII, 649. Diagram accompanying Farragut's general order of June 25, 1862 shows only 26 guns (*Ibid.*, 587). The chart sent to Welles by Porter, July 26, 1862, gives 27 guns (*Ibid.*, 646). The plan from the Craven papers has 59 guns in the diagram (*Ibid.*, 598).
22. *The Second Admiral . . .* by Richard West, Jr., 156.
23. *Loyall Farragut*, 273.
24. *O. R. Navies*, XVIII, 609, Farragut's report of July 2, 1862.
25. *Ibid.*, 762, log of the *Brooklyn*.
26. *Ibid.*, 711, Bell's diary.
27. *Ibid.*, 586, Farragut's general order, June 25, 1862.
28. *Ibid.*, 787, log of the *Oneida*.
29. *Ibid.*, 712-714, Bell's diary.
30. *Ibid.*, 750, 751, journal of the *Richmond*. For crowded appearance of *Richmond* in action see photograph in *Photographic History of the Civil War*, VI.
31. *Ibid.*, 757, 758, log of *Sciota*, and *Ibid.*, 798, log of the *Wissahickon*.
32. *Ibid.*, 712-714, Bell's diary.
33. *Loyall Farragut*, 276, 277, Farragut to his wife, June 29, 1862.
34. *O. R. Navies*, XVIII, 608-610, Farragut's report, July 2, 1862.
35. *Ibid.*, 588.
36. *Ibid.*, Farragut to Welles, June 28, 1862.
37. *Ibid.*, 590, Farragut to Halleck, June 28, 1862.
38. *Loyall Farragut*, 276, 277, letter to Mrs. Farragut, June 29, 1862.
39. *O. R. Navies*, XVIII, 619, 620, Fleet Surgeon Foltz's report, June 28, 1862, and *Ibid.*, 798, log of *Wissahickon*.
40. *Ibid.*, 608-610, Farragut's report, July 2, 1862, and *Ibid.*, 640, 641, Porter's report, July 3, 1862.
41. *Ibid.*, 591, 592, Farragut to Welles, June 30, 1862.
42. *Ibid.*, 640, 641, Porter's report, July 3, 1862.
43. *Correspondence of Gustavus Vasa Fox*, II, 123, 124. Craven, in his letter to Farragut of June 28, 1862, explains the incident as follows: "The *Kensington* arrived about noon with provisions, and the mortar boats have already besieged me with requisitions; as they appear to be pretty large, and I have no invoice of what the *Kensington* has on board, I send requisitions to you" (*O. R. Navies*, XVIII, 597).
44. "The Defense of Vicksburg" by S. H. Lockett, C.S.A., Chief Engineer of the Defenses, in *Battles and Leaders*, III, 483.
45. *O. R. Navies*, XVIII, 608, 610, Farragut's report, July 2, 1862.
46. *Ibid.*, 651.
47. *Ibid.*, 595, Farragut to Craven, June 28, 1862.
48. *Ibid.*, 597, Craven to Farragut, June 28, 1862.
49. *Ibid.*, 599.

50. *Ibid.*, 599, 600, Craven to Farragut, June 30, 1862, and *Ibid.*, 586, Farragut's general order, June 25, 1862.
51. *Ibid.*, 602, 603, Farragut to Craven, June 30, 1862. See West's *Second Admiral*, 156, which defends Craven; notes by Midshipman J. R. Bartlett of a conversation with Farragut in his cabin on June 30, 1862 (*O. R. Navies*, XVIII, 603, 604); and Farragut to Bell, July 3, 1862, in the Zabriskie Collection in Naval Academy Museum. This last letter, printed in *O. R. Navies*, XVIII, 607, 608, states, "I fear the Midshipman with his previous impressions magnified my remarks."
52. *O. R. Navies*, XVIII, 604, 605, Craven to Farragut, July 1, 1862.
53. *Ibid.*, 605, 606.
54. *Ibid.*, 606, Farragut to Welles, July 1, 1862.
55. *Loyall Farragut*, 276, 277, June 29, 1862.
56. D. D. Porter Papers, Library of Congress, Porter to Farragut, July 1, 1862.
57. *O. R. Navies*, XVIII, 714.

XI. MEETING OF THE FLEETS

1. *Loyall Farragut*, 282, Farragut to his wife, July 2, 1862. The *Benton* was a converted snag-boat; the others were 175 feet long, 51½ feet wide, and 6 feet in draft, with a casemate covered with 2½ inches of iron sloping at an angle of 35 degrees and armed with 13 guns (*Battles and Leaders*, I, 339). The guns were 32-pounders and 7 and 8-inch rifles.
2. *O. R. Navies*, XVIII, 728, log of the *Hartford*.
3. *Ibid.*, 751, journal of the *Richmond*.
4. *Ibid.*, 714, Bell's diary.
5. *Ibid.*, 714.
6. *Loyall Farragut*, 282, 283.
7. *Life of Charles Henry Davis* by Charles Henry Davis, Jr., 258, letter of June 30, 1862.
8. *O. R. Navies*, XVIII, 715. On July 4, Craven left the fleet, and went up the river on his way home, where he arrived too ill to report promptly at the Navy Department (*Ibid.*, 607). Both Davis and Lee tried to "convince him of his error, and that it would ruin him to go home" (*Ibid.*, 607, 608, Farragut to Bell, July 3, 1862). In 1863 he was given the command of the *Niagara* after being promoted to commodore. He then captured the *Georgia* but allowed the *Stonewall* to get away, for which he was court-martialed at the close of the war and sentenced to suspension from duty for two years with leave-pay for not trying "his utmost to destroy" the vessel. Farragut was president of the court. Welles set aside the finding as inconsistent, and in 1866 Craven became a rear-admiral.
9. See *David Glasgow Farragut: Admiral in the Making* by Charles Lee Lewis, 269-286.

10. *O. R. Navies*, XVIII, 751, 752, journal of the *Richmond*.
11. *Ibid.*, 608, Farragut's general order of July 3, 1862.
12. *Battles and Leaders*, I, 340.
13. *Twenty Years at Sea, or Leaves from My Old Log-books* by Frederic Stanhope Hill, 189, 190. The log of the *Hartford* for July 7 records a reconnaissance made by Davis and Farragut (*O. R. Navies*, 729). Hill may have been mistaken about the date.
14. *O. R. Navies*, XVIII, 624, Farragut to Welles, July 4, 1862.
15. *Ibid.*, 593, telegram of Halleck to Farragut, July 3, 1862.
16. *Diary of Gideon Welles*, II, 218, Jan. 8, 1863, and II, 314, May 26, 1863.
17. *O. R. Navies*, XVIII, 631, Farragut to Welles, July 6, 1862.
18. *Ibid.*, 631, Farragut to Bell, July 8, 1862.
19. *Ibid.*, 629, July 5, 1862, received by Farragut on July 8. Telegrams were sent by Cairo and thence by boat.
20. D. D. Porter Papers, Library of Congress, Farragut to Porter, July 8, 1862.
21. *O. R. Navies*, XVIII, 632, July 9, 1862.
22. *Ibid.*, 752, journal of the *Richmond*.
23. *Ibid.*, 675, Farragut to Welles, July 10, 1862.
24. *Ibid.*, 634, Farragut to Welles, July 11, 1862.
25. *Ibid.*, 753, journal of the *Richmond*.
26. *Ibid.*, 635.
27. Farragut's first wife and W. D. Porter's first wife were sisters.
28. *O. R. Navies*, XVIII, 635, Farragut to Bell, July 13, 1862.
29. *Ibid.*, 681, Farragut to Lieutenant Commanding J. H. Russell, July 13, 1862. Farragut did not receive Porter's letter of July 13, 1862, reporting on the bad situation below until after he had dispatched the two gunboats.
30. *O. R. Navies*, XVIII, 678-681, Porter to Farragut, July 13, 1862.
31. *Ibid.*, 645, Porter to Welles, July 26, 1862.
32. *Correspondence of Gustavus Vasa Fox*, II, 117, 118, Porter's letter of June 7, 1862.
33. The Henry E. Huntington Library and Art Gallery, Fox to Welles, Aug. 12, 1871.
34. *O. R. Navies*, XVIII, 673-674, George H. Preble to Farragut, July 10, 1862.
35. *Correspondence of Fox*, II, 124, 125, Porter to Fox, July 26, 1862.
36. *O. R. Navies*, XVIII, 635.
37. *Ibid.*, 636.
38. *Ibid.*, 595, Welles to Farragut, July 14, 1862.
39. *Ibid.*, 729, log of the *Hartford*.
40. Isaac N. Brown in *Battles and Leaders*, III, 572. See also *O. R. Navies*, XIX, 132. Brown gives the draft at 13 feet (*Battles and Leaders*, III, 575).
41. The *Tyler*, a small wooden gunboat, carried six 8-inch shell guns

and two 32-pounders (*Battles and Leaders*, I, 359). The *Queen of the West* was armed only with her ram.
42. *O. R. Navies*, XVIII, 652, telegram of Van Dorn to Davis, July 14, 1862.
43. *Ibid*, XIX, 41, Commander Walke's report of July 15, 1862, and the casualty list, *Ibid.*, 42.
44. *Ibid.*, 37-39, report of Lieut. Wm. Gwin, July 15, 1862.
45. *Ibid.*, 747, journal of the *Richmond*.
46. *Ibid.*, 705, 706, log of the *Hartford*.
47. *Ibid.*, 132, 133, papers of Acting Master's Mate Wilson, C.S.N.
48. *Ibid.*, 69, 70, Lieutenant Brown's report of July 15, 1862.
49. *Ibid.*, 65.
50. *Ibid.*, 3, Farragut to Bell, July 15, 1862, and *Ibid.*, 7, 8, Farragut to Davis, July 15, 1862.
51. *Life of Charles Henry Davis* by Charles Henry Davis, Jr., 263, 264, letter to his wife of July 16, 1862.
52. *O. R. Navies*, XIX, 747, 748, journal of the *Richmond*.
53. *Ibid.*, 8, general order of July 15, 1862.
54. *Ibid.*, 6, Davis to Welles, July 16, 1862.
55. Formerly she was the *General Sumter* of the Confederate navy, plated with railroad iron and mounting one gun (*Ibid.*, 747, 748, journal of the *Richmond*).
56. *Ibid.*, 8, 9, Farragut to Davis, July 16, 1862.
57. *Ibid.*, 711-713, Bell's diary.
58. *Ibid.*, 7, Davis to Welles, July 16, 1862.
59. *Ibid.*, 4, Farragut to Welles, July 17, 1862.
60. *Ibid.*, 713, Bell's diary.
61. *Ibid.*, 748, 749, journal of the *Richmond*.
62. *Ibid.*, 706, log of the *Hartford*.
63. *Ibid.*, 8, 9, July 16, 1862.
64. *Ibid.*, 9, July 16, 1862.
65. The act created four rear-admirals on the active list at an annual pay of $5,000, and nine on the retired list at $2,000; eighteen commodores, on the active list at $4,000, and seventeen, on the retired list at $1,800 (*Navy Register*, 1862). The four rear-admirals, in the order of seniority, were Farragut, Goldsborough, Du Pont, and Foote.
66. *O. R. Navies*, XIX, 9, 10, Davis to Farragut, July 17, 1862.
67. *Ibid.*, 10, 11, Farragut to Davis, July 17, 1862.
68. *Ibid.*, 12, Davis to Farragut, July 17, 1862.
69. *Ibid.*, 713, Bell's diary.
70. *Ibid.*, 4, Farragut to Welles, July 17, 1862.
71. *Ibid.*, VII, 584, Welles to Farragut, July 21, 1862.
72. *Ibid.*, XIX, 13, 14, Farragut to Davis, July 18, 1862 and Davis to Farragut, July 20, 1862; and *Ibid.*, 14, Farragut to Davis, July 19, 1862.

73. *Life of Charles Henry Davis* by Charles Henry Davis, Jr., 265, letter of July 18, 1862.
74. D. D. Porter Papers, Library of Congress, Commander W. B. Renshaw to D. D. Porter, July 19, 1862.
75. *O. R. Navies*, XIX, 80, 81, Farragut to Welles, July 20, 1862.
76. *Ibid.*, 16, Farragut to Bell, July 21, 1862.
77. *Ibid.*, 749, journal of the *Richmond*.
78. *Ibid.*, 44, July 20, 1862.
79. *Ibid.*, 714, Bell's diary.
80. *Ibid.*, 16, W. D. Porter to Davis, July 22, 1862, and *Ibid.*, 17, Farragut to Davis, July 22, 1862.
81. *Ibid.*, 18, Davis to Farragut, July 22, 1862, and *Ibid.*, 46, Ellet to Stanton, July 23, 1862.
82. *Ibid.*, 70, Brown's report, July 23, 1862. Brown states in *Battles and Leaders*, III, 578, that 8 were killed and 6 wounded.
83. *Ibid.*, 74, 75, July 22, 1862.
84. *Ibid.*, 16, July 21, 1862.
85. *Ibid.*, 714, Bell's diary.
86. *Ibid.*, 96-98, Farragut to Welles, July 29, 1862.
87. *Ibid.*, 18, Davis to Farragut, July 22, 1862; *Ibid.*, 16, July 21, 1862; and *Ibid.*, 46, Ellet to Stanton, July 23, 1862.
88. *Ibid.*, 56-58, Lieutenant S. L. Phelps to Flag-Officer A. H. Foote, July 29, 1862.
89. *Ibid.*
90. *Ibid.*, 62, 63, Farragut to Welles, Sept. 11, 1862. "Ramming" the *Arkansas* does not appear in Davis's letter to Farragut of July 21, 1862 (*Ibid.*, 16). There is no written report of Erben to Davis on record.
91. *Ibid.*, 19, Welles to Farragut, July 18, 1862.
92. Ellsworth Eliot, Jr. Collection, letter of July 22, 1862.
93. *O. R. Navies*, XIX, 715, Bell's diary.
94. *Ibid.*, 96-98, Farragut to Welles, July 29, 1862.
95. *Ibid.*, 19, Farragut to Davis, July 23, 1862.
96. *Ibid.*, 18, Davis to Farragut, July 22, 1862; *Ibid.*, 50, Davis to Williams, July 23, 1862; and *Ibid.*, 53, Davis to Farragut, July 24, 1862.
97. *Ibid.*, XXIII, 240, Davis to Welles, July 25, 1862, and *Ibid.*, XIX, 50, 51, Williams to Davis, July 23, 1862.
98. *O. R. Navies*, XIX, 53, Davis to Farragut, July 24, 1862.
99. *Ibid.*, 716, 717, Bell's diary, and *Ibid.*, 707, log of *Hartford*.
100. *Ibid.*, 54, Farragut to W. D. Porter, July 24, 1862.
101. *Ibid.*, 75, July 24, 1862.
102. *Ibid.*, 63, 64, Davis to Welles, Aug. 1, 1862.
103. *Ibid.*, 36, Welles to Farragut, July 25, 1862.
104. *Ibid.*, 5, 6, Aug. 2, 1862.
105. *Diary of Gideon Welles*, I, 72, Aug. 10, 1862.

XII. THE *ARKANSAS* AND BATON ROUGE

1. *O. R. Navies*, XIX, 98, Farragut to Welles, July 29, 1862.
2. *Ibid.*, 751, journal of the *Richmond*.
3. *Ibid.*, 98, 99, Commander W. B. Renshaw to Welles, July 29, 1862.
4. *Ibid.*, 100, Farragut to Lieut. George H. Preble, July 30, 1862.
5. *Ibid.*, 103, Farragut to Alden, July 31, 1862.
6. *Ibid.*, 101, Farragut to W. D. Porter, July 30, 1862.
7. *Ibid.*, 105, 106, W. D. Porter to Farragut, Aug. 1, 1862.
8. *Ibid.*, 106, 107, W. D. Porter to Butler, July 30, 1862.
9. *Ibid.*, 106, Butler to Farragut, Aug. 2, 1862.
10. *Ibid.*, 109, Butler to Farragut, Aug. 3, 1862.
11. *Ibid.*, 111, Farragut to W. D. Porter, Aug. 4, 1862.
12. *Ibid.*, 135, report of Acting Master's Mate Jno. A. Wilson, C. S. Navy.
13. *Ibid.*, 137, Gen. Van Dorn's report to Gen. S. Cooper, Sept. 9, 1862. Gen. Breckinridge (*Battles and Leaders*, III, 585) states that he took into action not more than 2,600 men.
14. *Ibid.*, 719, Bell's diary; *Ibid.*, 114, 115, report of Col. Thos. W. Cahill to Capt. R. S. Davis, Act. Asst. Adjt. Gen., Hdqrs. Dept. of the Gulf, Aug. 5, 1862; and *Ibid.*, 118, Lieut. F. A. Roe to Farragut, Aug. 6, 1862.
15. *Ibid.*, 719, Bell's diary.
16. *Ibid.*, 115, 116, Farragut to Welles, Aug. 7, 1862.
17. *Loyall Farragut*, 289, Farragut to his wife, incorrectly dated July 20, 1862.
18. *O. R. Navies*, XIX, 720, Bell's diary.
19. *Ibid.*, 137, 138, Gen. Van Dorn to Gen. S. Cooper, Sept. 9, 1862.
20. *Ibid.*, 131, Lieut. Read in the Jackson *Mississippian*. This is substantiated by Acting Master's Mate Wilson, C.S.N. (*Ibid.*, 133) and Gen. Butler's General Order No. 57 in New Orleans *Picayune*, Aug. 9, 1862 (*Ibid.*, 121).
21. *Ibid.*, 117, Aug. 6, 1862.
22. *Ibid.*, 123, 124, Porter to Flag-Officer Davis, Sept. 9, 1862, and *Ibid.*, 117, Porter to Welles, Aug. 6, 1862.
23. *Ibid.*, 115, 116, Farragut to Welles, Aug. 7, 1862.
24. *Ibid.*, 118, Aug. 8, 1862.
25. *Ibid.*, 120, Aug. 10, 1862.
26. *Loyall Farragut*, 289, incorrectly dated as July 20, 1862.
27. *O. R. Navies*, XIX, 60-62, W. D. Porter to Welles, Aug. 1, 1862.
28. *Ibid.*, 60, Davis to Welles, Sept. 12, 1862.
29. *Ibid.*, 63, Farragut to Welles, Sept. 11, 1862.
30. Ellsworth Eliot, Jr. Collection, Sept. 9, 1862.
31. *Diary of Gideon Welles*, I, 88, Aug. 20, 1862.
32. *Ibid.*, I, 145, Sept. 23, 1862.
33. *Correspondence of Gustavus Vasa Fox*, II, 124, 125, July 26, 1862.
34. *Ibid.*, 127, Aug. 4, 1862.
35. *Ibid.*, 132, Aug. 6, 1862.
36. *Loyall Farragut*, 290, 291, July 29, 1862.

37. Ellsworth Eliot, Jr. Collection, Farragut to his wife, July 22, 1862.
38. *O. R. Navies*, XIX, 721, Bell's diary. The *Oneida* soon departed for the Gulf, and was replaced by the *Itasca* (*Ibid.*, 143, 147).
39. *Ibid.*, 707, journal of *Hartford*, and *Ibid.*, 140, Farragut to Renshaw, Aug. 8, 1862.
40. *Ibid.*, 141, Farragut to Welles, Aug. 10, 1862, and *Ibid.*, 142, Resolutions of a Committee of Citizens, Aug. 11, 1862.
41. *Ibid.*, 144, Farragut to Welles, Aug. 10, 1862.
42. *Ibid.*, 708, log of the *Hartford*.
43. *Ibid.*, 147, Farragut to Welles, Aug. 11, 1862.
44. *Ibid.*, 148, Butler to Farragut, Aug. 11, 1862.
45. *Ibid.*, 148, 149, Farragut to Butler, Aug. 11, 1862.
46. *Ibid.*, 149, Butler to Farragut, Aug. 11, 1862.
47. *Ibid.*, 149, 150, Farragut to Butler, Aug. 12, 1862.
48. *Ibid.*, 708, log of the *Hartford*. This seems to have been a temporary commission. On March 13, 1863, Chief Clerk Wm. Faxon wrote Farragut from the Navy Department: "The President of the United States, by and with the advice and consent of the Senate, having appointed you a rear-admiral on the active list in the Navy from 16th of July, 1862, I have the pleasure to enclose herewith your commission, dated 9th of January, 1863, the receipt of which you will acknowledge to the Department" (*Ibid.*, 661). Among the seventeen commodores were Wm. D. Porter, Henry H. Bell, and Charles H. Davis. D. D. Porter and James Alden remained commanders (*Navy Register*).
49. *Navy Registers* for 1861 and 1862. Some of Farragut's former senior officers were retired as rear-admirals and commodores.

    According to *Regulations for the Uniform of the U. S. Navy*, July 31, 1862, the designation of rank on the sleeve of the rear-admiral's uniform was three stripes one quarter of an inch wide, alternating with three, three quarters of an inch wide, the upper one being narrow. Referring to the uniform of his rank, Farragut wrote, "I wish that uniform had been simply a broad stripe of lace on the cuff—say an inch and a quarter wide—with a narrow stripe of a quarter of an inch above it, and a little rosette with a silver star in the centre. The star is the designation of the admiral and therefore should be visible. The other uniforms were well enough—but this adding on stripes until they reach a man's elbow appears to me to be a great error" (*Correspondence of Gustavus Vasa Fox*, I, 332-334, Farragut to Fox, Apr. 22, 1863). *The Regulations for the Uniform of the U. S. Navy* of Jan. 28, 1864, however, stipulated that the sleeve of the rear-admiral should have eight stripes, one fourth inch in width. This was his uniform in the Battle of Mobile Bay, now in the National Museum, Washington, D.C.
50. *O. R. Navies*, XIX, 153, Aug. 13, 1862.
51. *Ibid.*, 247, 248, Farragut to Welles, July 31, 1862. The resolution was as follows: "Resolved by the Senate and House of Representa-

tives of the United States of America in Congress assembled, That the thanks of the people and of the Congress of the United States are due, and are hereby tendered, to Captain David G. Farragut, of the United States Navy, and to the officers and men under his command, composing his squadron in the Gulf of Mexico, for their successful operations on the Mississippi River, and for their gallantry displayed in the capture of Forts Jackson and St. Philip, and the city of New Orleans, and in the destruction of the enemy's gunboats and armed flotilla" (*Ibid.*, 248). This all originated in a letter from President Lincoln to Congress, May 14, 1862 (*Ibid.*, 246). The receipt of the thanks of Congress was acknowledged by Farragut, Aug. 12, 1862 (*Ibid.*, 248).
52. Ellsworth Eliot, Jr. Collection.
53. *O. R. Navies*, XIX, 147, Farragut to Welles, Aug. 11, 1862. The *Mississippi, Pensacola,* and *Portsmouth* were left for the protection of New Orleans; the gunboats *Itasca, Kineo,* and *Katahdin* and the *Essex* and *Sumter* were stationed at Baton Rouge. Other vessels which were not under repair at New Orleans went into the Gulf.
54. *Ibid.*, 708, log of the *Hartford.*
55. *Ibid.*, 152, 153. On Sept. 12, 1862, Farragut wrote Welles: "I would be pleased to know the views or wishes of the Department as to wearing the admiral's flag. Should we of the active list wear it at the main or mizzen? As I understood the law, I hoisted it in the main, but it will be quite as agreeable to wear at the mizzen, that being the invariable designation of a rear-admiral. I simply desire to conform to the views of the Department, having had no order on the subject" (*Ibid.*, 193). "The first rear-admiral's flag in our Navy was a plain blue flag, . . . and was first hoisted at the main on board the *Hartford* in 1862 by Rear-Admiral Farragut. . . . I have in my possession this flag, which was worn by Flag-Officer Farragut at the passage of the forts below New Orleans, and hoisted on the *Hartford* on his promotion to rear-admiral. Later the two stars were added to it. The admiral presented the flag to Lieut. D. G. McRitchie, U.S.N., who gave it to me in 1875" (Preble's *The Flag of the United States,* 670). This flag is now in the U. S. Naval Academy Museum.
56. *Loyall Farragut,* 292, 293, inaccurately dated Aug. 12 (for 14), 1862.

XIII. BLOCKADING THE GULF PORTS

1. *O. R. Navies,* XIX, 708, log of the *Hartford.*
2. *Ibid.,* 102-105, July 31, 1862.
3. *Ibid.,* 159, 163, Farragut to Commander W. M. Walker.
4. *Ibid.,* 708, log of the *Hartford.*
5. *Ibid.,* 163, 164, Aug. 20, 1862.
6. *Ibid.,* 96-98, Farragut to Welles, July 29, 1862.
7. *Ibid.,* 165, 166, Farragut to Welles, Aug. 21, 1862.
8. *Ibid.,* 167, Aug. 23, 1862.
9. *Ibid.,* 172, Aug. 31, 1862.

10. *O. R. Navies*, XVIII, 9, Welles to Farragut, Jan. 25, 1862.
11. *Ibid.*, 690, Bell's diary, and *Ibid.*, 40, Stations of Vessels of West Gulf Blockading Squadron, Feb. 25, 1862.
12. *O. R. Navies*, XIX, 104, 105, Hitchcock to Welles, July 31, 1862.
13. *Ibid.*, 101, Farragut to Capt. Henry Eagle, July 30, 1862, and *Ibid.*, 98, Farragut to Welles, July 29, 1862.
14. *Ibid.*, 105, Farragut to Welles, Aug. 1, 1862.
15. *Ibid.*, 242, Farragut to Welles, Sept. 29, 1862.
16. *Ibid.*, 169, Lieut. J. W. Kittredge to Welles, Aug. 26, 1862.
17. *Ibid.*, 202, 208.
18. *Ibid.*, 168, Farragut to Commander Henry French, Aug. 25, 1862.
19. *O. R. Navies*, XVIII, 653 et seq.
20. *O. R. Navies*, XIX, 267-286.
21. *The Flight from the Flag* by George W. Dalzell, 99.
22. *O. R. Navies*, I, 436-440, report of George H. Preble, Oct. 10, 1862.
23. *Ibid.*, 459, President Lincoln to the Senate of the United States, Feb. 12, 1862. "Oreto" was the English name of the vessel before she was commissioned a Confederate cruiser.
24. *Ibid.*, 431, Farragut to Welles, Sept. 8, 1862.
25. *Ibid.*, 455, Farragut to Welles, Oct. 18, 1862.
26. *O. R. Navies*, XIX, 178, Farragut to Alden, Sept. 6, 1862. In this letter it is revealed that Farragut thought the *Florida* was "the Laird's Gunboat built at London and commanded by Bulloch." In a letter to Preble, Sept. 5, 1862, he states that it was "gunboat No. 290" (*O. R. Navies*, I, 433). This was the *Alabama*.
27. *O. R. Navies*, XIX, 708, log of the *Hartford*.
28. *Loyall Farragut*, 293.
29. *Ibid.*, 295.
30. Ellsworth Eliot, Jr. Collection, Farragut to his wife, July 22, 1862.
31. *O. R. Navies*, XVIII, 631, Farragut to Bell, July 8, 1862.
32. Ellsworth Eliot, Jr. Collection, Oct. 10, 1862.
33. *O. R. Navies*, XIX, 162, Welles to Farragut, Aug. 19, 1862.
34. *Loyall Farragut*, 294, Sept. 3, 1862.
35. *O. R. Navies*, XIX, 172, Aug. 31, 1862.
36. *O. R. Navies*, I, 431, Farragut to Welles, Sept. 8, 1862.
37. *O. R. Navies*, XIX, 184, 185, Sept. 9, 1862.
38. *Loyall Farragut*, 294.
39. *Ibid.*, 293, Aug. 21, 1862.
40. *Life of Lord John Russell* by Spencer Walpole, II, 349-351.
41. *O. R. Navies*, XIX, 185.
42. *Ibid.*, 217, 227.
43. *Ibid.*, 227, September 24, 1862.
44. *Ibid.*, 224, Farragut to Welles, Oct. 28, 1862.
45. *Ibid.*, 78, May 21, 1862.
46. *Ibid.*, 77, 79.
47. *Ibid.*, 213, Sept. 19, 1862, and *Ibid.*, 253, Farragut to Welles, Oct. 15, 1862 (quoted also in *Loyall Farragut*, 295, 296).

48. *Ibid.*, 289, Oct. 9, 1862.
49. *Loyall Farragut*, 294, 295, and *O. R. Navies*, XIX, 242, 243, Farragut to Welles, Sept. 30, 1862.
50. *Correspondence of Gustavus Vasa Fox*, I, 318-320, Farragut to Fox, Oct. 11, 1862.
51. *O. R. Navies*, XIX, 184, 185, Fox to Farragut, Sept. 9, 1862.
52. *Ibid.*, 242, 243, Farragut to Welles, Sept. 30, 1862.
53. *O. R. Navies*, XVIII, 631, Farragut to Welles, July 6, 1862.
54. *O. R. Navies*, XIX, 253, Farragut to Bell, Oct. 5, 1862; *Loyall Farragut*, 293, Farragut to his wife, Aug. 21, 1862.
55. *O. R. Navies*, XIX, 162, Welles to Farragut, Aug. 19, 1862.
56. *Correspondence of Gustavus Vasa Fox*, I, 318-320, Farragut to Fox, Oct. 11, 1862.
57. *O. R. Navies*, XIX, 298, Welles to Farragut, Oct. 13, 1862.
58. *Life and Letters of Thomas Kilby Smith* by Walter George Smith, 316. *Loyall Farragut*, 391, tells the same story, but gives no names or definite dates. See *O. R. Navies*, XIX, 321-323 for official reports.
59. *O. R. Navies*, XIX, 241, Farragut to Capt. Henry W. Morris, Sept. 26, 1862.
60. *Ibid.*, 240, Farragut to Butler, Sept. 26, 1862.
61. *Ibid.*, 242, 243, Farragut to Welles, Sept. 30, 1862.
62. *Correspondence of Gustavus Vasa Fox*, I, 318-320, Farragut to Fox, Oct. 11, 1862.
63. *O. R. Navies*, XIX, 306, Farragut to Butler, Oct. 17, 1862.
64. Ellsworth Eliot, Jr. Collection, Farragut to his wife, Oct. 10, 1862.
65. *O. R. Navies*, XIX, 325, Farragut to Bell, Oct. 31, 1862. The original letter is in the Zabriskie Collection, U. S. Naval Academy Museum.
66. *Correspondence of Gustavus Vasa Fox*, I, 321, Fox to Farragut, Nov. 7, 1862. In *O. R. Navies*, XIX, 338, this same letter is dated Nov. 1, 1862.
67. *O. R. Navies*, XIX, 708, log of the *Hartford*.
68. *Loyall Farragut*, 306, 307.

XIV. DISASTERS IN THE GULF

1. *O. R. Navies*, XIX, 326-329, Buchanan to Farragut, Nov. 9, 1862. Buchanan was the nephew of Admiral Franklin Buchanan, C. S. Navy.
2. *Ibid.*, 346, 347, Farragut to Welles, Nov. 14, 1862. There is no authority for the statement in *Loyall Farragut*, 297, that Farragut came to New Orleans because of reports that Port Hudson was being heavily fortified.
3. *Ibid.*, 351, Ransom to Farragut, Nov. 18, 1862.
4. *Ibid.*, 384, Farragut to Welles, Nov. 29, 1862.
5. *Ibid.*, 299, 300, 306, Oct. 14, 1862.
6. *Ibid.*, 316, Butler to Farragut, Oct. 25, 1862.
7. *Ibid.*, 347, 348, Farragut to Acting Master Crocker, Nov. 15, 1862.

8. *Ibid.*, 386, Nov. 30, 1862.
9. *Ibid.*, 372, Farragut to Bell, Nov. 24, 1862.
10. *Ibid.*, 404, Farragut to Renshaw, Dec. 12, 1862.
11. Renshaw to D. D. Porter, Dec. (?), 1862, in Officers' Letters, Mississippi Squadron, Sept., 1862-Mar., 1863, Naval Records and Library, Navy Department.
12. *O. R. Navies*, XIX, 372, Nov. 24, 1862.
13. *Loyall Farragut*, 299, Nov. 27, 1862.
14. *Ibid.*, 300, Dec. 4, 1862.
15. *Letters of General Benjamin F. Butler*, II, 350, Nov. 17, 1862.
16. *Ibid.*, 526, 527, Dec. 10, 1862.
17. Zabriskie Collection, Naval Academy Museum, Nov. 25, 1862.
18. Naval Records and Library, Navy Department, Farragut Letter Book, Nov. 4, 1862-Dec. 29, 1863, notations on Ellison's letter of Dec. 26, 1862.
19. *O. R. Navies*, XIX, 340, 341, Halleck to Banks, Nov. 8, 1862, and *Ibid.*, 409, 410, Farragut to Bell, Dec. 15, 1862. See also the journal of the *Richmond*, *Ibid.*, 761. Mahan's *Admiral Farragut*, 201, is incorrect in stating that Banks arrived at New Orleans on Dec. 16, 1862; he arrived in the vicinity of the city on Sunday evening, Dec. 14 (*O. R. Navies*, XIX, 417).
20. *Ibid.*, 342, Nov. 11, 1862.
21. *Loyall Farragut*, 303, Dec. 16, 1862.
22. *O. R. Navies*, XIX, 417, Banks to Lincoln, Dec. 18, 1862.
23. *Ibid.*, 763, 764, journal of the *Richmond*; *Ibid.*, 415, Farragut to Welles, Dec. 19, 1862; and *Ibid.*, 417, 418, Banks to Halleck, Dec. 18, 1862.
24. *Ibid.*, 409, Dec. 15, 1862.
25. *Ibid.*, 421, Dec. 22, 1862.
26. *Ibid.*, 431, Dec. 29, 1862, and *Correspondence of Gustavus Vasa Fox*, I, 322-324, Dec. 23, 1862.
27. *O. R. Navies*, XIX, 409, 410, Farragut to Renshaw, Dec. 15, 1862.
28. *Loyall Farragut*, 300, Dec. 4, 1862.
29. *O. R. Navies*, XIX, 735, Bell's diary, and *Ibid.*, 437, 438, Farragut to Welles, Jan. 3, 1863.
30. *Ibid.*, 255-260, Oct. 8, 1862.
31. *Ibid.*, 489, 490, Jan. 5, 1863.
32. *Ibid.*, 447-450, Proceedings of Court of Inquiry, Jan. 12, 1863, and *Ibid.*, 446, 447, Farragut to Welles, Jan. 18, 1863. With the signal book of the *Harriet Lane* in Confederate hands, Farragut had to change the code. This he did by adding one to the numerical value of each signal (*Ibid.*, 499, Farragut to Bailey, Jan. 7, 1863).
33. *Ibid.*, 463, 464, General Order No. 28, Jan. 7, 1863.
34. *Ibid.*, 465.
35. *Ibid.*, 736, Bell's diary, and *Ibid.*, 504, Bell to Farragut, Jan. 11, 1863.
36. *Correspondence of Gustavus Vasa Fox*, I, 324, 325, Feb. 6, 1863.
37. *Ibid.*, II, 157, 158.
38. *Diary of Gideon Welles*, I, 231.

39. *Letters of General Benjamin F. Butler*, II, 577, 578, Jan. 13, 1863.
40. *Loyall Farragut*, 307, Farragut to his wife. The letter is incorrectly dated, for it could not have been earlier than Jan. 15, 1863. Cf. Farragut to Bell, Jan. 15, 1863 (*O. R. Navies*, XIX, 525). According to the journal of Semmes, the guns of the *Hatteras* were four 32-pounders, two 30-pounder rifles, one 20-pounder rifle, and one 12-pounder howitzer (*Ibid.*, II, 722). See also report of Semmes of May 12, 1863 (*Ibid.*, 684).
41. *Ibid.*, XIX, 737, Bell's diary; *Ibid.*, II, 20-22, Blake to Welles, Jan. 21, 1863; *Ibid.*, 683-685, Semmes to Secretary of Navy Mallory, May 12, 1863; *Ibid.*, 721, 722, journal of Semmes; and *The Flight from the Flag* by George W. Dalzell, 143-145.
42. *O. R. Navies*, XIX, 506, Jan. 15, 1863.
43. *Ibid.*, 525, Jan. 15, 1863.
44. *Ibid.*, 451.
45. *Ibid.*, 552, 553, Jan. 21, 1863.
46. *Ibid.*, 596, Feb. 3, 1863.
47. *Ibid.*, 618, Feb. 17, 1863.
48. *Ibid.*, 515.
49. *Ibid.*, 525, 526, Farragut to Bell, Jan. 15, 1863.
50. *O. R. Navies*, II, 667, journal of John N. Maffitt, C. S. Navy; *Ibid.*, 30, 31, Commander George F. Emmons to Commodore Hitchcock, Mar. 12, 1863; and *The Fight from the Flag* by George W. Dalzell, 100, 101.
51. *O. R. Navies*, XIX, 536, 613.
52. Ellsworth Eliot, Jr. Collection, Jan. 19, 1863.
53. Letter of Captain Jenkins, as quoted in Mahan's *Admiral Farragut*, 203, 204. It is made a part of a composite letter in *Loyall Farragut*, 307, 308.
54. *O. R. Navies*, XIX, 536, 537, Farragut to Alden, Jan. 17, 1863.
55. *Ibid.*, 577, Farragut to Welles, Jan. 24, 1863, and *Ibid.*, 578, 579, Banks to Halleck, Jan. 24, 1863.
56. *Ibid.*, 528, Jan. 19, 1863.
57. *Ibid.*, 481, Jan. 3, 1863.
58. *Ibid.*, 536, 537, Jan. 17, 1863.
59. Ellsworth Eliot, Jr. Collection, Jan. 26, 1863. Mrs. Farragut's letter to her husband is not extant. What she said about Porter may, however, be easily imagined.
60. *O. R. Navies*, XIX, 553, 554, Farragut to Welles, Jan. 29, 1863; and *Ibid.*, 564-566, report of Major O. M. Watkins, C.S.A., Jan. 23, 1863.
61. *Ibid.*, 600, Feb. 3, 1863.
62. *Ibid.*, 600, 601, Farragut to Hitchcock, Feb. 4, 1863.
63. *Ibid.*, 605, 606, Feb. 7, 1863.
64. *Ibid.*, 605, 606, Farragut to Bell, Feb. 7, 1863; *Ibid.*, 607, 608, Farragut to Welles, Feb. 12, 1863. *Loyall Farragut*, 305, incorrectly states that Farragut was on his way to the coast of Texas soon after the Galveston disaster, when he thus went aground.
65. *O. R. Navies*, XIX, 481, Farragut to Welles, Jan. 3, 1863.

66. *Ibid.*, 607, 608, Farragut to Welles, Feb. 12, 1863.
67. *Ibid.*, 609, Farragut to Commodore Smith, Feb. 12, 1863.
68. *Correspondence of Gustavus Vasa Fox*, I, 322-324, Farragut to Fox, Dec. 23, 1862.
69. *Loyall Farragut*, 309, Jan. 7, 1863.

XV. PASSING THE BATTERIES OF PORT HUDSON

1. *O. R. Navies*, XIX, 598, Farragut to Welles, Feb. 3, 1863.
2. *Loyall Farragut*, 309, Feb. 13, 1863.
3. *O. R. Navies*, XIX, 579, Jan. 24, 1863.
4. Jan. 8, 1863 (date of paper). See *O. R. Navies,* XIX, 551, Farragut to Welles, Jan. 21, 1863.
5. *Loyall Farragut*, 309, Feb. 1, 1863.
6. *O. R. Navies*, XIX, 543, Commander C. H. B. Caldwell to Farragut, Jan. 19, 1863. A full description of the mine is included.
7. *Admiral Farragut* by A. T. Mahan, 208, 209.
8. *O. R. Navies*, XIX, 584, Jan. 26, 1863.
9. *Ibid.*, 595, 596, Feb. 1, 1863.
10. *Ibid.*, 590, Feb. 4, 1863.
11. *Ibid.*, 615, Feb. 16, 1863.
12. *Ibid.*, 616, Feb. 17, 1863.
13. *Ibid.*, 637, Feb. 27, 1863.
14. *Diary of Gideon Welles*, I, 237.
15. *Loyall Farragut*, 310, 311, Feb. 17, 1863.
16. *Ibid.*, 310, Feb. 18, 1863.
17. *The Second Admiral* by Richard West, Jr., 215, 216.
18. *O. R. Navies*, XXIV, 383-386, Colonel Charles R. Ellet to D. D. Porter, Feb. 21, 1863.
19. *Ibid.*, 402-407, report of Major J. L. Brent, Feb. 25, 1863; *Ibid.*, 410-411, report of Colonel Wirt Adams, Mar. 1, 1863; and *The Second Admiral* by Richard West, Jr., 218, 219.
20. Quoted in *Admiral Farragut* by A. T. Mahan, 211, without citation of date or detail.
21. *O. R. Navies*, XIX, 640, Banks to Halleck, Feb. 28, 1863, and *Ibid.*, 644, Farragut to Welles, Mar. 2, 1863.
22. *Ibid.*, 650, Farragut to Bell, Mar. 5, 1863.
23. *Ibid.*, 651, Mar. 5, 1863 (a second letter).
24. *Correspondence of Gustavus Vasa Fox*, I, 327-329, Mar. 7, 1863.
25. *O. R. Navies*, XIX, 652, Farragut to Caldwell, Mar. 6, 1863.
26. *Ibid.*, 655, Farragut to Morris, Mar. 9, 1863.
27. *Ibid.*, 767, 768, journal of the *Richmond*.
28. *Putnam's Monthly* (October, 1908), V, 45-47, "Farragut at Port Hudson" by Loyall Farragut.
29. *Admiral Farragut* by A. T. Mahan, 211, 213. According to *Battles and Leaders*, III, 588, there were twenty-one heavy guns.
30. *O. R. Navies,* XX, 5, 6, Banks to Grant, Mar. 13, 1863, and *Battles and Leaders*, III, 588.

31. *O. R. Navies*, XIX, 768, journal of the *Richmond*, and *Ibid.*, XX, 5, 6, Banks to Grant, Mar. 13, 1863.
32. *Ibid.*, XIX, 668, 669. A memorandum of signals and further instructions, dated Mar. 13, 1863, accompanied the general order (*Ibid.*, 670). See diagram of Port Hudson (*Ibid.*, 669).
33. *Ibid.*, 665-668, Farragut to Welles, Mar. 16, 1863.
34. *Ibid.*, 768, 769, journal of the *Richmond*.
35. *Ibid.*, 665-668, Farragut to Welles, Mar. 16, 1863.
36. "Night with Farragut" in *War Papers and Reminiscences, 1861-1865, Commandery of Missouri, Loyal Legion*, I, 137.
37. *Putnam's Monthly* (October, 1908), V, 46-53, "Farragut at Port Hudson" by Loyall Farragut. See letter by Capt. Thornton A. Jenkins in *Battles and Leaders*, III, 566, footnote.
38. *Admiral Farragut* by A. T. Mahan, 213.
39. "Passing the Port Hudson Batteries," an address by Loyall Farragut, in *Personal Recollections of the War of the Rebellion*, edited by James Grant Wilson and Titus M. Coan, 317.
40. *Putnam's Monthly* (October, 1908), V, 46-52, "Farragut at Port Hudson" by Loyall Farragut.
41. *O. R. Navies*, XIX, 671, Capt. Palmer to Farragut, Mar. 16, 1863, and *Ibid.*, 665-668, Farragut to Welles, Mar. 16, 1863.
42. *Loyall Farragut*, 318, letter by Foltz.
43. Manuscript account of the passage of Port Hudson by Loyall Farragut, Ellsworth Eliot, Jr. Collection. The article in *Putnam's* was based on this manuscript. Cf. *Loyall Farragut*, 317.
44. J. W. Broom, 1st Lieut., Co. E, 49th Regiment, Tennessee Infantry, to Miss G. A. Brigham, Mar. 27, 1863, in Tennessee State Library.
45. *Life and Naval Career of Vice-Admiral David Glascoe* (sic) *Farragut* by P. C. Headley, 222-238, a letter written by "One on board the *Richmond*."
46. *The Independent* (Mar. 14, 1901), LIII, 589-598, "The Fight at Port Hudson: Recollections of an Eyewitness" by Thomas Scott Bacon, D.D.; and letter of Capt. T. A. Jenkins in *Battles and Leaders*, III, 566, footnote. J. R. Spears's *David G. Farragut*, 287, states that the Confederates had a locomotive headlight which they turned on the ships; but no authority is cited for the statement.
47. *O. R. Navies*, XIX, 709, log of the *Hartford*.
48. *Ibid.*, 672, Alden to Welles, Mar. 15, 1863.
49. *Ibid.*, 677, address of Capt. Alden to the officers and men of the *Richmond*, Mar. 22, 1863. Cummings died in New Orleans, Mar. 18, 1863.
50. *Ibid.*, 769, journal of the *Richmond*.
51. *Ibid.*, 672, 673, Mar. 15, 1863. An electric torpedo had been removed from the river by Capt. Caldwell of the *Essex* on Jan. 18, 1863 (*Ibid.*, 543, 544, Caldwell to Farragut, Jan. 19, 1863).
52. *Ibid.*, 676, Surgeon's report.
53. *Ibid.*, 686, 687, McKinstry to Farragut, Apr. 15, 1863.

54. *Ibid.*, 680, 681, Smith to Welles, Mar. 15, 1863. The claim of the Confederates that the *Mississippi* was set afire by hot shot fired from one of their batteries is not well founded.
55. *Ibid.*, 682, Surgeon's report, Mar. 15, 1863.
56. *Ibid.*, 685, Gen. Dodge to Gen. Hurlbut, Mar. 29, 1863.
57. *Ibid.*, 683, report of Surgeon Maccoun.
58. "Admiral Farragut's Passage of Port Hudson" by W. T. Meredith, in *Personal Recollections of the War of the Rebellion*, edited by A. N. Blakeman, 124.
59. Letter written from Port Hudson, Louisiana, Mar. 16, 1863, in Tennessee Historical Society, Nashville, Tenn.
60. *Life and Naval Career of Vice-Admiral David Glascoe* (sic) *Farragut* by P. C. Headley, 235, from a letter by "One on board the *Richmond*."
61. *O. R. Navies*, XIX, 665, Capt. C. S. Bulkley to Colonel Anson Stager, Mar. 15, 1863.
62. *Ibid.*, 697-699, Banks to Halleck, Mar. 21, 1863, and *Ibid.*, 699-700, Capt. Rowley to Maj. Myer, Mar. 22, 1863.
63. *Loyall Farragut*, 335.
64. *O. R. Navies*, XIX, 703, 704, Major-General Frank Gardner, C.S.A. to Major- General Richard Taylor, C.S.A., Mar. 16, 1863.
65. *Ibid.*, 686, Apr. 2, 1863.
66. *Ibid.*, 695, 696, Apr. 2, 1863.
67. *Correspondence of Gustavus Vasa Fox*, I, 331, 332, Apr. 2, 1863.
68. *Autobiography of George Dewey*, 104.

XVI. PATROLLING THE MISSISSIPPI

1. *O. R. Navies*, XX, 763, log of the *Hartford*.
2. *Ibid.*, 3, 4, Farragut to Welles, Mar. 19, 1863.
3. Letter of Mar. 17, 1863, as quoted in Mahan's *Admiral Farragut*, 224, 225.
4. *O. R. Navies*, XIX, 704, Major-General Frank Gardner, C.S.A., to Major-General Richard Taylor, Mar. 16, 1863.
5. *Ibid.*, XX, 4, Farragut to the Mayor of Natchez. The letter has been edited in *Loyall Farragut*, 337.
6. *O. R. Navies*, XX, 805, 806, Brigadier-General Bowen, C.S.A.
7. Notebook of D. G. Farragut, owned by Mr. George T. Keating.
8. *Loyall Farragut*, 337, 338; *O. R. Navies*, XX, 3, 4, Farragut to Welles; and *Ibid.*, 805, 806, report of Brigadier-General Bowen, C.S.A., Mar. 19, 1863.
9. *Putnam's Monthly* (October, 1908), V, 46-53, "Farragut at Port Hudson" by Loyall Farragut.
10. Ellsworth Eliot, Jr. Collection. In Farragut's official report the name of Loyall Farragut appears among those who were on the poop deck and "exerted themselves to render every assistance in their power" (*O. R. Navies*, XIX, 665-668).

NOTES 451

11. *O. R. Navies*, XX, 5, Farragut to Grant, Mar. 20, 1863, and *Ibid.*, 5, 6, Banks to Grant, Mar. 13, 1863.
12. *Ibid.*, 6, Mar. 20, 1863.
13. *Diary of Gideon Welles*, I, 249, Mar. 17, 1863.
14. *The Second Admiral* by Richard West, Jr., 210-212, and *The Mississippi Valley in the Civil War* by John Fiske, 218-220.
15. *O. R. Navies*, XX, 11, Porter to Farragut, Mar. 22, 1863.
16. *Ibid.*, 12, Farragut to Porter, Mar. 22, 1863.
17. *Ibid.*, 7, 8, Mar. 22, 1863.
18. *Ibid.*, 9, 10, Mar. 22, 1863.
19. *Ibid.*, 7-10, Mar. 22, 1863.
20. *Ibid.*, 8, 9, Mar. 22, 1863.
21. *Ibid.*, 14, Grant to Farragut, Mar. 23, 1863.
22. *Ibid.*, 12-18.
23. *Ibid.*, 23, Mar. 25, 1863. Porter had previously had a warm controversy with Ellet who contended that his flotilla was under orders of the War Department and the army and not under Porter's command. Hence the army rank which he and his officers bore rather than that of the navy. As late as Apr. 13, 1863 he was communicating officially with Secretary of War Stanton (*O. R. Navies*, XX, 51-53, and *The Second Admiral* by Richard West, Jr., 180).
24. *O. R. Navies*, XX, 23, Mar. 25, 1863.
25. *Ibid.*, 24, 25, Mar. 25, 1863.
26. *Ibid.*, 15, Grant to Farragut, Mar. 23, 1863, and *Ibid.*, 16, Farragut to Grant, Mar. 23, 1863.
27. *Ibid.*, 764.
28. *Ibid.*, 27, Farragut to Porter, Mar. 26, 1863.
29. *Ibid.*, 28, Porter to Farragut, Mar. 26, 1863.
30. *Ibid.*, 25, Farragut to Porter, Mar. 25, 1863.
31. *Ibid.*, 26, 27, Grant to Farragut, Mar. 26, 1863 (morning).
32. *Ibid.*, 27, Mar. 26, 1863 (morning).
33. *Ibid.*, 28, 29, Porter to Farragut, Mar. 26, 1863.
34. *Ibid.*, 37, 38, Porter to Farragut, Mar. 28, 1863.
35. *Ibid.*, 44, 45, Apr. 2, 1863, Welles to Porter.
36. *Loyall Farragut*, 344, Mar. 24, 1863.
37. *O. R. Navies*, XX, 764, log of the *Hartford*.
38. *Ibid.*, 28, Porter to Farragut, Mar. 26, 1863, and *Ibid.*, 37, 38, Mar. 28, 1863.
39. *Ibid.*, XIX, 390, 391, Farragut to Bell, Dec. 4, 1862.
40. Mar. 27, 1863, Ellsworth Eliot, Jr. Collection. Quoted with slight editing in *Loyall Farragut*, 355, 356.
41. Ellsworth Eliot, Jr. Collection, Apr. 17, 1863.
42. *O. R. Navies*, XX, 191, Farragut to Bell, May 15, 1863.
43. *Ibid.*, XX, 764, log of the *Hartford*.
44. Notebook of D. G. Farragut, owned by Mr. George T. Keating of New York.
45. *O. R. Navies*, XX, 48, Farragut to Welles, Apr. 6, 1863, and *Ibid.*, 39, Farragut to Porter, Mar. 30, 1863.

46. *Ibid.*, 48, Farragut to Welles, Apr. 6, 1863, and *Ibid.*, 294, Farragut to Welles, June 13, 1863.
47. *Ibid.*, 87, 88, Apr. 1, 1863.
48. *Ibid.*, 48, Farragut to Welles, Apr. 6, 1863.
49. *Ibid.*, 765, log of the *Hartford*.
50. *Ibid.*, 54, Farragut to Welles, Apr. 15, 1863.
51. *Ibid.*, 765, log of the *Hartford*, and *Ibid.*, 54, Farragut to Welles, Apr. 15, 1863.
52. *Ibid.*, 788, journal of the *Richmond*.
53. *Ibid.*, 765, log of the *Hartford* and *Ibid.*, 54, Farragut to Welles, Apr. 16, 1863.
54. *Ibid.*, 789, journal of the *Richmond*.
55. *Ibid.*, 56.
56. *Diary of Gideon Welles*, I, 274.
57. *Correspondence of Gustavus Vasa Fox*, II, 164, Fox to Farragut, Apr. 6, 1863, and *O. R. Navies*, XX, 121, 122, Welles to Farragut, Apr. 6, 1863.
58. *Correspondence of Fox*, II, 170, Apr. 17, 1863.
59. *Ibid.*, II, 175, Apr. 25, 1863.
60. *O. R. Navies*, XXIV, 626, 627, Porter to Welles, May 3, 1863, and *Ibid.*, 632, 633, Confederate reports, Apr. 29 and June 22, 1863.
61. *Ibid.*, 626, 627, Porter to Welles, May 3, 1863.
62. *Ibid.*, XX, 70, Farragut to Porter, May 1, 1863; *Ibid.*, 63, 64, Banks to Farragut, Apr. 23, 1863; and *Ibid.*, 69, 70, Farragut to Ellet, May 1, 1863.
63. *Ibid.*, 71, Farragut to Grant, May 1, 1863.
64. *Ibid.*, 767, log of the *Hartford*.
65. *Ibid.*, 790, journal of the *Richmond*; *Ibid.*, 76, signals; and *Ibid.*, 77, Farragut to Palmer, May 6, 1863.
66. *Cruise of the U. S. Flagship Hartford, 1862-1863 . . . from the private journal of William C. Holton* by B. S. Osbon, 68.
67. *O. R. Navies*, XX, 767, log of the *Hartford*.
68. *Surgeon of the Seas* by Charles S. Foltz, 283.
69. *Loyall Farragut*, 365, May 11, 1863.

XVII. THE SIEGE AND CAPTURE OF PORT HUDSON

1. *O. R. Navies*, XX, 179, 180, Farragut to Welles, May 12, 1863.
2. *Loyall Farragut*, 366, Farragut to his wife, May 12, 1863.
3. *O. R. Navies*, XX, 122, Welles to Farragut, Apr. 6, 1863.
4. *Ibid.*, 181, Farragut to Welles, May 12, 1863.
5. *Ibid.*, 191, Farragut to Bell, May 15, 1863.
6. *Ibid.*, 182, Welles to Farragut, May 12, 1863.
7. *Ibid.*, 277, Farragut to Welles, May 28, 1863.
8. *Ibid.*, 189, Farragut to Banks, May 15, 1863, and *Ibid.*, 186, Banks to Farragut, May 13, 1863.
9. *Ibid.*, 793, journal of the *Richmond*, and "The Capture of Port Hud-

son" by Lieutenant-Colonel R. B. Irwin, in *Battles and Leaders*, III, 593.
10. *O. R. Navies*, XX, 793, journal of the *Richmond*.
11. *Ibid.*, 213, 214, Banks to Farragut, May 28, 1863.
12. *Ibid.*, 212.
13. *Ibid.*, 212, May 26, 1863.
14. *Ibid.*, 221, Palmer to Porter, June 3, 1863.
15. *Diary of Gideon Welles*, I, 312, May 25, 1863.
16. Du Pont to Farragut, Mar. 9, 1863, Zabriskie Collection, Naval Academy Museum.
17. *O. R. Navies*, XX, 798, journal of the *Richmond*.
18. *Ibid.*, 217, Banks to Farragut, May 30, 1863.
19. *Forty-Five Years under the Flag* by Winfield Scott Schley, 45, 46, and *O. R. Navies*, XX, 799, journal of *Richmond*.
20. *Ibid.*, 227, June 11, 1863.
21. *Ibid.*, 228, June 12, 1863.
22. *Ibid.*, 229, 230, Banks to Farragut, June 13, 1863.
23. *Ibid.*, 269, to Major T. F. Willson, C.S.A., June 14, 1863.
24. *Battles and Leaders*, III, 595.
25. *O. R. Navies*, XX, 234, Farragut to Welles, June 15, 1863.
26. *Ibid.*, 298-300, June 15, 1863.
27. *Ibid.*, 325, 326, Farragut to Welles, June 29, 1863. Capt. Albert Stearns, U.S.A., who barely escaped capture, states that there were "about 300 Confederate cavalry" (*Ibid.*, 305, 306).
28. *Ibid.*, 239, 240, Farragut to Alden, June 19, 1863.
29. *Ibid.*, 83, Welles to Farragut, June 15, 1863.
30. Welles to Farragut, June 15, 1863, Ellsworth Eliot, Jr. Collection.
31. *O. R. Navies*, XX, 307, June 20, 1863.
32. *Ibid.*, 315, Farragut to Bell, June 25, 1863, and *Ibid.*, 312, telegram of W. H. Talbot, June 24, 1863.
33. *Ibid.*, 325, 326, Farragut to Welles, June 29, 1863, and *Ibid.*, 367, 368, Farragut to Welles, June 30, 1863.
34. *Surgeon of the Seas* by Charles S. Foltz, 287.
35. *O. R. Navies*, XX, 801, journal of the *Richmond*.
36. *Ibid.*, 271, Lieutenant-Colonel P. F. De Gournay to Major T. F. Willson, June 26, 1863.
37. *Ibid.*, 250.
38. *Ibid.*, 252, July 4, 1863.
39. *Ibid.*, 251, 329, July 4, 1863.
40. *Surgeon of the Seas* by Charles S. Foltz, 288.
41. *O. R. Navies*, XX, 252, 253, July 5, 1863.
42. *Ibid.*, 253, July 6, 1863.
43. *Ibid.*, 254, 255, to Porter, July 6, 1863.
44. *Life and Letters of Thomas Kilby Smith* by Walter George Smith, 319.
45. *O. R. Navies*, 256, 332, Farragut to Banks, July 7, 1863.
46. *Loyall Farragut*, 378, Palmer to Farragut, July 7, 1863.

47. *O. R. Navies*, XX, 803, journal of the *Richmond*, and *Ibid.*, 272, Colonel W. R. Miles, C.S.A. to Major T. F. Willson, July 7, 1863.
48. *Surgeon of the Seas* by Charles S. Foltz, 289.
49. *O. R. Navies*, XX, 334, Jenkins to Farragut, July 7, 1863.
50. *Ibid.*, 333, Farragut to Welles, July 28, 1863. Cf. *Henry IV, Part I*, V, 4, 104: "I could have better spared a better man."
51. *Battles and Leaders*, III, 595.
52. *O. R. Navies*, XX, 264, 265, Banks to Secretary of War, Apr. 6, 1863, and *Ibid.*, 272, Actg. Asst. Inspector-General C. M. Jackson to General Joseph Johnston, July 9, 1863.
53. *Battles and Leaders*, III, 599.
54. *O. R. Navies*, XX, 260, 261, Banks to Farragut, July 8, 1863, and *Ibid.*, 263, Jenkins to Farragut, July 9, 1863.
55. *Battles and Leaders*, III, 597.
56. *O. R. Navies*, XX, 774, log of the *Hartford*.
57. *Ibid.*, 340, 341, Farragut to Welles, July 10, 1863.
58. *Surgeon of the Seas* by Charles S. Foltz, 290.
59. *Battles and Leaders*, III, 598.
60. *O. R. Navies*, XX, 386, 387, July 13, 1863.
61. *Loyall Farragut*, 381, July 15, 1863.
62. *O. R. Navies*, XX, 393, 394, Porter to Farragut, July 16, 1863.
63. *The Mississippi Valley in the Civil War* by John Fiske, 247.
64. *O. R. Navies*, XX, 401, 427, and *Ibid.*, 423, 424, Farragut to Bell, July 28, 1863. Ten prizes had been taken in the Gulf during June and July, half of which were captured off Mobile Bay.
65. *Correspondence of Gustavus Vasa Fox*, I, 335, 336, July 10, 1863.
66. *Cruise of the U. S. Flagship Hartford, 1862-1863* . . . by B. S. Osbon, 68.
67. *O. R. Navies*, XX, 775, log of the *Hartford*.

XVIII. FARRAGUT HAS A FURLOUGH

1. *O. R. Navies*, XX, 433, H. H. Bell to Welles, Aug. 4, 1863.
2. *Ibid.*, 775, log of the *Hartford*, and *Ibid.*, 442, 443, Farragut to Welles, Aug. 10, 1863.
3. *Ibid.*, 804, journal of the *Richmond*.
4. *Ibid.*, 461, 468, 481.
5. *Ibid.*, 442, Capt. J. S. Palmer to Welles, Aug. 10, 1863, and *Loyall Farragut*, 385.
6. New York *Herald*, Aug. 10, 1863.
7. Joseph Henry to Mrs. Farragut, July 7, 1863, Zabriskie Collection, Naval Academy Museum, and George W. Cullum's *Biographical Register of the Officers and Graduates of the U. S. Military Academy at West Point, New York*, III, 125.

"A Scotch Traveller, who visited the United States, furnished the Edinburgh *Scotsman* the following anecdote: Mr. Osborn (President of the Illinois Central R.R.) told me a story of Admiral Farragut and his son. They were on the Mississippi, and Farragut's fleet was about

to pass Port Hudson, which was then held by the Confederates. Farragut's son, a lad of about 12, had been importuning his father that he might be sent to West Point, where the military cadets are educated. Old Farragut said: 'I don't know how that would do; I am not sure whether you would stand fire.' 'Oh! yes, father. I could do that.' 'Very well, my boy, we'll try; come up with me here.' The Admiral and his son went up together into the maintop; the old man had himself and the boy lashed to it, and in this way they passed Port Hudson. The boy never flinched while the shot and shell were flying past him. 'Very well, my boy, that will do; you shall go to West Point'" (*The Rebellion Record: A Diary of American Events*, "Rumors and Incidents," edited by Frank Moore, IX, 5). In spite of its many inaccuracies, this story may have some truth in it.
8. Farragut's remarks on Ellison's letter of Dec. 26, 1862, in Farragut's Letter Book, Nov. 4, 1862-Dec. 29, 1863, Navy Department, Naval Records and Library. Farragut makes no reference in his correspondence to his sister Elizabeth who married Celestin Dupont and resided at Pascagoula; she had four children: Eugenie, Zulme, Isadore, and Louis. She apparently had died before the outbreak of the war. (Letter from George G. Hall of June 12, 1942 to the author.)
9. Farragut to his wife, May 20, 1863, Ellsworth Eliot, Jr. Collection. Farragut's brother William had the following children: William J.; Glasgow; twins, Tenine and Pamelee, who married brothers by the name of Raby; and a daughter who married a Flotte. Both sons and the husbands of the daughters were in the Confederate Service. (Letter of Mr. George G. Hall of June 12, 1942 to the author.)
10. The New York *Herald*, Aug. 11, 1863.
11. *Ibid.*
12. *O. R. Navies*, XX, 443, Welles to Farragut, Aug. 11, 1863.
13. *Loyall Farragut*, 385, 386, Aug. 13, 1863.
14. *O. R. Navies*, XX, 491, Commodore Bell, Aug. 28, 1863.
15. George W. Childs to Mrs. Farragut, Aug. 27, 1863, Zabriskie Collection, Naval Academy Museum. Mrs. Farragut was "a cultivated person," "a great reader and well posted about current events and history"; "her command of language was unusually good" and she helped her husband "in his correspondence with officials and prominent citizens, writing out letters in long hand." (Letter of Mr. George G. Hall of Jan. 22, 1942 to the author.)
16. *O. R. Navies*, XX, 489-491, Farragut to Bell, Aug. 28, 1863.
17. *Ibid.*
18. *Diary of Gideon Welles*, I, 431.
19. *Ibid.*, 441, 442.
20. *Correspondence of Gustavus Vasa Fox*, I, 336, Farragut to Fox, Sept. 13, 1863.
21. *Diary of Gideon Welles*, I, 440, Sept. 21, 1863.
22. *O. R. Navies*, XX, 613, Farragut to Welles, Oct. 6, 1863.
23. *Ibid.*, Welles to Farragut, Oct. 7, 1863.

24. *Ibid.*, 629, 630, Farragut to Bell, Oct. 15, 1863.
25. *Correspondence of Gustavus Vasa Fox*, I, 337, 338, Farragut to Fox, Oct. 19, 1863.
26. *Diary of Gideon Welles*, I, 477.
27. D. D. Porter Papers, Library of Congress.
28. Oct. 30, 1863, Zabriskie Collection, Naval Academy Museum.
29. *Loyall Farragut*, 387, 388.
30. *Ibid.*, 388, 389. " 'Tis man's to fight, but heaven's to give success" is in Pope's translation of the *Iliad*, Book VI, l. 427. The other lines have not been located by the author.
31. *Memoir of Thurlow Weed* by Thurlow Weed Barnes, 346, 347, and *Abraham Lincoln: The War Years* by Carl Sandburg, II, 526.
32. *O. R. Navies*, XX, 691.
33. *Correspondence of Gustavus Vasa Fox*, I, 338, 339, Nov. 30, 1863.
34. *Naval Letters from Captain Percival Drayton, 1861-1865*, 38, Drayton to Mrs. L. M. Hoyt, Aug. 23, 1863.
35. *Ibid.*, 38, 39, Drayton to Mrs. Hoyt, Dec. 5, 1863.
36. *Battles and Leaders*, IV, 383 and I, 687.
37. Farragut to Porter, Jan. 17, 1864, Henry E. Huntington Library.
38. Mar. 21, 1864, Gideon Welles Papers, Library of Congress.
39. *O. R. Navies*, XXI, 796, log of the *Hartford*.
40. *Ibid.*, XX, 730, 731, Farragut to Welles from the Brooklyn Navy Yard, Dec. 23, 1863.
41. *Ibid.*, 751, Welles to Farragut, Dec. 30, 1863.
42. *Correspondence of Gustavus Vasa Fox*, I, 340, 341, Farragut to Fox, Jan. 3, 1864.
43. Jan. 4, 1864, Ellsworth Eliot, Jr. Collection.
44. *O. R. Navies*, XXI, 15, Farragut to Welles, Jan. 5, 1864.
45. *Ibid.*, 29, 30, Farragut to Welles, Jan. 13, 1864.
46. *Naval Letters from Captain Percival Drayton, 1861-1864*, 39-40, Drayton to Alexander Hamilton, Jr., Jan. 13, 1864.
47. *O. R. Navies*, XXI, 796, log of the *Hartford*.

XIX. WATCHFUL WAITING

1. *Correspondence of Gustavus Vasa Fox*, I, 341, 342, Farragut to Fox, Jan. 18, 1864.
2. *O. R. Navies*, XXI, 4, 5, Welles to Farragut, Jan. 3, 1864.
3. *Ibid.*, XX, 590, Bell to Goldsborough, Sept. 14, 1863.
4. *Ibid.*, XXI, 32, Bell to Porter, Jan. 15, 1864.
5. *Correspondence of Gustavus Vasa Fox*, I, 341, 342, Farragut to Fox, Jan. 18, 1864 and *O. R. Navies*, XXI, 45, Farragut to Welles, Jan. 20, 1864.
6. *O. R. Navies*, XXI, 39, 40, Farragut to Porter, Jan. 17, 1864.
7. *Admiral Franklin Buchanan* by Charles Lee Lewis, 208, and *Montgomery* (Alabama) *Daily Advertiser*, Mar. 8, 1863.
8. *O. R. Navies*, XIX, 632, Commodore R. B. Hitchcock to Captain Jenkins, Feb. 25, 1863.

NOTES 457

9. *Battles and Leaders*, IV, 401, "The Ram Tennessee at Mobile Bay" by Commander James D. Johnston, C.S.N.
10. *O. R. Navies*, XX, 705, and *Ibid.*, XXI, 35.
11. *Ibid.*, XXI, 886, Simms to Catesby Jones, Mar. 20, 1864.
12. *Ibid.*, XIX, 103, Hitchcock to Fox, July 31, 1862.
13. *Ibid.*, XX, 705, information on Confederate vessels of war at Mobile in hands of Union officers at various times, beginning July 31, 1862; *Ibid.*, XIX, 102, 718, 198-200, 423, 626-629, 632, 633; XX, 705, 735, 737; and XXI, 35.
14. *Ibid.*, XX, 314, Farragut to Welles, June 25, 1863.
15. *Ibid.*, XXI, 796, log of the *Hartford*, and *Ibid.*, 52, 53, Farragut to Welles, Jan. 22, 1864. The statement of "refugee McIntosh" mentioned in Farragut's report was probably that on page 35, *Ibid.*
16. *Ibid.*, XXI, 539, Major-General Canby to Major-General Halleck, Aug. 24, 1864; *Ibid.*, 36; and *Ibid.*, XIX, 103, 199, 629, 633. See also *History of the Confederate States Navy* by J. Thomas Scharf, 552. The report of Lieut. Charles S. Sargent, U.S.A. to Major-General Banks, Aug. 24, 1864, gives a detailed list after the capture of the fort (*O. R. Armies*, Ser. I, Vol. XXXIX, Part I, 419, 420). This includes the water battery and the Lighthouse Battery, and totals 46 guns, one of which was a signal gun.
17. *History of the Confederate States Navy* by J. Thomas Scharf, 552; *O. R. Navies*, XIX, 103, 199, 629, 633; and *Ibid.*, XXI, 36. Forty-six commissioned officers, eight hundred eighteen enlisted men, and twenty-six guns were captured (*O. R. Armies*, Ser. I, Vol. XXXIX, Part I, 403, Canby to Halleck, Aug. 9, 1864).
18. According to Lieutenant-Colonel and Chief Engineer V. Sheliha, C.S.A., "The distance from the water battery to the point at which the three lines of torpedoes commence is 226 yards" (*O. R. Armies*, Ser. I, XXXIX, Part II, 739). Mahan's *Admiral Farragut*, 259, states that the width was 100 yards. See note 24, chapter XXII.
19. *O. R. Navies*, XXI, 35, 36, Capt. Jenkins, Jan. 15, 1864, and *Ibid.*, XX, 828, Admiral Buchanan to Lieut. George W. Harrison, May 25, 1863.
20. *O. R. Armies*, Ser. I, XXXIX, Part II, 739, monthly report of operations for the defense of Mobile, Ala., for the month of July, 1864 by Lieut.-Col. and Chief Engineer V. Sheliha, C.S.A. Capt. L. J. Fremaux, C.S.A., wrote Maj.-Gen. D. H. Maury, June 2, 1864, that there were 86 torpedoes in the main channel (*O. R. Navies*, XXI, 900). Gen. Rains reported to Sec. of War Seddon, Aug. 15, 1864, that he placed 67 torpedoes there (*Ibid.*, 567). See also Surgeon Daniel B. Conrad's article in *Southern Historical Society Papers*, XIX, 81.
21. *O. R. Navies*, XXI, 372, 374, Myer to Farragut, July 13, 1864.
22. *Ibid.*, 52, 53, Farragut to Welles, Jan. 22, 1864, and *Ibid.*, 43, telegram of Bell to Farragut, Jan. 18, 1864.
23. *Ibid.*, 54, Bell to Welles, Jan. 23, 1864, and *Ibid.*, 796, log of the *Hartford*.

24. *Loyall Farragut*, 391.
25. *Letters of Drayton*, 41, 42, Drayton to Alexander Hamilton, Jr., Jan. 26, 1864.
26. *Ibid.*, 42, Drayton to Hamilton, Jan. 26, 1864.
27. Farragut to his wife, Feb. 4, 1864, Ellsworth Eliot, Jr. Collection.
28. *Ibid.*, Farragut to his son, Feb. 21, 1864.
29. *Loyall Farragut*, 218, Farragut to his wife, Apr. 11, 1862.
30. *Letters of General Benjamin F. Butler*, IV, 433, Butler to Brig.-Gen. George F. Shepley, June 21, 1864.
31. *Ibid.*, III, 357, Butler to Mrs. Farragut, Feb. 2, 1864.
32. *Ibid.*, IV, 306, 307, statement of General Butler, June 6, 1864.
33. Farragut to his wife, Feb. 1, 1864, Ellsworth Eliot, Jr. Collection. William and Glasgow were sons of Farragut's older brother, William. In this letter, Farragut curiously spells his nephew's name "Glasco." All his relatives in New Orleans and Pascagoula spoke French, and perhaps this was their French spelling of the name.
34. Feb. 19, 1864, Ellsworth Eliot, Jr. Collection.
35. *O. R. Navies*, XXI, 46, 62.
36. *Memoir and Correspondence of Charles Steedman, Rear Admiral, U.S.N.*, 4.
37. *Letters of Captain Percival Drayton*, 41, Drayton to Hamilton, Jan. 26, 1864.
38. *O. R. Navies*, XXI, 796, log of the *Hartford*.
39. Feb. 21, 1864, Ellsworth Eliot, Jr. Collection.
40. *O. R. Navies*, XXI, 80, 81, Drayton to Jenkins, Feb. 13, 1864.
41. *Drayton Letters*, 44, Drayton to Hamilton, Feb. 19, 1864.
42. *Ibid.*, 44, 45, Drayton to Hamilton, Mar. 2, 1864.
43. *Correspondence of Gustavus Vasa Fox*, I, 342-344, Farragut to Fox, Feb. 8, 1864.
44. *O. R. Navies*, XXI, 90, Farragut to Welles, Feb. 7, 1864, and *Ibid.*, 91, 92, Farragut to Banks, Feb. 11, 1864.
45. *Correspondence of Gustavus Vasa Fox*, I, 345, Farragut to Fox, Feb. 28, 1864; *O. R. Navies*, XXI, 80, 81, Drayton to Jenkins, Feb. 13, 1864; *Ibid.*, 93, 94; and *History of the Confederate States Navy* by J. Thomas Scharf, 553.
46. *O. R. Navies*, XXI, 103, 104, Maury to Seddon, Feb. 15, 1864.
47. *Drayton Letters*, 43, Drayton to Hamilton, Feb. 14, 1864.
48. *Correspondence of Gustavus Vasa Fox*, I, 342-344, Farragut to Fox, Feb. 8, 1864, and *Drayton Letters*, 43, Drayton to Hamilton, Feb. 14, 1864.
49. *O. R. Navies*, XXI, 94, 95, Farragut to Bailey, Feb. 19, 1864.
50. *Ibid.*, 104, telegram of Maury to General Polk, Feb. 19, 1864.
51. *Drayton Letters*, 43, 44, Drayton to Hamilton, Feb. 19, 1864.
52. *O. R. Navies*, XXI, 99, log of the *Octorara*.
53. *O. R. Navies*, XXI, 95, 96, Drayton to Jenkins, Feb. 24, 1864.
54. *Ibid.*, 96, 97, Farragut to Welles, Feb. 28, 1864. See *Southern Historical Society Papers*, XXXV, 174, 175, reprint from the Richmond

Times-Dispatch, Dec. 23, 1907, of a story that Farragut would probably have been ambushed and captured on Dauphin Island during the attack on Fort Powell, if mosquitoes had not forced the three Confederate soldiers to retire from the ambush before Farragut appeared. It makes an interesting story; but mosquitoes on Dauphin Island in February would hardly have been found.

55. *O. R. Navies,* XXI, 105-107, Marchand to Farragut, Feb. 18, 1864.
56. *Ibid.,* 113, Farragut to Palmer, Feb. 21, 1864.
57. *Correspondence of Gustavus Vasa Fox,* I, 345, 346, Farragut to Fox, Feb. 28, 1864.
58. *O. R. Navies,* XXI, 97, 98, Farragut to Welles, Mar. 1, 1864, and *Ibid.,* 101, log of the *Calhoun.*
59. *Ibid.,* 98, Farragut to Jenkins, Mar. 1, 1864.
60. *Ibid.,* 881, J. R. Eggleston to Commander Catesby ap R. Jones, Mar. 3, 1864 and Lieut.-Col. J. M. Williams to Col. G. G. Garner, Mar. 7, 1864.
61. *Loyall Farragut,* 392, 393, Farragut to his son, Mar. 2, 1864. This letter is in the New York Historical Society. It ends with "She [Aunt Gurlie] says that little Virginia Farragut, Will's little girl, is very well and a little beauty." This was the child who afterwards came to live with the Admiral's family, and eventually married George G. Hall.
62. *O. R. Navies,* XXI, 121, Farragut to Asboth, Mar. 1, 1864.
63. *Loyall Farragut,* 392, 393, Farragut to his son, Mar. 2, 1864.
64. *O. R. Navies,* XXI, 122, Farragut to Banks, Mar. 2, 1864.
65. *Correspondence of Gustavus Vasa Fox,* I, 347, 348, Farragut to Fox, Mar. 5, 1864.
66. *O. R. Navies,* XXI, 127, 128, Farragut to Palmer, Mar. 6, 1864.
67. *Ibid.,* 130, 131, Farragut to Welles, Mar. 9, 1864.
68. *Ibid.,* 881, Charles C. Simms to Catesby Jones, Mar. 5, 1864; *Ibid.,* 880, J. R. Eggleston to Jones, Mar. 3, 1864; and *Ibid.,* 886, Simms to Jones, Mar. 20, 1864.
69. *Drayton Letters,* 46, Drayton to Hamilton, Mar. 15, 1864.
70. *O. R. Navies,* XXI, 124, Farragut to Paymaster Bridge, Mar. 5, 1864.
71. *Correspondence of Gustavus Vasa Fox,* I, 348, Farragut to Fox, Mar. 5, 1864.
72. *O. R. Navies,* XXI, 126, 131, 130, 132, 135, 136.
73. *Correspondence of Gustavus Vasa Fox,* I, 344, Farragut to Fox, Feb. 8, 1864, and *Drayton Letters,* 43, Drayton to Hamilton, Feb. 14, 1864.
74. *O. R. Navies,* XXI, 144, Farragut to Jenkins, Mar. 17, 1864.
75. *Drayton Letters,* 47, Drayton to Hamilton, Mar. 20, 1864.
76. Mar. 8, 1864, Ellsworth Eliot, Jr. Collection.
77. *Correspondence of Gustavus Vasa Fox,* I, 345, 346, Farragut to Fox, Feb. 28, 1864.
78. *O. R. Navies,* 796, 797, log of the *Hartford.*

79. *Drayton Letters*, 48, 49, Drayton to Hamilton, Apr. 8, 1864.
80. *Loyall Farragut*, 393-395, Farragut to his wife, Apr. 4, 1864.
81. Apr. 9, 1864, Ellsworth Eliot, Jr. Collection.
82. *The Story of the Confederacy* by R. S. Henry, 341-347, and *The Second Admiral* by Richard West, Jr., 245-263.
83. *O. R. Navies*, XXI, 244, May 6, 1864.
84. May 7, 1864, The Henry E. Huntington Library.
85. *Drayton Letters*, 50, Drayton to Hamilton, Apr. 14, 1864.
86. *Ibid.*, 48, 49, Drayton to Hamilton, Apr. 8, 1864. "Mrs. ——" may have been Mrs. Norman Jackson, mentioned in Drayton's letter to Hamilton of Jan. 26, 1864 (*Ibid.*, 41, 42).

During Michael Hahn's campaign for governor of Mississippi, a meeting was held in Lafayette Square, New Orleans, where Clark Mills's statue of Jackson on the prancing horse is located. Six thousand school children were present. "Banners and bunting had inscriptions to Farragut, Banks, and Hahn as heroes of freedom and men of duty" (*Abraham Lincoln: The War Years* by Carl Sandberg, III, 12).

87. *Drayton Letters*, 50, Drayton to Hamilton, Apr. 14, 1864.
88. *O. R. Navies*, XXI, 172, Farragut to Welles.
89. *Ibid.*, 204, Drayton to Jenkins, Apr. 21, 1864, and *Drayton Letters*, 52, 53, Drayton to Hamilton, Apr. 22, 1864.
90. *Loyall Farragut*, 395, 396, Farragut to his son, Apr. 24, 1864.
91. *O. R. Navies*, XXI, 797, log of the *Hartford*.
92. *Admiral Franklin Buchanan* by Charles Lee Lewis, 215, and *O. R. Navies*, XXI, 892, Buchanan to Catesby ap R. Jones, Apr. 14, 1864.
93. *O. R. Navies*, XXI, 223, Farragut to Welles, Apr. 9, 1864.
94. *Ibid.*, 224, Farragut to Marchand, Apr. 11, 1864, and *Ibid.*, 224, 225, Marchand to Farragut, Apr. 14, 1864.
95. *Ibid.*, 911, 912, Maj.-Gen. Magruder to Sec. of War Seddon, Sept. 29, 1864, and *Ibid.*, 225, Marchand to Farragut, May 15, 1864.
96. *Ibid.*, 225, 226, Farragut to Welles, May 16, 1864.
97. *Ibid.*, 232, Farragut to Welles, June 9, 1864.
98. *Ibid.*, 219, Farragut to Welles, Apr. 30, 1864.
99. *Ibid.*, 270, Farragut to Marchand, May 10, 1864.
100. *My Fifty Years in the Navy* by Rear Admiral Charles E. Clark, 89-91.
101. *O. R. Navies*, XXI, 242, Farragut to Welles, May 3, 1864.
102. *The Second Admiral* by Richard West, Jr., 259-262.
103. *O. R. Navies*, XXI, 250, to Welles, June 9, 1864.
104. *Ibid.*, 897, to Catesby Jones, May 7, 1864.
105. May 3, 1864, Ellsworth Eliot, Jr. Collection.
106. *Admiral Farragut* by A. T. Mahan, 267, undated letter of Farragut to his wife, and letter of June 12, 1942 from George G. Hall to the author.
107. *Admiral Farragut* by A. T. Mahan, 268, undated letter.

XX. THE *TENNESSEE* ENTERS THE BAY

1. *O. R. Navies*, XXI, 244, 245, May 6, 1864.
2. *Ibid.*, 267, 268, Farragut to Welles, May 9, 1864.
3. *Ibid.*, 270, Farragut to Marchand, May 10, 1864.
4. *Ibid.*, 273, Marchand to Farragut, May 11, 1864.
5. *Loyall Farragut*, 400, Farragut to his son, May 12 and 13, 1864. The "Pinkham" sword was given to Farragut Hall, son of George G. Hall, by the executors of the estate of Loyall Farragut. He is now Colonel F. F. Hall of the Second Armored Corps, Camp Polk, Louisiana (Letter of George G. Hall of June 30, 1942 to the author).
6. *O. R. Navies*, XXI, 274, to Jenkins, May 13, 1864.
7. *Battles and Leaders*, IV, 402, "The Ram Tennessee at Mobile Bay" by Commander J. D. Johnston, and *O. R. Navies*, XXI, 935, log of the C.S.S. *Tennessee*.
8. *O. R. Navies*, XXI, 282, 283, stations of vessels in West Gulf Blockading Squadron, May 15, 1864, and *Ibid.*, 293, Capt. James Alden to Welles, May 22, 1864.
9. *Ibid.*, 291, Farragut to Commodore Wm. Smith, May 21, 1864.
10. *Ibid.*, 292.
11. *Loyall Farragut*, 400, May 21, 1864.
12. *Ibid.*, to Loyall Farragut, May 22, 1864.
13. *O. R. Navies*, XXI, 797, log of the *Hartford*.
14. *Ibid.*, 298, May 25, 1864.
15. *Drayton Letters*, 57, Drayton to Hamilton, May 25, 1864.
16. *O. R. Navies*, XXI, 311, Farragut to Gen. Asboth, May 30, 1864.
17. *Ibid.*, 298, 299, Farragut to Bailey, May 26, 1864.
18. June 3, 1864, Ellsworth Eliot, Jr. Collection.
19. *O. R. Navies*, XXI, 317, June 4, 1864.
20. *Ulysses S. Grant: The Great Soldier of America* by Robert R. McCormick, 106.
21. *Ibid.*, 123; *Coast Artillery Journal* (Mar.-Apr., 1941), LXXXIV, 113; and *Story of the Confederacy* by R. S. Henry, 294.
22. *Personal Memoirs of U. S. Grant*, II, 519.
23. *O. R. Armies*, Ser. I, XXXIX, Part II, 79, Grant to Halleck, June 5, 1864.
24. *O. R. Navies*, XXI, 323.
25. *Ibid.*, 344, Welles to Farragut, June 25, 1864.
26. *Ibid.*, XXVI, 379, 380, June 9, 1864.
27. *Ibid.*, 388, June 13, 1864.
28. *Ibid.*, 438, June 25, 1864.
29. *Ibid.*, 450, 451, June 30, 1864.
30. *Ibid.*, XXI, 321, 322, Farragut to Welles, June 7, 1864.
31. *Loyall Farragut*, 402, Farragut to his wife, June 9, 1864.
32. *Drayton Letters*, 58-60, Drayton to S. M. Hoyt, June 19, 1864.
33. *O. R. Navies*, XXI, 331, 332, Farragut to H. A. Wise, Chief of Bureau of Ordnance.

34. *Ibid.*, 331, Farragut to Lieutenant-Commander Fitzhugh, June 11, 1864.
35. *Ibid.*, 336, General Order of June 14, 1864.
36. *Ibid.*, 902, Buchanan to Jones, June 14, 1864.
37. *Ibid.*, 316.
38. *Drayton Letters*, 58-60, Drayton to S. M. Hoyt, June 19, 1864.
39. *O. R. Navies*, XXI, 339, June 18, 1864.
40. *Ibid.*, 333, 334, June 14, 1864.
41. *Loyall Farragut*, 396, May 28, 1864, and *Drayton Letters*, 61, 62, Drayton to Hamilton, July 3, 1864. The sword is now in the National Museum in Washington.
42. *O. R. Navies*, XXI, 339, 340, June 18, 1864.
43. *Loyall Farragut*, 398, June 25, 1864.
44. *Ibid.*, 402, June 21, 1864.
45. *Drayton Letters*, 60, 61, Drayton to Hamilton, June 25, 1864.
46. *O. R. Navies*, XXI, 348, Farragut to Palmer, June 27, 1864.
47. *Ibid.*, 903, 904, Page to Catesby Jones, June 26, 1864.
48. *Ibid.*, 353, 354, Farragut to Welles, July 2, 1864; *Ibid.*, 354, Drayton to Jenkins, July 1, 1864; *Ibid.*, 797, log of the *Hartford*; and *Ibid.*, 829, 830, log of the *Monongahela*.
49. *Ibid.*, 359, Drayton to Jenkins, July 3, 1864.
50. *Loyall Farragut*, 402, 403, July 6, 1864.
51. *O. R. Navies*, XXI, 904, 905, Gen. Maury to Gen. Cooper, July 7, 1864.
52. *Farragut and Mobile Bay—Personal Reminiscences* by J. C. Watson, paper read Dec. 16, 1916 to the Military Order of the Loyal Legion of the United States, Commandery of the District of Columbia. "The admiral assured me," wrote General James Grant Wilson, "that up to 1863 he had made a practice of taking a standing jump over the back of a chair on every birthday, adding, 'and I never felt old until my 62nd birthday came round, and I did not feel equal to the jump'" (*The Criterion* for Apr., 1902). That summer he was ill, while engaged in the siege of Port Hudson.
53. July 6, 1864, Ellsworth Eliot, Jr. Collection.

XXI. THE MONITORS ARRIVE

1. *O. R. Navies*, XXI, 904, telegram of General D. H. Maury to General S. Cooper, July 5, 1864.
2. *Ibid.*, 344.
3. *Ibid.*, 366.
4. *Ibid.*, 798, log of the *Hartford*.
5. *Ibid.*, 375, Farragut to Welles, July 15, 1864.
6. *Ibid.*, 799, log of the *Hartford*.
7. *Drayton Letters*, 63, 64, Drayton to S. M. Hoyt, July 14, 1864.
8. *O. R. Navies*, XXI, 397, 398.
9. *Ibid.*, 375, Farragut to Welles, July 15, 1864.
10. *Ibid.*, 378, 379, July 18, 1864.

11. *Ibid.*, XVII, 653, Feb. 18, 1864.
12. *Ibid.*, 656, 657, Welles to Bailey, Feb. 26, 1864, and *Ibid.*, XXII, 116, Welles to Farragut, Feb. 26, 1864.
13. *Ibid.*, 388, Canby to Farragut, July 26, 1864.
14. *Ibid.*, XXI, 377, Farragut to Bailey, July 16, 1864.
15. *Loyall Farragut*, 403, 404, July 20, 1864.
16. *O. R. Navies*, XXI, 386, Farragut to Canby, July 25, 1864.
17. *Ibid.*, 380, Canby to Sherman, July 20, 1864.
18. *Ibid.*, 388, Canby to Farragut, July 26, 1864.
19. *Ibid.*, 387, Farragut to Welles, July 26, 1864.
20. Farragut to Palmer, July 18, 1864, Zabriskie Collection, Naval Academy Museum. The postscript giving this information was not published with the rest of the letter in *O. R. Navies*, XXI, 378, 379.
21. *Ibid.*, 908, July 25, 1864.
22. *Ibid.*, 799, log of the *Hartford*.
23. *Ibid.*, 390, Commander T. A. M. Craven to Welles, July 29, 1864.
24. *Ibid.*, 398, July 29, 1864.
25. *Ibid.*
26. *Ibid.*, 900.
27. "Farragut and Mobile Bay—Personal Reminiscences" by Rear Admiral John C. Watson, U.S.N., War Paper No. 98 in Military Order of the Loyal Legion of the U.S., Commandery of the District of Columbia.
28. *O. R. Navies*, XXI, 394, Drayton to Jenkins, Aug. 1, 1864 and Drayton to Jenkins, July 31, 1864, and *Ibid.*, 936, log of the *Tennessee*.
29. *Ibid.*, 395, Farragut to Commodore Wm. Smith, Aug. 1, 1864.
30. *Ibid.*, Ser. II, Vol. I, Parts 1 to 4, *passim*. See also *Admiral Franklin Buchanan* by Charles Lee Lewis, 224.
31. *Loyall Farragut*, 404, July 31, 1864.
32. *O. R. Navies*, XXI, 401, Farragut to Jenkins, Aug. 2, 1864.
33. *Ibid.*, 390, Canby to Farragut, July 29, 1864.
34. *Ibid.*, 402, Farragut to Welles, Aug. 3, 1864
35. *Ibid.*, 799, log of the *Hartford*, Aug. 3, 1864, and *Ibid.*, 403, Farragut to Granger, Aug. 3, 1864.
36. *Drayton Letters*, 65, 66, Drayton to Hamilton, Aug. 3, 1864.
37. *O. R. Navies*, XXI, 399, 401, 402, 403.
38. *Ibid.*, 404, Farragut to Commander T. H. Stevens of the *Winnebago*, Aug. 4, 1864.
39. *Ibid.*, 404. One of the original diagrams is in the Manuscript Division of the Library of Congress.
40. *Ibid.*, 838, log of the *Oneida*, Aug. 4, 1864.
41. Aug. 4, 1864, Ellsworth Eliot, Jr. Collection. This letter is quoted in *Loyall Farragut*, 405, 406, accompanied by a photographic facsimile of the original letter. Mahan's *Admiral Farragut*, 266, 267, reproduces the letter with the curious error, "I am going into Mobile in the morning" instead of "I am going into Mobile Bay in

the morning." In reprinting the letter, we have capitalized the pronouns referring to God and have written the word "and" for "&."

XXII. FORCING THE ENTRANCE TO MOBILE BAY

1. *Admiral Farragut* by A. T. Mahan, 269, 270; *Loyall Farragut*, 412; *O. R. Navies*, XXI, 532, Capt. M. D. McAlester to Brig.-Gen. R. Delafield, Aug. 17, 1864; and *Ibid.*, 799, log of the *Hartford*.
2. *O. R. Navies*, XXI, 824, log of the *Manhattan*.
3. "Damn the Torpedoes . . .?" by Lieutenant Colonel Wilfrid Bovey, R. O. in *U. S. Naval Institute Proceedings* (Oct., 1939), LXV, 1446, is incorrect in stating that Farragut had eight sidewheelers in his attacking fleet. This article contains many errors of fact and makes a complete jumble of the first phase of the battle. Apparently the author did not examine the extracts from the logbooks in *O. R. Navies*, XXI; all his references are to *O. R. Armies*.
4. *O. R. Navies*, XXI, 405, 406, Farragut to Welles, Aug. 5, 1864, and *Ibid.*, 404, diagram of the Battle of Mobile Bay.
5. *Loyall Farragut*, 412. This states that he was "sipping his tea"; but a letter of Aug. 5, 1864 from Brooks to his wife, which was shown to the author by the daughter, Mary E. Brooks of Washington, D.C., states that it was "a cup of coffee." Brooks had previously been steward to Captain C. H. Bell and Commodore A. H. Foote. He had been with Farragut since the *Hartford* left New York the previous January.
6. *O. R. Navies*, XXI, 415-421, Farragut to Welles, Aug. 12, 1864.
7. Cf. The Chart of Mobile Bay, Alabama, published in 1856 (Furnished the author by Captain G. T. Rude, Director of U. S. Coast and Geodetic Survey).
8. *My Fifty Years in the Navy* by Rear Admiral Charles E. Clark, 96 Farragut had previously been in doubt as to where to fly his Admiral's pennant (*O. R. Navies*, XIX, 193).
9. *Naval Scenes and Reminiscences of the Civil War in the United States on the Southern and Western Waters* . . . by Rear Admiral H. Walke, U.S.N., 429.
10. *O. R. Navies*, XXI, 428, 429, Executive Officer L. A. Kimberly to Drayton, Aug. 8, 1864.
11. The logs of the ships are at variance as to the exact time. The log of the *Hartford* even disagrees in some details with Farragut's report to Welles of Aug. 12, 1864 (*O. R. Navies*, XXI, 415-421). Cf. *Ibid.*, 783, 784, 786, 794, 804, 805, 808, 819-823, 824, 828, 830-832, 835, 838, 839, 841, 844, 846-848, 852, 799, 800.
12. *Loyall Farragut*, 414, 415; *Battles and Leaders*, IV, 390, 407; *Battle of Mobile Bay* by F. A. Parker, 23; *Scribner's Monthly* (June, 1881), XXII, 306, letter of Sept. 6, 1880 by J. Crittenden Watson; and *Scribner's Monthly* (Feb., 1877), XIII, 542, "Farragut in Mobile Bay, Recollections of One Who Took Part in the Battle" by H. D. Baldwin, who was a signal officer on the *Port Royal*. Baldwin states that

Farragut ascended "the starboard main rigging," stopped just beneath the top, passed his arm through the "lubber's hole," and seized the foot of the pilot, Martin Freeman. When the signal quartermaster came up with a "hammock-lashing" to secure Farragut, he refused to be tied, by Freeman's advice, and went through the battle clinging to the pilot's foot. "To this day, 'old salts' smile over the poetical rendering of Farragut's position, as given by that worthy noncombatant, Ensign Brownell," he concludes. Cf. *U. S. Naval Institute*, VI, 303.

Acting Ensign Marthon, on the *Hartford* in the engagement, states (*Battles and Leaders*, IV, 407) that Farragut was lashed to the "port main rigging" about five or six ratlines up, and that he soon cast off the lashing and climbed up to the "futtock-rigging" where he "lashed himself" and remained during the action.

13. *Army and Navy Journal* (Jan. 7, 1865), II, 309, interview with Drayton. The quartermaster's name appears as Richard Knowles on a photograph in the Naval Academy Museum; as John H. Knowles in the *Photographic History of the Civil War*, VI, 242, and in *O. R. Navies*, XVIII, 616, 620, and 727.
14. *Scribner's Monthly* (Feb., 1877), XIII, 542, "Farragut in Mobile Bay, Recollections of One Who Took Part in the Battle."
15. *The Bay Fight: A Sketch of the Battle of Mobile Bay* . . . by Wm. F. Hutchinson, M.D. (Acting Assistant Surgeon on the *Lackawanna*), 14.
16. *Battle of Mobile Bay* by F. A. Parker, 25.
17. *Admiral Farragut* by A. T. Mahan, 276. Not in letters in *George Hamilton Perkins: His Life and Letters* by C. S. Alden.
18. The author found no explanation for Alden's not using his naval signal officers and men.
19. *O. R. Navies*, XXI, 508, copy of official signal message of Capt. E. A. Denicke to Maj. F. W. Marston, Aug. 5, 1864; *Ibid.*, 525, 526, report of Marston, Aug. 10, 1864; *Battles and Leaders*, IV, 387, 388, "Farragut at Mobile Bay" by Lieut. John C. Kinney, U.S.A.; and *Scribner's Monthly* (June, 1881), XXII, 199-208, "An August Morning with Farragut" by Lieut. John C. Kinney. Farragut's report of Aug. 12, 1864 states that the *Brooklyn* stopped before the *Tecumseh* was sunk (*O. R. Navies*, XXI, 417).
20. Notebook of D. G. Farragut in manuscript, owned by Mr. George T. Keating.
21. *O. R. Navies*, XXI, 404, Aug. 4, 1864.
22. *Battles and Leaders*, IV, 388, 391, footnote.
23. *O. R. Navies*, XXI, 508, copy of signal. The logbooks of the *Manhattan* and *Metacomet* record 7:30 as the time the *Tecumseh* sank; the logbook of the *Brooklyn* gives 7:25 and the *Richmond* 7:45; the *Hartford's* logbook and Farragut's report of Aug. 5, 1864 give the time as 7:40 (*Ibid.*, 824, 828, 783, 846, 799, 405). As usual, watches were at variance perhaps; but 7:30 agrees with the time series of the signals.
24. Notebook of D. G. Farragut in manuscript, owned by Mr. George

T. Keating. Without citing his authority, Mahan in his *Admiral Farragut*, 274, gives a portion of this incident. On 273, Mahan quotes from a "private letter" by Farragut, as stating, "I believe that the *Tecumseh* would have gone up and grappled with the *Tennessee*. Craven's heart was bent upon it."

"*Tecumseh* went down like a flash within 500 yards of Fort Morgan" (*Diary* of Ensign Philip H. Cooper, U.S.N. on *Richmond* in Battle of Mobile Bay, as quoted in *Life in Letters*, Nov., 1940, published by American Autograph Shop). "The open channel free of torpedoes between the black buoy and the fort was 500 yards wide" (*O. R. Navies*, XXI, 569, Lieut. F. S Barrett, in charge of torpedoes, to Lieutenant J. T. E. Andrews, Aug. 20, 1864). Capt. V. Sheliha stated that the width of the free channel was 226 yards (*O. R. Armies*, Ser. I, XXXIX, Part II, 739). "The *Tecumseh* is buoyed and lies very near Fort Morgan, say two or three hundred yards from the wharf, in a southwest direction, the pilots say in 7 fathoms water, with 3 fathoms over her" (*O. R. Navies*, XXI, 725, Farragut to Welles, Nov. 9, 1864). For expressions of doubt as to the *Tecumseh's* being sunk by a torpedo of the torpedo field, see *O. R. Navies*, XXI, 556, telegram of Gen. Maury to Secretary of War Seddon, Aug. 5, 1864; *Southern Historical Society Papers* (Sept., 1881), IX, 471, "The Battle of Mobile Bay" by Commander J. D. Johnston in answer to "An August Morning with Farragut" by Kinney in *Scribner's Monthly* for June, 1881; and *O. R. Navies*, XXI, 598, Capt. J. W. Whiting, C.S.A. to Gen. Maury, Oct. 4, 1864.

For fanciful story of conditions in *Tecumseh* after she went down, see *The Bay Fight* by W. F. Hutchinson, M.D., 17, 18. There is no record that divers ever examined the wreck. It has never been raised. In Aug. 1873, James E. Slaughter purchased the *Tecumseh* for $50, but on Aug. 15, 1876 a joint resolution of Congress refunded the money with interest. The resolution permitted future sale with provision that the bodies be removed for burial under supervision of the Secretary of the Navy. Robert Craven, son of Capt. Craven, wrote the Secretary, Sept. 22, 1876, that his father's body had never been recovered, that the family had been told various reports as to his going down inside the vessel, and that he had heard of the projected raising of the wreck and wished to communicate with the contractor. The Chart of Mobile Bay of Nov., 1864 placed the sunken *Tecumseh* about 450 yards northwest of the shore nearest Fort Morgan.

25. "The Battle of Mobile Bay in a Monitor" by Chief Engineer Harrie Webster, U.S.N., *War Paper, No. 14, Commandery of the State of California, Military Order of the Loyal Legion of the United States,* 12. The *Winnebago* was within a cable's length of the *Tecumseh* when she sank (*O. R. Navies*, XXI, 496, Commander Stevens to Farragut, Aug. 6, 1864).

26. "Battle of Mobile Bay" by A. D. Wharton, in Nashville *Daily American*, Sept. 13, 1877.

27. *O. R. Navies*, XXI, 579, Commander J. D. Johnston to Admiral Franklin Buchanan, Aug. 13, 1864. This letter, as printed in *O. R. Armies*, Ser. I, XXXIX, Part I, 446 and in *Southern Historical Society Papers*, VI, 224, reads, "the *Tennessee* was moved down to the middle of the channel just *outside* the line of torpedoes stretching across it." The original letter has disappeared. Dr. D. S. Freeman wrote the author, June 3, 1942, "I am exceedingly sorry to say that all the records of the Southern Historical Society that concerned events as remote as those in the publication of Volume 6 have been destroyed years ago."

"An instant before I had seen this noble vessel [*Tecumseh*] pushing on gallantly in a straight line to attack the enemy's ram *Tennessee*, which had apparently moved out to give her an opportunity" (*O. R. Navies*, XXI, 425-428, Drayton to Farragut, Aug. 6, 1864).

28. *Battle of Mobile Bay* by F. A. Parker, 26, and A. D. Wharton in Nashville *Daily American*, Sept. 13, 1877.

29. *United Service: A Monthly Review of Military and Naval Affairs* (Sept., 1892), new series, VIII, 262, article by Surgeon D. B. Conrad of the *Tennessee*.

30. *Ibid.* Conrad, a prisoner of war at Pensacola, talked with Pilot Collins. Cf. *The Monitor and the Navy under Steam* by Lieut. Frank M. Bennett, U.S.N., 206; *Battle of Mobile Bay* by F. A. Parker, 27. Dr. Wm. F. Hutchinson, who served on the *Lackawanna* in the battle, states in his *Bay Fight*, 18: "He [Craven] was partly out, when the pilot grasped him by the leg, and cried, 'Let me get out first, Captain, for God's sake; I have five little children!' The Captain drew back, saying, 'Go on, sir,' gave him his place, and went down with his ship, while the pilot was saved." A letter by two survivors, C. F. Langley and Gardner Cottrell, Acting Masters, written to Farragut, Aug. 6, 1864, states: "Captain Craven was seen on the turret by Mr. Cottrell just before the vessel sunk, and as he had a life-preserving vest on we have hopes that he reached the shore" (*O. R. Navies*, XXI, 490). "Craven, knowing that it was through no fault of the pilot, but by his own command, that the fatal change in her course had been made, stepped back, saying, 'After you, pilot' " (*Loyall Farragut*, 425). John J. P. Zettick, one of the rescued, was an acting ensign in charge of ammunition under the turret. He wrote that, when the ship was struck, her guns had just been reloaded. Lieutenant Kelly ordered, "Remain at your stations," but Zettick stated that he unbuckled his belt and let his sword and revolver drop on deck. He then climbed up into the turret which was deserted, and then out and on top "under the lea of the pilot house." He was carried down by the suction of the ship but, being an expert swimmer, was rescued by Nields' boat after three quarters of an hour in the water (*1862-1902, In Commemoration of Our 40th Anniversary* by M. F. Tobin, letter of Zettick, Oct. 16, 1899). John Ericsson, in "The Building of the Monitor" in *Battles and Leaders*, I, 735, declared that, if the pilot house of the *Tecumseh* had had an iron plate on top "let down into

an appropriate groove but not bolted down," Craven and others might have been saved. This was the arrangement he provided for the first and original *Monitor*. For an imaginative sketch of the sinking of the *Tecumseh*, see *Harper's Weekly* (Sept. 10, 1864), 581.

31. *O. R. Navies*, XXI, 492, list of officers and crew, and *Ibid.*, 490, names of the rescued men. The figure 114 was derived by checking earlier rolls and records of transfers and from lists furnished by the survivors (Copy of letter of June 29, 1938 from Capt. D. W. Knox, Officer-in-Charge, Naval Records and Library, to W. W. Dowling).

32. *O. R. Navies*, XXI, 442, Jouett to Farragut, Aug. 8, 1864; *The Battle of Mobile Bay* by F. A. Parker, 30; and a scrapbook sent the author by the daughter of Nields. Parker states that Nields was then a "mere boy," but he was twenty-five years old.

33. *Battles and Leaders*, IV, 408, "The Defense of Fort Morgan" by Brig.-Gen. R. L. Page, C.S.A.

34. Nashville *Daily American*, Sept. 13, 1877, Wharton's article. In quoting Wharton, *The Battle of Mobile Bay* by F. A. Parker, 30, substitutes for "their heads" the phrase, "the heads of that glorious boat's crew."

35. *O. R. Navies*, XXI, 508, copy of signal.

36. *Ibid.*, 445, 446, Capt. James Alden to Farragut, Aug. 6, 1864.

37. *Ibid.*, 783, log of the *Brooklyn*.

38. Loyall Farragut, 544. *History of the Parish of the Incarnation* by J. Newton Perkins states, "Farragut offered a prayer in substance: 'O God, my Maker, in this time of trial show me my duty to my country.' He seemed to hear a voice from above telling him to go forward. He obeyed the high behest of duty, and he conquered." *Admiral Farragut* by A. T. Mahan, 277, states that Farragut related the incident in his "later days." Watson relates, "We learn from letters to his family that he had found time to ask God for guidance, and he believed he heard a voice say, 'Go on!'" (Farragut and Mobile Bay—Personal Reminiscences" by Rear Admiral John C. Watson, U.S.N., War Paper, No. 98 in *Military Order of the Loyal Legion of the United States, Commandery of the District of Columbia*, read Dec. 16, 1916). General James Grant Wilson in "Recollections of Admiral Farragut" in *The Criterion* of Apr., 1902, declared, "His clergyman says: 'On that occasion, while the admiral was lashed in the rigging of the Hartford, he offered up a prayer in the following words: "O God, my Maker, lead me to do this day what is right and best for my country!" In answer to this prayer the admiral said he heard a voice from heaven, which seemed, in tones of thunder, to say, "Go forward!" He obeyed the voice and moved on to victory in the dear old *Hartford*.'"

39. *O. R. Navies*, XXI, 417, Farragut to Welles, Aug. 12, 1864. Out of first five torpedoes removed from channel after surrender of Fort Morgan one was still dry and dangerous. One of five more taken out was carelessly handled on shore and killed 5 men and wounded 9

(*Ibid.*, 616, 617, Farragut to Welles, Aug. 29, 1864). "The torpedoes in the channel were also harmless; owing to the depth of the water, the strong tides, and the imperfect moorings none exploded" (*Battles and Leaders*, IV, 409, article by Brig.-Gen. Page). "They had been planted so long that many leaked, only one out of ten remaining intact, and this fact explains why so many were run over by the Federal fleet" (*Southern Historical Society Papers*, XIX, 81, article by Dr. D. B. Conrad). "How it is that all the other vessels escaped from torpedoes is a mystery, for we see by the books captured at Fort Gaines that about 90 were planted on the 3d and 4th alone. I suspect that their harmlessness consists in the great difficulty of keeping the powder dry" (*Drayton Letters*, 67, 68, Drayton to Hamilton, Aug. 19, 1864). Quincunx arrangement is given in letter of Myer to Farragut, July 13, 1864 (*Ibid.*, 372, 374). Officers of *Richmond* and *Hartford* were said to have heard the primers snapping (*Battles and Leaders*, IV, 391 footnote).

40. There is no authority for this famous slogan in the official records and the personal letters of Farragut, Drayton, and other officers in the fleet. It seems to have first appeared in F. A. Parker's *Battle of Mobile Bay* (1878), 29. The next year, Loyall Farragut repeated it in the biography of his father, 416, 417. Lieut. J. C. Kinney in "An August Morning with Farragut" in *Scribner's Monthly* (June, 1881), 205, writes: "On board a war steamer the engines are directed by the tap of a bell, the wires connected with which lead to the quarter-deck. One stroke of the bell means 'go ahead'; two, 'stop'; three, 'back'; and four, 'go ahead as fast as possible.' Leaning down through the shrouds to the officer on deck at the bellpull, the admiral shouted, 'Four bells, eight bells, sixteen bells! Give her all the steam you've got.' " Kinney wrote an article for *Battles and Leaders* (1884), IV, 379-400, based on that in *Scribner's Monthly*, in which he writes: "As he [Farragut] passed the *Brooklyn,* a voice warned him of the torpedoes, to which he returned the contemptuous answer, 'Damn the torpedoes.' This is the current story, and may have some basis of truth. But as a matter of fact, there was never a moment when the din of the battle would not have drowned any attempt at conversation between the two ships, and while it is quite probable that the admiral made the remark it is doubtful if he shouted it to the *Brooklyn*" (391). "I was standing on the poop deck at the time, and heard the admiral shout, on the instant, it seemed: 'Damn the torpedoes! Full speed ahead, Drayton! Hard a starboard! Ring four bells! Eight bells! Sixteen bells!' I think he also called to Commander Jouett of the *Metacomet* to back, for she did so" ("Farragut and Mobile Bay—Personal Reminiscences" by Rear Admiral John C. Watson, U.S.N., War Paper No. 98, *Military Order of the Loyal Legion of the United States, Commandery of the District of Columbia*, Dec. 16, 1916). The Reverend Thom Williamson, Jr. writes in the *U. S. Naval Institute Proceedings* (Nov., 1939), LXV, 1676, that his grandfather, the late

Rear Admiral Thom Williamson (E.C.), U. S. Navy was standing near Farragut, and received from him the order, "Go ahead." He replied, "Shall I ring four bells, sir?" Farragut answered, "Four bells—eight bells—sixteen bells—damn it, I don't care how many bells you ring!" This incident, he declared, was related to him many times.

41. *U. S. Naval Institute Proceedings* (Dec., 1939), LXV, 1778, discussion by Rear Admiral Ammen Farenholt (M.C.), U.S.N. (Retired) of an incident related to him by the late Rear Admiral W. H. Whiting, U.S.N., acting ensign and one of Farragut's aides and an eyewitness.
42. *O. R. Navies*, XXI, 372, 374, Myer to Farragut, July 13, 1864, and *Battles and Leaders*, IV, 391 footnote.
43. *Southern Historical Society Papers* (Sept., 1881), IX, 471, "The Battle of Mobile Bay" by Commander J. D. Johnston, C.S.N.
44. *O. R. Navies*, XXI, 800, log of the *Hartford*, and *Ibid.*, 417, Farragut to Welles, Aug. 12, 1864.
45. *Ibid.*, 828, log of the *Metacomet*, and *Ibid.*, 442, Jouett to Farragut, Aug. 8, 1864.
46. *Ibid.*, 783, log of the *Brooklyn*.
47. *Ibid.*, 847, log of the *Richmond*.
48. *Ibid.*, 808, log of the *Lackawanna*.
49. *Ibid.*, 831, log of the *Monongahela*.
50. *Ibid.*, 806, log of the *Kennebec*.
51. *Ibid.*, 841, log of the *Ossipee*.
52. *Ibid.*, 838, log of the *Oneida*.
53. *Ibid.*, 479, Lieut. Charles L. Huntington to Farragut, Aug. 6, 1864.
54. *Ibid.*, 800, log of the *Hartford*.
55. *Naval Scenes and Reminiscences of the Civil War in the United States on the Southern and Western Waters . . .* by Rear Admiral H. Walke, U.S.N., 431.
56. *Battles and Leaders*, IV, 407, article by Acting Ensign Joseph Marthon.
57. *O. R. Navies*, XXI, 800, log of the *Hartford*.
58. *Ibid.*, 588-590, Lieut. J. W. Bennett to Secretary of Navy Mallory.
59. *Ibid.*, 587, 588, Lieut. P. U. Murphey to Admiral Buchanan, Aug. 15, 1864; *Ibid.*, 442, 443, Jouett to Farragut, Aug. 8, 1864; and *Prince and Boatswain* by J. M. Morgan and others, chapter on Jouett.
60. *O. R. Navies*, XXI, 505, Farragut to Welles, Aug. 8, 1864, and *Ibid.*, 507, Farragut to Welles, Sept. 8, 1864.
61. *Ibid.*, 558, Brig.-Gen. Page to Maj.-Gen. Maury, Aug. 6, 1864, and *Battles and Leaders*, IV, 409, "The Defense of Fort Morgan" by Brig.-Gen. Page. The casualty list appears to have been lost.
62. *O. R. Armies*, Ser. I, XXXIX, Part II, 786, 787, indorsement by Maj.-Gen. D. H. Maury on Lieut. F. S. Barrett's report of Aug. 20, 1864, and *O. R. Navies*, XXI, 598, Capt. J. W. Whiting, C.S.A. to Maj.-Gen. Maury, Oct. 4, 1864.
63. *Admiral Farragut* by A. T. Mahan, 288, 289.

XXIII. THE CAPTURE OF THE *TENNESSEE*

1. *Southern Historical Society Papers*, XIX, 74, article by Surgeon D. B. Conrad, C.S.N., reprinted from the *Winchester* (Va.) *Times*, Nov. 26, 1890; and *The United Service: A Monthly Review of Military and Naval Affairs* (Sept., 1892), new series, VIII, 261-270, "What the Fleet Surgeon Saw of the Fight in Mobile Bay" by Dr. D. B. Conrad. His statement that everything "standing as large as your little finger" had been swept clean from the decks of the *Tennessee* is an exaggeration. The smokestacks were not brought down until later.
2. *Ibid.*, 80, and *Admiral Franklin Buchanan* by Charles Lee Lewis, 242, 243.
3. *Naval Scenes and Reminiscences of the Civil War in the United States on the Southern and Western Waters* . . . by Rear Admiral H. Walke, U.S.N., 432.
4. Notebook of D. G. Farragut in manuscript, owned by George T. Keating. Mahan's *Admiral Farragut*, 281, states that Farragut said to Drayton, "As soon as the people have had their breakfasts, I am going for her," and cites Rear Admiral Kimberly, then first lieutenant on the *Hartford*, as his authority.
5. *Battles and Leaders*, IV, 407, article by Capt. J. C. Watson, U.S.N.
6. *O. R. Navies*, XXI, 418, Farragut to Welles, Aug. 12, 1864.
7. Palmer to Loyall Farragut, May 2, 1879, Ellsworth Eliot, Jr. Collection.
8. *O. R. Navies*, XXI, 831, log of the *Monongahela*.
9. *Ibid.*, 509, copy of signal.
10. *Loyall Farragut*, 424. See Report No. 1371, House of Representatives, 48th Congress, 1st Session for this recognition of Palmer's service: "In the late Civil War, as fleet-surgeon under Admiral Farragut, at the Battle of Mobile, he greatly distinguished himself by going from ship to ship to relieve the wants of the wounded, regardless of danger to his own person, and carried in person from the Admiral the orders which resulted in the capture of the rebel ironclad and the Admiral of the Confederate fleet." This was called to the author's attention in a letter of Feb. 3, 1942 from A. Kenny C. Palmer, the grandson.
11. *Admiral Farragut* by A. T. Mahan, 285, quoted from Palmer's diary. The author has been unable to locate the diary of Palmer.
12. *O. R. Navies*, XXI, 418, Farragut to Welles, Aug. 12, 1864. The original manuscript of Farragut's report is in the Zabriskie Collection in the Naval Academy Museum. In this, he wrote, "Then commenced one of the fiercest fights on record." This manuscript is of unusual interest as it shows how Farragut's secretaries edited his reports and other correspondence.
13. *Ibid.*, 831, log of the *Monongahela; Ibid.*, 473, Executive Officer O. A. Batcheller to Commander J. H. Strong, Aug. 5, 1864; *Ibid.*, 472, Strong to Farragut, Aug. 6, 1864; and *Ibid.*, 418, Farragut to Welles, Aug. 12, 1864.
14. *Ibid.*, 466, Capt. J. B. Marchand to Farragut, Aug. 5, 1864; *Ibid.*,

808, log of the *Lackawanna;* and *Ibid.*, 418, Farragut to Welles, Aug. 12, 1864.
15. *Admiral Farragut* by A. T. Mahan, 272, letter of Farragut to his wife without date. The letter also declares: "The illustrated papers are very amusing. Leslie has me lashed up to the mast like a culprit and says, 'It is the way officers will hereafter go into battle.' " Cf. *Frank Leslie's Illustrated Newspaper,* Sept. 10, 1864: "American Naval Officer Going into Action—New Style Invented by Commodore Farragut." See also "Farragut and Mobile Bay—Personal Reminiscences" by Rear Admiral John C. Watson, U.S.N., War Paper No. 98, *Military Order of the Loyal Legion, Commandery of the District of Columbia,* Dec. 16, 1916; and *Battles and Leaders,* IV, 407, article by Capt. J. C. Watson.
16. *O. R. Navies,* XXI, 800, log of the *Hartford,* and *Ibid.*, 418, Farragut to Welles, Aug. 12, 1864.
17. *Scribner's Monthly* (June, 1881), XXII, 208, "An August Morning" by J. C. Kinney.
18. *O. R. Navies,* XXI, 425-428, Drayton to Farragut, Aug. 6, 1864.
19. *United Service: A Monthly Review of Military and Naval Affairs* (Sept., 1892), new series, VIII, 265, article by Dr. D. B. Conrad.
20. *Loyall Farragut,* 426, 427, based almost verbatim on a letter from Drayton to Mrs. Farragut, Aug. 25, 1864, in Zabriskie Collection, Naval Academy Museum.
21. *The Battle of Mobile Bay* by F. A. Parker, 35, and *O. R. Navies,* XXI, 418, Farragut to Welles.
22. *O. R. Navies,* XXI, 664, Farragut to Welles, Sept. 27, 1864. Nicholson's report to Farragut of Aug. 6, 1864 says he fired six times at the *Tennessee* (*Ibid.*, 493).
23. *Ibid.*, 681, 682, Perkins to Farragut, Oct. 13, 1864. While passing the fort he fired 75 shells, and fired 52 solid shot at the *Tennessee.*
24. *Ibid.*, 579-581, Commander J. D. Johnston to Buchanan, Aug. 13, 1864. Dr. Conrad in *Southern Historical Society Papers,* XIX, 76, 77 has this gruesome account of the incident: "Suddenly there was a dull sounding impact, and at the same instant the men whose backs were against the shield were split in pieces. I saw their limbs and chests, severed and mangled, scattered about the deck, their hearts lying near their bodies. All of the gun's crew and the admiral were covered from head to foot with blood, flesh, and viscera. I thought at first the admiral was mortally wounded. The fragments and members of the dead men were shoveled up, put in buckets and hammocks." See also Johnston's article on the battle in *Battles and Leaders,* IV, 404.
25. *Southern Historical Society Papers,* XIX, 78, article by Conrad.
26. *O. R. Navies,* XXI, 579-581, Johnston to Buchanan, Aug. 13, 1864, and *Battles and Leaders,* IV, 401-406, article by Johnston.
27. *Battles and Leaders,* IV, 404. "Le Roy . . . was a perfect example of a gentleman of the old school. Once, when he was about to ram an

enemy's ship, an officer remarked to another standing near him: 'There goes Lord Chesterfield at the Reb. I'll wager he's getting ready to apologize now for being obliged to hit him so hard' " (*My Fifty Years in the Navy* by Admiral Charles E. Clark, U.S.N., 91). See also *O. R. Navies*, XXI, 475, 476, LeRoy to Farragut, Aug. 6, 1864.

28. *O. R. Navies*, XXI, 842, log of the *Ossipee*. According to Surgeon Conrad in *The United Service: A Monthly Review of Military and Naval Affairs* (Sept., 1892), new series, VIII, 267, "Two creatures dressed in blue shirts, begrimed and black with powder, rushed up to the wounded admiral and demanded his sword. His aide refused peremptorily, whereupon one of them stooped as if to take it anyhow; upon which Aide Forrest warned him not to touch it, as it would only be given to Admiral Farragut or his authorized representative. Still the man attempted to seize it, whereupon Forrest knocked him off the shield to the deck below. At this critical moment, when a fight was imminent, I saw a boat nearing flying a captain's pennant, and running down as it came alongside I recognized an old shipmate, Captain Le Roy. I hurriedly explained to him our position, whereupon he mounted the shield and, assuming command, he arrested the obnoxious man and sent him under guard to his boat. The sword was then given to Captain Giraud by Admiral Buchanan, to be carried to Admiral Farragut. Our flag, smoke-stained and torn, was seized by the other man and hastily concealed in his shirt bosom. He was brought before Captain Le Roy, and amidst the laughter and jeers of his companions, was compelled to draw it forth from its hiding place, and it was sent on board the flagship. These two heroes were said to be the correspondents of some New York and Chicago newspapers."

According to R. C. Bowles, in Richmond *Times*, Oct. 5, 1893, ". . . Mr. Forrest of Virginia, Master's Mate, learning that the ship was about to surrender, ran down and begged the admiral to give him his sword. He did not want Farragut to have it. He made no reply, but Mr. Forrest unbuckled the sword and threw it out of the porthole." According to Chief Engineer Harrie Webster in "The Battle of Mobile Bay in a Monitor," War Paper No. 14, *Military Order of the Loyal Legion of the United States, Commandery of the State of California*, 17, "By direction of our captain, the first lieutenant stepped aboard the ram, now alongside, and, seizing the rebel flag lying in the starboard scuppers, brought it aboard the *Manhattan* and tossed it into the turret through a gun port."

The flag of the *Tennessee* now is in the Naval Historical Foundation, Navy Department, given by Mrs. Larz Anderson, daughter of Commodore George H. Perkins. This flag together with that of the *Selma* and flags of Forts Morgan and Gaines were forwarded to Rear-Admiral H. Paulding, New York Navy Yard (*O. R. Navies*, XXI, 541). The author has been able to locate only the flag of the *Tennessee*.

Buchanan's sword, worn as Superintendent of U. S. Naval Academy and during his service in the Confederate Navy and surrendered to Farragut at Mobile Bay, was given by Loyall Farragut, after the war, to Buchanan's widow and presented to U. S. Naval Academy Museum, May 10, 1924, by Ensign Franklin Buchanan Sullivan, U.S.N.
29. *O. R. Navies*, XXI, 578, Buchanan to Secretary of Navy Mallory, Aug. 25, 1864, in postscript dated Sept. 17, 1864. Farragut's report to Welles, Aug. 12, 1864 (*Ibid.*, 418), is in error in stating that Johnston surrendered his sword and "that of Buchanan" to him on the *Hartford*.
30. *Ibid.*, 800, log of the *Hartford*. "I took her in tow and brought her to anchor near the *Hartford*" (*Ibid.*, 500, 501, Perkins to Farragut, Aug. 7, 1864).
31. *Battles and Leaders*, IV, 404, 405, article by Johnston.
32. *The United Service* (Sept., 1892), new series, VIII, 267.
33. *Loyall Farragut*, 427, 428, quoting from Palmer's diary.
34. *O. R. Navies*, XXI, 828, log of the *Metacomet*.
35. *Prince and Boatswain* by Rear Admiral Charles E. Clark and others, "Jim Jouett," 105.
36. *O. R. Navies*, XXI, 425.
37. Notebook of D. G. Farragut, owned by George T. Keating.
38. *O. R. Navies*, XXI, 406, 407, Farragut to Welles, Aug. 8, 1864, and *Ibid.*, 425-428, Drayton to Farragut, Aug. 6, 1864.
39. *Ibid., passim.*
40. *Admiral Franklin Buchanan* by Charles Lee Lewis, 219-245.
41. *O. R. Navies*, XXI, 442, 443, Jouett to Farragut, Aug. 8, 1864.
42. *Ibid.*, 590, Bennett to Secretary of Navy Mallory, Aug. 8, 1864.
43. *Loyall Farragut*, 422, 423, Farragut to his wife, Aug. 5, 1864.
44. *O. R. Navies*, XXI, 438.

XXIV. THE SURRENDER OF THE FORTS

1. Notebook of D. G. Farragut in manuscript, owned by George T. Keating.
2. *O. R. Navies*, XXI, 560, 561, Williams to Colonel G. G. Garner, C.S.A., Aug. 7, 1864, and *Ibid.*, 502, 503, Lieutenant-Commander J. C. P. de Krafft, U.S.N. to Farragut, Aug. 6, 1864.
3. *Ibid.*, 801, log of the *Hartford*.
4. Diary of D. G. Farragut, owned by George T. Keating.
5. *O. R. Navies*, XXI, 504, 505, Pomeroy to Lieutenant-Commander J. C. P. de Krafft, Aug. 6, 1864. Pomeroy listed 11 guns, though he thought another rifle was buried in the debris. De Krafft reported to Farragut, Aug. 6, 1864 (*Ibid.*, 503) that Pomeroy found 7 heavy guns and 6 fieldpieces. Gen Granger's report of Aug. 8, 1864 states that Fort Powell's "18 guns" were left in "excellent condition for immediate service" (*O. R. Armies*, Ser. I, XXXIX, Part I, 417).
6. *O. R. Navies*, XXI, 523, Aug. 6, 1864.
7. *Ibid.*, 439.

8. *Ibid.*
9. *Ibid.*
10. *Ibid.*
11. *Ibid.*, 801, log of the *Hartford*, and *Ibid.*, 414, Farragut to Welles, Aug. 8, 1864.
12. *Ibid.*, 414, to Farragut, Aug. 7, 1864.
13. *Ibid.*, 801, log of the *Hartford; Ibid.*, 414, Farragut to Welles, Aug. 8, 1864; and Diary of D. G. Farragut, owned by George T. Keating.
14. *O. R. Navies*, XXI, 562, telegram of Maj.-Gen. Maury to Secretary of War Seddon, Aug. 8, 1864, and *Ibid.*, 441.
15. *Ibid.*, 801, log of the *Hartford; Ibid.*, 414, Farragut to Welles, Aug. 8, 1864; and Diary of D. G. Farragut, owned by George T. Keating.
16. *O. R. Navies*, XXI, 563, Maj.-Gen. D. H. Maury to Adjutant and Inspector General S. Cooper, Aug. 9, 1864, and *Ibid.*, 566, Maury to Seddon, Aug. 12, 1864.
17. *Ibid.*, 566, Maury to Seddon, Aug. 12, 1864. Granger's report of Aug. 8, 1864 (*Ibid.*, 524) states that 818 prisoners and 26 guns were taken. Gen. Canby in a letter of Aug. 9, 1864 to Halleck (*Ibid.*) raises the total to 26 guns and 865 men.
18. Diary of D. G. Farragut, owned by George T. Keating.
19. *Loyall Farragut*, 423.
20. *O. R. Navies*, XXI, 440, Butler to Fox, Aug. 8, 1864, 2:30 P.M., and *Ibid.*, Butler to Lincoln, Aug. 8, 1864, 3 P.M. The first stated that the *Tennessee* was sunk, and did not mention the loss of the *Tecumseh*. The second stated that the *Tecumseh* was sunk by Fort Morgan. The first stated that Buchanan was captured; the second that he had lost a leg—an inaccuracy in the early Federal reports.
21. New York *Evening Post*, New York *Daily Tribune*, etc. of Aug. 9, 1864.
22. *Diary of Gideon Welles*, II, 100.
23. *Drayton Letters*, 67, 68, Drayton to Hamilton, Aug. 19, 1864.
24. *Ibid.*, 101. Cf. Note number 20.
25. *O. R. Navies*, XXI, 801, log of the *Hartford*.
26. *Ibid.*, 563, Page to Farragut, Aug. 9, 1864.
27. Diary of D. G. Farragut, owned by George T. Keating.
28. *O. R. Navies*, XXI, 523, Aug. 9, 1864.
29. *Ibid.*, 559, Aug. 7, 1864, and *Ibid.*, 562, Aug. 8, 1864.
30. *Ibid.*, 563, Maury to Adj. and Insp. Gen. S. Cooper, Aug. 9, 1864, and *Ibid.*, 566, Maury to Seddon, Aug. 12, 1864.
31. Diary of D. G. Farragut, owned by George T. Keating; *O. R. Navies*, XXI, 529, 530, Farragut to Welles, Aug. 16, 1864; *Ibid.*, 559, Lieut.-Col. Von Sheliha to Maj.-Gen. J. F. Gilmer, Aug. 6, 1864; and *Ibid.*, 565, telegram of Von Sheliha to Gilmer, Aug. 10, 1864.
32. Diary of D. G. Farragut, owned by George T. Keating, and *O. R. Navies*, XXI, 802, log of the *Hartford*.
33. Diary of D. G. Farragut, owned by George T. Keating.
34. *Loyall Farragut*, 463, Aug. 12, 1864.

35. *O. R. Navies*, XXI, 527, Farragut to Welles, Aug. 13, 1864, and *Ibid.*, 539, report of Commander Nicholson of *Manhattan* to Farragut, Aug. 26, 1864.
36. *Ibid.*, 530, telegram of Canby to Halleck, Aug. 17, 1864.
37. Diary of D. G. Farragut, owned by George T. Keating, and *Loyall Farragut*, 469, letter, n.d., to Mrs. Farragut.
38. *Drayton Letters*, 67, 68, Drayton to Hamilton, Aug. 19, 1864, and Diary of D. G. Farragut, owned by George T. Keating.
39. *O. R. Navies*, XXI, 535, 536, Farragut to Welles, Aug. 23, 1864, and *Ibid.*, 802, log of the *Hartford*.
40. *Ibid.*, 571, Page to Maury, Aug. 23, 1864; *Battle of Mobile Bay* by F. A. Parker, 43; *Battles and Leaders*, IV, 410, "The Defense of Fort Morgan" by Brig.-Gen. R. L. Page; and *Loyall Farragut*, 467, official report of Brig.-Gen. R. K. Arnold, U.S.A.
41. Page to Drayton and Brig.-Gen. Arnold, Aug. 23, 1864, Zabriskie Collection, Naval Academy Museum. Page, in *Battles and Leaders*, IV, 410, states that the white flag was hoisted at six o'clock.
42. *O. R. Navies*, XXI, 803, log of the *Hartford*, and Diary of D. G. Farragut, owned by George T. Keating.
43. *O. R. Armies*, Ser. I. XXXIX, Part I, 419, 420, detailed list by Lieut. C. S. Sargent, U.S.A., Aug. 24, 1864. Canby telegraphed Halleck that about "600 prisoners" and "60 pieces of artillery" were taken (*Ibid.*, 404). The Diary of D. G. Farragut, owned by George T. Keating, gives the number as 780 men and 40 officers. This may be an error, caused by confusion with reported captures in Fort Gaines. Cf. Note 17 above. Page, in *Battles and Leaders*, IV, 409, refers to "my garrison of 400 men." Page to Maury, Aug. 30, 1864, mentions "my limited garrison of some 400 effectives" (*O. R. Armies*, Ser. I, XXXIX, Part I, 439).
44. *O. R. Armies*, Ser. I, XXXIX, Part I, 404, Canby to Halleck, telegram of Aug. 1864.
45. *Battles and Leaders*, IV, 400, statistics.
46. Diary of D. G. Farragut, owned by George T. Keating, and *O. R. Navies*, XXI, 536, 537, Farragut to Welles, Aug. 25, 1864.
47. *O. R. Navies*, XXI, 541, 542, Aug. 26, 1864.
48. Notebook of D. G. Farragut, owned by George T. Keating.
49. *O. R. Armies*, Ser. I, XXXIX, Part I, 405.
50. Zabriskie Collection, Naval Academy Museum. Only an excerpt from this letter is published in *O. R. Navies*, XXI, 538.
51. *George Hamilton Perkins* by C. S. Alden, Aug. 24, 1864, 202, 203.
52. *Admiral Farragut* by A. T. Mahan, 252, undated letter.
53. *O. R. Navies*, XXI, 616, Farragut to Welles, Aug. 29, 1864.
54. *Drayton Letters*, 67, 68, to Alexander Hamilton, Jr., Aug. 19, 1864.
55. Diary of D. G. Farragut, owned by George T. Keating, Aug. 28, 1864.
56. *O. R. Navies*, XXI, 551.
57. Aug. 10, 1864, Zabriskie Collection, Naval Academy Museum.
58. *O. R. Navies*, XXI, 526, 527, Aug. 11, 1864.

59. Aug., 1864, Ellsworth Eliot, Jr. Collection.
60. *Diary of Gideon Welles*, II, 105, 106.
61. *O. R. Navies*, XXI, 542, 543, Aug. 15, 1864.
62. *Ibid.*, 544, 545, Sept. 4, 1864.
63. *Loyall Farragut*, 440, undated letter.
64. *O. R. Navies*, XXI, 543, Sept. 3, 1864. Similar recognition was given General Sherman for the capture of Atlanta.
65. *Ibid.*, 544.
66. Cf. Welles's *Diary*, Aug. 23, 1864, II, 114-116, for further expression of his grievances against the War Department because of its failure to give due credit to the navy.
67. *Frank Leslie's Illustrated Newspaper*, Sept. 3, 1864.
68. Aug. 20, 1864, I, 854.
69. *Ibid.*, Sept. 24, 1864, II, 70, 71. For Farragut's relations with Charles Folsom, see *David Glasgow Farragut: Admiral in the Making* by Charles Lee Lewis, 126-129, 132-134.
70. *Army and Navy Journal* (Sept. 3, 1864), II, 21. Published also in *Life and Naval Career of Vice Admiral David Glascoe* (sic) *Farragut* by P. C. Headley, 270-272.
71. *Harper's Weekly* (Sept. 10, 1864), 586.
72. Oct. 22, 1864, II, 133. Also in P. C. Headley's *Life and Naval Career of Vice Admiral David Glascoe* (sic) *Farragut*, 340-342.
73. *Army and Navy Journal* (Sept. 10, 1864), II, 42. Also quoted in this issue is an editorial on Farragut and Mobile Bay from London *Times*, Aug. 20, 1864.
74. *Ibid.* (Sept. 30, 1865), III, 92, letter of Apr. 28, 1865 to a friend in Washington.

XXV. FARRAGUT'S HEALTH FAILS

1. *O. R. Navies*, XXI, 612, Aug. 27, 1864, Farragut to Welles.
2. *Diary of Gideon Welles*, Aug. 29, 1864, II, 124, and Aug. 30, II, 127, 128.
3. *Ibid.*, Sept. 2, 1864, II, 133, 134.
4. *O. R. Navies*, XXI, 626, Sept. 5, 1864.
5. Welles to Farragut, Sept. 5, 1864, Naval Records and Library, Navy Department.
6. *O. R. Navies*, XXI, 545, Sept. 5, 1864.
7. *Ibid.*, 546, Sept. 19, 1864.
8. *The Story of the Confederacy* by R. S. Henry, 372.
9. *Correspondence of Gustavus Vasa Fox*, I, 345-351, Farragut to Fox, Sept. 5, 1864. "The admiral is not entirely well--nor will he be until he can enjoy a more tonic climate and better regimen. His brain wants rest and his muscles exercise. His liver needs a shaking. There seems to be an idea afloat that he may go North shortly. I have heard nothing from him on the subject—except frequent sighs for 'rest.' The rest I prescribe for him is to be taken in a wagon behind a pair of trotters, with Mrs. F. by his side—the temperature to be below 70—

and no navy in sight" (Dr. Lansdale to Dr. J. C. Palmer, Sept. 9, 1864, *Letters: Surgeon-General James C. Palmer*, Naval Records and Library, Navy Department).
10. *Drayton Letters*, 68, Drayton to Hamilton, Sept. 5, 1864.
11. *Ibid.*, 69, Sept. 8, 1864.
12. *Diary of Gideon Welles*, Sept. 15, 1864, II, 145, 146.
13. Sept. 22, 1864, Naval Records and Library, Navy Department.
14. Diary of D. G. Farragut, owned by George T. Keating.
15. *Ibid.*
16. *O. R. Navies*, XXI, 655, 656, Sept. 22, 1864.
17. Oct. 20, 1864, Ellsworth Eliot, Jr. Collection.
18. *O. R. Navies*, XXI, 644, 645.
19. *Ibid.*, 643, Sept. 15, 1864.
20. *Diary of Gideon Welles*, II, 159-161.
21. *Harper's Weekly* (Sept. 24, 1864), 609. A sketch by Wier accompanied the article.
22. Diary of D. G. Farragut, owned by George T. Keating.
23. *Life of Charles C. Davis* by Charles C. Davis, Jr., 312, 313.
24. Sept. 27, 1864, from Astor House, Zabriskie Collection in Naval Academy Museum. After Mobile Bay victory, Gen. Beauregard was afraid Farragut might be given the command off Charleston. "Renew rope obstruction near Sumter," he wrote Maj.-Gen. Sam Jones, commanding Dept. of Charleston, Aug. 30, 1864, "and put down new ones near mouths of Ashley and Cooper Rivers with proper pilings—Farragut may soon pay you a visit" (Cited in *A Calendar of Confederate Papers* by D. S. Freeman as printed in "O. R. s. 66, p. 617").
25. *Memoir and Correspondence of Charles Steedman, Rear Admiral, U. S. Navy*, ed. by A. L. Mason, 385.
26. *Diary of Gideon Welles*, II, 165, 166.
27. *Drayton Letters*, 71, 72, Drayton to Hamilton, Oct. 4, 1864; *Ibid.*, 61, 62, Drayton to Hamilton, July 3, 1864; *Ibid.*, 67, 68, Drayton to Hamilton, Aug. 19 and Sept. 5, 1864.
28. *Admiral Farragut* by A. T. Mahan, 250, 251, letter of Sept. 1864.
29. *Loyall Farragut*, 470, 471, Oct. 13, 1864.
30. *O. R. Navies*, XXI, 682, 683, Oct. 13, 1864.
31. *Ibid.*, 668, 669, Welles to Farragut, Oct. 1, 1864.
32. *Ibid.*, 657.
33. *Ibid.*, 690-692, Oct. 18, 1864.
34. Diary of D. G. Farragut, Oct. 18, 1864, owned by George T. Keating.
35. Oct. 20, 1864, Ellsworth Eliot, Jr. Collection.
36. *Correspondence of Gustavus Vasa Fox*, I, 351-353, Oct. 19, 1864.
37. *O. R. Navies*, XXI, 718, Oct. 28, 1864.
38. *Ibid.*, 718, 719, Sherman to Canby, telegram of Nov. 5, 1864, and *Ibid.*, 721, Halleck to Canby, Nov. 7, 1864.
39. *Loyall Farragut*, 471, Nov. 4, 1864.
40. *O. R. Navies*, XXI, 722, Nov. 8, 1864.
41. Diary of D. G. Farragut, Nov. 12 and 16, 1864, owned by George T. Keating.

42. *Political and Social History of the United States, 1829-1925* by Arthur M. Schlesinger, 224.
43. *Abraham Lincoln: The War Years* by Carl Sandburg, III, 203. A caricature appeared, entitled "The Democracy in Search of a Candidate," which portrayed Farragut in the rigging of the *Hartford*. "Oh, we are sinking!" cry several, who are trying to row out to him. "Who will save us! Man, in the shrouds, won't you?" Farragut replies, "Sheer off, you lubbers, or I'll give you a broadside. You're the same kind of craft as those we sunk in Mobile Bay." (*American Caricatures Pertaining to the Civil War*, Anon.)
44. *Abraham Lincoln: The War Years* by Carl Sandburg, III, 237.
45. Diary of D. G. Farragut, Nov. 19, 1864, owned by George T. Keating.
46. *O. R. Navies*, XXI, 724, Welles to Farragut, Nov. 9, 1864.
47. *Ibid.*, 735, Nov. 22, 1864.
48. *Ibid.*, 803, log of the *Hartford*, and *Ibid.*, 746, Fleet-Captain S. R. Franklin to Gen. Canby, Dec. 2, 1864.
49. *Loyall Farragut*, 474, Nov. 30, 1864.

XXVI. THE WAR ENDS

1. Diary of D. G. Farragut, *passim*, owned by George T. Keating, and *O. R. Navies*, XXI, 759, 760, Farragut to Welles, Dec. 13, 1864.
2. *O. R. Navies*, XXI, 803, log of the *Hartford*.
3. New York *Daily Tribune*, Dec. 14, 1864. The account of Farragut's arrival and reception is very much briefer in the New York *Evening Post* of the same date. There is an account of his arrival in the *Army and Navy Journal* (Dec. 17, 1864), II, 263. See also *O. R. Navies*, XXI, 776, 777, Drayton to Jenkins, Dec. 28, 1864.
4. *Life and Naval Career of Vice-Admiral David Glascoe* (sic) *Farragut* by P. C. Headley, 279.
5. *O. R. Navies*, XXI, 759, 760.
6. *Ibid.*, 764, Farragut to Welles, Dec. 21, 1864. Mrs. Farragut referred to the vessel repeatedly as the "dear old *Hartford*."
7. Dec. 15, 1864, Ellsworth Eliot, Jr. Collection.
8. *The Second Admiral* by Richard S. West, Jr., 274-283.
9. *O. R. Navies*, XXI, 776, 777, Drayton to Jenkins, Dec. 28, 1864.
10. *Loyall Farragut*, 478, 552. The Act of Congress of Dec. 21, 1864 created the rank of vice-admiral. One only was to be selected from the list of active rear-admirals, and he was then to be the ranking officer in the navy (Naval Records and Library, Navy Department). Farragut's commission was dated Dec. 21, 1864; *Loyall Farragut*, 552, says he was commissioned vice-admiral on Dec. 23, 1864. The commission is now owned by the family of George G. Hall. The author has not been able to learn the present whereabouts of his commission as a rear-admiral. See also *Army and Navy Journal* (Dec. 24, 1864), II, 277, and the *Navy Register* for 1865. See *Regulations for the Uniform of the United States Navy* (Washington, 1866).

11. *Army and Navy Journal* (Dec. 24, 1864), II, 281.
12. Dec. 20, 1864, Ellsworth Eliot, Jr. Collection.
13. *Life and Naval Career of Vice-Admiral David Glascoe* (sic) *Farragut* by P. C. Headley, 297-299.
14. There is no record of this, however.
15. Ellsworth Eliot, Jr. Collection.
16. *Ibid.*, n.d.
17. Dec. 14 and 27, 1864, Zabriskie Collection, Naval Academy Museum.
18. *Galaxy*, XII, 818.
19. *Life and Naval Career of Vice-Admiral David Glascoe* (sic) *Farragut* by P. C. Headley, 300. The total sum, collected and turned over to Farragut, was $51,130 (*Ibid.*, 306). According to the *Army and Navy Journal* (Feb. 11, 1865), II, 386, the morocco case and letter were transmitted to Farragut later. A pamphlet, entitled "Farragut Testimonial," which covers the details of the presentation is in the Public Library of the City of Boston. ". . . I see that the State of Ohio talks of making me a present of a home, etc.," wrote Sherman to his wife. "For myself I would accept nothing, but for you and the children I would be willing, especially if such a present were accompanied, as in Farragut's place, with bonds enough to give interest to pay taxes. My pay would not enable me to pay taxes on property." (*Sherman's Home Letters*, ed. M.A. DeWolfe Howe, 323).
20. *Loyall Farragut*, 476-478.
21. *Life and Naval Career of Vice-Admiral David Glascoe* (sic) *Farragut* by P. C. Headley, 308-312.
22. *O. R. Navies*, XXI, 776, 777, Drayton to Jenkins, Dec. 28, 1864.
23. *Diary of Gideon Welles*, II, 223.
24. *Drayton Letters*, 75, 76, Drayton to Alexander Hamilton, Jr., Jan. 21, 1865.
25. *O. R. Navies*, XXI, 776, 777, Drayton to Jenkins, Dec. 28, 1864. The answering article was written by Captain Jenkins or Brownell, according to Jenkins. It appeared in the *Army and Navy Journal* of Jan. 7, 1865.
26. *Army and Navy Journal* (Jan. 14, 1865), II, 322, 323.
27. *Battles and Leaders*, IV, 707.
28. *O. R. Navies*, XI, 640, telegram of Stanton to Grant, 9:10 P.M., Jan. 24, 1865.
29. *Ibid.*, 637, telegram of Welles to Parker, Jan. 24, 1865, and *Ibid.*, 645.
30. *Diary of Gideon Welles*, II, 230, and *Drayton Letters*, 76, Drayton to Hamilton, Jan. 26, 1865.
31. *Diary of Gideon Welles*, II, 232.
32. *Drayton Letters*, 77, Drayton to Hamilton, Feb. 1, 1865.
33. *Diary of Gideon Welles*, II, 233.
34. *Ibid.*, 235.
35. *Drayton Letters*, 81, Drayton to Hamilton, Mar. 26, 1865.
36. *Ibid.*, 77, 78, Drayton to Hamilton, Feb. 15, 1865.
37. *Abraham Lincoln: The War Years* by Carl Sandburg, IV, 87.
38. *Diary of Gideon Welles*, II, 251, 252.

NOTES 481

39. *Abraham Lincoln: The War Years* by Carl Sandburg, IV, 96. Farragut was present "in person as well as in sugar" (*Reveille in Washington* by Margaret Leech, 372). Both the Admiral and Mrs. Farragut attended the inaugural ball on the evening of March 6.
40. *The Criterion*, Apr., 1902.
41. For the Boston *Journal*, as quoted in *Loyall Farragut*, 480. See also *Battles and Leaders*, IV, 726, and *Drayton Letters*, 81, Drayton to Hamilton, Mar. 26, 1865. In the New York Historical Society is a copy of *Proceedings of the Court of Inquiry, relative to the Fall of New Orleans*. Published by Order of Congress. Richmond: R. M. Smith, Public Printer, 1864, on the title page of which is stamped the name and coat of arms of Farragut, containing the horseshoe and nail of his Spanish ancestors. The title page also contains the following: "Taken from the Rebel Senate, Richmond, Va., April 4, 1865 by Colonel E. Martindale, 81st Regt., U. S. Infry., etc. Presented to Vice-Admiral Farragut in whose honor this work was compiled." On the preceding page is the autograph of Admiral Farragut and the notation: "Gift of Wm. F. Meredith, Princeton, N.J., Apr. 30, 1932."
42. *The Second Admiral* by Richard S. West, Jr., 295, 296, and *O. R. Navies*, XXII, 176, log of the *Malvern*.
43. *Loyall Farragut*, 481, 482.
44. Anne C. Pierce to Albert Mordell, May 9, 1929, used by permission of Mr. Mordell.
45. John D. Gordon to Albert Mordell, May 27 and 31, 1929, and William C. Dickson to Albert Mordell, May 22, 1929, all used with Mr. Mordell's permission. For Farragut's reasons for remaining in the U. S. Navy, see *David Glasgow Farragut: Admiral in the Making* by Charles Lee Lewis, 288-292.

XXVII. ADMIRAL OF THE NAVY

1. A penciled note, Ellsworth Eliot, Jr. Collection.
2. *Abraham Lincoln: The War Years* by Carl Sandburg, IV, 389.
3. Typewritten "Reminiscences" by Loyall Farragut, Ellsworth Eliot, Jr. Collection.
4. Boston *Post*, July 7, 1865.
5. *Life and Naval Career of Vice-Admiral David Glascoe* (sic) *Farragut* by P. C. Headley, 338.
6. *Loyall Farragut*, 482-484. In an autographed copy of the poem, which Holmes wrote for Mrs. Farragut, now in the Zabriskie Collection in the Naval Academy Museum, the last four lines of the sixth stanza read as follows:

> "Shape not for him the marble form,
>   Let never bronze be cast,
> But see him through the battle-storm,
>   Lashed to his flag-ship's mast."

The poem was first published in the Boston *Evening Transcript*, August 1, 1865.

7. *Loyall Farragut*, 484, and Boston *Evening Transcript*, July 7, 1865. There is no record that Farragut saw Charles Folsom, then residing in Cambridge.
8. Address by Ex-Governor Alexander H. Rice in *A Memorial of David Glasgow Farragut from the City of Boston . . . Marine Park, South Boston*, 69, 70. When Farragut dined with Rice, he was Chairman, Naval Affairs Committee, House of Representatives.
9. *Life and Naval Career of Vice-Admiral David Glascoe* (sic) *Farragut* by P. C. Headley, 339, 340, and *Army and Navy Journal* (July 29, 1865), II, 773.
10. June 1, 1865, Zabriskie Collection, Naval Academy Museum.
11. *The Diary of Gideon Welles*, II, 396, Dec. 14, 1865.
12. On Feb. 16, 1866, President Johnson wrote Farragut a letter at 113 East 36th Street, New York. Farragut purchased this residence on Nov. 3, 1865 from John and Catherine Falconer for the sum of $33,000. After Loyall Farragut's death it was sold to J. P. Morgan for $45,000, and is now owned by Morgan's daughter, Frances T. Pennoyer (Letter of John P. Fox to Dr. John J. Loughlin, Sept. 25, 1942).
13. In February, Farragut received a letter from President Johnson, accompanying a copy of the Congressional Resolution of Thanks to Farragut and his officers and men for "their gallantry and good conduct in the action in Mobile Bay," which was passed on February 10.

    Farragut wrote Mrs. Farragut, Sept. 21, 1862, "As to prize money, I never count upon it. If any comes, well and good! But I am not so anxious to make money as I am to put an end to this horrid war" (*Loyall Farragut*, 294). Welles wrote, "Farragut, in his unselfish patriotism, which called out all his energies and all his time, was neglectful of self and fortune. He never received a dollar of prize money for the conquest of New Orleans, where more extensive captures were made than in any battle of the war" (*Galaxy*, Dec., 1871, XII, 832).

    After Farragut's death, prize money for New Orleans captures was paid his family, June 4, 1874, Aug. 21, 1875, and Aug. 15, 1884, totaling $54,115.43 (General Accounting Office). The author has been unable to learn how much prize money he received for captures made in Mobile Bay and elsewhere in the Gulf, though he was paid for the Mobile captures before Mar. 9, 1867 (*Army and Navy Journal*, Mar. 9, 1867, IV, 461).
14. *Diary of Gideon Welles*, II, 490, Apr. 24, 1866.
15. *Army and Navy Journal* (May 12, 1866), III, 605.
16. *Register of the Navy*, 1866. Regarding the admiral's uniform, Farragut wrote Jenkins, Aug. 8, 1866, "I think a silver star about two inches in diameter on the sleeve in place of the ordinary gold star which indicates the line officer with a ship engraved in the field of the centre would be sufficiently indicative of the rank. Any other

changes that the Dept. would think proper would be perfectly agreeable to me. I am unwilling to give up the anchor on the shoulder strap as it is the only indication of the profession" (Henry E. Huntington Library). See *Regulations for the Uniform of the United States Navy* (Washington, 1866).
17. *Diary of Gideon Welles,* II, 563.
18. *Army and Navy Journal,* III, 781, July 28, 1866.
19. *Army and Navy Journal* (June 30, 1866), III, 717, and *Scribner's Monthly* (Feb., 1877), XIII, 539.
20. *The Criterion,* Apr., 1902, "Recollections of Admiral Farragut" by General James Grant Wilson. Farragut and Drayton both told Gen. Wilson that Quartermaster Knowles lashed him to the rigging. Page's portrait is reproduced in *The Memorial History of the City of New York,* ed. by James Grant Wilson, IV, 566 and in *American Painters* by G. W. Sheldon. According to confidential printed letter signed by Peter Cooper, Hamilton Fish, and five other members of the committee, 250 gentlemen were expected to donate $100 each to the fund for purchasing the portrait (Copy of letter in New York Historical Society and another in Library of Congress). The author has been unable to learn the sum finally collected and paid Page. The letter to the Czar, accompanying the portrait was as follows: "The undersigned citizens of the United States of North America unite in behalf of their countrymen in offering to your Imperial Majesty the accompanying picture representing Admiral Farragut in the shrouds of the *Hartford* during the memorable battle of Mobile Bay, painted by William Page. We ask your acceptance of the same as a slight token of our appreciation of the sympathy manifested by your Majesty's Government and people during our war for the Union, and also as an appropriate recognition of the hospitable courtesies shown by the Civil Authorities and Naval Officers to the admiral and his comrades during their late visit to your Empire, whose continued prosperity is the earnest desire of your Majesty's grateful Friends" (*The Criterion,* Apr., 1902). The portrait, entitled "Farragut Triumphant," was placed in the Imperial Winter Palace, St. Petersburg. According to William Farragut Meredith, son of the poet William T. Meredith, in a letter to the author, July 13, 1942, "Page, unfortunately, made his own pigments and they had one fatal fault, all his paintings faded so that they became a blur after exposure of eight to ten years." Unless the portrait has been restored, it is of no value at present. On account of the war, the author has been unable to learn of its present condition and whereabouts. The copy of the portrait which Page painted for his family was presented in 1938 to the Historical Society of Western Pennsylvania (Letter of Mrs. George Stevens Page of Pittsburgh to the author, Sept. 15, 1942).
21. *Diary of Gideon Welles,* II, 588, 589, and *The Age of Hate* by George Fort Milton, 358.
22. *The Age of Hate: Andrew Johnson and the Radicals* by G. F. Milton, 361.

23. *Ibid.*, 362.
24. *Ibid.*, 363.
25. *Ibid.*, 367 and 728 note.
26. *Ibid.*, 369. See also *The Diary of Gideon Welles*, II, 588-596, and *Thaddeus Stevens* by John T. Morse, Jr., 281.
27. *The Age of Hate* by G. F. Milton, 386 and note 52, p. 730.
28. Mar. 16, 1867, Zabriskie Collection, Naval Academy Museum. In September, 1866, Farragut loaned his faithful steward, John H. Brooks, then a messenger in the Bureau of Navigation, $2,500 to build a house in Washington. He was to repay $40 per month with legal interest, all of which was duly paid (Farragut to Jenkins, Sept. 27, 1866 and Jenkins to Farragut, Sept. 28, 1866, Henry E. Huntington Library, and letter of the daughter, Mary E. Brooks, to the author, Jan. 15, 1942, who at that time resided in the house built by her father). John H. Brooks was a steward in the Navy from 1852 to 1865, and a messenger and then a clerk in the Bureau of Navigation until his death in 1897. He attended Captain Percival Drayton in his last moments when he died in Washington. Brooks named his sons Reginald Farragut Brooks and Percival Drayton Brooks.

XXVIII. THE EUROPEAN CRUISE

1. *The Diary of Gideon Welles*, III, 101.
2. *Ibid.*, 103, and *The Second Admiral* by Richard West, Jr., 312.
3. *Diary of Gideon Welles*, III, 104.
4. D. D. Porter had endeavored to secure this command (*Ibid.*, III, 563).
5. "In searching for information concerning the Farraguts, it was discovered that one of the admiral's ancestors was regent of Arragon and that his coat of arms was four stars, an anchor, and a horseshoe. 'How strange,' said Farragut to the present writer, 'that I should win for myself in the New World the right to assume the four stars and anchor, worn by my proud old Spanish ancestor many centuries ago" ("Recollections of Admiral Farragut" by General James Grant Wilson in *The Criterion*, April, 1902). See also *Army and Navy Journal* (Dec. 17, 1870), VIII for the same story quoted from "An Ex-officer of the Navy" in the New York *Herald*.
6. Welles's two youngest sons were attached to the *Franklin*, one as Farragut's private secretary and the other as a clerk to Capt. Pennock (*Diary of Gideon Welles*, III, 123).
7. The carrying of ladies on a man-of-war appeared "a great scandal to the old salts of that day,"—"a shocking innovation," which stirred up "great chatter" (*Surgeon of the Seas* by Charles S. Foltz, 300). Surgeon Foltz himself disapproved of it.
8. This account of Farragut's European Cruise is based on his journal as quoted in *Loyall Farragut*, 486 et seq., and on *Our Admiral's Flag Abroad: The Cruise of the Franklin* by James E. Montgomery, a

NOTES 485

  detailed account of 461 pages, which will be referred to as *Montgomery*.
9. The other vessels then belonging to the European Squadron were the *Canandaigua*, a wooden screw steamer of 2,130 tons and 10 guns; the *Ticonderoga*, a similar steamer of 1,533 tons and 5 guns; the *Onondaga*, a double turreted monitor of 1,250 tons, two 15-inch Dahlgrens and two 150-pounders; the *Shamrock*, a side-wheel double-ender of 974 tons and 4 light guns; the *Frolic*, a side-wheeler of 880 tons and 5 light guns; and the *Guard*, a storeship.
10. The Midshipmen's Practise Squadron was composed of the *Macedonian*, *Savannah*, and the *Dale*. On the *Dale* was Lieutenant W. S. Schley (*Forty-Five Years under the Flag* by Schley, 63).
11. *Loyall Farragut*, 487.
12. *Surgeon of the Seas* by C. S. Foltz, 303.
13. The *Dunderberg* was an ironclad ram frigate of wood iron-strapped with a tonnage of 5,090 and an armament of two 15-inch and eight 11-inch Dahlgrens.
14. *Montgomery*, 30.
15. *Loyall Farragut*, 489.
16. Farragut had previously met him in Washington.
17. *Surgeon of the Seas* by C. S. Foltz, 307. Grand Duke Constantine had shown great friendship and admiration for Matthew Fontaine Maury (*Matthew Fontaine Maury: Pathfinder of the Seas* by Charles Lee Lewis, 128, 162, 164, 166, 180, and 209).
18. *Loyall Farragut*, 491.
19. *Ibid.*, 492.
20. *Ibid.*, 493.
21. *Surgeon of the Seas* by C. S. Foltz, 314.
22. *Loyal Farragut*, 496.
23. *Montgomery*, 81, 84.
24. *Surgeon of the Seas* by C. S. Foltz, 315, 316. See *David Glasgow Farragut: Admiral in the Making* by Charles Lee Lewis, 265 for Farragut's acquaintance with Capt. Butakoff.
25. *Montgomery*, 90.
26. *Ibid.*, 93.
27. *Loyall Farragut*, 500.
28. *Ibid.*, 502.
29. *Montgomery*, 123.
30. *Ibid.*, 127.
31. For a copy of this letter, see *David Glasgow Farragut: Admiral in the Making* by Charles Lee Lewis, 338, note 46, and *Montgomery*, 127, and *Loyall Farragut*, 503 note.
32. *Montgomery*, 139.
33. *Ibid.*, 359.
34. *Ibid.*, 148.
35. *Ibid.*, 143.
36. It was reported that Farragut expressed the opinion that 15-inch

guns should "never be fired with more than 60 pounds of powder." "The English journals laid great stress on this remark, which we are by no means certain was ever made, as if forsooth Farragut were necessarily an infallible oracle on everything appertaining to naval warfare. If the admiral did make the remark attributed to him, he was mistaken, but we apprehend that sensible people will think no less of the first sailor of America because he is not thoroughly posted in the advances which have been made within the past few years. The 15-inch gun has been fired so many times with 100-pound charges that no one should think of using a smaller one, if it is desired to produce a maximum result" (*Army and Navy Journal*, Nov. 9, 1867, V, 181).

37. *Montgomery*, 169.
38. *Ibid.*, 188.
38. *Ibid.*, 201. Translation was made by Professor Werner of the College of the City of New York.
40. *Ibid.*, 201.
41. The name "Farragut" had its origin in "farradura," meaning horseshoe. A silver pitcher in the Admiral's cabin had this design on it as a coat of arms (Army and Navy Journal, V, 383, from a correspondent of the *Tribune*).
42. *Montgomery*, 212.
43. *Ibid.*, 244.
44. *Ibid.*, 251.
45. *Ibid.*, 261.
46. *Ibid.*, 267.
47. *Ibid.*, 270.
48. *Surgeon of the Seas* by C. S. Foltz, 324.
49. *Montgomery*, 309.
50. John J. Cisco to Farragut, Mar. 7, 1868; Cisco to Mrs. Farragut, Mar. 7, 1868; and Farragut to Cisco, Apr. 14, 1868, Ellsworth Eliot, Jr. Collection.
51. *Montgomery*, 319.
52. "Admiral Farragut" by Edward Kirk Rawson in *Atlantic Monthly*, April, 1892, LXIX, 489.
53. *Montgomery*, 339.
54. *Life of Henry Wadsworth Longfellow* by Samuel Longfellow, II, 444, and *Surgeon of the Seas* by C. S. Foltz, 330.
55. As an introduction to his poem, "The Bay Fight," Henry Howard Brownell used the following lines from Longfellow's "Saga of King Olaf":

> On the forecastle Ulf the Red
> Watched the lashing of the ships;
>   "If the Serpent lie so far ahead,
> We shall have hard work of it here,"
>   Said he with a sneer
> On his bearded lips.

See *War Lyrics and Other Poems* by Henry Howard Brownell (Boston, 1866). This introduction from the "Saga of King Olaf" does not appear in the version of the poem in *Loyall Farragut*, 441-457. "The Bay Fight" appeared in *Harper's Monthly* of Dec., 1864.
56. The original is in the Zabriskie Collection, Naval Academy Museum.
57. *Surgeon of the Seas* by C. S. Foltz, 330.
58. Typewritten "Reminiscences" by Loyall Farragut, Ellsworth Eliot, Jr. Collection.
59. Montgomery, 386.
60. *Ibid.*, 399.
61. *Ibid.*, 401.
62. *Ibid.*, 402.
63. *Fifty Years in Constantinople* by George Washburn, 12, 13, and "American Territory in Turkey: or Admiral Farragut's Visit to Constantinople, and the Extraterritoriality of Robert College," an address by R. E. Prime before the New York Society of the Order of the Founders and Patriots of America, Feb. 14, 1908. Publications of Society (1908-1914), 21-35.
64. Montgomery, 435.
65. *Ibid.*, 426.
66. *Ibid.*, 446.
67. *Army and Navy Journal* (Sept. 12, 1868), VI, 49, and *Ibid.* (July 27, 1867), IV, 781.

XXIX. "THE LAST SCENE OF ALL"

1. VI, 201, Nov. 14, 1868.
2. Nov. 10, 1868, Ellsworth Eliot, Jr. Collection.
3. New York *Herald*, Nov. 14, 1868.
4. *Ibid.*, Nov. 18, 1868.
5. *The Diary of Gideon Welles*, III, 468.
6. *Ibid.*, III, 469, 470.
7. Original letter of Nov. 30, 1868, Zabriskie Collection, Naval Academy Museum.
8. *Diary of Gideon Welles*, III, 501, Jan. 7, 1869.
9. VI, 257, Dec. 12, 1868.
10. *Daily National Intelligencer*, Mar. 5, 1869.
11. *Diary of Gideon Welles*, III, 542.
12. *Daily National Intelligencer*, Mar. 7, 1869.
13. *Diary of Gideon Welles*, III, 446, 551.
14. *Meet General Grant* by W. E. Woodward, 399.
15. *Diary of Gideon Welles*, III, 441.
16. *Ibid.*, 559.
17. *Ibid.*, 549, 559.
18. *Ibid.*, 556.
19. *Sixty Years* by George S. Boutwell, II, 212.
20. Fox to Welles, Aug. 12, 1871, Henry E. Huntington Library, and

The Second Admiral by Richard West, Jr., "The Grant-Porter Imbroglio," 326-334.
21. *Diary of Gideon Welles,* May 2, 1869, III, 582, 583. "I have done too much for Porter, who is incapable of gratitude, and is eaten up with selfish ambition" (*Ibid.,* III, 562).
22. *Army and Navy Journal* (Dec. 17, 1870), VIII, 281.
23. *The Galaxy* (Dec., 1871), XII, 831; *Admirals and Commodores,* Vol. I, Jan.-Mar., 1869, Naval Records and Library, Navy Department, for design of Farragut's uniform; and *Ibid.,* II, May 8, 1869, for Farragut's being permitted to retain old uniform, and his declining of offer of Port Admiral of New York. See also *Ibid.,* May 12, 1869, and *Regulations for the Uniform of the United States,* March 11, 1869.
24. *The Second Admiral* by Richard West, Jr., 323.
25. *Hamilton Fish: The Inner History of the Grant Administration* by Allan Nevins, 281, 282.
26. *The Second Admiral* by Richard West, Jr., 325.
27. *Loyall Farragut,* 539, 540.
28. Oct. 8, 1869, Zabriskie Collection, Naval Academy Museum.
29. James E. Montgomery, Farragut's secretary, to Rear-Admiral Thornton Jenkins, Nov. 22, 1869, Henry E. Huntington Library.
30. Dec. 7, 1869, Henry E. Huntington Library.
31. Porter to Rear-Admiral Thomas Turner, Dec. 23, 1870, D. D. Porter Papers, Library of Congress; Letter Books of Rear-Admiral Turner, New York Public Library; and letter of Admiral Turner to Secretary of Navy Robeson, Aug. 2, 1869, Naval Records and Library, Navy Department. The controversy between Farragut and Turner grew out of what Farragut considered a lack of personal and official courtesy shown him by Turner on his visit to California. Turner was in command of the Pacific Fleet at the time.
32. *Forty-Five Years under the Flag* by W. S. Schley, 67, 68.
33. "Recollections of Admiral Farragut" by Gen. James Grant Wilson, in *The Criterion,* Apr., 1902. In the Church of the Incarnation, there is a tablet in memory of Farragut on the left of the chancel with a likeness of the Admiral in bas-relief, modeled by Launt Thompson; this was erected by the Commandery of the Military Order of the Loyal Legion of the State of New York, as a tribute of love to their first Commander.
34. June 26, 1870, D. D. Porter Papers, Library of Congress.
35. *Loyall Farragut,* 541. Farragut's last flag, flown by the *Tallapoosa,* is in the Naval Academy Museum.
36. Diary of Gustavus Vasa Fox, in New York Historical Society.
37. *Army and Navy Journal* (Aug. 20, 1870), VIII, 9. *Ibid.* (Dec. 17, 1870), VIII, 281 contains an article which states that Farragut did not speak the last nine words of the statement which Butler quoted in his speech in Congress; namely, "Never raise that flag over me nor carry it before my coffin—that flag which has been imposed upon me by the man who expects to become my successor." See also Por-

ter's letter of Dec. 19, 1870 to Commodore Pennock, in D. D. Porter Papers, Library of Congress, and Pennock's reply to Porter, Dec. 21, 1870, in *The Second Admiral* by Richard West, Jr., 333. Porter also wrote Pennock, Aug. 12, 1870, a letter of sympathy for him and Mrs. Farragut. "He has conferred great fame upon the Navy," he wrote, "and we cannot do him too much honor. . . . I am still in hopes that his attack may pass off, though he would still have a continuation of his sufferings" (D. D. Porter Papers, Library of Congress). There is no record that Porter "honored" Farragut by attending the funeral ceremonies in either Portsmouth or New York.

Farragut's will of Dec. 11, 1869 bequeathed all his war trophies to his son Loyall and the house in New York to Mrs. Farragut, and divided the remaining estate equally between wife and son. The amount of the estate is not known as there was no inventory recorded (Certified copy of will from Clerk of the Surrogate's Court, County of New York, Sept. 28, 1942).

38. Diary of John H. Brooks, courtesy of his daughter, Mary E. Brooks.
39. *Army and Navy Journal* (Aug. 20, 1870), VIII, 9; *The Soldiers' Memorial* by Joseph Foster, *passim;* and letter of Jan. 25, 1942 from Edith M. Austin, Principal of the Farragut High School, Portsmouth, New Hampshire, to the author.
40. *Army and Navy Journal* (Aug. 20, 1870), VIII, 9.
41. VIII, 45.
42. *Ibid.*, VIII, 105, Oct. 1, 1870, and *Loyall Farragut,* 541.
43. *Ibid.*
44. *Ibid.*, VIII, 125, Oct. 8, 1870.
45. "Recollections of Admiral Farragut" by Gen. James Grant Wilson, in *The Criterion,* Apr., 1902.
46. The other dates on the monument are as follows: Virginia D. Farragut, born Nov. 24, 1824 and died Oct. 31, 1884; Gertrude Metcalfe Farragut (Loyall's wife), born Mar. 15, 1849 and died Feb. 23, 1896; and Loyall Farragut, born Oct. 12, 1844 and died Oct. 1, 1916.
47. Published in *Scribner's Monthly* (June, 1881), XXII, 261.

XXX. "WHAT WOULD FARRAGUT HAVE DONE?"

1. Letter of Feb. 12, 1900, Ellsworth Eliot Jr. Collection. See also *Army and Navy Register* (June 11, 1904), XXXV, 12, for ceremonies incident to laying the corner stone of Naval Academy Chapel, and *Navy Days* by W. E. Beard, in MS., for Dewey's address at dedication of marker at Farragut's birthplace near Knoxville, Tennessee, erected by Daughters of the American Revolution, May 15, 1900.
2. Aug. 20, 1870, VIII, 12.
3. *Forty-Five Years under the Flag* by Rear-Admiral Winfield Scott Schley, 50, 51.
4. *Memoirs of a Rear-Admiral* by S. R. Franklin, 185.
5. *A Memorial of David Glasgow Farragut from the City of Boston . . . Marine Park,* 66.

6. Jan. 1, 1880, XXX, 13, 14, review of Loyall Farragut's biography of his father.
7. *Admiral Farragut* by A. T. Mahan, 317, 318.
8. *Ibid.*, 319. The quotation is from Danton, and is, in English, "Audacity, more audacity, and always audacity." Mahan cites neither authority for this incident nor time and place.
9. *David G. Farragut* by J. R. Spears, 356, and *Famous American Naval Officers* by Charles Lee Lewis, 249.
10. "Farragut at Port Hudson" by Loyall Farragut in *Putnam's Monthly* (Oct., 1908) V, 46-53.
11. July 22, 1862, Ellsworth Eliot Jr. Collection.
12. Dec. 4, 1862, *Loyall Farragut*, 300.
13. *Ibid.*, 310, Feb. 18, 1863.
14. There is no foundation for Welles's statement that Farragut was christened "David" after David Porter in an Episcopal church in Newport (*Galaxy*, Nov., 1871, XII, 682). "The Admiral was never confirmed in the Episcopal church" (Letter of George G. Hall to the author, Jan. 27, 1941). But the day before his death he took the eucharist, and was buried with Episcopal rites (*Army and Navy Journal*, Aug. 20, 1870, VIII, 9). "When he was dangerously ill in Chicago, he desired to have a clergyman called, saying, 'He must be my pilot now.' At the time of his death he was a communicant of the Protestant Episcopal Church" (*Loyall Farragut*, 548). "We find upon examination of our records that Admiral Farragut, 113 East 36th Street, New York City, was listed as a parishioner of this Church in November, 1868. On March 18, 1870, we have a record that he was transferred, and that he died in Portsmouth, N.H., August 14, 1870. Dr. Montgomery, a former Rector of the Incarnation, delivered an address at the funeral service" (Letter of Aug. 28, 1942, to the author from Charles N. Kent, Clerk of the Vestry, Church of the Incarnation, New York).
15. "Personal Reminiscences of Admiral Farragut" by C. V. Anthony, in *Methodist Review* (Bimonthly), Sept.-Oct., 1894, LXXVI, 724-734 (Poole, LIV and 5th ser., X).
16. He contributed his first $500 of prize money to the erection of an Episcopal church at Hastings-on-Hudson (*Loyall Farragut*, 385). Farragut gave $1,000, according to *History of Zion Church Semi-Centennial* by Rev. George B. Reese, called to the attention of the author by a letter from Mrs. Edmund M. Devoe, of Hastings-on-Hudson, Apr. 20, 1942. The Rector of Grace Church, Hastings-on-Hudson, wrote the author, Jan. 20, 1942, that the gift was $1,000.
17. See *David Glasgow Farragut: Admiral in the Making* by Charles Lee Lewis, 140, 246-251, for Perry's treatment of Farragut.
18. Apr. 13, 1848, Naval Academy Museum.
19. *The Autobiography of Commodore Charles Morris, U. S. Navy*, 88 note.
20. *Army and Navy Journal* (Aug. 20, 1870), VIII, 11, and *Loyall Farragut*, 549, 545, 548, and 542.

21. His Bible with name and date, Jan. 1, 1827, is owned by Ellsworth Eliot, Jr. His Prayer Book is in the Chapel of the U. S. Naval Academy, to which it was presented, Jan. 23, 1938, by the Reverend C. G. Carpenter.
22. "Personal Reminiscences of Admiral Farragut" by C. V. Anthony, in *Methodist Review* (Bimonthly), Sept.-Oct., 1894, 724-734.
23. See *David Glasgow Farragut: Admiral in the Making* by Charles Lee Lewis, 177, 178, 253. Anthony (*op. cit.*) makes the statement that Farragut refused to believe that the moon governed the tides.
24. *Forty-Five Years under the Flag* by Rear Admiral Winfield Scott Schley, 50, 51.
25. Dec. 15, 1879, Zabriskie Collection, Naval Academy Museum. Sherman had been associated with Farragut before the war, when the latter was Commandant of the Mare Island Navy Yard (*Memoirs of General W. T. Sherman Written by Himself*, I, 154).
26. *Army and Navy Journal* (Aug. 20, 1870), VIII, 12.
27. "Recollections of Admiral Farragut" by Gen. James Grant Wilson, *The Criterion*, April, 1902.
28. *The Great Admiral* by Harry Lyman Koopman (1883).

APPENDIX: STATUES, PICTURES, AND POEMS

1. *Loyall Farragut*, 542, and *David G. Farragut* by J. R. Spears, 372.
2. The resolution was approved June 22, 1874, and the selection of the sculptor was left to the Secretary of the Navy, the General of the Army, and Mrs. Farragut (*Loyall Farragut*, 542). Admiral D. D. Porter was not included.

    Lieut. Hoxie, an engineer officer and friend of Loyall Farragut, met Miss Ream while she was working on the statue, and afterwards married her.
3. *Magazine of American History* (July, 1881), VII, 72. A reproduction is in *Harper's Weekly* (Apr. 23, 1881), XXV, 273.
4. Lucretia R. Garfield to Mrs. Farragut, Apr. 12, 1881, Zabriskie Collection, Naval Academy Museum.
5. *American Addresses* by Joseph H. Choate, 27-47. *The Memorial History of the City of New York*, ed. by James Grant Wilson incorrectly states that the unveiling was on May 26 (IV, 214). Spears' *David G. Farragut*, 372, incorrectly gives the date as May 21, 1881.
6. *Everybody's Magazine* (Nov., 1917), XXXVII, 37; *The American Architect* (Sept. 10, 1881), X, 117, 128; *Magazine of American History* (Oct., 1881), VII, 316 and VI, 389; *Scribner's Monthly* (June, 1881), XXII, 161-167; and *The Architectural Record* (Sept., 1911), 290, "Intimate Letters of Stamford White."
7. *Magazine of American History* (Oct., 1881), VII, 316.
8. *The Outlook* (Feb. 1, 1902), LXX, 318.
9. *A Memorial of David Glasgow Farragut from the City of Boston with an Account of the Dedication of the Farragut Statue at Marine Park, South Boston, June 28, 1893*, p. 36.

10. *Ibid.*, 71, 72. Russian naval officers visited Farragut's grave in Woodlawn Cemetery in May, 1893, and the Commander of the Russian Fleet made a "touching eulogy" (*Ibid.*, 36).
11. *Dedication and Unveiling of the Statues of Lincoln, Grant, Sherman, and Farragut . . . Memorial Day, 1900, passim*. A statue of Farragut is a part of the Union Navy Memorial at Vicksburg, Miss.
12. Letter of July 16 and Aug. 10, 1942 from Frederic Larrabee, Clermont, Iowa to the author; a pamphlet, *William Larrabee, Memorial Address* by William S. Kenyon; and New York *Times*, May 8, 1904.
13. *Review of Reviews* (Nov., 1900), XXII, 568. Reproduction is in *U. S. Naval Institute Proceedings* (May, 1927), LIII, 527.
14. See note 16, chapter XXX.
15. William Page portrait of Farragut is reproduced in *Memorial History of the City of New York*, ed. by James Grant Wilson, IV, 566, and in G. W. Sheldon's *American Painters*.
16. Catalogue of sale of paintings, Mar. 24, 1938, Parke-Bernet Galleries, New York. The portrait is now owned by Dr. John J. Loughlin of New York. A Farragut portrait was on the $100 Treasury Note, ser. of 1890; $500 3% registered bonds of 1898 (Spanish War Loan); and Navy Department checks. The engraving was by Charles Schlecht in 1873 (Letter to author from Director, Bureau of Engraving and Printing, Sept. 30, 1942). "The two most satisfactory oil paintings are to be seen at the Union League Club and University Club of this City" (Loyall Farragut to Paymaster Joseph Foster, Nov. 28, 1890 in *The Soldiers' Memorial* by Joseph Foster, "The Presentation of the Portraits of Whipple and Farragut," 26).
17. *Army and Navy Journal* (Mar. 9, 1867), IV, 461, and G. W. Sheldon's *American Painters*, 39, 42.
18. Reproduced in *Leslie's Weekly*, 1898, and Benson J. Lossing's *A History of the Civil War* (New York, 1895), 416.
19. Reproduced in *Putnam's Monthly*, V, 48.
20. *Rebellion Record* by Frank Moore, "Poetry and Incidents," V, 5, 6.
21. *Ibid.*, 18. George Henry Boker wrote the poems, "The Varuna" and "The Ballad of New Orleans."
22. *Loyall Farragut*, 251-260, and *War Lyrics and Other Poems* by Henry Howard Brownell (Boston, 1866).
23. *Loyall Farragut*, 441-457, and Brownell, *op. cit.*
24. *The Surgeon of the Seas* by C. S. Foltz, 321, and "Our Battle Laureate" in *The Atlantic Monthly* (May, 1865), 589.
25. Copies in New York Historical Society, one of which has a photo of Brownell in uniform pasted on inside of cover. For Farragut's humor, even during his last illness, see *Loyall Farragut*, 546.
26. *Loyall Farragut*, 457, 458.
27. *The Home Book of Verse*, ed. by Burton Egbert Stevenson (1918), 2507-2509. Different versions are to be found in *Army and Navy Journal* (Oct. 8, 1870), VIII, 128, and in *Loyall Farragut*, 459-460, where it is entitled "Farragut's Morn." In the Zabriskie Collection,

Naval Academy Museum is a proof sheet of the poem with the author's corrections and a letter of Sept. 24, 1889 to E. C. Stedman; this differs least from the version in Stevenson, which it may be assumed was approved by Meredith who was living when permission to reprint the poem was secured by Stevenson.
28. *The Battle of Mobile Bay* by F. A. Parker, 53-55.
29. *Harper's Weekly* (June 11, 1881), XXV, 381, 382.

INDEX

Abdul Aziz, Sultan of Turkey, 360.
Adams, Charles Francis, 344.
Agincourt, British ironclad, 346.
Alabama, 42.
Alabama, Confederate raider, 146, 156, 159, 161, 163, 255, 309, 316, 337, 344.
Albany, New York, 333.
Albatross, U.S. gunboat, 143, 171, 172, 176, 183, 192, 209.
Albemarle, Confederate ironclad, 241.
Albranca, Marquis de, 350.
Alden, Commander James, U.S.N., 23, 26-28, 35, 46, 80, 87, 93, 115, 116, 121, 129, 139, 155, 162, 177, 203, 208, 255, 261, 264, 266, 268, 269, 370, 426, 442.
Alexander II, Czar of Russia, 332, 483.
Alexander, William, 158.
Alexandria, Louisiana, 195-197, 199, 235.
Alexis, Grand Duke, 332.
Allatoona Creek, 245.
Alonzo Child, steamboat, 222.
Alton, Illinois, 333.
Amadis de Gaul, 305.
Anderson, Colonel C. D., C.S.A., 284, 285.
Anderson, Mrs. Larz, 473.
Anderson, Brigadier-General Robert, U.S.A., 327.
Ann, British steamer, 138.
Annapolis, Maryland, 19, 321, 336, 375.
Anthony, C. V., 384-386, 491.
Anthony, E., 395.
Antietam, Maryland, 141.
Arizona, U.S. gunboat, 145.
Arkansas, 111.

Arkansas, Confederate ironclad ram, 89, 108, 109, 111-129, 132, 140, 216, 241, 440.
Arkansas Post, 185, 186.
Arkansas River, 185.
Army and Navy Gazette (English), 296.
Army and Navy Journal (American), 294, 295, 315, 320, 332, 366, 367, 372, 376, 379, 389.
Arnold, Edward, 396.
Arnold, J. Loring, 395.
Arthur, U.S. bark, 137.
Asboth, Brigadier-General Alexander, U.S.A., 229, 231, 232.
Ashmun, Lieutenant, 323.
Atchafalaya River, 148, 165, 196, 201.
Atlanta, Georgia, 153, 294, 477.
Auburn, New York, 333.
Augur, Major-General Christopher C., U.S.A., 199.
Autrey, Colonel James L., C.S.A., 83.

Bailey, Captain Theodorus, U.S.N., 26, 27, 35, 36, 52, 55, 56, 59, 60, 69, 71, 77, 94, 255, 330, 376, 398, 427.
Bailey, Mrs. Theodorus, 330.
Bainbridge, Commodore William, U.S.N., 329.
Baker, Marion A., 70-72.
Baldwin, Acting Lieutenant, U.S.N., 29.
Baltic, Confederate gunboat, 222, 244.
Baltimore, Maryland, 142, 207, 211, 333.
Banks, Major-General Nathaniel P., U.S.A., 152-155, 158, 162,

Page 495

163, 165-167, 169-171, 173, 181, 185, 187, 193, 195, 197-202, 206-209, 213, 215, 218, 225-229, 234, 235, 237, 241, 248, 446, 460.
Banks, Mrs. N. P., 225, 226, 234, 235.
Barataria Bay, 31, 79.
Barnard, Brigadier-General John G., U.S.A., 7, 23, 37, 418.
Barnegat Light, 312.
Barnes, James, 10.
Barron, Commodore James, U.S.N., 386.
Bartlett, Midshipman John R., U.S.N., 417, 423, 437.
Batcheller, Midshipman O. A., U.S.N., 175.
Baton Rouge, Louisiana, 80-82, 85, 88, 94, 103, 121, 122, 124-126, 130, 131, 136, 154, 155, 162, 166, 169, 171, 173, 180, 181, 193, 203, 205, 208, 341, 443.
Bayou Sara, Louisiana, 171, 193, 199, 201.
Bayou Têche, Louisiana, 148, 160.
Beauregard, General Gustave T., C.S.A., 85, 94, 95, 478.
Belgium, 357.
Bell, Commodore Charles H., U.S.N., 4, 464.
Bell, Captain Henry H., U.S.N., 15, 17, 20, 26, 35, 45-47, 49, 52, 56, 59, 72, 73, 82, 83, 86, 87, 92, 93, 103-106, 108, 114-117, 121, 129, 144, 146, 149, 150, 152, 155-160, 163, 165, 167, 169, 191, 195, 198, 209, 210, 213, 215, 216, 221, 225, 227, 255, 398, 427, 442.
Belle Poule, French ship, 351.
Benjamin, Judah P., 41, 42.
Bennett, Lieutenant J. W., C.S.N., 281.
Benton, U.S. ironclad gunboat, 105, 107, 109, 113, 114, 118, 196, 437.
Berwick Bay, 31, 136, 209.
Bienville, U.S. gunboat, 246, 252, 261, 291.
Big Sunflower River, 186.
Biloxi, Mississippi, 21, 22, 240.
Bissell, George F., 394.
Black Hawk, U.S. gunboat, 189, 210.
Blair, Francis P., 334.
Blair, Montgomery, 6-9, 12, 13, 158.
Blake, Lieutenant-Commander H. C., U.S.N., 159.
Blanche, Confederate steamer, 138.
Boggs, Commander Charles S., U.S.N., 430.
Bohio, U.S. brig, 135.
Boker, George Henry, 492.
Bolton, Commodore William C., 386.
Bordeaux, France, 220.
Borie, Adolph E., 369, 371.
Boston, Massachusetts, 16, 17, 270, 330, 421.
Boutakoff, Vice-Admiral, Russian Navy, 342, 485.
Bowen, Brigadier-General John S., U.S.A., 192, 249.
Brady, Cyrus T., 282.
Brady, Matthew B., 395.
Branson, Lloyd, 395.
Brashear City, Louisiana, 197, 204.
Brazos, Texas, 108, 137,
Breckinridge, Major-General John C., C.S.A., 42, 97, 124-126, 441.
Breckinridge, Confederate gunboat, 430.
Bronx, U.S. revenue cutter, 312, 313.
Brooklyn, New York, 10.
Brooklyn, U.S. steam sloop, 16, 21, 22, 25, 26, 56-58, 60, 62, 63, 67, 72, 80-83, 88, 94-96,

98, 99, 101-104, 106, 109, 114, 121, 126, 130, 133, 135, 144, 147, 154, 155, 157, 159, 163, 167, 198, 199, 211, 218, 230, 243, 248, 257, 263, 264, 266, 267, 269, 270, 274, 280, 291, 302, 320, 376, 429, 430, 465, 469.
Brooklyn Navy Yard, 4.
Brooks, John H., 263, 375, 464, 484.
Brooks, Mary E., 464, 484.
Broom, Lieutenant, C.S.A., 181.
Brown, Lieutenant Isaac N., C.S.N., 111, 112, 118, 126, 438, 440.
Browne, Major W. R., C.S.A., 284.
Brownell, Henry Howard, 225, 265, 288, 397, 399, 421, 465, 480, 486, 492.
Brussels, Belgium, 357.
Bryan, Mayor of Baton Rouge, 81.
Bryant, William Cullen, 316, 367.
Buchanan, Admiral Franklin, C.S.N., 146, 156, 163, 194, 220, 221, 223, 224, 230, 241, 243, 247-252, 258, 272, 273, 275, 277-281, 293, 313, 316, 445, 472-475.
Buchanan, Commander Thomas McKean, U.S.N., 148, 160.
Buell, Major-General Don Carlos, U.S.A., 111.
Buenos Aires, Argentina, 206.
Buffalo, New York, 333.
Bull Run, Battle of, 2.
Burton, U.S. transport steamer, 83.
Butler, Major-General Benjamin F., U.S.A., 4, 28, 42, 45, 48, 50, 54, 64, 71, 72, 74-76, 78-80, 83, 84, 91-93, 109, 110, 125, 131, 132, 136, 140, 142, 143-146, 148-154, 284, 285, 292, 310, 315, 417, 488.
Butte-à-la-Rose, Louisiana, 195.
Buttre, J. C., 396.

Cable, George Washington, 68.
Cairo, Illinois, 5, 18, 78, 85, 190, 239, 438.
Caldwell, Lieutenant Charles H. B., U.S.N., 52, 83, 87, 169, 172, 449.
Calhoun, U.S. gunboat, 229, 230.
California, 373, 488.
Cambridge, Massachusetts, 329.
Canby, Major-General Edward R. S., U.S.A., 245, 248, 252, 256, 283, 287, 290, 299, 302-304, 308, 310.
Cape Canaveral, Florida, 18.
Caribbean Sea, 297.
Carlisle, Pennsylvania, 207.
Caroline, Confederate steamer, 145.
Carondelet, U.S. ironclad gunboat, 105, 112.
Carter, Doctor, 3.
Carthagena, Spain, 347.
Cayuga, U.S. gunboat, 36, 44, 52, 55, 56, 60-62, 67, 74, 125, 126, 130, 138, 159, 162.
Cedar Point, Alabama, 229.
Ceres, U.S. transport steamer, 83.
Chalmette, Louisiana, 67.
Chancellorsville, Battle of, 240.
Charles XV, King of Sweden, 343.
Charleston, South Carolina, 14, 42, 141, 146, 151, 167, 198, 200, 212, 215, 216, 230, 232, 234, 242, 304, 478.
Chase, Surgeon Charles, U.S.N., 4.
Chattanooga, Tennessee, 245.
Cherbourg, France, 337-339.
Chicago, Illinois, 333, 334.
Chickasaw, U.S. monitor, 246, 252, 254, 259, 261, 264, 265, 277, 283, 284, 302, 309.
Childs, George W., 213.
China, 16.
Choate, Joseph H., 316, 392.
Christian IX, King of Denmark, 343.
Church of the Incarnation, 488, 490.

498   DAVID GLASGOW FARRAGUT

Cincinnati, U.S. ironclad gunboat, 105, 113, 114, 118.
Cincinnati, Ohio, 333, 334.
Clark, Acting Ensign Charles E., U.S.N., 238, 239.
Clay, Cassius M., 340.
Cleveland, Ohio, 333.
Clifton, U.S. gunboat, 100, 150, 156, 214.
Clio, blockade runner, 144.
Coatzacoalcos, U.S. steamer, 84.
Coffin, Charles C., 324.
Cold Harbor, Virginia, 245.
Collingwood, Admiral Cuthbert, R. N., 29, 30.
Collins, John, 268, 467.
Colorado, U.S. steam sloop, 22, 26, 31, 35, 423.
Columbus, Ohio, 333.
Conrad, Surgeon D. B., C.S.N., 279, 467, 471.
Constantine, Grand Duke, 340, 485.
Constantinople, Turkey, 359-363.
Constitution, U.S. frigate, 390.
Continental Hotel, Philadelphia, 16.
Cooper, Adjutant and Inspector General Samuel C., C.S.A., 287, 367.
Copenhagen, Denmark, 343, 344, 379.
Corinth, Mississippi, 30, 42, 85, 94, 95, 111.
Coronado, Carolina, 348.
Corpus Christi, Texas, 136, 137.
Cotton, Confederate steamer, 160.
Craven, Robert, 466.
Craven, Commander T.A.M., U.S.N., 257, 267, 268, 282.
Craven, Captain T. T., U.S.N., 21, 25, 57, 62, 76, 80-82, 87, 101-106, 130, 144, 399, 429, 436, 437, 466, 468.
Crocker, Acting Master Fred, U.S.N., 142.

Cromwell, Oliver, 182.
Cronstadt, Russia, 339, 341, 342.
Crosby, Lieutenant Peirce, U.S.N., 121.
Croton Aqueduct, 3.
Cuba, 138, 142.
Cuba, blockade runner, 136, 144.
Cummings, Lieutenant-Commander A. Boyd, U.S.N., 177, 449.
Currier and Ives, 396.
Curtis, Major-General Samuel R., U.S.A., 111.
Cushman, Charlotte, 354.
Cuyler, U.S. gunboat, 160, 161, 163.

Dacotah, U.S. gunboat, 84.
Dahlgren, Rear-Admiral John A., U.S.N., 9, 200, 201, 203, 215, 230, 368, 417.
Dale, U.S. sloop, 374.
Dardanelles, 360, 361, 365.
Dauphin Island, 224, 229, 233, 254, 259, 284, 459.
Davidson, J. O., 396.
Davis, Charles Henry, Rear-Admiral, U.S.N., 2, 89, 94-96, 99, 100, 105-109, 111-123, 127-129, 150, 241, 304, 415, 416, 437, 440, 442.
Davis, President Jefferson, 41, 42, 65, 69, 72, 85, 101, 113, 119, 122, 201, 331, 433.
Dean, Charles, 329.
De Camp, Commander John, U.S.N., 46, 83, 87, 115.
Decatur, Commodore Stephen, U.S.N., 41, 377, 386.
Defiance, Confederate gunboat, 63.
Delaware River, 17, 159.
De Peyster, General J. Watts, 295.
De Ruyter, Admiral Michael A. Dutch Navy, 357.
De Sota, U.S. gunboat, 135.
Detroit, Michigan, 333.
Devoe, Mrs. Edmund M., 415, 416.

INDEX 499

Dewey, Admiral George, U.S.N., 59, 175, 178, 182, 208, 379, 381, 489.
Dix, Major-General John A., U.S.A., 337, 338.
Dobb's Ferry, New York, 3.
Dog River Bar, 221, 230, 232, 246.
Don, U.S. steamer, 321.
Don Luis I, King of Portugal, 346.
Donaldson, Lieutenant Edward, U.S.N., 83, 87.
Donaldsonville, Louisiana, 130, 203, 204, 207-209.
Donegal, blockade runner, 247.
Dorland, M. Ella, 415.
Douglas, Stephen A., 333.
Drake, Sir Francis, 346.
Draper, Henry, 3.
Draper, Collector of the Port S., 312.
Drayton, Captain Percival, U.S.N., 218, 220, 225, 228, 229, 232-238, 243, 244, 248-253, 255, 259, 264, 265, 269, 272, 274, 276, 279, 284-291, 300, 302, 305, 310, 313-316, 319-323, 381, 484.
Drayton, Brigadier-General Thomas F., C.S.A., 218.
Duganne, Colonel A. J. H., 314.
Duncan, Brigadier-General Johnson K., C.S.A., 39, 50, 52, 66, 74, 429.
Dunderberg, French monitor, 338, 485.
Du Pont, Rear-Admiral S. F., U.S.N., 5, 14, 19, 30, 167, 197, 198, 200, 214, 215, 218, 230, 419, 439.

Eaton, Lieutenant S. M., U.S.A., 196.
Edinburgh, Scotland, 358.
Edinburgh, Duke of, 359.
Egypt, 351.
Ellet, Brigadier-General Alfred W., U.S.A., 96, 99, 111, 118, 119, 165, 188, 451.
Ellet, Colonel Charles R., U.S.A., 188, 195.
Ellet, Lieutenant-Colonel John A., U.S.A., 188.
Emmons, Commander George F., U.S.N., 143, 161.
Emory, Major-General William H., U.S.A., 204, 206, 207.
England, 16, 141, 147, 338, 344, 346.
Erben, Lieutenant Henry, U.S.N., 120, 136, 440.
Ericsson, John, 467.
Essex, U.S. ironclad gunboat, 109, 118-121, 124-127, 130, 136, 163, 166, 169, 172, 175, 193, 199, 201, 209, 280, 390, 398, 443, 449.
Eugénie, Empress of France, 338, 348.
Evarts, William M., 366.

Farquharson, Colonel Robert, C.S.A., 179.
Farragut, Admiral David Glasgow, U.S.N., inactive at Hastings-on-Hudson, 1-4; appointed on Selection Board, 4, 5; selected to command the New Orleans expedition, 8-14, 418, 419; calls on Lincoln, 16; takes command of the *Hartford* at Philadelphia, and sails for the Gulf of Mexico, 17, 420, 421; arrives at Ship Island, 21; assembles his fleet, 22-24; gets his ships across the bars, 25-32; final preparations for running past Forts Jackson and St. Philip, 33-37, 40, 43; preliminary operations against the forts with the mortars, 44-54; fighting past the forts, 55-64; captures New

Orleans, 65-77; expedition up the river to Vicksburg and return to New Orleans, 78-90; returns to Vicksburg and runs the batteries to join Flag-Officer Davis, 91-111; the *Arkansas* episode, 111-134; receives the thanks of Congress, 109, 132, 442; promoted to rear-admiral, 116, 131, 439, 442; returns to the blockade of the Gulf ports, 135-147; losses in the Gulf, 148-164; returns to the Mississippi and forces his way past the batteries at Port Hudson, 165-182, 382, 383; his appearance, 172, 178, 233, 234, 238, 251, 280; patrolling the Mississippi from Port Hudson to Vicksburg, 183-197; siege and capture of Port Hudson, 198-210; goes home on leave, August, 1863, 211-220; famous saying about the best defense, 171; sword presented by the Union League Club of New York, 249, 462; watchful waiting at New Orleans and at Pensacola, 221-240; the *Tennessee* gets into Mobile Bay, 241-251; the monitors arrive in the Gulf, 252-262; famous saying about the Battle of Mobile Bay, 280; forces entrance into Mobile Bay, 263-272; captures the *Tennessee*, 273-282, 473; surrender of the Mobile Bay forts, 283-296; his health forces him to refuse command of expedition against Fort Fisher, 297-310, 477; he leaves for New York, 310, 311; official welcome in New York, 312-314; promoted to vice-admiral, 315, 479; presented a testimonial of $50,000 by New York merchants, 318, 480; welcomed home to Hastings-on-Hudson, 318, 319; emergency orders to James River, 321, 322; appointed president of a board on promotions, 322; purchases a house in New York, 482; at Lincoln's second inaugural, 323; at Richmond after its surrender, 324, 325; tours New England with family, 327-330; promoted to admiral, 331; portrait by William Page, 332, 483; other portraits and pictures, 395, 396, 492; poems, 295, 296, 328, 348, 355, 362, 377, 390, 393, 395, 397-403, 421; with President Johnson on his swing around the circle, 332-334; makes a remarkable European cruise, 336-365; at Grant's inauguration, 368, 369; revisits California with his wife, 371, 372; takes charge of Peabody funeral, 373; visits Portsmouth, 373, 374; last illness and death, 374, 375; funeral at Portsmouth, 375; funeral at New York, 376, 377; burial in Woodlawn Cemetery, New York, 377; his character, 379-383; his religion, 384-387, 468, 490, 491; his education, 388, 389, 485, 486; commemorative statues, 391-395; his oath of allegiance, 415; his uniforms, 442, 482, 488; his rear-admiral's flag, 443, 464; his last flag, 488; "lashed to the mast," 465; "Damn the torpedoes," 469; his coat of arms, 481, 484, 486; his prize money, 482, 490; and miscellaneous references, 425, 426, 427, 429, 435, 437, 454, 459.

INDEX 501

Farragut, Mrs. David Glasgow, 1, 3, 13, 15, 17, 26, 30, 49, 63, 70, 78, 80, 90, 95, 97, 103, 121, 127, 128, 130, 133, 139, 141, 146, 162, 165, 167, 184, 190, 191, 198, 203, 209, 211-213, 218, 225-227, 234, 258, 285, 303, 308, 310, 314, 318-322, 324, 327, 331, 333-336, 339-341, 343, 344, 348, 350, 353-357, 360, 361, 364, 366, 367, 371, 372, 374, 376, 377, 383, 384, 388, 422, 447, 455, 477, 481, 489, 491.

Farragut, Elizabeth, wife of Celestant Dupont, 455.

Farragut, Glasgow, 227, 458.

Farragut, Loyall, 1, 2, 15, 16, 139, 161, 167, 172-176, 180, 191, 211, 219, 226, 243, 258, 333, 360, 376, 377, 379, 382, 385, 389, 391, 392, 450, 454, 455, 461, 474, 489, 491.

Farragut, Lieutenant William, U.S.N., 455, 458.

Farragut, William, 227, 458.

Faxon, William, 369, 442.

Febrer, Mossen Jaime, 349.

Field, Cyrus W., 367.

Fish, Hamilton, 367, 369, 371, 483.

Florida, 42.

Florida, Confederate raider, 138, 139, 140, 141, 144, 146, 160, 161, 444.

Florida Reef, 23.

Folsom, Charles, 64, 295, 415, 482.

Foltz, Surgeon J. M., U.S.N., 35, 36, 47, 79, 174, 196, 205, 206, 336, 338, 340, 354, 359, 426, 430, 484.

Foote, Rear-Admiral Andrew H., U.S.N., 9, 14, 30, 31, 74, 78, 85, 89, 90, 119, 186, 439, 464.

Forbes, Captain, 145.

Fort Adams, 107.

Fort Barrancas, 310.

Fort Beauregard, 5.

Fort Constantine, 342.

Fort Donelson, 22.

Fort Gaines, 145, 146, 148, 164, 223, 224, 229, 230, 238, 255, 256, 271, 284, 286, 288, 295, 308, 469, 473, 476.

Fort Jackson, 6, 37-39, 44-46, 50, 52, 54-59, 63, 64, 74, 75, 92, 97, 98, 103, 110, 116, 132, 170, 216, 226, 241, 292, 418, 424, 428, 430, 435, 443.

Fort Lafayette, 316.

Fort Livingston, 31.

Fort Mifflin, 17.

Fort Morgan, 138, 145, 152, 213, 223, 224, 229-232, 238, 242, 243, 250, 253, 255, 256, 258, 263, 264, 266, 268, 269-274, 280, 283, 285-290, 295, 297, 299, 304, 466, 468, 473, 475.

Fort Pickens, 6, 243, 416.

Fort Pillow, 42, 43, 89, 95.

Fort Powell, 229, 238, 264, 285, 288, 459, 474.

Fort St. Philip, 6, 37, 38, 41, 44, 48, 50, 54, 56-59, 63, 64, 74, 75, 92, 97, 98, 103, 110, 132, 170, 216, 226, 241, 292, 418, 424, 443.

Fort Sumter, 4, 14, 327, 478.

Fort Walker, 5.

Fort Warren, 323.

Fortress Monroe, 20, 76, 77, 420.

Fox, Gustavus Vasa, 6-12, 18, 19, 23-31, 82, 84-86, 88, 89, 91, 93, 95, 100, 110, 124, 129, 130, 135, 141, 144-146, 151, 169, 181, 182, 194, 195, 210, 215, 218, 284, 286, 297, 299, 300, 308, 322, 374, 375, 417-419, 422.

France, 20, 296.

Franklin, U.S. steam frigate, 336-339, 342-350, 353-359, 361, 363-365.

Franklin, Rear Admiral S. R., U.S.N., 380.

Franklin, Benjamin, 306.
Freeman, Douglas Southall, 467.
Freeman, Martin, 265, 465.
Frolic, U.S. gunboat, 360, 485.
Fulton, steamer, 336.

Gabaudan, Edward C., 193, 196.
Gaines, Confederate gunboat, 223, 244, 281, 284, 287.
Galena, U.S. gunboat, 263, 266, 271, 281.
Galveston, Texas, 136, 138, 143, 148, 149, 154-167, 181, 198, 210, 218, 225, 232, 236, 303, 447.
Gardner, Major-General Frank, C.S.A., 202, 208, 209.
Garfield, President James A., 391.
Garfield, Mrs. James A., 391.
General Quitman, Confederate gunboat, 40.
General Rusk, Confederate steamer, 138.
Genesee, U.S. gunboat, 171, 172, 177, 199.
Georgia, 366.
Gerdes, Captain F. H., U.S. Coast Survey, 428.
Gettysburg, Battle of, 206, 209.
Gibraltar, 347, 356, 365.
Gierlew, Danish Consul at Tunis, 344.
Giraud, Lieutenant Pierre, U.S.N., 279.
Gladstone, William E., 359.
Glasgow, Scotland, 358.
Glasgow, U.S. gunboat, 230, 248-250, 310.
Goldsborough, Rear-Admiral Louis M., U.S.N., 30, 199, 221, 337, 368, 439.
Gordon, Brigadier-General George H., U.S.A., 324.
Governor Moore, Confederate gunboat, 40, 61, 430, 431.
Grace Church, Hastings-on-Hudson, 490.

Grand Gulf, Mississippi, 94, 107, 109, 168, 182, 184, 187, 188, 192, 194-196.
Grand Lake, Louisiana, 148, 197.
Granger, Major-General Gordon, U.S.A., 252, 259, 266, 284, 285, 288-290, 299, 304, 307, 308.
Granite City, U.S. gunboat, 239.
Grant, Sir Patrick, 355.
Grant, General U. S., U.S.A., 105, 107, 184, 185, 187, 189, 194, 196, 198, 199, 207, 235, 240, 242, 244, 245, 305, 310, 321, 322, 325, 331-333, 335, 366-370, 376, 392, 394.
Grant, Mrs. U. S., 335, 366.
Grant's Pass, 141, 229, 230, 264, 283.
Gravesend, England, 344.
Greeley, Horace, 3, 309, 334.
Green Point, Long Island, 5.
Grimes, Senator, 7, 417.
Grover, Major-General Cuvier, U.S.A., 199.
Guerrière, U.S. frigate, 376.
Guest, Lieutenant John, U.S.N., 74, 427.
Gulf of Mexico, 5, 7, 25, 31, 41, 47, 48, 111, 112, 124, 133, 134, 136, 145-147, 152, 154, 167, 221, 303, 443.
Gurlie, Mrs. (Nancy Farragut), 211, 227, 240.
Gurney and Son, photographers, 395.

Hahn, Michael, 460.
Hale, Senator, 13, 417.
Hall, George G., viii, 459.
Hall, Mrs. George G., viii, 459.
Hall, Colonel, F. F., U.S.A., 461.
Halleck, Major-General Henry W., U.S.A., 85, 95, 99, 100, 107, 111, 153, 166, 245, 248, 286, 305.
Halstead, Vice-Admiral, R.N., 337.

INDEX

Halter, R. E., 21.
Hamilton, Andrew J., 303.
Hamilton, Lady, 320, 379.
Hamilton, Philip, 4.
Hamlin, Dr. Cyrus W., 362, 363.
Hampton Roads, 17, 31, 50, 85, 108-110, 129.
Hancock, Major-General Winfield S., U.S.A., 368.
Harlow, Dr. S. Ralph, 420.
Harper's Weekly, 77, 295, 396.
Harriet Lane, U.S. gunboat, 23, 24, 46, 75, 78, 155-157, 160, 236, 238, 426, 427, 446.
Harrisburg, Pennsylvania, 207, 333.
Harrison, Lieutenant Napoleon B., U.S.N., 52.
Hartford, U.S. steam sloop, 15-17, 19-21, 24, 25, 33, 45, 46, 49, 51, 52, 55-58, 60, 62, 67-71, 81-83, 87, 88, 94-96, 98, 99, 105, 108, 111, 113-118, 121, 126, 130-133, 135, 139, 145, 147, 155, 163, 166, 169, 171-177, 180, 183, 184, 189-192, 196, 197, 200, 209-212, 214, 217-220, 225-231, 237, 243, 248, 252, 256-266, 269-279, 281, 284, 285, 291, 300, 310-315, 332, 390-399, 420-422, 429, 430, 443, 464, 469, 474.
Harwood, Captain A. A., U.S.N., 20, 293, 421.
Hass, Frederick de, 396.
Hastings-on-Hudson, New York, 1-3, 139, 212, 318, 319, 327, 394, 490.
Hatteras, U.S. gunboat, 137, 143, 158, 159, 256, 447.
Hatteras Inlet, 4.
Havana, Cuba, 20, 31, 137, 138, 144, 145, 199, 220.
Haynes's Bluff, Mississippi, 186.
Hazard, Captain S. F., U.S.N., 161.
Heginbotham, Captain Percival Drayton's clerk, 288.

Heisler, Lieutenant George, U.S.M.C., 71.
Hewitt, Captain, R. N., 147.
Higgins, Lieutenant-Colonel Edward, C.S.A., 424.
Hitchcock, Captain Robert B., U.S.N., 135, 154.
Hollins, Commodore George N., C.S.N., 41, 43, 49.
Holmes, Oliver Wendell, 323, 400, 481.
Hooker, Major-General Joseph, U.S.A., 323.
Horace Beals, U.S. barkentine, 422, 423.
Housatonic, U.S. steam sloop, 145, 232.
Houston, Texas, 150, 158.
Howard, Major, C.S.A., 193.
Hudson River, 3, 173, 234, 333.
Huger, Lieutenant T. B., C.S.N., 60.
Hull, Commodore Isaac, U.S.N., 329.
Hunter, Commander Charles, U.S.N., 138, 145.
Hunter, Surgeon L. B., U.S.N., 4.
Huntsville, Confederate ram, 222, 231, 241.
Hurlbut, Major-General Stephen A., U.S.A., 219.
Imperial, Mississippi River steamer, 210.
Indian No. 2, Confederate merchant steamer, 143.
Indianapolis, Indiana, 333.
Indianola, U.S. gunboat, 168, 181, 183, 184, 192.
Iroquois, U.S. gunboat, 35, 44, 45, 49, 56, 60, 81, 83, 98, 102.
Irving, Washington, 3.
Irwin, Lieutenant-Colonel R. B., U.S.A., 208.
Isabella, Queen of Spain, 348.
Isherwood, Engineer-in-Chief Benjamin F., U.S.N., 418.

Island No. 10, 31, 43.
Itasca, U.S. gunboat, 49, 52, 55, 59, 62, 81-83, 94, 223, 263, 271, 281, 287, 442, 443.
Ivanhoe, blockade runner, 251.
Ivy, U.S. tug, 194, 196.

Jackman, W. J., 396.
Jackson, Confederate gunboat, 40, 144.
Jackson, Andrew, 67, 460.
Jackson, Mrs. Norman, 225, 460.
Jackson, Mississippi, 90, 153, 196.
James River, 146, 321, 324, 325.
J. C. Kuhn, U.S. bark, 114.
J. D. Clarke, Confederate river steamer, 193.
Jenkins, Captain Thornton A., U.S.N., 161, 163, 166, 168, 172-174, 184, 196, 207, 208, 231, 253, 255, 259, 480.
Jessie Benton, 105-107, 109, 113, 114, 118, 196, 437.
John P. Jackson, U.S. gunboat, 100, 231.
Johnson, President Andrew, 327, 331-337, 366, 367, 482.
Johnston, Commander J. D., C.S.N., 267, 273, 277-279, 474.
Johnston, General Joseph E., 108, 196.
Joinville, Prince de, 296, 330, 345.
Jones, Commander Catesby ap Roger, C.S.N., 256.
Jones, Captain John Paul, 377.
Jouett, Lieutenant-Commander James E., U.S.N., 247, 255, 265, 270-272, 280, 282, 469.

Kanawha, U.S. gunboat, 136, 137.
Kane, Dr. Elisha Kent, 213.
Katahdin, U.S. gunboat, 36, 55, 98, 99, 110, 124, 130, 443.
Kautz, Lieutenant Albert, U.S.N., 58, 71, 73.

Kearsarge, U.S. steam sloop, 255, 256, 309, 336.
Kennebec, U.S. gunboat, 23, 26, 44, 56, 59, 75, 81, 83, 87, 88, 98, 99, 143, 263, 281.
Kennedy, John Pendleton, 354.
Kennesaw Mountain, Georgia, 245.
Kennon, Lieutenant Beverly, C.S.N., 60, 61, 430.
Kensington, U.S. gunboat, 114, 142, 149, 436.
Kentucky, 111.
Key West, Florida, 18, 19, 23, 28, 52, 220, 238, 243, 312.
Kimball, Chief Engineer James B., U.S.N., 88.
Kimberly, Rear Admiral Lewis A., U.S.N., 471.
Kineo, U.S. gunboat, 22, 26, 36, 49, 55, 63, 124, 130, 171, 172, 178, 199, 203, 209, 443.
Kinney, Lieutenant John C., U.S.A., 259, 266, 469.
Kittredge, Lieutenant John W., U.S.N., 137.
Kitson, Henry H., 394.
Knowles, Quartermaster John H., U.S.N., 173, 265, 465, 483.
Knoxville, Tennessee, 489.
Koopman, Harry K., 390.
Kossuth, Louis, 232.

Lackawanna, U.S. steam sloop, 169, 225, 242, 263, 265, 271, 275, 276, 281, 287.
Lake Borgne, 21, 31, 37.
Lake Pontchartrain, 31, 37, 66.
Lancaster, U.S. ram, 112, 188.
Larrabee, William, 394.
Law, Commander Richard L., U.S.N., 156, 157.
Laycock, The Reverend Doctor, 131.
Lee, General Robert Edward, C.S.A., 108, 141, 207, 240, 299, 384.

INDEX 505

Lee, Captain S. P., U.S.N., 81-83, 87, 94, 116, 120, 121, 297, 437.
Lenthal, Chief Naval Constructor John, U.S.N., 417.
Le Roy, Commander William E., U.S.N., 278, 472, 473.
Leslie's Weekly, 294, 396.
Lesoffsky (Lessovski), Rear-Admiral, Russian Navy, 218, 219, 339, 340, 341.
Lincoln, President Abraham, 5-7, 16, 69, 82, 85, 86, 139, 153, 182, 210, 214, 285, 286, 294, 303-305, 309, 310, 320-327, 394, 417, 418, 443.
Lincoln, Mrs. Abraham, 320.
L. L. Davis, Confederate merchant schooner, 152.
Lisbon, Portugal, 346, 356.
London, England, 344, 346.
Longfellow, Henry W., 359, 486.
Looker, Paymaster Thomas H., U.S.N., 372.
Loop, Henry Augustus, 395.
Lord Clyde, ironclad, R.N., 356.
Loughlin, Dr. John J., 492.
Louisiana, 26, 42, 125, 153.
Louisiana, Confederate ironclad ram, 40, 42, 50, 52, 53, 57, 63, 74-76, 118, 430.
Louisville, Kentucky, 333, 334.
Louisville, U.S. ironclad gunboat, 105, 114.
Lovell, Major-General Mansfield, C.S.A., 41-43, 66, 69.
Lowell, Robert, 397.
Loyall, U.S. steam tender, 274, 285.
Loyall, Margaret, 1, 424.
Luce, Captain Stephen B., U.S.N., 377.

Maccoun, Surgeon Robert T., U.S.N., 397.
Madrid, Spain, 348, 357.

Maffitt, Lieutenant John N., C.S.N., 138, 139.
Magruder, Major-General J. Bankhead, C.S.A., 155, 157.
Mahan, Captain Alfred Thayer, U.S.N., 381.
Mallory, Stephen R., Confederate Secretary of the Navy, 42.
Malta, 355, 356.
Malvern, U.S. gunboat, 325.
Manassas, Confederate ram, 24, 40, 41, 57, 59, 60, 135, 424, 429-431.
Manhattan, U.S. monitor, 246, 250, 252, 254, 256, 258, 261, 263, 264, 267, 274, 277, 473.
Manila Bay, 379.
Marchand, Captain John B., U.S.N., 236, 242.
Mare Island Navy Yard, 2, 9, 105, 415, 491.
Marion, Alabama, 153.
Marques de la Habana, Confederate steamer, 40.
Marsh, George P., 352.
Marston, Major Frank W., U.S.A., 259, 266.
Maryland, 141, 280.
Mason, James M., 5, 147.
Mason, John Y., 8, 9.
Massachusetts Volunteers, 155.
Matagorda, Texas, 136.
Matamoras, Mexico, 142, 144, 145, 152.
Maury, Major-General Dabney H., 229, 252, 272, 284, 287.
Maury, Matthew Fontaine, 485.
Maximilian, Emperor Ferdinand, 20, 365.
McClelland, Major-General George B., U.S.A., 7, 77, 108, 214, 417, 418.
McDougal, Senator, 16.
McIntosh, Commander Charles F., C.S.N., 63, 326.

McKean, Flag-Officer W. W., U.S.N., 8, 10, 17, 18, 21, 29, 74, 421.
McKinley, Alexander, Secretary to Farragut, 265, 288, 310.
McKinstry, Captain J. P., U.S.N., 178.
McRae, Confederate gunboat, 40, 60, 64, 72.
McRitchie, Lieutenant D. G., U.S.N., 443.
Meade, Major-General George G., U.S.A., 377.
Mediterranean, 217, 336, 356.
Meigs, Brigadier-General Montgomery C., U.S.A., 92.
Memphis, Tennessee, 42, 81, 85, 89, 94, 96, 99, 100, 107-109, 219.
Mercer, Captain Samuel, U.S.N., 12.
Meredith, William Farragut, 483.
Meredith, William T., 178, 401, 427, 483, 493.
Merrimac (Virginia), Confederate ironclad ram, 40, 45, 220, 221, 273.
Metacomet, U.S. gunboat, 244, 247, 259, 263, 268, 270-272, 280, 281, 284, 287, 460.
Mexico, 20.
Mexican War, 4, 8.
Miami, U.S. gunboat, 27, 131.
Micawber, Mr., 167.
Midnight, U.S. bark, 137.
Mignano, Duc de, 353.
Miles, Colonel William R., C.S.A., 202.
Miller, N.M., 395.
Mississippi, 153, 287, 366, 460.
Mississippi, Confederate ram, 68, 450.
Mississippi, U.S. steam frigate, 24-28, 33, 49, 55, 59-63, 81, 82, 86, 116, 133, 161, 163, 171, 173, 175, 178-182, 186, 225, 443.

Mississippi River, 2-6, 18, 21-25, 32, 36, 38, 41, 68, 70, 75-79, 82-86, 92, 94, 96, 109, 124, 128, 132, 134, 136, 140, 143, 147, 150, 152, 161-166, 169-171, 180-183, 186, 194, 199, 201, 209, 210, 216, 221, 239-244, 246, 257, 291, 422, 443, 454.
Mississippi Sound, 21, 136, 247, 256, 258, 283.
Mitchell, Captain John K., C.S.N., 12, 41, 50, 53, 63, 75, 321, 326, 431.
Mobile, Alabama, 21, 23, 41, 42, 76-82, 84-86, 92, 93, 108, 112, 124, 132, 135, 136, 143, 152, 153, 161, 162, 181, 198, 210, 216, 219-223, 229, 233, 234, 241, 245, 249, 252, 255-257, 281-289, 293, 296, 297, 299, 302, 306, 309, 313, 319, 342, 378.
Mobile Bay, 14, 18, 78, 81, 92, 131, 135-141, 144-147, 154-156, 159-165, 169, 194, 199, 219-224, 228-231, 233, 238, 241, 246, 250, 252, 255, 269, 281, 284, 285, 290-297, 301, 305, 308, 312, 316, 330-332, 382, 399, 402, 442, 471, 474, 478, 482.
Monarch, turreted battleship, R.N., 373.
Monarch, U.S. hospital ship, 108.
Monitor, U.S. ironclad, 5, 91, 468.
Monongahela, U.S. steam sloop, 169, 171-173, 178, 199, 203, 204, 208, 243, 248, 263, 271, 275, 277, 281, 287, 320.
Monroe, John T., 69, 73.
Montgomery, Alabama, 222.
Montgomery, U.S. gunboat, 138, 145.
Montgomery, Henry E., 375, 490.
Montijo, Countess, 348.
Moore, John W., 34.

INDEX 507

Moore, Governor T. O., 42, 65.
Morgan, Confederate gunboat, 223, 244, 271, 281.
Morning Light, U.S. ship, 162, 167.
Morris, Edward J., 360.
Morris, Commodore Henry W., U.S.N., 59, 71, 136, 169, 193, 206, 210.
Morro Castle, 20.
Mosher, Confederate tug, 58.
Motley, John Lathrop, 355, 357.
Muiron, French Navy, 351.
Murphey, Lieutenant P. U., C.S.N., 272, 280.
Myer, Colonel A. J., U.S.A., 224, 285.

Naples, Italy, 353, 354.
Napoleon III, 77, 158, 337, 351, 433.
Nashville, Tennessee, 22.
Nashville, Confederate gunboat, 222, 241, 287.
Natchez, Mississippi, 81-85, 95, 183.
Navy Register, 5, 8.
Nelson, Admiral Horatio, 29, 30, 53, 315, 316, 330, 346, 380.
New Carthage, Louisiana, 192.
New Ironsides, U.S. ironclad steam frigate, 141, 298.
New London, U.S. gunboat, 162, 209, 239.
New Orleans, 5-7, 12-14, 18, 21-24, 31, 32, 36-43, 46, 52, 61-98, 109-114, 116, 120, 122-125, 130-132, 135-137, 140-143, 147, 148, 150-152, 154-156, 158, 160, 161, 163, 165, 167-170, 173, 191, 193, 194, 196-198, 204-206, 208-210, 212, 216, 217, 221, 225-228, 233, 236, 237, 240, 241, 243, 246, 249, 252, 254, 255, 257, 258, 283, 286, 288, 291, 294, 296, 303, 305, 308, 310, 319, 325, 331, 336, 338, 342, 372, 378, 379, 383, 397, 416-418, 420, 421, 433, 435, 443, 445, 449, 460, 482.
New Orleans *Bee,* 65, 66.
New Orleans *Crescent,* 65, 66, 72.
New Orleans *Daily True Delta,* 65, 66.
New Orleans *Picayune,* 431, 441.
New York, 1, 3, 15, 190, 211, 212, 214, 216, 217, 220, 228, 230, 249, 296, 301, 304, 310, 313, 317, 318, 331-333, 336, 337, 356, 367, 373, 376, 391, 418, 464, 489.
New York *Daily Tribune,* 286, 314.
New York *Herald,* 47, 75-77, 212, 286, 316, 366.
New York *Journal of Commerce,* 166.
New York *Tribune,* 3.
New York *World,* 76, 77.
Newport, Rhode Island, 129, 490.
Niagara, U.S. screw steamer, 219, 437.
Niagara Falls, 174, 333.
Nice, France, 351.
Nichols, Commander Edward T., U.S.N., 46, 83, 87.
Nicholson, Commander James W. A., U.S.N., 277.
Niehaus, Charles Henry, 394.
Nields, Henry Clay, Acting Master, U.S.N., 268, 467, 468.
Nijni-Novgorod, Russia, 340, 341.
Norfolk, Virginia, 1-3, 8, 11, 12, 17, 45, 63, 139, 191, 226, 288, 309, 325.
Norfolk Navy Yard, 4, 5.
North Carolina, 227.

Ocean Queen, U.S. army transport, 84.
Octorara, U.S. gunboat, 96, 108, 223, 229, 263, 269, 281.
Oneida, U.S. gunboat, 36, 45, 50, 55, 60, 61, 72, 81, 82, 98, 102, 124, 130, 138, 161, 163,

508   DAVID GLASGOW FARRAGUT

261, 263, 271, 272, 281, 291, 320, 442.
O'Neill, photographer, 396.
Onondaga, U.S. monitor, 321, 485.
Opdyke, Mayor of New York, 309.
Opelousas, Louisiana, 195, 209.
Oreto (Florida), Confederate raider, 139, 161, 444.
Osbon, B.S., 35, 47, 51, 53, 55, 57, 58, 62, 421, 429.
Ossipee, U.S. gunboat, 238, 239, 263, 271, 278, 279, 281, 320.
Overend, W. H., 396.
Owasco, U.S. gunboat, 156, 167.

Page, Mrs. George Stevens, 483.
Page, Brigadier-General Richard L., 224, 250, 256, 268, 280, 284, 287-289, 313, 326.
Page, William, 332, 395, 483.
Paget, Vice-Admiral Clarence, R.N., 356.
Palmer, Surgeon James C., U.S.N., 264, 274, 280, 471.
Palmer, Commodore James S., U.S.N., 81, 87, 94, 116, 120, 129, 139, 147, 172-174, 176, 196, 201, 207, 218, 225-228, 252, 254, 255, 284, 288, 290, 304, 305, 310, 396.
Palmerston, Viscount, Prime Minister of England, 142.
Paris, France, 256, 337, 338, 392.
Parker, John C., 172.
Parker, Commander William A., U.S.N., 321.
Parsons, C. 396.
Parton, James, 317.
Pascagoula, Mississippi, 12, 21, 144, 152, 211, 227, 240, 245, 434, 455.
Pasley, Admiral Sir Thomas, 346.
Pass à l'Outre, 21, 24-27, 92.
Passaic, U.S. monitor, 302.
Patton, John, 394.

Paulding, Rear-Admiral Hiram, U.S.N., 2, 4, 5, 315, 473.
Peabody, George, 334, 335, 373.
Pearl River, Mississippi, 110.
Pelican Pass, 233.
Pemberton, Lieutenant-General John C., C.S.A., 196.
Pennock, Captain A.M., U.S.N., 1, 336, 337, 349, 351, 362, 374, 376, 489.
Pennock, Mrs. A. M., 337, 339, 341, 347, 349, 351, 360.
Pensacola, Florida, 18, 42, 85, 124, 131, 135, 143-145, 159, 163, 165, 210, 220, 221, 229, 231, 233, 237, 240-243, 250, 252, 257, 259, 280, 305, 310.
Pensacola, U.S. steam sloop, 16, 19, 23, 26-28, 53, 55, 59, 60, 62, 67, 68, 72, 86, 92, 116, 133, 138, 204, 225, 227, 429, 443.
Pensacola Navy Yard, 3, 108, 139, 163.
Perine, George E., 396.
Perkins, Lieutenant George H., U.S.N., 56, 60, 61, 69, 71, 265, 277, 290.
Perry, Commodore O. H., U.S.N., 377.
Persano, Admiral, Italian Navy, 364.
Petersburg, Virginia, 76.
Peter the Great, 340.
Petit Bois Pass, 258.
Phelps, Lieutenant S. L., U.S.N., 106, 119.
Philadelphia, Pennsylvania, 15, 16, 145, 207, 227, 333.
Philadelphia Navy Yard, 17.
Philippi, U.S. supply ship, 272.
Pierpont House, Brooklyn, 10.
Pilot Town, Louisiana, 26, 34.
Pinkham, Lieutenant Alexander B., U.S.N., 242, 461.
Pinola, U.S. gunboat, 49, 56, 60, 81, 94, 98, 102, 171.

INDEX 509

Pisa, Italy, 344, 352.
Pittsburgh, Pennsylvania, 333, 334.
Plaquemine, Louisiana, 165, 203.
Plymouth, England, 346.
Plymouth, U.S. corvette, 373.
Pomeroy, Acting Master G. P., U.S.N., 283.
Pontchatoula, 152.
Pope, Major-General John, U.S.N., 141.
Port Fire, U.S. steam tug, 330.
Port Gibson, 197.
Port Hudson, 148, 154, 155, 161-173, 180-184, 187-199, 203-210, 445, 449, 455, 462.
Port Mahon, Minorca, 349, 350.
Port Royal, South Carolina, 5, 6, 14, 19, 105, 218, 257, 301, 306, 307, 416.
Port Royal, U.S. gunboat, 263, 271, 281, 301, 320.
Porter, Commodore David, U.S.N., 9, 130, 360, 386, 387, 390, 398, 490.
Porter, Commander David Dixon, U.S.N., 6, 7, 9-12, 15, 17, 23, 26-28, 31, 37, 39, 44-54, 56, 64, 65, 72, 74-76, 78, 79, 86, 91, 92, 94-97, 100-103, 105, 108-110, 117, 119, 124, 127, 128, 130, 149, 150, 154, 157, 162, 168, 169, 185-196, 199, 201, 210, 214, 222, 230, 235, 239, 241, 242, 246, 252, 258, 307, 308, 315, 325, 336, 368-371, 373, 386, 416-419, 422, 425-430, 435, 442, 447, 451, 488, 489, 491.
Porter, Mrs. D. D., 218.
Porter, Commander William D., U.S.N., 109, 119, 121, 124-128, 216, 416, 438, 442.
Portsmouth, England, 376, 489, 490.
Portsmouth, U.S. ship, 56, 204, 423, 443.

Posniak, Colonel, Russian Army, 340.
Potomac, U.S. ship, 163, 418.
Potomac River, 4, 214, 256, 299.
Powhatan, U.S. steam frigate, 6, 417.
Preble, Lieutenant George Henry, U.S.N., 22, 110, 138, 139.
President, U.S. frigate, 41.
Profit Island, 166, 172.

Queen of the West, U.S. ram, 112, 118, 165, 167, 172, 183, 195, 439.

Rachel Seaman, U.S. mortar schooner, 142.
Radford, Rear-Admiral William, U.S.N., 321, 332, 367.
Rains, Brigadier-General Gabriel J., C.S.A., 224.
Ransom, Lieutenant George M., U.S.N., 148.
Randall, Postmaster General, 333.
Rawlins, Major-General John A., U.S.A., 333.
Read, Captain Abner, U.S.N., 208.
Read, Lieutenant Charles W. ("Savvy"), C.S.N., 60, 126, 127.
Read, Midshipman John H., U.S.N., 71.
Ream, Virginia (Vinnie), 391, 491.
Red River, 96, 109, 124, 125, 134, 153, 165, 167-171, 180, 181, 183, 186, 187, 189, 190, 192-196, 199, 235, 236, 239, 241, 242, 308.
Renshaw, Commander W. B., U.S.N., 29, 115, 117, 130, 143, 148, 149, 154-157, 162.
Rice, Alexander H., 329, 381, 393, 482.
Richmond, Virginia, 41-43, 107, 108, 152, 284, 285, 299, 321, 324.

Richmond, U.S. steam sloop, 16, 23, 28, 34, 35, 41, 46, 48, 49, 56, 58-60, 62, 68, 72, 81-83, 88, 93-96, 98, 106, 108, 112, 121, 124, 139, 147, 154, 163, 169, 171, 172, 176-180, 193, 199, 201, 205, 208, 211, 214, 221, 243, 247, 248, 259, 263, 270, 281, 310, 422, 423, 426, 428, 429, 436, 469.
Richmond *Examiner,* 284.
Ridgway, W., 396.
Rinaldo, Royal Navy, 147.
Rio Grande, 15, 135, 137, 143, 164, 233.
Ritchie, A. H., 396.
River Queen, Hudson River steamer, 333.
Robeson, George M., 371.
Robin, Augustus, 396.
Rodgers, Rear-Admiral John, U.S.N., 14, 215.
Rodgers (Rogers), William M., Assistant Engineer, C.S.N., 276.
Roe, Lieutenant Francis A., U.S.N., 53, 59, 62.
Rosas, Juan Manuel de, 206.
Ruric, Russian Navy, 341.
Russell, Boatswain's Mate George, U.S.N., 73.
Russell, Lord John, 142.
Russell, Lieutenant John H., U.S.N., 23, 46, 47, 87.
Russia, 354, 363, 365.

Sabine Pass, 136, 142, 162, 167, 181, 213, 215, 232, 303.
Sabine River, 239.
Sachem, U.S. gunboat, 196, 214.
Saint-Gaudens, Augustus, 391, 392.
Saint Mary's, U.S. sloop, 2, 415.
Sam Houston, U.S. schooner, 163.
San Francisco, California, 217.
San Jacinto, U.S. steam frigate, 5, 255, 312, 421.
San Juan d'Ulloa, 8.
Sand Island, 258.
Santee, U.S. ship, 137.
Schirmer, Lieutenant L. A., C.S.A., 205.
Schley, Rear Admiral Winfield Scott, U.S.N., 9, 201, 202, 373, 380, 388, 418, 485.
Scientific American, 246.
Sciota, U.S. gunboat, 44, 49, 51, 56, 81, 98, 102, 155, 159.
Scotland, 358.
Seaver, Acting Master James T., U.S.N., 272.
Second Manassas, Battle of, 141.
Seddon, James A., Confederate Secretary of War, 229, 287.
Selfridge, Captain T.O., U.S.N., 24.
Selma, Confederate gunboat, 223, 244, 270, 271, 280, 282, 473.
Selma, Alabama, 222, 308.
Seminole, U.S. gunboat, 263, 281.
Semmes, Captain Raphael, C.S.N., 2, 146, 255, 447.
Seward, William H., 6, 13, 304, 310, 327, 333, 336, 365, 416, 417.
Sheliha, Lieutenant-Colonel Von, C.S.A., 224, 466.
Sheridan, Major-General Philip H., U.S.A., 372.
Sherman, Brigadier-General Thomas W., U.S.A., 5, 200.
Sherman, General William T., U.S.A., 186, 187, 228, 229, 245, 286, 294, 297, 299, 305, 308, 310, 368, 372, 389, 394, 477, 480, 491.
Ship Island, 21, 23, 24, 27, 28, 31, 32, 34, 41, 42, 50, 74, 79, 131, 135, 139, 144, 152, 159, 163, 165, 210, 229, 230, 240, 422.
Shreveport, Louisiana, 183, 235.
Shubrick, Captain William B., U.S.N., 9.
Sickles, Major-General Daniel E., U.S.A., 291, 368.
Skaggs, E. H., 143.

Slidell, John, 5, 147, 433.
Smith, Lieutenant-General Edmund Kirby, C.S.A., 195, 235.
Smith, H. W., 396.
Smith, Rear-Admiral Joseph, U.S.N., 9, 135.
Smith, Captain Melancton, U.S.N., 51, 60, 178, 179, 181, 182, 391.
Smith, Brigadier-General Thomas Kilby, U.S.A., 207.
Smith, Commodore William, U.S.N., 163.
Smyrna, Turkey, 360.
Sodom, 153.
Soule, Pierre, 69, 72, 73.
Southwest Pass, 21, 25, 27, 137, 155, 158, 161, 163, 165, 211, 291.
Speedwell, U.S. steam tug, 376.
Spezia, Italy, 351.
Springfield, Ohio, 333.
Squella, Don Gabriel, 349, 350.
Squires, Captain M. T., C.S.A., 424.
St. Francisville, Louisiana, 82.
St. Louis, Missouri, 85, 210, 333, 334.
St. Petersburg, Russia, 339-342, 364.
St. Thomas, West Indies, 144.
Stanton, Edwin M., Secretary of War, 110, 317, 321, 323.
Stedman, E. C., 493.
Steedman, Captain Charles, U.S.N., 305.
Stevens, Lieutenant Henry K., C.S.N., 126, 127.
Stevens, Thaddeus, 331.
Stevens, Captain Thomas H., U.S.N., 376, 402.
Stevenson, Burton Egbert, 492.
Stevenson, Captain John A., C.S.A., 40.
Stockholm, Sweden, 343.
Stoddard, Richard Henry, 402.

Stonewall Jackson, Confederate gunboat, 430.
Stribling, Commodore Cornelius K., U.S.N., 312.
Stringham, Rear-Admiral Silas N., U.S.N., 4.
Sullivan, Franklin Buchanan, 474.
Sumner, Senator Charles, 331.
Sumter, Confederate raider, 2, 418.
Sumter, U.S. ironclad ram, 108, 114, 115, 119-121, 124, 130, 136, 443.
Susquehanna, U.S. steam frigate, 135, 136, 138, 160, 163.
Switzerland, U.S. ram, 188, 192, 195, 196.
Szymanski, Colonel, C.S.A., 61.

Tallapoosa, U.S. dispatch steamer, 374, 488.
Taylor, Lieutenant-General Richard, C.S.A., 183, 204, 205, 209, 235.
Taylor, President Zachary, 235.
Tecumseh, U.S. monitor, 250, 256-261, 264, 266-269, 280, 282, 285, 286, 293, 465-468, 475.
Tegethoff, Admiral, Austrian Navy, 364.
Tennessee, 42, 111, 153, 227.
Tennessee, Confederate ironclad ram, 221, 222, 230-233, 239-244, 246, 248-254, 257, 261, 267-281, 285, 287, 291-293, 308, 396, 466, 467, 471-473, 475.
Tennessee, U.S. gunboat, 80, 109, 126, 149, 203, 205, 207, 209, 210, 233, 236, 252, 279.
Tennessee River, 22.
Tenney, U. D., 395.
Terry, Major-General Alfred H., U.S.A., 321, 368.
Texas, 137, 142, 143, 147, 149, 153, 158, 159, 161, 164, 166, 216, 222, 233, 236, 239, 242, 247, 303, 304, 366, 447.

Thomas, Major-General George H., U.S.A., 368.
Thompson, Launt, 488.
Thornton, Lieutenant James S., U.S.N., 58, 139, 256.
Ticknor, George, 349.
Ticonderoga, U.S. gunboat, 339, 485.
Todd, Dr., 3.
Todd, Captain Alexander B., C.S.A., 97.
Toledo, Ohio, 333.
Totten, Brigadier-General James, U.S.A., 219.
Trent, English steamer, 5.
Tunis, 64, 352.
Turkey, 360, 361, 363.
Turner, Rear-Admiral Thomas, U.S.N., 372, 488.
Tuscaloosa, Confederate ram, 222, 231.
Tyler, U.S. gunboat, 112, 438.

Uhl, S. Jerome, 395.
Union League Club, 249, 492.
Union Point, 95.
U.S. Naval Academy, 16.
Usher, Colonel Roland G., U.S.A., 420.

Vandalia, U.S. sloop, 330, 376.
Van Dorn, Major-General Earl, C.S.A., 101, 113, 119, 122, 127.
Varuna, U.S. gunboat, 36, 55, 60-62, 430.
Velocity, U.S. schooner, 162, 167.
Venice, Italy, 352.
Vera Cruz, Mexico, 19, 214.
Versailles, France, 337.
Vicksburg, Mississippi, 42, 79-97, 98-101, 105-116, 121, 122, 128, 129, 134, 140, 148, 153, 154, 163-168, 182-190, 194-197, 199, 206, 209, 245.
Vicksburg, Confederate river steamer, 192.

Victor Emanuel, King of Italy, 352.
Victoria, Queen of England, 344, 359.
Victory, English ship of the line, 346, 379.
Vincennes, U.S. ship, 21, 41.
Virginia, 146, 240, 244, 366.
Volga River, 341.

Wainwright, Lieutenant J. M., U.S.N., 46, 156, 157, 162, 425-427.
Wainwright, Captain Richard, U.S.N., 17, 19, 20, 68, 87, 98, 131, 139, 426.
Walker, Captain W. W., U.S.N., 238, 239.
Warden, Rear-Admiral Read, R.N., 347.
Warley, Captain Alexander F., C.S.N., 61, 431.
Warrenton, Mississippi, 184, 188, 191, 192.
Warrior, Confederate gunboat, 57, 63.
Washington, D.C., 2-5, 12, 15, 16, 29, 77, 116, 117, 129, 132, 142, 152, 203, 212, 213, 221, 244, 285, 294, 305, 310, 315, 319, 321, 336, 370, 372, 419.
Washington Navy Yard, 420.
Washington *Daily National Intelligencer*, 76.
Washburne, E. B., 369.
Water Witch, blockade runner, 137.
Watson, Lieutenant J. C., U.S.N., 172, 225, 238, 250, 251, 258, 265, 275, 288, 310, 468.
Wave, U.S. gunboat, 239.
Waxholm, Sweden, 343.
Webb, Confederate ram, 168.
Webster, Engineer Harrie, U.S.N., 267.
Weed, Thurlow, 217, 304, 367.
Weir, J. F., 395.
Weitzel, Major-General Godfrey, U.S.A., 148, 324, 325.

INDEX 513

Welles, Gideon, 2-5, 7-9, 12-14, 18-21, 23, 28, 31, 37, 41, 42, 48, 50, 51, 74, 77, 78, 84, 86, 88, 89, 99, 100, 103, 107-111, 116-118, 121-127, 132, 135, 136, 139-144, 154, 159-163, 166, 177, 181, 190, 194, 198-204, 213-219, 231, 239, 244, 246, 252, 255, 256, 284, 286, 293, 297, 299-310, 314-322, 327, 330, 331, 333, 336, 366-372, 375, 416-419, 422, 425, 427, 433, 435, 437, 484, 490.
Welles, Mrs. Gideon, 219, 327, 331, 333.
West Gulf Squadron, 13, 15, 17.
West Florida, blockade runner, 142.
Westfield, U.S. gunboat, 49, 75, 150, 155-157, 160.
West Point, New York, 211, 212, 219, 333, 360, 366, 455.
Wharton, Lieutenant A.D., C.S.N., 267, 277.
White, Richard Grant, 392.
White, Stanford, 392.
Whiting, Rear-Admiral W. H., U.S.N., 470.
Wilcox, J. A. J., 396.
Wilkes, Captain Charles, U.S.N., 5, 163.
Wilkinson, John, 64.
Willard's Hotel, Washington, D.C., 15.
William G. Anderson, U.S. bark, 143, 163.

William, King of Holland, 358.
Williams, Lieutenant-Colonel J. M., C.S.A., 283.
Williams, Brigadier-General Thomas, U.S.A., 82-84, 87, 88, 94, 95, 100, 101, 107, 111-126.
Williamson, The Reverend Thom, 469.
Wilmington, North Carolina, 215, 300, 301, 303, 305.
Wilson, Brigadier-General James Grant, U.S.A., 324, 377, 390, 462, 468, 483.
Winona, U.S. gunboat, 22, 26, 27, 56, 59, 75, 98, 102, 138, 143, 203.
Winnebago, U.S. monitor, 246, 252, 254, 258, 261, 264, 265, 302, 402, 466.
Winslow, Captain John A., U.S.N., 256, 316.
Winthrop, William, 355.
Wissahickon, U.S. gunboat, 36, 44, 55, 60, 81, 98, 99, 102, 108.
Wolseley, General Viscount, 54, 64, 242.
Woodlawn Cemetery, New York, 376, 377, 391, 492.
Woodworth, Lieutenant Selim E., U.S.N., 144.

Yazoo River, 95, 96, 99, 108, 109, 111, 112, 122, 186, 222.
Yates, Lieutenant Arthur R., U.S.N., 265.

Zantzinger, Frank, 226, 227.

www.ingramcontent.com/pod-product-compliance
Lightning Source LLC
LaVergne TN
LVHW091526060526
838200LV00036B/504